SIDRAK AND BOKKUS
VOL. I

EARLY ENGLISH TEXT SOCIETY

No. 311

1998

They that in tyme of goddes soone shalbe
Shall they lyue as longe as wee
..ll suche of body as now ar we
..nt soo mekel shall they not be
And we are now of lenger lyfe
Than shall be thenne oþer man or wyff
ffor the worlde is stalworther
Thenne shalbe þenne and mighttyer
And þe erthe geues vs to
moore frute than hal then do
And þe plente that the erthe yeldes
Bothe in woode And in feldes
Is now of mekel moore mightt
Thenne hit shalbe thanne eet right
And the wynde is bryȝter nowe
Than shalbe thenne And to more prowe
fferfore ought we of right nature
lenger lyue And lenger endure
Than they that by the dayes Are
ffor febeler for thy shall they fare
ffor he that thenne lyue may
..v. yeere hit is a longe day
ffor euer shall men do bacward goo
Of lyff and of strenbthe also
But in wytt wyse they shall
And in maleys wt all
And of here bodyes lessyn ay
Be twyxe this and domes day
Telle me now soo mote thow pryue
how longe shall this worlde dryue

O man in erthe the presbyte
of god may knowe sane oonly he
hit is soo grete that wit hit ne can
Nowther Aungell beeste ne man
No neo thyng but hit be he

that wt god

Bodleian Library MS Laud Misc. 559, f. 42^v

þe kyng axide þidras J vnderstonde
Jf god made man wiþ his honde.

    An and al þat god him lent
    was made of his comandement
And who so vnderstonde can
A ful feble nature is in man
And of foule þing god him dighte
þe deuel to shende þwiþ & his mighte
ffor man þat so feble is
Is made to haue þat blis
þat pride caste þe deuelis fro
And þat is his sorowe & his woo
Of þe foure elementis god nam
And þof he made faire Adam
ffor his ende shulde at goddis wille
þe foure quarters of þis world fulfille
And for god it wiste bifore
þat man shulde synne aȝeinst his lore
And þat he shulde as þe vnwise
Not longe bileue in paradyse
þfore al oþ þing wolde he make
To mānes bihone for his sake
And many wormes he made also
als amptis flies and oþir mo
Sore to dere & bite man somtide
þat he ne falle noght in pride
But þat he him bipenke bi þis
hou feble a þing þat it is
þat he ne may not him self were
ffro so litel a worme þat may him dere
Of pismyres & gnennes men se may
hou þei be trauailinge al þe day
So besy shulde we be by right
To serue god wiþ al oure might

SIDRAK AND BOKKUS

A parallel-text edition from Bodleian Library,
MS Laud Misc. 559 and British Library, MS Lansdowne 793

EDITED BY

T. L. BURTON

With the assistance of
Frank Schaer, Bernadette Masters,
Sabina Flanagan, Robin Eaden,
and Christopher Bright

VOLUME ONE
INTRODUCTION, PROLOGUE, AND
BOOKS I–II

Published for
THE EARLY ENGLISH TEXT SOCIETY
by the
OXFORD UNIVERSITY PRESS
1998

Oxford University Press, Great Clarendon Street, Oxford OX2 6DP

Oxford New York

Athens Auckland Bangkok Bogotá Buenos Aires Calcutta
Cape Town Chennai Dar es Salaam Delhi Florence Hong Kong Istanbul
Karachi Kuala Lumpur Madrid Melbourne Mexico City Mumbai
Nairobi Paris São Paulo Singapore Taipei Tokyo Toronto Warsaw
and associated companies in
Berlin Ibadan

Oxford is a trade mark of Oxford University Press

Published in the United States
by Oxford University Press Inc., New York

© Early English Text Society, 1998

British Library Cataloguing in Publication Data
Data available

Library of Congress Cataloging in Publication Data
Data applied for

ISBN 0-19-722315-X

1 3 5 7 9 10 8 6 4 2

Typeset by Joshua Associates Ltd., Oxford
Printed in Great Britain
on acid-free paper by
Print Wright Ltd., Ipswich

IN MEMORY OF BASIL COTTLE

ACKNOWLEDGEMENTS

I am grateful to the Curators of the Bodleian Library and the Trustees of the British Library for permission to reproduce plates from the manuscripts in their care and for the opportunity to work in their libraries; similarly to the librarians of Trinity College, Cambridge, the Society of Antiquaries of London, Princeton University Library, and the Northamptonshire Record Office for permission to examine the manuscripts of *Sidrak* in their keeping and for the courtesy with which invariably I was treated. For help in locating the Brudenell fragment I am indebted to Sir Gyles Isham, Mrs Marian Brudenell, and Mr P. I. King; and for similar help in tracing the Robert H. Taylor manuscript I owe thanks to Mr P. N. Poole-Wilson, Ms Nancy N. Coffin, and Mr Robert H. Taylor.

Work on this edition, which has continued intermittently over many years, has been aided by generous grants towards research assistance from the Australian Research Council (formerly the Australian Research Grants Committee) and the University of Adelaide. The major part of the work has been carried out during periods of study leave from the University of Adelaide, during which I have enjoyed the hospitality of the Department of English Language and Medieval Literature at the University of Lancaster (1979–80), the English Faculty Library, Oxford (1984–85), the Huntington Library, San Marino (1989), and the Pontifical Institute of Mediaeval Studies, Toronto (1996). The enormous labour of typing the text and variants was shared initially by Joan Alvaro and Elaine Gregory; Jeanette Candlett took over after the first hundred-odd pages and completed the task with admirable cheer.

John Scattergood drew my attention many years ago to the need for a critical edition of *Sidrak*, and gave me invaluable advice on editorial procedure, along with much encouragement; he and the late Elizabeth Salter (examiners of my doctoral dissertation) both made helpful suggestions for improving my original edition of the Lansdowne manuscript. Pamela Gradon, Malcolm Godden, and Helen Spencer, for the Early English Text Society, have given careful thought to the many questions with which I have plied them, and I hope I have had the wit to benefit from their advice. Bernadette Masters made a detailed comparison between the English translations and the French original; her observations form the basis of many of my notes in the commentary. Robin Eaden collected marked words for the glossary (before word-processors simplified this laborious task) and made thoughtful suggestions for defining them. Sabina Flanagan collected the data from which were constructed the Linguistic Profiles reproduced in appendix 1. Frank Schaer checked the complete text of the two base manuscripts against microfilms of the originals, and is in no way to blame if I have persisted in erroneous readings against his advice; he also read through drafts of the introduction, commentary, and glossary with extraordinary care, made innumerable suggestions for improvement, and wrote section 6(c) of the introduction, dealing with the construction of a stemma for the English rhymed versions. Christopher Bright contributed several items to the notes on questions 96–111, and read the proofs of the whole edition with his customary care: his alertness has saved me from many errors and inconsistencies. A handful of kind friends helped me with linguistic difficulties: Susan Crane and Judy King (Old French), Gareth Lewis (German), Eleonora Toffolo and Tiziana Buxton (Italian). To all these, to the many others who gave me help on specific points acknowledged at the appropriate place, and to those whose contributions I may inadvertently have overlooked, and whose pardon I crave, I offer thanks long overdue. For any errors that remain I must accept sole responsibility.

To Basil Cottle, whose enthusiasm first drew me towards Middle English studies and who supervised my earlier edition of MS Lansdowne 793 (undertaken as a doctoral dissertation at the University of Bristol), but who did not live to see the publication of this edition, my debt is but faintly reflected in the dedication of this volume. For the unfailing support of my wife, Jill, who (in the days long before she became Director of the Centre for Applied Linguistics at the University of South Australia) herself typed the complete edition of the Lansdowne manuscript from which the present edition grew (and that on a manual typewriter) and who has encouraged me at every turn, and for the tolerance of our daughters, Rebecca and Sarah, for whom life without *Sidrak*—which they have never known—must have seemed at times a condition fervently to be wished, I know no inexpressibility topos sufficient to suggest my gratitude.

CONTENTS

VOLUME I

VOLUME II

PLATES

ABBREVIATIONS AND SHORT TITLES

1. SIGLA FOR MANUSCRIPTS AND PRINTED EDITIONS
(in English unless otherwise stated)

A   Society of Antiquaries of London 252
B   Laud Misc. 559, Bodleian Library
D   Brudenell (Deene) I.v.101, Northamptonshire Record Office
F   fr. 1160, Bibliothèque Nationale, Paris (French)
F2   fr. 24395, Bibliothèque Nationale, Paris (French)
F3   MS 11110, Bibliothèque Royale Albert Ier, Brussels (French)
G   Printed edition of Thomas Godfray
H   Harley 4294, British Library
L   Lansdowne 793, British Library
P   Taylor Medieval MS no. 3, Princeton University Library (olim Wrest Park MS 5; olim Meyerstein)
S   Sloane 2232, British Library
T   Trinity College, Cambridge, O.5.6
V   Printed edition of Anthoine Verard (French)

2. MANUSCRIPTS OF THE FRENCH *SIDRAC* CONSULTED IN THE PREPARATION OF THIS EDITION

Boston: Public Library, q. Med. 31 (G.31.60)
Brussels: Bibliothèque Royale Albert Ier
     11106
     11110 [= F3]
     11113
Cambridge: University Library, Gg.i.1 (54)
Copenhagen: Royal Library, Ny kgl. Saml. 2919
Dublin: Trinity College, B.5.1 (209)
Florence: Bibliotecca Medicea Laurenziana, Ashburnham 118
Florence: Bibliotecca Riccardiana, Ricc. 2758
London: British Library
     Add. 16563
     Add. 17914
     Egerton 751
     Harley 1121

Harley 4361
Harley 4417
Harley 4486
Royal 16 F.v
London: Lambeth Palace Library, 298
Lyon: Bibliothèque de la ville de Lyon, 948
Marseille: Ville de Marseille, Bibliothèque Municipale, 733
Montpellier: Bibliothèque Interuniversitaire de Montpellier, Section Médecine, 149
New Haven: Yale University, Beinecke Rare Book and Manuscript Library, Marston 260
Oxford: Bodleian Library
    Bodley 461 (*formerly* 2451)
    e Museo 34
Oxford: Corpus Christi College, 293A
Paris: Bibliothèque de l'Arsenal, 2320
Paris: Bibliothèque Nationale
    fr. 762
    fr. 1094
    fr. 1156
    fr. 1157
    fr. 1158
    fr. 1159
    fr. 1160 (= F)
    fr. 1161
    fr. 19816
    fr. 24395 (= F2)
    n.a.fr. 934 (fragment, f. 22)
    n.a.fr. 5237 (fragment, ff. 21–4)
    n.a.fr. 10063
    n.a.fr. 10231
    n.a.fr. 12444
Paris: Bibliothèque Sainte-Geneviève, 2202
Philadelphia: Library of the University of Pennsylvania, Rare Book Collection, Fr. 23
Rennes: Bibliothèque Municipale, 2435 (*formerly* 593)
Rome: Vatican Library
    Reg. Lat. 1141
    Reg. Lat. 1255
    Vat. Lat. 4793
    Vat. Lat. 5272

3. PUBLISHED WORKS CONSULTED IN THE PREPARATION OF THIS EDITION

This list contains (i) works devoted entirely to *Sidrac*; (ii) works cited more than once and referred to by author's name or short title. Details of other works consulted are given in full at the point of citation.

AE	*Adrian and Epictetus*, in Suchier: AE, q.v.
AR	*Adrian and Ritheus*, in Cross and Hill, q.v.
Arngart	*The Proverbs of Alfred*, ed. O. S. A. Arngart, 2 vols. (Lund, 1942, 1955)
Atkins	*The Owl and the Nightingale*, ed. J. W. H. Atkins (Cambridge, 1922)
AV	The Authorized [King James] Version of the Bible
Bartholomew	*On the Properties of Things: John Trevisa's Translation of* Bartholomaeus Anglicus De Proprietatibus Rerum: *A Critical Text*, ed. M. C. Seymour et al., 3 vols. (Oxford, 1975–88)
Bartoli	*Il Libro di Sidrach: testo inedito del secolo XIV*, ed. A. Bartoli (Bologna, 1863)
Beckers	Hartmut Beckers, 'Bruchstücke unbekannter Sidrach-Handschriften aus Münster, Düsseldorf und Brüssel', *Amsterdamer Beiträge zur älteren Germanistik*, 1 (1972), 89–110
Bosworth-Toller	*An Anglo-Saxon Dictionary Based on the Manuscript Collections of the Late Joseph Bosworth*, ed. and enlarged by T. Northcote Toller (London, 1898)

Burton [T. L. Burton]

'Additions'	'Fifteenth- and Sixteenth-Century Antedatings, Postdatings And Additions to O.E.D., M.E.D. and D.O.S.T. from "Sidrak and Bokkus"', *Notes and Queries*, 218 (1973), 369–75
'Crocodile'	'The Crocodile as the Symbol of an Evil Woman: a Medieval Interpretation of the Crocodile–Trochilus Relationship', *Parergon*, 20 (1978), 25–33
'*Daftness*'	'Defining *Daftness*', in *Medieval Literature and Antiquities: Studies in Honour of Basil Cottle*, ed. Myra Stokes and T. L. Burton (Cambridge, 1987), pp. 165–74

'Discoveries'   'Lexicographical Discoveries in the English
                      Sidrak', *Parergon*, NS 5 (1987), 71–93
'Drudgery'   'Drudgery, Bludgery, and Fudgery: Lexicography
                      for Editors of Middle English Texts', in *Lexico-
                      graphical and Linguistic Studies: Essays in Honour
                      of G. W. Turner*, ed. T. L. Burton and Jill Burton
                      (Cambridge, 1988), 19–30
'Hapax Legomena'   'Some Fifteenth-Century Hapax Legomena', *Die
                      Sprache*, 33 (1987), 112–13
'Idioms'   'Some Unnoticed ME Idioms Involving Chiefly
                      Reason and *Skill*, *Showing* and *Telling*', *English
                      Studies*, 68 (1987), 122–8
'Lansdowne'   '*Sidrak and Bokkus*: A Diplomatic Transcript of
                      MS. Lansdowne 793 (British Museum) with an
                      Introduction, Glossary and Notes (including sig-
                      nificant variants from the other English manu-
                      scripts).' 2 vols. Diss., University of Bristol, 1976
'Proverbs'   'Proverbs, Sentences, and Proverbial Phrases
                      from the English *Sidrak*', *Mediaeval Studies*, 51
                      (1989), 329–54
'Reproduction'   'Sidrak on Reproduction and Sexual Love',
                      Medical History, 19 (1975), 286–302
Words   *Words, Words, Words*, with illustrations by
                      Michael Atchison (Adelaide, 1995)
Bülbring   Karl D. Bülbring, 'Sidrac in England,' *Beiträge
                      zur Romanischen und Englischen Philologie* (1902),
                      443–78
Carmody   Francis J. Carmody, 'Brunetto Latini's *Tresor*:
                      Latin Sources on Natural Science', *Speculum*,
                      12 (1937), 359–66
Caxton's *Mirror*   *Caxton's Mirror of the World*, ed. Oliver H.
                      Prior, EETS ES 110 (London, 1913 *for* 1912)
Chancery Anthology *An Anthology of Chancery English*, ed. John H.
                      Fisher, Malcolm Richardson, and Jane Law
                      Fisher (Knoxville, 1984)
Collison   R. L. Collison, *Encyclopaedias: Their History
                      Throughout the Ages*, 2nd edn. (New York, 1966)
Coluccia   Rosario Coluccia, 'Confluenza di tradizioni scrit-
                      torie nel "Libro di Sidrac" salentino.' *XIV
                      congresso internazionale di linguistica e filologia*

	romanza, Napoli, 15–20 aprile 1974, Atti, ed. Alberto Varvari, iv (Naples and Amsterdam, [1977]), 605–17
Corser	Thomas Corser, *Collectanea Anglo-Poetica*, Part ii, Publications of the Chetham Society, 55 (Manchester, 1867)
Coxe	H. O. Coxe, *Catalogi Codicum Manuscriptorum Bibliothecae Bodleianae*, ii, fasc. 1 (Oxford, 1858)
Cross and Hill	*The Prose Solomon and Saturn and Adrian and Ritheus*, ed. James E. Cross and Thomas D. Hill, McMaster Old English Studies and Texts 1 (Toronto, 1982)
CT	*The Canterbury Tales*, in *The Riverside Chaucer*, q.v.
De imagine mundi	Honorius Augustodunensis, *De imagine mundi*, PL 172
De philosophia mundi	William of Conches, *De philosophia mundi*, PL 172
De rebus	*De rebus in oriente mirabilis* (Latin text of *Wonders of the East*, in Rypins, q.v., pp. 101–7)
DNB	*Dictionary of National Biography*, vols. 57 and 58, ed. Sidney Lee (London, 1899)
DOST	*A Dictionary of the Older Scottish Tongue from the Twelfth Century to the End of the Seventeenth*, ed. William A. Craigie and A. J. Aitken (Chicago, 1937–)
EDD	*The English Dialect Dictionary*, ed. Joseph Wright (London, 1898–1905)
Epistola Alexandri	Latin Text of the *Letter of Alexander the Great to Aristotle*, in Rypins, q.v., pp. 79–100
Elucidarium	The *Elucidarium* of Honorius Augustodunensis, in Yves Lefèvre, *L'Elucidarium et les lucidaires*, Bibliothèque des écoles françaises d'Athènes et de Rome, 180 (Paris, 1954) [also printed in PL 172]
Godefroy	Frédéric Godefroy, *Dictionnaire de l'ancienne langue française* (Paris, 1881)
Greimas	A. J. Greimas, *Dictionnaire de l'ancien français jusqu'au milieu du XIVe siècle*, 2nd edn. (Paris, 1968)

Hamelius   *Mandeville's Travels, Translated from the French of Jean d'Outremeuse. Edited from MS. Cotton Titus C. xvi in the British Museum*, by P. Hamelius, i, *Text*, EETS 153 (London, 1919 *for* 1916), ii, *Introduction and Notes*, EETS 154 (London, 1923 *for* 1916)

Hamilton   George L. Hamilton, review of 1st edn. of Langlois, q.v., in the *Romanic Review*, 3 (1912), 316–19

Haskins   Charles Homer Haskins, *Studies in the History of Mediaeval Science* (Cambridge, Mass., 1924)

Hastings   *Dictionary of the Bible*, ed. James Hastings (Edinburgh, 1909)

HLF   *Histoire Littéraire de la France*

Holler [William M. Holler]

  'Lapidary'   '*The Lapidary of Sydrac*: New Evidence on the Origin of the *Lapidaire Chrétien*', *Manuscripta*, 30 (1986), 181–90

  'Livre'   'Le Livre de Sydrac, Fontaine de Toutes Sciences, Folios 57–112', Diss., University of North Carolina, 1972 [an edition of the second half of BN MS fr. 1160]

  'Ordinary Man'   'The Ordinary Man's Concept of Nature as Reflected in the Thirteenth-Century French *Book of Sydrac*', *French Review*, 48 (1975), 526–38

  'Stone Lore'   'Unusual Stone Lore in the Thirteenth-Century *Lapidary of Sydrac*', *Romance Notes*, 20 (1979), 135–42

HRB   *The Historia Regum Britannie of Geoffrey of Monmouth, I: Bern, Burgerbibliothek, MS. 568*, ed. Neil Wright (Cambridge, 1985)

Index   Carleton Brown and Rossell Hope Robbins, *The Index of Middle English Verse* (New York, 1943)

Isidore

  De natura rerum   *De natura rerum*, in PL 83

  Etymologiae   *Etymologiarum libri xx*, in PL 82

James   M. R. James, *Catalogue of the Western Manuscripts in the Library of Trinity College, Cambridge*, iii, (Cambridge, 1902)

Kemble   John M. Kemble, *The Dialogue of Salomon and*

Saturnus with an Historical Introduction (London, 1848)

Ker   N. R. Ker, *Medieval Manuscripts in British Libraries*, i, *London* (Oxford, 1969)

Klibansky   Raymond Klibansky, Erwin Panofsky, and Fritz Saxl, *Saturn and Melancholy* (London, 1964)

Knudsen   *Sydrak. Efter haandskriftet Ny kgl. saml. 236*, ed. Gunnar Knudsen (Copenhagen, 1921)

LALME   Angus McIntosh, M. L. Samuels and Michael Benskin, *A Linguistic Atlas of Late Mediaeval English*, 4 vols. (Aberdeen, 1986)

Langlois   Charles-Victor. Langlois, *La Vie en France au moyen âge du XIIe au milieu du XIVe siècle*, iii, *La Connaissance de la nature et du monde*, revised edn. (Paris, 1927)

Latini   *Li Livres dou tresor de Brunetto Latini*, ed. Francis J. Carmody (Berkeley, 1948)

MED   *Middle English Dictionary*, ed. Hans Kurath et al. (Ann Arbor, 1952–)

Minervini   Vincenzo Minervini, 'Schede sulla tradizione manoscritta del Livre de Sidrach', *Annali Istituto Universitario Orientale Napoli, Sezione Romanza*, 19 (1977), 539–70

MLA   Modern Language Association of America

MO   *The Maister of Oxenford*, in Kemble, q.v.

Neckam   *Alexandri Neckam De naturis rerum libri duo. With the Poem of the Same Author, De laudibus divinae sapientiae*, ed. Thomas Wright (London, 1863) [Rolls Series 34]

Nichols [Robert E. Nichols, Jr.]

     'Earth Sciences'   'Sidrak and Bokkus on the Atmospheric and Earth Sciences', *Centaurus*, 12 (1968), 215–32

     'Medical Lore'   'Medical Lore from *Sidrak and Bokkus*: A Miscellany in Middle English Verse,' *Journal of the History of Medicine and Allied Sciences*, 23 (1968), 167–72

     'Procreation'   'Procreation, Pregnancy, and Parturition: Extracts from a Middle English Metrical Encyclopedia,' *Medical History*, 11 (1967), 175–81

     '*Sidrak*'   '*Sidrak and Bokkus*, now first edited from manuscript Lansdowne 793', Diss., University of Washington, 1965

Norton-Smith and Pravda
The Quare of Jelusy: ed. from MS Bodley Arch. Seld. B. 24 by J. Norton-Smith and I. Pravda (Heidelberg, 1976)

Odoric
[The Travels of Friar Odoric of Pordenone] *Cathay and the Way Thither*, trans. and ed. Henry Yule, rev. Henri Cordier, ii, *Odoric of Pordenone*, Hakluyt Society, 2nd series, 33 (London, 1913)

OED
The Compact Edition of the Oxford English Dictionary: Complete Text Reproduced Micrographically (Oxford,1971)
Electronic edition: *The Oxford English Dictionary Second Edition on Compact Disc* (Oxford, 1994)

OE Dicts
R. S. Cox, 'The Old English Dicts of Cato', *Anglia*, 90 (1972), 1–42

PL
Patrologiae Cursus Completus . . . Series Latina, ed. J.-P. Migne (Paris, 1844–64)

Pliny, *Nat. Hist.*
Pliny, *Natural History with an English Translation*, by H. Rackham et al., 10 vols., Loeb Classical Library (London, 1938–63)

Prophecies
Les Prophecies de Merlin, ed. Lucy Allen Paton, 2 vols., MLA Monograph Series (New York, 1926–7)

Renan and Paris
Ernest Renan and Gaston Paris, 'La Fontaine de Toutes Sciences du Philosophe Sidrach', *HLF*, 31 (Paris, 1893)

Riverside Chaucer
The Riverside Chaucer, 3rd edn., ed. Larry D. Benson, based on *The Works of Geoffrey Chaucer*, ed. F. N. Robinson (Boston, 1987)

Robinson
The Works of Geoffrey Chaucer, ed. F. N. Robinson, 2nd edn. (London, 1957)

Rypins
Three Old English Prose Texts in MS. Cotton Vitellius A xv, ed. Stanley Rypins, EETS 161 (London, 1924 *for* 1921)

Sarton
George Sarton, *Introduction to the History of Science* (Carnegie Institute, Washington), vols i and ii (1927–31)

Secreta
Three Prose Versions of the Secreta Secretorum, ed.

Robert Steele, with a glossary by T. Henderson, i, EETS ES 74 (London, 1898)

Segre   Cesare Segre, 'Su una fonte e sulla data del "Sidrac"', pp. 257–66 of 'Accopiamenti (forse) giudiosi,' in *Linguistica e filologia: Omaggio a Benvenuto Terracini*, ed. Cesare Segre (Milan, 1968), pp. 257–78

Sgrilli, *edizione*   *Il 'Libro de Sidrac' salentino: edizione, spoglio linguistico e lessico*, ed. Paola Sgrilli, Biblioteca degli studi mediolatini e volgari, NS 7 (Pisa, *c.* 1983) [not seen]

Sgrilli, 'Preliminari'   Paola Sgrilli, 'Preliminari all'edizione del Sidrac salentino', *Studi mediolatini e volgari*, 25 (1977), 171–200

SS   *Solomon and Saturn*, in Cross and Hill, q.v.

Steinberg   S. H. Steinberg, 'Encyclopaedias,' *Signature*, NS 12 (1951), 3–22

Steiner   Sylvie-Marie Steiner, *Le Livre de Sidrach: un témoinage de la diffusion enyclopédique au XIIIe siècle: édition critique d'après les manuscrits de Paris et de Rome* (Melun, 1994) [not seen]

Steinschneider   M. Steinschneider, 'Il Libro di Sidrach', *Il Buonarroti*, 2nd ser., 7 (Luglio, 1872), 240–1

Suchier: AE   *Das mittellateinische Gespräch Adrian und Epictitus nebst verwandten Texten (Joca Monachorum)*, ed. Walther Suchier (Tübingen, 1955)

Supplement   Rossell Hope Robbins and John L. Cutler, *Supplement to The Index of Middle English Verse* (Lexington, 1965)

Thouvenin   Georges Thouvenin, 'Note sur le *Sidrach*', *Romania*, 60 (1934), 242–9

Treanor   'Le Roman de Sidrac: Fontaine de Toutes Sciences', ed. S. Treanor, Diss., University of North Carolina, 1939 [an edition of the first half of BN MS fr. 1160]

Utley   Francis Lee Utley, 'Dialogues, Debates, and Catechisms', in *A Manual of the Writings in Middle English 1050–1500*, iii, ed. Albert E. Hartung (New Haven, 1972), Commentary 669–745, Bibliography 829–902 van Cleve Thomas Curtis van Cleve, *The Emperor Frederick II of Hohenstaufen: Immutator Mundi* (Oxford, 1972)

van Tol Johannes Fredericus Josephus van Tol, *Het Boek van Sidrak in de Nederlanden* (Amsterdam, 1936)

Vincent of Beauvais Vincentius Bellovacensis, *Speculum quadruplex sive speculum maius: naturale/ doctrinale/ morale/ historiale* (Douai, 1624; repr. Graz, 1964)

Vulgate *Biblia Sacra iuxta Vulgatam Versionem*, ed. Robertus Weber, 4th edn., rev. Roger Gryson (Stuttgart, 1994)

Ward H. L. D. Ward, *Catalogue of Romances in the Department of Manuscripts in the British Museum*, i (London, 1883)

Warner *The Buke of John Maundeuill: Being the Travels of Sir John Mandeville, Knight, 1322–1356: A Hitherto Unpublished Version from the Unique Copy (Egerton MS. 1982) in the British Museum*, ed. George F. Warner (Westminster, for The Roxburghe Club, 1889)

Warton Thomas Warton, *The History of English Poetry from the twelfth to the close of the sixteenth century*, ed. W. Carew Hazlitt (London, 1871)

Wells J. M. Wells, *The Circle of Knowledge: Encyclopaedias Past and Present* (Chicago, 1968)

White T. H. White, *The Book of Beasts* (London, 1954)

Whiting Bartlett Jere Whiting, with the assistance of Helen Wescott Whiting, *Proverbs, Sentences and Proverbial Phrases from English Writings Mainly before 1500* (Cambridge, Mass., 1968)

Wilson *Sawles Warde*, ed. R. M. Wilson, Leeds School of English Language Texts and Monographs 3 (Leeds, 1938)

Wyntoun *The Original Chronicle of Andrew of Wyntoun*, ed. F. J. Amours, iv, Scottish Text Society, 54 (Edinburgh, 1906) [C = MS Cotton Nero D.xi; W = Wemyss MS]

INTRODUCTION

1. THE AIM OF THIS EDITION

Sidrak and Bokkus is a Middle English verse adaptation of an Old French prose book of knowledge, cast in question-and-answer form, enclosed within a framing adventure story. Its astonishing contemporary popularity is shown by the number and distribution of surviving manuscripts (several dozen in French; seven in English, excluding fragments; others in Italian, Danish, and Dutch—see section 3 below, pp. xxxii–xxxiii); and the subtitle found in many of the French versions, 'La fontaine de toutes sciences', bears witness to its alleged authority. In spite of the work's obvious importance in the history of European thought, as an index of popular attitudes and beliefs in the Middle Ages (it covers just about everything from the visibility of the Deity and the power of devils to the cause of leprosy and the copulation of dogs—questions 2, 7, 65, 102), there is no published critical edition of the French original or of the English translation.

This edition sets out to fill the second of these gaps. Its purpose is to present full texts, in parallel, of the only two complete manuscripts of the Middle English poem, both from the second half of the fifteenth century: Bodleian MS Laud Misc. 559 (B), the shorter version, on the left-hand pages; British Library MS Lansdowne 793 (L), the longer version, on the right. The text is presented with textual notes and significant variants at the foot of the page, so that all the important textual information is directly before the eye; the remaining critical material will be found in the commentary, glossary, or appendices.

The decision to present the two versions in parallel texts has been made because this is the clearest and most convenient way to indicate the differences between the two schools of English manuscripts. It would have been possible, of course, to print a base text from only one manuscript, and to record variants from all the other witnesses against this single text. Such a method, however, although more economical in space, would have had two serious disadvantages: (1) it would have grouped together two distinct sorts of variant—those from manuscripts of the same school as the base text (generally minor differences in wording) and those from manuscripts of the opposite school (not infrequently indicating a different line of thought)—thus obscuring the differences between them; (2) it would have made reconstruction of the text of manuscripts from the opposite school a laborious and time-consuming business.

2. THE ORIGINS OF *SIDRAC*

Most of the French versions of *Sidrac*, from one of which the English *Sidrak* was translated, have two preliminary chapters. (For convenience I use the form *Sidrac* as a brief title for the work in any language, *Sidrak* or *Sidrak and Bokkus* specifically for the English versions.) The first of these chapters (hereafter called 'the Preface') purports to give a true history of the composition and transmission of the work; the second (hereafter 'the Prologue') gives a detailed account of the conversion of Boctus by Sidrac. Only the second is found in the English versions. The claims made in the Preface are summarized below.

Eight hundred and forty-seven years after the death of Noah, Sidrac, a descendant of Japhet, was born, and received from God knowledge of all things, past and future. Sidrac converted a heathen king, Boctus, by showing him a vision of the Trinity. Boctus plied Sidrac with innumerable questions, corporeal, spiritual, and scientific, and was so pleased with the answers that he had them recorded in a book. After the death of Boctus this book came into the possession of an eminent Chaldaean, who, prompted by the devil, attempted to burn it; however, God did not allow it to be lost in this way. After a long time it came into the possession of a king called Madyan. From him it passed to Naaman, commander of the King of Syria's cavalry, who cured his leprosy by bathing in the River Jordan [2 Kgs. 5]. There follows a blank period in its history, no more being heard of it till after the birth of Christ, but God did not wish that it should be entirely lost. Its next known owner was a Greek, an archbishop of 'Sabaste', called 'Ayouasilio'.[1] The archbishop had a clerk called 'Demytre' whom he sent to Spain to preach the faith, and who took the book with him. Demytre was subsequently martyred at Toledo. The book remained at Toledo, where it was found long afterwards (after the coming of the Church) and translated from Greek into Latin. The then King of Spain, hearing of the book, sent for it, read it, and set great store by it. 'Emyr elmomenym',[2] the Lord of Tunis, heard his messengers speaking of the book, and sent to ask the King of

---

[1] 'Probably St. Basil of Caesarea, whose younger brother Peter was Bishop of Sebaste in Armenia' (Ward, p. 903). Langlois makes the same identification, adding that the name, in Greek, means 'the holy king' (p. 218).

[2] 'i.e., Prince of the Faithful; but here used as a proper name' (Ward, p. 904); similarly Langlois, p. 218.

Spain for it. The latter had it translated from Latin into Arabic and sent the translation. Long afterwards, in the time of the Emperor Frederick II, some messengers visited the Lord of Tunis of the time, and found out that the source of his learning was a book [*Sidrac*] which had been sent to his ancestors by the King of Spain. Frederick, being greatly desirous to see the book, sent to the Lord of Tunis, asking him to send it to him; the latter, in return, asked the Emperor to send him a scholar who knew Latin and Arabic. A Brother Rogiers was duly sent, who translated the book back from Arabic into Latin, and returned to the Emperor, bringing his translation. There was, in the Emperor's court, a man called 'Todre le phylosophe', who bribed the Emperor's chamberlain to take a copy of it for him, so that he could study it secretly. After a while Todre sent his copy as a present to Albert, Patriarch of Antioch, who made use of it throughout his life. The Patriarch had a clerk called 'Johan Pieres de Lyons', who copied the work and took it back, once again, to the university of Toledo.[3] The Preface (in which this information is recorded) and the 'argument' (a brief summary of the subject matter of the questions) were written in the year 1243 (presumably in Toledo), by several scholars who considered the work spiritually profitable.

Several persons mentioned towards the end of this Preface are known historical figures, and are spoken of in an appropriate context: Frederick II, famed (amongst other things) for his intellectual curiosity and for 'the brilliant and precocious culture of his Sicilian kingdom', was Holy Roman Emperor from 1220 to 1250, and was known to maintain a correspondence with Muslim rulers and sages on philosophical matters;[4] Frederick's Arabic secretary, astrologer and confectioner, Theodore of Antioch, referred to in his letters as 'Theodorus philosophus noster', is presumably the 'Todre le phylosophe' who, according to the Preface, was well loved by the Emperor, and who obtained a copy of *Sidrac* by bribing the Emperor's chamberlain;[5] Albert, Patriarch of Antioch, to whom 'Todre' is said to have sent this copy as a gift, was indeed Patriarch of Antioch from 1226 to 1246 (having formerly been the Ghibelline Bishop of Brescia), and was present at the ecumenical council of Lyons in 1245;[6] moreover, the university of Toledo is known

---

[3] It appears to have been here that *Sidrac* was first (supposedly) translated from Latin into French; however, 'Ce passage est trouble dans tous les manuscrits' (Langlois, p. 219, n. 1).

[4] Renan and Paris, p. 289; Langlois, p. 203; Haskins, pp. 242–71; van Cleve, pp. 299–318. The comment on Sicilian culture under Frederick is from Haskins, p. 242.

[5] J. L. A. Huillard-Bréholles, *Historia diplomatica Friderici secundi*, i, *Préface et Introduction* (Paris, 1859), DXXIX–DXXXI; Ward, p. 905; Renan and Paris, p. 290; Langlois, pp. 203–4; Haskins, pp. 246–8; van Cleve, p. 310.

[6] Ward, p. 904; Renan and Paris, p. 290; Langlois, p. 204.

to have played a large part in the transmission of oriental works to the west.[7] However, a number of details combine to show that these persons are introduced merely as a name-dropping exercise, to lend an air of authenticity to a spurious history.[8] (1) It is impossible that *Sidrac* was composed as early as 1243, since it has been shown that it is indebted to Gossuin's *Image du monde* (see p. xlii below), which is known to have been written in 1246.[9] (2) It is unlikely that *Sidrac* was composed before the third quarter or perhaps even the end of the thirteenth century, since there is an apparent allusion (in a passage not found in the English *Sidrak*) to the subjugation of Antioch by Baybars in 1268;[10] since there is a possible allusion (likewise not found in the English *Sidrak*) to the fall of Saint-Jean d'Acre in 1291;[11] and since the earliest known manuscripts of *Sidrac* date from the beginning of the fourteenth century.[12] (3) No Hebrew, Greek, Latin or Arabic versions, such as are mentioned in the Preface, have ever been found, and there is no reason to suppose that *Sidrac* was not composed originally in French (although there has been some debate as to the dialect in which it was first written).[13] (4) Prefaces of this nature, some of them obviously fictitious, were not uncommon in the Middle Ages, and some of these, like that in *Sidrac*, make illicit use of the names of Frederick II and Theodore.[14] (5) Whatever the identity of the author, it is clear, from an examination of the sources he used (see p. lii below), that he had access

---

[7] Renan and Paris, p. 289; Langlois, p. 203; van Cleve, pp. 311–12.

[8] These brief comments are much indebted to Langlois's examination of the preface (pp. 198–213). He examines in detail, and rejects, several theories by previous writers as to the authorship and date of composition of *Sidrac*; I reproduce only his conclusions.

[9] Langlois, p. 211; Hamilton, p. 317.

[10] 'Il serait bien étrange, en particulier, que le sage Sidrac eût prédit si clairement la subversion d'Antioche par l'émir des Sarrasins du Caire si celui qui le fait parler n'avait rien su du sort que Bibars fit subir à cette ville le 19 mai 1268' (Langlois, pp. 212–13). Here Langlois disagrees with Renan and Paris, who feel there are no signs in *Sidrac* to show that, when it was written, Baybars had begun 'la série de ses foudroyants succès' (p. 311).

[11] Langlois, pp. 213, 273. The post-1291 dating is supported by Segre: see p. l below.

[12] Renan and Paris, p. 291; Langlois, p. 211.

[13] Renan and Paris (pp. 314–16) take the Provençal version of MS fr. 1158 as being, perhaps, the original; Langlois replies that several of the oldest manuscripts, particularly MS fr. 1160, contain 'des formes particulières à la langue qui était en usage au XIIIᵉ siècle dans les colonies franques de l'Orient latin' (p. 208). He goes on to argue, from internal evidence, that the author probably lived at one time in the Latin East.

[14] Works listed by Langlois (pp. 206–7) with prefaces naming Frederick and/or Theodore include the *Prophécies de Merlin* (see pp. xlviii–xlix below); two treatises on falconry, one in Arabic by 'Moamyn', one in Persian by 'mestre Tariph de Perse'; the *Regime du corps* of 'Maistre Alebrand' the Lombard; and the *Livre des neufs anciens juges de astrologie, especiaument quant as interrogations*.

to a collection of medieval religious, romantic, astronomical, geograph-
ical, and scientific works such as were kept in the libraries of religious
communities or of noblemen, and are sometimes found bound together
in one composite volume.[15] There is, therefore, no alternative but to
acknowledge the 'worthlessness as evidence' of the Preface of *Sidrac*,[16]
although it is not yet possible to indicate with certainty either the
identity of the author, or the exact time at which he wrote.

3. GENRE, POPULARITY, INFLUENCE, REPUTATION

(A) THE NARRATIVE FRAMEWORK; CLASSIFICATIONS OF THE WORK AS A WHOLE

What sort of a work is *Sidrac*? The Prologue gives the impression that
we are dealing with a religious romance or saint's legend: we have a
reputedly famous king as one of the chief characters; a hero, motivated
by religious faith, emerging triumphant in the face of incredible odds;
and an abundance of marvellous happenings treated with the utmost
baldness. It is with some surprise that readers of the English *Sidrak*, not
(as in the French versions) forewarned by a Preface, come upon the
questions that Bokkus puts to Sidrak, and find that they have been
deceived: this is no saint's legend but a collection of information and
dogma, cast in the form of question and answer, on theology, science,
morals and a variety of other subjects, enclosed in a narrative framework. A reading of the whole work makes it clear that the author's main
purpose is to inculcate the doctrine contained in the dialogue between
Sidrak and Bokkus; the romantic narrative serves only to whet the
reader's appetite at the outset and to give authority to the pronounce-
ments of Sidrak, which form the body of the work.

The generic mixture found in *Sidrac* has given rise to various different
classifications, the emphasis being placed sometimes on the narrative
framework, sometimes on the question-and-answer format, and sometimes on the breadth of subject matter of the main part of the work. These
different emphases are reflected in three corresponding modes of classification: (1) romance or history, (2) dialogue or catechism, (3) encyclopaedia or book of knowledge or philosophy; the classifications are modified not
infrequently by the addition of explanatory comments. The title *Sidrach le*

[15] Langlois, p. 214; Hamilton, p. 319.   [16] Hamilton, p. 317.

grant philosophe in some of the French printed editions (for example, those of Gaultier and Trepperel–Jehannot (see p. xxxii below), and cf. *Sydrac the Philosopher* in Trinity Coll. Camb. MS. O.5.6) and the common French subtitle *La fontaine de toutes sciences* indicate the early regard for *Sidrac* as a book of knowledge; and whereas in the English printed edition of Thomas Godfray the work is styled 'The *history* of kyng Boccus/ & Sydracke' (my italics), the writer of the prefatory comment has added that 'it may well be called a boke of philosofye/ that is to say a stody of wysdome' (see p. lxx below). Ward classes it with his 'allegorical and didactic romances' but describes it as 'a catechism of medieval science' (p. 903). Warton, evidently uneasy with the designation 'romance', calls it 'rather a romance of Arabian philosophy than of chivalry' (ii, 144). In *The Index of Middle English Verse* (entry 217) it is a 'didactic romance', a description altered in the *Supplement* to 'the didactic dialogue on morals and doctrines.' Nichols calls the English variously a 'metrical encyclopedia' or 'medieval romance and book of knowledge' and a 'miscellany in Middle English verse.'[17] Utley, in his revision of the original chapter IX in Wells's *A Manual of the Writings in Middle English* (where *Sidrak* was not mentioned), classes it amongst his 'catechisms on science and Biblical lore' and goes on to describe it as 'a comprehensive medieval encyclopedia . . . in dialogue form' (p. 745). It is evident that traditional methods of classification cannot deal with a mixed work such as *Sidrac*, since they inevitably draw attention to one aspect at the expense of the others; the work cannot be adequately categorized without the aid of comments explaining the relationship of the encyclopaedic body to the romantic framework and the consequent casting of the body of the work in dialogue form.

(B) THE DIALOGUE FORM

Dialogue as a literary form is of exceeding antiquity, as Utley points out with examples from Hindu, Sumerian, Egyptian, Akkadian, Greek, Latin, Hebrew, Old English, and Old French (p. 670). The use of dialogue as a vehicle for information and exposition (as in the body of *Sidrac*) belongs to a tradition descending, in the West, from Cicero. What we have here is not a Platonic dialogue in which a Socratic teacher 'draws out thought by suggestion and skilful questioning'[18] (cf., in the

---

[17] See 'Procreation', p. 175 (title and opening sentence); 'Medical Lore', p. 167 (title). Cf. the fuller description that follows in the opening paragraph of the latter: 'Ostensibly a romance . . . the work ultimately reveals itself as a compendious book of knowledge'. In '*Sidrak*' (p. xviii) Nichols records a number of other classifications not repeated here.

[18] See Elizabeth Merrill, *The Dialogue in English Literature*, Yale Studies in English, 42 (New York, 1911), 15.

Middle Ages, Boethius's *Consolation of Philosophy*); not a wit-contest or riddling match such as is found in the second (or second part) of the OE poetic dialogues of *Solomon and Saturn*;[19] not a discussion, dispute, or debate, such as the ME disputes of *The Owl and the Nightingale* and *The Thrush and the Nightingale* (there are reports of such debates between Sidrak and various of Bokkus's followers in the Prologue, 405/443 ff. and 703/761 ff., but their content is not recorded): we have here rather an expository or didactic dialogue in which one participant asks for, and the other supplies, information. This type of dialogue, or catechism, is distinguished from other kinds, as Utley remarks (p. 736), by a lack of conflict between the participants: one is cast as pupil, one as teacher; the pupil accepts the teacher's answer without argument and proceeds to the next question.

The popularity of such instructional dialogues in the Middle Ages is evidenced by the large number of them surviving, in manuscripts and printed editions, in a multiplicity of languages.[20] Here belong the various offshoots of the *Joca monachorum* tradition (Utley, p. 739), including in OE the *Prose Solomon and Saturn* and *Adrian and Ritheus* (see the recent edition of both these texts by Cross and Hill); in ME the *Questiones by-twene the Maister of Oxenford and his Clerk*, also known as *The Master of Oxford's Catechism* (a translation of the *Prose Solomon and Saturn*, published in Kemble's edition of the latter), *The Dialogue of Solomon and Marcolphus* (published in Antwerp in the late fifteenth century), and *The Demaundes Joyous* (published by Wynkyn de Worde in 1511); in Latin *Adrian and Epictetus* (see Suchier: AE), the Munich *Interrogationes*, the *Flores* of pseudo-Bede, and the *Dispute of Pippin and Albinus*; in German *Der Pfaffe Amis*. Other ME catechisms listed by Utley include *Ypotis*, an English version (of which fifteen manuscripts or fragments and a printed edition survive) of the story of *L'Enfant sage*;[21] various *elucidaria* derived (like much of *Sidrac*) from the

---

[19] Lines 179–506 in Dobbie's edition: *The Anglo-Saxon Minor Poems*, ed. Elliott Van Kirk Dobbie, The Anglo-Saxon Poetic Records, 6 (New York, 1942), 38–48.

[20] See Utley, 'Catechisms on science and Biblical lore' (pp. 736–45) and the bibliography to this section (pp. 894–902). For studies of the background and history of the various legends see also Kemble; L. W. Daly and W. Suchier, *Altercatio Hadriani Augusti et Epicteti Philosophi*, Illinois Studies in Language and Literature, 24, 1–2 (Urbana, 1939); *The Poetical Dialogues of Solomon and Saturn*, ed. R. J. Menner (New York, 1941); and Utley's 'The Prose *Salomon and Saturn* and the Tree called Chy', *Mediaeval Studies*, 19 (1957), 55–78.

[21] Over twenty versions of this dialogue, in several languages (including English), are collected in *L'Enfant sage (Das Gespräch des Kaisers Hadrian mit dem klugen Kinde Epitus)*, ed. Walther Suchier, Gesellschaft für romanische Literatur, 24 (Dresden, 1910).

Elucidarium (or *Elucidarius*) of Honorius Augustodunensis, 'a catechetical handbook written in, or shortly before, the year 1100, and in England',[22] and a few other pieces less well known. These works are all much shorter than *Sidrac*, but there are similarities: some of the questions are the same; the answers to these are sometimes the same or similar, sometimes completely different. A number of such correspondences and contrasts is pointed out in the commentary on the text. Medieval dialogues in French that may be compared with *Sidrac* include that of *Placides et Timeo* (considered by Renan and Paris to be greatly superior to *Sidrac*,[23] but resembling it in the lack of organization of the subject matter); and amongst several popular Latin dialogues, some of which were translated into French, Langlois mentions the 'Problems' of Aristotle, the *Questiones Naturales* of Adelard of Bath, the 'Commentaries' of Peter of Spain and the 'Questions' of Frederick II (p. 202).[24]

A common feature of such didactic dialogues is the gnomic or proverbial expression of some of the answers. Many such aphorisms in *Sidrak* are pointed out in the commentary to the text for the sake of comparison with sayings found in the better-known sapiential works in OE and early ME, such as the *Distichs of Cato*, the *Proverbs of Alfred* and the *Proverbs of Hending*, and with sayings from these and other works collected in Whiting's *Proverbs*.[25]

(C) THE ENCYCLOPAEDIC CONTENT

The Middle Ages saw the production of a remarkable number of works that endeavoured, in the ancient encyclopaedic tradition, to codify all knowledge in a manageable compendium.[26] Most of such works owed much, as regards organization or content or both, to Varro's

[22] Valerie I. J. Flint, 'The "Elucidarius" of Honorius Augustodunensis and Reform in Late Eleventh Century England', *Revue Bénédictine*, 85 (1975), 178–98, p. 179; see also Flint's 'The Chronology of the Works of Honorius Augustodunensis', *Revue Bénédictine*, 82 (1972), 215–42, pp. 219–20. On the names 'Augustodunensis', 'Inclusus', and 'Solitarius' by which Honorius is variously known see Eva Matthews Sanford, 'Honorius, Presbyter and Scholasticus', *Speculum*, 23 (1948), 397–425.

[23] 'Nous avons trouvé, dans Placide et Timeo, le germe d'un véritable esprit scientifique. Sidrach ne témoigne rien de semblable. La science que l'auteur y découpe avec minutie n'est que routine, tautologie, confusion. On voit bien ce qui pouvait sortir un jour de Timeo; rien assurément ne pouvait sortir de Sidrach' (p. 285).

[24] For a Latin text of Frederick's questions (many of which cover ground also treated in *Sidrac*) see Haskins, pp. 292–4; and, for an English translation, Haskins, pp. 266–7.

[25] The sententious matter in *Sidrak*, which includes many sayings not recorded in Whiting, is collected in Burton, 'Proverbs'.

[26] The brief account that follows draws on Collison, Sarton, Steinberg, Treanor, and Wells.

Disciplinarum libri IX and to Pliny's *Historia naturalis*, written in the first century BC and the first AD respectively. The Christian encyclopaedists reflected the attitudes of the early Church Fathers, particularly Augustine and Jerome, while still harking back to Pliny: 'The encyclopaedic literature of the Middle Ages has grown beyond Varro and Pliny only in that Christian theology was introduced as a fresh subject which directly and indirectly coloured every other topic. Otherwise Varro's formalistic arrangement according to the seven liberal arts remained the ground plan, and Pliny's notes the stock-in-trade of all subsequent encyclopaedias' (Steinberg, pp. 6–7). Capella's *Liber de nuptiis Mercurii et Philologiae*, one of the early (fifth-century) Christian encyclopaedias, was indebted to Pliny and Varro as well as to Solinus's *Collectanea rerum memorabilium* (or *Polyhistor*), of the third century, which was itself heavily dependent on Pliny. Cassiodorus, writing his *Institutiones divinarum et humanarum lectionum* in the sixth century, for the benefit of the Goths who now controlled Italy, made it clear that he wrote for 'the instruction of simple and unpolished brothers', not for the learned (Collison, p. 29). His Christian outlook is emphasized by his dealing with spiritual matters before the seven liberal arts. Isidore of Seville, in his *Etymologiae* of the following century (one of the most popular and influential encyclopaedias of the Middle Ages), returned to the system in which secular learning was treated before theology; but Hrabanus Maurus, Archbishop of Mainz, writing two hundred years later (in the mid ninth century), in his *De universo* (virtually a commentary on Isidore) restored theology to its place of prime importance as the first subject to be treated. After a period of comparative silence the twelfth and thirteenth centuries saw a resurgence in the compilation of encyclopaedias: Hugh of St Victor's *Didascalicon*, Lambert of St Omer's *Liber floridus*, Honorius's *De imagine mundi* and *Elucidarium* (see pp. xxviii above and xxxix–xli below), William of Conches's *De philosophia mundi* (see p. xlii below), Alexander Neckam's *De naturis rerum*, Abbess Herrad's magnificently illuminated *Hortus deliciarum*, Gervase of Tilbury's *Otia imperialia*, Alfonso X of Spain's *Grande e general estoria* (in Spanish), Bartholomew the Englishman's very popular *De proprietatibus rerum* (with its combination of systematic arrangement by subjects and alphabetical arrangement within some of the subjects—see pp. xxx–xxxii below), Thomas of Cantimpré's *De natura rerum*, Vincent of Beauvais's enormous *Speculum maius* (the last major encyclopaedia compiled specifically for religious communities), Gossuin's (or Gautier de

Metz's)[27] *Image du monde* (an adaptation of the *De imagine mundi*, written in French verse in 1246 and used by the author of *Sidrac*—see p. xlii below), and Brunetto Latini's *Li Livres dou tresor* (aimed at the secular audience of the Italian cultured classes—'what we should now call the "educated layman"' (Steinberg, p. 8)—, written in French, the language they used, and incorporating much material from Islamic and Arabic sources). This tradition culminates, in about 1315, in the anonymous *Compendium philosophiae*, which, with a return to the spirit of impartial enquiry of Aristotle, points the way to the modern scientific encyclopaedia.

It is to this tradition that the subtitle *La fontaine de toutes sciences* (as noted above) invites the reader to attach *Sidrac*. Specifically, as suggested in Treanor's tri-partite division of medieval scientific literature into (1) the writings of philosophers and technicians, (2) doctrinal books for clerics, and (3) translations and adaptations into the vernacular, aimed at the lay public, it is to the third of these classes that *Sidrac* belongs (pp. xi–xii). A few brief comparisons will suffice to show the differences in scope and organization between *Sidrac* and the encyclopaedias of Treanor's second class, of which Bartholomew's *De proprietatibus rerum* may be taken as a fair representative.

Angels are treated in several questions in the English *Sidrak*, as follows: questions 5, when they were created (the answer includes the pride and fall of Lucifer and his followers); 6, their functions (the answer details the nine orders and the function of each) ; 8, their shape and their knowledge; 141, those that receive the souls of the good into bliss; 158, how many God made, how many fell, how many were left in heaven; 232, whether they came from God's breath (with reasons why humans are superior) ; 269, the grief of guardian angels when people sin; 307, people's good and bad angels (partly repeated from 269); 308, their ability to don bodies of air in order to make themselves visible to humans. These questions are widely dispersed in the text; several of them have no connection with the questions on either side of them; there is some repetition in the answers. In Bartholomew, in contrast, the dogma concerning angels is all collected in one book (book ii), organized as follows: chapter 1, the etymology of the word for 'angel' in several languages; 2, the properties, abilities and understanding of angels in general; 3–5, symbols used to represent their properties and functions in words and painting; 6–18, the nine orders (divided into three hier-

---

[27] On the uncertainty concerning the author's name see Sarton, ii, 591 and Langlois, pp. 148–51.

archies), detailing the specific properties and functions of each hierarchy and each order; 19, evil angels, particularly Lucifer; 20, the properties of evil spirits in general.

Many questions in *Sidrak* deal with physiology and medicine (e.g., 30, 32–3, 59–60, 64–5, 75, 80, 85, 112, 170, 176, 185, 208–9, 217–18, 221–3, 228, 240–1, 247–51, 261, 265–6, 335, 367),[28] and whereas in Bartholomew these subjects are treated in two books set aside for that purpose (v and vii), in *Sidrak* they are, like those on angels, dispersed through the text, as indicated by the list above. The different quality of the answers may be gauged from a comparison between, for example, the sections in each concerning intestinal worms (*Sidrak*, Q. 251; Bartholomew, vii. 49): whereas *Sidrak* tells us only that worms in general are bred from and live off 'the mukke of the grettest metes/ That a man other woman etes' (B7541–2), Bartholomew describes in detail several different types of worm (according to the part of the intestine and the type of humour from which they are bred), their effect on the body, and methods of getting rid of them. The discussion of leprosy in each differs in the same sort of way. *Sidrak*, in two unconnected questions (65 and 112), tells us only (1) that women are the cause of the disease; (2) that it may be cured with a certain 'Oynemente of Philosofy' (B4024), which has a number of other equally astonishing properties. Bartholomew (vii. 64), with characteristic reference to named authorities, specifies four different types of the disease (elephantine, serpentine, vulpine and leonine); describes the signs and symptoms of leprosy in general and of each species in particular; discusses several possible causes (Sidrak's sole suggestion coming somewhat low on the list); admits that it is 'vnnethis curable but by Goddes *h*onde'; and offers a number of suggestions as to how it may, none the less, 'be somdel ihid and ilette, þat it distroye not so sone'. (Quotations from Bartholomew are taken from Trevisa's translation.)

The same difference in scope is observable in the treatment of most other subjects (cf., on the weather, the treatment of hail in *Sidrak*, Q. 122, and in Bartholomew, xi. 10). But the aims of the two works are, of course, different. It is not that the author of *Sidrac* sets out to tell us everything that is known about hail, and fails in the attempt, but that his intention is to reveal no more than 'whens and wherof' hail comes (4371–2/5335–6); the broader aim of Bartholomew is apparent from the more general nature of his chapter headings, 'De Grandine', 'De lepra',

---

[28] For further comments see Nichols, 'Procreation' and 'Medical Lore'; also Burton, 'Reproduction', pointing out several errors in the first of these articles and discussing more fully a number of other questions on the same general theme.

and so on. It is not the wording of the questions, but the grandness of the various subtitles given to *Sidrac*—which are not necessarily authorial—that leads present-day scholars to expect more from this work than the answers usually offer.

(D) POPULARITY AND INFLUENCE

It is evident, from the large number of manuscripts and printed editions surviving, in several languages, from the period of the twelfth to the sixteenth century, that *Sidrac* enjoyed enormous popularity in the late Middle Ages. The British Library alone has no fewer than eight complete French manuscripts, one Dutch manuscript, four different French printed editions, another printed edition in Italian, one in Danish and two in Dutch. The Dutch manuscript and seven of the French manuscripts are described by Ward (pp. 903–15); the eighth French manuscript and another fragment in French by Bülbring (pp. 445–7). The printed editions are listed under *Sydrach* in the *British Library General Catalogue of Printed Books*. The four French editions are those printed by Anthoine Verard (Paris, 1496?); Raulin Gaultier (Rouen, 1516); le veufve feu Jehan Trepperel et Jehan Jehannot (Paris, 1520? [Bülbring, p. 452, gives the date as 1528]); and Alain Lotrain et Denys Ianot (Paris, 1530? [a misprint in the BL *Catalogue* gives the name 'Ianot' as 'Tanot']). The first of the Dutch editions, printed by te Leyden (1495), is thought to be the earliest Dutch edition; the second is the modern edition edited by van Tol (Amsterdam, 1936), with the text taken from Bodley MS Marshall 28. The Danish edition, edited by Gunnar Knudsen, with the text from Hs. Ny kgl. Saml. 236, is also modern (Copenhagen, 1921). The Italian edition, *Il Libro di Sidrach*, was edited by A. Bartoli (Bologna, 1863).

Bülbring (pp. 447–55) notes the existence (in England and Ireland) of other French manuscripts in Lambeth Palace Library; the Bodleian Library (two); Corpus Christi College, Oxford; Cambridge University Library; Trinity College, Dublin; the Ashburnham Library (3); and several others mentioned in sale catalogues or catalogues of private collections, as well as four Italian manuscripts. In continental libraries there is a positive embarrassment of manuscripts of *Sidrac*, especially in French: 'Il a figuré dans toutes les bibliothèques princières du XIVe et XVe siècles. Il n'est guère de grande bibliothèque moderne qui n'en possède des manuscrits ou des incunables' (Langlois, p. 198). Langlois himself lists (pp. 215–17) about twenty examples of French manuscripts in Europe: of these Renan and Paris consider Bibliothèque Nationale

MS fr.1158 (written in Provençal) the earliest; Langlois himself believes MS fr. 1160 to be earlier. (The latter is the base text for the editions of Treanor and Holler, and that from which come most of the quotations in the commentary to the present edition). Langlois sorts these manuscripts into schools according to the number and grouping of the questions; his groupings are refined by Minervini, taking into account variants in the Prologue as well as the order and division of the questions. Further comment on these and other manuscripts is given in the introduction to Treanor's edition of MS fr. 1160. According to Holler, 'More than seventy manuscripts survive in French alone' ('Lapidary', p. 184, note 15), though not all of them are in European libraries. As for the printed editions, the earliest (published by Anthoine Verard) 'was republished in French at least six times before the middle of the sixteenth century' (Ward, p. 908).

I owe to Prof. John Scattergood the observation that copies of the French *Sidrac* were owned by important figures on the English political scene in the fourteenth and fifteenth centuries, notably Simon Burley (tutor to Richard II) and Robert de Roos, sometime Mayor of Bordeaux (1373) and Lieutenant for the Market of England (1380).[29]

It would be surprising if a work of such popularity had not exerted some influence over the thought and literature of its day. In the case of *Sidrac*, however (in Britain, at least), this influence appears to have been more nominal than actual: there are few quotations in English writings directly traceable to the work, and although there are occasional references to the name, it is not always clear whether our Sidrac is intended, or whether the reference is to Jesus, son of Sirach, the author of Ecclesiasticus. In the following quotation from the anonymous *Tale of Beryn*, for example (in which Geffrey describes Isope's wisdom to Beryn), the juxtaposition of 'Sydrak' and 'Salamonys sawis' makes it almost certain that the reference is to Ecclesiasticus, since The Wisdom of Solomon and The Wisdom of Jesus the Son of Sirach are placed next to each other in the (Vulgate) Old Testament:

> The .vij. sages of Rome, þou3 al ageyn hym were,
> The shuld be insufficient to make(n) his answere;
> ffor he can al langagis, Grew, Ebrewe, & latyne,

[29] For a list of Simon Burley's books see V. J. Scattergood, 'Two Medieval Book Lists,' *Transactions of the Bibliographical Society, The Library*, 23 (1968), 237 (item 4 is 'I liure de Sidrak'); Robert de Roos's will, in which he leaves to Elizabeth of Stapleton some money and 'unum librum de gallico qui vocatur Sydrak,' is published in full in *Publications of the Surtees Society*, 4 (1836), 178–80.

Caldey, ffrenssh, & lombard, yee knowe(n) wel fyne;
And all*e* maner (doctrine) þat men in bokis write;
In poyse, and philosophe, also he can endite.
Sevile (law), & Canoun, & (eke) al maner lawis;
Seneca, & Sydrak, & Salamonys sawis;
And the .vij. sciencis, & eke lawe of Armys,
Experimentis, & pompery, & al man*er* charmys,
As yee shull here(n) aftir, er þat I depart,
Of his Imaginaciouns, & of his sotill art.[30]

On the other hand, when the name 'Sidrac' appears at the end of a medical treatise, there can be no doubt that the reference is indeed to our *Sidrac*, in which there are many questions concerning medicine and physiology (see p. xxxi above), whereas Ecclesiasticus, though renowned as a book of wisdom, could scarcely be considered a treasury of medical knowledge:

This lytel boke compiled a worthi clerke called John de Burdeux for a frende that he had. after the descr*i*pcion of many oder diuerse doctours. that is to say. Bernarde Austyn. Plato. Tholome. Sidrac. Arystotell. Auycen. Galyen. and ypocras. & many oder diu*er*se acording to the same. (BL MS Sloane 989, the *Gouernale of Helth*)

The exalted company in which Sidrac's name appears here suggests that he was held in high esteem, even though a closer examination of the *Gouernale* reveals that most of the references are in fact to Avicenna and Galen: Sidrac's name is apparently used merely to add to the impressiveness of the list, but the author does not seem to think his name out of place beside those of the other formidable authorities. This bears out the comment of Renan and Paris on the popular influence of *Sidrac*: 'Presque ignoré des clercs, l'auteur est cité par les écrivains vulgaires sur le même pied qu'Aristote et les docteurs les plus autorisés' (p. 28).

A more flattering reference yet appears in the fifteenth-century Scottish poem, *The Quare of Jelusy*, in which the narrator's 'trety In the reprefe of Ielousye' begins with a veritable paean in Sidrac's praise:

The passing clerk, the grete philosophoure
Sydrake, enspirit of hevinly influence,
Quhich holdyn was into his tyme the floure
Of clergy, wisedome and intelligence,
Into his bukis declarith this sentence
To Bokas king, amang his doctrinis sere,

---

[30] *The Tale of Beryn*, ed. F. J. Furnivall and W. G. Stone, EETS ES 105, lines 2659-70.

Off Ielousy, and saith in this manere:

He clepith it foly of one ignorant,
The quhich euill humoris makith to procede,
As hert corrupt, or quho it list to hant,
Malancoly it raisith vp, but drede,
That lust of slepe, of mete or drink, of ded[e],
And wit of man confusith it all plane
With this hote feuir that is cotidiane.[31]

Here the conjunction of the names 'Sydrake' and 'Bokas king' confirms that the 'grete philosophoure' in question is our man; moreover, in spite of the claim by Norton-Smith and Pravda that the author of the *Quare of Jelusy* makes 'little use' of *Sidrac* (p. 69), a comparison of the second stanza quoted above with Q. 87 in our text, particularly lines 3397–406/ 4299–308, shows that in this instance at least there is a genuine debt (cf. F, Q. 90, 'Il i a autre maniere de ialousie qui ist de l'ordure dou cuer et de mauaises humors et qui durement et longuement s'asodent au cuer. Ce est la ialousie de fames qui est mult ardous et mult malicieuse, qui consume et confont le cuer et le met en perdicion et s'apelle folie, car le cuers s'art de mauaises pensees. Adonc les humors boillent et reflambent, donc le cors pert le mangier et le bo[i]re et son delit et son confort.').

Gower uses the name 'Sidrac' several times in his French work, the *Mirour de l'omme* (lines 2509, 3553, 16045, 22803, 23188), and it seems to have been generally accepted, without sufficient evidence, that these are all references to Ecclesiasticus.[32] Macaulay traces the first three of these references (on pride, on false seeming and on the care of one's reputation) to Ecclus. 10: 14, 40: 21, and 41: 15 respectively; he supplies no references for the last two occasions on which Sidrac's name is used, but the last of these (on the danger of listening to bad advice) is probably traceable to Ecclus. 37: 7–14. It is the penultimate occasion, however, that most concerns us. The passage, in Gower's *Mirour*, reads as follows (lines 22801–3): 'Rois doit la vérité cherir/ Sur toute chose et obeir,/ Ce dist Sidrac.' There is no such statement in Ecclesiasticus and the only passage that resembles it is chapter 10, verse 3: 'rex insipiens perdet

---

[31] *The Quare of Jelusy*, ed. Norton-Smith and Pravda, lines 318–30.
[32] Line references are to *The Complete Works of John Gower: The French Works*, ed. G. C. Macaulay (Oxford, 1899). 'The references of our author to "Sidrac" are to . . . 'The Wisdom of Jesus the son of Sirach' (Macaulay, p. 402, note on line 2509); 'Au XIVᵉ siècle, lorsque Gower dans son *Mirour de l'omme*, parle de Sidrac, c'est de l'Ecclésiastique qu'il s'agit' (Langlois, p. 211, note 1); 'Gower in his Mirour de l'homme refers to *Ecclesiasticus* as *Sidrac*, as others had done before him' (Hamilton, p. 318).

populum suum et civitates inhabitabuntur per sensum prudentium'. The correspondence is not entirely convincing: Gower's comment is somewhat closer to Sidrac's pronouncement, 'Les rois et les seignors doiuent estre primier loial de lor cors et de lor paroles et de lor iugemens' (F, Q. 407 = Q. 357 in this edition, 9747-50/11019-22), and it seems more probable that *Sidrac* is the source of this passage in Gower's *Mirour*. Moreover, although Gower's comments on pride are ultimately descended from Ecclesiasticus, it is noticeable that *Sidrac* treats the same subject in remarkably similar terms (in a passage not found in the English or in the shorter French versions):

> Sidrac, quant il d'Orguil treta,
> Dist et par resoun le prova,
> Orguil endroit de sa malice
> Fuist le primer apostata (Gower, *Mirour*, 2509-12)

> initium superbiae hominis apostatare a Deo
> quoniam ab eo qui fecit illum recessit cor eius
> quoniam initium peccati omnis superbia (Ecclus. 10: 14-15)

Ourgueil si est rachine de touz pechiez et de touz maux et si en vient inobedience. quant l'ome par son ourgueil refuse nostre signieur et ses commandemens (*Sidrac*, Q. 667, F2).

Evidently, *Sidrac* is here indebted to Ecclesiasticus, but who can assert with confidence that Gower's treatment is based on one of these rather than the other, since, as we have already seen, he apparently made use of both, and refers to them by the same name?

However, Gower makes no reference to *Sidrac* in his English writings and, though there are occasional correspondences between the subject matter of *Sidrac* and that of *Piers Plowman* or *The Canterbury Tales*, as, for example, in the passage on *lewte* in the answer to Q. 61 (cf. *Piers Plowman*, B. xi. 140 ff.) or that on true gentility in the answer to Q. 51 (cf. the Wife of Bath's tale, *CT* III (D) 1109-76), there is nothing to show that Langland or Chaucer is here borrowing from *Sidrac*, or that the work was used by any major writer of the Middle English period. Nevertheless, though *Sidrac* has had no discernible influence on literature in English, it remains a work of considerable interest to historians of science, of culture, and of language.

(E) CRITICAL RECEPTION

In contrast to the high reputation it evidently enjoyed in the Middle Ages, *Sidrac* has had a poor press from nineteenth- and twentieth-century critics, some of whom have expressed open contempt for the author's mentality and the work's lack of scientific value. Langlois, after wrestling with the problems of the Preface, appears to take some pleasure in giving his opinion of the author: 'C'était . . ., selon toute apparence, un sot. Aucune encyclopédie de notre moyen âge ne dépasse, en effet, celle-ci . . . en puérilité. Le style en est des plus misérables. . . . c'est une détestable logorrhée d'homme sans culture littéraire ni autre, qui s'adresse à des illettrés' (p. 21). Here he is in agreement with Renan and Paris (whose unfavourable comparison of *Sidrac* with *Placides et Timeo* has already been noted): 'Sidrach touche à toutes les questions des sciences naturelles; il n'en est pas une seul sur laquelle il apporte quelque trace d'esprit ou d'originalité. . . . La philosophie, pour notre auteur, ne s'élève pas au-dessus d'un grossier charlatanisme; il n' a pas même le soupçon de la science véritable, de son objet et de ses méthodes. . . . La chaîne des idées reçues empêche chez lui toute pensée originale. Un manque absolu de talent et de goût fait de son livre un des plus mal composés d'une époque où l'art de bien faire un livre était assez peu connu' (p. 317). Sarton, concurring with these views, remarks that *Sidrac* is 'perhaps the most puerile encyclopedia of the Middle Ages' (ii, 590); Carmody speaks of the work's 'unorganized agglomeration of details' (p. 359); and, more recently, Norton-Smith and Pravda have dismissed it as 'a bundle of drivel advertising as "inside knowledge"' (p. 69).[33]

Readers weaned on psychoanalytic criticism might find some justification for the lack of order in the questions by assuming that a part of the author's purpose is the realistic portrayal of the skittishness of the human mind in its flitting from one subject to another not related to it; to this one could object that without adequate indexing such disorder reduces the value of *Sidrac* as a work of reference. The Table of Contents in the French versions is better than no index at all; it is, however, of limited use, since it is arranged neither alphabetically nor by subject matter, but follows the order of the questions in the body of the work. In some of the English manuscripts (see p. xciii below) the situation is worsened by the total omission of the Table of Contents (as in B and T) or because (as in L and P) the Table consists solely of a verbatim repetition of the questions as put in the text and not (as in the more useful Tables of S and G) a summary of the subject matter of each question. Holler defends the 'apparently random arrangement' of the questions in *Sidrac* on the grounds that it 'reflects an important

---

[33] The last two references, like so much else in this edition, I owe to the kind offices of Dr Frank Schaer.

characteristic of the mind of medieval man who did not think in terms of the same categories we do', who 'saw the whole of creation as perfectly ordered' ('Ordinary Man', p. 527), and who, in consequence, did not look for the sort of categorization that we have come to expect of modern reference works; in other words, that to expect a systematic ordering of the material is to impose post-medieval presuppositions on a medieval work. But generalizations about 'the mind of medieval man' are no likelier to be accurate than generalizations about the mentality of any other age, and, like other forms of political correctness, they run the risk of patronizing the groups they set out to defend (in this instance by making medieval people appear like wide-eyed children). The encyclo-paedias of Vincent and Bartholomew show that systemization was by no means a post-medieval phenomenon; and Trevisa's translation of Bartholomew (from which I have quoted above) shows that expectations of systematic order were not confined to those who could read Latin.

But if *Sidrac* is so awful, why was it so popular? Or, to reverse the question, if it was so popular, why do most critics think it is so bad? (Holler is exceptional in considering that the answers 'radiate wisdom': 'Ordinary Man', p. 537.) Popularity is, of course, no guarantee of quality; but I do not think this is a sufficient answer. Part of the problem stems from the false expectations of present-day readers. Critics who complain of a lack of order and lack of indexing assume that *Sidrac* is intended as a reference work of the kind we are used to today, of which the encyclopaedias of Vincent and Bartholomew are medieval equivalents. Those who dwell on its lack of originality assume that its purpose is to record the latest developments in scientific research; those who are troubled by the generic mixture expect it to be *either* an adventure story *or* a book of knowledge, not both.[34] But *Sidrac* is evidently intended not as a journal of scientific research or a systematic encyclopaedia or a simple thriller: it is rather 'a kind of non-alphabetical encyclopaedia in the vernacular, in which everything gets mentioned somewhere';[35] the educational level of its intended audience is evidently low; and some repetition (as, for example, in the questions about angels, discussed above) and some inconsistencies (as between the answers to questions 34 and 287) are perhaps inevitable. It belongs, in short, to that class of sugared information transfer that has today come

[34] Since I have previously endorsed several of the objections listed here ('Lansdowne', ii, xxD–E) I cannot be excluded from the censure of having had false expectations.

[35] Derek Pearsall, *The Life of Geoffrey Chaucer: A Critical Biography* (Oxford, 1992), p. 80. Pearsall is in fact speaking of the *Roman de la Rose*, but the comment might justly be applied to *Sidrac*.

to be called (especially as applied to television programmes) 'infotain-ment'. Perhaps the worst that can be said of it in this light is that it aims low—and hits the target.

4. SOURCES AND ANALOGUES

The chief sources for the questions and answers in *Sidrac*, identified long ago by Hamilton (pp. 317–18) and Langlois (pp. 211, 269), are listed below.

1. The *Elucidarium* of Honorius Augustodunensis, the source for most of the theological material, to which (as Hamilton was the first to point out) the author 'owed the dialogue framework of his composition, and much of his information. . . . Beginning with one of the introductory questions on the omnipresence of God . . . down to the last questions on the Anti-Christ, Judgement Day, and the happiness of the blessed . . . the French work is dependent on its Latin model for the material, if not for the sequence and continuity of its questions' (p. 317). The full extent of *Sidrac*'s debt is shown in Lefèvre's edition of the *Elucidarium* (pp. 323–7); Table 1 below shows those questions in the *Elucidarium* to which the English *Sidrak* is ultimately indebted. (Significant differ-ences in treatment are indicated in the commentary on the text.)

Table 1: *Sidrak* and the *Elucidarium*

ELUCIDARIUM	SIDRAK	SUBJECT MATTER
	Prologue, lines	
i. 3	642–58/698–714	The Trinity likened to the sun
	Question no.	
i. 11	146	The three heavens
i. 13	1	God's foreknowledge
i. 21	3	God's presence felt by everything
i. 23	4	The chronology of the creation
i. 32–4	5	Satan's pride and his expulsion from heaven
i. 40	5	What became of Satan's followers
i. 48	7	The limits of devils' knowledge
i. 49	7	The limits of devils' power to do as they please
i. 54–5	8	The shape of angels
i. 56	8	The extent of angels' knowledge and power

Table 1 (*continued*)

ELUCIDARIUM	SIDRAK	SUBJECT MATTER
i. 57	115	Men created to take the place of the fallen angels
i. 62–3	9	How and why man was created
i. 65–7	9	Why animals were created
i. 68	10	Where Adam was created
i. 69	10	The location of paradise; the fruits that grew there
i. 70–1	10	The creation of Eve; she and Adam of one flesh and mind
i. 73	113	Why man was not made incapable of sin
i. 74–5	280	Reproduction without lust or pain in paradise
i. 79–80	10	Nakedness without shame in paradise
i. 90–1	10	How long Adam and Eve stayed in paradise
i. 93	11	Adam's life after he was expelled from paradise
i. 94–101	12	Adam's sin
i. 105–8	13	What Adam took from God
i. 109–12	14	Why Adam was not damned forever
i. 115–18	15	Why an angel was not sent to redeem him
i. 120	16	Why Christ was born of a virgin
i. 126–7	16	The conception and birth of Christ
i. 130–1	383	Christ's knowledge and power as a child
i. 132–4	381–2	Signs accompanying Christ's birth; their meaning
i. 137–9	384	Christ's teaching and baptism
i. 140	385	Christ's beauty
i. 142	386	Christ's death for obedience
i. 148	386	Why Christ died on a cross
i. 158	387	By whom Christ was killed
i. 161	387	Christ in hell
i. 166, 170	387	Christ on earth after the Resurrection
i. 172–3	388	The Ascension
i. 190	391	Bad priests and the Eucharist
i. 195	391	People who take communion unworthily
ii. 2	394	Sin is nothing
ii. 19	392	Rewards and punishments for priests in the next world
ii. 33	35	People who know nothing of God
ii. 34	34	When souls were created
ii. 42–3	277	The fate of children who die young

2. Gossuin's *Image du monde* (of which an English translation was printed by Caxton in 1481, under the title of the *Mirrour of the World*). The *Image* is named as the source for two sections in *Sidrac* not found in the English, those on the rebirth of knowledge after the Flood and on the origin of money (Langlois, p. 269), and for two that are in the English, Q. 74, on the inhabitants of India or of other islands, and Q. 150, on various springs and fountains of magical qualities (Hamilton, p. 317). Since, however, only four of the many peoples mentioned in Q. 74 appear in the *Image* (see the notes on lines 2875–80/3763–8, 2885–90/3773–8, 2993–6/3881–4, and 2997–3018/3885–3906), and that in a different order from their appearance in *Sidrac* (in contrast to Q. 150, which contains all the magical waters mentioned in the *Image*, and in the same order) it seems unlikely that the *Image* is indeed the source for Q. 74 (see the further discussion below). The indebtedness of *Sidrac* to the *Image* may, nevertheless, be greater than has hitherto been noticed (as suggested by Table 2, below); but since, on the other hand, a number of the topics that occur in the *Image* occur also, with similar treatment, in William of Conches's *De philosophia mundi*, of which the author of *Sidrac* also made use (see next item), it is often difficult to be certain which of the two works he is following.

3. Two works by William of Conches, the *De philosophia mundi* (at one time attributed to Honorius, and printed, together with Honorius's other works, in PL 172) and the *Philosophia secunda* or *Dragmaticon*.[36] The first is identified by Hamilton as the source of various questions in *Sidrac* on physiology and reproduction, such as those on the seven chambers of the womb (60), the mechanics of sight (241), the nourishment of the foetus (261), and the incapacity of young men to father strong children (367), besides a number not included in the English *Sidrak*; the second as the source of the questions on going grey and baldness (265 and 266). As shown in Table 2, however, there are many other chapters in *De philosophia mundi* on which the author of *Sidrac* may have drawn.

---

[36] There is only one printed edition of this work, entitled *Dialogus de substantiis physicis confectus a Guillelmo aneponymo philosopho* (Strasburg, 1567). The relationship between *De philosophia mundi* and the *Philosophia secunda* and the influence of William of Conches on later writers are discussed by Lynn Thorndike in *A History of Magic and Experimental Science during the First Thirteen Centuries of our Era*, ii (London, 1923), pp. 50–65.

Table 2: *Sidrak*, the *Image du monde*, William of Conches's *De philosophia mundi*, and Brunetto Latini's *Li Livres dou tresor*
(The numbering of sections in the *Image* follows that in the OF text; where this differs from that in Caxton's *Mirrour*, the numbering of the latter is given in square brackets.)

Sidrak	Image du monde	De phil. mundi	Livres dou tresor	Subject matter
1–3	i. 1			God's power
60		iv. 10		The seven chambers of the womb
113	i. 4			Why man was not made incapable of sin
116	i. 9–11 [i. 15–17]	iv. 1	I. civ	Formation of the world; its likeness to an egg; disposition of the elements; how the earth is held in place
117	i. 11 [i. 17]	iv. 3		Antipodeans
120	ii. 14 [ii. 24]		I. cvi. 1–2	The nature of air (how it holds birds aloft)
121	ii. 15 [ii. 25]	iii. 4	I. cvi. 3–4	Rain
122	ii. 15 [ii. 27]	iii. 8	I. cvi. 5–6	Hail
123	ii. 15 [ii. 27]		I. cvi. 7	Storms
124 130 }	ii. 15 [ii. 28]	iii. 10	I. cvi. 7–8	Thunder and lightning
125	ii. 16 [ii. 29]	iii. 15	I. cvi. 9 [?]	Wind
126	ii. 9 [ii. 19]		I. cv. 1–2	Watercourses like veins in the body
127	ii. 10, 13 [ii. 20, 23]	iii. 16		The saltness of the sea
128	ii. 10 [ii. 20]		I. cv. 4	Hot springs
131	ii. 9 [ii. 19]		I. cv. 1	The sea as the source of all waters
143	ii. 12 [ii. 22]			Earthquakes
144	iii. 3–5 [iii. 5–7]	ii. 30, 32		Eclipses of the moon and sun
145	ii. 17 [ii. 30]	iii. 12		Falling stars
147	i. 14 [i. 20]			The distance between earth and heaven
148	iii. 6 [iii. 8]			The effect of the movement of the heavens

Table 2 (*continued*)

Sidrak	Image du monde	De phil. mundi	Livres dou tresor	Subject matter
150	ii. 11 [ii. 21]			Waters with various magical qualities
152	i. 12–13 [i. 18–19]		I. civ	The earth's roundness
173	ii. 15 [ii. 25]			Clouds
201	iii. 1 [iii. 1, 3]			Day and night
223		iv. 8		The manufacture of semen
237	iii. 1, 2 [iii. 2, 4]			Stars not seen by day; the new moon
241		iv. 26		The mechanics of sight
247		iv. 19		Digestion
261		iv. 16		Nourishment of the foetus
312	ii. 8 [ii. 18]			The miseries of hell
316		iv. 22		Dreams
367		iv. 9		Impotence of the young

Carmody proposes (pp. 360–2) an unidentified Latin source, used in the *Image*, in William of Conches's *De philosophia mundi*, and in Brunetto Latini's *Livres dou tresor*, as the source for several of the meteorological sections in *Sidrac*, such as questions 116, 120–8, and 152. Since, however, these topics all occur in the *Image* and/or in *De philosophia mundi* (as shown in Table 2), and since the author of *Sidrac* uses each of these works elsewhere, it seems probable that his debt is in all instances to one of these rather than to this unidentified source. As indicated by Table 3 below, much of this and other material dealing with the natural world is covered also in other popular books of knowledge such as Pliny's *Natural History* (from which most later accounts derive), Isidore's *Etymologiae* and *De natura rerum*, Honorius's *De imagine mundi* (the source for the *Image*), Neckam's *De naturis rerum* and *De laudibus divinae sapientiae*, and Vincent's *Speculum naturale*; but the wording in *Sidrac* is nowhere close enough to suggest any of these, rather than the *Image* or *De philosophia mundi*, as the immediate source. (See further below, p. xlviii.)

Table 3: Some common topics in medieval encyclopaedias (cf. Table 2)

Sidrak Q. no.	Subject matter	Pliny, *Natural History*	Isidore, *Etym. & De nat.*	Honorius, *De imag. mundi*	Neckam, *De laud. & De nat.*	Vincent, *Speculum naturale*
121	Rain	II. xlii–iii	De nat. xxxiii	i. 59		iv. 45
122	Hail	II. lxi	De nat. xxxv	i. 60	De laud. iv. 188–93	iv. 48–9
124	Thunder	II. xlii–iii	Etym. xiv. 8; De nat. xxix	i. lvii	De laud. iii. 97–118	iv. 55
125	Wind	II. xliv–v	Etym. xiv. 11; De nat. xxxvi	i. liv	De nat. i. 18	iv. 26
127	Saltness of the sea	II. ciii	De nat. xlii	i. 45	De nat. ii. 1	v. 9
130	Lightning	II. xlii–iii	Etym. xiv. ix; De nat. xxx	i. 57	De laud. iii. 97–118	iv. 59
143	Earthquakes	II. lxxxi–ii	De nat. xlvi	i. 42–3	De nat. ii. 48	vi. 26–7
144	Eclipses	II. vii	Etym. iii. 58–9; De nat. xx–xxi	ii. xxxi	De laud. i. 502–11; De nat. i. 13	xv. 13–14

4. The *Secreta secretorum* (attributed to Aristotle). This is identified by Langlois as the source for a section on the four seasons in the amplified versions of the French *Sidrac* that does not appear in the English rhymed versions, and for the questions on warfare, only one of which (Q. 358, whether kings should appear personally in battle) appears in the English. It may also have been the inspiration for the question on the origin of fat (Q. 85). The differences in treatment between the *Secreta* and *Sidrak* are, however, rather more marked than the similarities (see 3325–52/4227–54n and 9769–94/11039–68n).[37]

[37] Several English translations of the *Secreta* are known, in both prose and verse: see

5. Albumasar's *Introductorium in astronomiam*, which is identified by Hamilton as the source of much of the astrological matter in *Sidrac*, for example the question on the influence of the planets and the signs of the zodiac on character (Q. 149).[38]

Many other possible sources and close parallels for passages in *Sidrac* have been noticed. Ward remarked (p. 905) that the episode of Bokkus's tower in the Prologue (20/28 ff.) 'is to some extent founded upon that of Vortigern's tower in the old Romance of Merlin', though it is hard to say whether the author of *Sidrac* took it from *Merlin* or got it directly from Geoffrey of Monmouth.[39] It has also been pointed out that Noah's book of astronomy and the mountain with magical herbs (191–290/214–326) both have parallels in the Indian *Kalīlah wa Dimnah* (made known to the West, under the title of *Directorium humanae vitae*, through John of Capua's Latin translation of a Hebrew version), the beginning of which contains an account of the mission of Barzōye to India to obtain for Khosrū Nūshīrvān, King of Persia (AD 531–79), a book that the latter had heard contained every kind of instruction.[40] Two similarities have been noticed between incidents in the Prologue to *Sidrac* and the story of the seven *sapientes* in *The Seven Sages of Rome*: in both, the ruler's advisers, faced with a difficult problem, ask for time in which to think up the answer (*Sidrak* 91/101 ff.; *Seven Sages* 2353 ff.); and in both, upon the failure of the official advisers to find the right answer, the situation is saved by an old man who knows what should be done (*Sidrak* 180/202 ff.; *Seven Sages* 2365 ff.).[41]

Lydgate and Burgh's Secrees of Old Philisoffres: A Version of the Secreta Secretorum, ed. Robert Steele, EETS ES 66 (London, 1894) and Steele's *Three Prose Versions of the Secreta Secretorum*. Van Tol points out (p. xxix) that some of the questions in the *Secreta* are indebted to Sir Michael Scot's *De secretis mulierum* (at one time wrongly attributed to Albertus Magnus).

[38] The British Library has two different editions (1489 and 1506) of the translation from the Arabic into Latin by Johannes Hispalensis, entitled *Introductorium in astronomiam Albumasaris*. I know of no English translation.

[39] For English versions of this episode see *Merlin, or The Early History of King Arthur: A Prose Romance*, ed. Henry B. Wheatley, I, EETS 10 (London, 1865), 27–8; *Merlin: a Middle-English Metrical Version of a French Romance*, ed. Ernst A. Kock, I, EETS ES 93 (London, 1904), 52–5; or *Of Arthour and Merlin*, ed. O. D. Macrae-Gibson, I, EETS 268 (London, 1973), 38–45. For Geoffrey's account see *HRB*, §§106–8 [VI. xvii–xix].

[40] The suggestion, first made by Italo Pizzi in 'Un Riscontro Arabo del Libro di Sidrac', *Raccolta di Studii Critici Dedicata ad Alessandro d'Ancona* (Florence, 1901), pp. 225–9, is repeated in van Tol, p. xxx. The relevant passage in John of Capua's *Directorium* may be found in the *École Pratique des Hautes Études, Bibliothèque . . . Sciences philologiques et historiques*, 72 (Paris 1869), 14–16.

[41] Van Tol, p. xxxi. Line references for the *Seven Sages* are from *The Seven Sages of Rome*, ed. Karl Brunner, EETS 191 (1933 *for* 1932), 106–18.

Two parallels have been noticed for the suicide by self-decapitation described in the answer to Q. 74, lines 2921–44/3809–32, both in the writings of Arab travellers in the Far and Middle East in the Middle Ages (see the note on these lines). There are also parallels (not previously noted) for the immolation of widows following the deaths of their husbands (see 2979–84/3867–72n): sutteeism appears in both *Mandeville's Travels* and Ibn Battuta's description of north-western India, and *Mandeville's Travels* has an exact parallel for the burial alive of widows with their dead husbands.[42] Ibn Battuta's travels cover the period 1325–54, and his writings are therefore too late to be regarded as a source for *Sidrac*; nevertheless, it seems reasonable to accept Thouvenin's assumption that the author of *Sidrac* was familiar with similar accounts from previous travellers in the East:

Si Ibn Battuta a rassemblé, le plus complètement, les observations des Arabes au cours de leurs navigations dans les mers du Sud, il n'en avait pas été le premier explorateur. Le *Sidrach* prouve qu'il circulait, bien avant lui, dans les milieux musulmans, des récits pareils concernant des spectacles aussi extraordinaires et des scènes d'une barbarie, qui avait plongé les marins arabes dans une grande stupeur. Que des échos, aussi précis, en soient parvenus au rédacteur du *Sidrach*, démontre plus les rapports de cet ouvrage avec l'Orient que tout ce qui avait été allégué jusque-là. (pp. 247–8)

A similar conclusion with regard to Africa is suggested by the description in *Sidrac* of the relationship between the crocodile and the trochilus, the nearest parallel for which is found some two hundred years later in Leo Africanus's *History and Description of Africa* (see 3212–46/4112–50n).

In addition to its account of the burial of widows *Mandeville's Travels* contains many other unnoticed parallels to passages in *Sidrak*. These parallels occur mainly (as might be expected) in the answer to Q. 74, concerning the earth's inhabitants. Although *Mandeville's Travels* is too late to be a source for *Sidrac*, the authors of both have evidently had access to the same sources or traditions. The collection of monstrous races and customs in *Sidrac* recalls similar lists in other medieval enyclopaedias and travelogues, and must raise the possibility that our

---

[42] Editors point out that Mandeville is here indebted to Friar Odoric of Pordenone, whose travels, covering the period 1316–30, are, like those of Ibn Battuta, too late to be considered a source for *Sidrac*. But the occurrence of the immolation of wives in *Sidrac* supports Thouvenin's contention (see below) that accounts of such customs were already in circulation before the reports of fourteenth-century travellers brought them wider renown. See further Odoric, pp. 166–7, n. 2.

author took this material from one such well-known medieval collection—the *Epistola Alexandri* or *De rebus in oriente mirabilis*, Vincent of
Beauvais's *Speculum naturale* (xxxi. 124–32) or *Speculum historiale* (i. 86–
93), or Isidore's *Etymologiae* (xi. 3)—or, indeed, that he went directly to
Pliny's *Natural History*, which is the source for most later accounts.

Comparisons, however, suggest that none of these works can have
been the source for this list of wonders in *Sidrac*. Whereas the list of
waters occurring in the answer to Q. 150 coincides, in both order and
detail, with that in the *Image du monde* (so that one may be confident of
our author's debt to the *Image* for Q. 150), there is no such coincidence
in the lists of monsters and monstrous customs. Of the fifteen items
listed in *Sidrak* (2861–3018/3745–906) only a few are found in any of
the other collections; in almost every instance the account in *Sidrak* is
either less or more detailed than the analogue, or else it has some
strikingly different details: see, for example, the notes on the ichthyo-
phagi (2869–74/3757–62), the Cyclopes (2875–80/3763–8), the pygmies
(2885–90/3773–8), the Cynocephali (2895–6/3783–4), and the Amazons
(2997–3018/3885–3906). The same is true of many of the answers in
Sidrac dealing with natural history. Although most of the same ground
is covered by classical writers and repeated by Vincent, and although
there are occasional passages that must be derived ultimately from
Aristotle or Pliny (see, for example, the argument about 'matter' versus
'shape and life', 7369–74/8455–60n, or the comments on the effect on a
child of its parents' thoughts at the time of its conception, 2483–8/
3363–8n), such passages are outnumbered by those where the resemblance to the earlier authorites is not strong, or where our author says
something entirely different (e.g., that fish never sleep; see 9737–42/
11009–14n and 10089–94/11385–90n). Unless he is showing unchar-
acteristic independence, it would seem that for much of this material our
author used at least one major source that is as yet unidentified.

Ward commented (p. 905) that some of the questions and answers in
Sidrac 'are of the same character as a portion of the French *Prophécies de
Merlin*' (a different work from the *Romance of Merlin* discussed above),
and the relationship between the two has been more closely examined by
Lucy Allen Paton in her edition of the *Prophecies* (ii, 233–9). After
pointing out the difference in the aims of the two works, Paton
compares several passages in which Sidrac and Merlin expound on
similar themes; of these, the following appear in the English *Sidrak*:
questions 47 (the future of the Church), 49 (the exercise of lordship),
197 (the extent of God's mercy), 233 (heavenly paradise), 269 and 307

(guardian angels), 303 (alms-giving), 310 (purgatory), 312 (hell), 363 (repentance, hope, and despair). The claim, in the Preface of the French *Sidrac* and in chapter 1 of the *Prophecies*, to have been translated from Latin into French at the command of Frederick II is a further similarity. But although there are obvious similarities in these passages, there are also notable differences, especially in the treatments of hell, repentance, and the future of the Church; moreover, for Sidrac's treatment of purgatory and hell the *Elucidarium* is the obvious source. Since neither *Sidrac* nor the *Prophecies* has yet been dated with precision, it is impossible to say which is indebted to which, if, indeed, there is a direct debt at all. Paton's conclusion, implying that there probably is not, seems eminently sensible: 'all that we can affirm is that the immediate influence of one production upon the other is possible, that the evidences of it are not very pronounced, and that such resemblances as exist between them may in general be accounted for by the practices and the prevailing thought of the period in which both books were written' (ii, 334).

There is a similar uncertainty concerning the lapidary section in *Sidrac*, which is not found in the English rhymed versions, although an English prose translation exists (see p. lxxxvii below and the note to line 10610/11954). Holler has argued that the lapidary in *Sidrac* is the source of the French verse lapidary usually known as the *Lapidaire Chrétien*, which is dated by Pannier to the second and by Baisier to the third quarter of the thirteenth century.[43] Holler's argument rests on two bases: (1) the two lapidaries contain passages that are found in no others; (2) whereas the author of the *Lapidaire Chrétien* refers frequently in these passages to an unnamed source or sources ('li livres de jadis', 'l'auctorité', 'l'escrit', 'li viés contes', etc.), the author of *Sidrac* 'never cites authorities in his work. His sole source is God, according to the book's first prologue' ('Lapidary', p. 184). From this Holler concludes that *Sidrac* is the earlier of the two works, and is in fact the unnamed source referred to in the *Lapidaire Chrétien*. But this is unconvincing. The author of *Sidrac* cannot name sources, because to do so would undermine the claim in the Preface that the book was directly inspired by God. This does not prevent his using the *Elucidarium* and the several other sources discussed above; and it seems probable that other sources

---

[43] Holler, 'Lapidary', *passim*; Léopold Pannier, *Les Lapidaires français* (Paris, 1882), p. 231; Léon Baisier, *The Lapidaire Chrétien, Its Composition, Its Influence, Its Sources* (Washington, D.C., 1936), p. 110. For a discussion of the content of the lapidary section in *Sidrac* see further Holler, 'Stone Lore'.

will in time come to light for those parts of the work that have appeared so far to be independent. If one of these lapidaries is the source for the other, the likelihood must be that it is the *Lapidaire Chrétien* (given its early dating by Pannier and Baisier) that is the source for *Sidrac* rather than vice versa. This is the view propounded by Cesare Segre, who suggests, however, that the lapidary in *Sidrac* (S) is derived from a third lapidary, the *Lapidaire de Philippe* (Ph), which is itself derived from the *Lapidaire Chrétien* (C). The arguments are, in brief, that: (1) S is shorter than Ph and contains nothing that is missing from Ph (of which the reverse is not true); (2) S and Ph both reproduce errors from C, including a double description of the colours of topaz; (3) the readings in Ph are demonstrably intermediate between those of C and S. Several examples are given in support of the last contention, of which one must here suffice: 'D'orient et d'Arabe vienent/cil que li sage a millors tienent' (C) → 'D'Orient et d'Arabe vienent li meillor' (Ph) → 'De Orient e de Arabe sunt les meillors' (S).[44] Segre argues further (pp. 255–6) that the Philip to whom Ph is dedicated is Philip the Fair (1285–1314), to whom a number of other works were dedicated. This accords well with the writing of Ph (a prose summary of C) in the early part of Philip's reign and with Langlois's later dating (after 1291) for the composition of *Sidrac* (see p. xxiv above).

Another work with which *Sidrac* has sometimes been linked (see p. xxxiii above) is the Wisdom of Jesus the Son of Sirach (or Joshua ben Sira), the longest of the books of the Apocrypha, more commonly known since the third century AD, because of its widespread use in churches, as Ecclesiasticus. The name Sidrac is by most commentators equated with that of Shadrach (spelt 'Sidrach' in the Vulgate Bible), who, with Meshach and Abednego, refused to worship Nebuchadnezzar's golden image: their faith saved all three from being consumed in the fiery furnace into which they were thrown as a result (Daniel, ch. 3). In the same way, it is pointed out, Sidrac refused to make sacrifices to Boctus's idol but survived the punishment that he thus drew on himself (355/393 ff.). Steinschneider, on the other hand, contends that, in spite of the similarity in name and history between Sidrac and Shadrach, the former should correctly be identified with Jesus, son of Sirach, the author of Ecclesiasticus (pp. 240–1). This hypothesis has not found favour with later writers, who insist on the identification

---

[44] Segre, p. 263. To avoid confusion with my use of F as a siglum for MS fr. 1160 I have substituted 'Ph' for Segre's 'F' as a siglum for the *Lapidaire de Philippe*.

with Shadrach;[45] since, however, there are indeed similarities between *Sidrac* and Ecclesiasticus, the connection cannot be summarily dismissed. Table 4 below shows a number of questions and answers in the English *Sidrak* that are reminiscent of passages in Ecclesiasticus.

Table 4: *Sidrak* and Ecclesiasticus

ECCLESIASTICUS (VULGATE)	Q. in SIDRAK	SUBJECT MATTER
6: 5–17; 19: 13–17	88	True and false friends
8: 4–5	105	Answering fools
9: 1	263	Jealousy
13: 25–29	92	Rich and poor
22: 7–22	372	Fools again
25: 17 to 26: 24; 42: 9–14	82, 86, 328	Women
30: 1–13	182	Children
31: 1–7	107	Avarice

In none of these cases is the resemblance so striking as to constitute direct quotation; moreover, the matter is mostly proverbial, so that its ultimate source is impossible to trace. None the less, it seems unlikely that medieval Christian readers, with their familiarity with Ecclesiasticus, would not have recognized the similarity: there may well be something, notwithstanding Langlois's assertion to the contrary (p. 199), in Le Clerc's suggestion that the subtitle by which *Sidrac* is sometimes known, *La Fontaine de toutes sciences*, is consciously reminiscent of the title *Trésors de toutes vertus*, which was sometimes applied to Ecclesiasticus and the Wisdom of Solomon.[46]

But it would be unwise to press the similarity between *Sidrac* and Ecclesiasticus to the point where one declared that Sidrac *is*, or is meant to represent, Jesus the son of Sirach; indeed, the attempt to identify Sidrac with any one figure is mistaken. Sidrac resembles the son of Sirach in being (reputedly) the originator of a book of wisdom that has been preserved by succeeding generations, but the latter, though he tells us that his life was at one time in danger, and speaks of being saved 'from the choking of fire on every side' (Ecclus. 51: 4, AV), is apparently speaking of verbal fire, and is not renowned, as is Shadrach, for having survived actual attempts to kill him because of his faith; equally, Sidrac resembles Shadrach in his refusal to worship idols in spite of dire

---

[45] See Ward, p. 903; Renan and Paris, p. 289; Langlois, pp. 199, 215.
[46] Victor Le Clerc, 'L'*Image du monde*, et autres enseignements', *HLF*, 23 (1856), 294.

punishment, but Shadrach, though described, along with his compan-
ions, as 'skilful in all wisdom, and cunning in knowledge, and understanding science' (Daniel 1: 4, AV), has left no known writings
embodying this wisdom; moreover, as van Tol points out (p. xxxiii),
the time in which Shadrach lived was about 400 years after the death of
Noah, whereas Sidrac's birth is placed (in the Preface) 847 years after the
same event. The likelihood must be, not that the author of *Sidrac* was
trying to identify his hero with any one character, but that, in order to
invest him with authority, he chose for him a name that would call to
mind other heroes famed for the qualities with which he wished to endow
his Sidrac, namely, courage and wisdom. The similarity in form between
'Sidrach' (the Vulgate form of Shadrach), 'Sirach' (in the patronymic of
the author of Ecclesiasticus), and the various forms of our hero's name is
self-evident; and if confirmation were needed of the probability of their
being confused, it is amply provided by Gower's use of the name 'Sidrac'
(see pp. xxxv–xxxvi above). It seems more sensible, in short, to assume
that the author consciously chose for Sidrac a name that he knew to be
ambiguous and that would allow its bearer the benefit of two distinguished reputations than to engage in necessarily inconclusive arguments
as to which of the two figures he intended to call to mind.

This review shows that only about a quarter of the questions
appearing in the English *Sidrak* have been traced to their sources. We
are not much nearer to identifying the remaining sources than when
Hamilton wrote in 1912; nothing has arisen to invite dissent from
Langlois's opinion that the author must have had access to an
ecclesiastical library, or at least to a manuscript containing an assortment
of medieval works of knowledge and travel (p. 214), one of those
manuscripts that is (as Derek Pearsall has said of the Auchinleck
manuscript) 'almost a library in itself'.[47]

5. THE ENGLISH RHYMED VERSIONS

There are eight known manuscripts (or fragments) of English verse
translations of *Sidrak and Bokkus*, and one printed edition. All but one
of the verse manuscripts (see A below) are mentioned in *The Index of
Middle English Verse* or its *Supplement*. The rhymed versions fall into
two schools: type I ('long') is listed under entry 772 in the *Index* and

---

[47] *The Life of Geoffrey Chaucer* (Oxford, 1992), p. 74.

Supplement; type II ('short' or 'abridged') under entry 2147. I give below physical descriptions of the various manuscripts, checked where possible by librarians in the collections where they are housed, together with an account of the contents of each manuscript. Approximate dates are given in the form 's. xv in.', 's. xv^2', etc., following the system explained in Ker, p. vii.

Type I versions

L: London, British Library, MS Lansdowne 793   s. xv^2
   (See Ward, p. 915; printed on the right-hand pages in this edition)

181 parchment leaves, size *c.* 285mm by 195mm, written space *c.* 195mm by 80mm. Collation: iv paper flyleaves, 1–22^8, 23^8 (lacks 6–8), iv paper flyleaves. Systematic quire signatures a–z (omitting i, u, w) in first half of quire, in red. Catchwords in black or red, as appropriate. The manuscript is written in one column, with (usually) 34 lines to a page, and with questions, headings, couplet pairings, and underlining in red, and is foliated in ink in the top right-hand corner. Initials from f. 161 onwards are in blue with red flourishing; before f. 161 they are marked for the rubricator but not executed. Pricking and ruling (in brown ink or crayon) for single bounding lines with double horizontals extended to edge of page at head and foot of text; an additional double horizontal beneath the text contains catchwords and quire signatures. British Museum in-house 19th-century red leather binding, gold-tooled with Lansdowne arms. Mr T. A. J. Burnett, (then) Assistant Keeper in the Department of Manuscripts, feels that, on palaeographical grounds, the manuscript 'can probably be assigned to the third quarter of the fifteenth century' (private communication, 19 May 1972); Ms Michelle Brown (who has kindly supplied many of the codicological details above) suggests mid-fifteenth century (private communication, 13 January 1997).

Marginalia: passim 'nota' and 'exemplum' in the scribe's hand; 1r top right, 'OOe'; 4r.12, maniculum in right margin; 11r.24–6, illegible scrawl in right margin; 21r.12–15, 'Jhon' in left margin with blotted mirror image in right margin of 22r; 35v bottom, 'Thomas Walker', 'John Walker', and other signatures; 41r top right, 'O Robert Webster'; 57r top right, illegible scrawl; 62v–63r bottom, pen trials; 66r right margin, pen trials; 71r right margin, scrawls and vertical lines; 76v.25 left margin, 'Nota' (not scribe's hand); 77r.5 'bene' (not scribe's hand);

78v left margin (landscape), recipe 'for ye Agyo Take half a hanfull of harttong & half a hanfull of sage & seth tham togeder in good ale & strene tham with ye ale & take a posset of ye ale & put yt to a quantyte of treacle & powd of a nutmeg & yes be profetabyll with good dyett'; bottom, 'Thys byth mad by me Thomas Walker' and two other signatures (the last a Webster [?]); 79r right margin and bottom, beginning of the same recipe; 80r bottom, 'Thys byth mad by me Thomas Walker the xvj day of Ianuarey in the year of our lord god Mccccxliij' witnessed by three others, 'Wyllam Qwathey' [?], 'Ihon Walker', 'Richard Wyntworrth' [?]; 87v bottom, questions repeated from text; 88v bottom, 'Johne Haumpoulle' [?]; 89r right margin, pen trials; 102v top right, 'liber'; bottom, 'I tell you playn of John Hanum [. . .]' [?]; 105r bottom, 'O lord of myghtys moste vnto the doe I crie trustinge in o lord thou wille [. . .] my wooss all though a wycked sinner I lye therfoe sayve o god of myghtys most'; 111v bottom, 'William Wylkensone'; 121r bottom, 'What hopist of [. . .]'; 122r bottom left, 'brodyr'; 124v bottom, 'Honor thy father and thy mother that thy deayes may be lounge in the land'; 135r bottom, 'When a man it [. . .]'; 145v bottom, scrawled alphabet; 146v bottom, 'necales Webister of ledisstone owis thys boke Iff ane man fynd it gef to hym agayn'; 147v bottom, 'Ihon Walker of beetton [? bretton] onis [? owis] thys boke if ane man fynd it gyf me It Agean And god gyf you [. . .] made by me Thomas Walker for ncoles Webyster of [. . .]'; 148r bottom, 'Thys byth made the xvj day of septembre In the yer of our lord god Mccccxli [. . .] Wytnes soth that I [? Wyllam Qwheathy . . .]'; 151r bottom, an alphabet followed by 'Harry bramam wrat thys whyt hys owen hand'; 156r bottom, an alphabet followed by 'In nomine patrys et fylyi et spiritus sancty amen harry bramam wrate thys wyht hys owen hand'; 162v–163r bottom, decorative 'W's; 170v bottom, the beginning of an alphabet; 172r bottom, names of [?] Thomas Walker, Thomas Cowpland, John Bolton, Robert Spynk, Garry Jacson, James Loueden, Thomas Tomson, John Best, Richard Hilborn; 181r bottom, 'Explicit Sydrak' repeated.

Contents: This is the fullest known English version of the work (the only complete version of type I), containing approximately 12,250 lines. (Ward's figure of 22,250 (p. 915), which is repeated in the *Supplement*, is clearly a slip of the pen or a misprint.)

The Prologue opens with a fourteen-line Introduction, starting with a prayer for God's assistance, '[F]adir and Sone and Holy Goost,/ As þou art Lord of mightes moost,/ Thre persones in Godhede,/ Now and euere this work now spede', and proceeding with the promise of 'Thinges þat ben not ofte in minde' and of 'questiouns many oone' that are 'asoiled . . . euerychoone'. The remainder of the Prologue (ff. 11.15 to 15v.22, lines 15–1006) is taken up with an account of the events leading up to the conversion of the heathen King Bokkus by the prophet Sidrak, which provides a narrative justification for the posing and answering of the questions that form the body of the work. The events related include the unsuccessful attempts of King Bokkus, 847 years after the time of Noah, to build a tower to defend his lands against those of his neighbour and enemy, Garaab of India; the advice of the astronomer Sidrak (on loan from one of Bokkus's dependent kings, Traktabare) to gather certain herbs from the Green Raven's Hill to destroy the spell that had apparently been put upon the tower; their battles with the inhabitants of, and their eventual capture of, the Green Raven's Hill; Bokkus's sacrifices to his gods in thanks for the victory; the refusal of Sidrak (who believed in the Trinity) to take part in these heathen ceremonies; Sidrak's defeat of Bokkus's chosen advisers in 'open desputacioun'; the destruction of Bokkus's idols by a fire from heaven, in answer to Sidrak's prayer; Bokkus's fury, and his reprisals against Sidrak; Sidrak's undaunted spirit, and his conversion of Bokkus by showing him a vision of the Trinity in a pot of water; further unsuccessful attempts by Bokkus's followers to discredit or destroy Sidrak; Bokkus's unshaken faith in Sidrak and in the Trinity, and his request that Sidrak should answer many things 'þat he him axe wolde.'

The Prologue is followed by a Table of Contents (ff. 15v.23 to 28v.28, lines 1007–900), headed 'Questiouns þat king Bokkus axed Sidrak and hou he answerid to hem.' There are 408 questions in this manuscript (which omits seven, numbers 43–9, of the 415 found in B), divided into four books, the first three containing (or intended to contain) 100 questions each, the last containing the remainder. The Table consists of a list of the various questions, in the order in which they are asked, and (except in some cases pointed out in the commentary) with the same wording as that used when they reappear later, at the appropriate point in the text. The questions are not arranged by subject matter, and the wording is not abbreviated, so that the Table will not serve as an index. The questions are numbered in red ink in the right-hand margin, and are designated 'chapter' (Ca°) rather than 'question'. The main body of the work, following the Table of Contents, consists of the answering of the questions (ff. 28v.29 to 179v.28, lines 1901–12198). The lines occupying ff. 170r.9 to 173v.8 (lines 11751–988) are misplaced in the manuscript: they should be preceded by the lines occupying ff.173v.9 to 176v.24 (11531–750), and are shifted in this edition to their correct position. There is some confusion, towards the end of the manuscript, as to which answer accompanies which question: the answer to Q. 405 is omitted; the answers to questions 406–12 precede the questions; the question for Q. 413 is omitted but the answer given; the correct order of question and answer is restored for the final two questions (414 and 415).

The narrative is concluded in four sections (numbered as chapters 109–12 of book 4) which relate the return of Bokkus to his own country, the successful completion of the tower under Sidrak's direction, the resulting conversion of King Garaab 'and manye a lond þereaboute' and their subsequent relapse into paganism after the deaths of Sidrak and Bokkus. There is a final prayer that God should save us from the 'wicked wiles' of the devil, 'And bringe vs into þat blisse/ Where þat none ende þerof isse;/ And þat it so be,/ Amen, Amen for charite.' Thereafter the scribe has written 'Explicit Sydrak' several times, in full or shortened versions, as if in relief at reaching the end of such a marathon. There are some scribbles on the reverse of the final folio, which I have been unable to decipher.

H: London, British Library, MS Harley 4294   s. xv²
    (See Ward, p. 918)

84 paper leaves, size *c.* 300mm by 195mm, written space *c.* 230mm by 85mm. Collation: i early paper flyleaf, 1–12⁶, 13⁶ + 1 leaf after 6, i parchment flyleaf, i paper flyleaf. No quire signatures. Catchwords remain in the middle of a quire on fols. 9v and 21v, at the end of a quire on fols. 60v and 72v, elsewhere in a quire on fols. 35v and 49v. The manuscript is written in one column, with 50–62 lines to a page and with questions and headings in red, and is foliated in pencil in the top right-hand corner. Ruling in brown ink for single bounding lines; horizontals not ruled. Remains of former gold-tooled brown calf bindings now form pastedowns in the modern BL binding. Mr T. A. J. Burnett feels that H, like L, 'can probably be assigned to the third quarter of the fifteenth century. It is possible that the Lansdowne MS may be as much as twenty years earlier than the Harley MS, but unfortunately in palaeography it is advisable to leave a margin of twenty-five years on either side of a date, so the result is inconclusive' (private communication, 19 May 1972); Ms Michelle Brown agrees that Lansdowne is earlier (private communication, 13 January 1997).

Marginalia: 1r top, '19 November, 1725'; throughout, in the same hand, comments usually indicating the subject of the question, or a topic in the answer. These are sometimes very brief, e.g., 'Jealousie' (Q. 87) and 'Freinds' (Q. 88), 9r ; sometimes fuller, e.g., 'How children come to be lepers' (Q. 65), 4v, 'When the poore is to giue place here to the rich and when not' (Q. 179), 33v; sometimes supplying a biblical quotation, e.g., 'Diues locutus est et omnes tacuerunt et verbum illius vsque ad nubes perducunt, Pauper locutus est et dicunt, quis est hic? Ecclesiast: 13:24 et 10:32' (Q. 92), 10v, top left; sometimes indicating a misreading of the text, e.g., 'An opinion that the soules of the Damned which were in Hell before the day of Judgment shall not be vnited with theire bodyes' (Q.271), 53r; sometimes supplying a missing question, e.g., that on tempests (Q. 123), 18r. In a different hand, 60v right margin, 'Misericordia In aeternitate Cantabo'.

End leaves: 80r, a poem in two columns, each of 28 lines, 'Wo worth . . .' in the left column, 'Blessyd be   . . .' in the right (see *Index* and *Supplement*, entry 4216); 80v, 'A Remedy for the swetyng syknes'; 81r, 'I am as lyght as any Roo' (*Index* 3782); 81v, 'I shall you tell of Crystes derlyng// Prey we all to the prynce of pece [?] Amice', and a poem (not entered in *Index* or *Supplement*, but printed in *Reliquiae Antiquae*, ed. Thomas Wright and James Orchard Halliwell, i (London, 1841), pp. 252–3) beginning 'He hathe myne hart everydele' and with the refrain 'Whatsoever ye thynk avyse ye wele'; 82r, some accounts, followed by 'Memorandum delyverd to John Mathew' and various comments in English and Latin, including 'Man remembre thy end and thou shalt never be shend' (*Index Supplement* 2072.4); also 'Ryght trusty and welbeloued' and 'Henry by the grace of god kynge'; 82v, 'A pen and ink outline of arms, a chevron between three roses; and the name of Ambrose is written three times on the same page' (Ward, p. 918).

Contents: The beginning of the work is lost from this manuscript. The first line of the remaining fragment, 'If þatt þou vnderstonde can' is equivalent to L3300, i.e. the fourth line of the answer to Q. 60. It is therefore impossible to say whether or not this version contained a Table of Contents in the same way as L. The division into books and the numbering of the questions are identical to those in L, except in a number of places where there are errors in L or H. (Books iii and iv are not, in fact, numbered in H, but the numbering of the questions restarts at 1 in each case, instead of continuing at 201 and 301. Book ii is labelled

Secundus.) The last line on f. 79v, 'That sanke from hem euery ny3t', is equivalent to L12224, and the remaining lines (62 in L) are lost.

In addition to the pages lost at the beginning and end of this manuscript, there are two other leaves lost, not noted in Ward's *Catalogue* or the British Library's *Catalogue of the Harleian Manuscripts*. These are: one leaf between ff. 8v and 9r (equivalent to L4171–290; 120 lines); one leaf between ff. 59v and 60r (equivalent to L9855–957; 103 lines). The total number of lines remaining in H is in the region of 8,750, so that, assuming it was originally the same length as L, about 3,500 lines have been lost on missing pages.

Type II versions

B: Oxford, Bodleian Library, Laud Misc. 559   s. xv^2
    (See Coxe, p. 402; printed on the left-hand pages in this edition)

153 parchment leaves, size *c.* 280mm by 200mm, ruled space *c.*185–8mm by 121–4mm. Collation: i modern paper flyleaf, ii parchment flyleaves (conjoint), 1–19^8, 20^7 (1 left), i parchment flyleaf, i modern paper flyleaf. Leaf signatures visible only in the second and third quires. Catchwords at the end of all gatherings except the second. The manuscript is written in one column, with 35 or 36 lines to a page, with questions in red; blue paraphs mark the beginning of each question and sometimes also the question number in the margin. The questions have not been filled in on ff. 70v–71r and 72r; from 78v onwards they are in a different hand from that of the rest of the text. Foliation (i, 1–157) is in pencil in the top right-hand corner, including flyleaves. Initials are in gold set in a red and blue surround, with green and gold leafy sprays. On the first page of the text of *Sidrak* (f. 3r) a space has been left, presumably for an illustration; the initial capital M is ornately decorated, with a border surrounding the whole page, in red, blue, green and gold. Pricking for the horizontal ruled lines is visible in the outer margins of the first quire only; prickings for the vertical bounding lines are visible in the top and bottom margins throughout. The ruling is in brown ink; frame ruling only is visible on ff. 78v–82v. The manuscript is in a standard Laudian binding, with Laud's coat of arms in gilt on both upper and lower cover; it has been quite extensively repaired. Date: Dr Martin Kauffmann, Assistant Librarian in the Department of Western Manuscripts at the Bodleian (to whom I am most grateful for supplying many of the codicological details above) dates the manuscript, on palaeographical grounds and from the style of

the decoration,[48] to the third quarter of the fifteenth century (private communication, 14 October 1996).

Marginalia and end leaves: Folios 1 and 2 contain names of members of the Wescott and Fowler families; Laud's own name appears at the bottom of f. 3r; the signature of Richard Wescott appears below the last line on f. 155r; and on the reverse of the last leaf (155v) there are various unintelligible notes in English and Latin, together with the signature of Robert Royse (which appears also on 154v).

Contents: This is the fullest known version of type II and has no pages missing. It contains just over 10,930 lines, i.e. about 1300 less than L. However, about 900 lines in L are included in the Table of Contents, which is omitted in B, so that the actual difference in the length of the body of the text is only 400 or so lines: this makes the terms 'long' and 'short' (for types I and II) somewhat misleading. The fourteen-line Introduction of L occupies only six lines in B: the opening invocation to the Trinity and the promise of answered questions are omitted. The opening couplet of B, which is roughly the same in all type II versions, reads 'Men may fynde in olde bookes/ Whosoo þat in them lookis'. The remainder of the Prologue is substantially the same as in L, one early difference being the naming of Bokkus's country (which is left unnamed in L) as 'Bectorye' (B10).

After the Prologue, the questions and answers begin at once, the Table of Contents being omitted. Of the questions and answers found in L only Q. 30 is omitted from B (it is supplied in this edition from T); many of the answers, however, are shorter than in L, though a few are longer (e.g. nos. 14, 23, 39). There are seven questions in B (nos. 43–9) not found in L, but common to all type II manuscripts, except where the relevant pages are lost. The questions and answers are not divided into books, but are numbered consecutively up to 400 (in fact B contains 414 questions, but this is obscured by errors in numbering). The order of questions, however (apart from the omission of one question and the addition of seven others, noted above), is identical to that in L, with the following exceptions: (1) the third and fourth questions in L are reversed in B alone, all other type II manuscripts having the same order as type I (see variants for B981–1008); (2) Q. 74, on the inhabitants of the world, is placed earlier in the type I versions than

---

[48] On the decoration see Otto Pächt and J. J. G. Alexander, *Illuminated Manuscripts in the Bodleian Library Oxford. Vol. 3: British, Irish, and Icelandic Schools* (Oxford, 1973), no. 1106.

in B and other type II versions (the placement in this edition follows type II); (3) the misplaced lines in L (L11751–988) are correctly placed in B and the other type II versions in which they appear. The conclusion of the narrative is more or less the same as in L, though slightly shorter. After the conclusion there is a twelve-line envoy, asking the reader to pray for 'Hughe of Campedene,/ That þis boke hath þoroghsought/ And vnto Englyssh ryme hit brought'.

T: Cambridge, Trinity College, MS O.5.6   s. xv ex.
  (See James, pp. 310–11)

69 vellum leaves, size *c.* 390mm by 265mm, written space *c.* 285mm by 225mm. Collation (after James): 1$^?$ (two left), 2^8 (lacks 8), 3^8 (lacks 1, half of 3 and 8), 4–5^8, 6^8 (lacks 1, 5), 7–8^8, 9^{10} (3, 4 are half leaves: 7 lacking), 10^8 (lacks 1, 7, 8), 11$^{?6}$ (lacks 6). No quire signatures. The manuscript is written in two columns, with 51 lines to a page, and with questions and question numbers in red, and is foliated in pencil in the top right-hand corner. The initial on f. 1 is in red, blue, green, and pink, with some gold; other initials in *Sidrak* (ff. 1r–37v) are in blue with red flourishing (those in the *Dicts and Sayings of the Philosophers*, which follows, are framed in gold, coloured in red, green, blue, and black). Ruling in brown ink for two columns with double outer and single inner bounding lines with two pairs of double horizontals at both head and foot of text. Original leather binding. Date: Bühler remarks of the *Dicts* (occupying ff. 38r to 64v in this manuscript): 'As the text is that of William Worcester's revision, the manuscript was written after March 1472.'[49] As to whether or not the first part of the manuscript, containing *Sidrak*, was written by the same scribe, or at the same time, Mr Bruce Purvis, (then) Assistant Librarian at Trinity College, writes: '*Sydrac* and the *Dicts* are written in very similar hands, but there are distinct differences in the formation of certain letters. . . . I would suggest that the two tracts were written by two different scribes, but the general style of the manuscript—the ruling of the pages, the textual layout, the decoration and the miniatures—suggests that both parts were undertaken in response to a single commission and that therefore they can be dated as exact contemporaries' (private communication, 7 June 1972). It seems safe, therefore, to assign this version of *Sidrak* to the fourth quarter of the fifteenth century, after 1472.

[49] *The Dicts and Sayings of the Philosophers*, ed. Curt F. Bühler, EETS 211 (1941 *for* 1939), p. xxvi.

Contents: The title 'Sydrac the Philosopher' appears on f. 1r, followed by the following prose preface: 'This boke is callid Sidrake grounded upon scripture the whiche was translated owte of Frenche in to Englishe compiled and made afore the Incarnacion of oure lorde Jhesu crist declaring sadde and notable wisedomes celestiall Instructiones and questiones for the helthe of mannes soule. With many othur vertuous and holsom thinges here after ensewynge, with a parcell of the seven sciencis.' The Introduction is the six-line version, as in B, with the opening prayer omitted. The Prologue is substantially the same as in B, and there is no Table of Contents. The questions and numbers are not divided into books, but are numbered consecutively to 304. The number of questions originally contained in this version cannot be determined, since there are several pages now missing and there are inaccuracies in the numbering of the questions left (e.g., jumps from 55 to 57 and from 179 to 190). The order of the questions (excluding those omitted or lost) is the same as in B, except in the following instances: (1) the third and fourth questions appear in the same order as in L; (2) Q. 30, which is omitted in B, is included in T, but precedes Q. 29; (3) Q. 42 (omitted in L) is numbered 43 in T, but follows Q. 58; it is the last question on f. 10*r (see note (3) below), and consequently the answer is lost. The conclusion to the poem is similar to that in B, although the envoy contains an extra couplet, 'ande that it mutte so bee/ Seith alle amen for charite'.

There are various pencilled notes in the Trinity manuscript concerning missing leaves, not all of them correct. An examination of this manuscript, and a comparison of it with other type II manuscripts, reveals the following: (1) There is a note at the bottom of f. 9v saying '1 leaf missing'. The question numbers show, however, that about sixteen questions are missing (from the latter part of Q. 30 to the beginning of Q. 46 in T numbering); the equivalent passage in B occupies about 400 lines (B1746–2156), and, since the pages of T contain about 100 lines per side (200 lines per folio), it can reasonably be assumed that there are two leaves missing between 9v and 10r. (2) A note at the bottom of 10v says '1 leaf missing'. This, however, is incorrect: no leaves are missing, in spite of a jump in the question numbers from 55 to 57: this is simply an error in the numbering of the questions. (3) Between the folios numbered 10 and 11 there is a half-folio, numbered 10*r. This is divided vertically, so that the right-hand column of 10*r and the left-hand column of 10*v are lost (containing about 100 lines). (4) The notes at the bottom of 14v ('1 leaf missing') and 30v ('1 leaf wanting') are correct. (5) There is one leaf missing between folios 34 and 35 (containing from the latter part of Q. 271 to the beginning of Q. 279 in T numbering, equivalent to lines 7745–948 in B), although there is no note to this effect.

Summary Table of Pages Missing in T

Between folios	Leaves lost	Equivalent lines in B	Lines lost
9 and 10	2	1746–2156	411
10 and 11	½	2389–2470	82
14 and 15	1	3293–3485	193
30 and 31	1	6724–6925	202
34 and 35	1	7745–7948	204

The total number of leaves lost is, thus, five and a half, representing a loss of about 1,100 lines. With the 7,400-odd lines remaining, this means that the full version of T must originally have contained about 8,500 lines, i.e. about 2,400 less than B. The bulk of the deficit is explained by the omission, in T, of 122 questions following T 282, which are included in both B and L (questions 272 to 393 in this edition, lines 8047–10464/ 9159–11788). That these questions are not lost, but intentionally omitted, is shown by the numbering in T, which proceeds from 282 to 283 without a break.

A: London, Society of Antiquaries of London MS 252   s. xv/xvi
(See Ker, p. 306)

78 paper leaves, size *c.* 305mm by 200mm, written space *c.* 190mm by 100mm. Collation: 1¹² (lacks 1, 12), 2¹², 3–5 lacking, 6¹² (lacks 2, 3, 10, 11), 7–9 lacking, 10–13¹², 14 lacking. Quire signatures at the end of each gathering except the first. Catchwords in black, underlined in red. The manuscript is written in one column, with 33 or 34 lines to a page, and with questions and question numbers in red. Initial capitals are marked for the rubricator but not executed, except for the opening M (black, with decorative plaits). No pricking or ruling is visible. Modern foliation in pencil in the top right-hand corner (1–77; a leaf omitted after f. 15 has been numbered 15*). Modern vellum binding (note inside front cover: 'Rebound by PRO, 1989'), with no flyleaves. Pamela Willetts, the Society of Antiquaries' manuscripts cataloguer (to whom I am indebted for several of these codicological details) points out that the former vellum covers (now preserved separately as MS 252*) 'were formed from an architectural plan, early sixteenth century, for a large (possibly collegiate) building. An inscription "Ann Reede hyr Book" occurs on these covers; fol. 1 of the manuscript is annotated "My Lady Ann Redes

boke"' (private communication, 16 October 1996). 'My Lady Anne Rede' has not been identified, but an index card at the Society of Antiquaries notes 'An Anne Rede, who could have been so described, except that she was a commoner, when married to her second husband, between 1551 and 1577. Buried at St. Margaret, Norwich.' Date: The late Professor N. R. Ker considered the manuscript to be 'very late in the century and perhaps even s. xv/xvi' (private communication, 13 Nov. 1972). The index card at the Society of Antiquaries gives the date as 'Late 15thc. according to Mill Stephenson, but poss. after 1500'.

Contents: The Introduction is the six-line version, as in B. The Prologue is substantially the same as in B, but there is one leaf missing between folios 10 and 11 (= B679–746). There is no Table of Contents. The questions are numbered consecutively as far as 381, but the remaining questions, and the conclusion to the poem, are lost. The total number of lines left is in the region of 5,000.

Summary Table of Pages Missing in A

Between folios	Leaves lost	Equivalent lines in B	Lines lost
10 and 11	1	679–746	68
21 and 22	35–36	1540–3910	2371
22 and 23	2	3979–4115	137
28 and 29	2	4522–4651	130
29 and 30	37–38	4719–7203	2485
After 77	7–8	10436–10934	499

This manuscript is remarkably similar to B, and they are obviously closely related, perhaps copied from the same exemplar. One striking similarity is the confusion concerning questions 380 to 389. In B and A the first eight of these ten questions are omitted, although the answers are given; the ninth question (388) is included and numbered (B 374 [number repeated], A 378); the tenth question (389) is omitted, but the answer is given. Thereafter, in each case, the questions are included and the numbering restarted, but with no numbers left out to account for the ten answers given in this section.

This is the only English verse manuscript not mentioned in the *Index* or *Supplement*.

S: London, British Library, MS Sloane 2232   s. xvi in. (1502)
    (See Ward, p. 919)

117 paper leaves, size *c.* 142mm by 102mm (duodecimo), written space *c.* 110mm by 70mm. Collation: iv paper flyleaves, i parchment flyleaf

(formerly a pastedown, pen trials on verso), 1^{10}, 2^{16}, 3^{12}, 4^{10} (wants 1, blank), $5-6^{16}$, 7^{14}, 8^{16}, 9^{10} (wants 10, blank), i parchment flyleaf (formerly a pastedown, pen trials on recto and verso), iv paper flyleaves. (I am grateful to Michelle Brown for supplying this collation.) No quire signatures. Catchwords at 25v, 37v, 62v, 92v, 108v. The manuscript is written entirely in black, frequently marred by blots and crossings out, in one column, with 24 to 33 lines to a page, some pages having two lines written as one long line (10v–11r, 12v–14v, etc.). Foliation in pencil in the top right-hand corner corrects an earlier brown-ink foliation that omitted f. 1. Ruling in brown ink or crayon. British Museum in-house 19th-century brown leather binding. The date (1502) is fixed by the colophon on f. 117r: 'Explicit quod Robertus Wakefelde. In vigilia ascensionis Domini iiij° die [4 minims]/ Anno Domini M° CCCCC^{mo} ij°'.

In the description of L in the British Library's *Catalogue of Lansdowne Manuscripts* (p. 183) there is a statement to the effect that 'Robert Wakefelde, whose name occurs at the end of the Sloane copy, was only the transcriber of the manuscript and probably the learned chaplain of King Henry VIII'. Since the author, or rather, translator, of *Sidrak* is named in B, T, and G as Hugh of Campdene, the first half of this assertion, that this Robert Wakefelde 'was only the transcriber' of S, would seem to be true; however, I do not think there is any justification for identifying this scribe with Henry VIII's chaplain, who happened to have the same name. According to the *Dictionary of National Biography* the Robert Wakefeld who was one of the king's chaplains first graduated in arts at Cambridge in 1513–14. Unless he did not go to Cambridge as an undergraduate until much later in life than is usual, he would have been very young in 1502, when S was written (between ten and thirteen years old, if one assumes a graduating age of between twenty-two and twenty-five). In 1527, Wakefeld wrote to the king concerning his proposed divorce. A comparison of the handwriting in this letter with that in S would settle the question as to whether they are both the work of the same hand; but I have been unable to ascertain whether or not the original copy of this letter still exists. However, the letter has been printed more than once,[50] and an examination of its language reveals no hint of the northern or north midland forms that characterize S (see p. xc below). Thus, unless Wakefeld's education and travel had wiped out all trace of his northern origin (*DNB* records that he became

---

[50] For example, (1) at the end of *Kotser codicis R. Wakfeldi*, printed by Thomas Berthelet (London, 1532); (2) in Appendix ix of Samuel Knight's *The Life of Erasmus* (Cambridge, 1726).

Professor of Hebrew at Louvain and taught also in Tübingen), or unless he made a point of writing to the king in London English, he cannot very well have been the man who wrote the Sloane manuscript.

End leaves: 1r–8v, Table of Contents, entitled 'Tabula sydrake', in a different hand (or style) from that of the poem; one blank folio, not numbered, between folios 8 and 9; 9r, four and a half lines in Latin and English prose concerning a woman who was 'in mysbeleve of the blessyd sacarment of the awter'; 9v, four lines of verse, 'No catell no care letitia/ No peny no ware duricia/ Spare & aye bare tristicia/ Spend & god wyll send alleluia' (see *Index* and *Supplement*, item 3209); seven lines of instructions, in Latin and English prose, for the preparation of a medicine, concluding, '& gyfe ye seke to drynke & he sall be holle wyt the grase of god probatum est'; the statement, 'Thomas genkenson a calfe ȝerly.'

Contents: Like the printed edition S begins with a Table of Contents (placed before the poem begins, not, as in L, after the Prologue). The Table, entitled 'Tabula sydrake' (see 'End leaves' above), consists of a list of the questions asked, or of the subject matter of the questions, in an abbreviated form, not (as in L) of a list of the questions in their full form. There is some confusion between the numbering of the questions in the Table and that in the text itself, since number 1 in the Table, 'of the trinite', refers to Sidrak's description of the Trinity at the end of the Prologue, which is not numbered as a question in the text. Fifteen questions (31–45) are omitted from the Table between the bottom of f. 1v and the top of f. 2r; thereafter the Table continues straightforwardly, but with many crossings out (notably on f. 7v), till the end of f. 8v. The last item, 'of ye knawlegyng' (numbered 243), is equivalent to the final question (Q. 415) in this edition.

The poem proper begins on f. 10r with the standard six-line Introduction for type II. The six lines following the Introduction (naming Bokkus's country as 'Bettorye', and dating him 847 years after Noah) are standard for type II; then, following the next couplet, 'The kyng Buccus hym byþoȝt / þat he walde haue a toure wroȝt' (which is common, in one form or another, to types I and II), the whole of that part of the Prologue dealing with the attempts to build the Tower, and the adventures on the Green Raven's Hill leading to the conversion of Bokkus (B15–635), is passed over with the following couplet: 'But of þis toure ouerpasse we nowe/ And speke of þinge of more prowe.' Thereupon, with an introductory couplet peculiar to this manuscript—'Buccus saide, "Sidrake now tell me/ Somwhat of the Trinite"'—S jumps to that section of the Prologue containing Sidrak's explanation of the Trinity by a comparison with the sun (B637–58). That done, S omits the remaining happenings of the Prologue dealing with the fury of Bokkus's followers and their unsuccessful attempts to destroy Sidrak (B659–908), and proceeds directly to the conclusion of the Prologue (B909–24), which acts as an introduction to Bokkus's questions.

The questions are not divided into books, but are numbered consecutively up to 243 (there are, in fact, 244 questions, but this appears as 243 owing to errors in numbering). The questions included, and their order, are the same as in B (except that questions 3 and 4 are not reversed) as far as B2386; thereafter S starts to omit some questions and to re-arrange the order of various others. One complete question and answer (Q. 139) appears twice in S, as Q. 81 and as Q. 202 (S 47r.1–18 and 100r.17–100v.8 respectively). After the answer to the final question, the conclusion to the story is compressed into the following fourteen lines:

> Sydrak, God forȝelde hit þe
> þe techinge þat þu hast taȝt me:
> Fro derkenesse þu hast me broȝt
> Vnto the lyȝt þat fayleþ noȝt;
> Now wote I mykel þinge
> þat I hade after grete longinge
> And now wote I what God may do
> To lyff and to þe soule also.
> God, Lorde of myȝtes moost,
> Fader and Sone and Holy Goost,
> Saue vs fro þe fendes wyles,
> For many oone þat shrewe bigylles;
> And brynge vs, Lorde, vnto þi blis,
> Wherof þat neuer nonn ende is. Amen.

The first eight of these lines are equivalent to B10853–60; then B10861–917, dealing with the return to Bokkus's kingdom, the completion of the tower, the conversion of Garaab, and the subsequent relapse, are omitted; and the remaining six lines are equivalent to B10918–22. Then follows the scribe's signature, with the colophon described above, the envoy being omitted. There are no pages missing, and the total number of lines included is about 6,000.

The characteristics that distinguish S from other manuscripts of type

II may be summarized as follows: (1) severe abbreviation of the Prologue, leaving only the explanation of the Trinity; (2) omission of large numbers of questions (not in one complete section, as in T); (3) different placing of many of the questions; (4) repetition of Q. 139; (5) omission of the concluding sections concerning Bokkus's return to his own country; (6) omission of the envoy; (7) inclusion of a Table of Contents (before the beginning of the poem) containing abbreviated forms of the questions or of the subject matter (cf. the printed edition).

P: Princeton, Princeton University Library, Robert H. Taylor Collection, Taylor Medieval MS no. 3 (olim Wrest Park MS 5; olim Meyerstein)

s. xv

39 parchment leaves, size c. 375mm by 265mm, written space c. 290mm by 170mm. Collation: ii paper flyleaves, 1^8 (lacks 1), $2–5^8$. Quire signatures (in a later hand than the text) on the first page of each gathering. Catchwords on ff. 15v and 23v. The manuscript is written in two columns, with 36 to 47 lines to a page, and with spaces left for the questions, which are omitted (except in the preliminary Table). Every eighth leaf is foliated in pencil in the top right-hand corner, counting [A]2 as leaf 1 and B1 as leaf 8. No coloured initials in ff. 1r–9v (Table of Contents); initials from 10r to 31v are in blue with red flourishing; from f. 32 onwards they are marked for the rubricator but not executed. Columns are pricked and ruled in pencil. Bound with *Brut Chronicle* (94 parchment leaves, ii conjugate paper blanks, followed by the paper paste-down) in 17th-century or early 18th-century panelled calf (rebacked after January 1979) with Wrest Park bookplate of Thomas, Earl de Grey.

Date: given in the ring catalogue as '15th Cent.'; it is difficult to be more precise.

Marginalia (difficult to decipher) on ff. 3v, 14r ('No myght haythe the body of hym self sykirly'), 21v ('O lorde god hou meruelouse . . .'), 24r (copying first three couplets of left column), 24v, 25r, 28r, 30v–32v, 37v ('Of gode clothyng . . .'); signature at bottom of 40v (first page of *Brut Chronicle*) identified on opening flyleaf by former owner E. H. W. M[eyerstein] as that of 'William Cecil (Baron Burghley, 1520–1598)'. This note is followed by a pencilled explanation: 'E. H. W. Myerstein, sold at Sotheby [c1953–4]'. An entry from a twentieth-century bookseller's catalogue pasted inside the back cover is followed by this note in pen: 'Ellis; March, 1923. Cat. no. 211'. Mark R. Farrell, the Curator of the Robert H. Taylor collection (to whom I am indebted for several of the codicological details above), indicates that 'Robert Taylor bought the book from Seven Gables on 5 December 1955 and bequeathed it to Princeton University in May 1985' (private communication, 6 November 1996).

Contents: P begins (like S and G) with a Table of Contents placed before the Prologue. The Table in P, however, differs from those in S and G in that it contains a list of the questions in their full form (as in L). The first 84 questions of the Table are lost on missing pages: f. 1 begins at Q. 85 in the Table (although the questions are not numbered in the Table in P). The poem proper begins on f. 5r with the standard six-line Introduction for type II, and continues, with no pages missing, until the end of the answer to Q. 182; the remainder of the work (B5853–10934) is lost. The lines extant in P amount to about 6,500.

This manuscript is listed in *Index* and *Supplement*, entry 772, as a type I version, and it does exhibit certain type I features, notably the placement of Q. 74 before Q. 63, and the inclusion of a Table of Contents consisting of a list of the questions with the full wording. But since, on the other hand, the placement of the Table before the Prologue, the giving of the short form of the Introduction and of the shorter form of those answers where type I is longer than type II, and the inclusion of questions 43–9 place it rather with the type II versions of entry 2147, I have classified it as type II and give variants from it against B rather than L.

D: Brudenell (Deene) MS I.v.101   s. xv in.

A fragment consisting of two vellum folios (conjoint), size *c.* 320mm by 260mm, written space *c.* 260mm by 160mm. The manuscript is written in two columns, with about 55 lines to a column. The questions, which are written in black, are indented, spaced off from the answers, and preceded by a paragraph mark in red; the answers begin with a capital letter in blue, with red flourishes. Date: The late Professor N. R. Ker writes: 'It is difficult to date a good set anglicana like this, but it could be about 1400 or it could be a little later than this, but I don't think much later. The long horizontal mark of abbreviation seems to me a distinctive feature' (private communication, 13 Nov. 1972). This makes the fragment by some way the earliest known manuscript of *Sidrak* in English. In the bottom left-hand corner of f. 1v, upside-down, is written, in seventeenth-century handwriting, 'Court Rolls of

Glapthorne'. The fragment was apparently used at one time as a wrapper for these manor court rolls.

Contents: The fragment contains about 440 lines, equivalent to B8336–775. There are twenty-two questions (apparently unnumbered), the first and last being incomplete, beginning at the sixth line of the answer to Q. 286, 'Whan he blew ferst on adam', ending with the seventh line of the answer to Q. 307, 'A wiked aungel he has also.' The centre pages, 1v and 2r, which appear to have been on the outside when the fragment was used as a wrapper, are so badly faded as to be, for the most part, illegible (even with the help of an ultra-violet lamp), although some words and even some whole lines can be made out. No variants from these faded pages (equivalent to B8445–660) are included in the apparatus to this edition.

The fragment is entered in *Supplement*, entry 2147, as 'Brudenell, Lamport Hall, Northants.' It belongs in fact to Mr Edmund Brudenell of Deene Park, Corby, Northants, and is in the keeping of the Northamptonshire and Huntingdonshire Archives Committee at the Northamptonshire Record Office. The Office was at one time housed at Lamport Hall before being moved to its present premises at Delapre Abbey, Northampton.

G: The Printed Verse Edition of Thomas Godfray

An edition of *Sidrak* was printed by Thomas Godfray in the first half of the sixteenth century. The British Library has one complete copy (Catalogue no. G 11228); a second copy, incomplete (C.13.a.20), in which the Table of Contents is defective and in which several questions and answers are supplied in handwriting (following the wording of Godfray's edition) where the printed pages are missing; and a fragment (C. 40.m.9. [17]) consisting of one page from the Prologue, dealing with Bokkus's idolatry. Bülbring notes that several copies (including the complete one mentioned above) are listed by Thomas Corser in his *Collectanea Anglo-Poetica*.[51]

Contents: The title-page contains the following portentous title, beneath which is a woodcut of 'Sidrack' and 'Kynge boccus':

The history of kyng Boccus /& Sydracke how he confoundyd his lerned men / and in ye syght of them dronke stronge venym in the name of the Trinite & dyd

[51] See Corser, p. 97. Bülbring notes also that there is mention, in W. C. Hazlitt's *Hand-Book to the popular, poetical and dramatic literature of Great Britain* (London, 1867), of another copy in the Britwell library ('Sidrac in England', p. 461).

hym no hurt. Also his diuynyte y*at* he lerned of the boke of Noe. Also his profycyes that he had by reuelacyo*n* of the aungell. Also his answeris to the questions of wysdome / both morall and natural wyth moche worldly wysdome contayned in noumber. CCC. lxv. translatyd by Hugo of Caumpeden / out of frenche into Englysche.

On the reverse of the title-page there is a preface by John Twyne,[52] the tone of which (unless it is mere publisher's hyperbole) gives some indication of the high regard in which *Sidrak* appears to have been held. It reads as follows:

John Twyne to the redar

The profyt and co*m*modite of this boke (O gentyl and curteys redar) is so euydent & open / that it nedythe no settyng out nor praysyng / for dowtful thynges comenly be praysyd or despraysed / be cause trewe iugment may be take*n* of them. but thynges of ope*n* goodnes nede no praysyng / for with theyr goodnes they prayse them selfe / as thou shalt fynd this boke / the whych to speke truly can not be suffycyently praysed. I had leuer ther fore (as Salust sayth of Carthago) hold my pese and to speke lytel of yt / but shortly to knowe somwhat of his matters in effect / he showeth of goddys workes ryght as the old & new testament in many volumes declareth. Also natural phylosophy express-yng the causes with euydent ensamples of moch moralyte in geuyng good counsel and a delect betwyx good and bades truly more euyde*n*t than euer dyd Plato / Arystotyles / or Cicero i*n* theyr manyfold workes / he shortly techeth moch knowlege of physyke the dyspocycyon of co*m*plexcyons the alteracyo*n* of ages with moch secresy of the yere / greatly of astronomy / course of heuyn / & planets with theyr respectes / breuely and playnly that that ypocras / Galyen or Ptholomy comprehendyd in great or iuste volumes. Also moch worldly experyence. Abundau*n*t in prophesyes / how the maners of me*n* shal alter and the world shalbe ended / with his iugment meruelus exhortyng the people to eschew the fylthynesse of synne / what paynes are ordayned for yt / and the ioyes of heuyn. Than is this boke necessary to al men. For it exhortyth to wysdome / good maners / ensamples hystoryis, wherfore it may well be called a boke of philosofye /that is to say a stody of wysdome. Than I counsayle euery man to rede this boke / or that cannot rede to geue dylygent eere to the reder for they shal fynde theri*n* great frute bothe to the soule and body.

Beneath the preface is a Table of Contents, beginning with a summary of the Prologue (not found in any of the manuscripts) and continuing with a list of the questions, or their subject matter, in abbreviated form (cf. S). The Table begins as follows:

[52] See *DNB*, 57 (1899), 402–3.

Here begynneth the table of this boke.

Fyrst the hystory of Boccus & Sidracke / how by the power of god he dystroyed his ydols / and by the counsayle of the aungel shewed hym the vmbre of the trinite / wherby he conuerted hym and all his host. Than gaue he hym enstructions / and answeryd to dyuers questions that he demaundyd of hym.

The questyons.

yf god be euer and euer shalbe.	The fyrst questyon.
where may it be that god of heuen may be sene	iii.
yf god be ouer al and euery where	iii.

The Table continues for a further ten sides, the last question, 'shall they remember them of theyr wyckednes' (numbered 362), being equivalent to the last question (Q. 415) in those manuscripts that have not lost their final pages.

After the Table, the poem begins with the six-line version of the Introduction common to the type II manuscripts, but, as can be seen from the transcript below, with some marked differences in wording:

Men may fynde in olde bokys
Who so therin lokys
Actes worthy of memory
Full of knowlege and mystery
Wherof I shall shew a lytell ieste
That befell ons in the Eest.

Thereafter the Prologue continues for 29 sides (about 930 lines), followed by the questions and answers, not divided into books, but numbered consecutively to 362. (The total number of questions is in fact 344, in spite of the figures 365, given in the title, and 362, given in the Table and the text.) The seven questions not included in the type I manuscripts (nos. 43–9) are included here; as in B and S, they are numbered 42–8. Several complete questions and answers that are included in all the manuscripts (except where the pages are missing) are omitted from G (e.g., nos. 17, 161, 255), and although certain groups of questions omitted from G overlap with groups omitted from S (e.g., nos. 255–70 omitted from G, 256–67 omitted from S), the general pattern of omissions in G is apparently independent: many questions omitted from S are included in G (e.g., nos. 239–45, 247–51). There are also some differences peculiar to G in the order of the questions (e.g., nos. 128–9, 338: in G these follow nos. 135 and 323 respectively).

The questions and answers are followed by the conclusion to the story (70 lines, roughly as in B), which is in turn followed by the envoy (12 lines, as in B), naming the translator as 'Hughe of caumpedene'. After the envoy is appended the note:

Thus endeth the hystory and questions of kynge Boccus and Sydracke. Prynted at London by Thomas Godfray. At the coste and charge of dan Robert Saltwode monke of saynt Austens at Cantorbury.
Cum priuilegio regali.

On the reverse of the last page there is a framed illustration of the coat of arms of St Augustine's monastery, Canterbury.

The date of Godfray's edition, which is not known, has given rise to much speculation, from the '?1510' of the *British Library General Catalogue of Printed Books* to the '?1530' of *Supplement* 2147. The originator of the 1510 theory is John Bagford: Ames, writing of Godfray's work, says, 'The first book may probably be, The history of king Boccus and Sydrache. . . . The copy which I saw had no date, but Bagford, in his MSS. adds, Cum privilegio regali, 1510.'[53] To this Dibdin, in his revision of Ames's work, replies: 'As *The History of Kyng Boccus and Sydracke* is, in reality, without date, I see no reason, upon the slender authority of Bagford, to affix to it the gratuitous date of 1510.'[54] Payne Collier claims that Godfray 'did not begin to employ a press until 1522';[55] but Bülbring (p. 460, n. 3) points out that this claim is groundless, since (1) the date 1522 is based on a letter of Erasmus to 'Christofer bysshop of Basyle' written in 1522, and printed by Godfray—but the printed copy is not dated, and may be later than 1522; (2) there is no evidence that Godfray's *Sydracke* was not printed before this letter in any case.

F. S. Isaac mentions three books of Godfray's to which dates can be assigned, all of them post-1530: 'Godfray issued only two dated books, the first complete edition of *Chaucer's Works* published in 1532, and *The maner of subvention for pore people in Hypres*, 1535. From internal evidence one book, Christopher St. German's *Answere to a letter*, can be proved later than 1535.' Isaac has no new material to offer on the date of Godfray's *Sydracke*, but notes that 'Robert Saltwood's name appears

[53] Joseph Ames, *Typographical Antiquities* (London, 1749), pp. 139–40.
[54] Joseph Ames, *Typographical Antiquities, augmented by William Herbert and now greatly enlarged, with copious notes* by the Rev. Thomas Frognall Dibdin, iii (London, 1816), p. 62. Bülbring (p. 59, n. 3) implies wrongly that Dibdin accepts Bagford's date.
[55] J. Payne Collier, *A Bibliographical and Critical Account of the Rarest Books in the English Language*, i (London, 1865), pp. 112–13.

among the signatories of the deed of surrender at the dissolution of the house in 1538.'[56]

Since the only dateable books printed by Godfray are all post-1530, and since there is no evidence (other than Bagford's unsupported assumption) that his *Sydracke* was printed a long time before any of these, it seems reasonable to follow *Supplement* 2147 in assigning to it the approximate date ?1530, at least until further evidence emerges.

6. RELATIONSHIPS OF THE ENGLISH RHYMED VERSIONS TO THE FRENCH AND TO ONE ANOTHER

(A) THE RELATIONSHIP OF THE ENGLISH TRANSLATION TO THE FRENCH

Since it was not possible for me to examine all the French manuscripts before deciding which one to use as the basis for a comparison with the English, I have used the earliest (F) as the basis of comparison and then attempted to see whether other French manuscripts are closer to the English than F. There are several questions to consider. (1) Where both schools of English manuscripts are shorter than F, are there other French manuscripts that omit the same passages as the English? (2) Where both schools of English manuscripts are longer than F, is there anything in other French manuscripts that could be the basis of the additional material in the English? (3) Where one school of English manuscripts is longer than the other, is there anything in any French manuscript that could be the basis of the additional material? (4) Are there errors in the English that are paralleled in any French manuscripts?

Whereas positive evidence in answer to these questions would be persuasive, negative evidence is necessarily inconclusive. One might reasonably suppose with regard to the second question (for example), if one found passages in French manuscript X corresponding to passages in the English that have no equivalent in F, that the English was translated from an X-type manuscript rather than from an F-type.

---

[56] F. S. Isaac, *English & Scottish Printing Types 1501–35, 1508–41* (Bibliographical Society, Oxford, 1930), p. 77. No date is assigned to *The maner of subvention* in the section on Godfray in *Hand-Lists of Books by London Printers 1501–1556*, Part ii (Bibliographical Society, London, 1896).

Failure to find such passages in the surviving French manuscripts, on the other hand, though it may suggest that such manuscripts never existed, is not proof that they did not. Nonetheless, it has seemed worthwhile to look at such evidence as I could find, negative or positive, in the attempt to answer these questions. I have accordingly attempted to look at all the French manuscripts I knew to exist (as listed on pp. x–xi above), comparing a few key passages in each with the equivalent passages in the English versions ('key' because they exhibit significant differences between the English versions and F; 'a few' because it was possible to spend only a short time looking at each manuscript). These passages are listed below, with the significant differences between the French and the English noted. The results must be treated with caution. The French manuscripts vary somewhat in both the number and ordering of the questions: I was not able to locate each question in all the manuscripts; in some cases a question I could not find might have been omitted, or might have been lost on missing pages; in others, it might have been present but not in the usual position, and I may have overlooked it unwittingly.

Q. 62: Envy. (Both schools of the English are longer than F.) There is no equivalent in F or other French manuscripts for the second half of the answer in the English, dealing with the tree of envy (see 2537–60/3419–42n).

Q. 89: No profit without work. (Both schools of the English are shorter than F.) The illustrative story about the two travellers, omitted from the English (see 3479–84/4379–84n), is standard in French manuscripts.

Q. 102: Copulating dogs (lost on missing pages in F). There are two types of answer in the French manuscripts: (1) a short answer containing the simile of the two pieces of iron (as in both schools of the English); (2) a longer answer (in the longer French manuscripts), omitting the simile but giving greater physiological detail (see 3810–18/4750–8n). It is reasonable to assume that the English translation derives from a manuscript of the first type (to which the evidence of other answers shows that F belongs, though it has lost this particular question).

Q. 103: Covetousness. (A difficult phrase in both the English and the French.) See 3826/4766n and appendix 3 for the various equivalents in the French manuscripts for the phrase *the devels grype/ þe deuelis gripe.*

Q. 145: Falling stars. (Both schools of the English are shorter than F, reducing three phenomena to one.) The treatment in F (see 4915–32/5897–5914n) is standard in French manuscripts.

Q. 172: Is there an original language? (Both schools of the English are shorter than F.) The extended treatment similar to the account in Herodotus (see 5627–30/6617–20n) is standard in the French manuscripts. In some of them, however (generally the same ones that give the longer answer to Q. 102), this passage is treated as two questions, the child appearing only in the second. In a few instances the experiment with the child is omitted (BL Harley 4486, Bodley 461, Ashburnham 118; also Copenhagen 2919, a very short answer, omitting also the fruit-tree image).

Q. 267: The planets and their signs. (An error in the English: the positions of Scorpio and Capricorn are reversed: see 7897,906,8/9003,12,14n.) Most French manuscripts in which I located this question agree with F in assigning Capricorn to Saturn and Scorpio to Mars. In several the question appears to be missing. In some there are anomalies: Rennes 2435 and Bodleian e Museo 34 omit Aquarius, give Saturn Capricorn and Taurus, and assign Taurus also to Venus. I found no parallel for the error in the English.

Q. 285: The responsibilities of the various planets for shaping different organs of the body. (The type I English manuscripts are longer than type II; both differ somewhat from F: see the several notes on lines 8293–328/9471–528.) I found no basis in any French manuscripts for the greater length of the answer in type I of the English. Most French manuscripts agree with F in having Mercury form the tongue, the penis, and the testicles (see 8315/9503–8n); some in which this question is included omit the section about the planets forming particular organs (e.g., Ste-Geneviève 2202, BN n.a.fr. 12444); Brussels 11110 gives Mercury 'la langue et le vit et les coulles'. It looks as if *sight* in the English (8315/9508) derives from a reading similar to this last, in which *vit* 'penis' was wrongly taken as deriving from *voire*.

Q. 338: The reproduction of birds. (The English answer bears no relation to that in F.) All French manuscripts in which I located

this question have an answer similar to that in F (see 9377–90/
10613–26n): in none is there support for the English answer.

What conclusions can be drawn from this limited survey? Positive
evidence is lacking: no French manuscripts have come to light that omit,
add, or treat differently from F the passages corresponding to the
omissions, additions, or different treatments in the English, or to those
places where one English version is longer than another. Of the negative
evidence (assuming that the English derives from a version such as one
of the surviving ones) questions 102 and 172 suggest that the English
derives from a French version of the shorter (earlier) type. These
questions, together with 89 and 145, suggest that the translator was
not afraid to omit material; question 62, that he was not afraid to add it;
question 338, that he was not afraid to ignore his source altogether and
to substitute an answer from elsewhere, or from his own invention.

(B) RELATIONSHIPS BETWEEN THE ENGLISH VERSIONS: THE WIDER PICTURE

The greater length of many of the answers to Bokkus's questions in the
type I English manuscripts raises several questions concerning the
relationships between the English versions: is type I an expansion of
type II? or is type II an abridgement of type I? or is each school derived
independently from the French? The last possibility may be swiftly
dismissed on account of the general similarity in wording between the
schools—it cannot be supposed that two separate adaptations were made
from the French which happened to have been expressed so similarly—
and because of errors found in both schools that are unlikely to have
been made independently and presumably derive from a common
English ancestor, e.g., 'love' for 'bone' in Q. 59 (see 2387–414/3267–
94n), an error occurring in all the versions that contain this question: L
(type I), BPG (type II). But the question of expansion or abridgement is
less easily solved.

Bülbring contends (p. 458) that the type I versions are expanded by
interpolations occurring throughout the text; the suggestion in *Index*
and *Supplement* 2147, on the other hand, is that type II is an 'abridged
version'. The lack of support in the surviving French versions for the
additional passages in the type I manuscripts supports Bülbring: as
indicated in the introduction to the commentary on the text (p. 717
below), where the answers in L are longer than in B there is rarely any
support for L from F; the comment on Q. 285 above suggests also that

there is no support from French manuscripts other than F. It may nevertheless be worth comparing some answers of substantially differing length in types I and II with the corresponding answers in F, to see in what ways the two types compare with the French. The text used for this purpose (as for the comparisons made in the commentary) is that of Treanor's edition, checked against a microfilm of the manuscript.

Q. 4: The first thing God made (1009–26/1991–2026); Treanor, Q. 5, pp. 70–1

Primiers fist Dieus un mult bel palais qui est apelés le regne dou ciel, apres, fist le siecle; apres, enfern. Mais en icel palais a il esleu un grant nombre des siens amis dont il vistront jamais puis que il seront eus. Itel nombre veut il faire des homes que des angles par humilite por ce que les homes et les angles aorassent un seul Dieu en trinite, pere et filz et saint esperit.

This answer in L occupies 34 lines, that in B only 16 lines. The type II version (as represented by B) differs little from the French except for the addition of some padding to assist the rhyme, such as 'vnto my lust', 'full of blisse and full of light', 'depe vndir vs'. Type I (L), however, differs from the French in two more important ways: (1) the contents of the heavens (the planets and stars) are enumerated and described; (2) the sorrows of hell and the joys of heaven, slightly stronger in B than in the French, are magnified still further in L.

Q. 105: Should fools be answered? (3871–92/4813–46); Treanor, Q. 107, p. 148

Ciaus qui folament parlent, on ne lor doit mie respondre se les paroles ne sont en son damage, car aucunes fois que les fols parlent d'aucuns homes solament et on ne set por cui il dient. Mais se il lor respondent tost sauront que por eaus a esté le dit et taisir vaut mieus et quant les saiges gens aucunes fois faillent et se reprendent meismes et se revertissent et se vergoingnent durement et quant on les reprent il se hontoient et se reconnoissent qu'il ont mal dist, les fols quant il parlent folament et on les reprent, il s'encorroissent et s'en felenissent durement et plus afferment et maintenent lour folie et si l'engendrent en mult de folies et pensees et raisons et plais et le taisir vaut miex que li repondres a tel gent se damage n'i est.

Here the type I answer is twelve lines longer than type II, the last fourteen lines of L taking the place of one couplet in B. The extra lines of type I are of a clearly moralizing kind: 'therefore one ought not to do this . . . therefore I advise every man to do that'. Neither the swords' points (or swords) of TSP (see variants for B3891) nor the two-edged swords of LH4836 are found in the French, but the one might well have suggested the other.

Q. 195: Unnatural eating (6159–82/7177–216); Treanor, Q. 201, pp. 217–18

Il i a assez de gent en ce siecle qui mangent autre gent et honteusement et faucement et desloiaument et n'entendez mie que la char de la gent mangent ciaux qui tollent d'autrui a tort. Il les manjent tous vis. Car il lor tollent le bien qu'il ont gaignié par le trevail et par la suor de lour char de quoi il devoient mangier et vivre et passier son tens en cest siecle. Il i a autre maniere de mangier la gent, car tous ciaux qui parlent mal de la gent et les font blasmer entre les autres gens, ciaux font si grant mal com se il manjassent lor char, et ciaux qui tuent la gent por le lor ou por noiant, vaudroit mieuz qu'il manjassent lar char de la gent et mult d'autres manieres.

Type I is longer than type II in three parts of this answer: (1) 6168/7186–8, three lines in LH for one in BT; (2) 6175–6/7195–200, six lines in LH for two in BT; (3) L7207–16, ten lines in LH, omitted entirely in BT. In each of these instances the extra lines in type I are in a didactic strain: (1) concerns what is or is not done virtuously; (2) concerns a failure to fear God and the regret with which such failure will be followed; (3) contains advice on the sort of food people *should* eat and the reverent manner in which it should be eaten.

In each of the three examples cited the type II answer is much closer to F; in no case is there anything in F from which the extra lines in type I are directly translated. Though one cannot discount entirely the possibility that there exists (or existed) in French an expanded school from which the type I English versions could have been translated, it seems more reasonable to assume that the original English version was of type II (which accords reasonably well with the early French versions) and that the type I English versions were expanded from type II, as Bülbring argued. Two other factors lend general support to this assumption: (1) the earliest surviving fragment of *Sidrak* in English, D (which antedates the other English manuscripts by half a century or more), is of type II—though this might be mere coincidence; (2) the extra lines in type I are often of a moralizing kind, as is evident from the passages discussed above; and that these passages are typical in this respect may be quickly confirmed by a look at other answers that are longer in type I than in type II. It is possible, of course, that an adapter went through type I striking out the passages of overt didacticism to leave us with type II; but an age which admired the prolixity of Lydgate, and which had seen Chaucer renounce whole sections of his work on the grounds of their lack of 'doctrine', admits more readily of an expander in the moralistic vein.

Another question to be considered is whether any of the surviving English versions were copied one from another. A few conclusions are immediately apparent from the number of questions contained in each, without reference to differences in wording: (1) none of the type II versions can have been copied from L since the latter lacks questions 43–9, which lends further general support to the belief that type II is not abridged from type I (the relevant pages are missing from H and A, but the evidence elsewhere shows that H belongs with L and A with B); (2) neither T nor S nor G can have been the exemplar for any of the other versions, since all of these omit many questions contained in the others and in one another. D, A, and P are in too fragmentary a state to allow conclusions as to whether any of the other versions were copied from any of them (A is in any case too late to have served as the exemplar for any except G and perhaps S), but there remains the possibility that B was the exemplar for the other type II versions (except D, which is too early) and/or for the type I versions. Both these possibilities, however, must be ruled out. The table following shows a number of lines missing from B that are present in the versions indicated, their absence from B showing that it cannot have been the source for any of these versions:

Lines missing from B	Present in these versions		Pages missing in these versions	
	Type I	Type II	Type I	Type II
L2589–90 [B1542/3]	L	TSPG	H	A
L2817–34 [B1769–86, *from* T]	L	TPG	H	A
L5413 [B4449, *from* T]	LH	TASPG		
L6157–8 [B5171/2]	LH	TPG		A
L7899–900 [B6830/1]	LH	SG		ATP

As may be seen from the table there are several omissions from B that eliminate it as a source for LH (I) and TSPG (II), but only one (B4449) that eliminates it as a source for A (II). This further confirms the closeness of A and B, and though neither can have been copied from the other (A's lateness ruling it out as a source for B), it seems probable, as suggested above, that they were both copied either from the same exemplar or from two manuscripts very closely related to each other.

As for the type I manuscripts, it is evident that H cannot have been copied from L, since L lacks the twenty-four lines numbered 3337–60 (supplied from H); conversely L cannot have been copied from H, since H lacks L7171–2 and L11639–40 and is, in any case, thought to be later than L on palaeographical grounds. But the closeness of these two manuscripts is attested by such errors as *eeres* and *eeris* for *hernes* (see 6650,1,5/7702,3,7n), and by the wrong placement of lines 11751–988 (see the description of these manuscripts on pp. lv–lviii above): these errors are common to LH but are not found in any of the type II manuscripts.

(C) (BY FRANK SCHAER) RELATIONSHIPS BETWEEN THE ENGLISH VERSIONS: STEMMA

Type I
L and H (as indicated above) self-evidently belong together. However, both independently preserve minor variations, each agreeing on occasion with the other witnesses where the second has a peculiar variation. The two are therefore mutually independent. (In view of their closeness L alone is cited in the ensuing discussion as representative of the type I text.)

Type II
Of the type II texts the one most closely related to L is P. L and P have many common readings (e.g., 105/119 besely B, dylygently G, ffast A, fastli T, *wanting* S, falsely LP; 190/212 and all hyse BG, & his AT, *om.* S, in al wise LP). Some of these readings are demonstrably inferior:

1446/2492 Goddis day is a thowsand yeere BATS, *wanting* G
day is] deth is hennes LP (li iors de Dieu est M ans F)

1773/2821 And as water in erth synkes TG, *wanting* BAS
as] al þe L, all P (car autresi [c]ome l'aigue aboiure la terre F)

2837/3723 And derkely answhere he shall BS, *wanting* A
derkely] mekely LP, merkly T, anone G (et le dira oscurement F)

3422/4324 And his whyle he tynes all BS, *wanting* AT
whyle] wille LP, tyme G (il . . . pert son tens F)

3473/4373 Forthy behoues pore traveyle smerte BSG, *wanting* AT
pore] to LP (si couient que les poures se trauaillent F).

As well as the additional lines in the type I text for which (as noted above) there is no evidence in the French, L has self-evidently inferior readings, e.g., 'seith Salamon' (7654) for 'shall Salamon . . . Say' (B6606–7). Similarly P has peculiar inferior readings, such as the rewriting of lines 1713–16/2761–4. Together with the previous evidence this suggests that L and P are not only mutually independent but together form an independent subgroup, descending from a lost (type II) subarchetype. This conclusion conforms to the theory of the primacy of the type II text (the contrary hypothesis would require that a medieval reader corrected these inferior LP readings with reference to a French text).

The subgroup BAT

These three witnesses share many readings; however, their common readings are often patently inferior, e.g.:

50–1/58–9 And iiij dayes lete þem þere reste/ The v^{the} day dede he hem calle BAT
   iiij dayes . . . The v^{the} day] þre dayes . . . The fourþe day LPG (les laissa reposser iij iors. Le quart ior F)

144/166 Of all prisounes þat was þe werste BAT
   werste] furst LP, fast G (ce fu la primiera prison dou monde F)

4401/5365 And exalten the hight BAST
   exalten the] exalaciouns þei LPG (cf. 4434,9,43/5399,403,7).

Such readings and further examples cited below demonstrate that BAT form an independent subgroup. Further support for this model is provided by the omission in BA of the wording of the question for numbers 380–7 and 389, although the answers are given. (The relevant pages are missing in T.) On the basis of the evidence so far we can posit a bifurcate stemma, with one of the two lines of descent from the archetype leading to LP, the other to BAT.

Each of the witnesses BAT individually preserves independent readings, as is apparent from the variants on any page (e.g., 196/220 baylye B] Armonie T; 477/517 om. B, but guaranteed by 'ou par la force de son Dieu' F; 773/839 om. A, but guaranteed by 'Tes offrandes iamais ne receurons' F; A also has a peculiar version of 759–62/823–8). This confirms (as argued above) that none of these witnesses descends directly from another. Their relationship can, however, be specified more exactly. The division BA vs. T etc. (as opposed to BT vs. A etc. or

AT vs. B etc.) is statistically favoured even on the analysis of trivial readings, and some of the readings common to BA are demonstrably inferior, e.g.:

7955/9065 hit angrith hym wel moore BA
  moore] sore LTS, *wanting* PG (durement F).

One further piece of evidence for the closeness of the link between B and A (to add to those pointed out in the description of A in section 5 above, p. lxiii) follows 134/148, where BA agree in omitting a rather obscure couplet found in the other type II witnesses (see the variants for B134/5) and preserved in expanded form in L149–54; a similar omission from BA, preserved in other type II witnesses as well as type I, is the couplet corresponding to L2589–90 (see the variants for B1542/3).

G

The position of G (from which variants are not given in the apparatus) is not immediately obvious. However, it is noteworthy that examination of shared readings over the whole of the text reveals no conclusive instance where a common LPG reading can be shown to be inferior to that preserved in the other witnesses. In addition there are a few cases where G agrees with what seems to be an inferior BAT reading, e.g.:

1614/2662 Thanne gothe she firste to ioye or blis BTG
  ioye] woo LPS (the context favours the latter reading)

1906/2956 There the deueles in pyne dwelle BG, *wanting* AT
  pyne] *om.* LP (la ou les dyaubles et les tenebres sont F)

568–9/614–15 Adam ooure fadir and put hym in/ Of þyn grace gost of lyff BATG, *wanting* S
  hym in] in him (*rh.* slim(e)) LP.

Though none of these readings is individually convincing, the balance of the evidence suggests that G belongs on the BAT branch of the stemma—assuming, that is, that the stemma is bifurcate. However, the possibility that it is trifurcate, with G on an independent third branch descending directly from the archetype, cannot be dismissed out of hand.

On occasion G uniquely preserves plausible and possibly archetypal readings:

4721/5697 For thre wonynges shall he fynde B
   wonynges] yles L, thyngis P, yones T, *wanting* AS, zones G

6851/7925 The herte reuerteth withall BA
   reuerteth] reuerdysse G, refresshiþ L, *wanting* PTS (reuerdist F): G's unique
   reading, an otherwise unrecorded word (but cf. OED *reverdure*, one example
   only, 1525), is evidently the original reading, echoing F.

G alone reads *fattest* for 'fairest' (plus grace F) at 9844,5/11120,1 and
thre for 'four' at 10162/11463.

S

S does not share the inferior reading of LP at 1446/2492 or the
apparently superior LP reading at 1906/2956 (both instances cited
above). These readings suggest that S belongs on the other branch of
the stemma. Further, S agrees with B's distinctive (and less original)
version of 1926–7/2976–7 against LPG (*wanting* AT, et son commande-
ment font ne lor demande autre que ceste petite chose F). On the other
hand, S does not share all the readings of BAT: for example, S at 1358/
2402 reads *fere* with LPG not *peere* with BAT; S (with LG) retains a
form of *feel* (touchies F) at 978/1958; S (with PG) retains the couplet
equivalent to L2417–18, which is omitted in BAT but guaranteed by the
French (et fera quanque home deura faire sans pechie F). Taken
together this evidence indicates that S is to be placed between G and
T on the BAT branch of the stemma.

   However, there are cases later in the text where S agrees with B
against T and the other witnesses, e.g., 1728/2776 *booke*, omission of Q.
30, B2180 *right*, 2203/3083 *wolde*, 2258/3138 *eyre*, 2526/3406 *vnclad*,
2547/3429 *course* (all instances where the witness of A is lacking), 7442/
8528 *nature*. Such agreements are in conflict with the previous model;
the explanation may be that the scribe of S changed exemplar at some
point before 1728/2776. The earlier and later components of S are
shown on the diagram as S1 and S2.

   A notable feature of S is the presence of plausible though not
necessarily original readings. Some may indeed be inherited from the
archetype, such as 1200/2240 *wille* (volente F), a reading that S shares
with T alone, the other witnesses having a form of *flessh*. However, there
are a number that appear uniquely in S, such as the very plausible
whepen 4383/5347 and *colres* 3342,4/4244,6. These may simply be
plausible guesses on the part of the scribe. Other readings, however,
although superficially plausible, prove not to be original, such as 1509/

2555 *no3t* (for *aught*: qu'il aient fait aucune chose F), or 3480/4380 *prounde* (i.e., *proude* with a superfluous flourish) for *prow* LPG, *avayle* B, *wanting* AT: que le preu soit apres F.

D

This witness is extant and legible in only two passages of a little more than 100 lines each; moreover, in the first the witnesses PTS and in part G are wanting, in the second PT and in part S. On this basis what can be determined about the stemmatic position of D is limited. That D does not belong in the subgroup BA is clear from over a dozen cases where D does not share the peculiar reading of BA, e.g., 8444/9644 *piself* LGD, *thy liff* BA; 8403/9603 *he kenned ilk a man* (*gaue man* G, *knewe euery mannes* BA) *cunning* DG (lor enseigna les ars et les mestiers F). There are two minor examples of an agreement between D and L: 8689–90/9895–6 *here* (rh. *were*) LD, *weere* or *woore* (rh. *soore*) BASG; 8370/9570 *kirnels* LD, *kyrnell* BAG. If these are significant, they narrow the location of D to somewhere between L and G; but on the basis of the evidence available it is impossible to locate D precisely on the stemmatic diagram.

D is also (like the other witnesses) stemmatically independent: it lacks 8419–20/9619–20, where the originality of the couplet is guaranteed by the French, and has other peculiar readings, so none of the other comparable witnesses can derive directly from D. This, together with the general absence of superior readings, suggests that D, in spite of its relatively early date, is not markedly superior to the other witnesses.

The archetype

There are a number of readings which suggest that all surviving witnesses descend from an exemplar (i.e., the archetype) that already contained copying errors. The most striking is *loue* for *bone* in all surviving witnesses to Q. 59 (see 2387–2414/3267–94n). In some other instances the wide divergences amongst the surviving witnesses suggest confusion or a lacuna in the archetype (see, for example, the text and variants for 52/60 and 191–2/213–14).

Whereas these readings demonstrate that the archetype was distinct from the translator's original draft, the presence of such errors is a source of confusion in the reconstruction of the stemma. The scribes frequently attempted to correct erroneous or garbled readings, so that coincidental agreements (i.e., shared readings not in accord with the postulated stemmatic model) are not uncommon. Moreover, it is uncertain whether a highly plausible reading, preserved perhaps in only a single manuscript, represents the anomalous survival of the archetypal reading or an inspired conjecture on the part of the scribe. Examples from G and S have been cited above; examples from other witnesses include:

259/289 the ravenys grene hill B] þe grene rauens hille LPGAT (la montaingne uert de corbeau F)

689/747 þe false forein L] Therefore BGAT, The devyll for ay P (la longaigne et la pulentie F)

1418/2464 His oone soone B
    oone] oo A, owne TSP, *om.* L, *wanting* G (j de ses filz F).

Another problem is the limited evidence available: apart from L and B all the manuscripts are physically defective (especially for the later part of the work), and the print omits some questions. Thus the amount of text for which all witnesses are simultaneously extant is fairly limited. Nevertheless, having been tested over the full extent of the text and with reference to the French original, this reconstruction of the stemmatic relations is presented with some confidence in its accuracy and consistency.

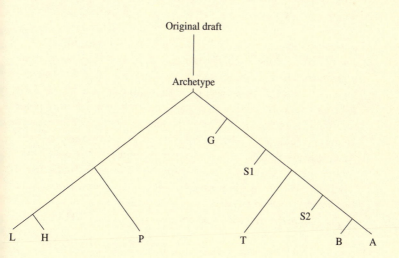

7. AUTHORSHIP OF THE ENGLISH
RHYMED VERSIONS

Practically nothing is known of the man who, we are told, 'brought'
Sidrac 'vnto Englyssh ryme' (B10930), other than his name, given to us
in four forms; *hughe of Campedene* (B), *hewe of Campedene* (T), *Hugo* and
Hughe of caumpedene (G). Two authorities tell us that he lived in the
reign of Henry VI (Warton, iii, 95; Corser, ii, 290), three others that he
was a much travelled and highly skilled linguist and translator. I quote
the latter three accounts in full:

(1) Hugonem Campedenum his nostris scriptoribus adiungere, hoc
    inter alia me mouet. Quum in remotioribus terris diu multumq*ue*
    studioru*m* gratia laborasset, & earum linguarum peritus admodum
    esset, uertendis opusculis ab uno sermone in alium operam
    diligentem impendit. Et inter cætera nonnulla, historiam de
    Boccho Maurorum & Getuliæ rege, ac de quodam Sydraco, e
    Gallica lingua in Anglicam loquelam transtulit. Liber incipit:
    Inuenire poterunt homines in ueteribus libris, &c. Opus habetur in
    Bibliopolarum officinis.[57]

(2) Hugo Campedenus natione Anglus, vir multarum linguarum peri-
    tus, quas vt perdisceret, exteras regiones varias peragrauit, vna cum
    artium liberalium, & Philosophiæ studijs, sermonem locorum
    semper addiscens. Vnde, quantum hactenus inuenio, nihil fere de
    suo in lucem emisit, sed tantum aliena in Anglicum vel Latinum
    sermonem vertit. Vt inter cætera quidem e Gallica in Anglicam
    linguam transtulit Historiam de Bocomaurorum & Getuliæ Rege,
    Librum vnum. *De quodam Sidracio*, Librum vnum. Inuenire poter-
    unt homines in veteribus. Et hæc aliquando Londini typis mandata
    dicuntur. Quid autem aliud scripserit, vel quando vixerit, nescio.[58]

(3) 'Campedenus [Hugo] qui postquam magnam Christiani orbis
    partem perlustravit, linguarum Europaearum peritissimus evasit.
    Transtulit e Gallico idiomate in Anglicos rhythmos *Historiam de
    Boccho Maurorum et Getuliae rege, ac de quodam Sydracho astronomo;
    in quo 400 quaestiones cum Sydraci responsis*, lib. I . . . [Here follows

---

[57] John Bale, *Scriptorum illustrium maioris Britanniæ . . . Catalogus*, ii, Basileae, 1559,
p. 85.
[58] Joannes Pitseus, *Relationum Historicarum de Rebus Anglicis* or *De Illustribus Angliæ
Scriptoribus*, Paris, 1619, App. 1, p. 865.

the full title as in Godfray's edition, a note of Twyne's preface and of the colophon] . . . Tempus quo floruit me latet'.[59]

These are the assertions; but no evidence is given for the first (that Campdene lived in the reign of Henry VI), and the only work that can be cited in support of the second (his reputation as a translator) is *Sidrak and Bokkus* (which Pitseus, the author of the second account quoted, had evidently not seen, since he takes it to be two separate works, one about each character).

Since Chipping Campden, in Gloucestershire, is the only recorded place in England to have been known as *Campedene* or *Caumpedene*,[60] it seems reasonable to suppose that this is the place referred to in Hugh's surname. Nichols mentions several Hughs who were owners or part-owners of the manor at Campden from the Norman Conquest to 1427, any of whom might have been called Hugh of Campden, but of whose literary pretensions we know nothing; also two Campdens at Oxford University in the fourteenth century, neither of whom, however, was called Hugh ('*Sidrak*' pp. xv–xvi). There is, however, no evidence that our Hugh was himself a Gloucestershire man, as opposed to having merely inherited the name from an ancestor who was; and he seems destined to remain nothing but a name.

8. ENGLISH PROSE VERSIONS

(1) MANUSCRIPTS: BODLEIAN LIBRARY, MS DIGBY 194

This long, slender, paper manuscript (298mm x 95mm), contains nineteen different works or fragments in one collection, the last of which (ff. 153r–155v) is a fragment of *Sidrak* in English prose (Bülbring, pp. 472–3). The questions and answers, beginning in the middle of no. 494 and continuing to the end of no. 521, have no equivalent in any of the English metrical versions. Questions 494–5 deal with astrological matters; the remainder, equivalent to questions 509–33 in F, form a small lapidary dealing with the 24 most precious stones (see above, p. xlix, and 10610/11954n).

---

[59] Thomas Tanner, *Bibliotheca Britannico-Hibernica, sive de scriptoribus, qui in Anglia, Scotia, et Hibernia ad saeculi XVII*, London, 1748, p. 148.
[60] See A. H. Smith, *The Place-Names of Gloucestershire*, Part i, English Place-Name Society, 38 (Cambridge, 1964), p. 237; Eilert Ekwall, *The Concise Oxford Dictionary of English Place-Names*, 4th edn. (Oxford, 1960), p. 84.

The eighteen other pieces (all in Latin) with which the *Sidrak* fragment is bound consist of a number of astrological tracts including (nos. 1, 5, 6, 7) several works of, or inspired by, Albumasar, to whom the author of the original *Sidrac* is indebted for some of his information on astrology (see above, p. xlvi); 'the precepts of Messahala', and works derived from, or connected with it (nos. 10, 11, 12, 14); and various other oddments.

(2) PRINTED VERSIONS

1. British Library General Catalogue of Printed Books, C.38.a.8:

'Here be certayne Questyons of Kynge Bocthus of the maners, tokyns, and condycions of man, with the answeres made to the same by the Phylosopher Sydrac.
(The Propertyes of a good Horse.)'
R. Wyer: (London, 1535?) 12°.
Twelve leaves, without pagination, Register A–C. Sig.Ciij is incorrectly marked Biij.

This delightful booklet contains twenty-three questions asking what is signified by various physical characteristics (e.g., freckles [or pimples], baldness, a hairy chest) and what indications of character there are in various parts of the body (e.g., eyes, nose, lips, hands, feet etc.). These questions (beginning 'The kynge asked by what maners/ tokyns/ and fassyon myghte a man knowe the maners and condycyons of good folkes and of euyl') correspond to nos. 922–45 in F2; they do not appear in the shorter French versions and have no equivalent in the English rhymed versions. They are followed by a section of one and a half pages entitled 'The Propertyes of a good horse' (see 10137–52/11437–52n). The fragment ends with two and a half pages of proverbs and aphorisms, e.g., 'Two wyues in one house,/ Two cattes and one mouse/ Two dogges and one bone,/ Shal neuer accorde in one' (cf. Whiting D333).

In addition to this booklet, which may be seen at the British Library, Bülbring (pp. 475–8) mentions two other fragments (the present whereabouts of which are unknown) both of which are recorded in Dibdin's enlarged edition of *Typographical Antiquities* (p. 201):

2. 'The Boke of Demaundes, of the scyence of Phylosophye and Astronomye, Betwene Kynge Boccus and the Phylosopher Sydracke.'

The description in Dibdin runs as follows:

On the reverse are portraits of these distinguished characters; behind the former is an apparently female attendant. This tract has neither preface nor introduction: but it consists of twenty-four questions with their answers in prose; and is very different from Godfray's edition of Boccus and Sydracke in verse; although this latter consist of questions and answers (362 in number) also, on the reverse of sign.D.ij. we have the following curious specimen of the work:

'The king asked—might a man number the drops of the water of the sea or the gravel of the earth? Sydracke answereth—'And the world were greater than it is a M. times and a M, and were all firm earth, and that it dured a M. times a M. year going, and were all inhabited with folks—the day and the night be xxiiij hours—and every hour is a M.lxxx points—and in every point were born a M.M. times men, and as many women—and they were all full of *heer*—and for euery heer should have a M.M. times drops of water of the sea—yet the drops of the sea water, and yet the misericord and mercy of God is more than the one and the other—or all other things that be in the world, or were or shall be unto them that seek to have it or deserve it.'

The impression contains D in fours, and has the following colophon on the reverse of D iiij. *Printed by Robert Wyer dwellynge at the Seynt John Euangelyst in Seynt Martyns Parysshe in the duke of Suffolkes Rentes be syde Charynge Crosse*. In the collection of Mr. Heber: formerly in that of Latham.

The question quoted by Dibdin is equivalent to Q. 156 in the English rhymed versions (160 in F). The wording of this prose translation is significantly closer to F than that of the rhymed versions.

3. 'A Booke of Medicines of King Bocchus. Printed by Robert Redman. Quarto.'

Bülbring suggests (pp. 477–8) that this fragment may be based on one of two sections in the French versions which are not found in the English: either the section beginning with nose-bleeds (F questions 451–78) or that dealing with the medicinal value of herbs (F questions 534–83).

The existence of these several fragments suggests that there was at one time a complete version in English prose; the different treatments of Q. 156 in the prose and metrical versions suggests, however, that the translations were independently made.

9. LANGUAGE

Most literary texts in English dating from the latter end of the fifteenth century are likely to have become sufficiently standardized linguistically to conceal the area of origin of both their authors and their scribes. So it is with the surviving manuscripts containing all or part of the verse *Sidrak*. Linguistic Profiles of all eight manuscripts, compiled from responses to the questionnaire printed in *A Linguistic Atlas of Late Mediaeval English*, are reproduced in appendix 1, but (with the exception of S, which shows marked regional characteristics in spite of its late date, and which the editors of *LALME* place in Nottinghamshire),[61] none of the manuscripts has proved possible to locate with any confidence.

A more fruitful line of enquiry with literary texts dating from the latter end of the fifteenth century may be the extent to which their language accords with that of the emerging standard of the official documents produced by Chancery.[62] An examination of the two base manuscripts, B and L (see appendix 2), shows that, in spite of a few differences in orthographic preferences, the language of both accords reasonably closely with that of the documents published in the *Chancery Anthology*. Whereas L has a distinct preference for *þ* as against *th* (in, for example, the definite article, the 2nd person singular pronoun, and the 3rd singular present of verbs), and is more inclined to use *ʒ* (e.g., in *aʒein* and *aʒe(i)nst*), B generally prefers *th* (except in the 3rd singular present of verbs, where *th* and *þ* are more or less evenly distributed) and avoids *ʒ* (preferring *y* or *g*); where L generally prefers *i* to *y* (*him, þei, rein, veines,* present participle in *-ing(e)*, etc.), B generally prefers *y* (*hym, they, rayn, veynes, -yng*); L prefers *it*, B *hit*; L *shal*, B *shall*. Of these spellings only L's conservatism in its predilection for *þ* and its use of *ʒ* is at odds with Chancery preferences: the other forms are all more or less evenly distributed in Chancery documents.

In all other instances where there are sufficient examples in the lines examined, B and L agree with each other and with Chancery. All prefer the forms *and, but, if, not* (though B and L contain a number of *-ght* forms, mainly in rhyme), and *suche*; they prefer *-aun-* to *-an-* (*comaund-, aungel-*, etc.), *-d-* to *-th-* or *-þ-* (in forms of *gader, togeder*, etc., but not *whether*, where all three prefer *-th-* or *-þ-*), *-e-* or *-ee-* to *-ea-* (*erthe, grete* or *greet, see* for *sea*, etc.), and vowel + *gh* to (lengthened) vowel alone (except in *high* and *dry*, where both B and L prefer forms without *gh*—although a

---

[61] See i, 116 and 231. My reservations about *LALME* are discussed at length in 'On the Current State of Middle English Dialectology', *Leeds Studies in English*, NS 22 (1991), 167–208. They are by no means dispelled by Michael Benskin's detailed reply in the same issue (pp. 209–62).

[62] See the *Chancery Anthology*; also John H. Fisher, *The Emergence of Standard English* (Lexington, 1996).

high proportion of these occur in rhyme); they prefer *e* to other vowels in unaccented syllables such as noun plurals and possessives, 3rd singular present of verbs, preterite and past participle of weak verbs, comparative and superlative adjectives, and the final syllable of words such as *after*, *(n)ever*, and *other*; they prefer *-e* or zero inflection for infinitives, present plurals, and strong past participles; they prefer *be-* forms to *are* for the present plural of the verb *to be*; and their preferred form of negation is auxiliary + *not* + main verb (although proclitic *ne* and verb + *not* are significant minor variants in both B and L).

But whereas the manuscripts of *Sidrak* hold few surprises in spelling, accidence, or syntax, they are rich in lexicographical material that has been largely neglected in the compilation of the major historical dictionaries. A search for quotations using the electronic version of OED produces fourteen quotations from MS Laud Misc. 559; these are to be found (with equivalent line references added from this edition) s.vv. *cast*, *v.*, 73 (B408); *crave*, *v.*, 2.d. (B181–2); *even*, *a.*, 15.c. (B507); *fere*, *v.*[1] *Obs.*, 2.b. (B30); *ghostly*, *a.*, 4 (B400); *grass*, *n.*[1], 2.a. (B98); *imagery*, 2 (B324); *incoming*, *vbl. n.*, 2 (B23); *Ind*, 1.c. (B9, quoted from Warton); *little*, *a.*, 7.a. (B5); *mocking*, *vbl.n.* (B164); *overcast*, *v.*, 1.a. (B536); *parliament*, *n.*[1], 2 (B482); *pine*, *v.*, 5.a. *intr.* (B528). These are all taken from the first ten folios; with the exception of *little*, none is in common use in MnE in the sense in which it is used here. It looks as if the reader of the Laud MS had been instructed to look only for rare or obsolete usages, and got no further than (or was not asked to read beyond) the Prologue.

Godfray's printed edition was treated differently. An electronic search produces thirty-two quotations, all from the letters *W–Z*; they are taken from throughout the text, not merely from the Prologue, and they include usages current in MnE (such as *we*, *pron.*, 1.f. 'used indefinitely in general statements in which the speaker or writer includes those whom he addresses, his contemporaries, his fellow-countrymen, or the like') as well as rare and obsolete forms and uses (such as *wem*, *v. Obs.*, 3, 'to spot or stain with sin or impurity'). It is evident that a different policy prevailed towards the end of the alphabet: a different text of the poem was used, and it was used with much greater thoroughness. I have come across one stray quotation, not thrown up by electronic search (because the source is given incorrectly as Douce (instead of Laud) MS 559, without further title): this is under *file*, *n.*[4] *Obs.*, and is taken from the body of the poem (B7377), not from the Prologue. It is not easy to see how this quotation came to be included.

Sidrak is not listed in the 1954 *Plan and Bibliography* for MED, and was evidently not used in the compilation of the early fascicles, the only quotations from it in these being taken over from OED (e.g., that for *file*, noted above, s.v. *file*, n. (2)). From *lom-* onwards, however, MED has made extensive use of Nichols's edition of MS Lansdowne 793 and of his articles deriving from it, and L is well represented in quotations thereafter. There remains a wealth of lexicographical matter in those manuscripts of *Sidrak* that have not been available to the editors of MED; I have attempted to cover this material in the glossary to this edition and in the lexicographical articles listed on pp. xii–xiii above.

10. EDITORIAL POLICY

(A) TRANSCRIPTION

The layout of the base manuscripts is preserved unless there is good reason for altering it. Their indentation is retained, showing the usual two-line indent and the occasional one-line half-indent of L compared with the varying two- or three-line indent of B. The questions and headings, which appear in red in the manuscripts, are here reproduced in italics; marginalia are omitted. Abbreviations in the manuscripts are silently expanded; strokes and other occasional punctuation marks, including full stops found frequently with numerals, are removed; capital letters are provided at the beginning of each line and otiose capitals removed. *God* is capitalized only when used of the Trinitarian Deity by believers; pronouns referring to him, and the words *heaven*, *hell*, and *paradise*, are not capitalized. Punctuation is sparingly supplied: subordinate clauses, especially non-defining relative clauses and temporal and conditional clauses are generally given commas; co-ordinate clauses are allowed to stand without punctuation except when their number is excessive.

In the manuscript of L a space has been left for a decorative capital at the beginning of each new paragraph before f. 161, a small letter in the left-hand margin indicating for the rubricator the capital required. In the transcript these capitals are silently supplied, except where the marginal letter is omitted or incorrect.

Word division is normalized according to the following system: individual words run together in the manuscripts are silently separated; compounds written as separate words in the manuscripts but now normally written as one word are silently joined together; hyphens and apostrophes are avoided.

Since the numbering of the questions differs in each manuscript, and since both base manuscripts contain errors in numbering, an editorial question number (for ease of referencing) is supplied in this edition, in parentheses to the right of each question. For the convenience of scholars wishing to consult the originals the manuscript numbering is reproduced uncorrected in the left margin. The question numbers are reproduced in the abbreviated form used in the manuscripts, i.e. 'Ca.° j°' etc. for L, 'Qo. 7ᵃ' etc. for B. (The first six questions in B are unnumbered. The superscript 'a' after the number is sometimes omitted in the manuscript, but is retained throughout in the transcript for the sake of consistency. The superscript abbreviation used in the manuscript for *Questio* is ignored.) Folio numbers are supplied in the margins in the usual way. Where the transcription does not follow the sequence of lines in the manuscript, the line number is given as well as the folio number at the point at which the transcript moves to a different place in the manuscript. Thus 'f. 51r/15' in the margin of L at the beginning of question 74 indicates that this question, which is placed earlier in L than in B (see the notes to lines 2560/3442 and 2855/3743 ff.), begins in L at line 15 on folio 51r. There is no Table of Questions in B parallel to that occupying lines 1009–1900 in L (indeed none of the shorter manuscripts contains such a Table at this point in the text, although S begins with a Table in summary form); the incomplete Table of Questions reproduced in the B text here is supplied from P, where it occurs at the start of the manuscript, the first eighty-four questions being lost on missing pages.

(B) EMENDATIONS

The policy here is generally conservative. The intention is to produce an intelligible copy of each of the two complete manuscripts (one from each school) with unquestionable errors corrected: there is no attempt at what has come to be regarded as the dubious practice of constructing an archetype for each school or a hypothetical common original. Emendations are therefore made only where one of the base texts is defective or nonsensical. Even where comparison with the French suggests that the reading in the base manuscripts derives from a mechanical error (e.g. *loue* for *bone* in B2387/L3267, where the French has *os*; *eeris* for *he(e)rnis* in L7702, where the French has *ceruelle*), the text is allowed to stand provided that it makes sense, and the error is noted in the commentary.

Emendations to the base texts are made usually on the basis of readings from another manuscript of the same school. Occasionally, however, one of the base texts is emended on common-sense grounds when the resulting emendation alters the text less than it would be altered by the introduction of a reading from another manuscript. Thus in B2473 the word *they* is supplied in preference to the adoption of a reading from one of the other manuscripts. Emendations are sometimes supported from the French: this is not meant to imply that the scribe of either of the base texts had direct access to a French MS, but to suggest a reason why this emendation is likely to be correct.

(c) VARIANTS

Variant readings are recorded only when they make a significant difference to the sense or where they are of some textual or linguistic importance. The aim is to provide not an exhaustive list of differences from which the text of each manuscript can be reconstructed but an indication of the important ways in which the meaning of the other manuscripts differs from that of each of the base texts. The following types of variant (which are very frequent) are generally considered insignificant and are therefore excluded: alternations between definite and indefinite article and between *this/that*, *these/those*, etc.; minor variations among prepositions (*in/on/upon*, etc.); inversions of word order that do not affect the sense; omission or inclusion of optional articles, optional relative and possessive pronouns, redundant subject and object pronouns, repeated prepositions, auxiliary *do/did/gan*, etc., common intensifying adverbs such as *full/well/right/all*, line fillers such as *also*, *eke*, etc.; minor variations among verb tenses (*sent/hath sent*, *came/were come*, preterite/historic present, etc.) and inflexions (3 pl. prt. in *-en/*uninflected, etc.); obvious minor errors in manuscripts other than the two base texts.

Synonyms are treated as follows: individual variants that make little or no difference to the general sense (*ay/euer*, *blithe/glad*, *call/clepe*, *deuel/fende*, *dwell/liue/wone*, *grete/moche*, *hest/bidding/comaundement*, *place/stede*, *poison/venom*, *suffer/thole*, etc.) are ignored; instances in which there is some agreement amongst the variants from the manuscripts of the shorter versions against the reading in B and which may therefore be considered textually important (as in the variants for B5, 88, 111, etc.) are recorded; forms which are of some particular linguistic interest (e.g. forms of *kilth* for *cold*, B4368, 4374, 4380, etc.) are recorded.

Variants which would otherwise be excluded on any of the grounds mentioned above are included in particular instances where they are textually helpful for some reason (e.g., where a variant from the shorter school agrees with the longer and vice versa) or where (atypically) they change the sense enough to warrant notice. Capitalization in the variants is as for the text. Punctuation is omitted except where direct speech begins or ends within a variant.

Variants against L are taken from H, the only known manuscript of the longer version apart from L itself. H is defective at the beginning: its text does not begin until L3300. Variants against B are taken from all the known manuscripts of the shorter version (A, D, P, S, T), but not from the printed edition (G). To save space, variants against B are spread out across both left- and right-hand pages; variants against L (of which there are far fewer) follow, after a separating line, at the foot of the right-hand page.

The normal order of citation for variants against B is TASP, but this order is sometimes varied—especially when a variant is incorporated into the text of B or used as the basis for an emendation—in order to give the form closest to the usual spelling in B; thus, for example, in B1097 the form *Ceraphyn* is supplied from A, being closest to the form *Ceraphyns* originally appearing in B1090. Parentheses are used within variants as a shorthand way of indicating differences between two similar variants. In such cases the word or comment in parentheses refers to the word immediately preceding; thus in the variants for B3179 the words 'ne (*om.* P) maye froo blenke (slenke S) TSP' indicate that TSP share the reading 'ne maye froo blenke' (spelling from T) except that *ne* is omitted from P and *blenke* is replaced in S by *slenke*. Where a variant would otherwise suggest a misrhyme the rhyme word is given in parentheses, preceded by '*rh.*'; thus the A variant for *wode* in B7546 is given as 'stere (*rh.* addere)', indicating that *stere* in A rhymes with *addere*, the latter not being entered as a variant in its own right since its appearance in rhyme position results merely from an inversion of word order (which does not affect the sense) in the preceding line.

TEXT

f. 3^r

Men may fynde in oolde bookes—
Whosoo þat in them lookis—
That men may mooche here;
And þerfore, yff þat yee wolle lere,
I shall teche yoow a lytill ieste   5
That befelle oonys in þe Este.

There was a kynge þat Boctus hyght
And was a man of moche myght.
His londe lay be grete Inde:
Bectorye hight hit as wee fynde.   10
After þe time of Noee even
Viij^{te} hundred yeere fourty and seven
The kynge Boctus hym bethought
That he wolde haue a citee wrought
The rede Iewes fro hym [to] spere   15
And for to mayntene his were
f. 3^v   Ayenst a kyng that was his foo
And hathe moste of Inde longyng hym too:
His name was Garaab the kyng.
Boctus tho preved all þis thyng   20
And smartly a toure beganne he
There he wolde make his citee;

[F]adir and Sone and Holy Goost,   f. 1ʳ
As þou art Lord of mightes moost,
Thre persones in Godhede,
Now and euere this worke now spede.
Men forsothe mowen hereyn fynde   5
Thinges þat ben not ofte in minde;
Or who þat liketh it to heere,
Miche good þerinne may he leere.
A litile þing I wole ȝou telle
Of þinges þat heretofore felle: 10
Herynne ben questiouns many oone
And asoiled ben euerychoone;
And in þe Eest cuntre it fel
As þise clerkes knowen wel.
   Ther was a king þat Bokkus hight: 15
   He was a man of miche might.
His lond lay bi þe greet Inde
And marchid to it as we finde.
After þe time of Noe euene
Viijᶜ ȝere fourty and seuene   20
Thus king Bokkus him biþoght
þat he wolde haue a citee wroght
The rude Iewis from him to spere
And for to maintene wel his were
Aȝenst a kyng þat was his foo   25
þat miche of Ynde longed vnto:
His name was Garaab þe king.
But Bokkus þo purueide al þing
And smertly a tour bygan he
þere he wolde make his citee,   30

prowe S.   15 to] *from* TAP, *om.* B.   18 And . . . longyng] That moche of
Ynde longid P;   moste] moche TA;   hym too] thertoo T.   20 preved]
purueyed P; þis] his T.   21 he] to hye A, hye P.

1 Fadir] Adir (*gap for rubricator, not completed*) L.   4 worke] *possibly*
werke L.

And hit was right at þe incomyng
Of Garabys lond, the kynge.
The masons with grete laboure   25
Beganne to worche vpon the towre
And alle þat þey wroughten on day
On night was hit doone away.
On morn, whan Boctus hit herde,
Hee was wroþe þat hit soo ferde   30
And dyd hit all newe begynne:
Att even, whan they shulde blynne
Off werke whenne þey wente to reste,
In þe night was alle doune keste.
Well vij monthis þus they wrought   35
And in þe night avaylid hit nought.
　　Boctus was wrothe wonderly
　　And callid his folke þat was hym by.
　　'Councellith me, lordynges,' seyde hee,
'How I may beste make þis citee.'   40
They seyde, 'Sir, sendith anoon
After yooure phelosopheres euerychon
And þe astronomers of yooure londe:
Of hem shall yee goode counsayll fonde.'
Anoon þer he after þem sente   45
And gadered þem to his entente;
And whanne þat they were gadered þere,
Foure score and ix masteres þere were.
The kyng receyved them with þe beste
And iiij dayes lete þem þere reste;   50
The v^{the} day dede he hem calle
And whanne þey came, he seyde to them alle,
'Lordynges, I shall telle yoow nowe
Why þat I sente after yoow.
I am þe grettest kyng, ywys,   55
That vnder þe sonnerysyng is:
Alle þe kynges of this contre

f. 4^r

23 And hit] Thatt A;　　incomyng] commynge TP.　　　　30 þat] whanne TA.
32 Att] And P.　　　33 whenne þey wente] and go P.　　35 Well] þis P;　　þus] om.
P.　　　36 in . . . hit] alle myght availe TA, al ne myght availe right P.　　44 goode]
no TAP;　　fonde] wande TAP.　　　46 And] That T, They AP;　　to his entente] and
after went TA, fast and to hym wente P.　　49 receyved] welcomyd P.　　50 iiij]

Euene at the incomyng
Of Sire Garaabis lond, þe kyng.
þe werkemen with greet labour
Bygan to worche on þe tour
And al þat þei made on the day   35
On þe night it was done away;
And whanne king Bokkus þis herd,
He was wrooþ that it so ferd
And made hem newe it newe begynne.
And at euen, whanne þ[ei] shulde blynne   40
Of her werke and wende to reste,
At night it was adoun ycast.
Aboute vij monthes þus þei wroght
And al it might availe hem noght.
    Bokkus waxe wroth þo wondirfully   45
    And clepid his folke þat stood him by.
'Counseileþ me now,' quod he,
'Hou may best make þis citee.'
'Sire,' seide a lord, 'sendith anoon
Aftir ȝoure philosophurs euerichoon   50
And after þe astronomyes of ȝoure lond:
Of hem ȝe shullen ȝour counceil fond.'
Anoon þe kyng after hem sent
And þei comen to him present;
And whanne þei weren gadrid yfere,   55
Foure score and nyne maistres þer were.
þe king resceyued hem with chere prest
And þre dayes made hem to rest;
The fourþe day he dede hem calle
And seide in haste to hem alle,   60
'Lordinges, I shal telle ȝow now
Whi þat I sente after ȝow.
I am þe grettest kyng, iwis,
þat vndir þe sunne living is,
For alle þe kinges of þis cuntre   65

thre P.   51 v^the] iiij P;   dede] lete P;   calle] alle P.   52] To speke with
hym in his halle P.   55 grettest] worthiest P.

    40 þei] þᵘ L.

At my comaundement will þey be,
All but Garab, the kyng
That in Inde is he lordyng.   60
He ayenseith my comaundement
And not cometh to my parliament:
Of hym may I not wroken bee,
For to his londe is wikked entree;
But men haue councellid me   65
For to make þere a citee.
Masounes and stoone I thedyr brought
And vij monþes þeron þey wrought
Right in þe enteryng of his londe
For to meke hym to my honde;   70
And all þat þey on þe day wrought
In þe night turned hit to nought.
And iff Garab haue hit herde
Of my worke howe hit ferde,
He woll say I haue noo myght   75
A citee in his londe for to dight.
Therefore yooure wittes hereon leye
And I praye yoow þat yee me seye
How I may, after my wyll,
This toure and þe citee to fulfill: 80
For me were leuer wroken be
Of Garab that dispisith me
Thanne name of all þe worlde to bere;
And by my god I woll yoow suere
That I shall for yooure goode dede   85
Aquyte yoow rychely yooure mede.'

f. 4ᵛ   'Sir,' seyd they, 'greueth yoow noon yll:
Wee shall asay to doo yooure wyll
Soo þat yee shull wroken be

And be fulfillyd of yooure citee.   90

But wyll ye vs respite yeue
Xl dayes, by yooure leve,

58 my] om. T.   62 not cometh] wull not come P.   67 thedyr] dide to be P.
70 meke hym] make hym right P;   my] his T.   71 þey] I P;   on þe] on o T,
oon P.   74 my] owre TAP.   76 citee] toure TAP.   80 to] om.

At my comaundement redy be,
Saue Garaab, þe grete kyng   f. 2ʳ
Of Ynde is maister and lordyng:
For he wiþseith my comaundement
And nil not come to my parlement.   70
Of him I may not wroken be:
Into his lond is wikked entre;
But men haue now counseiled me
Forto make þere a grete citee.
Masouns and stones I þidre broghte   75
And vij monthis þeron þei wroghte
Right in þe entre of þis londe
Forto make him bowe to myn honde;
And al þat þei on þe day wroghte
At night it turned al to noghte.   80
And if Garaab þerof haþ herd
Of oure werke hou it ferd,
He wole seie I haue no mighte
A tour in his lond forto dighte.
Herto ȝoure wittes loke ȝe leie   85
And I preie ȝou ȝe me seie
Hou þat I may, after my wille,
þis tour with þe cite to fulfille:
For me were leuere vengid be
Of Garaab þat þus despisiþ me   90
þan name of al þe world to bere;
And by my god I wole ȝou swere
þat I shal for ȝoure good dede
Ful richely quite ȝou ȝoure mede.'
      'Sire,' quod þei, 'greue ȝou noþing   95
      And we shullen do oure kunnyng
So þat ȝe shal venged be
Of Garaab king and his meyne
And make þe cite at ȝour wille
And do ȝoure list boþe lowde and stille.   100
But wole ȝe, lord, vs respite ȝeue   f. 2ᵛ
Firste fourty daies, bi ȝoure leue,

TA.   85 for yooure goode] you for youre TA.   86 yoow rychely] riȝt wele
A;   yoow] om. T, ffull P.   87 greueth yoow noon] lettith nothinge TAP.
88 asay] fonde TAP.   90 of] om. P.   92 by yooure] and we P.

Tyll wee oure arte haue ouerseen
How yooure toure shall be made ayen,
And þanne shall we do oure myght   95
To make hit stonde boþe day and nyȝte,
A place þeryn for to be
With many a grasse and many a tree
And with the water of þe ryuer.'

He comaundeth on all maner   100
That þey were seruyd richely
That day as his owne body.

Astronomeres forsothe they woore
That were eldest men of loore:
They wrought besely in theire arte   105
Euerychon on his parte.
And when xl dayes were comyn and goon,
They come byfore the kyng anoon.
He askyd them how they had wrought.
'Sir,' quod they, 'dysmay yoow nought: 110
Make yoow glad and mery also
And yooure desyre yee shall come to.
Withynne a xv nyghtes, shall yee se,
Comaunde yooure masounys redy to be—
Suche a tyme as wee shall you say—   115
Stone vppon yooure toure to lay:
Therefore loke yee þey be redy
And we woll echone stonde þerby.'
Full gretely thanked hem þe kyng
And grete ioy had he off theyre tydyng.   120

f. 5ʳ   Tho came þe day þat þey hadde sette:
                              The masounes were all redy fette

94 yooure] the P.   95 þanne] so P;   we do] be don T.   97 þeryn] om.
P.   103 forsothe] om. TAP;   they] there TA, all they P;   woore] add ful
hoore T.   104 That . . . men] And olde men and wise P.
105 They] That TAP;   besely] fastli T, ffast A, falsely P.   106 Euerychon] So
dyde they all P.   107 comyn and] om. TAP;   goon] past P.   108 anoon] in
haste P.   111 mery] blithe TAP.   112 And] For P.   113 xv nyght]

Til we oure art haue oueresen
þat ȝoure tour may be made aȝen,
And þanne we shullen do oure might 105
To make it stonde boþe day and night
And a rome place wiþynne to be
Of diuerse herbes and trees manye,
And of watir a faire ryuere
Ȝe shullen haue þerynne withouten were.' 110
'Þanne,' quod þe king, 'if it be þus,
Ȝe shullen be to me leef and desirus,'
And comaundid þat þei serued were
Of þe beste in al manere
As wel as his owne body: 115
'Loke þei be plesid by and by.'
And alle þise astromyes were
þe eldest men þat weren owhere:
þei wroghten falsely in her art
And trouþe from falshed þei gan depart. 120
    And whanne þe xl daies were agoon,
þei come bifore þe king anoon.
He axed hem how þei had wroght.
'Sire,' þei seide, 'dismaye ȝow noght:
Make ȝou right bliþe and glad also 125
And ȝoure desire ȝe shal come to.
Sire, withynne þis fourteniȝt loke ȝe
Comaunde ȝoure masouns redy be—
Suche a time as we shal ȝou seie—
Stones redy forto leie: 130
Loke þat thei be sone redy
And we shullen alle be hem by.'
Greet þanke þei hadde þo of þe king
And greet ioye [he] had þo of her tiþing.
    Thanne came þe day þat þei had set: 135 f. 3ʳ
    þe masouns weren alle þidre yfet

fourtenyght P;   shall ye see] comawnde ye P.   114 Comaunde] All P.
116 Stone] Stone and morter P;   yooure] the TAP.   117 Therefore . . . þey] And
dothe hem all ther P.   118 And] For P.   119 gretely] hyly P.
120 grete] om. P;   tydyng] seyyng A.   122 redy] thider P.

    107 a rome] arome L.   134 he] þei L.

And þe masteres yede wythalle
To beholde them þat werke shalle.
With grete ioy they begonne   125
And wrought ay till down was þe sonne;
And whanne hit to þe nyght drough,
The masters bade þat light enough
Were sette vppon the werke all nyght
That hit were not withowten lyght.   130
They yeden home all þat þere were
And came ayen on morowe there:
The kynge was tho well nere wode
Whan he sawe þat hit not stoode.

Anon he did call þe clerkys   135
And sayde, 'Bene these þe goode werkys
That yee me hyght for to doo?

By þat god þat I obeye too,

Aquyte I shall alle yooure dede!
For yooure workes yee shall have mede: 140
Bynde yee hem ffote and hande!'
This worde ouerspredde alle þe lande.
There were þey in prison threst:
Of all prisounes þat was þe werste.
     For of this toure the word ran   145
     And to Garab hit cam:
     Whan he hit herde, grete ioy he hadde
And his herte þerof was gladde.
A letter he made to Kyng Boctus

123 wythalle] with hem all AP.   124 beholde] se AP, serue T;   werke shall]
wroughtyn on the walle P.   126 till down was] while thei had TP.   127 drough]
fast drough P.   132 ayen] to werk A.   134/5 *add* Also the tresoure of his hoorde
/ Also wide yede the worde T, And for the tresoure of his horde / That so wyde sprang the
word P.   138 obeye] lowte AT, leue P.   139 alle yooure] youre aldris P.

And þise maistris ȝede wiþ hem ful soone
To se hem worche þat þidre shulde come.
With miche ioye þo þei begunne
And wroghte while þei had sunne;
And whanne it to þe night drow,   140
þise maistres bad þat light ynow
Shulde on þe werke be set al niȝt
And þat it were not wiþoute light.
þei ȝeden home alle þat þere were
And comen aȝein on þe morwe in fere.   145
    Thanne þe king was welny wood
Whanne he sawe þe werke not stood;
And for þe cost of his tresour
Him þoghte it gret dishonour,
For wondre wide spronge þe worde   150
þat his tresour and his horde
Was ywasted al in vaine,
Whereof his enemyes weren ful faine.
þe king cleped to him his clerkes
And seide, 'Ben þese ȝoure good werkes   155
þat ȝe behiȝten me forto do?
Whi han ȝe done me þus vnto?
Now, by þe god I leue vpon,
ȝe ben fals euerichone!
I shal quite ȝou ȝoure mede: 160
For ȝoure seruice ȝe shal be dede!
Bindeþ hem faste, fote and hond!'
þis noise spronge þorghout þe lond.
þere were þei in prisoun þurst
And of alle prisouns þat was þe furst.   165
    Fer of þis tour the word ran
    And to king Garaab þis word cam:
Whanne he it herde, greet ioye he made   f. 3ᵛ
And in his herte he was ful glade.
A lettre he made tho to King Bokkus   170

141 yee hem] ham fast P.   142 ouerspredde all þe] spradde into his TA, sprong in all his P.   143 threst] caste P.   144 werste] ferst P.   145 For] Sere P;   ran] name T, came P.   146] Vnto Garab that grete man P;   Garab] add anon A.   147 grete] om. P.   148 his . . . was] in his herte he was ful TA; his . . . gladde] in his hert grete ioy he made P.

And sente hit hym, that spake alle þus: 150
'Wee, Garab, of Inde kyng,
To þe, Boctus, sende gretyng.
We haue vnderstondyng well
Of þy wyll and of þy werke somdele,
Of þe citee þat þou woldist dyght;   155
Butt thou haste þerto noo myght,
Neyþer by arte ne by engyne,
For to brynge hit vnto a fyne.
But wylt þou sende to my feere
Thy doughter, that to þe is soo dere,   160
I shall yeve þe leve þerto
To make þat thou desirest soo.'
This came to Boctus the kyng
All in scorne and in mokkyng.
Boctus þought his herte shulde blede   165
Whenne he herde the letter rede:
As he þat was so wode and kene
The messangere dyd he slee for tene.
Thanne dyd he in his londe crye
Iff ther were ony, lowe or hye,   170
That cowde hym councell of þat þynge—
How he might brynge hit to endynge,
That ylke citee with þe toure—
He shulde with full grete honoure
Yeve hym his doughter vnto wiff,   175
With all his tresoure in his lyff.
Wele twoo dayes after his crye
The kynge sate ful heuely
For he ne wyst what for to doo.
Thanne came an olde man hym to   180
And sayde, 'Sir, I woll not crave
Yooure doughter ne yooure tresoure to haue;
But woll yee do me some good,
And I shall amende well yoowre mode
And teche yoow howe yee shall ontake   185

f. 5ᵛ

---

150 hit] to T;   that] this letter P.   151 Wee] I P.   155 þe] thi P.
158 unto a] to no P.   164 mokkyng] hethynge T, hatyng P.   165 shulde] *om.*
A.   167] And he was so wode in tene P;   As] And TA.   168] That the
messanger he did sleyne P.   170] Yf any man myght they aspye P.   173 ylke]

And sente it him, þat spake right þus:
'We, Garaab, of Ynde lord and kyng,
To þe, King Bokkus, sendiþ greting.
We haue vndirstonding right wel   175
Of þi wille and of þi werke somdel,
Of þe citee þat þou woldest dighte;
But þou ne hast now þerto mighte,
Nouþer bi art ne bi engine,
Forto bringe it to a good fine.   180
But wilte þou sende me to my fere
þi doghter, þat is to þee so dere,
þanne shal I ȝeue þe leue therto,
To make þat þou desirest now so.'
    This letter come to Bokkus þe kyng   185
Al in vanite and in greet scorning.
Bokkus þoghte his herte shulde blede
Whanne þei to him þis letter gan rede,
And he as a man wood and kene
þe messagere slowh for tene.   190
þanne dide he in his lond to crie
If þere were any, lowe or hie,
þat coude counseile him of þat þing—
How he mighte bringe it to ending,
þat same citee wiþ the tour—   195
He wolde ȝeue him wiþ greet honour
His owne doghtir to his wyue,
Wiþ half his tresour, bi his lyue.
    The þridde day aftir þe cry
    þe king sat ful drerily   200
For he ne wist what to do.
þanne came an olde man him to
And seide, 'Sire, I wil not craue   f. 4ʳ
Ȝoure doghter ne tresour forto haue;
But I wole þat ȝe do me good,   205
And I shal sumwhat mende ȝour mood
And telle I wole and vndirtake

thick P.   174 shulde with full] wolde geue hym with P.   175 Yeve hym his]
His owne P.   177 his] this TAP.   178 sat ful heuely] rose ful erlie T;
heuely] drerelye A, drerefully P.   179 do] done P.   180 hym to] sone
P.   183 woll] I wull that P;   some] om. P.

Youre toure and yooure citee to make.'
   The kyng anoon swhore by his god
   That he on leved and trowed
   He shoulde so yelde hym his seruyce
That hit shoulde lyke hym and all hyse.   190

f. 6ʳ

'Sir,' he seyde, 'a messangere muste fare
Vnto þe kyng Tractabare

And prayeth hym, for yooure seruise,
þat he yeve yoow leve on all wyse

To have the boke of astronomye   195
That whilom Noe had in baylye.
Thorough þe aungell was made þat boke
And Noee his oon sone hit toke;

And soo hit hathe goone, I warne yoow,
That Tractabare hit hathe nowe.   200

Prayeth hym also þat he yoow lene,
For þe love þat is yoow betwene,
His astronomer, Sydrak:
He shall vndo yoow all þe pak—
All yooure wyll yee shall have doo,   205
So þat Sidrak come yoow to.'
   Anon þe kynge a letter dyd make
   And to a messenger hit did take,
   And vnto Tractabare he sente
Full ryche and grete present,   210

And prayeth hym that he lene wyll
That boke and Sydrak hym vntyll.

And Tractabare that messengere

189 seruyce] avyse P.   190 hit] he A;   and all hyse] in all wyse P.   191 a
. . . fare] now be ware T, lett oon fare A, wirke wysely and ware P.   192 Vnto] And
sendith to TAP;   kyng] om. P.   193 for yooure seruise] as ye can best devise
A.   194 yeve yoow leve] wull lene you P.   195 To have] om. TP.
196 baylye] Armonie T.   198 oon] om. P.   199 soo . . . goone] Sir therfore
P.   201 he] he wulle hit P.   203 Sydrak] good Sidrake T.   204 vndo . . .
pak] hit you shew and what P;   pak] werke T.   205 yee shall have] he shall mow

ȝoure citee and tour forto make.'
    The kyng þo swore an oth
þat he shulde neuere to him be loth: 210
He wolde so ȝelde him his sise
þat it shulde like him in al wise.
'Sire,' he seide, 'take hede to me.
For ȝe shullen sende to king Traktabare
And preie him hertly þat he wil   215
Sende vnto ȝow, wiþ good wil,
For al ȝoure good seruise—
And þat he faile in no wise—
þe worþi book of astronomye
þat Noe hadde in balye.   220
For an aungel made þat book
And Noe to his sone it took;
And so it is ifalle now,
As I purpos to warne ȝow,
þat Traktabare þe king   225
Hath it in his keping.
And preie him it ȝow lene,
For þe loue is ȝow bitwene,
His astronomyere, Sidrak;
And he shal vndo to ȝou al þe pak,   230
And all ȝoure wille ȝe mowe do,
So þat Sydrak come ȝow to.'
    Anoon þe king dide a letter make
    And to a messagere let it take,
And to king Tractabare him sente   235
With ful riche and greet presente,
And preieþ him sende him þe book   f. 4ᵛ
þat Noe to his sone bitook,
And also Sidrak, þe greet clerke
þat kunnyng is in mannes werke.   240
þe king Tractabere with good chere

TA, may be P.   206 yoow to] thertoo T.   207 a . . . make] withoute lettyng
A;   a letter did] did haste T, dide lettres P.   208] A messanger sentt vnto
þat kyng A;   to . . . did] letters a messanger lete T, a messager lete P.
209 Tractabare] hym also A;   he] thei T, hym P.   210 Full . . . grete] Many a
rich and worthy A;   grete] a good TP.   211 wyll] me shall T, hym shall A, you
shall P.   212 hym vntyll] withalle TAP.

Resseyved with full mylde chere
And seyde, 'Fayre sir, welcome to me: 215
Grete ioye I have þat I nowe see
That my lord and my ffrende, Boctus,
Sendiþ to me these letterys þus.
A boke to lene he prayeth me
That in olde tyme had Noee: 220
That booke can telle hym, with skyll,
Someþynge þat is in an hill,
That whoso might come þerto,
He myght all his will doo.
My ffader wente vp vnto þe hill   225

f. 6ᵛ   But he myght neuer come þertyll;
But Boctus is of moche myght
And he woll with hem fight
That vpon the hill woone:
He shall have his wyll soone.'   230
He sente hym his boke and Sydrak

And a letter þat þus spak:

'Vnto oure lord and ooure frende,
The Kyng Boctus, vnto whos hande
Wee oblege that we have eche dele,   235
Wee, Kyng [Tractabare], gretith wele.
Wete yoow that we sende yoow vnto
Oure booke and ooure clerk alsoo,
And þanke yoow mochill of yooure sendyng.'
A glad man was Boctus þe kyng   240
Whan Sydrak bifore hym come:
Anoon [he] by þe honde hym nome
And tolde hym anon all his caas
And how that hit befallen was.
'Sire,' quod Sidrak, 'that londe, iwys,   245
Euerydele iwycched is.
There shall neuer man spede

---

214 with full] hym with P.   215 Fayre sir] Beau sir TA, Messanger P.
217 Boctus] now Boctus T.   218 these] this T, his A, *om.* P;   letterys] letter
T.   221 telle] ken P.   222 Someþynge þat is] Sum thyngis that arn P.
223 þerto] hem to P.   233 lord] louer T;   frende] kynde frende P.   234] To

Resceiued gladly þe messagere
And seide, 'þou art welcome to me:
Greet ioye I haue here þe to se.
And hou is it þat Kyng Bokkus,   245
Mi lord, sendiþ his lettris þus?
A booke to lene him he preieþ me
þat in oolde time had Noe:
þat booke can teche him vntil
Some þinges þat ben on an hil,   250
þat whoso mighte come hem to,
He might all his wille do.
Mi fadir wente vp to þat hil
But he mighte neuere come þeretil;
But Kyng Bokkus is of miche mighte: 255
I wote he wole wiþ hem fighte
þat vpon þat hil doþ wone,
And he shal haue his wille sone.'
He sente his book and Sydrak
Vnto þe king þat I of spak;   260
And his letter he sent wiþal,
As 3e hereafter here shal:
    'To oure lord and to oure frende,
    Kyng Bokkus, we sende
3oure request eueridel,   265
And also we grete 3ou wel.
Wite 3e, we sende 3ow to
Oure book and oure clerke also,
And þanke 3ou miche of 3oure sending.'
Glad was Bokkus þe kyng   270
Whanne Sydrak bifore þe king cam: f. 5ʳ
Faire bi þe honde he him nam
And telde him eueridel of his cas
And al hou it bifallen was.
'Sire,' quod Sydrak, 'þat lond, ywis,   275
Euerydel biwicched is.
þerynne shal neuere man spede

Kyng Botous we sende P.   235 that] vs and that P.   236 Wee] And I P;   Kyng]
om. P;   Tractabare] *from* ATP, Garab B.   237 that we] welle I P.   240 was] than
was T.   241 Whan] And A.   242 he] *from* TAP, hym B.   243 anon all] eche
a dele P;   his] þe A.   244 that hit befallen] beffallyn (befallem T) hym itt AT.

Vpon þat londe to doo noon dede
That off shall come any bounte,
But þat wychecrafte for[d]o be;   250
And I shall hit wele fordo.'
'Leve Sidrak,' quod he, 'do þanne soo.'
  'Sir,' quod Sidrak, 'we fynde
   In this booke that was Noees mynde
    That an aungell came hym to   255
Fram his God that sente hym soo,
And tolde hym þat he myght fynde
An hyll farre in þe londe of Inde
That hyght the ravenys grene hill;
And hathe þe name for þis skyll,   260
That Noee sente þe raven þere
Owte of þe arke to seche euerywhere
Iff he sawe any drye londe.

He fell on carayne that he fonde

And wolde not come away.   265
The dowue vpon that oþer day
Founde londe and came ayen blyve
With a braunche of grene olyve.

That hill of lengthe is, as we reede,
Foure iorneys and iij on brede.   270
Folke þere dwellith, of sely chere,
Made of body as wee be here;
But here visages for to loke on
Bene as houndes euerychon.
By the londe of Femenyne, as hit tellis,   275
Lyeth hit, ther no man in dwellis.
On þat hill soo been woxen

f. 7^r

---

248 dede] nede T.   250 fordo] for to B, ffordo A, fordon TP.   252 Leve . . .
he] 'Now gode,' quod the kyng P.   253] 'Sir kyng, we ffynde,' quod Sidrak tho
A;   Sir] Sir kynge TP;   fynde] fynde hit P.   254] This boke that Noe had long
agoo A;   mynde] in mynde T, wit P.   256 that] he P.   259 ravenys grene]

Vpon þat lond to do good dede;
þerof shal neuere come bounte
Til þe wicchecrafte fordone be;   280
And I shal, Sire, þat wel fordo.'
'Leef Sydrak,' quod þe king, 'þanne do so.'
  'Sire king,' quod Sidrak, 'we finde
    In Noes boke þat makeþ minde
þat þe aungel come him to—   285
Bi Goddis bidding it was do—
And tolde him þat he might finde
An hil fer in þe londe of Ynde
þat hatte þe grene rauens hille;
And haþ the name for þis skille: 290
Noe sente þe rauen forto se
If ony lond mighte owhere be.
He fond an hille, as I rede,
And þereon lay a carein dede:
He fel vpon þat foule carein,   295
þat of flesshe was wonder barein.
þe raven þere abood stille þo;
Aȝein þe shippe nolde not go
And nolde not come þerfro away.
A culuer he sente þe secounde day: 300
He fond lond as blyue
And come aȝen wiþ grene olyue;
A faire braunche in hir mouth she broght
For of no carein roght she noght.
þat is on lengþe as we rede   305 f. 5ᵛ
Foure iorneies and thre in brede.
þerynne woneþ folke of wondre chere,
Ymade of body as we ben here;
But her visages to loke vpon
Beth liche houndes euerichon.   310
Bi þe lond of Femynyne, as men telliþ,
It lith, þerynne as no man dwelliþ.
And on þat hille waxeþ, iwis,

reversed TAP.   262 arke] ship P.   265 not] nott from itt A.   271 Folke]
For P.   272 Made] More P.   275 Femenyne] Femynynes T.   276 Lyeth]
Nygh P;   ther] clere and T, *om.* P;   in] *om.* P.   277 soo been woxen] þer is
growyng A.

Of dyuers erbis xij thowsan:
The iiij thowsand mow goode doo,
And iiij thowsand been evyll þerto;   280
The iij^{de} fourth, whoso vndirstode,
To man done neyþer evel ne goode.
Vij maner waterys bene þeron
And all they gader in tyll oon:
Tho dewith the erbys and doth hem spryng;   285
And if yee wyll have yooure desiryng,
Laboure þe erbys for to wynne
And sethen þat yoow neuer blynne
To doone all þat in yooure power lyys
And ouercome yooure enemyes.'   290
The kyng made ioy whan he herde þis
And swhore—'Soo have I euer blisse'—
His good and his tresoure to forlese all:
Of thos erbys have [h]ee shall.
Redy on þe þrydde day,   295
He and his folke wente her way:
Vnto þe hyllwarde they hem spedde
And Sidrak he with hym ledde.
The xiij^{the} day came they tyll
A valey att the foote of þe hill;   300
There dyd he hem iij dayes abyde,
The iiij^{the} beganne vp for to spede.
But þe folke þat dwellith þere
Herde wele that þey comyng were:
Styfly they agaynst hem ranne   305
And faughte with hem and ouercame.
Vnto þe valey ayen þey turned
And v dayes there soiourned
And syþen wente hem vp ayen.
They of þe hill with all theyre mayn   310
Faught with hem full hardely
And ayen discomfytet þem fully:

f. 7^v

Xij þousand of diuerse herbis:
þe iiij þousand mowen good do,   315
And oþer iiij þousand beth yuel vnto;
The þridde iiij, who hem vndirstood,
þei mowen do nother yuel ne good.
Vij manere of watris beþ þeron
And alle þei gadriþ in to oon: 320
þei deweþ the herbes and makeþ hem springe;
And if ȝe wole haue ȝoure willynge,
þise herbes ȝe mote fonde to wynne;
And þanne þar ȝow neuere blynne
To do al þat ȝoure herte on lyes   325
And ouerecome alle ȝoure enemyes.'
    The king made ioye whanne he herd þis
    And swoore, so euere he haue blis,
His tresour and his good to forsake al:
Of þise herbes haue he shal.   330
Redy on the thridde day,
He and his meine tooken her way:
To þe hille þei hem spedde
And Sydrak with him þe kyng ledde.
þe xiij day þei come vntil   335
A vale of þe foot of þe hil;
þre daies þere þei gan hem rest,
While þei gadred herbis of þe best.
But þe folk þat woned þo þere,   f. 6ʳ
Whanne þei herde þat þei come were,
Stilliche aȝenst hem þei hem nome   340
And faughte wiþ hem and hem ouercome.
To þe valey aȝein þo þei torned
And v daies þere þei soiourned
And sith þei wente vp aȝein.   345
And þei on þe hil wiþ al her main
Fauȝte aȝein wiþ hem ful hardily
And of hem hadde þe victory:

yee B, he TA, Y P.   298 he with hym] with ham they P.   301 he] they
P;   abyde] lye A, lende T, to lende P.   302 beganne] *repeated* B;   for to
spede] to hye A, to wende T, wende P.   304 wele] telle P.   305 ranne] name
TP.   310 They of] On P.   311 Faught] Efte they faught P;   full] efte ful
TA.   312 ayen] efte T, anon P.

Vnto the dale ayen þey wente
And after grete socour they sente.
Whanne þey were come, they hem spedde   315
Ayen þat þey were at þe dede,
And þoo þat on þe hyll were
Discomfited they for euermore.
And vij dayes they dwelled stille
And hadde all þe hill at þeyre wille.   320
 Boctus was heþen and knewe nought
 God of heven that hym wrought:
 He trewed all in idolatrye
And in fals ymagerye.
Sidrak trowed on þe Trynyte   325
And his comaundementes helde he.
The kyng Boctus, where he yeede,
His mawmettis with hym he dyd lede.
And vppon þe xviij day
That þey vppon the hyll had lay   330
And here warre was all doone,
The kynge lete dyght a pavylon
And his go[d]dys furth did fette
And echon in his stede sette.
All were þey sette on a molde,   335
Bothe of syluer and of goolde;
And amonge all þere was oone,
Richest of hem euerychon,
Of gold, siluer, and perre:
Aboven all hyest stode he   340
And was moste holden lefe and dere
Amonge xxx^ti þat þere were.
Bestis forthe þe kyng let take,
Sacrafise off hem for to make.
He takeþ Sidrak by þe honde   345
And oþer lordes of þe londe,
And to þe pavilion they goon.
They comaunded to brynge anoon
A shepe that were fatt enough:

f. 8^r

316] Agayn there they bene had P. 318 Discomfited they] Discomforted hem P. 319 vij] viij P. 320 at þeyre] to P. 329 þe xviij] another P. 330] Ther whilis they theron lay P. 333 goddys] from TAP, goodys B.

To þe dale þo aȝein þei wente
And after greet socour þe king þo sente. 350
Whanne þei were come, þei gan hem spede
To fighte aȝein as þei dede,
And þei þat on þe hil wore
Discomfited weren for euermore.
And viij daies þei dwellid stille 355
And hadde al þe hille at her wille.
    Bokkus was heþen and knew noght
    God of heuene þat him had wroght,
For he bileued al in ydolatrie
And in falshede of ymagerie. 360
Sydrak bileued on þe Trinite
And his comaundement wel helde he;
But King Bokkus, whereeuer he ȝede,
Hise mawmetis he dide wiþ hym lede.
þanne it bifel on anoþer day, 365
As þei on þe hil lay
And her werre was al idoon,
þe king lete sette vp a paviloun
And hise goddes forþ doth fette,
And euery god in his stede was sette. 370
Alle þei weren imade of molde,
Boþe of siluer and of golde;
But among hem alle þere was oon   f. 6ᵛ
þat was richest of euerichon,
Of gold, of siluer, and of perre; 375
And aboue alle oþere hiest stood he
And moost was had in reuerence
Of alle þe xxx in his presence.
þe king made beestis to take
And of hem sacrafice make. 380
He took Sydrak bi þe honde
And oþer lordes of his londe,
And to þe pauiloun þei gan goon.
þe king comaundid to bringe anoon
A sheep þat were fat inow; 385

340 all] al other P.   341 lefe and dere] in honoure T, in ffere A, in ore P.
348 They] He TA, The kyng P.
    363 King] *repeated* L.

He toke a knyff and þere hit slough   350
Before hym þat soo hye stoode
And offred vnto hym þe bloode;
And echeon slow oon at þe laste
And abowte þe pavylyon hem caste.

Sidrak wondred in his herte   355
And angred soore of theyre werke.
The kyng sayde to Sidrak, 'Vpryse
And vnto god make sacrafise.'
Sidrak answherid with grete yre
And sayde, 'þat shall I neuer, Syre;   360
But sacrafise shall I make him to
That made heuen and erthe also,
Erthe, eyre, sonne, and see,
And all þat euer þeryn be:
That made bothe Adam and Eve,   365
He is þe God þat I on beleue.'
The kyng was wroth þere he stode
And axed hym with evell moode,
'Whatt canst þow be my goddis say?
Are they not goode and verrey?'   370
'Sir,' quod Sidrak, 'trowe me to,
They ben wyked and false also;
The devel in þem dwellyng is
That begyleþ þe, ywys.
Neuer honoure do þem vnto,   375
But I rede þe þow hem fordo.
For a badde godde I hym take
That a mannys herte canne not make:
Vnto þe deþe rather wold I goo
Or I accordyd to any of tho.'   380
The kyng was wroþe of his seyyng
And did his god before him brynge;
And whenne þey were byfore hym brought,

f. 8ᵛ

350 þere] he P.   353 oon] a shepe P.   355 herte] þouȝtt AP.
356 angred] tene T, greuyd P;   theyre werke] þat they wrouȝtt AP.   357 vnto
god] to oure goddis P.   360 I] *om.* P.   361 him] hem P.   363 sonne]
add and mone P.   364 þeryn] in erthe P.   368 evell] angry P.   371 trowe

And þe king anoon it slow
And bifore his god þat so hie stood
To him he offrid vp þe blood;
And euery man slowh oon at þe leste
And aboute þe paviloun þei it keste. 390
þus þei worshipped her goddis alle:
For such miche meschif haþ falle.
 Sydrak wondrid in his þoght
  And was greued sore of þat þei wroght.
þe king seide, 'Sidrak, vp þou rise 395
And to þis god make þi sacrifice.'
Sydrak answerde wiþ greet ire
And seide, 'þat shal I neuere, leue Sire;
But I shal make a sacrifice him to
þat made heuene and erthe also, 400
Erþe, eir, sunne, mone, and þe see,
And alle þinges þat euere þerinne be:
He þat made Adam and Eue,
He is þe God þat I on leue.'
þe king was wrooþ þere he stood 405
And axed Sidrak with egre mood,
'What canst þou by my goddis seie? f. 7ʳ
Ne be þei not good and verreie?'
'Sire,' quod Sydrak, 'bileeue me to,
For þei be wikked and false also; 410
þe deuellis wonnyng in hem is
þat begileþ þe and thine, ywis.
Neuere do þou worshipe efte hem vnto,
But I rede þat þou hem soone fordo.
A better god I rede to þee þou take 415
þat in þis world of noght þe gan make;
For to þe deeth raþer wolde I goo
þan worshipe do to any of thoo.'
The king was wrooþ wiþ his seieng
And made his god bifore him bring; 420
And whanne þei were bifore him broght,

me to] Y sey no P. 377–8] To a bettir God Y rede the take / That the of nought
this world can make P. 379 rather] or T, er P, om. A. 380 Or . . . to] Then I
shulde worship P. 382 god] goddes A. 383 þey were] he was T.

He sayde, 'Sidrak, disdayne þe nought
Sacrafyse to make anoon　　　　　　　　　　385
To soo ryche a god as he is oon.'
'Sir,' he saide, 'my sacrafise
Shall be to God, þat high iustice
That made man, and man not hym.
But þis is þe develis owne lym:　　　　　　　　390
The devyll vnto þanke itt takes
Alle þe worshipp þou hym makes.
And þerfore, by þe rede of me,
Alle þese mamettys, lett þem be!'
　　Nowe was þe kynge angred soore　　　　　395
　　That his goddis dispised woore,
　　And seide to Sidrak, 'Telle þou me,
Thy god þat þow clepiste, what is he?'
'Sir, I shall yoow telle, ywys:
O God of gostely substaunce is,　　　　　　　400

And þe angelis of heven light,
þat bene so nobyll and soo bright
As þe sonne is vij folde,
Have ioye on hym to beholde.'
The kynge lete calle þan[n]e ij of his　　　　　405
That in here lawe were holden wys
For to despute with Sidrak,
But he caste hem all abakke
And ouercome all here reason
Right in open disputacion.　　　　　　　　410
'Pray þow þy god,' quod þay, 'vnto
And we wyll to ooure praye also,
And we shall see soone tokenyng
Who shall sonnest have his axyng.'
These ij yeden furst at laste　　　　　　　　415
And her god encensid faste
And sette hem on kneys hym before
And seide, 'Lord god, thyn oore!
Lete neuer this wycche with his sawe

---

384 disdayne] ne deyne TAP;　　þe] he P.　　　390 owne] skyn and T, *om.* AP.
391 vnto þanke itt] of the thankyng P.　　　392] Whan þou hym worshipist and ioye
makis P.　　　393] But I rede thou do be me P.　　　394 mamettys] mahoundis
TA.　　　395 angred] tened TA, agrevid P.　　　400 of] a TP.　　　401 And]

þe king seide, 'Sidrak, ne denie þe noght
To make þi sacrifice here anoon
To suche a riche god as þis is oon.'
'Sire,' quod Sidrak, 'my sacrifice   425
Shal be to God, þat hie iustice
þat made man, and man noght him.
But þis god is þe deuelis lim:
The deuel to þanke he it takith
Al þe worshipe þat ʒe him makith.   430
And þerfore, bi rede of me,
Alle þise helle houndes, let hem be!'
    Tho was þe king agreued sore
þat hise goddes despised so wore,
And seide, 'Sidrak, now telle þou me,   435
þi god þat þou callist on, what is he?'
'Sire, I shal ʒou telle, ywis:
My God a goostly substaunce is
So þat þe aungel of heuene light,
þat ben so noble and so bright,   440
More þan the sonne by vij folde,
Ʒit haue þei ioye on him to biholde.'   f. 7ᵛ
    The kyng dide calle two of hise clerkis
    þat weren wise of her werkis
Forto dispute wiþ Sydrak,   445
But he broghte hem sone to wrak
And ouercome hem in her resoun
By open desputacioun.
'Preie þou,' quod they, 'god vnto
And we wole preie oure god also,   450
And we shal soone se tokeninge
Who shal haue sonnest his axyng.'
    These clerkes wenten forþ in hast
And her god encensid fast
And on her knees sette hem him bifore   455
And seide, 'Lord god, now þin oore!
Lat neuere þis wicche wiþ his sawe

That P.   404 Have] Ʒit haue they P.
call A, dide calle then to men P;   calle] com T;   405 lete . . . two] ijᵒ clerkis lett
406 here] om. P.   411 þy] om. A.   þanne] þa three minims e B.
TA.   415 ij] om. P;   furst] forthe TP.   413 see] be P.   414 sonnest] erste
                                          419 wycche] wickid P.

Ouercome þe ne þy lawe.'   420
The devell thanne to hym spake:
'Smertly,' quod he, 'take Sidrake
And brennith hym and do hym shame
But he worship wyll my name.'
They arose Sidrak to take,   425
And he satte his prayeres to make
And sayde, 'Lord God, full of myght,
That made boþe day and nyght,
Thow arte God of Noee,
Of Abraham, Isaac, and of me: 430
I beseche þe, Lorde dere,
That byfore this folke now here
Hem shewe þy powere anoon right,
And þat þe devill haue no myght
Noughwhere þe maystry to wyn   435
There þy name is namyd in.'
Whanne he hadde made his orison,
A fyre came from heven adown
And brente to pouder, þere þey stoode,
Theyre goddes þat þey called soo goode   440
And þoo men alsoo
That Sidrak to take wolde have goo;
An hundred twenty and moo
That stode abowte all brent they þoo,

And vnnethes scaped þe kyng   445
That he ne hadde that same endyng.
Owte of her god the devell ran
And caste a crye that euery man
Hadde suche drede þat he ne wiste
What he dyd ne [what] hym lyste.   450

Now hathe þe kynge his witte nere teynt,
Whanne he sawe his god þus brente.

421 to] withynne TAP.   425 They] Theise twoo T.   426 And] As P.
427 full] om. P.   431 dere] so dere P, entiere T.   433 Hem Thou P.
435 Noughwhere] Now here P.   440 called] held AP, helden T.   441 men]

f. 9ᵛ

Ouercome þe, Lord, noþer þi lawe.'
 The deuel þanne withynne him spak:
'Smertly,' he seide, 'ȝe take Sidrak   460
And brenneth him and do him shame
But if he wole worshepe my name.'
þanne roos þei vp Sydrak to take,
And he knelid his preiers to make
And seide, 'Lord God of might   465
þat madest boþe day and nyght,
Lord þou art and God of Noe,
Of Abraham, Isaac, and of me:
I beseche þe, Lord so dere,
þat bifore þise folk now here   470
þou shewe þi powere anoon right,
And þat þe deuel haue no might
Ne ȝit þe maistrie forto wynne
In þe place þi name is nempned ynne.'
 And whanne he had made his orisoun,   475 f. 8ʳ
A fire fro heuene came adoun
And brente to poudre, þere þei stood,
Her goddis þat þei helde so good
And þo men forsoþe also
þat Sydrak to take wolde haue go;   480
And an hundrid and twenty eke
þat stoden to loke on þe smeke
Alle weren brente wiþouten doute
þat to God of heuene weren stoute.
Vnneþe escaped þenne þe kyng   485
þat he ne had þe same endyng.
Out of her goddis þe deuel þo ran
And made suche a cry þat euery man
Hadde suche drede þat he ne wist
Whidre to fle for þe greet mist   490
þat was isprad aboute hem tho:
No wondre þogh þei weren ful woo.
 The kinges witt was almost shent
Whanne he sawe hise goddis so brent.

tway men T, euery man in fere P. 447 god] mametis A. 450 what] *from*
TAP, nothyng B. 451] The kyngis witte for wo was ny went P. 452 god]
goddes AP.

He lete take anoon Sydrak
And bounde his handis byhynde hys bakke
And dyd hym kepe also styll   455
Tyll he of hym wolde doo his will.
Thereafter lay he all thore
Vij dayes and somdele moore
That of þe worlde had he noo light,
For þey hadde nere teynte all his sight.   460
    Sidrak þus in prison lay
    Tyll hit befelle on þe ix^{the} day
    That the kynge hym bethought
And sawe þat he myght spede nought,
Ne of counsayll hadde noo man   465
To fulfille þat he beganne.
All þe wisest dede he þore
Of his hoste to come hym byfore
And saide, 'Lordynges, yooure counsayll nowe:
What shull we doo? What þynkeþ yowe?   470

He þat hathe vs hedyr brought
And after his counsayll we have wrought,
Ayenste ooure grete god he hathe misdoone,
And he is brente þorow his treson;
And we ne canne not wite, iwys,   475
Wheþer þorough wicchcrafte hit is
[Or þrough his goddes my3tt.]
Therfore councellyth me aright
And loke how we shullyn fare
In this straunge londe whereyn we are.'   480
Anoon forthe þey wente
And kepte a grete parliamente.
Thanne þere was oone þat þus spake:
'I shall telle yoow: this Sidrake,
That makyth þe kynge þis werke begynne   485
And brought vs hedyr for to wynne,
And withouten hym may hit nought
To an eande oure purpose be brought—

456 wolde do] had done P.   457] He was in hold þus kepte ffast A;   he] thei
TP.   458] Tyll seven dayes was all past A.   459–60] *om.* A.   459 he]
thei TP;   light] myght P.   460 nere. . . sight] almoost tynt here light P;   his]
hur T.   462 befelle] was P.   470 yowe] ye now P.   476 Wheþer

He dide do take anoon Sidrak   495
And bounde hise hondes behynde his bak
And kepte him forsoþe stille
Til he wolde his wil fulfille,

Viij dayes fully

In grevous torment pinefully.   500
   Thus Sydrak in prisoun lay
   Til it was þe nynthe day;
þanne þe kyng him byþoghte
And sawe þat he might spede noghte,
Ne of counseile had no man   505
To fulfille þat he bigan.
þe wisest men of his londe
He dide do come to his honde:
He seide, 'Sires, ȝoure counseil now: f. 8ᵛ
What shullen we do? Hou þinke ȝow?   510
He þat haþ vs hidre ibroght
And bi his counseil we haue wroght,
Aȝeinst oure grete god he haþ mysdon,
And he is ibrent þorgh his treson;
And we ne conne not wite, iwis,   515
Wherof þat wicchcraft made now is,
Or wheþer it is þorgh his goddis might.
Wherfore counceileþ me aright
And loke hou þat we shullen fare
In þis lond þat we now are.'   520
Anoon þei alle forth wente
And made a ful greet parlemente.
Vp stirte oone and to þe king spak:
'I shal ȝow telle of þis Sidrak,
þat made þe kyng þis werk bigynne   525
And broghte vs here forto wynne,
And wiþouten him now may noght
Oure purpos to þe ende be broght:

þorough] Wherefore P.
P;   his] his owne T.   477] *from* A, *om.* B;   Or þrough his] Othir hit is thorow
481 Anoon] *add* togedre A.   480 straunge] fremeth T, onkouthe P.
483 þus] thoo TA, there P.   482 kepte] helde P, helden TA;   a grete] *om.* P.
                               484 this] of P.   487 And] For P.

Thorough hym have we eke teynt
Oure god þat þe fyre brente.   490
Neuerþelese, I rede þat wee
Soo þat he delyuered be;
And whanne we have þat we have sought
And into owre contre brought
And wroken of ooure enemyes,   495
Than shall þe kynge, if he be wyse,
Do hym drawe and brynge to dede
As ooure god was þorough his rede.'
All assentid they gladly þerto
And all þey toldyn þe kyng soo.   500
Anon þe kyng chese hym [t]enne
Of his altherwysest men
And beden hem to Sidrak goo;
And sayde hym how þe kynge was woe
That he shulde lye long soo,   505
And þat he shulde his wyll doo
And foryeven hym even and odde
That he hadde doone ayenst his godde.
Sidrak answherid anoon thus:
'Grete yee well þe kyng, Boctus,   510
And seye hym, as God me save,
That I wyll noo foryeuenesse have
Of nought þat I haue doone amys.
Yff [God þat in] heven is
On his godde shewid his powste,   515
What woll he foryeve þat me?
But sey hym, if hit be his will
That I his seruise woll fulfill,
In God of heven trowe [he] shall
And his comawndement doon all;   520
And his grace and his mercy
I shall him shewe opynly.'
Anoon the messengere[s] þens wente

f. 10ᵛ

489 have . . . teynt] we ben al shent P.   490] For oure goddis bein al tobrent
P.   492 Soo] Doo TP, Se A.   494 And] And be P.   495 And] Yf we be
P.   499 gladly] om.P.   501 tenne] from TAP, þenne B.   502 his
altherwysest] all the wysest P.   503 beden] diden T.   505 long] om. T, in
prison A;   long soo] ther so long P.   506] Hym forthought swithe strong
P.   507 even and odde] more and lasse P.   508 godde] add trespasse

þorgh him oure god is forshent
þat was wiþ wilde fire ybrent.   530
Neuereþelesse, I rede þat we
Ordeine þat he deliuered be;
And whanne we þus haue ywroght
And to oure countre ben ybroght
And yvengid of oure enemyes,   535
þanne shal þe king, if he be wys,
Todrawe him and bringe him to deed
As þat oure god was þorgh his reed.'
    [Th]anne þei sentid all þerto
    And þe king graunted also.   540
The kyng chees to him ten,
þe wisest of alle his men,
And made hem to Sidrak go;   f. 9ʳ
And seide to him þat þe king was wo
þat he hadde leine þere so longe: 545
It forþoghte him swiþe stronge;
And þat he wole forȝeue al þe wite
Done to his god and þe despite.
Sidrak answerde anoon þus:
'Gretiþ wel now King Bokkus   550
And seie him, also God me saue,
þat I nile no forȝeuenesse haue
Of noght þat I haue do[n]e amis.
If God wole, þat in heuene is,
For on his god is shewid his pouste,   555
What wolde he forȝeue þat me?
But seiþ to him, if it be his wille
þat I shal his seruice fulfille,
In God of heuene bileue he shal
And hise comaundes done al;   560
And his grace and his mercy
Shal shewe to him apertly.'
    Anoon as þe messagers weren ywent

P.   509 anoon] om. P.   514 God þat in] from TAP, þat in God B.
516 he] ye P.   519 he] from TAP, I B.   522 opynly] appertli TA, propirly
P.   523 messengeres] messengere B;   þens] om. TA, forthe P.

536 þe] repeated (2nd þe marked for deletion) L.   539 Thanne: T om., h obscured
by blot L.   553 done: n very faded L.

Vnto þe kyng, þat them sente,
And tolde hym what answhere they had.   525
The kyng was wroþe and hem badde
That he shulde oþer dayes nyne
In prison leve and þere pyne.
Thanne þe ix dayes were goone also,
The kyng sente ayen hym too   530
The same bodyes, lasse ne moore,
That he hadde sente to hym byfore;
And he his answhere on hym layde
The same þat he erste had sayde.
Whanne þe kyng sawe at þe laste   535
That his travaylle þus was ouercaste
And þat he was a redeles man
And withoute hym nought ne can,
He lete brynge hym anoon right
And made hym all þe ioye he myght.   540

f. 11ʳ

Sidrak anoon byfore þe kyng
Sayde, 'Sir, by God þat made all þynge,
The nedis that þow haste to do
Shall neuer endyng come vnto
But thow wylt trowe in God of right,   545
That all þyng made by his might;
And yff þat þow wilte hym see,
Opynly I shall hym shewe þee.'
The kyng saide, with wordis grym,
'Let se, þanne, do shewe me hym: 550
And he be suche as þow hym preches,
I shall trowe as þow me teches.'
And anoon, whanne þat herde Sidrak,

With þat anoon he drowe hym abak

527 he shulde] they shuld done hym P.   528 þere] thole P.   530 too] *from*
TAP, twoo B.   531 bodyes . . . moore] men hit wore P.   533 his answhere]
the same message P.   534] That before had he to hem seide P.   535 sawe]
bethought hym P.   536 þus was ouercaste] was all lost P.   537 And . . . was]
For he was but P.   538 nought ne] no rede he P.   542 þat made] of TA
545 right] light TP.   546 all . . . by] of nought all made P.   548 Opynly]

To þe kyng, þat hem hadde ysent,
And telde þe answere þat þei hadde,   565
þe king was þenne wroþ and hem badde
þat he shulde oþer daies nyne
Ligge in prisoun and suffre pyne.
And whanne þe nyne daies weren ago,
Aȝein þe king him sente vnto   570
þe same lordis, boþe lesse and more,
þat he hadde sente him tofore;
And he his answere aȝein on hem leide
þe same þat he tofore had seide.
And whanne þe king sawe at þe laste   575
þat his trauaile was al in waste
And þat he was a redeles man,   f. 9ᵛ
And þoruȝ a wile he made him þan
Afore him to be broght right
And made him feyned ioye as tite.   580
þanne seide þe king Sidrak vnto,
'How þenkest wiþ me now forto do?'
He answerid anoon to þe king
And seide, 'Bi mighti God liuing,
Al þing þat þou hast to done   585
Shal neuere ending come þerone
But þou wilt bileue in God of light,
þat made al þing of his might;
And if þat þou wilt him see,
I shal shewe him apertly to þe.'   590
    The king seide, wiþ wordes grym,
    'Haue ido, and shewe me him!
And if he be such as þou prechist,
I shal bileue as þou me techist.'
And whanne þat Sidrak herde him þus seie,   595
He þankid God with herte verreie
And drowe him a litel tine abak,
þis good clerke called Sidrak,

Appertli TA, Apert P.   549 saide] answerid P.   550 þanne do] anon thou
P.   551 hym] me P.   552 trowe] levyn and don P.   553] And whanne
þat Sidrake harde hym sei that T, Whan that he herd anon Sydrak P.   554 With þat
noon] om. P; hym] add a litill P.

594 shal] repeated L.

And sette hym on his kneys at þe laste;   555
His eyen vp to hevyn he caste
And his prayer þanne made he:

'Lord God, full of pytee,

And herest all þat calle þe too
And madest heven and erthe alsoo   560
And aungelis full of clerte
Also full of wysdam for to be—
Lucifer in pride gan fall
For lorde he wolde be of all,
And þow, Lord, hym caste adown   565
Into helle, þat fowle prison—
And madest eke off erthe and slyme
Adam, ooure fadir, and put hym in
Of þyn grace gost of lyff,
And madest Eve vnto his wiff: 570
Lorde, also wytterly,
I beseche þe inwardly
That þow me grace down sende
These wykked folke for to amende,
Soo þat I have noo blame   575
For þat I worshipp thy holy name.'
    Whan that he hadde made his orison
    An aungell came from heven adown
    And sayde to Sydrak, 'Be þow gladde!
For God hathe herde þat thou badde   580
And hathe herde also þy boone.
This kynge þow shalt conuerten soone;
Thow shalt ouercome, þat warne I the,
The devyll and his pouste:
God hathe grauntid the þat might   585
And his grace in þe is light.
Thow shalte right soone, in a throwe,
[A party] of Goddis might to hym showe:

f. 11ᵛ

---

555 at þe laste] downe P.   556] And prayed God with devocyon P
557–8] And God full of mercy and of pite / That madist bothe lond and see P
559 herest all] all that P.   560 erthe] helle P.   562 full] om.P.   567 And
. . . eke] Then madist thou P.   568 fadir] forne fadir P.   570 vnto] to bene P

And on his knees he dressid him fast
And hise yȝen vp to heuene he cast   600
And his prayere þanne made he,
As here ȝe may boþe rede and see:
   'Lord God almighti, ful of pite,
þat liuest and regnest in þi glore
And heerist alle þat clepen þe to   605
And madest heuene and erþe also
And aungels ful of charite
And so ful of wisdom forto be—
But Lucifer in pride gan falle
For þat he wolde be lord ouere alle,   610
And þou, Lord God, þrewe him doun   f. 10ʳ
Into helle, þat foule prisoun—
þanne þou madist of erþe and slim
Adam, oure firste fadir, and puttist in him
Of þin holy grace a goost of lyf,   615
And madest Eue to be his wyf:
Now, Lord God, als witterly,
I beseche þee inwardly
þat ȝe ȝoure grace doun to me sende
þise wikked folk forto amende,   620
So þat I here haue no blame
And þat þei may worship þin holy name.'
   And whanne he had made his orisoun,
   An aungel come from heuen doun
And seide to him, 'Sidrak, be glad!   625
For God haþ herd al þat þou bad
And haþ ygraunted þe þi bone.
þis king þou shalt conuerte right sone;
þou shalt ouercome, I warne it þe,
Fully of helle þe deuels pouste: 630
God haþ ygraunted þe, of his might,
His grace, whiche is in þe light.
þou shalt sone, wiþinne a þrowe,
A party of his might him shewe:

571 also] now also T.   576 For... worshipp] And that they trust in P.   580 þat]
alle that T, the all þat A.   581 herde also] graunte the T, grawntyd the P.
583 þat warne I the] hem all parde P.   584 devyll] add of helle P.   585 þat] the
TA, thy P.   586 right] om. TAP.   588 A party] from TP, A partt A, Apertly B.

How he þe worlde fyrst began
And why þat he made man   590
And of þe comyng of Goddis Soone,
That in erthe shall with yow wonne,
And of Antecrist withalle

And how þe worlde endid be shall.

An erþen potte þou lete þe fette   595
And vppon iij stakes thou hit sette
In þe name of þe Trinite,
Oon God and persoones three.
Do fill that potte with water clere
And þanne calle þe kynge þe nere: 600

Goddis grace than shalt þow see
And shewe hit hym, and soo shall hee.'
The aungell anoone wente his way
And he dyd as he herde hym say:
He callid þe kyng and sayde, 'Sire,   605
Woll yee see þat yee desyre?'
The kyng [was] full wroth, iwys,
And sayde, 'Do shewe me which he is:
Wheþer is better wolde I see,
Owre god þat þow brente or hee.'   610
f. 12ʳ   Sidrak toke iij stakys anoon
               And sette an erthyn pot þeron
               And dyd hit with water fyll.
He lokyd þerin, with grete will,
And he clepid the kyng hym to   615

589 he] *om.* P.   600 þanne calle] thow take P.   602 hee] be P.   604 he
herde hym] the angell dide P.   607 was] *from* TA, *om.* BP.   608 And sayde]
om. P.   614 grete] gode P.

Hou he þe world first bigan 635
And whi þat he made man
And of þe comyng of Goddes Sone,
þat shal in erþe for a time wone;
And of Anticrist telle þou shal,
þat shal haue a grete fal, 640
And hou þat þe world shal ende
þorgh Goddes might, whan he shal sende
Hise aungels into erþe lowe
To warne þe peple in a þrowe
Of Goddis greet veniaunce, 645 f. 10ᵛ
þat shal be ful greet grevaunce
To hem þat shullen dampned be.
þis is soth, as I telle þe.
Anoon an erthen potte do fette
And vpon iij stakes do it sette 650
In the name of þe Trinite,
Oo God and persones thre;
And fille þat potte with water clere
And þanne take þe king þe nere
And shewe him þere, wiþ mylde mode, 655
þe King þat is so milde of mode.
þorgh Goddes grace þere shal he se
þe Lord þat þou bileuest to be.'
Anoon þe aungel wente his weie
And he dede as he herde him seie: 660
He clepid þe king and seide, 'Sire,
Wole ȝe see þat ȝe desire?'
þe king was ful wrooþ, ywis,
And seide, 'Shewe me what he is:
Wheþer is þe bettir, þat wolde I see, 665
Oure god þat þou brentist or he.'
    Sydrak toke iij stakes anoon
    And sette an erþen potte þeron
And ful of watir he dide it fille.
He lokid þerynne, wiþ milde wille, 670
And he callid þe king him to

665] *misplaced at foot of page, marked for insertion in correct place* L.

And seyde, 'Beholde hereyn, loo!'
The kynge behelde and þanne sawe he
The noumbre of þe Trynyte
That of might is altermooste,
Fadir and Sone and Holi Goste,   620
In heven as þey syttyng were,
And aungellis hem stode bifore
Syngyng as þey were wonne
Praysyng to þe Fadir and to þe Sonne,
The Sone to þe Holy Gost also   625
And þe Holi Goste to hem twoo.
Whanne þe kynge hadde sey that sight,
He was full ioyfull and full light:
Hym þought that he was in heven;
His gladnesse cowde he not neven,   630
And tolde Sidrak how he ferde
And saide to hym, þat alle herde,
'I trowe in þy God, ywis,
And in all þat of hym is
Or euer was or euer shall be;   635
But I þe pray, telle þou me,
Thatte I þe better may trowe þeron,
How þenne these iij be in oone.'
'Sir,' he seyde, 'I shall yoow shewe
In what maner yee shall hem knowe.   640
Iff yee vnderstonde conne,
Se ye on the skye the sonne:
Thre thynges þer are þeryn
And no man may hem twyn.
Oon is þe sonne properly   645
That ye se vpon þe skye;
Anoþer is þe cleerete
That lite yeveth bothe yoow and me;
And þe hete soo is þe thirde
That wyde is in þis worlde ykyd.   650

f. 12ᵛ

616 hereyn] here and se P.   618 noumbre] vmbris P.   622 stode] *om.* P.
624 Praysyng] Herienge TA, Worshipyng P.   625 The Sone to] And P.
626] Worshipyng with hem bothe to P.   634 þat] that euyr P.   635–6] S *begins*
again with Buccus saide, 'Sidrake, now tell me / Somwhat of the Trinite.'   635 euer
(2)] yet P.   638] How arn they than iij mon P.   638/9] *add* Nota hic de

And seide, 'Biholde hereyn, lo!'
þe king bihelde and þere sawh he
Almighti God in Trinite
þat is God of mightes moost, 675
Fadir and Sone and Hooly Goost,
As þei in heuene sittinge were,
And alle þe aungels bifore hem þere
Singing wiþ honour as þei euere done, f. 11ʳ
þe Fadir lowting to þe Sone 680
And þe Sone to þe Holy Goost also
And þe Hooli Goost to hem bo.
  Whanne þe king hadde seen þis sight,
  He was ful ioyful and ful light:
He þoghte þat he was in heuene; 685
His ioye coude he not neuene.
He telde Sidrak hou it ferde
And seide to him, þat al it herde,
'Sydrak, I bileue in þi God, ywis,
And in all þing þat his wille is 690
And euere was or euere shal be;
But I preie þee þat þou telle me,
þat I þe bettir bileue þeron,
Hou þat þei thre ben alle in oon.'
'Sire,' he seide, 'I shall ȝow showe 695
On what manere ȝe shal hem knowe.
And if þat ȝe vnderstonde konne,
On þe sky ȝe mowe se þe sonne
þat þer be þre þinges þerynne
þat no man may departe atwynne: 700
Oone is the silf sunne propurly
þat ȝe seen vppon þe sky;
þe secounde is her faire clerte
þat he ȝeueþ to ȝou and me;
And also þe hete is þe thridde 705
þat in þe world so wide is kidde.

Trinitate T.   640 shall hem] mow hit P.   644 hem twyn] parte hem atwyn P.
648 lite] it TA, *om.* P;   yeveth] shewith P;   bothe] to SP.

---

675 mightes] mightest L.

By þe sonne I vndirstonde
The Fader, þat alle þynge hathe in honde;
And þe Sonne by þe cleerte,
For of þe Fadir comyn is he;
The Holi Goste by þe hete.   655
Thes been þre that be full grete
And all þre ben God but oon,
As þow mayst se the sonne vpon.'

Boctus is now thanne soo blyve
  Thatt he ne can hit well discryve,   660
  And he cried and high spake:
'I trowe on þy God, Sidrakke:
Thre persoones and oon clepe I God.
All to late have I on hym trowid!
The goddis þat my ffaders were   665
And myn auncetours me byfore
Forsake I here for euer and ay
For hym that all thyng may.'
Whanne the folke that vnderstode,
They were wroth as they were wode   670
And swhore þat Sidrak shulde dye
For ought that any man cowth sey.
Somme wente forth by ther oon
And ffor þe kynge made grete moone
And sayde, 'Alas, þat he was bore!   675
Oure kyng hath his wyt fforlore.'
Herewithall they came hym to
And seyde, 'Sir, þow haste misdo.
Full wrothe now be þy meayne—
All þat shulde þe levest be—   680
That þow haste a wych trowyd
And reneyed þy grete godd
That þy ffadir and þyn auncetours all

f. 13ʳ

---

655 by] betokenyth P.   656 be full grete] that I grete TASP.   659–908] *om.*
S.   660 well] halfe TAP;   discryve] kithe TP.   661] For on hym he cryed and
spak P.   663 oon clepe I] o verray P.   666 me] here P.   667 euer] ones
P.   668 For] And cry on P.   670 as they were] and waxyn P.   673] Sum
for the kyng made grete mone P;   wente forth] drowen hem TA.   674] And sum

'By þe sunne mowen ȝe vndirstonde
þe Fadir, þat haþ al þing in honde;
And also þe Sone bi þe cleerte,
For of þe Fadir comen is he;   710
And þe Holy Goost bi þe hete.
þise ben alle iliche grete
And alle thre nys God but oon,   f. 11ᵛ
As þou maist see þe sunne vpon.
Here is ensample faire and clere: 715
Of þi bileue be not in were.'
    Now is Bokkus so blithe
    þat he ne can it descryue,
And to him criede and spak:
'I bileue in þi God, Sidrak,   720
þat ben þre persones and oo God.
To late I haue on hem ytrowed!
And þe go[d]des þat my fadres wore
And myn auncetris herebifore
I forsake here for euere and ay   725
For him þat alle þinges do may.'
And whanne þe folkes þat vnderstood,
þei weren wrooþ as þei weren wood
And seide Sydrak shulde deie
For ought þat any man koude seie.   730
þenne wente some by hem alone
And for þe kyng maden greet mone
And seide, 'Allas, þat he was bore!
Now haþ the king his witt forlore.'
And herwiþal þei come him to   735
And seide, 'Sire, þou hast mysdo.
Ful wrooþ now ben þi meyne—
Alle þat shulde þe leuest be—
þat þou hast a wicche trowod
And renneied þine owne god   740
þat þi fadir and auncetris alle

---

seide, 'Alas, what hathe he done?' P.   675 þat] that euer P.   679–746] *page missing* A.   681 a wych trowyd] to a wicche turned T.   682 grete god] god so gode P.

---

723 goddes] goodes L.

Holden full dere and wolden on call.
Now haste þou hym thorough thyn assent　　　685
Confounded and in fyre brente.'
The kyng saide to hem alle bedene,
'Yee wote not what yee mene!
Therefore I haue forsaken
And to Godde of heven me taken:　　　　　690
Loste I have þe derke nyght
And founde I have þe sonnelight.
Yee been of this mater lewed
But Sidrak hit hathe me fayre shewed—
The noumbre of þe Trinite—　　　　　　695
And þat owre ffaders and wee
Haue trowed in goddis fals and badde
And a febyll lyfe haue wee hadde.
But now have I hym in mynde
That bothe may loose and bynde.　　　　700
In this lawe, sothe to say,
Therinne woll I boþe lyve and deye.'
　　The folke abakke hom drowe,
　　　As þoo þat were wroþe enowe.
　　They chosen iiij men of alle þe oste　　705
That wysest weren and cowde moste
For to holde a disputacion
Ayenst Sidrak and his reason.
These iiij bifore the kyng wente
And seyde, 'Sir, yee be blente:　　　　710
This wiche with his wichcrafte
Hathe yooure wittis from yoow rafte.
Sir, do hym come, for we woll now
Dispute with hym byfore yow.'
Bothe þey grauntyd at þe laste　　　　715
And to despute beganne faste.
They shewid him theire false lawe
And he fordidde hit in a throwe:
He destroyed with reason

f. 13ᵛ

688 not] neuer all P.　　689 Therefore] The devyll for ay P.　　690 Godde
of heven] oder God T;　of heven] om. P.　　691 Loste I have] I haue forsake
P;　　Loste] Leten T.　　692 founde I have] Y take me to P;　founde] taken T.
693 mater] thinge full TP.　　695 noumbre] ombre P.　　704 wroþe] wode P.

Holden ful dere and wolden on hem calle.
þou hast now þorgh þin owne assent
Confoundid and in [fire him brent].'
    [T]he king seide to hem alle bidene,   745
    'Ȝe witen ful litel what ȝe mene!
þe false forein [I] haue forsake   f. 12ʳ
And to oon ful dere God I me betake:
I haue lefte þe derke night
And take me to þe sunnes light.   750
Of þis þing we weren ful lewid
Til Sydrak had to me it shewid—
þe noumbre of þe Holy Trinite—
And þerfore oure fadris and we
Bileued on goddis false and badde   755
And a feble lyf we haue ladde.
But now I haue him in mynde
þat may boþe bynde and vnbynde;
And in his lawe, soþe forto seie,
I wole now boþe lyue and deie.'   760
    þenne al þe folke abak hem drow,
As men þat weren wo inow,
And chees iiij men of al þe oost
þat weren wisest and cowde moost
Forto holden open desputacioun   765
Aȝenst Sidrak and his resoun.
And þise iiij to þe kyng hem wente
And seide, 'Sire, ȝe ben foule blente
For þis wicche wiþ his wicchecraft,
þat fro þi bileue haþ the rafte.   770
Sire, make h[i]m come forth now:
Despute we wole bifore ȝow.'
And boþe þei grauntid at þe last
And to despute þei bigunne fast.
    Thei shewid to Sidrak her fals lawe   775
    And he concludid hem in a þrawe;
And he destroied bi good resoun

712] Hathe (He hathe P) made yow alle bidafte TP.

744 *line unfinished* L.   745 The] he *with erroneous* w *in margin for rubricator*
L.   747 I] ȝe L.   766 Aȝenst] And ȝenst L.   771 him] hem L.

All theyre false opynyon.   720
Wrothe away þey yeden right
For ayenste him þey hadde noo might.
Whenne þey ouercomen wore
And þey myght doo noo moore,
They wente anoon forth and fette   725
Of starke poyson a gobet
And came to Sydrak þer he stode
And sayde, 'þow seyest þy god is goode:
Darst þow, in þe name of hym,
Drynke this gobet of venym?   730
For if he be trewe and woll þe were,
Hit ne shall þe noþyng dere.'
'Be God,' quod Sydrak, 'þat yee wene
Ne may not avayle yoow a bene.
Venym of addyr or of snake   735
That I in Goddis name take
Ne may greue me right nowght:
Take hit hedyr that yee have brought!'
The venym in his honde toke hee
That all þe folke abowte myght see   740

And sayde, 'Yee þat have not trowed,
Yee shall se what is my God.'

Hee dranke þat venym anoone right
And was sownde, hoole, and light.
Alle þe folke þat þere gadered was   745
Hadde grete wonder of þat caas;
The kyng was full glad þerfoore
And loved God moche þe moore.
Anoon cam fallyng from heven
A grete þonder and a leven   750
f. 14ʳ   And smote þese iiij vnto þe grounde
Starke dede in a stounde.

Her goddis and her false opinioun.
þanne þei wroþly awey gan turne
Sighed and sorwed, and weile and morne.   780
But whan þei ouercomen wore   f. 12ᵛ
And aȝein Sidrak might do no more,
þei wenten forþ anoon and fet
Of verre venym a greet goblet
And come to Sidrak þere he stood   785
And seide, 'þou seist þi god is good:
Darst now, in þe name of him,
Drinke þis gobet of foule venim?
And he be trewe, he wole þe were
þat it ne shal noþing þe dere.'   790
'By God,' quod Sidrak, 'þogh ȝe myswene,
It may not availe ȝou a bene.
þe venim of addre or of snake
In my Goddes name I wole it take:
It shal greue me right noght.   795
Take it me þat ȝe haue broght!'
þe venim in his hond þo toke he
þat alle þe peple might it wel se
And to hem þat aboute him stood
Sidrak seide, wiþ mylde mood,   800
'Ȝe shullen see, or I hennes meve,
Hou my God saueþ hem þat on him leue.'
He drank þe venim anoon right
And aftir was hole, sounde, and light.
þe folke þat þidre gadrid was   805
Hadden greet wonder of þat cas;
And þe king was glad wonder sore
And loued God miche þe more.
    Anoon come falling fro þe heuene
    A greet þondre and a leuene   810
And smote þe iiij men to þe grounde
þat tempted God in þat stounde
In preving of his greet might.
þei wende Sidrak haue slain right
In þat stounde amonge hem alle;   815 f. 13ʳ

P.   746 Hadde grete] So hadden T.   747 A begins again.   751 þese iiij]
the iiij maystris P.

Thanne was þe folke afrayed soore
And þey seyde, all þat þere woore,
'Hadde Sidrakkis god not trewe be,   755
He hadde brosten þat wee hadde se;
And þese iiij þat hym þought dispite
Ne hadde not be dede so tyte.'
    Whanne þe devell was owtelopen
That in þe brente ymagis before was cropen,   760

He and his felowes lopyn efte
Into oþer ymages þat were lefte;
And þey alle at þe laste
Vpon þe kyng a crye caste
And seide, 'Boctus, þow haste þy wytte   765
Forlore—and soo semyth hit
Whanne þow chaungest all thy lawe
And trowest on a wycches sawe.
As þow haste now forsaken
And to wycchecrafte þe ytaken   770
And we shall alle forsaken þe,
Shall noon of vs þy frende be:
Thy sacrafice wee shull forsake;
On þy goodis we shall do wrake;
All þy bestes shull we sloo   775
And help ayenste þe þy foo;
And we shall vs haste bly[v]e
Oute of þy kyngdame the to dryve;
Alle þy childryn slee we shall
And oþer of þy kynne withall;   780
And þyselve, soþe to say,
An evyll deþe shall þou deye.
Bot þow wolte scape all þis
And byleve styll in blis,

   755 trewe] verrai TAP.   757 iiij] *add* maistris P;   hym þought] sought his
P.   759–60] Whan þe ffendes sawe þis caas / Thatt in þe mametes had dwellyng
place A.   760 þe . . . before] his breth god T, here brest god P.   761–2] *om.*
A.   761 He] That devill T.   762 ymages] *om.* P.   763 And] Anon A,
But P.   769 As] And vs all P; now] *om.* P.   771 we . . . forsaken] shull we

But veniaunce sone on hem gan falle.
þanne weren þe folke affraied sore
And alle þei seiden þat þere wore,
'Nadde Sydrakes god good and verray be,
He hadde tobroste, he might not fle;   820
And þise iiij þat þoghte his god despite
Caused hem þat þei weren dede so tite.
For whanne þe deuels weren outlopen
And out of oure goddis cropen,
Whanne þei weren brent al in fere   825
þat weren to vs so leef and dere,
Ʒit he and his fel felawes lepen efte
In some ymage þat weren lefte.'
And alle þei at þe laste
Vpon þe king a greet cry caste   830
And seide, 'Bokkus, where is þi witt?
It semeþ þou hast forlorn it
Whanne þou chaungest al þi lawe
And bileuest on a wicches sawe.
þou hast now vs alle forsake   835
And to þe wicchcrafte þe bitake
And we shullen alle forsaken þee,
Ne none of vs shal þi frende be:
þi sacrifice we shullen forsake
And on þi goodis we shullen do wrake   840
And alle þi beestis we sholen slo;
Aʒenst þe we sholen helpe þi fo
And we shullen vs haste bliue
Out of þi kingdom þe forto driue;
Alle þi children sle we shal   845
And manye of þi kingdom wiþal;
And þiself also, soth to seie,
A shameful deth þou shalt deie.
But and þou wilt scape al þis,   f. 13ᵛ
Leue þi wicchecrafte, I þe wis,   850
And leeue on þin olde loore:

now P.   773] *om.* A.   774/5 And thy riches from the I take *added in margin* A.   776 help . . . þe] of they frendis make P.   777 blyve] *from* TAP, blyþe B.   782 shall þou] we shall don T, we shull do the P;   deye] dawy P.   783 scape] forsake T, forsakyn and skape P.   784 blis] owre blisse T, thi blis P.

f. 14ᵛ

Ayensay all þat þow haste sayde   785
And all that thyn herte is on leyd
And do breke þe yondir pott atwoo
His wicchecrafte soo to fordoo;
And þe water at þe last
Vndyr þy houndes fete þow cast   790
And sythens Sidrak doo þow brenne,
That all þis woo haþe brought þe ynne.'
The kyng and alle þat þere wore
Of þis þynge were wonder soore
And abasshed were somdele.   795
Sydrak that behelde full wele
And sayde, 'Sir, dysmay þe nought:
On God of heven be alle þy thought.
Lete þe devell have noo pouste
With his engyne to fasten on þe,   800
For þou shalt see anoon right
I shall destroye hym and his might.'
A betyll in his honde he nam
And to þe fals goddis cam.
Hee stode and seyde alle an hye,   805
'In his name þat is almighty
I shall yoow breke þis day
And þe devell dryve away.'
With his betill he leyde vppon
And brake the idolys euerychon.   810
Whan þe devyll sawe noo more
That his dwellyng myght be þoore,
Hee and alle his companye
Beganne thens þanne for to hye;
And an hedews crye þey cast,   815
Whan the idole all tobrast.
An erthedyn they maade anoon,
As þe folke þought euerychon,
That þe erthe sanke and downe wente;

785 Ayensay] Wicchecrafte hit is P.   786 that . . . on] thyn hert thou hast theron
P.   787–8] And thow woldist one pot breke anon / All his wicchecrafte were fordon
P.   790 houndes] *om.* T.   794 wonder] wondrid P;   soore] feere T.
798 alle] *om.* T.   805 stode] spake A.   807 yoow] *om.* P;   þis] this ilke
P.   809 betill] betillis A.   810 idolys] mamettis P.   812 his . . . be] he

It shal availe þe miche þe more.
It is but wicchecrafte þat Sidrak seide,
þogh þou þin herte þeron hast leide.
þerfore do breke ȝonder potte anoon,   855
þat Sidrakes wicchecraft were fordoon,
And þe water þerof swiþe now caste
Vndre þin houndes feet faste;
And þanne Sidrak do þou brenne,
þat al þis harlotrie þe dide kenne.'   860
    Tho þe king and alle þat þere wore
    Of þis þing wondride ful sore
And weren abasshid gretly somdel;
And þat byheld Sidrak ful wel
And seide, 'Sire, dismay þe right noght: 865
Euere on God of heuene lat be þi þoght.
Lat þe deuel neuere haue no pouste
Wiþ hise gynnes to fasten on the,
For þou shalt see anoon right
I shal destroye þe deuel and his might.'   870
    A greet betille he toke in honde anon
And to þe false ymages he wente soon.
Bifore hem he stood and seide on hy,
'In his name þat is almighti
I shall ȝou tobreke þis same day   875
And þe deuels I shal driue away.'
Wiþ his betille þo he leide on
And brake þe false maumetis euerichon.
þanne þe deuel sey þat no more
His dwelling place might be þore,   880
He and al his company
Bygunne hem þus forto hy.
A grisely cry þanne vp þei caste,   f. 14ʳ
Whanne þe maumetis al tobraste.
þe deuels made an erþe[dy]n anoon   885
So þat þe folkes sawe it euerichoon
þat þe erthe sanke and doun wente;

dwellyng myȝtt haue A.   814 thens þanne] hem henseward P.   816 idole]
ydollis T, mamettis P.   817 erthedyn] erthe dyde P. .   818 As þe folke] So that
folke saw and P;   As] Alle T.

885 erþedyn] erþen L.

f. 15^r

Thundyr and lyghtyng also þey sente;   820
Hayle and rayne also was þore
That the folke abaysshed soore;
And þe kynge of alle þe oste
Was abaysshed althermoste.

    Sidrak sawe the kynge in drede   825
    And anoon to hym he yeede
    And sayde, 'Sir, discomforte þe nought:
Goddis myght, þat all hathe wrought,
Is strenger than þe devell of helle;
And þerfore of þese wordes felle   830
Drede þe not but comforte þe:
Ouer vs soone his grace shall be.'
Down came an aungell bright
All abowte with moche light
And seyde, 'Sydrak, take with þyn honde   835
The water þat in þe potte doþe stonde:
On þe iiij sydes of þe hows hit caste
All the whyle that hit woll laste
In þe name of þe Trinite;
And sithens thenne þe stakes thre   840
Bete faste togedyr hem to
And þe devell shall renne þerfroo.'
Sidrak dyd as þat he badde
And anoon they feyre wedir hadde.

Anoþer aungell þey sawe comyng   845
And a swherde in his honde brennyng
And smote þe devell and hym shente
And þe idole all tobrente.
Alle þe folke þat þere wore
That wolde not convertid be afoore,   850
Whenne they had herde of þat sight,
They turnyd vnto God anoon right.

---

827 discomforte] discomffite A.   828 Goddis . . . all] God that alle thynge T.
830 þese] his P.   832 his] Goddis P.   835 take] *om.* P.   837 iiij] *om.*
A;   sydes] walles TAP;   of þe hows] aboute A, thou P.   840 thenne] of
TAP.   841 to] tho A.   842 renne] fle P.   845 þey sawe comyng] ther
com goynge T, þer came discendyng A, was commawnde P.   846] Bryngyng

And þondre and lightnyng also þei sente,
Haile and reyn to greue hem sore,
And baisshid þe folk þat þere wore; 890
And þe king of al þe oost
Was abaisshid alþermoost.
   [S]ydrak sawe þe king in drede
   And to him anoon he ȝede
And seide, 'Sire, discomforte þe noght: 895
For Goddis might, þat al haþ wroght,
Is strenger þan þe deuel of helle;
And þerfore of þise wordes felle
Drede þe not but comfort þee:
For over vs shal his grace euere be.' 900
Adoun come þere an aungel bright
And ouereshone hem wiþ greet light
And seide, 'Sidrak, with þin handes
Take þe water þat in þe pott standis
And all þe while þat it wole last 905
In þe iiij corneris of þe hous it cast
In þe name of þe Holy Trinite;
And þanne aftir þe stakis thre
Bete faste togidre þe maumetis two
And þe deuel shal fle hem fro.' 910
   Anoon Sidrak dide as he bad
And sone faire wedir þanne þei had,
Ioying þerof and in herte glad
And of chere wondre sad.
Anoþer aungel come fleyng, 915
þat bare a swerde al brennyng:
He smote þe deuel þat he was shent   f. 14ᵛ
And þe false maumetes al tobrent.
þanne alle þe peple þat þere were
And þat noþing ȝit conuerted nere, 920
Whann þei hadde isen þat sight,
To God þei torned þanne anoon right.

a swerde all brennande P.   847 devell] develis P.   848 idole] mamettis
P.

893 Sydrak] ydrak (*gap for rubricator, not completed*) L.

f. 15ᵛ

Boctus þe kyng, whanne he þat sawgh,
A lytyll began for to lawgh:
In his herte he was blithe   855
And Sidrak he axed swhythe,
'Lieue Sidrak, now telle me
What signifieth þe stakes þre
And þe potte of erþe alsoo
That þe water þow puttest into,   860
And why þow soo þe water caste
And bete togedyr þe stakes faste.'
'Sir,' he seyde, 'þe stakes thre,
They signifie the Holy Trinite,
Fader and Sone and Holy Gost,   865
That ben o God as þow well wost.
By þe erthen potte I take
This worlde that [God] of erthe did make.

The iij stakes the potte vp bare
And þe worlde, be þow wel ware.   870

The water þat in þe potte was doone,
That signifieth Goddis Sone,
That in þis worlde born shall be
Of a mayden pure and fre.
And þat Sone shall all with right   875
Distroye þe devell with his might.
Vppon þe crosse he shall be doone
And dye ayenst the tyme of noone;
In erthe shall he graven be
And aryse withynne dayes iij.   880
Thorogh þat deþe shall he call
Adam and his frendes all
Owte of woo and of caare,

860 That] And A;   þe ... into] thou didist thi water in do P;   puttest into] madest
in doo TA.   864 Holy] om. P.   868 God] from TAP, om. B;   did] wolde
P.   869–70] om. A.   870 And] So dothe God P.   876 with] and all P.

Whanne Bokkus þe king þis sawe,
In his herte he was ful fawe
And of his chere he was right bliþe   925
And axede Sidrak als swithe,
'Leef broþer, telle þou me
What signifieþ thise stakes thre
And þe potte of þe erthe also
þat þou didest þe watir in do,   930
And whi þat þou þe watir so cast
And bete togidre þe stikkes fast.'
  'Sire,' he seide, 'þe stakes þre
  Bitoken þe Holi Trinite,
Fadir and Sone and Hooli Goost,   935
þat is oo God wel þou woost.
By þe erthen pott I vndirstonde
þe Lord þat is al weldande:
þis world he made at his wille
Mankinde þerwiþ forto glade and fille;   940
Wiþ the fruites þerof shulde springe
Mankindis hunger refresshinge.
þe þre stakes þe pott vp bar
Bitoken God, þerof be war,
þat al þe world bereþ vpright   945
þorgh his grete vertu and his might.
þe watir þat in þe p[o]tte was done,
It bitokeneþ Goddis Sone,
þat in þis worlde born shal be
Of a clene maide pure and fre.   950
And þilke Sone shal with right   f. 15ʳ
Destroie þe deuel and his might.
Vpon þe cros he shal be done
And deie aȝenst þe time of none;
He shal in erþe grauen be   955
And rise to lijf wiþynne daies thre.
þorgh þe deeth he shal calle
Adam and hise frendes alle
Out of her woo and of her care,

878] And suffre deth and passion A.

———

947 potte] pitte L.

That now in þe develis bondis aare.
The water þat I at þe laste   885
Abowte þe iiij wallis caaste
Betokeneþ iiij men þat shall þo
In iiij sides of þe worlde goo;

And many men shall þanne wyte.
And eche of þem his booke shall write,   890
Thorough whiche confounde þey shall
The devill and his power all.
The stakys þat I togedir smote
Made grete dene as yee wele wote:
That was in token of hem þoo   895
That with Goddis Sone shall goo
And shull his descipeles be.
They shull preche of þe Trinite,
And þe voys of þem shall wende
Ouerall to þe worldis ende;   900
For þey shull the folke preche
And the right beleve hem teche.
Many on that þen is bore
Shull they call that is forlore;

And that bene in right beleve   905
Goddis Soone hem shall foryeve
All that they have doon amys
And brynge hem to heven blys.'
Boctus liked these wordis well
And is now knowyng somedell   910
Thoroughowte Sidrakkes loore
And in þe feith hym strenkþith more

f. 16ʳ

884 now] *om.* P;   bondis aare] handis ware P.   887 þo] goo AP.   888 sides] partis A;   goo] to P, to and ffroo A.   889] And many a contre shall þey visite A, Full many a man that shall wete P.   890 eche of þem] euery man P.   892 power] werkis A.   895 þoo] all A.   899 voys] noyse P.   904 call . . . forlore] aduertise þat els were lore A.   909 S *begins again.*   910] As Y now know

þat in þe deuels hond now are.   960
    And þe water þat I at the last
Aboute þe iiij corners cast
Bitokeneþ [iiij] men þat shullen wende,
Preching þe ioye þat neuere shal haue ende,
Sente of God þe world aboute   965
Into þe foure parties wiþouten doute,
As many a man wel shal wite.
And eche of hem his book shal write,
þoruȝ þe whiche confound þei shal
The deuel and his power al.   970
    The stakes þat I togidre smoot
Bitokeneþ the greet dole, I wel woot,
þat shal be for taking of hem tho
þat shal wiþ Goddis Sone þan go
And shullen hise disciples be.   975
And þei shullen preche þe Trinite,
And the noise of hem shal wende
In eche countre to þe worldes ende;
For þei shullen to þe peple preche
And þe riȝt weie of bileue teche.   980
Many oone þanne shal be borne
Shullen weile for hem þat shal be lorne
For þei nolde bileeue right
In Goddis vertu and his might;
þerfore bi riȝtwise iugement   985 f. 15ᵛ
þei shullen to peyne and turment.
    And þo þat ben in right bileue
Goddes Sone shal hem forȝeue
Al þat þei haue here doo mys
And bringe hem into ioye and blis.'   990
    Kyng Bokkus liked þise wordes wel
    Of his techyng euerydel
And wondre ioyful was of his lore
And strengþed in oure feith þe more

---

sumdele P.   911 Thoroughowte] Thorow P, Through the vertu off A.   912 þe]
his P;   strenkþith] streyneth T, stablishte A.

---

  963 iiij] my L.   969 confound] confoundid L.   977 noise] *possibly* uoise
L.

And Goddis name right lefe he hadde
And was in þe feythe full sadde.
Thenne desyred he for to here   915
Many thynges þat he wolde lere
And prayde Sydrak hym telle shulde
Thynges that he axe wolde.
Sydrak answherd full blythely,
'Axe what þow wolt hardely.'   920
The kyng axid hym anoon
These questions by oon and oon
That bene wretyn in this boke,
And vnto hem grete kepe he toke.

913 right] more A;   right lefe] the levere TS, to hym leuer P.   915 Thenne]
That P.   919 answherd] saide S, sore he seide P.   920 þow wolt] ȝe will ser
S.   922 These] Many S.   924 kepe] hede P, ȝeme S.

And þe more loue to God he had 995
And in þe feith contynued right sad.
þe king desired þan forto here
Many þinges þat he wolde lere
And preide Sidrak him telle shulde
þinges þat he him axe wolde. 1000
He seide he wolde ful bleþeli:
'Axe what þou wilte, Sire, hardely.'
The king axede him anoon
þise questiouns bi oone and oon
þat ben ywriten in þis booke, 1005
And to hem greet heed he tooke.

*Questiouns þat King Bokkus axed Sidrak and hou
he answerid to hem: Liber Primus.*

Ca.º jº	The firste þing þanne axede he:	(1)
	If God was euere and euere shal be.	1010
Ca.º ijº	The king axide if it might bene	(2)
	þat God of heuene might be sene.	
Ca.º iijº	Also þe king axede him þere	(3)
	If God be oueral and euerywhere.	
Ca.º iiijº	'Whiche was now þe firste þing	(4) 1015
	þat euere God made?' axede þe king.	
Ca.º vº	Also þe king Sydrak bisoght	(5)
	To telle whanne aungel was wroght.	
Ca.º vjº	The king axith, 'Wherof serueth	(6) f. 16ʳ
	þe aungels þat in heuene dwellith?'	1020
Ca.º vijº	The king axede if deuels also	(7)
	Al þing woote and al þing may do.	
Ca.º viijº	'Of what shap ben aungels and of what þing	(8)
	Kunne þei and knowe þei?' axede þe king.	
Ca.º ixº	The king axede Sidrak, I vnderstonde,	(9) 1025
	If God made man wiþ his honde.	

Ca.° x°   The king askid, or he furþer ȝede,   (10)
           [Wher] God made Adam and in what stede.

Ca.° xj°   The king axede, 'Whidre wente Adam   (11)
           Out of paradys whanne he cam?   1030

Ca.° xij°   'Dide Adam any oþer synne [þan] þat   (12)
           But brake Goddes heste and þe appel at?

Ca.° xiij°   'What was it þat Adam from God refte   (13)
           And how shal he ȝelde it him eft?

Ca.° xiiij°   'Lorne for euere whi was he noght   (14) 1035
           Siþen he so grete synne wroght?

Ca.° xv°   'Why nolde God an aungel sende   (15)
           Or a man Adam to amende?

Ca.° xvj°   'Whi shal God be bore, þou me telle,   (16)
           Of a maide, and she a maide dwelle?'   1040

Ca.° xvij°   The king axede, for he wolde lere: (17)
           'Hou longe lyuede Adam here?

Ca.° xviij°   'Whi is deth clepid deth, tel þou me,   (18)
           And how many dethes þat þer be?

Ca.° xix°   'Sendiþ God man ought to seie   (19) 1045
           On what deeþ þat he shal deie?

Ca.° xx°   'Whanne soule fro þe body shal shede,   (20)
           Hou wendiþ þe soule to oþer stede?

Ca.° xxj°   'Now wolde I wite wheþer wore   (21)
           Soule or body made bifore.   1050

Ca.° xxij°   'Wheþer spekeþ, wite wolde Y—   (22)
           The soule of man or þe body?

Ca.° xxiij°   'The soule þat a goost is oon   (23)
           And haþ nouþer flesshe ne boon
f. 16ᵛ   Ne noght takiþ ne ȝeueþ þerfro,   1055
           Hou may it þole wele or woo?

1027–8] *misplaced at foot of page, marked for insertion after* 1026 L *table.*
1028 Wher] *from* 2218, þat L *table.*   1031 þan] *from* 2299, *om.* L *table.*
1032 Goddes] *from* 2300, goddest L *table.*

Ca.° xxiiij°   'Who is more lord of þe tweie—   (24)
                     þe soule or þe body?–þou me seie.

Ca.° xxv°   'Whereaboute, so God þe spede,   (25)
                     Haþ soule in man his woning stede?   1060

Ca.° xxv[j]°   'Whi is þe soule no lenger lefte   (26)
                     In þe body whanne þe blood is byreft?

Ca.° xxvi[j]°   'I preie þe now þat þou me seie   (27)
                     Whi it is þat folke so deie.

Ca.° xxvii[j]°   'Hou [mowen] men wite þat it so is   (28) 1065
                     þat God made man to heuen blis?

Ca.° xxix°   'Siþen we of Goddis liknesse be,   (29)
                     Whi mowen we not do as dide he?

Ca.° xxx°   'Where bicomeþ the blood al   (30)
                     Of man when he die shal?   1070

Ca.° xxxj°   'Whanne þe fire slakid is,   (31)
                     Where bicomeþ [it]?—Telle me þis.

Ca.° xxxij°   'Whi dieþ not þe body thore   (32)
                     Or þat he lese half his blood and more?

Ca.° xxx[iij]°   'Of what complexioun telled may be   (33) 1075
                     þe body and of what nature is he?

Ca.° xxxi[iij]°   'Weren soulis made at þe firste for ay   (34)
                     Or ben þei made ȝit euery day?

Ca.° xxx[v]°   'Mowen þei haue any excusing   (35)
                     þat of God knoweþ [no]thing?   1080

Ca.° xxxv[j]°   'Shal a man ought elles do   (36)
                     But þat God comaundeth him to?

Ca.° xxxv[ij]°   'Hou many worldis beþ of alle   (37)
                     And hou now doth men hem calle?

Ca.° xxxvii[j]°   'Is God of greet ȝilding to tho   (38) 1085
                     þat in his seruice here aright go?

1061–5 q. nos. xxvj–xxviij] *final digits lost in binding* L *table.*   1065 mowen] *from*
2773, *om.* L *table.*   1072 it] *from* 2836, *om.* L *table.*   1075–85 q. nos. xxxiij–
xxxviij] *final digits lost in binding* L *table.*   1080 nothing] *from* 2918, al thing L *table.*

Ca.° xxxix°   'The peple þat in þe time shal be   (39)
                   Of Goddes Sone whan comen is he
f. 17ʳ   And shullen þei after comounly
                   Bileue alle in him stedfastly?   1090

[Ca.°] xl°   'What comaundement, bi þi leue,   (40)
                   Shal Goddis Sone his peple ȝeue?

[Ca.°] xlj°   'þe blisfullest þing, aftir þi witte,   (41)
                   And worþiest and fairest, whiche is itte?

[Ca.°] xlij°   'þe foulest and þe perilousest þing to se   (42) 1095
                   And most accursed, what may þat be?

[Ca.°] xliij°   'Shal any man good do   (50)
                   His kyn and his frendis to?

[Ca.°] xliiij°   'Now I preie þe þat þou telle me: (51)
                   Gentillesse, what may þat be?   1100

[Ca.°] xlv°   'Hou may it be colde eche ȝere   (52)
                   Whanne þe weder is faire and clere?

[Ca.°] xlvj°   'May a man oght by any þrowe   (53)
                   þe good men fro þe wikked knowe?

[Ca.°] xlvij°   'The truþe þat was here bifore   (54) 1105
                   Of false mamettes þat þere wore,
                   Shal it euere arered be
                   So strong as was in tyme of me?

[Ca.°] xlviij°   'Whi was it not Goddis wille   (55)
                   þat man might not lyue a weke with a fille?   1110

[Ca.°] xlix°   'Deieth þe riche men also   (56)
                   As other pore men here do?

[Ca.°] l°   'Shullen men deme þe riche also   (57)
                   As þat men þe pore here do?

[Ca.°] lj°   'May þe wikked als wel for ay   (58) 1115
                   Haue Goddis loue as þe good may?

[Ca.°] lij°   'Hou may þe childe, þat ful of loue is,   (59)
                   Come out of þe modres wombe?—Telle me þis.

1091–1158] Ca. *om. before q. no.* L *table.*   1113–14] *misplaced at foot of page,
marked for insertion after* 1112 L *table.*

[Ca.°] liij°   'May any womman bere mo   (60)
               Children in her attones þan two?   1120

[Ca.°] liiij° 'Whiche is þe best þing þat may be   (61)
               þat man may haue?—Telle þou me.

[Ca.°] lv°   'The werste þing, so God þe saue,   (62)
               Whiche is it þat man may haue?

[Ca.°] lvij°   'Telle me ȝit an axinge newe: (63) 1125 f. 17ᵛ
               Hou may a man be feiþful and trewe?

[Ca.°] lviij° 'Hardynesse of man and drede,   (64)
               Wherof come þei, so God þe spede?

[Ca.°] lix°   'Wherof may it to man bifalle   (65)
               þat he haue meselrie or scalle?   1130

[Ca.°] lx°   'Weren alle þinges of Goddis making   (66)
               Made firste at þe bigynning?

[Ca.°] lxj°   'Telle me now, aftir þi witt: (67)
               þe fruites of þe erþe, who norisshiþ it?

[Ca.°] lxij°   'þe beestis þat haue no witt,   (68) 1135
               Hou wexe þei rage?—Telle me it.

[Ca.°] lxiij° 'What beest is it, as þat ȝe fynde,   (69)
               þat lyueþ lengest in his kynde?

[Ca.°] lxiiij° 'Fedith God al þing   (70)
               þat is in erþe of his making?   1140

[Ca.°] lxv°   'Fisshes, foules, and bestis echone,   (71)
               Haue þei soules or haue þei none?

[Ca.°] lxvj°   'They þat in þe time of Goddis Sone shal be,
               Shullen þei liue as longe as done we?   (72)

[Ca.°] lxvij° 'Telle me now here, or þou gange: (73) 1145
               Hou longe shal þis worlde here stande?

[Ca.°] lvj°   'Lyue any men in þe world mo   (74)
               þanne on þe erthe þat we on go?

                    1147–8] *precede* 1125 L *table.*

f. 1ra

'Whens comyth ther fathede and why   (85)
That a man hathe in his body?

'Shall men wymmen chastysyn and wysse   (86)
With betyng when they done amys?

'What thyng is gelosy to know   (87)   P5
And why in gelosy is man sone throw?

'Shall a man loue his frende   (88)
And fonde to holde hym in his honde?

'May a man loue his frende so   (89)
And no trauayle haue thereto?   P10

P1–724] *from preliminary table, questions not numbered* P, *not in* BAST.

[Ca.°] lxviij°   'Whi ben some blake in toun   (75)
             And some white and some broun?   1150

[Ca.°] lxix°   'Tel me now, par companye: (76)
             Wherof comeþ felonye?

[Ca.°] lxx°   'Þe beestes þat God in erþe haþ wroght,   (77)
             Of oo colour whi be þei noght?

[Ca.°] lxxj°   'Thei þat eten and dr[i]nken more þan nede is,   1155
             Wheþer do þei—wel or amis?   (78)

[Ca.°] lxxij°   'Which is þe beste þing of þe man   (79)
             And þe worste?—Telle, if þou can.

Ca.° lxxiiij°   'Wheþer ȝeueth a man more kunnyng—   (80)   f. 18ʳ
             Hote mete or colde in etyng?   1160

Ca.° lxxv°   'How may a man fle felonye   (81)
             And wraþþe and malenncolye?

Ca.° lxxvj°   'Wheþer to haue is more bate—   (82)
             Loue of wommen or her hate?

Ca.° lxxvij°   'A man þat is in hele and ȝing,   (83) 1165
             Hou wraþiþ he him for litel thing?

Ca.° lxxviij°   'Hou may a man blamles be   (84)
             To loue a womman and him she?

Ca.° lxxix°   'Whennes comeþ þe fatnesse and why   (85)
             þat a man haþ in his body?   1170

Ca.° lxxx°   'Shullen men chastice wymmen and wisse   (86)
             Wiþ betyng whan þei done amisse?

Ca.° lxxxj°   'What þing is ielosie to knowe   (87)
             And whi is man ielous somme þrowe?

Ca.° lxxxij°   'Shal a man loue his frende   (88) 1175
             And fonde to holde him in his hende?

Ca.° lxxxiij°   'May a man his profite do   (89)
             And no trauaile haue þerto?

1155 drinken] *from* 3991, drunken L *table.*   1159–77 *q. nos.* lxxiiij–lxxxiij *for*
lxxiij–lxxxij L *table.*

'Shall men do gode or almysdede   (90)
Vnto peure men that haue nede?

'How shal a man hym conteyne   (91)
When he is the folk betwyne?

'Is a riche man the lasse worthy   (92) P15
That he forlesys his gode holy
Or a poure man worthy the more
Thow richesse on hym is waxed hore?

'The wyckyd maner of man that Y se   (93)
And wyckid custome, whiche may they be?   P20

'Sythyn iren is so harde and starke   (94)
And fyre to wyrche with moche carke,
How was furst made and wrought
Tongis, hamer, and the stocke?

'Dothe they amys that all day swere   (95) P25
By here god that is so dere?

'Shall a man of his body   (96)
In all thyngis be chast holy?

'Whom shall a man loue withall to go   (97)
And what company fle fro?   P30

'Whedir is bettir, so God the saue—   (98)
Richesse or pouerte for to haue?

'Shall a man honoure that are nygh do[m]e (99)
Ilyke a riche man or a grome?

'Delite the pore men ham in pouerte also   (100) P35
As the riche in here riches do?

'Shall a man make his roos   (101)
Ought of anythyng that he doos?

'Why are houndis fast that done here kynde (102)
More then any other bestis that men fynde?   P40

'He that of othir mennys wyuys couetous is (103)
[Or] of his gode, do he not amys?

P33 dome] done P *table.*   P42 Or] *from* B3820, Where P *table.*

Ca.° lxxxiij° 'Shullen men do good and almesdede (90)
     To þe pouere þat haue nede?   1180

Ca.° lxxxiiij° 'Hou shal a man gouerne him (91)
     Amonge þe peple withoute grim?

Ca.° lxxxv° 'Is a rich man þe lasse worþi (92)
     þat he forlesiþ his good holi
     Or a pore man worþi the more 1185
     þouȝ richesse on him woxen wore?

Ca.° lxxxvj° 'þe wikkid maners of man þat I se, (93)
     Wherof come þei?—Telle þou me.

Ca.° lxxxvij° 'Siþen yren is so hard and stark (94)
     And man to worche it haþ gret cark, 1190
     Hou was first made and wherwith
     Tongis, hamers, and þe stith?

Ca.° lxxxviij° 'Do þei amis þat alday swere (95) f. 18ᵛ
     Bi her god, whatso þei here?

Ca.° lxxxix° 'Shal a man in his body (96) 1195
     Be chaaste in alle þinges holi?

Ca.° lxxxx° 'Wiþ whom shal a man loue to go (97)
     And whom shal he fle fro?

Ca.° lxxxxj° 'Wheþer is better, so God þe saue— (98)
     Richesse or pouert forto haue? 1200

Ca.° lxxxxij° 'Shal a man worshipe, telle þou me, (99)
     Yliche riche and pore þat ȝe here se?

Ca.° lxxxxiij° 'Deliteþ þe pore men in pouert so (100)
     As riche men in her richesse do?

Ca.° lxxxxiiij° 'Shal a man ought make his boost (101) 1205
     Of þat he doth in any coost?

Ca.° lxxxxv° 'Whi ben houndes fastned þat doth her kinde (102)
     More þan oþer bestes þat men finde?

Ca.° lxxxxvj° 'He þat of anoþer manis wif coueitous is (103)
     Or of his good, [doþ he] not amis? 1210

1179 *correct q. nos. resume* L *table.* 1210 doþ he] *from* 4760, þat he do L *table.*

f. 1rb

'May no man ascape the dethe   (104)
For rychesse and myght and oþer dede?

'[Is hit goode to answhere] ay   (105)   P45
Hem that spekyn foly all day?

'Of all cunnyngis that thou can,   (106)
Whiche is most greuous to man?

'They that trayuayle for to wynne   (107)
And can not lyue, why nill they blynne?   P50

'In what maner may hit ryse   (108)
That men become folis and vnwyse?

'Is the soule or the body wo   (109)
When eyther shall parte other fro?

'Whedir shall a man holde more—   (110)   P55
An olde man or a yong that wore?

'Why reyneth hit in o yere more   (111)
Than in another and wherefore?

'May ony man with connyng of clergy   (112)
A mesell hele of mesilry?   P60

'Why ne had God man so wrought   (113)
That he ne had synnyd nought?

'Is hit gode to haue intermettyng   (114)
Ageyns ilke a man or ageyns al thyng?

'Telle me now as for what sake   (115)   P65
That God wolde this world make.

'How was the world made as hit is   (116)
And how holdis hit?—Tell me this.

'Is ther any folke more than we   (117)
That of the sonne haue the clarite?   P70

P45 Is hit goode to answhere] *from* B3871, Sithe God to ham answerid P *table.*

Ca.° lxxxxvij°   'May not a man þe deth escape here   (104)
                     þorgh ȝiftes or preiere in any manere?

Ca.° lxxxxviij°   'Is it good to answere ay   (105)
                     Hem þat speken folily alday?

Ca.° lxxxxix°   'Of al þe kunnynge þat we here can,   (106) 1215
                     Whiche is most grevous vnto man?

Ca.° C°   'þei þat trauaillen forto wynne   (107)
                     And kunnen not lyue, whi nyl þei blynne?'

Libro Secundo

Ca.° primo   'On what manere may it rise   (108)
                     þat men bicomen fooles and vnwise?   1220

Ca.° ij°   'Is þe soule or body woo   (109)
                     Whanne þat oone shal parte þe oþer fro?

Ca.° iij°   'Wheþer shal a man holde wiþ more—   (110)
                     Oolde or ȝonge wheþer it wore?

Ca.° iiij°   'Whi reineth it in oo ȝere more   (111) 1225
                     þan in anoþer?—Telle me wherfore.

Ca.° v°   'May any man with kunnyng of clergie   (112)   f. 19ʳ
                     Hele a mesel of his meselrie?

Ca.° vj°   'Whi ne had God man so ywroght   (113)
                     þat he ne hadde isynned noght?   1230

Ca.° vij°   'Is it good to haue entirmeting   (114)
                     Aȝeinst euery man of eche þing?

Ca.° viij°   'Telle me now as for what sake   (115)
                     þat God wolde þis worlde make.

Ca.° ix°   'Hou was þe world made as it is   (116) 1235
                     And hou holdiþ it?—Telle me þis.

Ca.° x°   'Is þer any oþer folk þan we   (117)
                     þat haue of þe sunne cleerte?

'How long may the world be,   (118)
How brode, and how riche is he?

'Why shall God clenlyke also   (119)
The folk of this world vndo?

'The fowlis that in the eyre flye,   (120)   P75
How are they bore on lofte so hye?

'Among all tell me ȝit: (121)
The reyne that fallys, whens comyth hit?

'Haile shouris that fall all so,   (122)
When and whereof come tho?   P80

'When[s] are the tempestis all   (123)
That somtyme among us falle?

'Tell me now, for hit is wondir: (124)
Of what thyng comyth the thondir?

'The wynde that blowith by londe and se,   (125)   P85
Whereof euyr may hit be?

'How issues watris of hillis hy   (126)
That semyd bettir to be dry?

'The watir that is in the see,   (127)
f. 1ᵛᵃ   Why is hit salte?—Tel me.   P90

'Telle me now, yf thow wote: (128)
How oute of the erthe spryng watris hote?

'Among all other telle me one: (129)
Whereof comyth the brymstone?

'Whereof may hit euer be,   (130)   P95
The leame that we as fyre se?

'The watris that ebbyn and flowen also,   (131)
Whens comyth they? Whidir is that they go?

'Hyllis and rockis, were they nouȝt   (132)
Made furst whan the world was wrought?   P100

P73 clenlyke] clense lyke P *table*, clenly B4295.   P81 Whens] *from* B4383T,
When P *table*.

Ca.° xj°   'Hou longe may þe world be   (118)
And brode and þicke?—Telle þou me.   1240

Ca.° xij°   'Whi shal God clenly also   (119)
þe folke of þis world fordo?

Ca.° xiij°   'þe foules þat in þe heir fflie,   (120)
Hou ben þei borne on lofte on hye?

Ca.° xiiij°   'Amonge alle oþre telle me right: (121) 1245
þe reyn þat falleþ, whens cometh it?

Ca.° xv°   'þe haile stones þat fallen also,   (122)
Wherof and whens cometh tho?

Ca.° xvj°   'Whennes beþ the tempestis alle   (123)
þat somtyme among vs falle?   1250

Ca.° xvij°   'Telle me now, for it is wondre: (124)
Of what þing cometh þe thondre?

Ca.° xviij°   'þe winde þat blowiþ bi lond and see,   (125)
Wherof euere may it be?

Ca.° xix°   'Hou renneþ watir from hilles [hye]   (126) 1255
þat semeth bettir to be drie?

Ca.° xx°   'The watir þat is in the see,   (127)
Whi it is salt telle þou me.

Ca.° xxj°   'Telle now me, if þou woot: (128)
Hou springeþ of þe erþe þe water hoot?   1260

Ca.° xxij°   'Among alle oþer telle me oone: (129)   f. 19ᵛ
Wherof cometh þe brimstone?

Ca.° xxiij°   'Wherof euere may it be,   (130)
þe lightnyng þat we as fire se?

Ca.° xxiiij°   'þe watris þat ebben and flowen alweie,   (131) 1265
Whens come þei and whider goo þeie?

Ca.° xxv°   'Hilles and roches, weren þei noght   (132)
Ymade whanne þe world was wroght?

1255 Hou renneþ] *written as one word, marked for separation* L *table*;   hye] *from* 5409,
drie L *table*.

'Shall the deuyl come any more   (133)
In the worlde as he was byfore?

'Whan Noe shuld to the Arke go   (134)
And of ilke a best toke with hym to,
Why wolde he thycke bestis take   P105
As scorpions, addris, and snake?

'Whereof comyth the gold   (135)
That is in mannys hold?

'Charboklis and other stonys mo,   (136)
Whereof comyth they so?   P110

'Of the world telle thou me   (137)
How many londis therin be.

'Might any man in dry lond welle   (138)
Go the londe abowte ilke a dele?

'Might any man sayle nyght and day   (139) P115
That had the wynde with hym ay
So long that his ship gan rente
At the turnyng of the firmament?

'Why made God man and not to be   (140)
As yong, ioly, and of postee,   P120
Riche and long lyf had hym lente,
And at his dethe to blysse haue wente?

'Whilk are the angelis, telle me this,   (141)
That receyuyn mannys sowle to blis?

'I pray the, Maister, thou me saye   (142) P125
Whiche were bettir of the tweye—
Gode werkis withoute chastite
Or wyckid workis [and] chast to be.

'What thyng euer may hit make,   (143)
The erthedyn that dothe the erthe quake?   P130

'Whereof are—tell me yf thou conne—   (144)
Eclips of the mone and of the sonne?

P107–8] *written as one line* P *table;*   gold] l *inserted above line* P *table.*   P128 and]
from B4818, othir P *table.*

Ca.° xxvj°   'Shal þe flood come any more   (133)
                  In þe world as was bifore?   1270

Ca.° xxvij°   'Whanne Noe shulde to þe shippe goo   (134)
                  And of euery beest took wiþ him two,
                  Whi wolde he yuel beestis take
                  As scorpiouns, addres, and snake?

Ca.° xxviij°   'Wherof euere cometh the golde   (135) 1275
                  þat is in manye a mannes holde?

Ca.° xxix°   'Charbokelis and oþer stones moo,   (136)
                  Wherof may þei come, all þo?

Ca.° xxx°   'Of þis world telle þou me   (137)
                  Hou many londes þereynne be.   1280

Ca.° xxxj°   'Mighte any man on drie lond wel   (138)
                  Go aboute þe world euerydel?

Ca.° xxxij°   'Mighte any man saile night and day   (139)
                  þat hadde þe winde with him ay
                  So longe þat þe ship cam vnrent   1285
                  To þe torning of þe firmament?

Ca.° xxxiij°   'Whi made God man not to be   (140)
                  Euere ȝonge and iolyf and of pouste,
                  Riche and longe lyf him haue lent,
                  And at his deth to blisse haue went?   1290

Ca.° xxxiiij°   'Whiche beþ the aungels, telle me þis,   (141)
                  þat resceiueþ a mannes soule to blis?

Ca.° xxxv°   'I preie þe, Sidrak, þou me seie   (142)   f. 20ʳ
                  Whiche were better of þe tweie—
                  Good werkes withouten chastite   1295
                  Or euel werkes and chast to be.

Ca.° xxxvj°   'What þing euere may it be,   (143)
                  þe erthequake?—Telle þou me.

Ca.° xxxvij°   'þe clipsis of þe mone and sunne,   (144)
                  Wherof be þei?—Telle, if þou kunne.   1300

1281–2] *repeated* L *table.*

'Sterris that men se downe falle,   (145)
How fal they and where become they all?

'Tell me now, or we ferther fare,   (146) P135
How many heuenys that ther are.

'Telle me now: how hye is heuyn   (147)
Aboue the erthe for to nemyn?

'The firmament that we ouyr vs se,   (148)
Of what may they be?   P140

'Tell me now of what myght   (149)
The planetis are and what they hight.

'Tel me this onys ʒit: (150)
How many maner of watris ther be.

'Now woll Y wetyn of the se   (151) P145
How many seis that ther be.

'Why hathe God made the worlde all   (152)
Rownde abowte as a balle?

'Why is the mone colde of kynde   (153)
And sun whote, as we fynde?   P150

'Now Y pray the, tell me this: (154)
Whiche is the most thyng that is?

'Whethir may grauell of the erthe more be (155)
Or dropes of the watir ouyr the se?

'Might the erthe ouʒt grettir told be   (156) P155
Or watir dropis of the see?

'Now wold Y wete wyttirly   (157)
How many sterris ere on the sky.

'Canstow of angelis telle me ought   (158)
How many God of heuene wrought,   P160
And how many he lefte therinne,
And how many fill for synne?

Ca.° xxxviij°	'The sterres þat men se doun falle, I preie the, where bicome þei alle?	(145)
Ca.° xxxix°	'Telle me, or we ferþer fare, Hou many heuenes þat þer are.	(146)
Ca.° xl°	'Telle me ȝit, wiþ mylde steuene: Hou ferre is it vnto þe heuene?	(147) 1305
Ca.° xlj°	'Þe firmament þat we here se, Of what might may it be?	(148)
Ca.° xlij°	'Telle me ȝit anoon right Of þe planetis, what þei hight.	(149) 1310
Ca.° xliij°	'Þis oone þing telle þou me: Ho[u] many maners of water þer be.	(150)
Ca.° xliiij°	'Now wole I wite ȝit of the Hou manye sees þat þer be.	(151)
Ca.° xlv°	'Whi made God þe world al Rounde as it were a bal?	(152) 1315
Ca.° xlvj°	'Whi is þe mone colde of kinde And þe sunne hoot, as we fynde?	(153)
Ca.° xlvij°	'Now I preie the, telle me þis: Which is þe most þing þat is?	(154) 1320
Ca.° xlviij°	'Wheþer may grauel more be Or dropes of water of þe see?	(155)
Ca.° xlix°	'Might erþe ought gretter ytolde be Or water dropes of þe see?	(156)
Ca.° l°	'Now wolde I wite witterly Hou many sterres ben on þe sky.	(157) 1325
Ca.° lj°	'Canst þou of aungels telle me oght Hou manye God of heuene wroght,	(158)
Ca.° lj°	And hou many be lefte þerynne, And hou many fel out for synne?	1330 f. 20ᵛ

1312 Hou] *from* 6072, hony L *table.*   1313–14] *misplaced at foot of page, marked
for insertion after* 1312 L *table.*

'Whiche are the most—beest or man   (159)
Of fowle or fysh that swym can?

'Of all the world tel me ȝitte: (160) P165
The delectablyst stede, whiche is hitte?

'Whethir is the hardier—that gothe be nyght (161)
Or he that gothe be daylyght?

'Whiche is most pruesse and best—   (162)
That in towne or in fforest?   P170

'Yf a man haue an yll wyfe   (163)
Or be poure or be of ffebill lyfe
Or he haue a wem in a lyme,
Shall a man vpbrayden hym?

'Shall we ilke a man worship do   (164) P175
And all here wille do also?

'Shall he ought forgetyn be   (165)
That to lykyng hathe seruyd me?

'May a man hym ought withholde   (166)
Fro wymmen that hathe hem in holde,   P180
That he no lechery do
When he hathe grete wille therto?

f. 2ra

'The grettist delite that is   (167)
Whiche is hit?—Telle me this.

'Tel me now that yf a man   (168) P185
Shall owght delite hym with a woman.

'Yf an oost and another mete,   (169)
Shall he anon on hym shete?

'Whiche membris of a man now ar tho   (170)
That he worst myght forgo?   P190

'Wherefore tonge and tethe [a]r þo
That a man may worst forgo?

'The furst instrument, h[o] made hit   (171)
And how came hit in his witte?

P191 ar] or P *table, question not in* B.   P193 ho] he P *table,* who B5595.

Ca.° lij°   'Wheþer be moo—of beestis or of man   (159)
    Or of foules or fisshes þat swymme can?

Ca.° liij°   'Of al þe worlde telle me it: (160)
    þe delictablest stede, whiche is it?

Ca.° liiij°   'Wheþer is hardier—he þat goþ anight   (161) 1335
    Or he þat gooþ bi þe daylight?

Ca.° lv°   'Whiche is more prowesse and best—   (162)
    þat of þe towne or of þe forest?

Ca.° lvj°   'If a man haue an yuel wyf   (163)
    Or poure or be of feble lyf   1340
    Or haue a wem in any lym,
    Shal a man vpbreide it hym?

Ca.° lvij°   'Shal men euery man worshipe do   (164)
    And al her wille do þerto?

Ca.° lviij°   'Shal he oght forȝeten be   (165) 1345
    þat to my wille haþ serued me?

Ca.° lix°   'May a man oght him wiþholde   (166)
    From a womman þat haue him wolde,
    þat he no leccherie do
    Whan he haþ greet wil þerto?   1350

Ca.° lx°   'þe grettest delite þat is,   (167)
    Whiche is it?—Telle me þis.

Ca.° lxj°   'Telle me now if þat a man   (168)
    Shal delite him oght with a womman.

Ca.° lxij°   'If an oost anoþer mete,   (169) 1355
    Shul eiþer on other anoon shete?

Ca.° lxiij°   'Whiche membre[s] of þe man be þoo   (170)
    þat he mighte werst forgoo?

Ca.° lxiiij°   'þe firste instrument, who made it   (171)
    And hou come it in his witt?   1360

    1337 prowesse] *altered from* proweste L *table.*   1357 membres] *from* 6561, membre L *table.*

'He that is dombe and defe and se ne may,   (172)   P195
What speche in his hert thynkith he ay?

'Why are sum clowdis in the sky   (173)
White and sum blake thereby?

'May no creaturis that God wrought   (174)
Wite Goddis wille ne his thought?   P200

'3it wite Y wolde, yf Y may   (175)
Yf a man shall worship God allway.

'Whereof may hit be and why   (176)
That they sumtyme wepyn blythely?

'What [maner] of folke are men holde to   (177)   P205
In this world worship to do?

'The largist man, whiche is he   (178)
That now in this world may be?

'Shall a poure man ought in werre   (179)
Put hym a riche man before?   P210

'Is hit no synne a man to ete   (180)
Eche a thyng that he may gete?

'Shall a man another grete   (181)
All day whan he may hym mete?

'How shall a man his childryn 3eme   (182)   P215
So that he may hem aftir queme?

'Whethir shall a man more loue haue till—   (183)
His wyf or his chylde be skylle?

'Yf Y had no fadir borne   (184)
Ne no modir me beforne,   P220
How shuld Y haue borne be
In this worlde, or here se?

'He that hathe full the shappe   (185)
In the modir, by what happe
Is hit sumtyme brought to nought   P225
And may not forthe on lyfe be brought?

P205 maner] *from* B5715, folk P *table.*

Ca.° lxv° 'He þat is dombe and deef and may not se, (172)
In his herte what speche þinkeþ he?

Ca.° lxvj° 'Whi ben somme clowdis of þe sky (173)   f. 21ʳ
White and some blake þerby?

Ca.° lxvij° 'May no creatour þat God wroght (174) 1365
Knowe Goddis wille ne his þoght?

Ca.° lxviij° 'Now wolde I wite, if I may, (175)
If man shal worshipe God al day.

Ca.° lxix° 'Wherof may it be and why (176)
þat yȝen somtyme wepen bleþely?
                                            1370

Ca.° lxx° 'What manere of folke ben men holden to (177)
In þis worlde worshipe to?

Ca.° lxxj° 'þe largeste man, whiche is he (178)
þat in þis worlde now may be?

Ca.° lxxij° 'Shal a pore man owghwhore (179) 1375
Putte him a riche man bifore?

Ca.° lxxiij° 'Is it any synne a man to ete (180)
Al þing þat he may gete?

Ca.° lxxiiij° 'Sal a man anoþer grete (181)
Al day whan he him mete?
                                            1380

Ca.° lxxv° 'Hou shal a man hise children ȝeme (182)
So þat þerafter þei may him queme?

Ca.° lxxvj° 'Wheþer shal a man more loue haue til— (183)
His wif other his children bi skil?

Ca.° lxxvij° 'If I hadde no fadir yborne (184) 1385
Ne no moder me biforne,
Hou shulde I borne haue ben
Or þis worlde here haue sen?

Ca.° lxxviij° 'The childe þat haþ ful þe shappe (185)
In the moder, by what happe
                                            1390
It is somtyme broght to noght
And may nat aliue forþ be broght?

f. 2rb

'Wymmen that in this worlde are here,　　　(186)
Are they alle of o manere?

'Yf thy frende haue wyf or meyne　　　　(187)
And hem ought mysdo that thou se,　　　　　P230
Shalt thou vnto thy frende say
[And] his wyf and his meyne bewray?

'Yf a man anythyng shall do,　　　　　　(188)
Shall he hym ought hast therto?

'Shall he that any gode can　　　　　(189) P235
In this worlde loue ylke a man?

'The folke of this worlde echon,　　　　(190)
Are they comyn aftir on?

'Do men honour the riche echon　　　　(191)
And vnto the pore right non　　　　　　　P240
[In] that other world also
As men that in this world do?

'Shall the fadir bere any burdon grym　　(192)
From his sone or he from hym?

'They that sle men and fordo,　　　　(193) P245
Takith they here synne hem onto?

'Whiche is more sorow, as thynkith the—　(194)
That thow hyrist or that thou may se?

'Myght any folke now fynde　　　　　(195)
Onythyng that etyth other ayenst kynde?　　P250

'Whiche is the worst of the thre—　　(196)
Murther, thefte, or baratour to be?

'Foryeuyth God with a gode chere　　(197)
All the synnys that a man dothe here?

'Why trauaylith a man so　　　　　(198) P255
In this worlde as that men do?

P232 And] *from* B5960, *om.* P *table.*　　　　P234 hast] helpe hast P *table.*
P241 In] *from* B6053, And P *table.*

Ca.° lxxix° 'Wymmen þat ben in þis world here,   (186)
            Ben þei alle of oone manere?

            'If þi frende haue wif and mayne   (187) 1395
            And oght be mys þat þou maist see,
Ca.° lxxx° Shalt þou to þi frende seie   f. 21ᵛ
            And his wyf and mayne bewreie?

Ca.° lxxxj° 'If a man anyþing shal doo,   (188)
            Shal he him haste þerto?
                                                               1400

Ca.° lxxxij° 'Shal he þat any good can   (189)
            In þis world loue euery man?

Ca.° lxxxiij° 'þe folke of þis world echone,   (190)
            Ben þei comouuly of wille oone?

Ca.° lxxxiiij° 'Do men honour þe riche echone   (191) 1405
            And to þe pouere man right none
            In þat other world also
            As men in þis worlde here do?

Ca.° lxxxv° 'Shal þe fader bere any gilte   (192)
            For þe sone þogh he be spilte   1410
            Or þe sone for him
            For hise fauȝtis vgly and grim?

Ca.° lxxxvj° 'þei þat slee men and fordo,   (193)
            Take [þei] her synne hem vnto?

Ca.° lxxxvij° 'Whiche is more sorwe, as þinketh þee—   (194) 1415
            þat þou herest or þat þou maist see?

Ca.° lxxxviij° 'Might any man folke now fynde   (195)
            þat etith anyþing aȝenst kynde?

Ca.° lxxxix° 'Whiche is þe worste þing of þise þre—   (196)
            Morther or þefte or baratour to be?   1420

Ca.° lxxxx° 'Forȝeueþ God wiþ good chere   (197)
            Alle þe synnes þat a man doth here?

Ca.° lxxxxj° 'Whi trauailleþ a man so   (198)
            In þis world as some men do?

            1414 þei] *from* 7126, *om.* L *table.*

'Telle me now, withoutyn mysse: (199)
Whiche is the merkist thyng that is?

'The gode werkis and the ille   (200)
That a man dothe of his wille,   P260
Whedir come they of God hym to
Or of hymselfe that dothe hym so?

'Where hidith hym the day from the nyght (201)
And the nyght fro the daylight?

'How holde the planettis all   (202) P265
On the sky that they ne falle?

'How may men know the ouris aright   (203)
And the poyntes of the day and nyght?

'All the sterris vp on hy,   (204)
Turne they aboute on the sky?   P270

'Shall euyr in this world now be   (205)
Warre and contake as men now se?

'Wrattheth God hym ought for mannys dethe
f. 2va   Whatso he dey, gode or quede?   (206)

'Tel me now, for Y am [in] were: (207) P275
Whiche is the dygnyste day of the yere?

'3it wolde Y wite more   (208)
Why slepe was made and wherefore.

'The holsummyst stede, aftir thy witte,   (209)
Of all the worlde, whiche is hitte?   P280

'Whiche folke ar they, as thow wenyst,   (210)
That the worlde now most susteynes?

'Whether is hyer, as ye thynke—   (211)
Law of londe or the kyng?

P273 Wrattheth] Wratthe they P *table*, Wratheth B6435.   P275 in] *from* B6457,
om. P *table.*

Ca.° lxxxxij° 'Telle me now, wiþouten mysse: (199) 1425
               Wich is þe derkest thing þat isse?

Ca.° lxxxxiij° 'þe good wor[k]es and þe ille   (200)
               þat a man doth of his wille,
               Wheþer come þei of God him to
               Or of himself þat doth hem so?   1430

Ca.° lxxxxiiij° 'Where hideþ the day him fro þe night   (201) f. 22ʳ
               And þe night fro þe daies light?

Ca.° lxxxxv°   'Hou holdeþ þe planetes alle   (202)
               On þe sky þat þei ne falle?

Ca.° lxxxxvj° 'Hou may a man knowe þe houres aright   (203) 1435
               And þe pointes of þe day and night?

Ca.° lxxxxvij° 'Alle þe sterres vp an hy,   (204)
               Torne þei aboute on þe sky?

Ca.° lxxxxviij° 'Schal euere in þis world be   (205)
               Werre and contekke as men now see?   1440

Ca.° lxxxxix° 'Wreþeth God him ought for mannes dede   (206)
               What deeþ so he die, good or quede?

Ca.° C°   'Telle me, for I am in a were,   (207)
               þe worþiest day of þe ȝere.'

Liber Tercius

Ca.° primo   'Now wolde I wite more   (208) 1445
               Whi sleep was made and wherfore.

Ca.° ij°   'þe holsomest stede, whiche is it   (209)
               Of al þe world, after þi witt?

Ca.° iij°   'Whiche folke ben þei, as it semeth,   (210)
               þat þe worlde now moost susteneth?   1450

Ca.° iiij°   'Wheþer is best, to thi seming—   (211)
               þe lawe of þe lond or þe king?

1427 workes] wordes L *table*, werkes 7307.

'May a man in ony manere   (212) P285
Any worldly gode haue here
That he ouyrall may with hym bere
And the wight not hym dere?

'Yf t[w]ey togedir haue louyd strong   (213)
And sithen are asondir long   P290
And come togedir as they efte wore,
May they loue togedir as they did before?

'How may a man loue a womman right   (214)
Or she hym for his sight?

'A man that light conciens beris   (215) P295
And by his god falsely sweris
Often fals thyngis for the nonys,
Is he ought forswore but ones?

'He that any gode techith here   (216)
Vnto folk, hem to lere,   P300
Shall any grace come hym to
More than shall do othir to?

'Thought that man thynkith all day,   (217)
Whereof euyr come hit may?

'Why than fallith the folk all so   (218) P305
Of wyckid euyll as men seith ham do?

'Whiche is the perlyoust leme   (219)
That manis body hathe in hym?

'Whiche is the sykerist art of alle   (220)
And the most perile therin may falle?   P310

'How is a man sumtyme iolyf   (221)
And light of body as the l[i]fe?

'May a man a child not getyn ryf   (222)
Eche tyme that he tochith his wyf?

'What is hit and what gederith hit to,   (223) P315
Mannys kynde that gothe hym fro?

Ca.° v°   'May a man in any manere   (212)
                 Any worldly good haue here
                 þat he may wiþ him ouereal bere   1455
                 And þerwiþ noþing him ne dere?

Ca.° vj°   'If tweie togidre loued haue stronge   (213)
                 And after ben asondre longe
                 And comen togidre aȝein faire and wel,
                 May þei loue togidre trewely and lel?   1460

Ca.° vij°   'Hou may a man loue a woman right   (214)
                 Or she him tofore þe sight?

                 'A man þat light conscience berith
Ca.° viij°   And by his god falsly swerith   (215)   f. 22ᵛ
                 Of ten false þinges for þe nones,   1465
                 Is he ought forswore but oones?

Ca.° ix°   'He þat any good techiþ here   (216)
                 To þe folke, hem forto lere,
                 Shal any grace come hem to
                 More þan it shal to oþer do?   1470

Ca.° x°   'þoght þat a man þinkeþ alday,   (217)
                 Wherof euere it come may?

Ca.° xj°   'þe wickid yuel þat folk ouereþrowe,   (218)
                 Wherof cometh it?—Canst þou knowe?

Ca.° xij°   'Whiche is þe p[eril]ousest lym   (219) 1475
                 þat mannes bodi haþ in him?

Ca.° xiij°   'Whiche is þe sikerest crafte of alle   (220)
                 And þat most perelle may in falle?

Ca.° xiiij°   'Hou is a man somtyme iolyf   (221)
                 And light of body, iocounde of lyf?   1480

Ca.° xv°   'May a man gete a child, bi þi lyf,   (222)
                 Euery time þat he touchiþ his wyf?

Ca.° xvj°   'What is it and hou gadreþ it so,   (223)
                 Mannes kynde whanne it goþ him fro?

1475 perilousest] *from* 7853, plenteuousest L *table*.

'Is a man holden therto   (224)
To loue his childryn and gode hem do?

'Enchauntementis and sorcery,   (225)
Avayle they ought or ar they foly?   P320

'Whiche is the wightyest best that is   (226)
And most of sauour?—Tell me this.

'Whethir of the twey may be   (227)
Heyer—the londe or the see?

'Wherof snaylis comyn, witen Y wolde,   (228) P325
And whi they to the erthe hem holde.

'How slepe thes oolde men all so   (229)
As this yong childryn do?

'Yf God had man so mochill wrought   (230)
As all the worlde, myght [h]e [n]ought   P330
[Haue] stonde ageyn God and right
Thorow vertu of his myght?

'What shulde the world haue bene and howh (231)
Had God not ordeyned hit as hit is nowh?

'Where the angell of God his brethe came   (232) P335
As dide the sowle furst of Adam?

'Now wolde Y wite blithely of this: (233)
What thyng is heuynly paradis?

'The fayrest thyng in this world fre   (234)
That God made, whiche may hit be?   P340

'Whethir ought thou loue more for thy prow— (235)
That loue the or that thou louyst now?

'Whiche are the dygnest wordis that may be (236)
And gres and stonys, as thynkith [th]e?

'Why may no man the new mone se   (237) P345
Vntil hit in the est be?

P330 he nought] be thought P *table*, he nouȝtt B7038.   P331–2] *in reverse order,*
marked for correction P *table.*   P331 Haue] *from* B7039, And P *table.*   P342 loue]
God loue P *table.*   P344 the] *from* B7156, me P *table.*

Ca.° xvij°   'Is a man holden therto   (224) 1485
                 To loue hise children and good hem do?

Ca.° xviij°   'Enchauntementz and sorcerie,   (225)
                 Availe þei oght or be folie?

Ca.° xix°   'Whiche is þe wittiest beest þat is   (226)
                 And moost of sauour?—Telle me þis.   1490

Ca.° xx°   'Wheþer of þe lond or þe see   (227)
                 Is hier?—Telle þou me.

Ca.° xxj°   'Wherof comeþ snailes, wite I wolde,   (228)
                 And whi þei to þe gresse hem holde.

Ca.° xxij°   'Hou slepe these olde men now so   (229) 1495
                 As þise ȝonge children here do?

Ca.° xxiij°   'If God had man so miche ywroght
                 As al þe world, might he ought   (230)   f. 23ʳ
                 Haue ystonde aȝenst God aright
                 þorgh þe vertu of his might?   1500

Ca.° xxiiij°   'What shulde þe world haue be and how   (231)
                 Nad God imade it as it is now?

Ca.° xxv°   'Wheþer þe aungels of Goddis hond cam   (232)
                 As dide first þe soule of Adam?

Ca.° xxvj°   'Now wolde I bleþeli wite þis: (233) 1505
                 What þing is heuenli paradis?

Ca.° xxvij°   'þe fairest þing in þis world to se   (234)
                 þat God made, whiche may it be?

Ca.° xxviij°   'Wheþer shalt þou loue more for þi prow— (235)
                 þat loueþ þee, or þat þou louest now?   1510

Ca.° xxix°   'Whiche ben þe worþieste þinges three—   (236)
                 Is it not worde, grasse, and stoon, as þinkeþ the?

Ca.° xxx°   'Whi may man þe newe mone not se   (237)
                 Til þat she in þe west be?

1511 þinges] *hole in MS. between* n *and* g L *table.*

'Shalt thow thy concell [tell] ylke a dele　　　(238)
To thy frende that thou louyst wele?

'Whiche are wymmen of most profite　　　(239)
To a man to haue with his delite?　　　　　　　P350

'The quakyng that a man is inne　　　(240)
Somtyme, whereof may hit begynne?

'When a man seith a thyng,　　　(241)
Whethir hit geue the ye ought in seyng
Othir hit receyuyth inward thereto　　　　　　P355
The shappe that hit sy also?

'How may a man spekande be　　　(242)
Be hym alone, as thynkith the?

'May with takyng of the se　　　(243)
Anythyng amenusid be?　　　　　　　　　　P360

'Whethir shall men loue one or other—　　　(244)
Child of the sustir or of the brothir?

'Tel me now, yf that thou can,　　　(245)
The perlioust thyng that is in man.

'Of all the flesshis thou may gete　　　(246)　P365
Whiche is the holsomyst to ete?

'The mete that a man shall leuyn by,　　　(247)
How departith hit in his body?

'How shulde a man of his throte wynne　　　(248)
A bone or a row thyng stycand inne?　　　　　P370

'The muk that gothe eche a man fro,　　　(249)
Tel me whi hit stynkith so.

'Tel me now, Y pray the, this:　　　(250)
Why a mannys vreyne so salte is.

'Whereof euyr wormys brede　　　(251)　P375
In man and how they hym fede?

f. 3ᵣₐ

P347 tell] *from* B7213, *om.* P *table.*　　　P376 and] *repeated* P *table.*

Ca.° xxxj°	'Shalt þou þi counseil telle eueridel To þi frende þat þou louest wel?	(238)	1515
Ca.° xxxij°	'Whiche beþ þe wymmen of moost profit To man to haue wiþ his delit?	(239)	
Ca.° xxxiij°	'þe quaking þat a man somtime is ynne, Wherof comeþ it or may it begynne?	(240)	1520
Ca.° xxxiiij°	'Whan a man seeþ a thing, Wheþer ȝeueþ þe yȝe ought in seing Or it resceyueþ inward þerto þe shappe þat it seeþ so?	(241)	
Ca.° xxxv°	'Hou may a man spekinge be Aloone bi himself, as þinketh þe?	(242)	1525
Ca.° xxxvj°	'May þe water in the see Anyþing ymenvsed be?	(243)	
Ca.° xxxvij°	'Wheþer shullen men loue oone or oþer— þe childe of þe sister or of þe broþer?	(244)	1530
Ca.° xxxviij°	'Telle me now, if þat þou can, þe perilouseste þinges þat ben in man.	(245)	
Ca.° xxxix°	'Of alle þe ff[le]sshes þat men may gete Whiche is þe holsomest forto ete?	(246)	f. 23ᵛ
Ca.° xl°	'þe mete þat a man lyue shal by, Hou departiþ it in his body?	(247)	1535
Ca.° xlj°	'Hou schulde a man out of his þrote wynne A bone or a þorne stikynge þerynne?	(248)	
Ca.° xlij°	'þe mukke þat goo[þ] euery man fro, Telle me why it stinkeþ so.	(249)	1540
Ca.° xliij°	'Telle me now, I pray þe, þis: Whi mannes vrine so salt is.	(250)	
Ca.° xliiij°	'Wherof comeþ wormes and brede In man, and hou do þei hem fede?	(251)	

1533 fflesshes] *from* 8523, ffisshes L *table*.   1539 gooþ] *from* 8591, good L *table*.

'How many maistris, and whiche ar tho,   (252)
That man myght worst forgo?

'Whethir shall in heuyn haue more blis—   (253)
Childryn, that cowde not do amys,   P380
Or they that for God of here wylle
Toke the gode and lete the ille?

'How may a man, in what manere,   (254)
Ouyrcome the wille of this world here?

'How long aftir was made Adam   (255) P385
That Lucyfer from heuen downe cam?

'Whiche is the fayrest lyme, and why,   (256)
That a man hathe in his body?

'How may the wynde be felid so wele   (257)
And hit is sene neuer a dele?   P390

'How may the fire men make   (258)
And no man may hit holde ne take?

'Whethir shall be before God more dignyte—
Maydynhede or virginite?   (259)

'Whethir of lechery may more—   (260) P395
Man or womman, and wherefore?

'A womman with childe heuy,   (261)
What norish hit in here body?

'Shall a mannys wyf be shent therfore   (262)
Yf she do amys owhere?   P400

'Is hit gode to mannys lyf   (263)
To be gelous of his wyf?

'Shall a man anothir trow ilke a dele   (264)
That he thynkith on hym euyll or wele?

'How may yong men greyhorid be   (265) P405
And olde men not, as sumtyme men se?

'Whereby euer comyth hit to   (266)
That som men be balde also?

              P391 may] may me P *table.*

Ca.° xlv°   'What crafty men ben tho   (252) 1545
               þat man myght werst forgo?

Ca.° xlvj°   'Wheþer schal in heuene haue more blisse—   (253)
               þe children, þat coude not doo amisse,
               Or þei þat for God wiþ good wille
               Dide þe good and lefte þe ille?   1550

Ca.° xlvij°   'Hou may a man, ʒit wolde I lere,   (254)
               Wiþstonde his wille in þis world here?

Ca.° xlviij°   'Hou longe was it after þat Lucifer fel   (255)
               þat Adam was made?—þou me tel.

Ca.° xlix°   'Whiche is þe fairest lym, and why,   (256) 1555
               þat man haþ in his body?

Ca.° l°   'Hou may þe winde be felt so wel   (257)
               And may be seen neuere a del?

Ca.° lj°   'Hou may men a fire make   (258)
               And no man may it holde ne take?   1560

Ca.° lij°   'Wheþer shal bifore God worþier be—   (259)
               Maidenhede or virginite?

Ca.° liij°   'Wheþer of leccherie haue more—   (260)
               Man or womman, and wherfore?

Ca.° liiij°   'A womman wiþ childe greet and heuy,   (261) 1565
               What norissheþ it in her body?

Ca.° lv°   'Shal a man shende his wif þerfore   (262)   f. 24ʳ
               If she do mys bifore men thore?

Ca.° lvj°   'Is it good to mannes lyf,   (263)
               A man to be ielous of his wyf?   1570

Ca.° lvij°   'Shal a man leeue anoþer euerydel   (264)
               þat he þinkeþ of him, yuel or wel?

Ca.° lviij°   'Hou mowe ʒonge men greihored be   (265)
               And olde men noght, as we somme see?

Ca.° lix°   'Telle me ʒit þis skil: (266) 1575
               Whi some be balled wite I wil.

               1546 man] *inserted above line* L *table.*

'How are planettis in signes ay,   (267)
And what compleccyons are they?   P410

'How gothe gode sowlis to heuyn to dwelle (268)
And wyckid to the pyne of helle?

f. 3rb
'Angrith hit to the gode angelis ought   (269)
Whan a man a synne hathe wrought?

'Shull they that are dede any more   (270) P415
Come ageyne to this worlde owere?

'Tho that to paradis or to helle go,   (271)
Shull they neuer come therfro?

'Whi gon not the gode that arne wise   (272)
Vntill erthely paradise?   P420

'Whethir is the sowle heuy or lyght,   (273)
Grete or smalle, merke or bright?

'Gode sowlis that from the body gone,   (274)
Whidir wendith they anon?

'May no man in heuene be   (275) P425
But he purgatory furst se?

'Sithe God sendith sum to helle   (276)
And sum to heuene for to dwelle,
Whereto shall he the dome queme
And whan shall he than deme?   P430

'Yong chyldren, that can no reson,   (277)
Shull they dole ought dampnacion?

'Whedir in that other world may be   (278)
Ony hous, towne, othir cite?

'Shall they be dampnyd, canst thou sey,   (279) P435
Childryn of hethyn men that day?

'Yf no syn had done Adam,   (280)
Shulde all that folke that of hym cam
With flesh and with felle as they are sene
Euer in paradis haue bene?   P440

P413 hit] hit ought *with* ought *partially erased* P table.

Ca.° lx°   'Hou ben þe planetes in signes ay,   (267)
             And of what complexioun be þay?

Ca.° lxj°   'Hou goon soules to heuen to dwelle   (268)
             And some to þe peyne of helle?   1580

Ca.° lxij°   'Greueþ it þe good aungel ought   (269)
             Whan a man haþ synne wrought?

Ca.° lxiij° 'Shullen þei þat ben deed heretofore   (270)
             Come into þis world any more?

Ca.° lxiiij° 'Þo þat to paradys or to helle goo,   (271) 1585
             Shullen þei euere come out þerfro?

Ca.° lxv°   'Whi gon not þe soules þat ben wys   (272)
             Vnto þe erthely paradys?

Ca.° lxvj°   'Wheþer is þe soule heuy or light,   (273)
             Greet or smal, derke or bright?   1590

Ca.° lxvij° 'Good soules þat fro þe body goon,   (274)
             Whider wende þei so sodeinly anoon?

Ca.° lxviij° 'May no man in heuene be seen   (275)
             But he in purgatorie firste haue been?

Ca.° lxix°   'Siþen God sendith some to helle   (276) 1595
             And somme to heuen forto dwelle,
             Wherto shal he þan þe dome deme
             And whom shal he þan queme?

             'Ȝonge children, þat kunne no resoun,   (277)
             Shullen þei haue dampnacioun?   1600

Ca.° lxx°   'Wheþer in þat oþer world may be   (278)   f. 24ᵛ
             Ony toun, hous, or citee?

Ca.° lxxj°   'Shullen þei be dampned, canst þou me seie, (279)
             Heþen mennes children þat doth deye?

Ca.° lxxij° 'If no synne hadde idoo Adam,   (280) 1605
             Shulde alle folk þat of him cam
             Wiþ flesshe and felle as þei ben
             Euere in paradys haue ibeen?

1599 *q. no. om.* L *table: all q. nos. in table erroneous hereafter.*

'Whan watir helid the world ilke a dele,   (281)
Helid hit paradis as wele?

'Of what erthe made God Adam   (282)
Whan he into this worlde came?

'Tho that at the dome shull dey   (283) P445
And haue not seruyd to helle the wey
Neither to helle as ty3t may not go,
How shall hit befall of tho?

'Why may not men the sowle yse   (284)
As men done me and the?   P450

'Whedir to make [God] furst began—   (285)
Sowle or body of the man?

'Whedir the soule be made kyndly   (286)
Of engendure of the body?

'Where sowlis were made at onys for ay   (287) P455
Or ar they made 3it euery day?

'Whan sowle come to the body also,   (288)
On whiche half gothe hit in therto?

f. 3ᵛᵃ 'A wyf with childe that dethe gothe to   (289)
And the childe dey in here also
And oute of here nought ne may,   P460
Where gothe the childe is sowle away?

'Who namyd furst al thyng   (290)
And techid hem here connyng?

'Whi euyr hit be and wherefore   (291) P465
That som men are lasse and sum more?

'Whethir is hit more perill to haue—   (292)
Hete or colde thyself to saue?

'The esyest folk oute of wo   (293)
In this worlde, whiche ar tho?   P470

'Deryd a man ought vnto   (294)
That wyckid fadir and modir hathe allso?

P451 God] *from* B8293, *om.* P *table.*   P458 hit] *inserted above line* P *table.*

Ca.° lxxiij°   'Whanne watir hilled þe world eueridel,   (281)
                      Dide it hille paradys as wel?   1610

Ca.° lxxiiij°   'Of what elde made God Adam   (282)
                      Whanne he into þis world cam?

Ca.° lxxv°   'þo þat at þe dome shal deie   (283)
                      And haue not to helle serued þe weie
                      Ne to helle as tite mowen not goo,   1615
                      Hou shal it bifalle of alle thoo?

Ca.° lxxvj°   'Why may men þe soule not see   (284)
                      As men may doo thee and me?

Ca.° lxxvij°   'Wheþer to make God first bigan—   (285)
                      þe soule or body of þe man?   1620

Ca.° lxxviij°   'Wheþer þe soule be made kindely   (286)
                      Of engendring as þe body?

Ca.° lxxix°   'Were soules ymade at ones for ay   (287)
                      Or ben þei made ȝit euery day?

Ca.° lxxx°   'Whan soule comeþ to body also,   (288) 1625
                      Whiche weie gooþ it in þerto?

Ca.° lxxxj°   'A wif wiþ childe þat deeþ gooþ to,   (289)
                      A[nd] þe childe die in hir also
                      And out of her noght ne may,
                      Wher gooþ þe childes soule away?   1630

Ca.° lxxxij°   'Who [n]amed first al þing here   (290)
                      And [t]aughte men her vertues sere?

Ca.° lxxxiij°   'Whi euere it be and wherfore   (291)
                      þat somme men ben litel and some more?

Ca.° lxxxiiij°   'Wheþer is it perilouser to haue—   (292) 1635 f. 25ʳ
                      Hete or colde þiself to saue?

Ca.° lxxxv°   'þe esiest folk out of woo   (293)
                      In þis world, whiche ben tho?

Ca.° lxxxvj°   'Shal it any harme to a childe do   (294)
                      þat haþ wikked fader and moder also?   1640

1628 And] *partially erased* L *table.*   1631 named] n *erased* L *table.*
1632 taughte] *initial* t *erased* L *table.*

'Shall a man helpe his frende vnto   (295)
Or his neyghboure that hathe to do?

'Whethir is bettir or lasse to spille—   (296) P475
A man to speke or holde hym stille?

'Whethir ought wyser to be—   (297)
A yong man or an olde, as thynkith the?

'Tel me now ȝit, I pray the,   (298)
What skynnys thyng delite may be.   P480

'Whiche is the delectablist sight   (299)
That is vndir sonnelight?

'Whi made God, as thou may se,   (300)
On mannys body here to be?

'What skynnys appull was that   (301) P485
That oure fadir Adam ate?

'Whi come they this worlde vnto   (302)
Dombe and defe also?

'Profiteth the folk vnto   (303)
The almysdedis that they here do?   P490

'A domesman synnyth he ought   (304)
That demys hym that [i]ll hathe wrought,
Or synnyth he ought withall
That the dome fullfille shall?

'Tho that arne dombe and folis iborne   (305) P495
And dothe ille, shull they be forlorne?

'Why lerne thes children so   (306)
Wel more then olde men do?

'Angelis that with God are dere,   (307)
Kepith they mannys sowle here?   P500

'How may angelis, that is no body,   (308)
Shew hym to man opynly?

P492 ill] all P *table*, evill B8698.

Ca.° lxxxvij°   'Shal a man helpe his frende   (295)
                 Or his neighbor þat he fint kynde?

Ca.° lxxxviij°   'Wheþer is better and lesse ille—   (296)
                 A man to speke or holde hym stille?

Ca.° lxxxix°   'Wheþer ought wiser forto be—   (297) 1645
                 Ʒonge men or elde, as þinkeþ the?

Ca.° lxxxx°   'Telle me now, I preie the,   (298)
                 What þing þat delite may be.

Ca.° lxxxxj°   'Which is þe confortablest sight   (299)
                 þat is vnder þe firmament bright?   1650

Ca.° lxxxxij°   'Whi made God, as þou maist see,   (300)
                 On mannes body heer to be?

Ca.° lxxxxiij°   'What kynnes appel þenne was þat   (301)
                 þat oure forme fader, Adam, at?

Ca.° lxxxxiiij° 'Whi come some þis world vnto   (302) 1655
                 Dombe iborne and deef also?

Ca.° lxxxxv°   'Profiteþ ought þe folke vnto   (303)
                 þe almesdedes þat þei here doo?

Ca.° lxxxxvj°   'A domesman synneþ he ought   (304)
                 þat demeþ hem þat yuel han wroght,
                 Or synneþ he ought also wiþal   1660
                 þat þe dome fulfille shal?

Ca.° lxxxxvij°   'þo þat ben fooles and dombe borne   (305)
                 And doon ille, shullen þei be lorne?

Ca.° lxxxxviij° 'Hou lerne þise children so   (306) 1665
                 More þan þise olde men do?

Ca.° lxxxxix°   'Angels þat ben wiþ God dere,   (307)
                 Kepe þei mannes soule here?

Ca.° C°   'Hou may aungel, þat is no body,   (308)   f. 25ᵛ
                 Shewe him to man here opunly?'   1670

f. 3vb

'Has the deuelis peris ay euerwere   (309)
Of that the folke mysdo aywhere?

'How is the fyre on that manere   (310) P505
Purgatory that men calle here?

'How many sowlis shull ther than wende   (311)
To hevyn aftir the worldis ende?

'What thyng is hit that men calle helle   (312)
And [how] come sowlis therin to dwelle?   P510

'They that in helle haue here dwellyng,   (313)
Wote they or know they anythyng?

'The gode that go to heuene as tit,   (314)
Come they now into ioy parfite?

'May sowlis ought shew hym tille   (315) P515
Here frendis eche a tyme that they wille?

'Dremys that men dremyn anyght,   (316)
Whereof come they to mannys sight?

'Whan God made furst treis for mankynde,   (317)
Was ony fruyte that tyme thereinne?   P520

'What [day] and in what tyme was hit   (318)
That Adam was made?—Tell me 3it.

'Whiche was the man that altherfurst   (319)
Drank wyne or wyne wist?

'Whan the f[lod]e ouyr alle the world ran,   (320) P525
Made God new fruyte vnto man?

'Where sate Noes ship on londe   (321)
Whan the flode was withdrawande?

P510 how] from B8854, om. P table.   P516 Here] to here P table.   P521 day]
from B8985, om. P table.   P525 flode] from B9013, fruyte P table.

Liber Quartus

Ca.° primo	'Telle me ʒit oo þing, I þe pray:	(309)
	If deuels awaiten on men alday	
	Forto reherse al her blame	
	þat þei heraftir may worche hem shame.	
Ca.° ij°	'Of purgatorie telle me ʒitt:	(310) 1675
	What is it, by thi witt?	
Ca.° iij°	'How many soules shullen wende	(311)
	To heuene after þe worldes ende?	
Ca.° iiij°	'What þing is it þat men calle helle	(312)
	And hou come soules þere to dwelle?	1680
Ca.° v°	'þei þat in helle haue her dwelling,	(313)
	Wote þei or knowe þei anyþing?	
Ca.° vj°	'þe good þat wendiþ to heuen tite,	(314)
	Come þei anoon to ioye parfite?	
Ca.° vij°	'May soules ought shewe he[m] tille	(315) 1685
	Her frendes whan þei wille?	
Ca.° viij°	'Dremes þat men dremen anight,	(316)
	Wherof comeþ it to mannes sight?	
Ca.° ix°	'Whanne God made first trees for mankynne,	(317)
	Was any fruit þat tyme þerynne?	1690
Ca.° x°	'What day and what tyme was it	(318)
	þat Adam was made?—Telle me ʒit.	
Ca.° xj°	'Which was þe man alþerfirst þat knew	(319)
	Wyne and dranke it?—Telle me trw.	
Ca.° xij°	'Whanne þe flood over al þe world ran,	(320) 1695
	Made God þanne newe fruit to man?	
Ca.° xiij°	'Where sat Noes ship on londing	(321)
	Whanne þe flood was wiþdrawing?	

1685 hem] *from* 10157, he L *table.*

'Whan Noe fro the ship went tho,   (322)
Came he this worlde strange vnto?   P530

'Whereof euyr may hit be   (323)
That a man hathe in his hert pite?

'Tho that loue delite and rest,   (324)
Whethir do they—worst or best?

'Shall men haue pite on al tho   (325) P535
That ly in pyne and wo
And delyuerith hym also
Yf that men may come therto?

'Whedir is bettir, as ye thynke—   (326)
Wyne or watir for to drynke?   P540

'When man hathe talant for to fight   (327)
With som that stondith in his sight,
How may he than holde hym stille
And ouyrset the wyckid wille?

'Why haue wymmen al the wo   (328) P545
Of the world and the ioy also?

'Shall a man that curteys be   (329)
Ofte comme his frende to se?

'Is hit holsum for to ete   (330)
Al thyng that men may gete?   P550

'Whiche ar tho that make rous most   (331)
Of all men that thou wost?

'Why may me nought clowdis in somer se   (332)
So thycke as they in wynter be?

'Why are childryn when they borne are   (333) P555
So vncunnyng as bestis ware?

'Tel me now, yf that thou can: (334)
Wherof comyth nature within man?

'Whereof may hit come to,   (335)
The fnesyng that men fnese so?   P560

P556 ware] w *inserted above line* P *table.*

f. 4ʳᵃ

Ca.º xiiij º   'Whanne Noe fro þe shippe went þo,   (322)
               Came he þis world straunge to?   1700

Ca.º xv º   'Wherof euere may it be   (323)
               þat a man hath pite?

Ca.º xvj º   'þilke þat loue delite and rest,   (324)   f. 26ʳ
               Wheþer do þei—werst or best?

Ca.º xvij º   'Shullen men haue pitee of alle þo   (325) 1705
               þat liggen in peine and woo
               And deliuere hem also
               If þat men mowen comen þerto?

Ca.º xviij º   'Wheþer is it better, as þe þinke—   (326)
               Wyne or water forto drinke?   1710

Ca.º xix º   'Whanne a man is willy forto fighte   (327)
               Wiþ somme þat stondiþ in his sighte,
               Hou þanne may he holde him stille
               And ouercome þat wicked wille?

Ca.º xx º   'Whi haue wymmen al þe woo   (328) 1715
               Of þis world and þe ioye also?

Ca.º xxj º   'Shal a man þat curteis is   (329)
               Goo visite his frende often siþes?

Ca.º xxij º   'Is it holsom forto ete   (330)
               Al þing þat man may gete?   1720

Ca.º xxiij º   'Whiche ben tho þat boosten most   (331)
               Of alle men þat þou woost?

Ca.º xxiiij º 'Whi mowen not men clowdis see   (332)
               In somer as þikke as þei in wynter be?

Ca.º xxv º   'Whi ben children whanne þei borne are   (333) 1725
               More vnkunnynge þan bestes are?

               'Telle me now, if þou can: (334)
               Wherof cometh nature in man?

Ca.º xxvj º   'Wherof may it come also,   (335)
               þe fnesinge þat men fnesen so?   1730

1727–8] *bracketed and numbered with preceding question* L *table.*

'Whiche elementis of all that are   (336)
Might a man hire worst or best forbere?

'Wynde blowand fast with all the mayne,   (337)
Why deyeth hit for a shoure of rayne?

'Why hathe foules in hem no nature   (338) P565
As bestis to make here engendure?

'Whiche is starker of the tway—   (339)
Wynde or water?—Thow me say.

'Why deyes a man so lyghtly   (340)
And haue othir peynes so longly?   P570

'Whethir felis the sorow or the wo—   (341)
Sowle or the body when they partyn onto?

'Tel me now in what manere   (342)
A man shall lyuen in this world here.

'Shall a man owght drede quytly   (343) P575
Hym that is his ennemy?

'Shall a man ought rygourously   (344)
Bere hym ageyns his ennemy?

'Whiche are moe worthier of the twey—   (345)
Riche or poure?—Thou me say.   P580

'Shall a man that in gode stede be   (346)
To seke a bettir remew his se?

'Shall a man loue and haue hym by   (347)
Hem that ille spekis commynly?

'May ony man forgetyn welle   (348) P585
His owne contre ylke a dele?

'Whedir is bettir tel a dede—   (349)
Sleyght or strength at nede?

'Yf a man aske another a skylle,   (350)
Shall he anon answere hym tille?   P590

P576 Hym] Drede hym P *table*.   P590 anon] anothir anon P *table*.

Ca.° xxvij°   'Whiche elementis of alle þat ere   (336)
Might a man best forbere?

Ca.° xxviij°   'Wynd blowing wiþ al þe mayn,   (337)
Whi deieþ it for a shour of rayn?

Ca.° xxix°   'Whi haue foules in hem no nature   (338) 1735
As haþ bestes for engendrure?

Ca.° xxx°   'Which is þe strenger of þe tweie—   (339)   f. 26ᵛ
Winde or watir?—þou me seie.

Ca.° xxxj°   'Whi dieþ a man so smertly   (340)
And anoþer pyneþ so grevously?   1740

Ca.° xxxij°   'Wheþer feliþ the sorwe and woo—   (341)
Soule or body whan þei parte atwo?

Ca.° xxxiij°   'Telle me now in what manere   (342)
A man shal lyue best in þis world here.

Ca.° xxxiiij°   'Shal a man ought drede greetly   (343) 1745
Him þat is his enemy?

Ca.° xxxv°   'Schal a man oght fersely   (344)
Bere him aȝenst his enemy?

Ca.° xxxvj°   'Whiche ben more worth of þe tweie—   (345)
Richesse or pouert?—þou me seie.   1750

Ca.° xxxvij°   'Shal a man þat in good stede dwelle   (346)
Go seke a bettir?—þou me telle.

Ca.° xxxviij°   'Shal a man loue and haue him by   (347)
þat vse to speke yuel comounly?

Ca.° xxxix°   'May a man forȝete þe cuntre   (348) 1755
Where he was borne?—Telle þou me.

Ca.° xl°   'Wheþer it is bettir to a dede—   (349)
Sleight or strengþe at nede?

Ca.° xlj°   'If a man axe anoþer a skile,   (350)
Shal he answere anoon him tile?   1760

'Shall a man onythyng lette   (351)
Of anothir to aske his dette?

'Whethir is hit to man more semly—   (352)
Faire visage or faire body?

'How shall a man ledyn his lyf   (353) P595
That fyndith anothir hawntyng his wyf?

f. 4rb
'Shall men for tene or for lesyng   (354)
Blame God of heuen in onythyng?

'Shall a man serue ylke a man   (355)
Of suche as that he can?   P600

'Whiche is the saueroust thynke   (356)
Of all that are, at thy w[e]nnyng?

'Of what manere and of what bounte   (357)
Owith kyngis and lordis to be?

'Kyngis or lordis, shull they ought fayle   (358) P605
To bene hemself in batayle?

'Swet that comyth of the body,   (359)
How comyth hit, whereof, and why?

'Whiche are the beste hewes that are   (360)
Of clothyng men for to were?   P610

'Sum men grene a gode hue calle: (361)
Whiche is the grenost thyng of alle?

'S[ey] me now, so haue thow blis: (362)
Whiche is the fairest thyng that is?

'Whiche is bettir at the dede day—   (363) P615
Repentaunce or hope of blisse for ay?

'Shall a man wepe and make ille chere   (364)
For a man that dyeth here?

'Came ther ȝit from that other worlde anythyng (365)
That of hevyn or of helle tolde any tydyng?   P620

Ca.° xlij°   'Shal a man anyþing lette   (351)
                      Of anoþer to axe his dette?

Ca.° xliij°   'Wheþer is it to men more semely—   (352)
                      Faire visage or faire bodi?

Ca.° xliiij°   'How shal a man lede his lyf   (353) 1765
                      þat fint anoþer haunting his wyf?

Ca.° xlv°   'Sullen men for tene or for lesing   (354)
                      Blame God in heuene for anyþing?

Ca.° xlvj°   'Shal a man serue euery man   (355)
                      Or suche þing as þat he can?   1770

Ca.° xlvij°   'Whiche is þe souerinest thing   (356)   f. 27ʳ
                      To man or beest, to þi wening?

Ca.° xlviij°   'Of what manere and what bounte   (357)
                      Ought kinges and lordes forto be?

Ca.° xlix°   'Kinges and lordes, mowen þei faille (358) 1775
                      To ben hemself in bataile?

Ca.° l°   'Swoot þat cometh of þe body,   (359)
                      Hou cometh it, wherof, and why?

Ca.° lj°   'Whiche ben þe beste colours þat ben (360)
                      Of cloth to were for to be seen?   1780

Ca.° lij°   'Siþen men grene a good hewe calle, (361)
                      Whiche is þe grennest þing of alle?

Ca.° liij°   'Seie me now, so haue þou blisse: (362)
                      Whiche is þe fairest þing þat isse?

Ca.° liiij°   'Wheþer is better aftir synnyng ay— (363) 1785
                      Repentaunce or hope of blisse?—Me say.

Ca.° lv°   'Shal a man wepe and make yuel chere (364)
                      For his frende whan he dieth here?

Ca.° lvj°   'Come euere any man here to dwelle (365)
                      þat of heuene and helle cowde telle?   1790

'Shall a man anythyng say   (366)
Whan he shall to slepe lay?

'Why may barnes not getyn also   (367)
Strong childryn as yong men do?

'Of all batayles that are in londe   (368)   P625
Whiche is the strengist to withstonde?

'All that euer is in this worlde here and there, (369)
Shull they be dede and hens fare?

'How lithe a childe, tell me this   (370)
In the modris wombe whan hit is?   P630

'How shall a man shewen his skile   (371)
When he shall do medisyne hit tille?

'Shall his witte tell a wyse man   (372)
Among sympill men that lytill can?

'Tell me now of wy[n]es tite   (373)   P635
Why sum are rede and sum white.

'Haue fowles or bestis ony spekyng   (374)
Or vndirstond they onythyng?

'Whethir helpith hit the soule more—   (375)
That a man dos here before   P640
Or that a man aftir dos for hym
Whan that he is dede and dym?

'Fysshis that swymmen here and there   (376)
In watir, slepe they euermore?

'Of all that in the worlde be   (377)   P645
The fayrest fowle whiche is he?

'Whiche is the fayrest beest that is   (378)
And that a man [m]ought ne mys?

'Tel me ȝit o thyng mo: (379)
The fayrest horsis, whiche ar tho?   P650

f. 4va

P635 wynes] wyves P *table*, wynys B10029.   P648 mought] nought P *table*, myȝt
B10124.

Ca.° lvij°   'Shal a man anyþing seie   (366)
              Whan he to sleep shal him leie?

Ca.° lviij°   'Whi may not ȝonge men gete also   (367)
              Stronge children as olde men do?

Ca.° lix°   'Of alle batailles þat ben in londe,   (368) 1795
              Whiche is werste to vnderstonde?

Ca.° lx°   'Alle þat in þis world borne are,   (369)
              Shullen þei alle bi deeþ fare?

Ca.° lxj°   'Hou lieth a child, telle me þis,   (370)
              In þe modres wombe whanne it is?   1800

Ca.° lxij°   'Hou shal a man shewe his wil   (371)
              Whan he shal his tale tel
              Afore wise men and grete
              Or iugges þat in dome sete?

Ca.° lxiij°   'Shal his witte telle a wise man   (372) 1805 f. 27ᵛ
              Among hem þat no good can?

Ca.° lxiiij° 'Telle me now of wynes tite   (373)
              Whi somme is reed and some is white.

Ca.° lxv°   'Haue foules and beestes any speking   (374)
              Or vnderstonding of anyþing?   1810

Ca.° lxvj°   'Wheþer helpeþ the soule more—   (375)
              þat a man dooth here bifore
              Or þat a man doth after for him
              Whanne þat he is deed and dim?

Ca.° lxvij°   'Fisches þat swymmeþ here and þore   (376) 1815
              In water, slepe þei neueremore?

Ca.° lxviij° 'Of alle þat in þe world be   (377)
              þe fairest foule whiche þinkeþ the?

Ca.° lxix°   'Whiche is þe fairest beest þat is,   (378)
              As þinkeþ the, wiþouten mis?   1820

Ca.° lxx°   'Telle me ȝit oo þing moo: (379)
              þe fairest horsis, whiche ben tho,
              And surest on to ride
              By dale or downe in ech tide?

'Whiche ar the bestis, so God the saue,   (380)
That most vndirstandyng haue?

'When Goddis Sone shall borne be,   (381)
By what tokyn shall men hit se?

'Telle me now, as shall befalle: (382) P655
What sygnyfieth the tokenys alle?

'Whan he is borne a childe, shall he   (383)
Be commendid more than othir be?

'Whan he is borne, as that we telle,   (384)
Where shall he in coste dwelle?   P660

'ʒit wolde Y wote more of the: (385)
Shall Goddis Sone a faire man be?

'Tel ʒit, yf thou can say,   (386)
Why hit is that he wolde dey.

'Ho shall hym sle and by whos rede   (387) P665
And how long shall he be dede?

'Shall he into heuyn [stye]   (388)
Alone into company?

'Shall Goddis Sone, that is hym dere,   (389)
Ony hous in erthe haue here?   P670

'Shall his body euer dwelland be   (390)
In erthe so that men mow hym se?

'Shall eueryche a man haue myght therto   (391)
His body for to makyn also?

'Shall they before the Trynyte   (392) P675
Ouʒt more than [oþer] worshipid be?

'Why shall they ilke a day be uone   (393)
To make the body of Goddis Sone?

P667 stye] *from* B10331, *om.* P *table.*   P676 oþer] *from* B10420, *om.* P *table.*

Ca.° lxxj°   'Whiche beeþ the beestes, so God þe saue,   (380) 1825
               þat of vnderstonding most haue?

Ca.° lxxij°   'Whanne Goddes Sone shal here born be,   (381)
               By what tokene shal men it se?

Ca.° lxxiij°   'Telle me now, I pray thee: (382)
               What signifieþ þe tokenes þat we see?   1830

Ca.° lxxiiij° 'Whanne he is borne, shal not he   (383)
               Of kunnynge more þan other be?

Ca.° lxxxvj°   'Whanne Goddes Sone is borne, þou me telle,   f. 28ʳ/19
               In what contre shal he dwelle?   (384)

Ca.° lxxxvij° 'I wolde wite ȝit more of thee: (385) 1835
               Shal Goddes Sone a faire man be?

Ca.° lxxxviij° 'Telle me ȝit, I þee preie: (386)
               Whi shal Goddes Sone deie?

Ca.° lxxxix°   'Who shal him slee and by what reed   (387)
               And hou longe shal he be deed?   1840

Ca.° lxxxx°   'Shal he also to heuene stie   (388)
               Wiþouten more companye?

Ca.° lxxxxj°   'Shal Goddes Sone, þat is him so dere,   (389)
               Haue castell or hous in erþe here?

Ca.° lxxxxij° 'Shal his body euere dwelling be   (390) 1845
               In erthe so þat men mowe it se?

Ca.° lxxxxiij° 'Shal euery man haue might þerto   (391)
               His body forto make also?

Ca.° lxxxxiiij[j]° 'þilke þat haþ might þerto   (392)   f. 28ᵛ
               þat body forto make also,
               Shullen þei bifore þe Trinite   1850
               More þan oþer worshipped be?

Ca.° lxxv°   'Shullen preestes euery day be boun   (393)   f. 27ᵛ/29
               To make þe body of Goddis Soun?

1833–52] *follow 1876 in L table, with questions numbered accordingly.*   1850 *q. no.*
lxxxxiiij] *final digit lost in binding L table.*   1853–76] *follow 1832 in L table, with*
questions numbered accordingly.

'Telle me now: what thyng is synne,   (394)
That man shall be borne inne?   P680

'By what signe shall men se   (395)
Whan Goddis Sone shall dede be?

'When Goddis Sone shall in erthe dwelle,   (396)
Of what vertue shall men of hym telle?

'Shall his dissiplis ought also   (397) P685
W[ir]che myraklis as he shall do?

'Whethir hopis þou ilke a day be mo   (398)
Borne to the world or go therefro?

'Shull they neuer haue ende   (399)
Ne no wo that to hevyn wende?   P690

f. 4vb

'Tho that are in helle faste,   (400)
Shull they no mercy haue ne no reste?

'[Th]o that in heuyn shall be,   (401)
Shull they clad or nakid be?

'Whan God to deme come shall   (402) P695
Quyk and dede and the world all
And al shall dey, whiche are he
That shall than on lyue be?

'Where shall be borne that fals profite   (403)
That all the worlde in erthe shall bete?   P700

'What day shall hit on befalle   (404)
That Goddis Sone shall deme vs alle?

'What tyme shall he come thereto   (405)
For to deme the world also?

'How shall he come, in what manere,   (406) P705
When he shall come to deme vs here?

'Shall his crosse be present   (407)
Whan he shall yeue his iugement?

P686 Wirche] Whiche P *table*, Doo B10528.   P687 þou] *inserted above line* P
table.   P693 Tho] *from* B10597, So P *table*.

Ca.° lxxvj°   'Telle me now: what þing is synne,   (394) 1855
                  þat man shal be lorn ynne?

Ca.° lxxvi[j]°   'Bi what signe shullen men see   (395)
                  Whanne Goddis Sone shal deed be?

Ca.° lxxviij°   'Whanne Goddes Sone in erthe shal dwelle, (396)   f. 28ʳ
                  Of what vertu shal men him telle?   1860

Ca.° lxxix°   'Schullen hise disciples also   (397)
                  Do miracles as he shal do?

Ca.° lxxx°   'Wheþer hopist þou euery day be mo   (398)
                  Borne into þe worlde or goo þerfro?

Ca.° lxxxj°   'Shullen þei neuere haue none ende   (399) 1865
                  Ne no woo þat to heuene wende?

Ca.° lxxxij°   'Tho þat ben in helle faste ibounde,   (400)
                  Shullen þei mercy ne reste haue no stounde?

Ca.° lxxxiij°   'þei þat in heuene shullen haue her see,   (401)
                  Shal þei cloþid or nakid be?   1870

Ca.° lxxxiiij°   'Whanne God to þe dome come shal   (402)
                  Quike and deed and þe world al
                  And alle shullen be deed, whiche is he
                  þat shal þanne alyue be?

Ca.° lxxxv°   'Where shal Antecrist born be,   (403) 1875
                  þat trouble shal eche citee?

Ca.° lxxxxv°   'What day shal it on bifalle   (404)   f. 28ᵛ/5
                  þat Goddes Sone shal deme vs alle?

Ca.° lxxxxvj°   'What tyme shal he come þerto   (405)
                  For to deme þe world also?   1880

Ca.° lxxxxvij°   'Hou shal he come and in what manere   (406)
                  Whan he shal come to deme vs here?

Ca.° lxxxxviij°   'Shal his crosse be þere present   (407)
                  Whanne he shal ȝeue his iugement?

          1857 *q. no.* lxxvij] *final digit lost in binding* L *table.*

'Whan he the folke shall deme also,   (408)
How shall he shew hym theym vnto?   P710

'Shall hys mynysters with hym be   (409)
In the dome to heren and se?

'How shall God the dome do   (410)
And what shall he seyn hem to?

'Shall eche man tha[n] know well   (411) P715
That he hathe done here ylke a dell?

'Whan all is done the dome so harde,   (412)
What shall be done aftirward?

'What shall betyde then and how   (413)
Of this worlde there we are now?   P720

'Shall the gode haue leue thertille   (414)
For to do all what they wulle?

'Shall they than remembir hym ought   (415)
Of wyckidnesse that they haue here wrought?'

LAUD (B) (cont.)

f. 16ᵛ   *The furste thyng thenne asked he:*   (1)   925
                Yf God was ay and ay shulde be.
                   'God hadde neuer begynnyng
                   Ne never shall have endyng:
                   Or he heven or erthe wroght
                Or onythyng to werke brought,   930
                Thanne wiste he wele he shulde hem dight
                And all þorow his owne myght;
                And or he made an aungell to be,
                The noumbre of hem well wiste he,
                Of man and beste and ilke a dele,   935
                Of fowle, of fyssh, all wiste he wele;
                And what dethe echon shuld haue
                And which shoulde her soulis saue
                And which they were þat shulde be forlore,

P715 than] that P *table,* þanne B10771.   P724] *followed by* Summa question-
narum tabule Sydrac CCCCxvj P *table.*
   925–1054 *first six questions not numbered* B.   927 God] *add* he saide A.
930 Or] Her P.

Ca.° lxxxxix°	'Whanne he þe folke shal deme also, How schal he shewe him hem to?	(408)	1885
Ca.° C°	'Shullen hise ministres with him be In þe doome it to here and see?	(409)	
Ca.° Cj°	'Hou shal he þe dome do And what shal he seie hem to?	(410)	1890
Ca.° Cij°	'Shal eche man knowe eueridel þat he haþ done here, yuel or wel?	(411)	
Ca.° Ciij°	'Whanne al is done þat dome so hard, What shal be done afterward?	(412)	
Ca.° Ciiij°	'What shal betide þanne and how Of þis worlde þere we be now?	(413)	1895
Ca.° Cv°	'Shullen þe gode leue þere stille Forto do al þat þei wille?	(414)	
Ca.° Cvj°	'Shullen þei þanne remembre hem ought Of wickedness þat þei here wroght?'	(415)	1900

Ca.° Primo	*The firste þing þanne axede [he]:* *If God was euere and euere shal be.*	(1)

'God had neuere begynnyng
Ne neuere shal haue ending,
And or þat heuen or erthe wroght   1905
Or any oþer þing to werk broght,
He wiste wel he shulde hem dighte   f. 29ʳ
And al þorgh his owne mighte;
And or he made aungel forto be,
þe noumbre of hem wel wiste he,   1910
Of man, of beest, and of eeuerydel,
Of foule, of fisshe, of al he wiste wel;
And what deth euerich shal haue
And whiche shulde her soules saue
And whiche þei were þat shulde be lore,   1915

1901 he] *from table* 1009, *om.* L.

All togedyr he wiste bifore,   940
And her wordis and here þought—
God hadde he ellis be nought.
And be all togeder of his makyng
Ne was he amendid noþyng
Ne enpeyred shoulde he nought   945
Have bene though they had bene vnwrought:
He was and is and euer shall be,
And euer alike of oon pouste,
And ouer all is his myght.
And iij hevenes hathe he dight: 950
That oon is bodely that wee se;
That oþer gostely þere aungelis be;
The þridde there God hymselue is.
They that ther be is moche blis:

There shall þe rightwos loke hym on,   955
Whanne þat þis world is all agoon.'

The kyng asked wheþer hit myght ben   (2)
That God of heuen might be sene.
    'Visebyll is God, that warne I the,
    And inuisebill soo eke is he,   960
    For all þynge may he see

f. 17ʳ And he ne may not seen be,
For that þat is of bodely makyng
May not se noo gostely thyng;
But gostely thyng þat is in blis   965
May se gostly thyng þat is.
Butt whan Goddis Sone so dere
Into erthe is comyn here
And þe folke shall walke betwene,
He and his werkes shall be seene.   970
That shall be mooste of Goddis myght

943 togeder] þat was A.   944 amendid] to amende S.   948 euer alike]
onliche P.   954] Ther ioy is ay and eternall blis A;   They . . . is] There that
ther is ful T, þere þen is þe S.   956 all agoon] ffordoon A.   964 not]

Al togidre he wiste bifore,
And her wordes and her þoght—
And elles had he God be noght.
And of al togidre his makyng
Ne was he amendid noþing   1920
Ne empeired shulde he haue be noght
þogh þei hadde alle ben vnwroght,
For he was and is and euer shal be,
And euere iliche of oo pouste,
And ouer al is his might.   1925
And þre heuens he haþ dight:
þat oon is bodily þat we see;
þat oþere goostly þere aungels be;
The þridde to vnderstonde is
þere God regneþ in his blis.   1930
þat blis is wiþouten ende:
Wel is him þat þider may wende
þere shal he se God face to face.
To hem it is an endeles grace,
For whan þis world haþ an ende,   1935
Alle rightwise men þider shal wende.'

Ca.° secundo   *The king axide if it might bene*   (2)
                   þat God of heuen miȝte be sene.
                       'God is visible, þat warne I the,
                        And eke invisible so he,   1940
                   For al þing he may se   f. 29ᵛ
                   And he may not ysen be,
                   For he þat is of bodily makyng,
                   He may se no goostly þing;
                   But gostly þing þat is in blis   1945
                   May see goostly þing þat is.
                   But whanne Goddis Sone so dere
                   Is man become in erthe here
                   And shal walke þe peple bitwene,
                   He and hise werkes sholen be.sene,   1950
                   For he shal be a goost of Goddis might

---

neuer T.   966 gostly] bodely A, ony bodely P;   þat] what itt A.
969] Amonge the peple shall walke in londe A.   970 seene] vndirstonde A.
971 mooste] gost SP.

That in a mayden shall alight
Body to take of þat virgine
And shall be boore withowte pyne;
And he shall do as man shall doo,　　　　　　975
Saue synne that may not hym vnto,
And God almyghty shall he be.
Hym shull men here and see
And butt if he body toke,
Shoulde no body on hym loke.'　　　　　　　980

Yet asked the kynge wel moore　　　　　　(3)
Whether God be oueral and euerwhore.
　　'Neuer yete ne made God noþing
　　Thatt it ne hadde of hym felyng,
　　Forwhi suche as we be nowe　　　　　　985
Fele hym and I shall [s]ay the howe:
Wee leven here, wexe, and goo—
That comyth hym eche a dele froo;
And euery frute is of hym felyng
That euery yeere is newe growyng;　　　　　990
The hevenes þen fele hym also—
They turne euer as he bad hem do;
Sonne and mone and sterris bright,
All fele they hym and his myght,
For euer faste abowte þey goo　　　　　　995
Till þey came þere they came first fro;
The erthe hym felis, if þou hit levis,
For euery yeere his frewte hitt yevis;
Wynde and see hym felys, iwys,
And whenne althermost tempest is,　　　　1000
Att his byddyng and his wyll
Hit withdrawyth, and þat is skyll;
The dede hym fele on þe same wyse,

972 That] Thatt he A.　　　973 Body] Redy S.　　　975 as] alle a T, al as S, so as
a P.　　　976] Save oonly syn excepte hym ffro A;　　vnto] cum too TSP.
978 here] here feill S, worship P.　　　981–1008] *follow* 1009–26 B, TASP *as* L.
981] The kyng axid off Sidrak þer A.　　　986 say] fay B.　　　987 wexe and goo] in
wele and wo P.　　　988 hym . . . froo] off hym and off no moo A;　　eche a dele] eche
day P.　　　989] And with frute be we felande T, And by þe fruyt ar we hym felande SP,

þat shal here in a maide light
And oure flesshe to take of þat virgine
And shal be born wiþoute pyne;
And al as a man he shal do,   1955
Saue synne may not come him to,
And almi3ti God shal he be.
And men shal here him fele and see
And but if he a body took,
þere shulde no body on him look,   1960
For noon erþely þing þat is
May not see þe Godheed, ywis.'

Ca.° iij°   *Also þe king axide him þere*   (3)
    If God be ouereal and euerywhere.
      'Neuere 3it made God noþing   1965
      þat it ne haþ of him feling,
For suche as we be now
Shullen fele him, and I shal telle þe how:
We lyuen here and in þe wey goo—
þat cometh euery day him fro;   1970
þe erthe also is him feling,
For he beriþ euery 3ere newe fruit waxing;
Heuene feliþ him also,
Euere tourninge aboute as he bad hem do;
Sunne and mone and sterris bright,   1975   f. 30ʳ
Alle þei felen him and his might,
For euere faste aboute þei goo
Til þei come þere þei come first fro;

Winde and see him feliþ, ywis,
And whanne alþermoost tempest is,   1980
At his biddinge and his wille
þei wiþdrawen and holden hem stille;
Deth him feleþ on al wise,

As ffrute and corn han also ffelyng A.   990 newe] renwed by A, now SP;
growyng] waxande TSP.   992 euer] *om*. AS.   998 euery yeere] eche aire
T.   1002 Hit withdrawyth] Withdraweth hem TA, Withdrauen hem S, Withdraw
they ham P;   þat is skyll] biddeth hem stille T, ease be and still A, holde hem styll
SP.   1003 þe same] all SP.

For at his wyll they shall vpryse;

The bestis þat in erthe goo,   1005
They fele hym for þey dee alsoo
As he yave hem kynde to be;
And þerfore ouerall his he.'

'Which was now the firste thynge   (4)
That God made?' asked þe kynge.   1010
  'Sir,' quod Sidrak, 'vnto my lust
  A full fayre palys made he fyrst
  Full of blisse and full of light
That þe kyngdome of heven hight;

Sethens made he þe worlde þus   1015
And sethen helle depe vndir vs.
In heven his frendes he lete;
His ffoes to helle falle full depe.

Man made he þanne, as was his will,
The noumbre of aungelis to fulfill   1020
Instede of hem þat fallen were
And shulde in heven come no moore.
Aungell and man shall feris be,

1006 for þey dee] I wote S;   dee] don TP.   1007 be] do A.   1008 And
þerefore] Forwhy as Y seide P;   he] *add* and no moo A.   1011 my] me SP;
lust] lyst S.   1014] Therin aungelle bene faire and bright P.   1015 þus] alle

For at his wille þei shullen rise;
Helle him knoweþ also, iwis,   1985
For he mote ȝelde aȝein alle his;
þe beestes þat on erthe goo,
þei felen him euermore also
And as he ȝaf hem her kynde to be
He kepeþ hem oueral by his pouste.'   1990

Ca.º iiijº   'Whiche was now þe firste þing   (4)
                    þat euere God made?' axed þe king.
                      'Sire,' quod Sydrak, 'I þee telle shal:
                      He made þe courte celestial,
                      A paleys ful of ioye and light   1995
                      And moost of plesaunce to þe sight;
                      The planetes and þe sterres seuene
                      To enlumine wiþ the heuene;
                      þe cercles and þe speres nyne
                      And other sterres forto shyne;   2000
                      Who þat cowde her cours wel knowe,
                      þe planetes, as þei stande arowe:
                      Firste Saturnus, þat stant so ferre,
                      And Iubiter, þat goodly sterre,
                      Mars, god of armes, and þe sunne   2005
                      To voide awey alle skies dunne,
                      Goddesse of loue, Dame Venus,
                      And aftir hir Mercurius,
                      þe mone wiþ hir hornes pale,   f. 30ᵛ
                      þe erthe wiþ many an hil and vale;   2010
                      And aftir þat, who liste to knowe,
                      Ordeined helle, þat stant so lowe,
                      For Lucifer þere to abide
                      Wiþ wicked spirites for her pride;
                      And man he made only by grace   2015
                      Forto occupie his place
                      With þe cherachies thre
                      In þat heuenly faire citee,
                      Eternaly þe Lord to preyse

thus TASP.   1017 lete] hath ordeyned A.   1018] In helle his ffoos with
sorowe distreyned A;   depe] depere B, theke T, skete SP.   1021 fallen were]
ffillen beffore A.   1023 feris be] in ffeere soiour A.

For oon God worshipen he

Thatt is God of myghtys mooste,   1025

Fader and Sone and Holi Goste.'

The kyng ʒit Sidrak besought   (5)
To telle whenne aungeles were wrought.

'Whanne God sayde by noo word but oon,

Thanne aungelis were made anoone.   1030

Lucyfer hymselue gan se,

That ffeyrest of all was hee:

In pryde soone he ganne fall

And despised þe oþer all—

Hee was also goode, hym þought,   1035

As God hymselue, þat hym wrought.

Some of þe aungeles turned hym vntoo

And þought well hit myght be soo;

Maystryes to make he hem hight

Aboven other aungellis þat were bright.   1040

Owte of þat place was he caste:

An owre myght he not þerinne laste,

For hit was noo right þat he

Ayenst his lorde shoulde have be.

Shoulde he þanne ony parte have in þat blisse?   1045

And for þat ferde he amys

And all þat were of his assente.

But summe with hym to helle wente

And summe into the þykkest ayre

That o[f] ioye [haue] noon [e]spaire: 1050

They ne may noo mercy have

Ne ffor pride no mercy crave.'

1024 God] *add* boþe S, bothyn P;   worshipen he] they worshippe and honour A.
1025 God] his God P.   1029 by noo word] do now P.   1030 Thanne] All S,
And P;   anoone] ichon S.   1038 Soo] do P.   1041 place] paleis SP.
1042] Into helle at the laste P.   1044] That ageyn his lord wold be P;   be] pouste
A.   1045] Thereffore fferde he amys A;   Shoulde] Or S;   he þanne] *om.*

Whiche þat list him so hie to areise 2020
With his aungels to be fere
Ful ferre aboue þe sterris clere,
þorgh his powere, whiche is diuine,
In þat heuenly cristaline
Where, as clerkes can disserne, 2025
Is ioye ay lastinge and eterne.'

Ca.° v°

Also þe king Sydrak besoght (5)
To telle whan aungel was wroght.
'God seide a word, as was his wille,
Heuene wiþ aungels to fulfille 2030
And ful sodeinly anoon
Aungels weren made euerychon.
But whan Lucifer himself gan se,
þat of alle oþere fairest was he,
In pryde sone he gan to falle 2035
And wilned to be lord ouere alle,
For he was als good, him þoght,
As God himself, þat him had wroght.
Some of þe aungels torned hem to
And þoghten þat it myghte wel be so; 2040
To make hem maistres he hem behight
Aboue alle aungels þat be so bright.
Out of þat palys soone God him cast   f. 31ʳ
Into þe deep pitte of helle at last,
For it was no right þat he 2045
þat wolde aȝeinst his lord be
Shulde haue any parte of þat blis,
þerfore sodeinly he gan it mys.
And alle þat weren of his assent
Anoon wiþ him to helle some went 2050
And somme into þe þikke eyre
þat of þat ioye beeþ in dispeire,
For þei mowen no mercy haue
Ne for pride þei mowen noon craue.'

TSP.   1046] Exclude vtterly ffrom ioy and blis A.   1049 þykkest] *om.*
P.   1050] Thatt vnto ioy shall neuer repeire A;   of] *from* TSP, oo B;   haue]
from S, is BTP;   espaire] *from* TSP, dispaire B.   1052 no mercy] may þai none S,
they wull non P.

The kyng asked, 'Wherof serue þey,   (6)
The aungeles þat in heven are ay?'
   'The aungellis þat now in heven been   1055
   Shull neuer wyll to doo synne,
   For þey fell not away
Butt in blis shall bene ay.
And to echon God yafe, ywys,
Ordyr and office in his blis.   1060
Of aungellis is þer o maner
That vnto folke tellith here,
Bothe in water and in londe,
The grete thynges of Goddis sonde.
Anoþer maner þere is also   1065
That tellyth connyng folke vnto,
Be itt lowde, be itt stylle,
The smale bodyes of Goddis will.
The iij þer is that hight Pouste
And off suche office bene he: 1070
Lordshippes ouer deuellis they have
And comaunde hem as man his knave
That þey ne may ne not þey canne
Ouermoche evell do to man.
And oþer hight Principalte: 1075
Masters ouer good spirites they be
And comaundith hem to fulfille
Goddis seruice vnto his wille.
Yett is þere oon that Virtutes hyght,
That techeth men to goo aright.   1080

Anoþer þer is yete of might:
Domynacions theyre names hyght,

f. 18^v

1057 fell not] shull neuer falle P.   1066 connyng] comyng P, comune S.
1068 bodyes] bedes SP.   1072 man his] here P.   1074 to] no P.

Ca.° vj°

(6) 2055

The king axede, 'Wherof serueth
þe aungels þat in heuene dwelleth?'
　'Aungels þat ben in heuen wiþynne,
　þei sholen neuere haue wil to synne
For þat þei fel noght þerfro away;
þerfore in blisse þei shullen be ay.   2060
And to echone God 3af, iwis,
Ordre of office in his blis.
þe firste is Archaungel, withouten were,
þat telliþ to þe folke now here,
Boþe in water and lond,   2065
þe grete þinges of Goddis sond.
Anoþer manere of aungel þere is also
þat telliþ the comoun peple to,
Be it lowde, be it stille,
þe smale sondis of Goddis wille.   2070
The þridde ordre is Pouste;
Of suche ordre made was he
þat lordship ouer deuels þei haue
To helpen many oon to saue
þat þei mowen not ne not can   2075
To myche yuel do to no man.
þe fourþe is now Principate   f. 31ᵛ
And maister of good spiritis he hate
And comaundeþ hem to fulfille
Goddis seruice to his wille.   2080
þe fifþe ful faire Vertues highte:
þei tellen men to arighte
In vertues lyf hem to gouerne
And yuel fro good to discerne
So þat þei mowen herafter wynne   2085
þe endeles ioye þat neuere shal blynne.
The sixte is of power grete
As men may here þise clerkes trete:
Dominacioun men hem calle;
His power is ouer alle.   2090
þei rule and gouerne mankynde,
þat ofte to God ben vnkinde.

1075 And oþer] Anothur TAS;　　hight] hy of P.　　'1078] The commawndement of
Goddis wille P.

Be obedient the oþer tofore
In here subieccion bene thore.

Yete ther is oon, of the high Trone is he: 1085
Therevppon is Goddis see.
By hem vsith God an high
His iugementes to iustefye.

And an ordyr is þer yete of all
Thatt [Cherubyns] wee hem call;   1090
Many creaturis of skyll
Be þat order subiecte vntyll,
For full besely þey se
In þe mirrowre of Goddis cleerte,
And þey knowe of þeyre natures   1095
The pri[uet]es of creatures.

Yete is ther [Ceraphyn] above:
They brenne all in Goddis love
Moore thenne all oþer be,
And they been of suche dignite   1100
That noon oþer spirite is
Betwixe hem and God in blis.'

1083–4] The oþer affore be obedientt / Vnto hem att her commaundementt A.
1085 of] *om.* S;   of the] that P;   high . . . be] Trone hight he TSP, Trone namyd
be A.   1087 vsith God an] God sitte vpon P.   1088 to iustefye] to certeffie A,
full grisli TS, to geue full greselye P.   1090 Cherubyns] *from* TASP, Ceraphyns

Of obedience þei ben oþer bifore
In her subieccioun ouere more;
So shulde þe peple suget be   2095
Eche to oþer in her degree.
þe seuenþe is Thronns, as I saie þee,
And þervpon is Goddis see;
And by hem vsith God an hy
Hise iugementis ful rightwisly,   2100
Whiche shulde cause euery man
To do þe good þat he can
And cause him eke to ȝerne þe blis
þat aungels forfetid for her mys.
The viij ordre ȝit shullen we calle   2105
Cherubyn among þise oþere alle;
And manye creatures, bi Goddis wille,
Ben suget þat ordre tille
For þe greet blis þat þei see
In þe mirrour of Goddes clertee;   2110
And þei knowen bi her natures   f. 32ʳ
þe priue þinges of creatures
þat shal hem herafter repreue
But þei her fautis þe sonner leue
And amende her misgilte   2115
þat her soules be not spilte;
And þanne mowen þei surely wende
Into þat ioye þat haþ noon ende.
There is ȝit þe laste of alle:
Seraphyn þise clerkes calle.   2120
And þei ben ful hie aboue
Euere brennynge in Goddes loue
More þan alle þe othre be,
And ben suche of dignite
þat noon oþer spirit þer nis   2125
Bitwene hem and God in blis.
So þei þat ben in loue brenning
To God here hertly desiryng

B.   1091 of] repeated B.   1092 Be] Arne of P;   subiecte] subieccious
P.   1093 se] be P.   1095 þeyre] þe S, all P.   1096 priuetes] priuetees
S, priuete AP, princes BT;   of] of alle TAP.   1097 Ceraphyn] from TASP,
Cherubyn B.   1098 brenne all] er brennand SP.

f. 19ʳ *Qo. 7ᵃ*   *The kynge askyd ȝiff ffendes also*   (7)
                          All thynges woote and all may doe.
                                'Sir,' quod Sidrak, 'wee fynde   1105
                                That devellis been of angellis kynde
                                And for þey of þat nature were,
                          Of full grete connyng they are;
                          And þerfore þey be more gostely
                          Thanne manne that hathe body,   1110
                          Therfore they can moore þanne man;
                          Also þey rather began.
                          But of thynge þat there is comyng
                          Be they nooþynge knowyng.
                          Thynge that I have do, or þow,   1115
                          They þerof wote well ynow.
                          Of euyll wyll and evyll þought,
                          Thereof wote þe devyll right nought
                          Ne none but Godde alone wote he
                          Of euery herte the pryuyte.   1120
                          The devyll may weele evyll doo,
                          But goode have they no wyll vnto;
                          And ȝit may they not fulfill
                          To doone in evill all here wyll,
                          Nee more have þey myght vntyll   1125
                          Thanne goode angellis hem licence wyll.'

    1109 þerfore] *om.* P;   more] most P.   1113 þat . . . comyng] þou hast nott yitt
done A;   comyng] commande TP.   1114] Theroff can þey tell noon A;
knowyng] wetande TP.   1115 þow] now P.   1119 Ne none] *om.* A;   wote]

And from þis worlde departid to be
To regne wiþ him in his glore,   2130
Whanne þei ben deed and hens goon,
þei shullen in þat ioye euere woon
þe whiche ioye can no man telle,
Clerke write, ne tunge spelle,
Herte þinke, ne here here,   2135
To hem þat on þis manere
Enhablen hem, bi Goddes grace,
To come to þat holy place.
And þus, sire king, euere preie we
þat Goddes faire face þere we may see.'   2140

Ca.º vijº   *The king axede if deuelis also*   (7)
                 Al þing woote and al þing may do.
                      'Sire,' quod Sidrak, 'we finde
                      þat deuels ben of aungels kynde
                 And for þei of þat nature were,   2145 f. 32ᵛ
                 Of ful greet kunnyng þei ere;
                 And for þei weren more goostly
                 þan man in his body,
                 þerfore þei kunne more þan man
                 And also þei raþer bigan.   2150
                 But of þinges þat ben comyng
                 Thei ne ben noþing knowing,
                 But þinges þat we done now,
                 þerof þei witen wel ynow.
                 But of yuel wille and yuel þoght,   2155
                 þerof wote þe deuel noght
                 Ne noon but God aloone woot he
                 Of euery manis herte þe priuite.
                 þe deuels mowen wel yuel do:
                 To God haue þei no wille to;   2160
                 And ȝit þei mowen not fulfille
                 To do yuel at her wille,
                 Ne no more haue þei mighte til
                 þan þe good aungel hem þole wil.'

for that wote T, all knowith A.   1122 But goode] For God P;   vnto] to doo
Γ.   1124 evill] *add* is P.   1125] No more myȝtt haue þey nott to greue
A.   1126 hem . . . wyll] will geve hem leve A;   licence] thole TSP.

Qo. 8ᵃ   'What shappe haue aungeles and what thyng   (8)
             They can and may?' askyd the kyng.
                  'On oo wyse than have þey even
                   The lykenesse of God of heven,   1130
                  For bodilese they bene and bright,
             Full of fayrenesse and of light,
             And þere is noþynge in kynde
             That they ne wote ne haue in mynde.
             No wonder though they knowyng be—   1135
             All thynge in God they see;
             And alle that they have wyll vnto,
             Withowte greuaunce they may hit doo.'

f. 19ᵛ

Qo. 9ᵃ   The kynge asked Sydrak his frende   (9)
             Yff God made man with his hand so hende.   1140
                  'Man and all þat God hym lente
                   Was made by his comaundemente
                   And, who vndirstonde can,
             A febyll nature is in man
             And of foule thynge God hym dyght   1145
             To shende þe devill and his myght;
             For man, þat soo febyll is,
             Than is made vnto þat blis
             That pryde caste the devell froo:
             That is his sorowe and his woo.   1150
             Of the iiij elementis God began
             And thereof he made Adam
             For his kynde, att Goddys wyll,
             Shulde iiij sides of þe world fulfille;
             And for God wiste before   1155
             That man shulde synne ayenst his loore
             And that he shulde as an vnwyse
             Not longe beleave in paradyse,
             All other thynges wolde he make

1129 On] Now P;   oo] no A;   even] resemblaunce A.   1130 The] To the
A;   of heven] as in substaunce A.   1131 bodilese] bodyes P.   1139 Sydrak
his frende] I vndurstonde T;   his frende] þan A.   1140 man . . . hende] with
his honde man A;   hand so hende] honde T, hende S.   1143] om. P.

Ca.º viijº   'Of what shap ben aungels and of what þing   (8) 2165
Kunne þei, knowe þei?' axede þe king.
    'On no wise þan haue þei euene
    þe liknesse of God of heuene:
Wiþouten bodi þei ben and bright,
Ful of fairhede and of light,   2170
And þere ne is noþing in kynde
þat þei ne witeþ and haþ in mynde.
For no wonder þogh þei knowing be,
For al þing in God þei mow see;
And al þat þei haue wil to,   2175
Wiþouten greuaunce þei mowen it do:
Thanne sueþ it wel þei knowe al þing
þat is vnto Goddis plesing.'

Ca.º ixº   þe king axide Sidrak, I vnderstonde,   (9)   f. 33ʳ
If God made man wiþ his honde.   2180
    'Man and al þat God him lent
    Was made of his comaundement
And, whoso vnderstonde can,
A ful feble nature is in man
And of foule þing God him dighte   2185
þe deuel to shende þerwiþ and his mighte;
For man, þat so feble is,
Is made to haue þat blis
þat pride caste þe deuelis fro,
And þat is his sorowe and his woo.   2190
Of þe foure elementis God nam
And þerof he made faire Adam
For his kinde shulde, at Goddis wille,
þe foure quarters of þis world fulfille;
And for God it wiste bifore,   2195
þat man shulde synne aȝeinst his lore
And þat he shulde as þe vnwise
Not longe bileue in paradyse,
þerfore al oþer þing wolde he make

1144/5 add And filthe shall from hym come P.   1148 Than] That P.
1151 began] nam TS, toke A, made man P.   1152 made Adam] Adam shope
A.   1154 sides of] sithes T.   1157 shulde] add not T.   1159 All] And
SP.

To mannys behofe and for his saake.   1160
And many wormes made he alsoo
As emptis, ffleis, and other moo
Man to greve and byte in som tyde,
That he not falle into pryde;
And þat he thynke by this   1165
How febyll a creature he is
That he may not hymselffe were
For soo lytyll þat hym may dere.
Of empte and irayn se men may
How they ben travelyng all a day: 1170
So besely shoulde we be with right
God to serue with all ooure might
For vnto oure delite made he
All thynge thatt wee may se,
And wee and they were made also   1175
Vnto God worshipp to doo.'

f. 20ʳ

Qo. 10ᵃ   *The kynge askẹd, or he forth nam:*   (10)
        'In what stede made God Adam?'
        'In Ebron, as God wolde hit have,
        There he was dede and leyde on grave.   1180
        Thanne was he sette in paradyse,
A fayre place þat in the este is:
There is ioy and grete delyte
And treis of many kynnes ffruyte
And ech frute thanne is of myght   1185
After thatt God hathe hem dyght.
Some frute þer is that, iff a man
Hadde oonis hit etyn, neuer after þan
Ne shulde have hungyr neuer moore;
And another is than thore   1190
That is called the frute of lyff
That is goode for man and wyff,
For whoosoo eteth of that tree

1161 made he] *om.* P.   1162 emptis] myres SP.   1163 greve] dere TSP.   1166 creature] þinge þat SP.   1167 were] astertt A.   1168 For] Fro TAS;   þat . . . dere] a þing þat doth hym smertt A.   1169 empte] myre S, myren P;   irayn] wormys P.   1171] So shulde we doo with all riȝt S;   besely] besi TP.   1175 wee . . . made] man made was P.   1177 forth] furthere TS, þens A;   nam] cam A.   1180 dede and] *om.* T.   1181 sette in] sent into P.

To mannes bihoue for his sake. 2200
And many wormes he made also
As amptis, flies, and oþir mo
Boþe to dere and bite man somtide,
þat he ne falle noght in pride
But þat he him biþenke bi þis 2205
Hou feble a þing þat it is
þat he ne may not himself were
For so litel a worme þat may him dere.
Of pismyres and irennes men se may
Hou þei be trauailinge al þe day: 2210
So besy shulde we be by right
To serue God wiþ al oure might
For to oure delite made he   f. 33ᵛ
Alle þinges þat we mowen see,
And we and þei weren imade also 2215
Almighti Godhed worshipe to do.'

Ca.º xº   *The king axide, or he ferþer ȝede,* (10)
      Wher God made Adam and in what stede.
'In Ebron, as God it wolde haue,
þere he was deed and leide in graue.
þo was he putte in paradys, 2220
A faire stede þat in þe est is:
þereynne is ioye and greet delite
And trees of manye diuerse fruite
And euery fruite of diuerse might 2225
As God ordeined hem and dight.
Somme fruite þer was þat, if a man
Had oones eten þerof, neuere after þan
Ne shulde he sore hungre more;
And anoþer fruit is thore 2230
þat is yclepid þe fruit of lyf
And he is good for man and wyf,
For whoso eteth þe fruit of þat tree,

1182 is] lis T.   1183 delyte] dedute T.   1184 kynnes] maner S, dyuers
?.   1185–86] *om.* P.   1185 myght] grete myght T.   1187 þer is] *om.*
?.   1188 hit . . . after] ete and neuer or P;   neuer] than T.   1189] Sore an
hungrid shuld he neuer be P;   have] a man S;   neuer] *om.* S.   1190] Anoþer
her is eke thore A, Another is and that hight he P.   1193 of] the fruyte of P.

Shall neuer sike ne olde bee.
Whanne Adam was theder broughte,   1195
There was Eve thanne of hym wrought.
Soo were they nakyd, as we fynde,
Of oon fflessh and of oon kynde
For they shoulde be, where that they wente,
Of oon fflessh and of oon assente: 1200
God made hem such that they not synne,
The moore mercy vnto wynne.
And whan that God hadde Adam maked,
He and Eve were bothe naked,
But therof shamed they hem nought   1205
Vnto the synne that they hadde wrought;
Whan they of the appell hadde beten a bytte,
f. 20^v Eche shamed of other also tytte
For they sawe hem thanne vncladde
Off clothyng and grace that they hadde.   1210
And in paradyse they woore
Vij owres and no moore:
The iij^{de} owre after his makyng
Yafe Adam name to all thynge;
The vj^{te} owre ete his wiff   1215
Of the appyll that made all the stryff;
The vij^{the} Adam the appell bote
And was chased owte foote hoote—
The aungell came anoon hastyng
With a shuerde of fire brennyng: 1220
With the fyre beset he there
The walles of paradyse that were
Soo that no man þerinne shulde wone
Vnto the comyng of Goddis Sone—
After his dethe he shall fordoo   1225
The fyre that the aungell brought therto
And Adam and his frendes all
Vnto heven lede hym withall.'

1197 nakyd] made ASP.   1199 where that] er S.   1200 fflessh] will
TS.   1201 soche that they not] sothe withoute P;   not] myȝt S.   1202 vnto
after to SP.   1206 the . . . hadde] tyme they had syn A, þai hade synne SP
1210 Off . . . that] The clothe of grace forlorne P.   1214 Yafe . . . to] God gaue to
Adam P.   1215–16] om. P.   1215 ete] add Eue S.

Syke ne oolde shal he neuere be.
And whanne Adam was þidre broght,   2235
þanne was Eue of him iwroght.
þanne weren þei naked, as we finde,
And of oo flesshe and of oo kinde
For þei shulde be, where þei went,
Of oo fleisshe and of oone assent: 2240
God made hem suche, withoute synne,
þe more mercy after forto wynne.
And whanne þat God had Adam maked,
He and Eue weren boþe naked,
But þerof shamed hem right noght   2245
Til þat þei hadde synne ywroght;
And whan þei hadde of þe appil bite,   f. 34ʳ
Eiþer shamed of oþer as tite
For þei sawe hem so vnclad
Of cloþing of grace þat þei had.   2250
And in paradys þei wore
Seuene houris and no more:
þe þridde houre after his making
Adam ȝaf name to alle þing;
þe sixte hour eet his wyf   2255
Of þe appel þat made all þe stryf;
þe seuenþe hour Adam þe appel boot
And was chased out anoon fote hoot—
þere come an aungel anoon flienge
Wiþ a firy swerd al brennyng,   2260
And wiþ the fire he bisette þere
þe wallis of paradys þat were
So þat no man þerynne shal wone
Til þe comyng of Goddis Sone;
For after his deth he shal fordo   2265
þe fire þat þe aungel broghte þerto
And Adam and hise frendes shal
With him lede into heuen al.'

1217 vijᵗʰᵉ] add houre ASP, viij houre T.   1218 And] Therefore P;
foote] full P.   1219 hastyng] ffast hyyng A, goande TS, glydande P.   1220 of
fire] bright P;   brennyng] brennand TSP.   1226 therto] tho P.   1227 all]
shall P, he shall TS.   1228 hym] hemTAP;   withall] he shall A.

Qo. 11ᵃ   The kyng asked, 'Whider wente Adam   (11)
                 From paradyse whenne he ouȝte cam?'   1230
                      'Whanne he came owte, he wente anoon
                      There he was made, into Ebron.
                      An hundryd yeere there ladde he is lyff
                 And gate childryn by his wyff;
                 But for Caym, that was soo fell,   1235
                 Hadde his brother slayn, Abell,
                 Adam came his wyff not nere
                 Thereafter in an hundred yeere
                 For angere that Abell was slayn.
                 Thanne badde the aungell hym goone agayn   1240
                 And knowe his wiff as he should doo,
                 And sayde that God hym badde soo,
f. 21ʳ   For cursed of God was Caym
                 And alle the sede that came from hym,
                 And of the cursed sede and lorn   1245
                 Wolde not Goddis Sone be born.
                 Thanne yede Adam and Seth gate he,
                 Of whose sede Goddis Sone shall be.
                 And wete thow, sir, that from Adam
                 Vnto the tyme that Noe came   1250
                 Neuer fell on erthe noo rayn
                 Ne noo [raynebowe] was there sayn:
                 Flessh that tyme no man ete
                 Ne dranke wyn, rede ne swhete;
                 The weder was all that tyme there   1255
                 Fayre as somers day hitt were
                 And plente was of all thynge
                 Tyll mannys synne hit made lettyng.'

Qo. 12ᵃ   'Dyd Adam ony other synne þanne that   (12)
                 He brak Goddis heste and þe appel ate?'   1260
                      'Nay, he did noon othyr synne
                      But a gretter myght he not begynne,
                      For he coveytyd God to be:

1233 there] *om.* P.   1235 for] as sone as TA, soon so S, whan that P.
1239 For angere] And fourtene P;   angere] tene TS.   1245 and (2)] that was
P.   1247 Seth] sithe P;   shall] *add* borne S.   1249 sir] well P.
1251 Neuer] Nouther T.   1252 raynebowe] *from* TASP, wynde blowyng B.

Ca.º xjº   *The king axide, 'Whider went Adam*   (11)
                        Out of paradys whan he cam?'   2270
                          'Whanne he come out, he wente anoon
                          þere he was made, into Ebron;
And an C ȝere þere he ladde his lyf
And bigate children by his wyf.
But whanne Caym, þat was so fel,   2275
Hadde islayn his broþer Abel,
Adam come his wyf not nere
After þat tyme an C ȝeere
For anger þat Abel was so slaine;
Til þe aungel bad him go againe   2280
And knowe his wyf as he shulde do,   f. 34ᵛ
And seide þat God bad him so,
For of God acursed was Caym
And al þe seed þat come of hym,
And of þat cursed seed and forlorne   2285
Goddes Sone wolde not be borne.
þanne ȝede Adam and Seeth gat he:
Of him God wolde borne be.
And wite þou wel, sire, þat fro Adam
Til þat time þat Noe cam   2290
Neuere in erþe fel no reine,
Ne no reinbowe was yseine:
Fleisshe þat time no man eet
Ne no wyne God wexe leet;
þe weder was þat time euere fair to see   2295
As now is somere in any cuntre
And plente was of al þing
Til mannes synne made letting.'

Ca.º xijº   *'Dide Adam any oþer synne þan þat,*   (12)
                         But brake Goddes heste and þe appil at?' 2300
                          'Nay, he dide noon oþer synne:
                          A gretter miȝte he not begynne,
                          For he coueited God forto be

1254 Ne . . . rede] Ne wyne that waxe gode TS, Wyne ne wax god P, Ne wyn þer was noon
A;   ne swhete] non lete TP, ne bade S, to gete A.   1255 that tyme there] tyme off
the yere A.   1256 hitt were] is here P.   1261 Nay] *add* he seide P.

Therfore of that appyll ete hee.
There shoulde noo creature of witte   1265
His makers byddyng ouersett.
Iff thow before God now were
And some aungell seyde to the there
That thow behynde shouldest se
Or the worlde fordone shulde be,   1270
And God the badde loke on hym faste
And nowhere ellis thyn eyen caste,
Goddis byddyng thow shuldest fulfill
And lete all the worlde spyll.
For though Adam cowthe noo goode,   1275
Byforn God sometyme he stode
And behynde he loked as vnwyse:

f. 21^v Therfore loste he paradise.

In that oone synne þat he did
Vij synnes þerinne weryn hid: 1280
Firste pride, for that he
Desired Godis like for to be;
Inobedience the other also,
For he brake that God hym bade do;
Covetous the iij^{de} wolde greve,   1285
For he covetyd more than God wolde geve;
Sacrelage the fourthe synne
That Adam was loken inne,
For he tooke on hym thore
That God for[b]ade hym beffore;   1290
The v^{te} may be called by reason
Goostely fornycacion,
For his verry spouse he forsoke
And to the develis councell hym toke—
Therfore his right spousall he brak   1295
And in advoutry hy[m]selff stak;
The vj^{te} to manslawter hym drowe
Whenne that he hymseluen slowe;

1265 There shoulde] And for that skylle shall P;   noo . . . witte] noþing as by reason
A.   1266 byddyng] body P;   ouersett] to ffordoon A.   1269 se] a se
P.   1275 For though] Forthi TAS.   1280 þerinne] þen S, so P.
1282 Godis] Godde T;   like] lyckenesse P.   1283 the other] he synnyd P.
1285 wolde] thatt moch doth A.   1286 wolde geve] gaiff hym leve S.

And þerfore þe appul eet he;
And þere shulde no creature þat haþ witt   2305
His creatours comaundement oueresitt.
For if þou now bifore God were
And aungel seide to þee there
þat þou shuldest behynde þe see
Or elles þe worlde fordoon shulde be,   2310
And God bad þe loke in him faste
And nowher ellis þin yȝe to caste,
Goddes heest þou shuldest fulfille
And lat al þe world spille.
And for þat Adam cowde no good   2315   f. 35ʳ
Bifore God whanne he stood,
He loked behinde him vnwisely
And loste þe ioye of paradys sodeinly;
And in þat oo synne þat he did
þe vij synnes weren yhid: 2320
The firste was pride, and for þat he
Desired lyke to God to be;
Inobedience þe toþer also,
For he brake þat God him [bade] do;
Couetise þe þridde wole greue,   2325
For he coueited aȝenst Goddes leue;
Sacrilege was þe fourþe synne
þat Adam was ycombred ynne,
For it was an holy stede
þere þat he his synne dede;   2330
The fifte may be cleped bi resoun
Spiritual fornicacioun,
For his verre spouse he forsook
And to þe deuels counseil he him took
(For mannes soule is Goddes wyf: 2335
þerfore in avoutrie he ledde his lyf);
þe sixte to mansleing he drowh
Whanne þat he himself slowh;

1290 forbade] *from* TASP, forfade B.   1292 Goostely] Softly P.   1294 coun-
cell] *om.* P.   1295] Therffore he brak his riȝtt spousall A.   1296 hymselff] hy
selff B, hym TS, sore he P;   hymselff stak] he gan fall A.

2313 Goddes] Goddest L.   2324 bade] *om.* L.

Gloteny the vij^{the} was
Whanne he putte hym in þe same caas   1300
To ete the appel, as his wyff badde,
That hym God forbedyn hadde:
Therfore in that appel etyng
Was synne enough and trespasyng.'

Qo. 13^a

'What was that fro God Adam refie   (13) 1305
And how shall he hit yelde hym efie?'
  'Adam f[ro] God moch toke
  That tyme thatt he hym forsoke:
  All þat he shoulde in erthe have wrought
That Adam should furth have brought—   1310
That is, that they shulde have ouercome
The devill and fro hym his myght have nome
As the devill dyd Adam
And in hym all þat of hym cam.

f. 22^r

But for his synne was moche moore   1315
Thanne was alle þe worlde, þerfore
Behoved hym more ayen to yelde
(And this hadde he not in welde)
Or fynde a man that more be
Thanne alle þe worlde: this was not he,   1320
And þerfore eteth he his brede
In swhynke and swhete tyll he be dede.'

Qo. 14^a

'Forloren for ay why was he nouȝt   (14)
Whenne he soo grete a synne had wrouȝt?'
  'For hit behoveth nedely to stonde   1325
  That God hathe ordeynd beforehonde.
  God ordeynd att the begynnyng
  That [of] Adam and his ofspryng

1300 þe same] that SP.   1304 and trespasyng] as me thynke TS, off þat
mysdoyng A, withoute lesyng P.   1305 fro God] God from T.   1307 fro]
from TASP, for B.   1309 All] And S;   shoulde in erthe have] had in erth A;
erthe] the T, you (?þou/?þo) S, *om.* P.   1310 That] For P;   have] *om.* P.

And glotonye þe seuenþe was
Whanne þat he putte him in þat cas 2340
To ete þe appul, as his wyf him bad,
þat tofore God forboden him had:
Wherfore in þat appul eting
Was synne inowh to my seming.'

Ca.° xiij° 'What was it þat Adam from God refte (13) 2345
And hou shal he ȝilde it him efte?'
  'Adam fro God miche took
  þat time þat he him forsook,
For al þat euer God wroght,   f. 35ᵛ
For mankynde it was forþ broght: 2350
þerfore he shulde in þat stounde
þe deuels myȝt haue wiþstonde,
For as þe deuel ouercome Adam
So he doth alle þat of him cam.
For Adams synne was so grete, 2355
As þese clerkes wel wete,
þat him bihoued greet peine to haue
If euere his soule God shulde saue;
But for his synne was miche more
þan was in any oþer man tofore, 2360
þerfore him bihoued amendis to ȝelde
(And þat had he noght in his welde)
Or finde a man þat it might do:
In al þis world þer was noon tho,
And þerfore he eet his breed 2365
In swynke and sweet til he was deed.'

Ca.° xiiij° 'Lorne for euere whi was he noght (14)
Siþen he so grete synne wroght?'
  'For it bihoued nedely to stonde
  þat God hadde ordeined biforehonde. 2370
God ordeined at þe biginning
þat of Adam and of his ofspring

1311 have] *om.* P. 1312 fro . . . nome] his power ffordone A; fro hym] *om.*
P; have nome] bynome S, nomyn P. 1321 eteth] ete TAS, yete P.
1322 be] was TASP. 1325 nedely to stonde] to vndurstonde T. 1328 of]
from SP, *om.* B; his] of his P.

Shulde the ordre of aungeles be chosen,
Be fulfilled and owte losen;   1330
And after, whanne Adam hadde forthought
And angred þat he hadde soo wrought,
Mercy anoon might he noone take,
For he myght noon amendys make.
And ȝif God hadde foryoven hym þis   1335
And putte hym ayen to blis
That aungell was caste owte byfore
For a þought and for no moore,
Thanne hadde God not be rightwosse
So soone to forgeve þat he did amys.   1340
Iff a man founde anon
In a myre a ryche stoone
That were foule and noþynge clene,
He shulde hit wayssh, as I wene,
And in tresoure hit not lay   1345
Vnto þe filthe were all away;
But Goddis Sone, that more shall be
f. 22ᵛ   Thanne alle þe worlde, shall dye on tre
Amendes for Adam to make
And of hym his penaunce take: 1350
Soo shall he come owte of helle
And amonge Go[d]des chosen dwelle.'

Qo. 14ᵃ   'Why wolde not God a aungel sende   (15)
            Or a man Adam to amende?'
                'Bought aungell man and made hym fre,   1355
                His vnderling thenne shoulde he be;
                And man in erth was made here
            For to be aungellis peere
            And iff aungell the kynd nam
            Off man and a man becam,   1360
            Thenne were aungellis of lesse pouste
            Thenne God hem made ffyrste to be.

1329 aungeles] God T, Goddis SP;   be] *om.* SP;   be chosen] ffulffill A.
1330] That for pride to hell ffill A;   losen] of losen T.   1340] Withowte
recompence ffor his dede amys A;   So . . . forgeve] Forthi in synne TSP; þat . . .
amys] grete wreke lis T, wreche h *(remainder lost in binding)* S, that wrecchid is P.
1342 myre] slough TSP.   1347 more] bettur S.   1350 of hym] ffor hym A,
hym fro TP, hym out of S.   1352 Goddes] *from* TASP, goodes B.

Shulde þe ordris of God chosen be
And noght forlorne, as I seie thee:
And after, whanne þat Adam forþoght 2375
And repentid þat he had so wroght,
For he mighte none amendis make,
þerfore mercy mighte he none take.
And ȝif God had forȝeue him þis
And yputte him aȝein to blis 2380
þat aungels were ycast fro bifore
For a þoght and for no more,
þanne had God not ben rightwis. f. 36ʳ

For if a man fonde anoon 2385
In a podel a precious stoon
þat were foule and noþing clene,
He should wasshe it al bidene
And in tresour not it leie
Til þe felþe were aweie; 2390
Thus Goddes Sone most precious
þan al þe world shal deie for vs
And amendis for Adam make
And out of his penaunce aȝen him take:
So shal he come out of helle 2395
And among Goddes chosen dwelle.'

Ca.º xvº   'Whi nolde God an aungel sende (15)
Or a man Adam to amende?'
   'Hadde aungel man boght and made him fre,
His vnderling þanne shulde he haue be; 2400
þerfore man in erþe was made here
For to be aungels fere
And if aungel þe kinde nam
Of man and a man bicam,
þanne were aungel of lesse pouste 2405
þanne God hem made firste forto be.

1353–1635 *questions numbered* 14–23 (*for* 15–24) *with* 19 *om.* B.   1356 vnderling]
vnderloute S, owne derlynge T;   thenne] that T.   1357 And] A P.
1358 peere] fere SP.   1359 nam] toke vppon A.   1360 becam] beganne P.

2384] *line left blank* L.

For man ayen myght no man wyn,
For all were they loken in oon syn:
Forthy shall Goddis Sone of myght   1365
In a clene mayden light;
Oure kynde shall [h]e in hir take
And off ij kyndis a man make:
God and man bothe shall he be,
And off his manhode shall he   1370
Begyle the devill for evermore
As he dyd the man therbefore.'

Qo. 15ᵃ   'Why shall God be bore, me tell,   (16)
             Of a mayde, and she a mayde shall dwelle?'
                  'Sir, on þre manere we hit fynde   1375
                  That God on erth made mankynde:
                  Fyrst made he man and yafe hym lyff
             That noþer cam of man ne of wyff;
             Wymman of man than oonly he nam,
             As Eve, þat he made of Adam;   1380
             The thridde maner than shall be
             Whanne God hymselue, of his pouste,
f. 23ʳ   Shall lyght in erthe into a woman
             Withouten knowlechyng of man;
             And seth þe worlde furste began   1385
             Hathe God yloked for a man
             That shall best doone his will
             And his comaundementes to fulfill,
             And of his kynde shall chosen be
             A clene mayden and a free   1390
             That shall be withowtyn synne
             And all vertues here withynne.
             Hir fadyr shall hire son be,
             And of his doughter shall be noryshed he:
             Spered shall he be in hir bright   1395

1363 For man ayen] Of man to geyne P.   1367 he] from ASP, be B;   hir] erithe
S.   1368 off ij kyndis] to kyndes of P.   1369 bothe] so P.   1372/3 add
And (For P) of mankynde shal he not twynne / Save that he shal neuer doo synne SP.
1376 God] he A.   1379 Wymman] Man TASP; than] om. S; oonly] om. A;   nam]

And man aȝenst man might not wynne,
For alle þei were loken in synne:
þerfore shal Goddes Sone of mighte
In a clene maide alighte,   2410
And he shal in hir oure kynde take
And two kindes in oo man make:
God and man shal he bothe be,
And of his maidenhede shal he
Begile þe deuel for euermore   2415
As þat he dide man bifore;
Fro mankynne shal he not twynne   f. 36ᵛ
And ȝit he shal neuere do no synne.'

Ca.° xvj°   'Whi shal God be bore, þou me telle,   (16)
                 Of a maide, and she a maide dwelle?'   2420
                    'Sire, on þre maneres we fynde
                 þat God in erthe made mankynde:
                 First he made man and ȝaf him lyf
                 þat nouther come of man ne wyf;
                 Womman of man oonly he nam,   2425
                 As Eue, þat he made of Adam;
                 The þridde manere þanne was þis,
                 Whan God, þorgh myght and pouste his,
                 Shal lighte in erthe in a womman
                 Wiþouten knowing of any man;   2430
                 And sithen God þe world first bigan
                 He haþ tenderly euere loued man,
                 For he shal best do his wille
                 And hise comaundementis fulfille;
                 And of his kinde shal chosen be   2435
                 A clene maide faire and free
                 þat shal be wiþouten synne
                 And of alle vertues fulfilled wiþynne.
                 Hir fadir shal hir sone be,
                 And of his doghter his moder she: 2440
                 þe ȝatis shitte, he shal lighte

gan A.   1382 his] om. S.   1385–6] om. S.   1386 God] om. T;   for a]
vnto TA, vnto no P.   1387 doone] do affter A.   1393–4] om. A.   1394 of]
om. P;   shall . . . he] inorished bee T, his maide she S, his modir shal be P.   1395 And
(om. SP) sperid yates shall he (be) in hur light TSP, The Holy Gost shall in hir aliȝtt A.

And dwelle there ix monþes right,
For the ix orderes shall be fulfilled
Of aungellis that in heven were spylled
With mannes kynde that shall be born
And forthe have comen herebeforn.   1400
He shall also, þorow his myght,
Be boren of þat maydyn bright,
And she of childe berynge
Shall be wemmyd of nooþynge;
For the sonne his light casteþ   1405
Thorow the glas that hoole lasteth
And comeþ owte as he furst was
Withoute wemmyng of þe glas:
Soo shall God in that mayden descende
And owte of her body wende,   1410
And she beleven mayden ryght
As the glasse for þe sonne bright.'

Qo. 16ᵃ   *The kyng asked, [for] he wolde lere:*   (17)
                        'How longe leved Adam here?'
               'Nyne hundryd yeere levyd Adam   1415
               And whanne he to his age cam
               And hym thought the dethe was hende,

His oone soone the wey he kende
To paradyse and badde hym goo
To the aungell that drofe hym þerfroo,   1420
And prayde hym to sende anon right
The oyle of mercy that he hym hight
To hele the evell that hym so [d]ered
Whanne he hym drofe owte with a shuerde.
To paradyse his soone he spedde hym than   1425
And wanne that he thedyr came,
He wolde inne and nought he myght.
The aungell stode redy in his sight:
He prayde hym his fader to sende

And dwelle in hir ix monþes righte,
For þe ix ordres he shal fulfille
Of aungels þat beþ in heuene stille.
Wiþ mannes kinde he shal be borne   2445
And saue soules þat shulde be lorne.
He shal also, þorgh his might,
Be borne of a maide bright,
And þe maide after his bering
Shal be wemmed of noþing;   2450
For right as þe sunne his light cast   f. 37ʳ
þoruȝ þe glas and is hool and fast
And cometh out as he firste was
Wiþoute enpeiryng of þe glas,
So shal God in þat may lende   2455
And also out of hir body wende,
And she bileue a maide bright,
As þe sunne þorgh þe glas doþ light.'

Ca.° xvij°   þe king axide, for he wolde lere: (17)
'Hou longe liued Adam here?'   2460
   'Nyne hundrid ȝere lyued Adam
   And whan he vnto eelde cam
And him þoghte þat deeth was hende,
His sone Seeth þe weie he kende
To paradys and bad him goo   2465
To þe aungel þat drof him þerfro,
And preide to sende him anoon right
þe oyle of mercy þat he him hight
To hele þe yuel þat him derde
Whan he drof him out with a swerde.   2470
To paradys þe weie his sone nam
And whan he to þe ȝates cam,
He wolde in and not ne might.
But þe aungel stood redy in his sight:
He preide him his fader to sende   2475

in elde bicam S, wolde became P;   his] þat A.   1417 hende] ny hande P.
1418 oone] oo A, owne TSP.   1421 prayde . . . sende] pray hym he seyde P.
1422 hym] me P.   1423 dered] *from* ATSP, fered B.   1425 To] The way to
S;   he . . . than] yede þan A, name TSP.   1426 wanne that] as sone as A;   thedyr]
To Paradise T, ate gates S, at the gatis P.   1428 stood] *add* þere S;   his] *om.* S.

Thynge þat might his disease amende.   1430
Thre kernellis the aungell yafe hym þere
And badde hym to his father hem bere
And bydde hym in his mowth hem ley
Whatte tyme þat he shall deye,
And sey hym oone of these thre   1435
Shall waxe and his hele be;
And Goddis comaundemente is soo,
V dayes and an halfe be therto.
The soone came and the kernell brought
And seyde, "Father, drede yoow nought: 1440
After v dayes and an halffe shull yee
Bene heled, so the aungell seyde me."
Adam herde and sighed soore
And wiste whatte the v dayes wore
And seyde, "Myn hele is not soo neere: 1445
Goddis day is a thowsand yeere."
And the iij kyrnellis in his mouthe he caste
And yelde the goste atte the laste.
Anone the devill thedyr came
And with grete ioye the soule name   1450
And into helle with hym hit drowgh,
There hit suffered woo enowgh.

f. 24ʳ

Be the ix hundred yere
That Adam was levyng here
Ix orderys of aungellis I take   1455
That Adam lete from Eve his make.
Of echon of the kyrnelles thre
At Adams mouthe sprange a tre,
And there shall dye vppon oon of thoo
Goddis Soone, and Adam brynge owte of woo.   1460
By the v dayes and an halfe is vnderstonde
V C yere and v thowsande.'

Qo. 17ᵃ   '*Why is dethe called dethe, tell thou me,*   (18)
             And how fele dethes that ther be?'

1430 his disease] hym S;   disease] hele TAP.   1434 Whatte] Whan A, þat ilke
SP;   he] his fadir TA.   1444 whatte the] wel thoo TA, that P.   1445 not]
om. P.   1446 day] dethe P;   is] is hens P.   1448 atte the laste] tho in haste P.
1449 devill] fendes S;   thedyr came] þer cam yn A; came] name P.   1450] And

Thing þat might his sore amende.
þre kirnels þe aungel took him þere
And bad him to his fader hem bere
And bid him in his mouth hem leie
þe same tyme þat he shal deie,   2480
And seie him þat oon of the þre
Shal wexe and his hele be;
For Goddis comaundement so
Fyue daies and a half shal be þerto.
þe sone come and þe kernels broght   2485 f. 37ᵛ
And seide, "Fadir, drede þe noght:
After fiue daies and an half shul ȝe,
þe aungel seide, helid shullen be."
Adam herde þat and siked sore:
He wiste what þe fyue daies wore   2490
And seide, "Myn hele is not so nere:
Goddes deth is hennes v Ml ȝere."
þe iij kernels þo in his mouth he cast
And ȝelde vp þe goost at þe last.
Anoon þe deuel þider cam   2495
And wiþ greet ioye þe soule nam
And it into helle wiþ him drowh,
And þere suffred wo and sorwe ynowh.
By þe nyne hundred ȝere
þat Adam was lyvinge here   2500
þe ix ordres of aungels I take
þat Adam lost for Eue his make.
Of eche of þe kirnels thre
At Adames mouth sprang a tree,
And þere shal deie vp oon of tho   2505
Goddis Sone, and bringe Adam out of woo.
Bi þe v daies and an half I vnderstonde
Fyue hundrid and fyue þowsande.'

Ca.° xviij°   'Whi is deth cleped deth, telle þou me,   (18)
            And hou many deeþis þat þer be?'
                                      2510

---

toke the soule ffurth with hym A, And toke the sowle of Adame P.   1451 with hym]
he P;   hym] þaim S.   1456 lete from Eve] lefte for euer and P;   from] for
S.   1461 and an halfe] om. P;   is] I ASP.

'For bitternesse is deth callid dede   1465
  And for Adam, thorow evell rede,
   A bitter bete of the appell he bote,
That drofe hym into swhynke and shwote.
And thre maner of dethes ther is:
Oon that nought ripe ne is,   1470
As of children that be yonge—
They fele noo grete peyne in dyyng;
Another deth there is also
That is bitter to come vnto,
As yonge men whan hem liketh beste   1475
And dethe cometh on hem as faste—
Bitternesse he suffreth and woo
Er the goste departe hym froo;
Gostly dethe the thridde hit is,
There the sowle is euer dede fro blis.   1480
And all thre to man they cam
For the synne that did Adam;
And iff that synne ne hadde be wrought
Manne ne shulde haue dyed nought.'

Qo. 18ᵃ   *'Sendeth God ought man to seye*   (19) 1485
             Of what dethe he shall dye?'
             'Nay, he sendith to noo man
f. 24ᵛ   But to hym that so moche can
That hathe in mynde of the dethe
And of werkes that beste bethe,   1490
Soden dethe shall he not deye
For he shall goo the sekyr weye.
And the goode that trowen aright
In God of heven and his myght
And werke as they ought to doo,   1495
To what deth that they go too—
Wheþer he be slayn with swherde or knyff
Or with wylde bestes lese his liff
Or in water drenchid be

1465 is] is itt B, is TASP.   1466 for] *om.* P.   1472 fele] thoile S, dole
P.   1475 whan] that P.   1476 cometh] be SP;   as] *om.* SP.   1481 all]
om. S.   1482 synne that did] trespas of olde T.   1485 ought . . . seye] to man
any knowlechyng A.   1486 he shall dye] shall be his endyng A;   he] that man

'For bitternesse is deeþ cleped deed
And for þat Adam, þorgh yuel reed,
A bitter bit of þe appul he boot,
þat drof him into swink and swoot.
And þre maneres of deeþis þer is: 2515
Oon þat noght ripe ne is,
As of children þat beeþ ȝynge
þat suffre litel peyne in her deyinge;
Another deth þer is also   f. 38ʳ
þat is bitter to come to,   2520
As a ȝonge man whan him likeþ best
And þe deeth be on him fest—
He suffriþ bitternesse and woo
Or þe goost may departe him fro;
Goostly deth þe þridde is,   2525
Whan þe soule is deed fro blis.
And alle þre to man þei cam
For þe synne þat dide Adam;
And if þat synne ne had be wroght
Man ne shulde haue deied noght.'   2530

Ca.º xixº   'Sendiþ God man oght to seie   (19)
                   On what deeth þat he shal deie?'
                        'Nay, he sendith to no man;
                        But he þat so miche can
                   þat haþ menyng of þe deed   2535
                   And worcheþ after þe best reed,
                   On sodein deth shal he not deie
                   For he shal go þe siker weie.
                   And þe goode, þat bileuen aright
                   In God of heuene and his might   2540
                   And worcheþ as þei ought to do,
                   To what deeþ þat þei goo to—
                   Slain eiþer wiþ swerd or knif
                   Or wiþ wilde bestis lesiþ her lyf
                   Or in water drenchid be   2545

T.   1488 to hym] he TASP.   1489 in mynde] menynge TAS, amenyng P;
dethe] dede TASP.   1490 And werkis of (atte S) the (*om.* AS) beste rede TAS, And
werke euer Goddis rede P.   1497 Wheþer he be] Thoughg they were P;   he be]
om. TAS.   1498 his] theire T, thy A, þai S, here P.

Or hangid hye vppon a tre   1500
Or of some foule aventure
May thanne the liff noo lenger endure—
Wykked deþe is noon of þis
In the sight of God and of his;
For theyre goode dedes more and lesse   1505
And Goddis owne rightwisnesse
May not be lorn in Goddis thought,
Forthy suche dede ne dereth nought.
And if they hadde done aught amys
Thorow ffeblenesse that in hem is,   1510
All shall b[e] foryeven of that dede
For the sharpe deth that they to yede.
But he that in God troweth nought
Ne of his comaundement nothynge wrought,
What may itt hym avayle   1515
That he hathe grete travayle
And paynes stronge or he dye?
And sethen men euer hym bye
What dethe so he dyeth he this
Wykked deth and shorte hit is.'   1520

'Whenne the soule from þe body shall passe,   (20)
Howe wendes þe soule into other place?'
f. 25ʳ   'The soule wendith ffro the body,
            Wenne he dyeth, full prevely;
            But whenne hit is owte goon,   1525
There comyth ayenst hit anoon
A companye of helle hyne
With moche sorow and moche pyne,
And vnto helle they hit bere
With many peynes hit to dere.   1530
But after the tyme of Goddis Soone,
That he is come into erthe to wone,

1502 thanne] _om._ T, hem SP.   1503 þis] theise TASP.   1504] _om._ T, His
good dedis he shall nott lese A.   1506] God rewardith off his riȝtwisnes A.
1507 May . . . lorn] No good dede A.   1508] Is nott fforgete þat they haue wrouȝtt
A;   Forthy] _from_ PTS, For they B;   dede] _om._ P.   1509 aught] noȝt S.
1511 be] _from_ TASP, b B;   of] _om._ TSP.   1514 of] _om._ TSP, affter A;
nothynge] nought ne T, noȝt S, hathe not P.   1516 hathe] that hathe had P.

Or hie hanged vpon a tre
Or somme of foule aventure
Whan he þe lyf no lenger may dure—
Wicked deth is none of þise
In Goddis sight be no wise;   2550
For her goode dedes more and lasse
And Goddes owne rightwisnesse
May noght be lorne in Goddes þoght,   f. 38ᵛ
Wherfore such deeþ ne dredeth noght.
And if þei hadde oght doo amys   2555
þorgh febelnesse þat in hem is,
Al shal be forȝeue to þe dede
For þe sharp deth þat he to ȝede.
But he þat in God bileueþ noght
And his comaundement haþ noght wroght,   2560
What may it him availe
þat he haþ so grete trauaile
And hard þrowes longe or he deie?
Suche ben worþi, as I þe seie,
What deth so þei deie, ywis,   2565
A wickid deth to hem it is.'

Ca.º xxº   'Whan soule fro þe bodi shal shede,   (20)
                 Hou wendith þe soule to oþer stede?'
                   'The soule wendeþ fro þe body,
                     Whanne he dieth, ful prively;   2570
                 But whan it is out ygoon,
                 þere comeþ aȝenst him anoon
                 A companye of deuels of helle
                 Wiþ greet crye and greet ȝelle,
                 And wiþ hem þei wole it bere   2575
                 With many peynes to do it dere.
                 But after þe time of Goddis Sone,
                 þat he is come in erþe to wone,

1517 paynes strong] throwes long TASP.   1518] Grete peynes or many a day lye
A;   euer hym bye] him faili lye T, hym fayr (fairely P) leye SP.   1519 he (1)]
om. P.   1521–2 q. no. om. B.   1521 passe] shede TS.   1522 þe
soule] itt A;   place] stede TS.   1527 hyne] houndis A.   1528] With
grete noyse and grete sownys A;   sorow] ioye TP, noys S;   pyne] dyne TSP.
1532 come . . . wone] into erth come A.

Of ledyng ther shall be maneres thre
Soules to lede there they shull be.
Oon is if a man haue here   1535
Trowed as Goddis Sone hym shall lere
And Goddis comaundementis have wrought
And owte of the right feyth erred nought:
Whanne his lyfe owte of the worlde wendith
And his sowle fro the body tendith,   1540
Of aungellis a grete company
Gaderen hem with grete melody

And take the soule with pley and songe
And thanken God euer amonge;
Vnto heven therwith they wende   1545
There to dwelle withouten ende.
Another maner of ledyng there is:
If a man haue do amys
And will not his lawys fulfille
But all his lyfe hathe doon yll,   1550
And ayenste he dye shall
He repentyth hym of all
And to God mercy cries,
Whenne the soule from the body flies
A goode aungell hit takyth in haste   1555
And deliuerith hit to a wikked gaste
And he shall hit forth lede
Payne to suffre for his misdede;
But whanne that he hathe beten hit withall
And suffered that he suffer shall,   1560
The goode aungell hym takes away
And ledeth hit to ioye for aye.
The þridde maner if man or wyff
In sinne have euer ladde here lyff
And Goddis worde wolde not fulfille   1565
But didde all her hertis will,

f. 25ᵛ

1537 Goddis] his SP.   1539 owte . . . wendith] in þis worlde endes SP;
wendith] pretendith A.   1540-3910] *pages missing* A.   1542 grete] *om.*
S.   1542/3 *add* Vnto hym that his kepar was / Where that he wente in ilke a cas
T, Vntil hym that his keper was / And in fowndyng in ylke a cas P.   1545 therwith

Soules shullen be led in þre maners
Somme to ioye and some to peynes.   2580
One is if a man haue here
Yliued as Goddes lawe him lere
And hise comaundementȝ haue wroght
And out of þe right wey yerrid noght:
Whanne his lyf in þis world haþ ende   2585
And þe soule fro þe bodi shal wende,
Of aungels a greet companye   f. 39ʳ
Gadrid togidre wiþ melodie
And goon wiþ him þat his keper was
To saue it alwey in euery cas,   2590
And take þat soule wiþ pley and song
And þanken God euere among
And into heuene þerwith þei wende
þere to dwelle wiþouten ende.

Anoþer manere of leding þer is   2595
þat if a man haue ido amys
And wole not Goddis lawe fulfille
But al his lyf haþ done ille,
And aȝeinst þat he deie shal
He repentith him of al   2600
And to God mercie doth crie,
Whanne þe soule fro þe bodi flie
A good aungel it takeþ in hast
And deliuereþ it to a wicked gast
And he shal it forþ lede   2605
To suffre peyne for his mysdede;
And whanne he haþ his peine al
Fulfilled and no more suffre shal,
The good aungel takiþ him away
And ledeth him to ioye for ay.   2610
þe þridde manere if man or wif
Haue euere in synne lad her lyf
And Goddis hest not fulfille
But dide after her owne wille,

they] that hit with hem S.   1549 his] Goddis P.   1552 of] of his euel dedes
S.   1555 hit . . . haste] in hast hit takis anon P.   1556 gaste] gost sone
P.   1559] Bot when hit hais the paynes all S;   beten hit withall] hit botenyd alle
P.   1563 if] of T.   1564 sinne] add that T.

Deuelis take that soule anoon
Whanne hit is owte of the body goon
And berith hit to peyne of helle
Withouten ende therynne to dwelle.'   1570

Qo. 20^a   'Now wolde I wete whether wore   (21)
                Sowle or body made byfore.'
                    'The body is furste made full fayre
                    Of ffuyre, water, erthe, and eyre;
                    And the iiij complexions that are   1575
                In man of this iiij they are.
                And whanne the body is made also,
                God of his grace comeþ therto
                And blewe in hym the gost of liff
                And syth of hym made a wyff.   1580
                Lord and syre he bade hym to be
                Of all in erthe that he myght se;
                But whanne he the appill tooke,
                Clothyng of grace he forsoke:
                Thatt hym angred sythens soore   1585
                As that ye haue herde before.'

Qo. 21^a   'Whiche spekeþ, wete wolde I—   (22)
                The soule of the man or the body?'
                    'No myght ne hathe body
                    Of hymselue sekerly   1590
                    To speke, ne goo, ne nought to do,
                But that the soule yevith hym to.
f. 26^r   Men seen ofte hit betydith
                That a man on high hors rideth
                And he hym gydeth to and froo   1595
                The way that he will to goo;
                And the hors, as he muste nede,
                Gothe as the man will hym lede:
                Also the body hathe noo myght
                Of speche, of goyng, ne of sight,   1600

1567 take] kepe S, kepyn P.   1573 full] clere and P.   1578 grace] merci
T.   1583 tooke] chese TSP.   1548 he forsoke] ther he les S;   forsoke]
forlese TP.   1588 or] or ellis T.   1591 go] grone T.   1594 high] an
TSP.   1595 gydeth] wisses STP.   1596 to] he S, he shall T, *om.* P.

Deuels kepeþ the soule anoon 2615
Whanne it is fro þe bodi goon
And beriþ it to þe peyne of helle
Wiþouten ende þerwith to dwelle.'

Ca.° xxj°   'Now wolde I wite wheþer wore (21)
   Soule or body made bifore.'
      'The body is first made clere and fair 2620   f. 39ᵛ
      Of fire and watir, erthe and air;
And þe iiij complexiouns þat ere
In man of þise iiij þei were.
And whanne þe body was made also, 2625
God of his grace come þerto
And blewe in him a goost of lyf
And sithen made of him a wyf,
And lord and sire made him to be
Of al þat he in erthe might se; 2630
But whan he þe appel ches,
Clothing of grace he forlees:
And þat angrid him ful sore
As ȝe haue herd bifore.'

Ca.° xxij°   'Wheþer spekiþ, wite wolde I— (22) 2635
   þe soule of man or þe body?'
      'No might ne hath þe body
      Of himself sikerly
To speke, ne go, ne noght to do,
But þat þe soule him ȝeueþ to. 2640
Men seen ofte it betide
þat a man may on hors ride
And he him ruleþ to and fro
þe weie þat he wole haue hym to go;
And þe hors, as he mote nede, 2645
Gooþ as þe man wole him lede:
Also the body haþ no might
Of speche, of goyng, ne of [s]ight,

1597 he muste] hym bihoues S.

2618 Wiþouten] Wiþ oute outen L.   2648 sight] might *marked for correction* L.

Ne of noothyng that he doo shall,
But of the soule itt cometh all.
The body is of the erthe wrought
And shall rote all to nought,
Therfore is he of fekyll nature   1605
Ayenste þe soule, that euer shall endure;
And the body is nooþynge
Vnto the soule but an helyng.
Thow seest well, whanne þe soule is goon,
A foule caren is the body oon   1610
That speke ne stere may
Sith the soule wente away.
And for all thynge of the soule is,
Thanne gothe she firste to ioye or blis;
And thanne is of the soule euerydele   1615
That the body dothe ille or wele.'

Qo. 22^a

'A sowle that a gooste is oon   (23)
And [hath] nouther fflesshe ne boon
Ne nouȝt takeþ ne geueth therfro,
How may hit thole wele or [w]oo?'   1620
    'Gost is soule, the sooþe to say,
    And neuer more ne may hit deye:
    Ete ne drynke ne will itt nought,
    And hit is swhyffte as ony thought;
    Felte ne yseye may hit not be,   1625
    Ne noo stede may hit ocupye.
    But whanne the liff comes to an ende
    And the soule shall fro the body wende,
    He[ld h]e Goddis comaundemente,
    A clothe of grace hym shall be sente;   1630
    Haue he be wikked ouerall,
    A clothe of sorowe to hym come shall,
    Thorough whiche clothyng sofere shall he
    Ioye other payne whether hit be.'

f. 26^v

1604 rote all] rote awey TS, alwey turne P.   1605 fekyll] febill P.
1611 may] nought ne may TSP.   1612 wente] is wente TSP.   1614] Than
she furste the doer is T;   Thanne goth she] That he go P;   ioye] woo SP.
1618 hath] he B, haues T, hais S.   1620 woo] *from* TS, doo B.   1621 Gost]
A gost SP, No goost T.   1624 swhyffte as ony] also (as P) swifte as TSP.

Ne of mouth þat he do shal,
But of þe soule it cometh al.   2650
þe body is of erthe ywroght
And al shal roote awey to noght
For þat he is of brutil nature
Aȝeins þe soule þat euer shal dure;
And þe body is nothing   2655 f. 40ʳ
To þe soule but an hillyng.
þou seest wel, whan þe soule is goon,
A foule carein is þe body oon
þat speke ne meue noght ne may
Whanne þe soule is went away.   2660
And for al þing of þe soule is,
þanne gooþ she first to woo or blis;
And þanne it is of þe soule eueridele
þat þe body doth yuel or wele.'

Ca.° xxiij°   'The soule þat a goost is oon   (23) 2665
                 And haþ noþer flesshe ne boon
                 Ne noght takeþ ne ȝeueþ þerfro,
                 Hou may it suffre wele or woo?'
                     'A goost is þe soule, soth to seie,
                      And neuere more may it deie: 2670
                 Ete ne drinke ne wole it noght,
                 And it is as swift as þoght;
                 Felte ne seen may it not be,
                 Ne no stede may it occupe.
                 But whan þe lyf comeþ to þe ende   2675
                 And þe soule shal fro þe body wende,
                 If he kepe Goddes comaundement,
                 A clooþ of grace shal him be sent;
                 And if he haue be wicked oueral,
                 A clooth of sorowe him couere shal.'   2680

1625 yseye] om. P.   1629 Held he] Heled be B, Halde he S, Holde P, And he kepe
T.   1631 Haue] And if T.   1632 to hym come] ouercom hym T, hym
ouercome P.   1633 sofere] sorow P.

2659 meue] perhaps mene L.

Qo. 23ᵃ   '*Who is more lord of þe twhey—*   (24) 1635
                       Soule or body?—Thou me say.'
                           'The body moore lorde is
                               That ledyth the soule ofte amys,
                               But a moore perell shall abyde
                       The soule, if that evill betyde.   1640
                       As if ther were now yonge men twey
                       Goyng togedyr in theyre wey
                       And that oone be bolde and hardy,
                       That oþer a cowarde that gothe hym by:
                       The cowarde thynketh, as he goys,   1645
                       "If there come ayenst vs ony ffoys,
                       This hardy man shall me were
                       So they shall not me dere."
                       Thus goth the cowarde hardely.
                       The hardy thynkeþ, "What shall I?   1650
                       This coward that gothe with me,
                       If ought come butt goode, he woll fle
                       And I shall suffre the brunte at nede."
                       Thus gothe the hardy man in drede.
                       All thus hit fareth witterly   1655
                       Betwyxte the soule and the body:
                       The body seythe, "I woll have quyte
                       All my wyll and alle my delyte.
                       Whanne I am dede, erthe shall I be:
                       What reccheth me what falleth of the?"   1660
                       The soule seythe, "A felowe I lede
                       That me bereth febill felowrede,
                       For whanne ther cometh any aduersite,
                       I shall sofere and not he."

f. 27ʳ   Thus is the soule in perell ay   1665
                       For that the body holdes play.'

Qo. 25ᵃ   '*Whereabowte, soo God þe spede,*   .   (25)
                       Hathe soule in man his wonyng stede?'
                           'In the body and euerywhere
                           Abydes the soule, and blode be there.   1670

1640 that] ony T, hit S.   1642 togedyr in theyre] in a perellous TSP.
1644 gothe] stondis T.   1645–50] *om.* P.   1646 ony] oure S.   1650 hardy]
add man TS.   1651 This] *add* is a TSP.   1653 brunte] woo TSP.
1654 man] *om.* P.   1657 have quyte] a quyte P.   1660] What (Who P) thar

Ca.° xxiiij°   'Who is more lord of þe tweie—   (24)
        þe soule or þe body?—þou me seie.'
        'The body þe more lord is
        þat lediþ the soule ofte amis,
        But þe more perelle it shal abide   2685
        þe soule, if þat it yuel betide.
        As þogh þer were ȝonge men tweie
        Going in a perilous weie
        And þat oone be bolde and hardy,   f. 40ᵛ
        þe toþer a coward þat goþ him by: 2690
        þe coward þinkeþ, as he goos,
        "If aȝenst vs comeþ many foos,
        þis hardy man shal me were
        So þat me þei shullen not dere."
        þus gooþ the coward ful sory.   2695
        þe hardy þenkeþ, "What shal I?
        This is a coward þat gooþ by me:
        If oght but good come, he wole fle
        And I must suffre þat come nede."
        þus gooþ the hardy man forþ in drede.   2700
        Al þus it fareþ euer truly
        Bitwene þe soule and þe body:
        The body seith, "I wole haue tite
        Al my wille and my delyte.
        Whan I am deed, erþe shal I be: 2705
        What dar I rekke what comeþ of me?"
        þe soule seith, "A felowe I lede
        That bereþ me febil felowrede,
        For and þer come any aduersite,
        I shal suffre it and noght he."   2710
        þus is þe soule in perel ay
        For þe body loueþ play.'

Ca.° xxv°   'Wheraboute, so God þe rede,   (25)
        Haþ soule in man his woning stede?'
          'In þe body for euermore   2715
          Woneþ the soule, if blood be thore.

reke what is of mee TSP.   1662 febill] *om.* P.   1663 whanne ther cometh]
com TS.   1667ff. *correct q. nos. resume* B   1667 Whereabowte] Whethuroute
T;   spede] rede TS.   1670 Abydes] Wonnes TSP.

Blode is vessel of the soule sothely
And of the blode is the body,
And thereas the blode ne is noothyng,
There hathe the soule noo wonnyng,
As in tethe, in here alsoo,   1675
In nayles, and in hyde therto.
3if thow say, lyfe is in tho
For they may fele whoo dothe hem woo,
Therto is a answhere goode,
For in her rotes styketh blode: 1680
Pare hem and clippe hem when thow will
And come the rotes nought vntill,
Shull they neuer feele a dele
Whether thow doste hem woo or wele.'

Qo. 26ª   '*Why is þe soule noo lenger lefte*   (26) 1685
                In the body thenne þe blode is refte?'
                'Also hit fares, nother more ne lesse,
                  But as a ponde þat in ffyssh is:
                Yf a man a goter make
                The water fro the ponde to slake,   1690
                The water rennes small and smalle
                Vnto hit be ronnen all;
                Thenne lythe the ffyssh of þat ponde
                Betyng ageynes the drye londe,
                And for the water is from þem away,   1695
                Therfore they moste nedes deye.
                Of the soule hit fares also:
                Whenne the blode is ronnen therfro,
                Euer as the blode is oute rennyng
                Soo is þe soule enfebelisshyng;   1700
f. 27ᵛ   And whenne the blode is oute euerydell,
                The sowle no lenger likes wele
                In that body for to dwelle

    1671 vessel of] the selle for P;   sothely] Forthi TSP.   1677] Thei may not
fele who do þem woo T;   lyfe] hit P.   1678] And therfore lif is not in thoo
T;   they] hit P;   whoo] hit P.   1679–80] *om.* T.   1680 in . . .
styketh] þair rootes towches S, ther the rotis tochid P.   1681 and clippe hem] *om.*
P.   1682 nought] *om.* P.   1683 neuer] *om.* P.   1687 lesse] mynne
TSP.   1688 in ffyssh is] fisshe is ynne TSP.   1692 ronnen] renne oute P.

Blood is vessel of þe soule forþi
And of þe blood is the body,
And if þer be of blood noþing,
þanne haþ the soule no woning, 2720
As in teeþ and in heer also,
In nailes and in skyn þerto.
If þou seie, þe lijf is in þo f. 41ʳ
For þei mowen fele who dooþ hem wo,
þerto lieth an answere good, 2725
For þere þe rotes toucheþ blood:
Pare hem and clippe hem at wille
And come þe rootes noþing tille,
And þei sholen fele neuere a del
Wheþer þou doost hem woo or wel.' 2730

Ca.º xxvjº 'Whi is þe soule no lenger left (26)
In þe body whan þe blood is out reft?'
'Also it fareþ, as I þe mynne,
As a pole þat fisshe is ynne:
If a man a goter make 2735
þe watir out of þe pole to slake,
The water renneþ smal and smal
Til it by ronne out al;
þanne lieth þe fisshe of þe ponde
Abidinge þere on þe londe, 2740
And for þe water is al aweie,
þenne bihoueþ hem nedely to deie.
Of þe soule it fareþ so:
Whanne þe blood renneþ him fro
And al þe blood is out renninge, 2745
So wexiþ the soule a feble þinge;
And whanne þe blood is out euerydel,
þe soule no lenger likeþ wel
In þat body forto dwelle

1694] Dryand ayenst the londe P. 1695 from þem] alle TP, also S.
1696 Therefore they moste] Thanne the fisshe muste T, þaim bihoues S, Then behouyth
hem P; nedes] nedelynge T, nedely to S, nedelyche to P. 1698 is ronnen] it
rennes T, hit rennyth P. 1699 Euer] And P; rennyng] rennande TSP.
1700 enfebelisshyng] enfeblisshande S, feblishande T, of febill sonde P. 1701 is
oute] om. P.

But departes also snell;
For his nature forleses he soo   1705
As ffyssh whenne the water is them fro.'

Qo. 27ᵃ   *'I praye þe now that þow me say*   (27)
How hit is þat folke soo dey.'
   'Man dyes on many wyse:
      Some whenne that here dayes hyes   1710
That God hem sette fulfilled are,

Thenne byhouith hym nedely to fare.

Somme of outerage that they do,
As of mete and drynke also,
And destroyes here nature   1715
Soo þat þey may not endure:
Vnderstande that no man may
Ouer Goddes terme lengthe a day,
But with outerage men may lette
The terme that God hathe sette.   1720
Summe dye in batayll and in fiȝte
With staffe or swhirde þat falles liȝte,
And on other wyse also
Moo thanne I can telle vnto.'

Qo. 28ᵃ   *'How may man wete þat hit soo is*   (28) 1725
That God made man to his lykenesse?'
   'We fynde of antiquite
      In booke that somtyme hadde Noe
That whenne God of heuen kynge
Hadde made bestes and all thynge,   1730
Thenne sayde oon of þe persoones þre
That are in the Trinite,
"Now all thynge is made bothe more and lesse,
Make we man to ooure lykenesse."

1704] *om.* T.   1705 soo] thoo TSP.   1710 here] *om.* TS;   hyes] hise
TS, hase P.   1712 Thenne . . . nedely] Bothe behouyth he nedis P.
1713] *om.* P.   1715 nature] *add* tho P.   1716/17] *add* For to lyue no
lengir here P.   1718 lengthe] live T.   1720 hathe] hath hym T, hym hathe P,
has many S.   1722 þat] as S, hit P;   liȝte] riȝt S.   1724] There dyen many

But parteth þerfro, as I the telle;   2750
For his nature he leseþ þo
As fisshe whanne water is þerfro.'

Ca.° xxvij°   *'I preie þe now, þou me seie*   (27)
                       Whi it is þat folke so deie.'
                          'Man deieþ on manye wise: 2755
                          Somme, forsothe, whanne þei done rise—
                       þe time þat God him sett here   f. 41ᵛ
                       Fulfilled is day and ȝeere,
                       þanne bihoueþ him nedely to wende
                       Whanne of þe tyme comen is þe ende.   2760
                       Some deie of outrage þat þei doo,
                       As of mete and drinke also,
                       And destruien her nature
                       So þat þei mowen not endure:
                       Ȝit vnderstonde þat no man may   2765
                       Ouere Goddes terme lengþe a day,
                       But wiþ outrage man may lett
                       þe terme of God him haþ sett.
                       Somme dien in bataile and in fight
                       Wiþ staff or swerd þat [s]leeþ light,   2770
                       And in oþer wises also
                       Mo than I can telle to.'

Ca.° xxviij°   *'Hou mowen men wite þat it so is*   (28)
                       þat God made man to heuen blis?'
                          'We finde in antiquite   2775
                          In bookes þat somtime hadde Noe
                       þat whanne God of heuen king
                       Had made bestis and al thing,
                       þanne seide oone of þe persones þre
                       þat ben in þe Trinite,   2780
                       "Now al þing is made more and lesse,
                       Make we man to oure liknesse."

nen mo P;   vnto] yow too TS.   1727 of] of grete T;   of antiquite] in Antyoe
?.   1728 booke] bokis TP;   that somtyme] when P.   1730 bestes and] of
estis P.

2770 sleeþ] fleeþ L.

f. 28^r

And forthy he sayde, "Make wee,"   1735
To vnderstonde that there are three;
And that he sayde is noo lesyng:
Thanne are we vnto hym lykyng.'

Qo. 29^a   'Sythen we of Goddis lykenesse be,   (29)
Why may we not do as didde he?'   1740
'In Goddes lykenesse we are diȝt
And therfore hathe he yoven vs miȝt
Abouen yche other creature
That he made here for to dure;
And for that lyknesse soo knowe we   1745
All thynges that in erthe be.
Wee canne swhynke, worche, and wynne,
And we knowe almesse from synne;
And creatures may we take
And oure seruauntis of hem make;   1750
And all other thynges that are nought
Vnto Goddis lyknesse wrought
Have noo myȝte ne kunnyng þerto
To doo þynges that we doo,
Ne comaunde vs noȝte þey ne may   1755
As we doo hem euery day.
But though we be of his lykenesse,
We may not neuertheles
Be as stronge and wyse as he
For his handyworke than ar we: 1760
He is maker of all thyng
And we be of his makyng.
He is þat lord þat may vs save
For the lykenesse þat we have:
Yff that we do noȝt ill,   1765
Angelis noumbre we shall fulfill;
For other lykenesse then [h]ys
Were not worthi to that blysse.'

1738 vnto hym lykyng] like hym as me thinke TSP.   1739–45] *follow* 1768
T.   1746–2156] *pages missing* T.   1747 Wee] Som P.   1749 And] Al
P.   1753 kunnyng] comyng P.   1763] He is lorde and we knave SP
1767 hys] his SP, ys B.

And for he seide, "Make we,"
We vnderstonde þat þere were þre;
And þat he seide is no lesing;   2785
þanne be we like him by his making.'

Ca.º xxixº   'Siþen we of Goddis liknesse be,   (29)
                  Whi mowen we not doo as did he?'
                  'To Goddis liknesse we ben dight:
                  þerfore he haþ ȝouen vs might   2790
Aboue eche oþer creature   f. 42ʳ
þat he made here forto dure;
And for þat liknesse so knowe we
Alle þinges þat in erthe be.
We kunne worche besily and wynne   2795
And almesdede knowe fro synne;
Alle creatures we mowen take
And seruauntes of hem to vs make;
And all oþir þing þat is noght
To Goddis liknesse here iwroght   2800
Haþ no knowing ne might þerto
To do al þing þat we here do,
Ne comaunde vs not þei ne may
As þat [we] done hem euery day.
And þogh we be of his liknesse,   2805
ȝit we mowen not neuereþelesse
Be as stronge and as wijs as he
For his handwerke þanne be we:
He is maker of al thing
And we ben of his making.   2810
He is lord and we knaue
And for þe liknesse þat we haue,
If þat we do noþing ille,
Aungels noumbre we shullen fulfille;
For oþer liknesse þan his   2815
Beþ not worþi to þat blis.'

['*Where becomes the blode alle*   (30)
Of man when he deye shalle?'   1770
      'Godde made blode of water right
         And the bodi of the erthe he dight;
And as water in erth synkes
And the erthe the water drinkes
For to mayntene alle thynges   1775
That wexis and in erthe springes,
Also mayntenes witterli
The blode that is in mannis body.
And whan the soule departe shall,
The blode he berys with hym alle;   1780
And whanne the hete is fro hym sente,
The blode is into the water wente;
And the bodi that is drie
And ripe may not longe lie
That it ne drinkes the blode alsoo   1785
As erthe wil the water doo.']

['*When the fyre slekkede is,*   (31)
Whider bicomes hit?—Tell me thys.']
      'Off the sunne þe fyre is right:
         Thereof he hath bothe hete and light   1790
And, be hit slekned, he shall goo
To the sonne there he cam fro.
Thou seest the sonne, þat light makes
And heete also there hit ontakes,
Oute whenne he from vs wente,   1795
Alle the hete that he lente
And the liȝte of hym also
All hathe he hym taken vnto
And ledes with hym that he brought:
Fro hym departe may hit not.   1800
Also when fuyre is quenchid here,
He withdraweth him on þat ilke manere
Vnto þe nature for to go
Of the sonne þat he came froo.'

f. 28ᵛ

1769-86] *from* T (preceding 1739), *om.* BS.   1773 as] all P.   1776 and . . .
springes] on erthe spryngyng P.   1778 that . . . mannis] all that is in the P.
1780 he . . . alle] is colde as is the walle P.   1781 hete] *from* P, herte T.
1783 And] And than P.   1787-8] *from* S, Of what complexion may be / The body

Ca.° xxx°   'Where bicomeþ the blood al   (30)
                Of man whan he deie shal?'
                   'God made blood of water right
                      And þe body of þe erthe dight;   2820
                   And al þe water into erthe sinketh,
                   And al þe erthe þe water drinketh
                   For to maintene al þinge
                   þat waxeþ in the erthe springinge.
                   Also God mainteneþ witterly   2825 f. 42ᵛ
                   þe blood þat is in my body.
                   And whanne þe soule departe shal,
                   He bereþ the blood wiþ him al;
                   And whanne þe hete is from him went,
                   þe blood is into water sent;   2830
                   And þanne þe body þat is drye
                   And rype may not longe lye
                   þat it ne drinkeþ þe blood also
                   As þe erthe þe water do.'

Ca.° xxxj°   'Whanne þe fire slakid is,   (31) 2835
                Wher bicomeþ it?—Telle me þis.'
                   'Off þe sunne þe fire is right:
                      þerof haueþ it hete and light
                   And bi þe slaking shal goo
                   To þe sunne þere he come froo.   2840
                   þou seest þe sunne, þat light makeþ
                   And hete þerof þat we takeþ,
                   And whanne he is fro vs went,
                   Al þe hete þat he sent
                   And þe light of him also   2845
                   Al aȝein he takeþ him to
                   And ledeþ wiþ him þat he broght
                   And fro him may it departe noght.
                   Also whanne fire is slaked here,
                   He wiþdraweþ him on þe same manere   2850
                   To þe nature forto go
                   Of þe sunne þere he come fro.'

and of what nature is he B.   1790 he hath] haue we P.   1791 And . . .
slekned] Be the slakande P.   1794 ontakes] out takes S.   1795 Oute] On
nyght P.   1800 Fro] For P.   1802 withdraweth] drawith P.

Qo. 31ᵃ   'Why dyeth not the body there   (32) 1805
                 Whanne he hathe loste halfe his blode and moore?'
                      'Though the blode be halfe away,
                         The body may ʒit nought deye;
                 For the heete of the soule, iwysse,
                 That the blode mentenande is   1810
                 Departes nought so liʒtly,
                 And I shall telle þe forwhy:
                 The lytill blode þat there is lefte
                 Makes þat the soule is hym not refte
                 For hit mayntenes the soule styfly   1815
                 And þe soule þe blode in the body.

                 The weyke þat in a candel is,
                 Whenne hit begynneth for to mysse,
                 The fuyre quenchis and is away.
                 Also is hit the sothe to say: 1820
                 Of the blode the weyke I make
                 And by the fuyre the soule I take;
                 Whenne þe blode awaye is all,
                 The soule no lenger dwelle shall;
                 But whill þe blode confortes hym soo,   1825
                 But other euel hyt fordo,
f. 29ʳ   [D]yes he not soo liʒtly
                 But holdeth hym on lyue forthy.'

Qo. 32ᵃ   'Of what complexion may be   (33)
                 The body and of what nature is he?'   1830
                      'Off nature of the erthe, hit is tolde,
                         And his complexion is colde;
                 And thenne is he maked yare
                 Of foure elementis þat are:
                 Of the erthe is the flesshe   1835
                 [And the blood of waiter nesshe];
                 Of the ayere the soule maked [was]
                 And of fuyre the hete hase:

1815 styfly] sofly S.   1816 in] and SP.   1818 for to mysse] to do amys
P.   1820 the sothe] her SP.   1827 Dyes] Syes B.   1828] But only
holdith hym so fastely P.   1831 nature] the mater P.   1833 yare]

Ca.° xxxij°   'Whi deieþ not þe body þore   (32)
Or he lese half his blood and more?'
    '[T]hogh þe blood be half aweie,   2855
    Ʒit þe body may not deie;
For þe hete of þe soule, ywis,
þat þe blood mayntened by is
Departeþ not so lightly,   f. 43ʳ
And I shal telle þee forwhi: 2860
For þe litel blood þat þere is lefte
Makeþ þat þe soule is not birefte
For it mayntneþ þe soule stifly
And þe soule þe blood and þe body.
Ensample þerof þou maist se   2865
As I here shal shewe to þee:
þe weike þat in þe candel is,
Whanne it byginneþ for to mys,
þe fire slakeþ and is aweie.
þus it is here for to seie: 2870
Of þe blood þe weike I make
And by þe fire þe soule I take,
And whanne þe blood awey is al,
þe soule no lenger dwelle shal;
But while þe blood comfortiþ him so,   2875
In peyne he langwissheþ and in woo
And deieth he not so lightly
As if of blood he were empty.'

Ca.° xxxiij°   'Of what complexioun may be   (33)
þe body and of what nature is he?'   2880
    'Off þe kinde of þe erthe, it is tolde,
    And al his complexioun is colde;
For he is made, withouten les,
Of the iiij elementes:
For of þe erthe is þe fleisshe   2885
And of þe water his blood neisshe;
Of þe eyr his soule made was
And of þe fire þe hete he has.

---

there P.   1836] *from* SP, *om.* B.   1837 was] *from* SP, is B.

2855 Thogh] hogh (*gap for rubricator, not completed*) L.

Soo fflessh is of erthes kynde
And blode of the water, as we fynde: 1840
Bothe ar they colde of kynde to fonde;
But soule, þat is of Goddis sonde,
That oughte to be clene and fayre
And is hot of kynde of the ayre.
That soule wones in the blode   1845
And hetes hit and dothe hit goode;
And þe blode hetes, sothely,
All the lemes of thy body.'

Qo. 33ᵃ   'Were soules made at þe firste for ay   (34)
           Or they ben made ȝit euery day?'   1850
           'All thyng þat euer God thought
              To make, all were at onys wroght;
           That is to say, at the begynnyng
           That he before sawe all thyng
           And oon comaundemente made he   1855
           All þat was or shall be.
           But I say not þat they were
           In the lymmes þat þey now are:
           All thyng were in hem spered
           Vntyll they came into þis worlde;   1860
           Thenne he shapes here figure
           Euerychon after here nature.
           But for he comaunded all to be
f. 29ᵛ   At ones, forsothe, say we
           That at ones made he all thynge   1865
           Of his worde and his biddyng.'

Qo. 34ᵃ   'May they haue ony excusyng   (35)
           That of God ne wote noothyng?'
           'They that ne knowe not here
              Ne hym to knowe wyl not lere,   1870
           At the day of dome shall he
           Knowe hem for noon of his meyne;

1842 sonde] onde S, honde P.   1847 sothely] forþi SP.   1855 And] Att
S.   1858 lymmes] lykenesse P;   þey now] thou P.   1859 spered]
sprede S.   1861 he shapes] they shappid P.   1866 and his biddyng] at his
begynnyng P.   1869 that] add of God P.

Siþen þe flesshe is of þe erthes kynde
And blood of water, as we fynde,   2890
Boþe þei beþ colde of kinde to fonde;
But soule, þat is of Goddis sonde,
He oughte to be clene and faire
And is hote of kinde of aire.   f. 43ᵛ
þat soule wonneþ in þe blood   2895
And hetiþ it and doth it good;
And þe hete of þe blood, truly,
Norissheþ alle þe lymes of þe body.'

Ca.° xxxiiij°   'Weren soules ymade for ay   (34)
At þe firste or day be day?'
                         2900
'Al þing þat God þoghte to make,
Al at oones þei weren ishape;
þat is to seie, at þe biginning
He sawe at oones al thyng
And at oone comaundement [made] he   2905
Al þat was and euere shal be.
But I seie not þat þei ware
In þe liknesse þat þei now are:
Alle þinges weren in him sperd
Til þei come into þis midlerd;   2910
þanne he shapeþ her figure
Eche after her nature.
But for he comaunded al for to be
Al at oones, for þat seie we
þat al at oones he made al þing   2915
Of his worde at þe biginning.'

Ca.° xxxv°   'Mow þei haue any excusing   (35)
þat of God woot noþing?'
        'Thei þat of God knowe noght here
Ne him to knowe wole not lere,   2920
At þe day of dome shal [he]
Knowe hem for none of his meine;

2895 þat] þat þe L.   2905 oone] *preceded by* one *marked for deletion* L;   made]
om. L.   2921 he] *om.* L.

And they þat trowe and wil not do
The werke þat falleþ hem vnto,
That sympely hem vnderstonde   1875
As sympyll men that ar in londe,
Ȝyf they be dampned therfore,
Turmented shul they not be therfore;
And þey that have goode knowlechyng
Of God and do not his biddyng,   1880
Fro pyne they may not hem defende
But they here hem amende.'

Qo. 35ᵃ   'Shall a man ouȝt elles do   (36)
               But that God comaundeth hym to?'
                  'God hathe kyndely made man   1885
                  To serue hym in all þat he can
               And his comaundement to doo
               And the deuel to hate alsoo;
               And as we lordshipp woll craue
               Of all thyng and here seruyse woll have,   1890
               So woll God in all wyse
               Aske and haue oure seruyse,
               That we trowe on hym stedfastly
               And worshipp hym with ooure body
               And love hym aboue all thyng,   1895
               For we are alle of his makyng.'

Qo. 36ᵃ   'How many worldis are of all   (37)
               And how do men hem call?'
f. 30ʳ   'Gostly worldis are there twoo
                  And two bodely also: 1900
               That oon gostly heuen is,
               There aungelis are and all blisse
               And the goode generacion
               Of Adam þat shall after come;
               That other goostly then is hell,   1905
               There the deueles in pyne dwelle.
               The twoo bodely is in ooure sight,

1877 therfore] therfore to B.   1878 therfore] tofore S.   1882 here] rather
P.   1890 here] other P.   1901 heuen is] is hevyn ywis P.   1904 þat . . .
come] shall hereafter wonne SP.   1906 pyne] om. P.

And þo þat leuen and wole not do
þe werkes þat hem fallen to,
þat simpely hem vnderstonde   2925
As simple men þat ben in londe,
If þei dampned shal be þerfore,   f. 44^r
Turmentid shul þei not be sore;
And þei þat haue good knowing
Of God and do not his bidding,   2930
þei mowen not fro peine hem defende
But if þei hem here amende.'

Ca.° xxxvj°   'Shal a man oght elles do   (36)
               But þat God comaundiþ him to?'
                  'God haþ kindely made man   2935
                  To serue him in þat he can
               And his comaundement forto doo
               And þe deuel tisement to hate also;
               And as [w]e lordship wole craue
               Of al þing and he[r] seruice haue, 2940
               Also God wole in al wise
               Haue of vs seruise
               And bileue on him stedfastly
               And worshipe him principally
               And loue him ouer al þing,   2945
               For we ben of his makyng.'

Ca.° xxxvij°   'Hou many worldes ben of alle   (37)
               And how doþ men now hem calle?'
                  'Goostly worldes þere ben two
                  And two bodily also: 2950
               Goostly heuene oone is, iwis,
               þere aungels ben ful of blis
               And þere þat þe good generacioun
               Of Adam herafter shal woun;
               þat oþer goostly þanne is helle,   2955
               Where þat deuels yn dwelle,
               þe two bodily ben in oure sight,

2933-4] *supplied in right margin* L.   2939 we] þe L.   2940 her] he L.

As sonne and moone, day and nyght,
And other thynges þat we see
That vs yeues here claryte;   1910
That oþer there vs not wante:
Men may that riȝt feele with hande,
As the erthe, that all takes,
And ooure wombe, þat nought forsakes.
And fro þe bodyly that are   1915
Vnto the gostely for to fare,
Whether hit be lowe or hye,
Is but a twynkelyng of an eye.’

Qo. 37ᵃ   ‘*Is God of grete yeldyng to tho*   (38)
            That right in his seruyse here goo?’   1920
            ‘In all the worlde ys no man
            That may thynke ne telle can
            The goode ne the honoure in many wyse
            That God yeues man for his seruyse
            That in hym trowes and in his might   1925
            And agayn synne is redy to fight.
            And his comaundementes has he:

            “Do goode and lete the euel be.”

            His Soone shall he sente here downe
            To dye for mannys saluacion: 1930
            They that his seruyse have in mynde,
            In his blisse they shall hit fynde,
            For he shall hem worshipp more
f. 30ᵛ   Thanne ony aungell that is þore.’

Qo. 38ᵃ   ‘*The folke that in the tyme shal be*   (39) 1935
            Of Goddes Sone whenne comen is he
            And after, shall they comenly
            Trowe in hym stedfastly?’
                ‘All shall they here trowthe in hym ley—
                His owne folke that is to say—   1940

1911 there] þar S, dar P;   vs not] not of vs P.   1912] For men not fele hit in
hande P.   1923 The . . . honoure] That God the honourith P.   1924 That
God yeves] And God ioyeth P.   1926] And his commawndementis dothe aright P.

As sunne and mone, day and night,
And oþer þinges þat we se
þat ȝeueþ to vs her clerte;   2960
Of þe toþer þar vs not wante
For men mowe fele it with her hande,
As þe erþe, þat al takith,   f. 44ᵛ
Oure dede bodies not forsakith.
And fro þe bodily þat are   2965
To þe goostly forto fare,
Wheþer it be lowe or hie,
It is but a twincling of an yȝe.'

Ca.° xxxviij°   'Is God of greet ȝelding to tho   (38)
                 þat in his seruise here aright go?'   2970
                    'In al þe world is no man
                    þat may þenke ne telle can
                 þe good and þe honour in any wise
                 þat God ȝeueþ to man for his seruice
                 þat bileueþ on him and his might   2975
                 And hise comaundementȝ kepiþ aright.
                 And a short comaundement haþ he
                 Comaunded bothe to þee and me:
                 To doo þe good þat we may
                 And leue yvel night and day.   2980
                 His Sone he shal here sende adoun
                 To die for manis saluacioun
                 And þo þat seruice haue [in] mynde,
                 In his blisse þei sholen it fynde,
                 For he shal worshipe hem more   2985
                 þan any aungel þat is thore.'

Ca.° xxxix°   'Þe peple þat in þat time shal be   (39)
                 Of Goddes Sone whanne comen is he,
                 [And] shullen þei [after] comounly
                 Bileue in him al stedfastly?'   2990
                    'Alle þei shullen in him her truþe leie—
                    His owne peple, þat is to seie—

1927] A short commawndement hathe he P.   1934 ony aungell] alle the angelis P.

2983 in] om. L.   2989 And . . . after] from table 1089, þan . . . alle L.

But all shull they gederid be
Of ferre speche and of fer contre;
But they shull not euerychone
Have comaundement after oon.
The comaundement, as men shall se,   1945
Of Goddis Soone shall ay oon be;
After hym his ministres twelve
Shall commaunde the folke theyreselue;
But they that come after tho
That instede of mynestres shall goo,   1950
They shal wel biholde and fynde
The febelnesse of mannes kynde,
And lighter comaundement for that skyll
Shall þey make the folke vntyll.
And euery nacyon shall wene þat he   1955
Be better then ony other be,
But of theym shall at þe fyne
Be as of a grete gardyn
There many trees inne stonde
And all be they frute berande: 1960
The tre þat beste frute beres—
Be they appeles or be þey peres—
And plenteuouseest of beryng
And beste of sauour in etyng,
That tre shall þe gardyner   1965
Moste loue and serue in tyme of yeere.
Also they that shal beste beleue
In Goddis Sone and here herte hym yeue
And best shall here in erthe do,

<table>
<tr><td>f. 31^r</td></tr>
</table>

f. 31ʳ   Whenne tyme comes therevnto,   1970
They shull moste worshipped be
In heuen bifore the Trinite.'

Qo. 39ᵃ   'What comaundement, by thy leue,   (40)
              Shall Goddis Sone his folke yeue?'
                   'Hit shall be loue and abstinence   1975
                   And charite and patience

    1942 ferre . . . fer] sere . . . sere S, dyuers . . . dyuers P.   1957 shall] shall be
P.   1958 Be as of] As dothe by P.   1961 beste] the furst P.
1964 etyng] tastyng P.

Alle þei sholen ygadred be
Of diuerse speche in diuers cuntre;
But þei shullen not euerichone   2995
Haue comaundementȝ after oone.
þe comaundement, as men sholen see,   f. 45ʳ
Of Goddis Sone þanne shal it be;
After him his ministres twelue
Shullen comaunde þe peple þe[m]selue;   3000
But þei þat come aftir tho
þat sholen instede of ministris go,
þey shullen wel biholde and fynde
þe feblenesse of mankynde,
And liþer comaundement for þat skile   3005
þei sholen make þe peple vntile.
And euery nacioun shal wene þat he
Is bettir þan any oþirs be,
But of hem shal be a fyn
As men done bi a greet gardyn   3010
þat many trees be ynne stonding
And alle þei ben fruit bering:
þe tree þat best fruit bers—
Be þei applin, be þei pers—
And most plentevous of bering   3015
And of best sauour in eting,
þat tre shal þe gardenere
Moost loue and serue in time of ȝere.

Also þei sholen most iworshipped be
In heuene bifore þe Trinite.'   3020

Ca.° xl°   '*What comaundement, bi þi leue,*   (40)
           Shal Goddis Sone his peple ȝeue?'
           'It shal be loue and abstinence
           And charite and pacience

3000 þemselue] þe selue L.

And þat no man other do
That he wolde not were don hym to.
God hymselfe, for mannes love,
Shall sende his Sone from aboue   1980
And shall suffere abstinence
And sufferaunce and pacience
And bitter dethe at the laste
His folke oute of pyne [to] caste;
And whoso beholdes these foure thynges,   1985
All godenes oute of them sprynges,
For he þat goode loue hathe in God
Loue in himselue is not alode;
And he þat haueth abstinence
And charite and patience   1990
And hathe þe loue of God withall,
At the laste he yelde hit shall.'

Qo. 40ᵃ   'The blisfullest thyng, after þy witte,   (41)
                   And dyngnyest and fayreste, whyche is hit?'
                        'Soule, þere [hit] is goode, of man,   1995
                          Of all thyng þat I can,
                   Hit is þe fayreste þynge þat may be;
                   For brighter þenne þe sonne is he,
                   And dygnyere thynge is ther nought
                   Of all þat God in erthe hathe wrought;   2000
                   For of Goddis brethe hit cam,
                   When God brethed vpon Adam;
                   Therfore aungeles are sente þerto
                   To kepe here in all þat they may do.
f. 31ᵛ   Also the blisfullest hit is   2005
                   For hit is ordeyned to the blisse
                   There neuer ende shall be
                   Of ioye, of blisse, of game, and gle;
                   And God yafe hit all thynge
                   To serue man his blessyng;   2010
                   Thenne is hit blesfullest in tho
                   And dignieste and fayrest also.'

    1984 to] *from* SP, *om*. B.   1988 Loue] Lyfe P;   alode] so gode P.   1995 hit]
from SP, *om*. B.   2001 brethe] honde P.   2002 brethed] bleew SP.
2003 sente] set P.   2007 There . . . ende] For neuer ende ther P.   2009 hit] to SP.

And þat no man to oþir do 3025
þat he wolde [not] were idone him to.
God himself, ffor mannes loue,
Shal sende his Sone fro aboue
And here shal suffre abstinence
And eke haue charite and pacience 3030
And bitter deth atte laste f. 45ᵛ
His peple out of peine to haste;
And whoso biholdeþ þese iiij þinges,
Al goodnesse out of him springes,
For he þat good loue haþ in God, 3035
Loue on himself is not al od;
And he þat haþ pacience
And charite and abstinence
And haþ þe loue of God wiþal,
At þe laste to God he ȝelde shal.' 3040

Ca.° xljº   *þe blisfullest þing, bi þi witt,* (41)
      And worþieste [and fairest], which is it?'
     'Soule, þere it is good, of man,
      Of al þing þat I reken can,
It is þe fairest þat may be; 3045
Brighter þan the sunne is she,
And worþier þing is þer noght
Of al þat God in erþe haue wroght;
For of Goddes sonde it cam,
Whan God blewe on Adam; 3050
For aungels ben putte þerto
To kepe hir in al þei mowen do.
Also þe blisfullest þing it is
For it is ordeyned to þat blis
þer neuere ende shal be 3055
Of ioye and blis, game and glee;
And God ȝaf to al þing
For to serue man his blessing;
Thanne is þis þe blisfullest þing
þat is here in erþe woning.' 3060

3026 not] *om.* L;   to] to be L.   3042 and fairest] *from table* 1094, *om.* L.

Qo. 41ᵃ   'The fouleste and the perelousest thyng to see   (42)
                     And moste waryed, which may hit be?'
                              'Wykked soule of man, ywysse,   2015
                              Is the fouleste thyng þat is.
                     Soo hardy herted man is noon,
                     And he a wyked soule sawe oon
                     In the right lykenesse of hit,
                     That he ne sholde lese his witte.   2020
                     Also hit is perilose
                     For hit gothe to a vylen howse
                     There perell is and moche woo
                     There hit neuer shall come froo.
                     The moste waryed is hit ay   2025
                     [For] Goddes Sone on domesday
                     Byfore aungeles all thore
                     Shall wary hit for euermore;
                     And of the pyne that hit shall to
                     Angels and archangels also   2030
                     Shall have bothe ioye and blisse
                     For þat hit punyshed is.'

Qo. 42ᵃ   'The goode soules, shall they ought   (43)
                     For wyke haue dolour and thought?'
                              'The goode soules, whenne þe wykkyd spylle, 2035
                              Shall be alle of Goddis wille;
                     An whenne they the dome haue sene
                     Of hem þat ageynes God haue bene—
                     That they ar dampned from Goddis face—
                     That shall be here solace.   2040
f. 32ʳ   For þe dome shall be rightwosse
                     That shall be youe vnto his enemyouse;
                     And whenne þey are in all here pyne
                     Amonge other of helle hyne,
                     The goode soule blithe shal be   2045
                     In here pyne hem on to se
                     As we haue game to beholde
                     The ffissh to swhymme in water colde.'

2018 sawe] haue P.   2026 For] from SP, Byfore B.   2032 punyshed is]
hathe done amysse P.   2038 þat ageynes God] then ageyne P.   2039 from]
before P.

þe foulest and þe perilousest þing to see (42)
And most acursed, what may þat be?'
    'Wicked soule of man, ywis,
      Is þe foulest þing þat is.
So harde hertid man is þer noon, 3065 f. 46^r
And he loked a wicked soule [on]
In þe right liknesse of it,
þat he ne shulde lese his wit.
Also it is perilous
For it goþ to a vilens hous 3070
Ful of perelles and miche wo
þere þat it shal neuere come fro.
And þe moost cursedist þing is ay
For Goddis Sone at domesday
Bifore alle hise aungels þore 3075
Schal acorse it for eueremore;
And of þe peine þat it shal to
Aungels and archaungels also
Shullen haue boþe ioye and blis
For þat it haþ idone amys.' 3080

3066 on] *om.* L.

Qo. 43ᵃ   ['*Wheþer is better, so God the saue—*   (44)
                   Heele or seekenes for to haue?']   2050
                        'Hele of soule is goode to wynne
                           To kepe hit oute of dedely synne;
                   For whenne hit is hole and fayre,
                   Of heven blisse hit shall be heyre
                   And his dwellyng by God shall be   2055
                   For his hele and his bonte.
                   Yif thow haddes now a knyght
                   That were stronge to stande in fight
                   And were holden bolde and hardy,
                   Hym þow woldest holde the by   2060
                   And þow shuldest into fight;
                   And were he seke and oute of myght,
                   Noughwhere thow woldest hym lede
                   But þereas þow shulde stonde in drede.
                   Also hit is of soules hele: 2065
                   God woll not with soule deele
                   That febyll is and seke in synne
                   But yf he woll therof blynne.
                   Aneniste the helthe of body
                   To goode men say I sekerly,   2070
                   Is better hoole then seke to be
                   For in goodenesse his heele vseth he;
                   And they that lyue in synne and woo,
                   Sekenesse is beste vnto tho:
                   For the pyne of here sekenesse   2075
                   They shall synne ȝit the lesse
f. 32ᵛ   And withdrawe hem þerfro
                   That in heele sholde not do soo.'

Qo. 44ᵃ   '*What pouer is hit, þat wolde I lere,*   (45)
                   That God hathe yeuen to soule here?'   2080
                        'God hathe yeuen euery soule vnto
                           A kyngdome for to gete also

_____

    2049–50] *from* S, Hele of soule is goode to wynne / To kepe hit oute of dedely synne
B.   2058 to stande] and stoute P.   2061 into] stonde in P.   2062 oute
of] of no P.   2063 Noughwhere] *om.* P.   2064] þere þe shulde bistand drede
S, Ther he shulde bestadde withoute drede P.   2070 I] hit P;   sekerly] witterly
SP.   2078] *om.* P.   2082 gete] ȝeme SP.

That, yf he kepe hit aright,
His kynges sete shall be dight
Byfore God in heven blisse,   2085
And God shall say to hym this:
"Come, my dere sone, to me:
The kyngedome tha I betaught the
Hast þow soo kepte in all thynge
That þow art worthy to be a kynge;   2090
Therfore þow shalt crouned be
Byfore my Faderes mageste."
The soule for the kynge take I,
And for the kyngedom þe body;
And the comaundement of euery goode kynge   2095
In his londe shulde be doo withoute gaynsayynge.
Therfore, whatsoo the soule will,
The body shulde hit do with skyll;
And but the body do also
As the soule hym redes to do,   2100
Bothe togeder thenne shall be caste
Into the fuyre at the laste.'

Qo. 45ᵃ   'Sith Goddis Sone, that to erthe is sente,   (46)
               Is agayn to heuen wente,
               Shall ony astromyour leue here   2105
               In this worlde þe folke to lere?'
                  'Whenne God so vp shall stye
                  Vnto his Fatheres companye,
               His xij minystres leue he shall
               That in erthe hym walked withall.   2110
               A holy howse amonge hem all
               Shull they make þat they shall calle
               Goddes house, and soo shall hit be   f. 33ʳ
               For theyreinne shall goode men mowe se.
               After them shall other come also   2115
               That there comaundemente shall doo
               A while whil hit laste may,

2083 kepe] helpe P.   2088 betaught] behight P.   2096 withoute gayn-
sayynge] me þinke SP.   2102 fuyre] add of hell SP.   2107 God] Goddis Sone
P.   2110 walked] werke P.   2114 goode men] men God SP;   mowe] now
P.   2115 After] of P.

And they shall from day to day
Wexe riche and of grete might;
And for here richesse anone right   2120
The lawe that Goddes Soone hem lefte
And his xij mynistres efte
Febely thenne shull they holde,
But for richesse shall all be solde;
And God shall destroye them tho   2125
For here synne and for here woo.
And they shull kunne grete maistry
Of the arte of astronomye,
And wyse men shull they holden be;
But coueytyse shall shende here gle.'   2130

Qo. 46ª   'Goddes house þat shal be tolde,   (47)
              Whoo shall hit kepe and haue in holde?'
                 'Forsothe Goddis Soone hymselfe
                 Shall amonge his disciples xijᵉ
              Comaunde oon to kepe right,   2135
              And stone of stones shall he hight:
              He shall hit kepe þat nought shall wante;
              Sythen shall hit goo from hand to hand.
              But after the tyme þat Goddis Sone
              Is comen into erthe for to wone,   2140
              A thowsand yeere then shall begynne
              In the worlde to sprynge synne
              Agaynes God and his lore
              And shall be worse thenne byfore.
              After that shall men se   2145
              Two grete douues shall borne be
              That Goddes lawe forther shall
              And mistrowthe destroye all:
f. 33ᵛ   That oon douue shall be callid mendere
              And þat other amonaster.   2150
              In the worlde þey shal be bolde
              And pore men they shall be tolde.

2120 here] thy P.   2127 they] then P;   kunne] comme P.   2135 kepe]
kepe hit P.   2139 þat] of P.   2146 douues] dowues S, dowuys P.
2148 mistrowthe] mynestris P.   2150 amonaster] A monaster B, amonester S, a
mynestrere P.

The goode shall loue hem inwardly;
The wyked shall drede hem wonderly
And worshipp hem with drede and sawe   2155
For they shall haue of hem grete awe.
Campyons þey shall be stronge
In faythe to holde and fordo wronge:
Goode kepers shall they be
Of Goddis house and his mayne.'   2160

Qo. 47ᵃ   *'That no gode dothe but holdeth hym inne,*   (48)
              Whether doth he—almesse or synne?'
                  'He þat dothe no goode ne euyll dedes,
                  The lif of bestes right he ledes;
              And that dose euel, he dothe synne;   2165
              And he þat of goode woll blynne
              And dothe not there he may hit do,
              He dothe euel and synne also.
              For yf a man were honger bestad
              And gladly wolde of mete be fedde   2170
              And he by an orcheyarde go
              And sethe mekell froyte thereinne therto
              And dies for defaute of mete
              And of the froyte woll not ete,
              He dothe evill and amysse   2175
              For his owne defaute hit is.'

Qo. 48ᵃ   *'Lordshipp, whether shall hit be—*   (49)
              Stoughte or stourne or of þyte?'
                  'Lordship is of Goddis will
                  Lawe and right to fulfill;   2180
              And but menne might iustyse fynde,
              Men shulde be of fysshes kynde:
              The stronge shulde þe ffebull ete
              And the grete the smale þat they might gete.
              And lordshipp aughte stowte to be   2185 f. 34ʳ
              And stalworthe and of powste,

2154 wonderly] vttrely P.   2157 T *begins again.*   2158 In] The TP.
2164 lif . . . right] right life best T.   2165 synne] noo synne BS.   2170 fedde]
stadde P.   2171 go] gange TSP.   2172] There he sees mekull frute hange
TSP.   2178 or (1)] and T.   2179 of] *om.* TSP.   2180 right] iustice
TP.   2181 menne] right T.

With right and skyll the wykked to deme,
And pese amonge the folke to yeme.
A lytel Goddes Sone byforne
A kyng shall in erthe be borne: 2190
He shall be profete or he dye
And he shall say in his prophecie,
"Blessed be they God vnto
That dome and rightwosnesse shal do."
Ʒif a wykked man be reynt   2195
And of wykkednesse be ateynte,
The lorde may deme hym of his right
And foryeve hym of his might;
But yf he eftesoonis do amys,
Of the dome worthy he is.'   2200

'Shall any man gode do   (50)
His kyn and his frendes vnto?'
'Iff thy kynne goode men wolde be
And they haue grete nede to the
And haue forloren by myschaunce   2205
The goode that shulde hem avaunce,
Thow shalte hem helpe and goode hem do
And counsell hem and rede hem also.
If they be of wykked lyf,
Be hit man, be hit wyff,   2210
And they be in wrecchednesse
Thorowe here owne wykkednesse—
Also some that are of euel mode,
He dothe ille to hym þat dothe hym goode:
That men dothe all hit is lorn   2215
In a purse that is totorne.
What helpes wax for to take
And a cerge therof to make
And byfore a man hit light
That is blynde and hathe noo sight?   2220

2195 reynt] rent S, reyned P, arayned T.   2201–2 *q. no. om.* B.
2203 goode] *repeated* P;   wolde] *om.* TP.   2204 grete] ony T;   grete nede to]
defaute of P.   2206 The goode that] Thenne thi goode T.   2211/12 wrec-
chednesse/wykkednesse] *reversed* P.   2214 ille to hym] amys T, yll S, euyll P;
hym (2)] hem TS, no P.   2215 men . . . is] mony is all P;   all hit is] to þem is alle

Ca.° xliij° 'Shal any man good do   (50)
      Hise kyn and his frendes to?'
      'Iff þi kyn good men be
      And þei haue nede to þee
      And haue forlorne þorgh mischaunce 3085
      þe good þat shulde hem avaunce,
      þou shalt hem helpe and good [do]
      And counseile hem and reede also.
      If þei be of wicked lyf,
      Be it man, be it wyf,   3090
      And þei be in wickednesse
      þorgh her owne wrecchidnesse—
      And somme þat ben of yuel mood,
      þei done hem yuel þat done hem good:
      þat men done al is ylorne   3095
      In a purs þat is totorne.
      What helpeþ it wexe to take
      And a tapre þerof make
      And bifore a man it light   f. 46ᵛ
      þat is blinde and haþ no sight? 3100

T.   2216 In] As mony put in T, That is in P. 2218 cerge] candill T, taper
P; to] do P.

 3087 do] *om.* L.

f. 34ᵛ

To suche a man helpes nought
The light that is byfore hym brought:
Also hit is lorne for to shewe
Any goodnes byfore a shrewe.'

Qo. 49ᵃ

'Now I praye the to telle me: (51) 2225
Gentilnesse, what hit may be.'
　'Gentrye thenne is power
　　And richesse that a man hase here
Of londe, of rente, and of ffee,
And comyn is of antiquite;   2230
And who that hathe for to dispende
For moste gentyll is he kende.
And somme are riche men of goode
And are chorles kynde of bloode:
A riche man m[en] calle hym oon   2235
But gentilman is he noon.
And he þat riche is wonderly
And a nobil man of his body,
Curteys and wyse and holden fre,
A grete gentilman is he.   2240
And though he be a pore man
And amonge men bere hym can
As of norture in boure and halle,
A gentilman men shall hym calle.
And alle of pore men we cam,   2245
As of Eue and Adam.'

Qo. 50ᵃ

'How may hit be colde euery yeere   (52)
Whenne þe weder is fayre and clere?'
　'The [weder], whenne that hit is fayre,
　　The colde comes downe from þe eyre   2250
And into the erthe he dryues þore
The heete þat hette the erthe byfore;
And soo is the heete all away—
On wynters dayes, that is to say.
And whenne the weder ys troubeled, thykke,   2255

2231 who . . . for] that in coste has T, in costis to P.　　2233 somme] *om.* P.
2234 chorles] clerkis P.　　　　　　2235 men] *from* SP, may B, men may T.

> To suche a man helpiþ it noght
> þat light bifore him be broght:
> Also it is lorn forto shewe
> Any goodnesse to a shrewe.'

Ca.º xliiijº

'Now I preie þat þou telle me: (51) 3105
Gentilnesse, what may it be?'
>   'Gentilnesse þanne is powere
>   And richesse þat a man haþ here
>   Of londes, of rentis, and of fee,
>   And is ycome out of antiquite;   3110
>   And in coostes haþ to defende
>   þat him of malys wolde shende.
>   And some ben riche men of good
>   And ben cherles bi kynde of blood:
>   A riche man men clepen hym oon   3115
>   But gentilman is he noon.
>   And he þat is riche wondirly
>   And noble man of his body,
>   Curteis and wijs and holden fre,
>   A ful greet gentilman is he.   3120
>   And þogh he be a pore man,
>   And he among men hym bere can
>   As of norture in boure and halle,
>   A gentilman men shal him calle;
>   For of pouer men alle we cam,   3125
>   As of Eue and oure fader Adam.'

Ca.º xlvº

'How may it be colde eche ȝere   (52)
Whanne þe weder is faire and clere?'
>   'The wedre, whanne it is fair,
>   þe colde comeþ adoun fro þe air   3130
>   And in to þe erthe he driueþ thore
>   þe hete þat hett þe erþe bifore;
>   And so is þe hete al away   f. 47ʳ
>   On winter daies, as I the say.
>   And whanne þe wedre is troubled right,   3135

2237 wonderly] worthely P.   2249 weder] *from* STP, *om.* B.   2250 colde]
kilthe T.   2252 hette] he hete T.   2255 whenne] *om.* P; thykke] right P.

The colde may not downe light;
And the sonne of his might

Chaufis þe eyre vppon þe night.
So may hit here be warme tolde
And summetyme in fayre weder colde.'   2260

Qo. 52ᵃ   'May a man by oony throwe   (53)
              The goode men fro þe wykked knowe?'
                  'Gode men hemselfe kythe
                  For of vysege ar they blythe
              And here eyen ar ful bright   2265
              And louely they are of sight
              For the goode lyf þat they are inne
              And be sekyr oute of synne;
              And for they lyue so chastely,
              Swhete wordis haue they comenly.   2270
              The wyked of euyll will þey be
              And louryng ar they on to see:
              Of stabulnesse haue þey noothyng;
              Oute of mesure is here laughyng;
              Smerte goyng they haue also   2275
              And they are full selden in roo;
              And the wykkidnesse of her herte
              In worde in werke they shewe as smerte.'

Qo. 53ᵃ   'The trouthe þat was herbyfore   (54)
              Of false ydoles that there woore,   2280
              Shall hit euer reysed be
              Soo sterke as was in tyme of me?'
                  'Chylder þat shall come of the,
                  In God of heuen here truthe shal be
              And here childer yit also;   2285
              But they that shall come of hem tho
              Shull turne vnto þe wykked lawe
              That was before the olde dawe.
              And they shall make a cite:
              Thereinne shall a toure be   2290

   2256 colde] kilthe T.   2258 eyre] erthe TP;   þe night] hight P.   2261 by
oony throwe] ought vmbithrowe T.   2264 vysege] vsage P.   2265 ar ful] ar
than T, þai ar S, that are so clere P.   2272 louryng] lourid T, lewde P.

þe colde may not adoun light;
And þe sunne of his mighte
Chaufeþ þe erthe vpon þe nighte.
So may it be here warme ytolde
And somtime in faire wedir colde.'   3140

Ca.º xlvjº   'May a man oght be any þrowe   (53)
                    þe good men fro þe wicked knowe?'
                      'Gode men hemsilf kithe
                        þat of visage ben blithe
                    And her ey3en þat ben bright,
                    And louely þei ben of sight   3145
                    For þe good lyf þat þei ben ynne;
                    And þei ben out of deedly synne;
                    And for þei lyue so chastly,
                    Swete wordes þei haue comounly.   3150
                    þe wicked of yuel wille þei be
                    And lourdeins one to see:
                    Of stablenesse haue þei noþing;
                    Out of mesure is her leighing;
                    Smert going þei haue also   3155
                    And miche yuel hapte to do;
                    And þe wickednesse of her herte
                    In werke and worde þei shewe smerte.'

Ca.º xlvijº   þe truþe þat was here bifore   (54)
                    Of false mawmetis þat þer wore,
                    So stronge as was in time of me   3160
                    Shal it euere arered be?'
                      'Children þat shal come of þe,
                        In God of heue[n] her truþe shal be
                    And her children 3it also;
                    But þilke þat shal come of hem þo   3165
                    Shal torne into wicked lawe
                    þat was tofore bi olde dawe.   f. 47ᵛ
                    And þei sholen make a citee
                    And þerynne shal a tour be;   3170

2274 laughyng] lechinge T, lackynge S, lachyng P.   2276 in roo] onwoo T.

3164 heuen] heue L.

And that toure shall haue thore
Foure and fourty stagis bifore;

f. 35ᵛ

And þereinne shall regne a kyng
Of all þe worlde moste maysterlyng.
And an ymage he shall do dight   2295
After his fader and lyke hym right,
And all folke shall he make go to
That ymage worship for to do.'

Qo. 54ᵃ

'Why was hit not Goddis will   (55)
That man leved a wyke with oon fill?'   2300
        'Honger oon of the paynes is
        For synne that Adam dyd amis.
And man was made so, yf he wolde,
That he euer lyue sholde
Withoute trauayle and withoute woo;   2305
But that he was fallen fro
Might he nought agayn com to
Withoute trauel and wo also,
And trauel sholde hym nought lyst
But yf he hadde hunger and thriste.   2310
And honger and thriste, colde and hete,
[And] oþer paynes men with mete,
Sholde nothyng man þerof have wyste
Hadde þe man nought synned furste.
And with honger and thriste may   2315
Glotony be don all away;
And for to meve in mannis thought
The gloteny that Adam wrought
And þat synne to wassh away
Kyndely man hongers euery day.'   2320

'The ryche men, dye they alsoo   (56)
Lightly as þe poore men doo?'
        'Ryche and poore that men fynde,
        Alle made God hem of oon kynde.
Otherwhile waxith the pore riche   2325

2292 stagis] stakis P.   2300 man] *inserted above line* B.   2311 colde and
hete] kelith and hetyth P.   2312 And] *from* P, Noon B, No T, Ne S;   men] that
men P;   mete] metith P.   2318] *om.* P.   2321-2 *q. no. om.* B.

And in þat tour he shal haue
Xliiij stages his body to saue.
And þerynne shal regne a king
And al þe world maistiryng;
And an ymage he shal do dight   3175
After þe liknesse of his fadres sight,
And al þe folke he shal make go to
þat ymage worshipe forto doo.'

Ca.° xlviij°   'Whi was it not Goddes wille   (55)
    þat a man might not lyue a weke with a fille?'   3180
      'Hvnger oon of þe peynes it is
      For synne þat Adam dide amis.
And man was made so, if he wolde,
þat he euere lyue sholde
Wiþouten traueile, wiþouten woo;   3185
But þat he was ifalle þerfro
Mighte he not come aȝen þerto
Withoute woo and trauaile also,
And traueile he shulde not list
But if he hadde hunger and þrist.   3190
And hunger and þrist, coolde and hete,
And oþer peines þat me wiþ mete,
Man shulde noþing þerof haue wist
Nad Adam synned first.
And wiþ hunger and þrist may   3195
þe synne of glotonye be done away;
And forto meue in manis þoght
þe glotonye þat Adam wroght
And þat synne to wasshe away
Kindly him hungreþ euery day.'   3200

Ca.° xlix°   'Deieþ the riche man also   (56)   f. 48ʳ
    As oþre pore men here do?'
      'Riche and pore þat men fynde,
      God made hem alle of kinde.
Somtime wexeþ the pore riche   3205

3174] *repeated with* maistering *for* maistiryng L.

f. 36ʳ

And the riche pore euen aliche:
Vp and downe catel is brought
But kynde of man chaunges nought.
Honger, thruste, hote, and colde,
Ioye and sorow manyfolde,   2330
Slepe, wake, ete, and drynke,
And many maner other þynge,
These have þe poore men as well
As riche, and of kynde euerydell;
But þe poore, by reason,   2335
Are of strenger complexion
Thanne þe riche, that woll hem fede,
That dothe here trauel and here dede.
But whenne hit comes to the deede,
Than is there non other rede   2340
But bothe alyche shall they fare,
Riche and poore, whatso they are.'

Qo. 56ᵃ

'*Shall man deme the ryche also*   (57)
As men the poore doo?'
        'Men shall þe ryche deme with right   2345
        Sterker then any poore wight;
And euer þe richer tha he be,
And he misdo ayens þe,
The moore penaunce shall he bere—
Sholde noo richesse with right hym were.   2350
And yf men deme þe riche soore,
The poore shall hem drede þe more;
But for þe pore mannys dede
Hathe þe riche man nothing drede.
And also God rewarde ne can   2355
The riche more þanne þe poore man,
And demes bothe rightwosly
After þat they are worthy:
Also sholde men deme þe queke,
Riche and poore, all inlyke.'   2360

2326 euen aliche] and wriche T, and bryche SP.   2335 by] bi grete T.
2336 strenger] starker TSP.   2337 fede] fynde P.   2338 dede] kynde P.
2346 Sterker] More hard P.   2357 bothe] More T.   2360 inlyke] is lycke P.

And þe riche pore, sikerliche:
Vp and doun catel is broght
But kinde of man chaungeþ noght.
Hunger and þrist, hete and colde,
Ioye and sorwe manyfold,   3210
Slepe and wake, ete and drinke,
And many kynnes oþer þinke,
þis haþ the pore men as wel
As þe riche, and of kinde euerydel;
But þe pouere, bi resoun,   3215
Beþ of strenger complexioun
þan þe riche, þat hem wel fede,
þat done no trauaile ne daies dede.
But whan to hem come is deth
And shullen leue vp wynde and breeþ,   3220
Boþe yliche sholen þei fare,
Riche and pore, whatso þei are.'

Ca.° l°   'Shullen men deme þe riche also   (57)
                   As men þe pouere here do?'
                      'Men shullen þe riche deme with right   3225
                      More harder þan any pore wight;
                   And euer þe richer þat he be,
                   And he misdo, as I seie the,
                   þe more penaunce shulde he bere—
                   þere shulde no ricchesse with right him were. 3230
                   And if men deme þe riche sore,
                   þe pouere shal drede miche þe more;
                   But for þe pouere mannes dede
                   þe riche man haþ no drede.
                   And as God not rewarde can   3235 f. 48ᵛ
                   þe riche more þan þe pouere man,
                   He demeth boþe rightwisly
                   After þat þei ben worþi;
                   þerfore shulde men deme þe quike,
                   Riche and pouere, alle ylike.'   3240

[*'May þe wicked als wele for ay*   (58)
Haue Goddes love as þe goode may?']

f. 36ᵛ   'A wyked man þat hathe don synne
                         And of wikkednesse woll blynne
And crye mercy and do no more,   2365
He shall with God be hadde in oore.
The good are Goddes where the go;
The wyked ar fallon hym fro.
Yif a man haue a thynge forloren
That he loued well byforne   2370
And he may hit after fynde,
That shall be hym more in mynde
And more sholde he therof be gladde
Thenne of all that other that he hadde.
By man fares God also: 2375
Yif man ayenste hym misdo
And hit dedely synne be,
Fer from God fallyn is he;
But if he wol mercy craue,
Sekerly he shall hit haue,   2380
For therof is God full fayne
And then fyndes he hym agayn
And of his fyndyng is he blithe
And forthy grete loue he woll hym kythe.
Thus may þe wykked as well all daye   2385
Haue Go[d]des [loue] as the goode men may.'

Qo. 58ᵃ   'How may þe chylde, þat full of loue is,   (59)
                 Come oute of þe moderes wombe?—Telle me this.'
                         'God, that all hathe made of nought,
                         Moo wondres hathe he wrought   2390
And also he hathe pouer þerto
That oon body in that oþer to do,
As hathe he might hit oute to brynge
For at his will is all thynge.
Whenne tyme comes þat woman shall   2395
Be delyuered of that she gothe withall,

2361–2] *from* S, *om.* B.   2366 in oore] more T.   2378 Fer] For S
2386 Goddes] goodes B;   loue] *om.* B.   2387–2488] *om.* S
2387–8] The goode soule shall it ought / For the wicked haue dole or thought T

Ca.º ljº

'May þe wicked als wel for ay (58)
Haue Goddis loue as þe good may?'
   'A wicked man þat haþ do synne
   And of wickednesse wole blynne
And crie mercy and do no more, 3245
He shal of God bi loued þe more.
þe goode ben Goddis where þei go
And þe wicked ben fallen him fro.
If a man a þing haue lore
þat he loued wel bifore 3250
And he may it after fynde,
þat shal him be more in mynde
And more shulde þerof be glad
þan of al þe toþer þat he had.
þus fareþ God by man also: 3255
Whan he aȝein him haþ mysdo
And it dedly synne be,
Fer fro God þanne fallen is he;
But if he wole mercy craue,
Sikerly he shal it haue, 3260
And þerof is God ful fain
Whanne he fyndeþ him aȝain
And of his finding he is bliþe—
Greet loue to man euere he doþ kithe.
þus may þe wikked als wel alday 3265
Haue Goddes loue as þe gode men may.'

Ca.º lijº

'Hou may þe child, þat ful of loue is, (59)
Come out of þe modres wombe?—Telle me þis.'
   'God, þat al haþ made of noght f. 49ʳ
   And manye wondres he haþ wroght, 3270
And as he haþ power þerto
þat oon body in þat othir do,
So haþ he might it out to bring
For at his wille is al þing.
Whanne time comeþ þat womman shal 3275
Be delyuered of þat she gooþ wiþal,

2389–2470] half page (outer column) missing T.   2390 hathe] that P.   2392 oon]
om. P.

f. 37ʳ

All the ioyntes of here body
Open and enlarges them kyndely,
All saue oon the chine before.
And in that tyme the childe is bore,   2400
As a lykenesse of dethe that ware;
But soone so þat body bare
The ayre hathe sauoured þat is here,
The bones, that febely may stere,
Begynne for to drye anon   2405
And waxes harde and falles to bon,
And all þe liththes that were vpon
In the woman agayn are cropen—
Herkyn, I shall telle þe hough:
Yif a man his fynger drowe,   2410
The ioynt wolde opyn and vndo
And sethen crepe ayen vnto;
So fares woman after childyng
Thorow the grace of heuen kynge.'

Qo. 57ᵃ

'May ony woman bere mo   (60) 2415
Childeren here at oones þenne twoo?'
    'A woman may bere kyndely
    Vij at oones in here body
For the matrice of woman,
Yif thow vnderstonde can,   2420
Hathe vij chambres and no mo
And ichon is spered other froo
And she may haue in yche of tho
A child and with vij goo,
Yf Goddes wyll be firste þerto   2425
And the kynde of woman also.
Yf hote of kynde be the woman
And hathe grete lykyng to man,
Oon chambir or two or thre
Of tho that in her matrice be   2430
Of grete will open theragayn
That a man haue by here layn:

2399 All saue oon] Allone saue P;   chine] chyn P.   2401 of dethe] as der
P.   2402 so] om. P.   2403 sauoured] savours P.   2404] That the bony
all mow stire P.   2405 Begynne] They begyn P.   2406 and] as I

Alle þe ioyntes of hir body
Openeþ and largeþ kindely,
Echoone saf þe þe chin bifore.
And in þat time þe childe is bore   3280
As a sykenesse of deeþ bi ware;
But as sone as þe body bare
Haþ sauered þe eir þat is here
And þe feble bones gynneþ stere,
þanne þei bigynne to drie anoon   3285
And wexen hard and fallen to boon,
And alle þe ioyntes þat weren open
In þe womman aȝein ben cropen—
Herken and I shal telle þe howh:
If a man his finger drowh,   3290
þe ioynte wole open and vndo
And siþen crepe aȝein þerto;
So fareþ wymmen after childing
þorgh þe grace of heuene king.'

Ca.° liij°   'May any womman bere mo   (60) 3295
                              Children in hir attones but two?'
                              'A womman may bere kindely
                              Seuene at ones in her body
For þe matrice of womman,
If þat þou vnderstonde can,   3300
Haþ vij chaumbres and no mo
And eche is departid othir fro
And she may haue in eche of þo   f. 49ᵛ
A childe and wiþ seuene goo,
If Goddis wille be first þerto   3305
And þe kinde of womman also.
If hoote of kinde be þe womman
And greet liking haþ to man,
Oon chaumbre or two or thre
Of þilke þat in hir matrice be   3310
Of greet wille open þeraȝein
Whan þat a man haþ by hir lein:

2415–16 q. no. 57 for 59 B.   2423] om. P.

—————

3300 H begins.

f. 37ᵛ

The sede falles in hem anoon
And they close ageyn ychon
And yf that seede acordaunce fynde,　　　2435
Hit waxith forthe in his kynde;
And if that other chamberes be
Open and hit be þat she
Knowe man efte that ilke night
Or on morowe by daylight　　　2440
Or the secunde day lette here nought
And the seede be therinne brought,
They speryn to and holdyn faste
And noryshen childeren at the laste;
And soo longe they shall be born　　　2445
Latter than other are toforn
As they were gotyn sunderly.
But vnderstande nought forthy
For at euery tyme þat a man
Knoweth fflesshly a woman　　　2450
That the sede rote in here take:
Many thynges may lettyng make;
But hit behoues that he and she
Be bothe togeder atempre.
For yf a man a lecchor be　　　2455
And hauntes [many] as men se,
The seed of hym is of no myght
For febulnesse of foulyng right.
And yif a man be holdyn longe
That he not to woman gange　　　2460
And sethen dothe as ye wote,
The sede of hym is thenne so koet,
Whenne hit is to here chamber brought,
Hit brennes and wastes all to nought.
And if the man be atempre　　　2465
And the woman not so be
But brennyng hote and of grete will,
f. 38ʳ　　Yit the seede shall in her spille.

2436 waxith] worchit P.　　　2441 Or] And P;　　lette her] letter P.
2452 lettyng] lette makyng P.　　2454 atempre] of oo tempre P.　　2455 a
lecchor] lecherous P.　　2456 many] *from* P, *om.* B.　　2462 koet] whote
P.　　2465 atempre] of gode tempre P.　　2467] Brennyng hete a grete while P.

þe seed falleþ in hem anon
And þei closen aȝein echon
And if þat seed acordaunce finde,   3315
It wexeþ ferþer in his kinde;
And if þat þe oþere chaumbres be
Open and it be so þat she
Knowe a man ofte þat same night
Or on þe morwe bi þe daylight   3320
Or þe secounde day, latter noght,
And þe seed be þerynne broght,
þei closen and holden faste
And children norisshen at þe laste;
And so longe þei shullen be vnbore   3325
As þe seed of oþer weren sowe bifore
As þei weren geten wonderly.
But vnderstonde not forthi
þat same time þat a man
Knoweþ flesshely a womman   3330
þat seed in hir roote take:
Many þinges may letting make;
But it bihoueþ þat he and she
Be boþe togidre of oone tempre.
For if a man a lecchour be   3335
And haunte many as men may se,
[The seede of hym is of no myȝt
For febilnes of folowind riȝt.
And if a man wiþholde hym long
That he nat to woman gang   3340
And do siþen as ȝe woote,
The seede of hym þan is so hote,
þan whan it is to his chambre brouȝt,
It brenneþ and wastiþ all to nouȝt.
And if þe man be of a tempre   3345
And þe woman nat so be
But brennyng hote of grete wille,
Yet schal þe seede in hir spille.

3316 wexeþ] werkeþ H.   3321 latter] lette her H.   3327 wonderly]
sonderly H.   3337–60] from H, om. L.

And yif they bothe be of oon tempure,
Heere sede shall in here chamber dure   2470
And festen therinne and norisshen faste
And come vnto man at the laste.
And yif [they] at here geder comyng
Be glad and blithe in all thyng,
Of glad sembelant the childe shall be   2475
As they were bothe at asemble;
Yf they assemble hem wroþly,
Wrothly shal be the childe, sothely;
Yf that oon be glad, that other nought,
And a childe be betwene them wrought,   2480
The childe shall sumtyme be blithe
And sumtyme grete felnesse kythe;
And yf that hit befalle soo
That the ton of hem two
Have ony man gretely in thought   2485
Whenne the sede is to his chambyr brought,
The seede may lykenesse take in caase
Of hym that in here thought soo was.'

Qo. 60ᵃ   'Whiche is þe beste thyng þat may be   (61)
       Or man may have?—Telle þat to me.'   2490
       'Leaute is the beste thyng
       That is vnder heuen kyng
For whoso hathe with hym leaute,
He is lever then other thre
To God and hymselue also   2495
And his euen Cristen vnto.
All thynges are loued therby
And God loveth hit sekerly;
The aungels that in heuen are
For [leaute] might not fall in care   2500
For the other that fill oute
For they were proude and stoute;

And if þei be boþe of tempure,
Here seede schal in his chambre dure   3350
And fasten þerin and wex fast
And come to man at last.
And if þei togidre at þe bygynnyng
Be liþe and glade in all þing,
Of glade semblant þe childe schal be   3355
As þei were boþe at þe semble;
And if þei assemble hem wroþely
The childe schal be such, sikerly;
And if þat oon ben glad and þat oþer nouȝt
And a childe bitwene hem wrouȝt,]   3360
þe childe shal be somtime bliþe
And somtime greet felnesse kiþe;   f. 50ʳ
And if þat it bifalle so
þat þe oone of hem two
Haue any man gretly in þoght   3365
Whanne þe seed is to his chaumbre broght,
þat seed may take liknesse, percas,
Of him þat her þoght in was.'

Ca.° liiij°   *'Which is þe best þing þat may be*   (61)
þat [man] may haue?—Telle þou me.'
  'Leute is þe best þing   3370
  þat is vnder heuene king
For he þat haþ wiþ him leute,
He is trewe aȝeinst þre:
To God and to himself also
And eke his even Ċristen vnto.   3375
Alle þinges ben loued þerby
And God loueþ it most truly;
þe aungels þat in heuen are
For leute might not falle in care   3380
Wiþ þat oþer þat fellen out
þat weren vnbuxom and prout;

leall ayenste T, leel anentes S, trew as anemptis P;   thre] thee T.   2498 sekerly]
forthi TS, truly P.   2500 leaute] *from* STP, mirthe B.   2501 For the] With
that T, With tho P.   2502 proude] onlele TS, vntrew P;   stoute] prowte P.

3370 man] *from* H, om. L.

f. 38ᵛ

The grete flode askaped Nooe
For the godenesse of his leaute;
The prophetes, that may not lye,   2505
By trowthe tellen here prophecie;
By trowthe Goddis Sone of might
Shall into a maydyn light;
By leaute shall he dye also,
Adam and his to lowse oute of woo;   2510
For trowthe shall many a goode man
Be deliuered to martirdam.
Leute is as worthi and bright
As the sonne, þat shewes vs light,
That euer holdes, withoute lette,   2515
The right way that God hym sette;
And sith all is ordeyned for leute,
Then is hit beste, as thynkes me.'

Qo. 61ᵃ

'*The worste thynge, soo God þe save,*   (62)
Whiche is hit þat man may have?'   2520
   'The worste thyng and mooste foly
     That man may have then is envye
For hit engendereth coueytyse
And treson in many wyse.
For enuye that aungeles hadde   2525
Vnto God the were vnclad
Of grace and of blisse also
And therfore they felle to woo.
For envye Adam vnwyse
Was dryven oute of paradise   2530
And coueytyse, nought for to lye,
She is the doughter of envye:
She worches many man fol woo
And ful late do sum goo

2506 trowthe] leaute SP, hur lewte T.   2507 trowthe] leaute SP, the lewte P.   2510 his] alle his TP;   lowse] bryng P.   2511 trowthe] lewte TSP.   2512 to] fro P.   2513 as worthi] a thinge light T. 2514 shewes] gevith TSP.   2520 hit . . . may] that a man may in hym T. 2526 vnclad] ongladde TP.   2529 vnwyse] on his wyse P.   2531 coueytyse]

þe greet flood scaped Noe
For þe goodnesse of his leute;
þe prophetes, þat mowen not lye,   3385
By leute tellen her prophecie;
By leute Goddes Sone of might
Shal in a maide sodeinly alight;
By leute he shal deie also,
Adam and hise to lisse of wo;   3390
For leute shal many a good man
Be deliuered to martirdam.
Leute is as worþi and bright
As þe sunne, þat ʒeueþ vs light,
þat euer holdeþ, withoute lett,   3395   f. 50ᵛ
þe right weie þat God him sett;
And siþen al is ordeined for leute,
þanne is it þe beste, as þinkeþ me.'

Ca.° lv°   '*þe werste þing, so God þe saue,*   (62)
               Which it is þat man may haue?'   3400
                  'The werste þing and moost folye
                   þat man may haue it is envie
               For it engendriþ couetise
               And tresoun on many manere wise.
               For envie þat aungels hadde   3405
               To God þei weren made vngladde
               Of grace and of blisse also
               And for þat þei felle in to woo.
               For envie Adam, þat was vnwys,
               Loste þe ioye of paradys   3410
               And couetise, not forto lye,
               She is doghtir of envie:
               Sche worcheþ many man woo
               And ful late doþ somme to goo
               To here Goddis diuine seruice,   3415
               þat is euery Cristen mannes gise,

covetid P.   2532 She is the] So vs his P.   2534 ful . . . sum] at the last she
dothe hym P.

———

3390 of] or H.   3409 vnwys] so wise H.   3412 She] So H.

And somme by the nekke to hange	2535

And somme by the nekke to hange   2535
Tha might, wolde they in peace gange, . . .
Somme man is þat may se

f. 39ʳ

His neighbor go freer than he:
He hathe envye and fallis light
In coueytyse and withoute right.   2540
What envye is, yif thow wilte here,
Listen and thow mayst lere:
Hit is a tre þat sprynges wyde
And the rote of hir is pride;
The body soo is evel wyll,   2545
That in mannys herte is stylle;
The bowys, that wyde course make,
Is rancoure of herte and hate;
The floures of that ilke tre
Are pale and lene on to se   2550
For yche envyes, as I wene,
Comenly bene pale and lene;
The frute of this tre then is
Bothe sorow and eke blisse—
Blysse of his neighbors care   2555
And sorow of his welfare.
Has ony man in medyl erthe here
A worse tre growyng in his herbere?
That therof comes euerydell
Is wykked and euel and nothyng well.'   2560

Qo. 62ᵃ   *'Telle me ȝit an askyng newe:*   (63)
         How may a man be lele and trewe?'
         'Lightly may a man be trewe, I trowe:
           Furste tha he God of heue[n] do knowe
That hym made of nought also   2565
And at his will hym may fordo
And trowe stedfastly that he
Was ay and withoute ende shal be

2535] By the necke to hangyng faste P.   2536] So endith couetise at the laste
P.   2537 Somme . . . þat] Envye is wrothe when he P.   2538 freer] ferther T,
fairer SP.   2540 withoute right] with onright TS, in onright P.   2542 thow
mayst] I shall the TSP.   2545 soo] of that tre so P.   2546 mannys] many
P;   is] lithe P.   2547 The] In T;   that] of that tre that P;   course] *om.*
TP;   make] betake P.   2548 Is] In P, The T.   2550 Are pale] Pale hede T,

And somme by þe nekke hange
þat nolden here in pees gange.
Somme man haþ envie, as we may se,
Whanne his neighebor is better þan he: 3420
He haþ envie and falleþ light
In couetise wiþ vnright.
What it is, if þou wolte lere,
Listneþ to me and I shal þe lere:
It is a tree þat springeþ wide   3425
And þe roote of hir is pride;
And þe body is yuel wille,
þat is in mannes herte stille;
þe bowes, þat with þe wynde shake,   f. 51ʳ
Is rancour of herte and hate;   3430
The floures of þis same tree
Ben pale and leene vpon to see
For eche envious, as I wene,
Comynliche is pale and lene;
þe fruit of þis tree þanne is   3435
Sorwe and care and eke blis—
Blis of his neighebores yuel care
And sorwe of his welfare.
Lo haþ any man in myddilerde
A werse tree growynge in his ȝerde?   3440
What þat comeþ þerof euery del
Is wikked and bad and noþing wel.'

Ca.° lvij°   'Telle me ȝit an axinge newe: (63)   f. 53ᵛ/19
How may a man be feiþful and trewe?'
'Lightly may a man be trewe   3445
If he of heuene truly knewe
And God þat him made of noght also
And at his wille him shal fordo
And bileue stedfastly þat he
Was euere and biþoght shal be   3450

Is pale hide P.   2661 yche] thycke P.   2553 The] In T.   2557 erthe
here] erde TSP.   2558 herbere] yerde TSP.   2561–854] follow 3028 P.
2563 I trowe] om. TSP.   2564 heuen] heue B;   do know] knewe TSP.
2566 at . . . may] that is hym shall sone P;   may] shalle T.

3443 ff.] follow 3916 LH.

And holde well the comaundemente
That is [Sone], when he down is sente,   2570
Shall in erthe geve man vnto
Ageyns God and man also

f. 39^v

And do goode and euel lete be
And coueytyse and enuye fle
And take vnto hym patience   2575
And charite and abstinence—
For whoso hathe these thre,
Iwis, a feythfull man is he.
And sithen for his leute
In heuen may he crowned be   2580
With aungeles bifore God almyght
There euer is day withoute nyght.'

Qo. 63^a   *'Hardynesse of man and drede,*   (64)
    Wherof com they, soo God þe spede?'
      'Hardynes and drede of man,   2585
      Whens they come telle I can:
They com of þe complexion,
And I shall telle þe reson.
Thou wost well þat mad men were
Of the foure elementes that ere   2590
(Saue that God gaue hym gooste)
And after man hathe in hym moste—
Of wete or drye, hoote or colde—
Shall his complexion be tolde;
And yif these iiij euen be   2595
Deeled in man, þan shall he
Be nother coward ne hardy:
Lyston, and I shall telle þe why.
Yf colde not ouercome the hete
Ne the drye ouercome þe wete   2600
Ne hete þe colde ne wete þe drye,
The herte of that man shall lye
For the euennesse of hym tho

2570 Sone] *from* PT, *om.* BS.   2573 euel] wicke T, the wyckid P, ill S.
2578 feythfull] leal TS, full trew P.   2581 almyght] of myght T.
2583–668] *om.* S.   2590 that ere] of the eyre P.   2591 Saue . . . gaue hym]
Gaue . . . saue that P.   2592 after man hathe] aftirward hauys a man P.

And holde wel þe comaundement
þat his Sone, whanne he is doun sent,
Shal ȝeue man in erþe vnto
Aȝeinst man and God also
And do good and lat yuel be   3455
And lete envie and coueitise fle
And take to him pacience
And charite and abstinence—
For whoso haþ thise þre   f. 54ʳ
A feithful man may he be.   3460
And sithen for his lewte
He may in heuen crowned be
Wiþ aungels bifore God almight
þere euere is day and neuere night.'

Ca.º lviijº   'Hardinesse of man and drede,   (64) 3465
                 Wherof come þei, so God þe spede?'
                   'Hardinesse and drede of man,
                     Whereof þei comen telle I can:
                 þei comen of þe complexioun,
                 And I shal telle þee by what resoun.   3470
                 þou woost wel þat men made were
                 Of þe foure ellementȝ that ere
                 And þerto God ȝaue him goost;
                 And aftir a man haþ in him moost—
                 Of weet or drie, hete or colde—   3475
                 His complexioun shal be tolde;
                 And if þise iiij euene be
                 Delid in man, þanne shal he
                 Be noþer coward ne hardy:
                 Listen, and I shal telle þe why.   3480
                 If colde ouercome not þe hete
                 Ne þe drie ouercome not þe wete
                 So þat þe hete, colde, weet, and drye
                 In the herte of man euene lie,
                 For þe euenhede of hem þo   3485

2596 Deeled] Glyde P.   2601 þe (1) and (2)] ne TP.   2603 euennesse]
evenhede T, euende P.

3478 Delid] Delite H.

f. 40ʳ

And stire nother to ne fro;
And yf the hete the colde ouergo   2605
And the drye the wete also,
The body begynnes for to qwake
And þe herte to stere and shake
And for heete is hardy anoon
And dredes nought that he lokes on;   2610
Yf colde be maister ouer the hete
And ouer the drye þe wete,
The body we[x]eþ colde at nede
And the herte nesshe and full of drede.'

Qo. 64ᵃ   'Where may hit man befall   (65) 2615
            To have the meselry and þe skall?'
              'Meselry and skalle also,
                Of the woman come þey bothe two.
            A woman þat is hote of kynde,
            And a man here in here floures fynde,   2620
            The floures are bothe hote and drye:
            And the man þenne by here lye
            And gete a chylde perauenture,
            That chylde shall of right nature
            Outher be skalled or mesell,   2625
            The nature hit is so fell
            That hit in the woman takes
            Of a blode that hit all makes:
            Menstruum þat blode we call
            That bredyth meselry or skall;   2630
            And whill hit regnes in woman
            Hit is foly to come to man.
            But a man shall knowe his wyf
            In entente to gete a lyfe
            To worship God þat hym wrought;   2635
            And whenne she is with childe brought,
            He sholde come nere here no more
            Tyl þat she delyuered wore,

2612 And] Or P.   2613 wexeþ] weyeþ B.   2615 Where] Wherof T.
2616 and the] or T.   2617 skalle also] shabbe forsothe P.   2618 þey bothe
two] thoo T;   two] om. P.   2620 here (1)] om. P.   2622 þenne] om. T.
2627 hit] om. TP;   takes] so takis P.   2628 a . . . all] blode that is alle þat T;

Stire it shal neiþer to ne fro;
And if þe hete þe colde ouergo
And þe drie þe weet also,
þe body begynneþ for to quake
And þe herte to stere and shake   3490
And for þe hete he is hardy anoon
And dredeþ not he lokeþ vpon;
And if þe colde be maister ouere þe hete   f. 54ᵛ
And ouer þe drie also þe wete,
þe body wexeþ colde at nede   3495
And þe herte neisshe and ful of drede.'

Ca.° lix°   'Wherof may it to man bifalle   (65)
                 þat he haue meselrie or scalle?'
                    'Miselrie and scalle also
                  Of þe womman come boþe two.   3500
                A womman þat is hoote of kinde,
                And a man in hir flouris finde,
                þe floures beþ bothe hote and drie;
                And if þe man þanne by her lie
                And gete a child perauenture,   3505
                þat childe shal of right nature
                Ouþer be scalled or be missel.
                þe nature of hem it is so fel
                For þat þat in a womman flakeþ
                þe kinde of hem a blood it makeþ: 3510
                Menstruum þat blood we calle
                þat bredeþ bothe miselrie or scalle;
                And þe while it regneþ in womman
                It is folye to dele wiþ hem þan.
                But a man shal knowe his wyf   3515
                In suche atente to gete a lyf
                To worshipe God þat him wroght;
                And whanne sche is wiþ childe broght,
                He ne shulde come at hir no more
                Til þat she deliuered wore,   3520

a blode that] o blode P.   2632 come to man] dele than with ham P.   2634 a] a
gode P.   2636 whenne] om. T.   2637 nere here] ahendere P.

3509 flakeþ] falliþ H.

Ne fourty dayes after nought:
Suche heste the aungell to Noe brought.'   2640

Qo. 65ᵃ   'Were all thynges of Goddes makyng   (66)
                Made furste at the begynnyng?'

f. 40ᵛ   'God made of his myght all thyng
                        Of his worde and his biddyng
                But alle creatures that he forth brought   2645
                At oon tyme ne made he nought
                For hit were agayn kynde, me thought,
                A thyng þat of mater is wrought
                But yif the mater were before
                Ere þat thyng therof made wore: 2650
                For longe is stoone and tre
                Or the house maked be.
                Also fynde I, God hit wote,
                Vermen made of mannes swote,
                As lysse and other wormes moo   2655
                And somme of mannes flessh also
                And of mannes flessh hem fede,
                As wormes that in handes brede.
                The sharnbod ys of mouke of neete
                And þat is a worme right grete;   2660
                Of houndes come hounde flyes to,
                And wormes of wykked ayre also;
                And if that thynge liter be
                Then that [they] cometh of, thenkes me
                That God at the begynnyng   2665
                Made not at oones all thyng;
                And all thyng he made, ywys,
                Vnto the leste worme þat is.'

Qo. 66ᵃ   'Telle me now, after þy wytt: (67)
                The froyte of erthe, how noreshith hit?'   2670
                        'All the frute in erthe growes
                        And þat men vpon þe erthe sowes,

2647 kynde me] my P.   2654 Vermen] Wormes TP;   mannes] moomys
P.   2657 flessh] they P.   2658 As] Ande T;   wormes] armys
P;   handes brede] gravis wormys fede P.   2659-60] And in mucke wormys be /
That of the dunge bredyn be P.   2659 sharnbod] scarbode T;   mouke] mylke
T.   2660 þat . . . right] this a worme lawely T.   2661 hounde flyes] howndes
lise T.   2663 that] theise T, the P;   thynge liter] thynges latter TP.

> Ne fourty daies afterward noght:
> Suche heest þe aungel to Noe broght.'

Ca.° lx°   'Weren alle þinges of Goddes making   (66)
      Ymade firste at þe bigynnyng?'
        'God of his might made al þing   3525
        Of his worde and his bidding
      But alle þe creatures þat he forþ broght   f. 55ʳ
      At oo time þanne made he noght
      For it were aȝenst kinde, in my þoght,
      A þing þat is of mater ywroght   3530
      But if þat mater were bifore
      Or þat þing þerof ymade wore:
      For longe tofore is stone and tree
      Or þe hous ymaked bee.
      Also finde I, God it woot,   3535
      þat wormes be made of mannes swoot,
      As lijs and oþer wormes moo
      And somme of mannes flesche also
      And of mannes flesshe þei hem fede,
      As wormes þat in hondes brede.   3540
      Scarbod is a mvk of neete
      And þat is a worme resonably grete;
      Of houndes comeþ houndes flies too,
      And wormes of wicked eir also;
      And if þise þinges latter be   3545
      þan tho þat þei comen of, þanne þinketh me
      þat God at the bigynnyng
      Made noght attones al þing;
      And alle þinges he made, ywis,
      To þe leest worme þat is.'   3550

Ca.° lxj°   'Telle me now, aftir þi witt: (67)
      þe fruites on erþe, who norissheþ it?'
        'Al þe fruit þat on þe erthe growiþ
        And þat men vpon þe erthe sowiþ,

2664 that they cometh of] that cometh of hem B, that thei came of as T, they come of P.
2669 S *begins again.*   2670 how] who T.   2671–88] *om.* S.   2672 þat
. . . þe] man that in P.

3529 my] his H.   3537 As lijs] and lyeþ H.   3541 a] as H.

All noreshith God of his myght
And þerfore hathe he hem dight
The foure elementes to fynde   2675
Ichon norture in his kynde.
The erthe sustinaunce to hem taketh;

f. 41ʳ   The [eyre] norissh[eþ] hit and makeþ;
The water hit fedeth and grene makeþ;
Of fuyre and hete waxyng hit takeþ.   2680
These foure make rype euery frute
Whereof men haues here delight—
Right as thow shuldest sethe a meete
Foure thynges behoueth the to gete:
Fuyre and water, ayere and vessell,   2685
Ellis be hit not sothen well.'

Qo. 67ᵃ   *'The beste þat ne haveth noo witte*   (68)
How waxe they rageous?—Telle me ȝitt.'
'God made euery beste after his kynde
And to yche gaue wit after his kynde   2690
And euery thyng hathe knowlechyng
Aftyr his wytt of some thyng
And þat wit may sone away
In maner þat I shall the say.
A man may reken and fynde soone   2695
The xxvij day of the moone
The tyme of Iune right esterly
A sterre hym shewes in the skye
And be hit night or be hit day,
Yf a beste hit biholde may   2700
Or the vmbere in water anyȝt,
He shall wax rageouse anon right;
And yf hit man or beeste then bote,
Hit sholde become rageous fot hote.'

2676 norture] norturith P.   2677 sustinaunce] susteyneth and TP;   hem]
yeme T.   2678 The eyre] *from* T, They B, The erthe P;   norissheþ] norissh
B.   2680 fuyre . . . hit] the hete his waxyng he P;   and hete] hete and T.
2683 thow shuldest] he shulde T, he so shulde P;   a] his P.   2684 the] hym T,
ham P.   2688 ȝitt] itt T.   2689 S *begins again*;   kynde] mynde P.
2690 after his] and S;   kynde] mynde TS.   2691 thyng] kynde TP;   hathe] as P.
2692 of] and P.   2695] *om.* P.   2696 xxvij] xxviij TP.   2696/7 *add* Yf

Al norissheþ God of his might 3555
And for þat he hem haþ dight
þe iiij elementes ordeined hem to finde
Eche to norisshe hem in her kynde.
þe erþe sustineth and taketh;
þe eir norissheþ it and maketh; 3560
þe watir it fediþ and makiþ it grene;   f. 55ᵛ
And þe hete of þe sunne doiþ it sustene.
þise iiij make rype euery fruit
Wherof men haue here greet delit—
Right as oon shulde seeth his mete 3565
Iiij þinges bihoueþ him þerto gete:
Fire and water, eir and vessel,
Elles beþ þei not sothen wel.'

Ca.º lxijº   'þe beestis þat haue no witt, (68)
    Hou wexe þei rage?—Telle me it.' 3570
    'God made euery beest after his minde
    And to eche ȝaf witt after his kinde
And euery kinde haþ knowleching
Aftir his witt in somme þing
And þat wit may sone away 3575
In manere þat I shal þe say.
A man may rekene and finde sone
þe xxviij day of þe mone
In time of Iune riȝt hesterly
A [s]terre him sheweþ on þe sky 3580
And be it night, be it day,
If a beest it biholde may
Or þe shade in þe water anight,
It shal wex mad anoon right;
And wheþir it man or beest be, 3585
It shal become woode, as I seie the.'

thou vndirstonde conne P.   2697 Iune] I *five minims* j P.   2698 A sterre]
After T.   2701 vmbere] nombre T, shadow P.   2702 rageouse] wode P.
2703 then bote] be P.   2704] Hit shall be wode as Y tolde the P;   fot]
om. T.

3580 A sterre] *from* H, Afterre L.

Qo. 68^a   '*What beste is hit, that yee fynde,*   (69) 2705
                That lengeste leueth in his kynde?'
                   'An eron leves lengest throwe
                   Of all the bestes tha I knowe:
                The eron euery day woll flye
                Into the eyre vpright hye   2710
                Hyer þan ony man may hym se
                And fressh and newe becomes he;

f. 41^v   And in longe lyfe he kythes
                That he fresshes soo fele sythes.
                The edder also hathe longe lyff   2715
                And vnder erthe he dwelles ryff
                And vnder stones and vnder brynkes
                And the colde of the erthe he drynkes;
                His hyde he newes euery yere
                And becomes yonge and fayre: 2720
                Be he not slayne with beste ne man,
                A thousand yere wel lyue he can;
                And when a M^l yere is gone,
                Horne on his hede waxith oon
                And soone after begynnes he   2725
                A fyre dragon for to be.
                But all fare they not soo:
                Some dye or they come þerto
                And some ar slayn here and þere
                And elles all to feele þer were.'   2730

Qo. 69^a   '*Fedeth God al thyng*   (70)
                That is in erthe of his makyng?'
                   'God made al thyng for goode
                   And all he sendes lyues foode:
                Frute in erthe and flessh on londe   2735
                And fyssh of water and of sonde
                To mannes foode is ordeyned all
                And þerby he lyue shall.
                Beestes eke are fedde also
                Of that the erthe gyves hit froo: 2740

2707 throwe] thorow P.   2714 soo] to P.   2717 vnder (2)] in
TSP.   2718 colde] kilthes T, kelthe P;   erthe] eyre T.   2720 yonge]
new P.   2725 soone] smert SP.   2726 fyre] feyre T.   2736 and of]

Ca.º lxiij º   'What beest is it, þat ȝe fynde,   (69)
                  þat liueþ lengest in his kynde?'
                        'An eerne lyueþ lengest þrowe
                           Of alle þe beestis þat I knowe: 3590
                        þe eerne ech day wole fliȝe
                        Vp into þe eir right hiȝe
                        Hiȝer þan any man may see
                        And freisshe and newe bicomeþ he;
                        And þe lenger lijf he lyueþ   3595 f. 56ʳ
                        þat he in þe eir so him chaungeþ.
                        The addre also haþ longe lijf
                        And vnder þe erþe he dwelliþ rijf
                        And vnder stones and vnder brinkes
                        And of þe colde of þe erthe he drinkes;   3600
                        His skyn he newiþ euery ȝere þenne
                        And bycomeþ ȝonge and fair to kenne
                        And if he be not slayne with beest ne man,
                        A þousand ȝeere wel lyue he can:
                        And whanne a þousand ȝeere is goon,   3605
                        An horne in his heed wexeþ anoon
                        And sone aftir bigynneþ he
                        A firy dragoun forto be.
                        But alle fare þei not so:
                        Somme deien or þei come þerto   3610
                        And some ben slayne here and þere
                        And ellis al to fele ther were.'

Ca.º lxiiij º   'Fedith God al thing   (70)
                  þat is in erthe of his making?'
                        'God made al þing to good   3615
                           And to alle he sendeþ lyues food:
                        Fruit in erþe and fleisshe in lond
                        And fisshe in water, þoruȝ his sond,
                        To mannes nede is ordeined al
                        And þerby he lyue shal.   3620
                        And so ben beestis fedde also
                        Of þat þat comeþ þe erthe fro:

thorow his P.   2737 mannes] many P.   2739 eke] so TP.   2740 the
. . . hit] it geuys the erthe P.

Foules somme of the erthe are fed

And some of the water here lyf is ledde;

The fissh lyues by his mete
For ychon will other eete;
The worme in þe erthe also;   2745
And all hem sendes God vnto:
All þoo þat he lyf hathe lente,
Alle hathe he mete vnto them sente.'

f. 42ʳ

Qo. 70ᵃ   'Fysshe and foule and bestes ychone,   (71)
                  Have þey soules or have they none?'   2750
                     'Ryʒ[t]ly soules for to say
                        Is suche that may neuer dye
                  For yeue the body do well here,
                  The soule shal be aungels feere;
                  And þat is called soule of skyll   2755
                  That [God] yaue oonly man vntyll.
                  Therfore euery other creature
                  Is vndyr man by right nature
                  And for that man shall mayster be
                  Ouer all beestes, therfore shall he   2760
                  Haue soule þat moste wisdom can—
                  Elles were beeste lyke to man.
                  Beestes and foules and ffysshes all
                  Haue noo soule rightly to calle.
                  Yf thow say, as som men doo,   2765
                  All that lyuen han soule þerto
                  Thorow whiche soule the body steres,
                  Eeteth and drynketh, seeth and heeres,
                  Hit is noo soule—hit is but an oonde
                  That God hathe lente hem of his sonde: 2770
                  For noo goode ne can þey doo
                  But that men hem norisshes to—
                  Thenne have they wit of mannes leryng

2745 erthe] *add* is fed TSP.   2747 þoo . . . lyf] that he yf euer P;   þoo þat] that
euer TS.   2751 Ryʒtly] Ryʒly B, Lyghtly P;   soules] soule haue thei non
T.   2752 may] it maye TSP.   2756 God] *from* TSP, *om.* B.

Foules of þe heir somme ben fed
On careins where þei be led
And some in þe water feden hem so   3625
As þei may best come therto;
And þe fisshe lyueþ by his mete
For þe grete the smale wole ete;
þe worme of þe erþe is fed also   f. 56ᵛ
Of suche as God sendeþ þerto   3630
For to alle þat he haþ lijf lent
To hem alle he haþ mete sent.'

Ca.° lxv°   *'Fisshes and foules and beestis echoone,*   (71)
Haue þei soules or haue þei none?'

'A soule, truly forto seie,   3635
Is suche þat it may neuere deie
For if þe body do wel here,
þe soule shal be aungels fere;
And he is clepid soule of skile
For God ȝaf it man vntile.   3640
For euery oþer creature
Is vnder man bi right nature
And for þat man shal maister be
Ouer alle beestis, þerfore shal he
Haue soule þat most wisdom can—   3645
Elles were beest lich to man.
Bestis and foules and fisshes alle
Han no soule rightly to calle;
And if þou seie, as men do,
Alle þat lyuen han soule þerto   3650
þorgh whiche þe body sterith,
Etith and drinkeþ, spekiþ or herith,
It is no soule but an oonde
þat God haþ lente hem of his sonde:
For no good kunne þei do   3655
But þat men hem norissheþ to—
þanne haue þei witte of manis lerninge

2757 other] *om.* P.   2770 God . . . his] comith thorow Goddis P.   2772 men
hem] God T.

3649 as] of H.   3652 and] or H.

But of hemself haue þey nothynge.
Yif witte of hemselue wore,   2775
Here soule were of myght þe moore
But here soule, that I [onde] call,
Whenne þe body dede shall fall,
Hit fares as a[n] oonde of mouthe:

Whenne hit is oute, hit is no man couthe   2780

But vanyssheth in þe ayre away
And noo lenger endure ne may.'

f. 42ᵛ *Qo. 71ᵃ*   *'They that in tyme of Goddes Soone shal be,*   (72)
                      Shall they lyue as longe as wee?'
            'All suche of body as now ar we   2785
              But soo mekel shall they not be;
And we are now of lenger lyfe
Than shall be thenne oþer man or wyff
For the worlde is stalworthere
Thenne shal be þenne and mightyere   2790
And þe erthe geues vs to
Moore frute then [hit s]hall then do.
And þe plente that the erthe yeldes
Bothe in woode and in feldes
Is now of mekel moore might   2795
Thenne hit shal be thanne with right
And the wynde is byggere nowe
Than shal be thenne and to more prowe;
Therfore ought we of right nature
Lengere lyue and lenger endure   2800
Than they that by the dayes are
For febolere forthy shall thay fare.
For he that thenne lyve may
A C yeere, hit is a longe day;
For euer shall men downward goo   2805

2777 I onde] eche coude P;   onde] on do B.   2779 an oonde of] dothe oute
of thy P;   an] as B.   2782 ne] they P.   2785 All] *om.* TP;   of] a
P.   2789 is] is now more P.   2790 and] a P.   2791 geues] semyth
P.   2792 frute] frotthe P;   hit shal] hal B.   2797 byggere] sterker
TSP.   2799 of right] be of oure P.   2802 febolere] flebleloker S, febilloker

But of hemself haue þei noþinge.
And if þe witt of hemself wore,
Her soule were of might þe more   3660
But her soule, þat I oonde calle,
Whanne þe body is deed, shal falle:
It fareþ as an onde of thi mouth   f. 57ʳ
For it is to no man kouth;
For whan þe word is out spoken   3665
And þe soun awey is cropen,
It vanissheþ in þe eir away
And no lenger it dure may.'

Ca.° lxvj°   'þilke þat in þe time of Goddis Sone shal be,   (72)
Sholen þei lyue as longe as done we?'   3670
    'Ye, suche of body as now ben we
    But so miche shullen þei not be;
And we ben now of lenger lijf
þan shal be þanne man or wyf
For þe world is stalworthier   3675
þan it shal be þanne and mightier
And þe erþe now ȝeueþ vs to
More fruit þan it shal þan do.
And þe plente þat þe erþe ȝeldis
Boþe in wode and in feeldes   3680
Is now of miche more might
þen it shal be þenne wiþ right
And þe winde is strenger now
þan it shal be þenne, as I telle ȝow;
þerfore we oght of right nature   3685
Lenger to lyue and lenger to dure
þan þei þat in þilke daies are
For febloker þei shullen fare.
For he þat may þanne gange
An hundred ȝere, he lyueþ lange;   3690
And euere men sholen dounward goo

P.   2803 thenne lyve may] may þen (them T) gange STP.   2804 hit is a
longe day] he levith to (om. S) lange TS, than lithe he longe P.   2805 downward
goo] lasshe to P.

3671 as now] anow H.   3677 now] om. H.

Of lyff and of strenkthe also
But in wytt wax they shall
And in maleys withall
And of here bodyes lessyn ay
Betwyxe this and domesday.'　　　　　　2810

Qo. 72ᵃ

'Telle me now, soo mote thow þryfe:　　　(73)
How longe shall this worlde dryve?'
　　'No man in erthe the prevyte
　　Of God may knowe, saue oonly he:
Hit is soo grete that wit hit ne can　　　2815
Nowther aungell, beeste, ne man,
Ne noothyng but hit be he
That with God be full pryve
And that he loues alþermoste,
As his Sone or the Holi Goste,　　　　2820
For they with hym ar alle oon
In Godhede, or ellis wot hit noon.
For euery erthely man wol not
Telle to euery man his thought
Nor his will of priuete　　　　　　2825
Butte he pryue with hym be;
Also reserues God hym to
Many thynges that he wolde doo
That he woll of noo knowlechyng
Gyue to man ne to noo thyng　　　　2830
But to his owne Sone oonly
For he is nexte and moste hym by.
And that tyme that Goddis Soone
Shall a man in erthe here woone,
Men shall hym aske yif the worlde here　　2835
Shall endure vij thowsand yeere;
And derkely answhere he shall
And saye, "Yee and moore withall";
For of the Faderes priuete
Of the moore shall noon þe wysere be.　　2840

f. 43ʳ

2806 lyff] stryf P.　　2812 dryve] lyve T.　　2813 the prevyte] ne may neven
TS, may may ne mene P.　　2814] The privite of Godde in (of SP) heven
TSP.　　2815 wit] *om.* P.　　2817 hit be] oonly P.　　2822 wot hit] *om.*
P.　　2823 erthely] *om.* P.　　2831 owne Sone oonly] Sone on hye P.

Of body, of lyf, þe febler be tho
But in wit wexe þei shal
And in grete malice encrese withal
And of her bodies lasky ay   3695
Bitwene þis and domesday.'

Ca.° lxvij°   'Telle me now, or þou gange: (73)   f. 57ᵛ
                  Hou longe shal þis world stande?'
                     'No [man] may in erþe neuene
                  þe priuetes of God in heuene: 3700
                  It is so greet þat iwite it ne can
                  Nouþer aungel, beest, ne lyuynge man,
                  Ne noþing but it be he
                  þat God woot right prive may be
                  And þat he loueþ alþer moost,   3705
                  As his Sone and þe Holy Goost,
                  For þei ben euere wiþ him aloone
                  In Godhede, and ellis wote it none.
                  For to eche erthely man wole he noght
                  Telle his priuete and his þoght   3710
                  Ne noþing of his secrete
                  But he priue wiþ him be;
                  Also God reserueþ him to
                  Many þinges þat he wole do
                  þat he wole of no knowleching   3715
                  To no man ȝeue ne to no þing
                  But to his owne Sone oonly
                  For he is next and moost him by.
                  And in þat time þat Goddis Sone
                  Shal man here in erthe wone,   3720
                  Men sholen him axe if þis world here
                  Shal dure seuene þousand ȝere;
                  And þanne mekely answere he shal
                  And seie, "ȝe and mo wiþal";
                  For of þe Fadris priuete   3725
                  No mo shal þe wiser be

2837 derkely] merkelye T, mekly P.   2838] om. T.   2840 noon þe] no man
P.

3699 man] from H, om. L.   3704 God woot] wiþ God H.

We fynde well that God of heuen
Hathe made planetes vij
The worlde to kepe day and nyght
And ichon yeues þat is his myght;
And eueriche is assigned to   2845
A thousand yere to kepe also
And whan ichon hase on this wyse
A thousand yeere doon his seruyse,
Thenne shall oon God fulfill
The worlde lenger at his wyll.   2850
For as þe planetes gouernoures be,
Also hem gouernes he;
And for he is abouen all
Wot not but he what shall befalle.'

f. 43ᵛ   *Qo. 73ᵃ*   *'Lyue any men in the worlde mo*   (74) 2855
Oute of the erthe þat we on goo?'
    'Syre, iles ar many in the see:
    A Mˡ CCCC and two þere be.
Sume are enhabited men withall
And summe not ne not ne shall.   2860
There is suche as men wone inne
Of ooure likenesse more ne mynne
And of heighte but handfulles thre:
Here berdes hangen to here knee;
Here here doune to her helis is;   2865
Of flessh they fede them and of gryse;
Here bestes are right small euerychon;
And speche they haue by hem all oon.
Another ile is by the see
And thereinne small men there be: 2870
A spanne longe ar they and no moore;
All by ffysshe lyue they thore;
In the water ar they by liȝt

2843 The] In P.   2844 yeues] gevyn T, gyue P;   myght] riȝt S.
2847 this] his P.   2849 oon] ouer TS, euer P.   2852 hem] then P.
2854 not] non TSP.   2855–3028] *precede* 2561 P.   2856 þat] thanne
T.   2858 and two] *om.* P.   2865 Here here] The herrer P;   helis] pepill
P.   2866 they fede them] fishe T;   gryse] fissh S.   2870 small . . . be] ben

But þe Sone [and] þe Holy Goost,
þe whiche two he loueþ moost.
We finde wel þat God of heuene
Haþ imade planetes seuene   3730
þe world to kepe bi day and night   f. 58ʳ
And eche þing gouerneþ þorgh his might;
And eueriche ben assigned here
To kepe fully a þousande ȝere
And whan þat eche of hem on þis wise   3735
Haþ done a þousand ȝere his seruise,
Ȝit shal þanne God fulfille
þe world lenger after his wille.
For right as planetes gouernours be,
Whanne þei haue done, þanne gouerne wole he; 3740
And for he is aboue hem alle
Woot noon but he what shal befalle.'

Ca.º lvjº   '*Lyue any men in þe world mo*   (74)   f. 51ʳ/15
                  þan on erthe þat we on go?'
                  'Sire, þer ben many yles in the see   3745
                  A M¹ CCCC an two þer be.
                  Somme ben enhabited men wiþal
                  And some not ne neuere shal.
                  þere ben somme þat men ben ynne
                  Of oure liknesse more ne [m]ynne   3750
                  And of heighte but handfulles þre
                  And han berdes to þe kne;
                  þe heer of her heed is to her heelis;
                  Of fleisshe þei feden and of gris;
                  Her beestis ben right smale echone;   3755
                  A speche þei haue bi hemself aloone.
                  Anoþer yle is in þe see
                  And þerynne ben right smale meyne:
                  þei ben a spanne longe and no more
                  And al wiþ fisshe þei liuen thore;   3760
                  In þe water þei ben be daylight

(ar SP) smale meyne TSP.   2871 no] *om.* S.   2873 liȝt] daylight P.
_____

  3727 and] *from* H, of L.   3743–916] *precede* 3443 LH.   3743 Lyue] Haue
H.   3745 in the see] *om.* H.   3750 mynne] *from* H, blynne L.
3758 right] but H.

And vppon londe ar they by ny3t.
3yt there oþer yles be   2875
With men as grete as wee
With oone eye in the frunte, no moore,
And vs with twhoo they drede soore:
They ete flessh and with the felles
Clothe they hem and with nought elles.   2880
Yit ther is another also:
The folke that longes thervnto
Are telid ri3t as a shepe ychone
And they lyue of ffysshe alone.
3it is there oon of ooure shapnesse   2885
But they are wel mykel lesse
And they are euer in fight and were
Agaynes a grete man[er] of foule þat is þere:
In colde wynter the foules grete
Take they and holde hem for here mete.   2890

f. 44ʳ

Another is there 3ytt ny3 hande
There is a maner fowle dwellande:
Though they were on fuyre brought
Brenne ne sholde here fetheris nought.
Another folke is there, fayre to fonde: 2895
They haue faces lyke an hounde.
3it is there folke in a contre
And of febill beleue they be:
On þe sonne and mone they trowe
And sacrifise they make summe throwe.   2900
But whenne they sacrifise shall make,
Somme will his beste frendes take
And praye hem company to bere
Atte the sacrifise he shall do there.
Thenne shall he lete make a fuyre   2905
That be brennyng full sure;
Thenne shall he crye, þat all men may here,
"For loue of the sonne dere"

2877 frunte] forehede T.   2878 drede] drevyn P.   2882] In whiche alle the
peple that þere goo T.   2883 telid] tailed TSP.   2888 maner] from TS, man
B, mayny P.   2891 is there 3ytt] yle ther is P.   2895 folke] foule P;   to
fonde] and sounde TSP.   2897 in] dwellyng in P.   2900 they make] hem
makith T, they make hem P.   2902] Here beste frendis they wul take P.

And on þe londe þei beþ anight.

But ȝit, sire, oþer yles þer be   f. 51ᵛ

Wiþ men also greet as we

With one eyȝe in þe front and no more   3765

And vs wiþ two þei dreden sore:

þei eten fleisshe and wiþ the fellis

þei cloþen hem and wiþ noght ellis.

Anoþer yle þere is also

And þe folke þat longe þerto   3770

Ben tailed riȝt as a shepe echone

And þei lyuen be flesshe aloone.

And some þer ben of oure liknesse

But þei ben ful miche lesse

And þei ben euer in fight and were   3775

Aȝein a manere of folke þat is þere:

In colde winter þe foules grete

Takeþ hem and holdeþ hem for her mete.

Anoþer yle þer is, to vnderstonde,

And þerynne is a manere of foule dwellande   3780

And þouȝ þei were in fire broght

þe feþeres of hem brenne sholde noght.

Anoþer folke þer is, fair and sounde,

þat han visage like an hounde.

Anoþer folk þere is in somme cuntre   3785

And of þe feble bileue þei be

And on sunne and mone þei trowe

And sacrifice þei make to hem somme þrowe.

But whan þei shole sacrifice make,

Her beste frendes þan wole þei take   3790

And preie hem companye him to bere

Of þe sacrifice he wole do þere.

Thanne shal he do make a fire

And make it to brenne faire and clere;

þanne shal he crie, þat all may here,   3795

"For loue of þe sunne, þat is so dere"

903 praye] _om._ S;   bere] make P.   2904] At that sacrefice parte to take P.
905 he] one of them P.   2906 sure] shire TS, clere P.   2908 dere] so dere
ˉSP.

———

3772 aloone] and bone H.

(Or the mone, whether hit be,
Or an ymage made of tre)   2910
"Hoppe I in this fyre al hote
For my meryte well I woote."
Thus hymselue þere he brennes
And þe deuel hys soule wynnes;
And þo þat bere hym company   2915
Anoone shall do þe same foly.
That other folke aboute bedene
Sitte till they be brente all clene;
And þenne shall they asshes take
And relekes shall they therof make.   2920
Another londe ther is also
That sacrifise the deuel vnto
Of here bodyes and are full blithe:
They lete make a sharpe sythe
In lykenesse of an horssho   2925
And þat shall haue haftes twoo;
By þe here shall he hanged þenne be
Hye on lofte that men may se:
The sithe in his nekke shall men ley,
The haftes in his hondes tway,   2930
And he shall crye, as man of rage,
"For the loue of this ymage
That is my god this shall I do,"
And kerve his owne nekke [on twoo].
The hede hangeth stylle on hye;   2935
The body falleth hastely.
That body shal be take with wynne
And done owte all that is þerinne
And salted as they woll hit haue
And by that ymage do þat graue.   2940
Vpon that graue shall wreten be
His owne name and how þat he
Made to þat ymage his sacryfyse
And on what day and in what wyse.

f. 44ᵛ

2911 Hoppe I] I wol lepe P;   al] so TS.   2912 well] hit is well P
2915 And] All P.   2918 brente] brought P;   all] om. T.   2919 þenne] anon
P;   they] add her at S.   2932 this] his T.   2934 on twoo] from T, vnto B
atwo SP.   2938 owte] abought T.

(Or þe mone, wheþer it be,   f. 52^r
Or an ymage ymade of tree)
"I wole hoppe in þis fire al hoot
For my merit wel I woot."   3800
þus [hym]self þere he brenneþ
And to þe deuel his soule bikenneþ;
And þat beren him companye
Anoon sholen do þe same folie.
þat oþir folke aboute bydene   3805
Shullen sitte til þei be brent clene;
þanne wole þei her askes take
And þerof þei sholen relekes make.
Anoþer lond ther is also
þat makeþ sacrifice þe deuel to   3810
Of her bodies and beþ ful bliþe:
And þei lat make a sharpe sithe
In þe liknesse of an horse sho
And [it] shal haue haftes two;
þanne shal he [by] þe [here] hanged be   3815
Hie on lofte þat alle men mowen see:
þe sithe in his nekke men sholen leie
And þe heftes in hise hondes tweie
And he shal crie, as a man in rage,
"For þe loue of þis ymage   3820
þat is my god þis shal I doo,"
And þanne kerue his owne necke atwo.
þere hangeþ the heed stille on hy
And þe body falleþ hastily.
The body shal be taken þenne   3825
And done out al þat is þerynne
And þenne, þe body forto saue,
By þe ymage þei wole it graue.
Vpon þat graue shal writen be
His owne name hou þat he   3830
Made to þe ymage his sacrifice   f. 52^v
And on what day and on what wise.

Another maner there is 3ytt   2945
Of folke, that are of lytill wytt:
Whenne the[y] sacryfise shall make,
An high tre they shall lete take
And do hit steken in a plase
With many abowte makyng solace   2950
And aboute þat ilke tree
Foure naaked swhirdes shal sette be,
The poyntes vpwarde euerychon.
Thenne shall he be taken anoon
That the sacrifise shall do   2955
And bounden fote and honde also
And vpdrawyn shall he be
To þe ouermeste ende of þat tre.
There shall he crye the folke vnto,
"In worshipp of god þis I do."   2960
They lete slakke þat they drawe with
And on the same swherdes downe he falleþ
As most nedes on them lyght
And gothe to þe devel anoone right.
Thanne shall the body men take   2965
And in a fayre place hit wake
Twhoo dayes; and þat whyle shal be
A crye made in all þat contre
That suche a man made sacrifise
And 3if any are so wyse   2970
To come pray hym ony boone,
Haste hem and come þeder soone
Or he to his graue be brought
For of here bed shall they wante nought.
Thenne summe come vnto þat stede   2975
And vnto hym make here bede
And at here goddis fote shall he
Afterwardes grauen be.

2947 they] *from* PTS, thenne B.   2948 lete] goon T, *om.* P.   2949 do . . . a]
to stike it in that T;   steken] set P.   2950] And many men shall make solace
P.   2952 naaked . . . sette] swerdes shall naked T.   2956 And] Shall be P;
also] *om.* P.   2957] And vppon hy shall he drawyn be P.   2958 ouermeste]
hyest P.   2960 God] oure goddis P;   I] is P.   2961] Thei slake the rope
that thei hym with drowe T, þai slake þat þai with hym drowe S, They that sey vp hym

Anoþer manere þere is ȝit
Of folke, þat ben of litel wit:
Whanne þei sholen sacrifice make,   3835
An hie tree þei shul doun take
And make it stike in a place
And manye one aboute making solace
And aboute þat same tree
Foure naked swerdes shullen sett be,   3840
þe pointis vpward euerichone.
þanne shal he [be] taken anone,
He þat þe sacrifice shal do,
And foote and honde bounde boþe two
And drawen vp shal he be   3845
To þe ouermeste ende of þe tree.
þere shal he crie þe folke vnto,
"In worshipe of my god þis I doo."
þanne slakeþ the roope þat him vp drowh
And þanne he falleþ sharpe inowh: 3850
Vpon þe swerdes he doth light
And gooþ to the deuel anoon right.
þanne shullen men þat body take
And in a faire place it wake
Two daies; and þilke while shal be   3855
A cry ymade in al þe countre
þat suche a man made sacrifice
And if þat any man is so wise
To come and praye him any bone,
Haste him and come þider sone   3860
Or he to his graue be broght
For of her bone þei shal faile noght.
þanne comeþ somme to þat stede
And maken þere to him her bede
And at her goddis foote shal he   3865   f. 53ʳ
Aftirward ygrauen be.

---

drough P.   2962] Ande (Then P) he fallith sharpe enowe TSP.   2963] Vpon
the swerdes behouyth hym to (*om.* S) lighte TSP.   2966 hit] done hit P.
2977 here] his P.

3836 An] Ani H.   3842 be] *from* H, *om.* L.   3846 ouermeste] ouereste
H.   3862 of] þei or H.

Yit is a contre furþermore
That whanne a man is dede þore,   2980
And he haue wyff, thenne shall she
All qwykke by hym grauen be
And also þe man by þe wyff,
Yf she rather lese here lyff.
And other folke þere ben and that   2985
Woll ete for dente hounde and catt.
Another þer is whenne he wyff shall wedde,
He dare not with here go to bedde:
The firste night woll he blethly
Yif another man leve to ligh here by   2990
For he seyth hit is perell of lyff
To towche furste a wedded wyff.
Another folke ther be, well fedde,
But they woll no wyff wedde:
They say þat noo wyfe may ne can   2995
Holde here trewly to oon man.
Yit ther is oon þat men calle
Londe Femenyne amonge hem alle,
All of wymmen and noo man,
For no man þerinne live can   3000
That is passed v yeere of elde

f. 45ᵛ Ouer v dayes hymselue to welde.
But in foure sesons in þe yeere
Men and they comen in fere
And haue with hem felowred.   3005
They loke not after sybred.
Viij dayes fare they thus and no moo
Or the men departe them froo;
And if ony a childe haue
And so be hit be a knave,   3010
They shall hit kepe and norissh hit well
Fyue yeere but more noo dele
And þenne shall they dryue hit soone

2979–82] *om.* P.   2984 rather] furste T, or he P.   2985 And other]
Another TS;   and] than T.   2987 Another . . . he] And when he that is P.
2989 woll he] but he yeue T, will he geve S, he geuyth P.   2990 Yif] *om.* TSP;
another man leve] Another yifte T, A gifte to another man P.   2991 he . . . of] it is
perilouse he seithe to T;   of] to his P.   2992 towche] twyche P.
2993 Another] And other P;   be] is that is P.   2994 woll no] nyl neuer T, will

Ʒit þer is a contre ferþermore
And whanne a man is deed thore,
If he haue a wijf, þanne shal she
Al quik by him buried be   3870
And also þe man by þe wijf
If she raþer þan he lese þe lijf.
Anoþer folke þer is þan þat
þat wole ete hounde and cat.
Anoþer whanne he his wijf shal wedde,   3875
He dar not wiþ hir goo to bedde:
þe firste night he ʒeueþ blethly
Leue to anoþer man to ligge hir by—
He seiþ it is a perel to a mannes lyf
To touche first a weddid wyf.   3880
Anoþer folk þer is and wel yfedde
But þei wole no wyf wedde:
þei sein þat no wyf may ne can
Holde hir euer to oone man.
Ʒit þer is oon þat men calle   3885
Lond Feminin amonge hem alle,
Al of wymmen and of no man,
For þerynne no man lyue can
þat is past fyue ʒere of elde
Ouþer fiue daies himself to welde.   3890
But in foure times of þe ʒere
Men and þei wendiþ togidre þere
And han wiþ hem felashipe
And of sibred þei take no kepe.
þus þei faren viij dayes and no mo   3895
Or þe men departe hem fro.
If any of hem a childe haue,
If it be so it be a knaue,
þei shul it kepe and norisshe wel   f. 53ᵛ
Fiue ʒere and no more no del   3900
And þanne wole þei driue it sone

neuer SP.   2996 trewly] euer T, *om.* P.   2998 Femenyne] Femynye S,
Femynem P.   2999 of] are P.   3002 Ouer] And S.   3004 comen in
fere] gadder full nere T, wende togedir there P.   3007 they] *om.* T.   3009 ony
a] they ony P.

3887 man] moo H.

Into þat londe þere þe men do wone.
They swhynke and till here mete bedene   3015
And ouer hem they have a qwene
That comaundes as qwene shall do
And holdeth hem in pece also.
Contrees ar ther many moo
And longe hit were to telle all þoo;   3020
But of these some shall mete
At the comyng of the false prophete.
But many a man shall there furst be lorn
For a kynge ȝit shal be born
That shall þe worlde do seke by mynde   3025
And shall do wriȝte þat men fynde;
And many of tho shall he spyll
And of other here londes fill.'

Qo. 74ᵃ   'Why are somme men blake in toune   (75)
          And sum whyte and sum browne?'   3030
'In thre maners hit comyth to
That a man is coloured soo.
Oon þat is here kynde,
As we in ooure bokes fynde:
For yif the man broun be   3035
And þe woman as well as he
And þey togeder haue comonynge,
Hit ough[t] to be broun þat childe ynge;
f. 46ʳ   Yif that oon be broun, þat other whyte,
And they assemble with grete delyte,   3040
Whos sede of moste delite festes
Whenne hit in þe chambir restes,
To þat sede shall þe chylde be
Likenyd moste in shapp and blee.
Anothir skele ȝit ther is: 3045
Yif a man be fedde amys
And pore be and porely goo,

3014 do] in TSP.   3015 here mete bedene] albedene P.   3017 That] as
P;   comaundes] *add* hem TSP; qwene] when they P.   3018 pete also] pees
ande roo TSP.   3019 Contrees] Certeyn T.   3020 all] of TP.   3023 a
man] *om.* TP; lorn] borne P.   3024] With hym shall holde furst beforne P.
3025 do] to T, *om.* P.   3026 do wriȝte] be ywrete T.   3028 londes] lande T; fill]
fulfille P.   3031 comyth] semyth P.   3033 Oon þat is] In his P; here] thorugh

To þe londe þere þat þe men in wone.
For her mete þei swinken bidene
And ouere hem þei haue a quene
þat kepeþ hem as quene shulde do   3905
And holdeþ hem in pees and rest also.
Contrees þere ben many moo:
Longe it were to telle of thoo;
But of þise somme shal mete
With þe comyng of þe false prophete.   3910
But firste þere shullen manye be ylore
For a king þat shal be ybore:
He shal seke þe world bi mynde
And shal do write þat men finde;
And manye of þise he shal spille   3915
And of oþer her londis fille.'

Ca.° lxviij°   'Whi ben somme blake in towne   (75)   f. 58ʳ/13
                  And some white and some browne?'

                      'In þre maneres it cometh to
                        þat a man is icoloured so.   3920
                  Oone is þorgh kynde,
                  As clerkes in her bokes fynde:
                  For if þe man broun be
                  And þe wijf as wel as he
                  And þei togidre haue engendrure,   3925
                  It oght to be broun of nature;
                  And if þat oon be broun and þat oþer white
                  And þei assemble wiþ grete delite,
                  Whos seed of moost delite festneþ
                  When it in þe chaumbre resteþ,   3930
                  Of þat side shal þe child be
                  Most yliche of shap and ble.
                  Anoþer skile ȝit there is:
                  If þat a man be fed amis
                  And porely ete and porely goo,   3935

TSP.   3035 broun] borne S.   3036 woman] wife TP.   3037 comonynge]
engendred T, engendrure S, engendure P.   3038 ought] ough B, aȝt S, oweth TP;
þat childe ynge] natured T, of nature SP.   3041 festes] feste P.   3042] And hit
be clene and honeste P.   3043 sede] syde T.   3044 in shapp and] and sharpe of
T;   in] and P;   and] of P;   blee] lee S.   3047 pore] poreli T;   be] ly P.

Hit makeþ hym not coloured soo
As that he sholde [be] with right
And he were kepte day and nyght.   3050
The thridde skyll hit is also
The londe and þe ayre therto:
For euer the hotter þat the londe is,
The brouner is the folke, ywys;
The coldere land, the whitter ay   3055
For here hyde is [not] brente away.'

Qo. 75ᵃ   *'Telle now, per company:*   (76)
         Whereof cometh felony?'
       'Wykked humours make malacoly
         And þat engendereth felony.   3060
The wykked humours kyndell smerte
And glowes oþerwhyle abowte the herte
And chaufeth hit as a fyre
And maketh hit marke and blakke for yre;
And þat merkenes answhers þenne   3065
Vpon the brayn panne;
And whanne the braynnes be marked soo,
A grete dele of witt they forgoo
And smyte anoon into þe felony
And þat maketh þe herte to dry;   3070
And whanne þat the humours sese
And of here brennyng is relese,
The herte restes and stille lendes
And þe derkenesse from hem wendes:
The lymes are ly3tere euerichon   3075
f. 46ᵛ   And in goode poynte bycome anoon.'

Qo. 76ᵃ   *'The bestes that God in erthe hathe wrought,*   (77)
         Of oon hewe why ar they nought?'
       'For they of Goddis liknesse not be
         Diuerse coloures hauen he   3080

3048–51] *om.* P.   3049 be] *from* TS, *om.* B.   3052 therto] alsoo TP.
3054 folke] man T.   3055 coldere] colde T;   ay] man aye T, for ay P.   3056 hyde]
hede T, sede P;   not] *from* TS, *om.* B, no P.   3061 kyndell] kyndely TSP.
3062 oþerwhyle] humwhile T, *om.* P.   3064 marke] derke P.   3066 Vpon]
Vppe vntill T, Vp vnto S, Vntille P;   brayn] harne T, horne P.   3067 braynnes]
harnes TP.   3070 þat] *om.* S;   to] so TSP.   3071 sese] gyn sease P.

þat makeþ him feble coloured also
Oþerwise þan he shulde be wiþ right
And he were fed wel day and night.
The þridde skile it is also   f. 58ᵛ
þe lond and þe eir therto: 3940
For euere þe hatter þe lond is,
The brouner is þe folk, iwis;
þe colder lond, þe whitter ay
For her hide is not brent away.'

Ca.° lxix°   '*Telle me now, þer companye:*   (76) 3945
Wherof comeþ felonye?'
　　'Wicked humers makeþ malencolie
　　And þat engendreþ felonye.
þe wicked humours ben kyndly smert
And gloweþ somwhile aboute þe hert   3950
And enchafeþ it as fire
And makeþ it derke and b[l]ak for ire;
And þat merknesse answeriþ þenne
Vp into þe herne panne;
And when þe hernes beþ imerked so,   3955
A greet dele of witte þei done forgo
And smyteþ anoon in felonye
And þat makeþ þe herte so drye;
But whan þe humours done sees
And of her glowinges ben in pees,   3960
þe herte restith and stille lendith
And þe merkenesse fro him wendith;
And þe lemes lightne euerichone
And in good pointe bicomeþ anone.'

Ca.° lxx°   '*þe beestis þat God in erþe haþ wroght,*   (77) 3965
Of oo colour whi ben þei noght?'
　　'For þat þei Goddis liknesse haue noght,
　　þerefore of dyuers colours þei ben wroght

3072 brennyng] gloweynge T, glowande P;   is] *om.* P.   3074 derkenesse] merkenes
TSP.   3075 are lyȝtere] ar liȝt S, lighten T, lightly P.   3078 oon] one maner
T.

3952 blak] bak L, black H.   3966 oo] *om.* H

And for they on þe grounde hem fede
Dyuerse herbes to here mete I rede.
Som ar colde and somme ar hote
And somme drye and som wete
And yf a beeste, when hit greses   3085
And gothe etand in þe lesues
That moost is hoote and drye also,
The ȝynge shall blake hewe come vnto;
And yf the mooste parte be hote,
Rede shall the ȝyng be, God hit wote;   3090
And be they moyste, hit shall be gray;
And be they colde, whyte for ay;
And [yf] þat a beste fynde
In a plase herbes of sere kynde
And þe bestes fede hem of hem alle,   3095
Of diuerse hewe the beeste shall falle;
And after that the beeste moste etes,
Moste of hewe þe beste getes.
And of all bestes fareth hit soo,
Wylde and tame, where þey goo,   3100
And all hathe God dight this thynge
At his wyll and at his ordeynyng.'

Qo. 77^a   'That ete and drynke moore thenne nede is,   (78)
              Whether do they—well or amysse?'
                    'He that etes moore thenne nede is   3105
                    And moore thenne his kynde wolde, ywys,
              He dothe harme his body to
              And synne vnto his soule also
              And distruccyon of mete dothe he
              That oþer withall myȝt fed be;   3110
              Agayn God suche a man is
              Worse þenne a beeste, iwysse.
f. 47^r God ordeyned man hym to fede
              After þat his kynde haue nede

3081 hem fede] frete SP, ete T.   3082 I rede] *om.* TSP.   3085 greses]
grete is TP.   3086 in þe lesues] on the gres TP.   3087 That moost is] Yf the
most parte of the gresse be P.   3088 ȝynge] yonglyng P.   3090 ȝyng] yonlyng
P.   3093 yf] *from* PTS, *om.* B.   3094] Herbes that ben of sondri kynde
T.   3095 þe bestes] she TP;   hem (1)] hur TP.   3096 beeste] beistes S,

And for þei on þe grounde doiþ frete
Diuerse herbes to her mete.   3970
Some ben colde and some ben hote
And some drie and some wote
And if a beest, whan it greet is   f. 59ʳ
And gooþ eting on þe gris
þo þat ben moost hote and drie tho,   3975
þe ȝonge shal blak hewe come to;
And if þe moost parte of þe herbes be hote,
Rede shal þe ȝonge be, God it wote;
And if þei be moist, þei shal be gray;
And if þei be colde, white for ay;   3980
And if þat a beeste do finde
Herbis on a place of diuerse kinde
And she fede hir of hem alle,
Of diuerse colour þe ȝonge shal falle;
And þat þei moost of ete,   3985
Moost of colour þe ȝonge shal gete.
Of alle beestis it fariþ so,
Wilde and tame, whereeuer þei go,
And God haþ dight al þis thing
At his wille and his ordeining.'   3990

Ca.º lxxjº   *þei þat eten and drinken more þan nede is,*   (78)
               Wheþer done þei—wel or amis?'
                    'He þat etiþ more þan he sholde
                    And more þan his kynde wolde,
               Harme he doth his body to   3995
               And synne to his soule also
               And distruccioun of mete doþ he
               þat oþer þerwith yfedde mighte be;
               And aȝeinst God suche a man is
               Werse þan a beest, ywis.   4000
               God ordeined a man him to fede
               After þat his kinde haþ nede

yonge T, yonglyng P.   3097 the beeste moste] she moste of TP.   3098 beste]
yonge T, yongelyng P.   3100 þey] it T.   3102 at his] *om.* P.
3103–4] Doo thei well or doo thei mys / That eten and drinken more than nede is T.
3105 nede is] he sholde TSP.   3107 ywys] *om.* TSP.   3112 beeste] *add* he is
T, *add* forsothe P.   3113 hym] *om.* T.

And þe remenaunte soo to saue   3115
Vntyll after he myster haue;
And a man þat is wyse
Shall ete ones on the day or twyse.
A man þat etes at a meele
Whill hym þynkes þat he is wele   3120
And lay efte abouen moore
Er þat be defied bifoore,
His stomak soore acombris he
And þe hete þerinne sholde be;
And soo his kynde he brynges doun   3125
And hymselue to corupcion,
And his witte in þat is lesse
Thanne a beeste þat etes gresse.
For ther is nother hors ne kowe,
Whanne þat he hathe eten ynowe,   3130
Thatte woll ete ony more
Tyll efte þat hym hongere soore;
And sythen a dowme beste dothe hit,
Moore shulde a man þat hathe wit.

Therfore, I say, amysse þey doo   3135
That ete moore than nede is to.'

Qo. 78ᵃ   'Whiche is þe beste thyng of a man   (79)
                 And the worste that thow reken can?'
                 'The beste thynge of man, iwysse,
                 And þe worste þe tonge hit is.   3140
                 For his tonge a man may gete
                 Siluer and goolde, drynke and mete,
                 Loue and worshipp and fauoure
                 And enhaunsynge of honoure;

3121 efte] oftyn P.   3122] Eer the other defied wore T, Er that he defyed there
P.   3123 soore acombris] encombreth TP.   3125 he] om. P.
3126 hymselue] so torneth it T.   3130 Whanne] Iwhanne B, Fro TS, Fro the tyme P;

And al þe remenaunt forto saue
Til he þerof mister haue;
And a man þat is wys   4005
Shal ete ones a day or twys.
A man þat eteth at a mele   f. 59ᵛ
Til him þinke þat he is wele
And leith sone aboue more
Or þat be defied bifore,   4010
His stomak encombreþ he
And þe hete þat þerynne shulde be;
And so his kinde he bringeþ doun
And himself to corrupcioun,
And his witt in þat is lesse   4015
þan a beest þat etith gresse.
For þer is neiþer hors ne cow
þat, whanne he haþ ete inow,
þat wole ete any more
Til efte þat him hungred sore;   4020
And siþen þat a beest dooþ þus,
More shulde a man þat feleþ his pous
Distempred and is not wel at ese
Ete mesurably, his God to plese;
For þei þat han her resoun and witt   4025
Han þe miche more nede to gouerne it.
þerfore, I seie, amys þei do
þat etith more þanne mister is to,
Ouþer drinke, wheþer it be:
I rede þou lerne wel þis of me.'   4030

Ca.° lxxij°   'Which is þe best þing of þe man   (79)
                     And þe werste?—Telle, if þou can.'
                         'The beste þing of man, iwis,
                         And þe werste þe tunge it is
                     For wiþ his tunge a man may gete   4035
                     Siluer and golde, drinke and mete,
                     Loue and worshipe and fauour
                     And encresing of miche honour;

þat] thens T;   he] they P.   3132 efte þat hym] that he after T.   3133 dowme]
om. P.   3137 ff.] follow 3246 S.   3141 gete] om. S.   3144 enhaunsynge]
avaunsyng P.

Also for the tonge he may   3145
Haue shame and vylonye all day
For suche wordes may a man say
That perauenture may make hym daye.
The tonge hathe nother golde ne fee
f. 47ᵛ   But moche honoure maketh he;   3150
And the tonge ne hathe noo boon
But yt dothe breke many oon;
Also, well were hit þe wyll,
Hit myght speke þe goode as þe ill.'

Qo. 79ᵃ   'Whether yeueþ a man moore cunnyng—   (80) 3155
                Hote metes or colde etyng?'
                   'A man þat vseth hote metes,
                      He chaufeth the body when he etes;
                The senewes norishith hit therby
                And alle þe veynes of the body;   3160
                Hit warmeth the braynes and þe herte
                And makeþ hem of wittes smerte.
                Colde mete dothe nought þerto
                But keles senewes and veynes also
                And stere the humors wykked and ill   3165
                And þe herte holdeth stille

                And tho kele mannys witte;
                Forþy nedly behoueth hit,
                Whenne þe wittes are so colde,
                That they the lasse connyng holde.'   3170

Qo. 80ᵃ   'How may a man fle felony   (81)
                And wraþþe and malencoly?'
                   'Fyrst shall a man haue in his thought
                      God, that hym haue made of nought,
                And thanke hym in all sake   3175
                That after his lykenesse he wolde hym make.

3147 a man] he T, hit P.   3159 hit] he T, she P.   3161 Hit] He TP,
braynes] hernes T, veynes P;   and] of P.   3166 And þe herte] That the hete T,
That hote mete P.   3167 kele] seeke S.   3172 wraþþe] wrathehede T.

And also for þe tunge he may
Haue shame and vilanye alday 4040
For suche wordes it may seie f. 60ʳ
þat it may make him to deie.
þe tunge haþ neiþer gold ne fe
But ȝit miche merþe makeþ he;
And þe tunge haþ no boon 4045
But he do breke many oon;
And also, and it were his wille,
It might speke good and leue ille.'

Ca.º lxxiijº 'Wheþer ȝeueþ a man more kunnyng— (80)
Hoote mete or colde in eting?' 4050
'A man þat vsith hote metis,
It enchawfeþ him whan he etis;
The synewis norisshiþ he þerby
And alle þe veynes of his body;
It warmeþ the brayne and þe herte 4055
And of wittes makeþ hem smerte.
Coolde metis doth noght þerto
But keleþ synwes and veynes also
And steriþ the humours most to ille
þat hote metes wolde kepe stille 4060
In good temperure wel and fyn
And from yuel make it declyn;
For whan a man fediþ his body
And eteþ colde mete gredily,
It keleþ þe brayn and þe herte 4065
And þe witt it makeþ derke;
And whan þe wittes ben so keled,
þe lesse kunnynge þei haue feled.'

Ca.º lxxiiijº 'Hou may a man fle felonye (81)
And wratthe and malencolye?' 4070
'First shal a man haue in his þoght
þe Lorde, þat made him of noght,
And þanke him of his grace and might
þat to his liknesse he wolde him dight

3174 God] Hym TP.   3176 hym] it T.

─────────

4058 keleþ] kepeth H.

And he sholde hym beþynke also
Of the dethe þat he shall to,
That noo man may hit withstonde.
Also shall he hym bythenke in londe   3180
How God hathe youen to many
Maym and sekenesse of body
And to somme rotyng of lyme,
And what heale he gave to hym.
Ete and drynke after skyll   3185
And slepe as þat reason woll:

f. 48ʳ   That euel wylle ouercome he shall
That h[ym] steres to greue withall.
And soo may he felonye
Ouercome and malancolye.'   3190

Qo. 81ᵃ   'Whether to have is more hate—   (82)
Love of wymmen or theyre hate?'
            'A goode woman is goode to loue
And holde vnto mannes behove
For of goode woman comes nought,   3195
Nother in worke ne in thought,
But goode and worshipp where she goose
And eke a name of full goode loose;
For but goode trouthe and lawe
Dothe she ay to here felawe;   3200
And suche a woman loue men shall
And doo worshipp and honour withall.
A wyked woman shall men hate
And fle from here in way and gate
And yf men may not fle here, styll   3205
Fond to flee here wykked wyll:
For men shall neuer haue but foly
Of wykked wymmannes company

3179 may hit withstonde] ne (om. P) maye froo blenke (slenke S) TSP.   3182 Maym]
Mayne P.   3185 Ete] Etynge T.   3186 as] alle alle T, aftir P.   3187 he]
om. P.   3188 hym] from TSP, he B;   greue] grete T.   3189 he] he fle
P.   3190] And ouercome the malyncoly P.   3191–246] precede 3137 S.
3193 goode (2)] om. P.   3195 of] a P.   3198 eke a name] ekynge T, ekened

(For holy writ to vs witnesse   4075 f. 60ᵛ
þat God made man to his liknesse).
And he shulde biþenke him also
þat he shal deie and hens goo:
From þat may no man him blenke.
And also he shulde him biþenke   4080
Hou þat God haþ ȝeue to many
Flesshe and boon, skyn and body,
And to some roting of lym,
And what hele he ȝaf to him.
Ete and drinke aftir skile   4085
And slepe al þat resoun wile
And so wel ouercome he shal
þe yuel þat he is stired wiþal.
And so may he felonye
Ouerecome and malencolye.'   4090

Ca.º lxxvº   'Wheþer to haue is more bate—   (82)
                Loue of wymmen or her hate?'
            'A good womman is to loue
            And cherised to manis byhoue
        For a good womman coueiteþ noght,   4095
        Neiþer in werk ne in þoght,
        But worshepe God where she goos
        And encresing of good loos;
        And truþe aftir Goddis lawe
        Doth she euere to hir felawe;   4100
        And suche a wommen men loue shal
        And do hir worshipe and honour wiþal.
        A wikked woman men shal hate
        And flee from hir in þe gate
        And if þou may not flee hir at þi wille,   4105
        Algates flee her wicked wille,
        For men shullen neuer haue but folie
        Of wicked wommannes companye;

S;   name of] *om.* P.   3199 goode] *add* and TS.   3200 Dothe] Bothe P;
ay] any S.   3204 here] hem P;   way and] the TP.   3205 styll] felle P.

4107 but] wiþ H.

And oþerwhyle skathe, perel, and blame
And amonge men mekel shame.   3210
Here maners are full of euel vyce
For she is lyke a cocatryce,
That is a beste that men of telles,
And in þe water moste he dwelles.
He hathe a grete hede and a longe   3215
And many tethe crokyd and wronge
And twhyse in the yeere shall nede
Aboute his tethe wormys brede;
And whenne he feles hem also,
The londe shall he þenne drawe to;   3220
And he agayn the sonne alday
Lye and gape as wyde as he may.
Thenne cometh a foule that God wolde make,
The wormes oute of his tethe to take.

f. 48ᵛ

The mouthe of his hede is dyght   3225
Shapyn as an ele ys right:
The foule crepith in as nyce
Into the mouth of þe cokadryce

And þe wormes eteth ychone.

The cocatrice feleth anoon   3230

That the wormes destroyed be:
Anoon here mowthe closeþ she
And wolde þat foule destroye for his mede
That hadde doon here þat goode dede.
The bridde feles here euel will   3235
And wote þat she wolde hym spyll:
With his bille, þat is sharpe bifore,
The cocatryce he smytes soore
In þe mouthe agayne þe palate ·
And she openeth þe mouthe with that.   3240

3209 oþerwhile skathe] vmwhile scape TP.   3211 full] *om.* P;   euel] *om.* T,
wicked S, foule P.   3212 cocatryce] cokentrice P.   3217 twhyse] thries
T.   3218 Aboute] But in P.   3221 he] lye SP, ligge T;   alday] allewey
T.   3222 Lye] *om.* TSP.   3223 wolde make] made T.   3224 tethe]

And some wole shape peril and blame   f. 61ʳ
And doo many men miche shame.   4110
For her maners ben ful of vice
And she is like a coketrice,
þat is a beest þat men of telle,
And in þe water most wole dwelle.
He haþ a greet heed and a long   4115
And many croked teeþ and wrong
And twies in þe ȝere þer shal nede
Aboute his teeþ wormes brede;
And whan he feleþ hem crawling þo,
He shal drawe þe lond vnto   4120
And ligge aȝeinst þe sunne alday
And gape as wide as he may.
þanne comeþ a foule wiþoute make
And þe wormes out of his teeþ he take;
And þe mouth on his heed is dight   4125
Liche a rounde hole right:
þis foule fleeþ wiþ al his might
Into þe cokatrice mouth right
As he gapeþ aȝein the sunne,
þise wormes to pike out if he kunne;   4130
And þe wormes euerichone
He pikeþ hem out by oone and one.
And whan þe cokatrice þis feleþ
(þat sadly fastned ben her teeþ
And þat þe wormes distroyed be),   4135
þanne faste hir mouth closeþ she
And wolde ete þat foule for his mede
þat haþ done him so good a dede.
þe brid feliþ hir yuel wille
And woot þat she wolde hir spille   4140
And wiþ his mouth sharpe bifore
þe cokatrice he smyteþ sore
In þe mouth aȝeinst þe palat   f. 61ᵛ
And she openeþ her mouth wiþ þat:

hede T.   3225 ele ys] Elis T.   3227 as nyce] alle nyce T, that vyce P.
3232 Anoon] And P.   3233 destroye] ete TSP.   3234 That] That so T;
here þat] for hur T.   3237 bille] mouth TP;   soore] thore T.

  4111 vice] "vice" of L.   4124 he] doþe H.   4131 And] And anon H.

The bridde shoteth [out] in haste
And forthe fleeth he away faste.
Suche seruice yeldes a wykked woman
For his goode dede vnto man
And þerfore bothe loude and styll   3245
Shall men fle here wykked will.'

'A man þat is in hele a[nd] ȝynge,   (83)
How wrappes he for lityll thynge?'
'I shall say þe how and why:
The herte is lorde of the body   3250
And þe body is his warden
And his seruant with all his mayn
For al þat lykes þe herte vnto
Lykes vnto þe body also.
The eyen are gyderes of the herte;   3255
The eres are messangeres smerte;
The tonge as avokate is she;
The fete his supportoures be;
The handes are his knyghtes twoo;
The hertis castell is þe hede also;   3260
The braynes are chastylene
þat of the herte all ye[m]es fayne.
Yf the herte a worde here nowe,
Be hit skathe, be hit prowe,
He may hit not wete ne knowe   3265
But his messengere hit hym shewe;
And yif the tydyngys hym lyke,
He reioyseth hym wondirlyke
And all his men haue ioye and blisse
Of that the herte soo ioyfull is.   3270
But whenne þe messengere tellith hym onythyng
That towcheþ wrath or euel þynge,
He steres and quakeþ wroþfully
And all his men are þenne sory:

f. 49ʳ

3241 out] *from* STP, *om.* B.   3243 seruice] wyse P.   3244 For] For alle
TP.   3245 bothe] Y rede you P.   3246 Shall men fle] Fle from P.
3247–8 *q. no. om.* B.   3247 and] *from* ST, a B.   3249 how] *om.* P.
3255 The eyen]   The men T, Thes P;   gyderes] syoures T, Gyours P.
3256 eres] yen P;   are] arne his P.   3257 as] *om.* TSP.   3258 suppor-
toures] somers TSP.   3259 twoo] levid T, lede S, lewde P.   3260 also] *om.*

þanne sheteþ the brid forþ in haste   4145
And fleeþ forþ awey faste.
In suche wise ʒildeþ a wicked womman
For alle hise gode dedes to a man
And þerfore men shulde lowde and stille
Flee ech wommanes wicked wille.'   4150

Ca.° lxxvj°   'A man þat is in hele and ʒing,   (83)
Hou wraþþeth he him for litel þing?'
        'I shal þe seie hou and why:
        þe herte is lord of þe body
And þe body is his wardayn   4155
And his seruaunt wiþ al his mayn
For al þat likeþ þe herte to
It liketh to þe body also.
þe men beth gouernours of þe herte
And þe eeren messageris smerte;   4160
þe tunge avokett is she
And þe sighte his sonde be;
þe hondis beeþ hise knightes two;
þe hertes castel is heed þerto.

If þe herte heere a worde,   4165
Be it yuel, be it goode,
He may it not wite ne knowe
But his messangere it him showe;
And if þat þe erande him like,
He reioyseþ him wonderlike   4170
And alle þe membris haue ioye and blis
Of þat þe herte so ioyful is.
But whan þe messageris tellen him to
Anyþing þat is yuel do,
He steriþ and quakeþ wrothfully   4175
And alle hise membres ben sory

TSP.   3261 braynes] harnes T, hertis P.   3262 yemes] yeves B, yemiþe T,
ʒemes S.   3263 a worde here] geue a word P.   3267 tydyngys] tytanne
P.   3272 þynge] tythynge TSP.   3273 wroþfully] wrongfully T.

4150 wommanes wicked] reversed H.   4162 þe] his H.   4163 þe] His
H.   4168 messangere] messengers H.   4171–290] page missing H.

Alle are þey wrothe and qwake also   3275
As they wote hymselfe doo;
His enemyes are blythe þerfore
And on his men are gleand soore.
Yf the herte be sterke and wysse
And loueth þe castell þere he lyes   3280
And his men woll se vntill
And here skathe not norissh will,
Blame and charge and wraþþe withall
Vpon hymselfe take hit he shall
And holde hym faste and harde agayn;   3285
His men shull reste þenne and be fayn
Yif his foes ouercome be
That hathe recouered his meyne.
And ȝif the herte be febyll and vayn,
His enemyes brennes hym agayn   3290
And he hathe no myȝt to withstonde
Here asawte hym asayland;
And his men are febull as he
And sopheres not here aduersite
But to misdo þey stere hem smerte   3295
And al the skaþe lettes be þe herte
For the body may take no skathe
f. 49ᵛ   But yf þe herte fele hit rathe.'

'How may a man blameles be   (84)
                 To loue a woman and hym she?'   3300
               'Loue togeder they may well
                 As in God withouten cele
For God togedyr hem feste louely
And of bothe made oon body
And for frute sholde b[e]twyxe hem twoo   3305
Goddes name worship doo
For they sholde eyther loue other in blisse
As þe comaundement of God is.

3275 þey] wrathe P.   3278 gleand] glowande SP, gloweynge T.
3280 loueth] leuys P;   lyes] is T.   3281 vntill] hym tille P.   3283 wraþþe
withall] the wrath all TP.   3285 and (2)] *om.* T.   3286 men] man P;
þenne] *om.* P.   3287] And that is for ouyrcomyn be P;   Yif] And TS.
3288 recouered] rered TSP.   3289 vayn] feyn P.   3290 brennes hym]
bryngis he P.   3292 asawte] assente TS;   hym] hem P.   3293–485] *page*

And alle þei ben wrooþ and quake also   f. 62ʳ
As þei knowen himself do;
Hise enemyes ben bliþe þerfore
And on hise membres ben glowyinge sore.
If þe herte be strong and wys   4180
And loueþ the castel þere þat he is
And hise membres wole seie him vntil
þat þeire skaþe þei norisshe wil,
Blame and charge and þe wreche al   4185
Vpon himself take he shall
And holde him and harde again;
Hise men shullen reste and be fain
And hise foon ouercome be
þat haue rerid his meyne.   4190
And if þe herte be feble and fein,
Hise enemyes bringeþ him agein
And he haþ no might to wiþstande:
þere asaute is to him seilande.
And hise men ben as feble as he   4195
And þoleþ not her aduersite
But to misdo þei stere hem smerte
And al þe scathe betideþ the herte
For þe body may take no scathe
But if þe herte fele it rathe.'   4200

Ca.º lxxvijº   'Hou may a [man] blameles be   (84)
                    To loue a [womman] and him she?'
                    'Loue may þei togidre wel
                    Vertuously, as I the tel,
                    And togidre festen hem louely   4205
                    And of boþe make oo body
                    And for þe fruite bitwene hem two
                    To Goddis name shal worshipe do
                    And for þat eche shulde loue oþer in blis
                    As þe comaundement of God is.   4210

missing T.   3293 febull as] febeler than P.   3294 here] *om.* P.
3296 lettes be] betechith P.   3302 cele] cel S, dele P.   3303 hem feste]
fastenyd he P.   3305 betwyxe] btwyxe B, be betwyne P.   P.   3306 doo] to do
P.   3307 eyther . . . in] loue other in loue and P.

    4201–2 man . . . womman] *from table* 1167–8, *reversed* L.

Of loue þere is another maner
As þe worlde forgeues here,   3310
As a man to loue his wyff
For here fayrenesse and here goode lyf,
For richesse and for here beaute
And with that in here may be:
A man, yf he a goode wyf haue   3315
That hym bothe can guyde and saue
And ys of goode maners withall,
The world will that he loue here shall;
And for thes skeles shall woman
After þe worlde agayn loue man.   3320
But otherwyse who þat loue wyll
Of these vertues hathe neuer a dele:
Mykel to blame they are forthy
For they loue vnskylfully.'

Qo. 84ᵃ 'Whennes comeþ þe fatnesse and why   (85) 3325
          That a man hathe in his body?'
               'Of ffleumes þat in þe body rennes
               Cometh fattenesse, whoso hem kennes.
          And ȝif the flewmes be swhete,
          Thorough the body they shote   3330
          And þe hete of other thynge
          Slee they and hemselue sprynge
          And lordship they haue anoon
          Ouer the humours euerychone;
f. 50ʳ   And whenne þat they lorde are,   3335
          The swhettenesse of hem turneth yare
          Vnto grece: thenne gedereth þat
          And makeþ soo þe body fatte.
          Yf the flewmes be salte withynne,
          The fflessh and þe body they brenne   3340
          And ffelowshipp anoon þey take
          Vnto colours yelow and blake;
          And whenne they in lymmes and veynes are spred

3312 fayrenesse] godenes P.   3313 beaute] lewte P.   3315 yf he] that
P.   3316 hym . . . guyde] wynnes bothe hym P;   guyde] wyn S.
3318 will . . . here] wele here loue P.   3320 worlde] worde P.   3321] But so
loue other wele P.   3322 of] And of P;   hathe neuer] haue no P.

Of loue þer is anoþer manere   f. 62ᵛ
As þe world forȝeueþ here,
As a man to loue his wijf
For hir fairnesse and hir good lijf,
For hir ricchesse and hir leute   4215
And for þe vertues in hir may be:
A man þat a good wijf haue
And þat him boþe wynneþ and saue
And is of good manere wiþal,
þe worlde wole þat he hir loue shal;   4220
And for þise skilles shal a womman
After þe world aȝein loue man.
But whoso loueþ oþer wel
And of þise vertues haþ no del,
It is more lust þan resoun   4225
As is shewed in many a toun.'

Ca.° lxxviij°   *'Whennes comeþ fatnesse and why*   (85)
               þat a man haþ in his body?'
       'Off flewmes þat in þe body renne
       Comeþ fathed, whoso hem kenne.   4230
And if þe flewmes be swete,
þorgh þe body sone þei shete
And þe hete of othir þing
Sle þei and hemself spring
And lordshipe þei haue anoon   4235
Ouer þe humours euerichon;
And whan þat þei lord are,
þe swetnesse of hem torneþ ȝare
Into grese: þanne gadreþ þat
And maketh so the body fat.   4240
And if þe flewmes be salte wiþynne,
þe flesshe and þe body þei brenne
And felowred anon þei take
Into colours ȝelowe and blake;
And whanne þei in lymes and veines sprede   4245   f. 63ʳ

3330 body they] bodies þat S.   3334] Ouercome the lyuers euerychon P.
3340 they] *om.* P.   3341 ffelowshipp] felaundir P.   3343 they] hit P;   are]
om. P.

And the colours with hem ledde,
As longe as they thereinne dure   3345
They reue þe body the n[or]ture
And holdeth hit soo lene alway
That hit noo grece gader may.
Therfore hit is goode to many oon
To lete the flewmes oute of hem gon,   3350
For a man myght be slayne forthy
Or make grete skabbe on his body.'

Qo. 85ᵃ   *'Shall men wymmen chastyse and wisse*   (86)
                 With betyng whenne they doon amisse?'
                 'Goode wymman to deele withall,   3355
                   Here misdede shall be but small;
                 And yf that she has ought misdone,
                 She repentes her anoon
                 And shryues here of þat misdede:
                 Menne shall here þanne chastyse and lede   3360
                 With fayre wordes and with softe
                 And shall no man mone here ofte.
                 Whenne wykked woman hathe miswrought,
                 She ne shames right nought
                 But vauntes therof astyte   3365
                 And hathe þerof grete delight.
                 Yf men here blame þat she did soo,
                 Eftesoones shall she worse doo;
                 Yf men here vnbroyde or bete,
                 The lesse she shall here foly lete.   3370
f. 50ᵛ   Thou shall here warne twyes or thryse
                 With fayre wordes, yf thow be wyse,
                 And with gyfte and fayre hetyng:
                 And she wol not leue for þat thyng,
                 Men shall here leue and from here goo—   3375
                 For helpeth man noon other woo
                 Vnto woman that wykked woll be
                 For of fendes wyll is shee

3344 ledde] lede SP.   3345 thereinne dure] endure P.   3346 reue] renne
P;   norture] *from* SP, nature B.   3350 hem] here P.   3351 forthy] therby
P.   3359 shryues] shoues (?shones) S.   3360 þanne] *om.* P.   3362 mone
here] move S.   3364 shames] yeuyth therof P.   3365 vauntes] vanytes P;
þerof] hir of þat S, here thereof P.   3368 Eftesoones] Anothir tyme P.

And þe colours wiþ hem lede,
So longe as þei þeryn dure
þei reuen þe body of norture
And holdeþ it so lene alway
þat it no greece gadre may.   4250
þerfore it is good to many oon
To late þe flewmes out of him goon,
For a man might be slayn þerby
þorgh swelling of his body.'

Ca.° lxxix°   'Shullen men chastise [wymmen] and wisse   (86) 4255
                    Wiþ beting whan þei done amisse?'
                'A good womman to dele wiþal,
                  Hir mysdede shal be bot smal;
                And if she haue oghte mysdone,
                She repentith hir ful soone   4260
                And shameþ of hire misdede:
                Suche men shul wel chatise and lede
                Wiþ faire wordes and wiþ softe
                And no man shal mene her ofte.
                And whanne a wicked womman haþ miswroght,   4265
                She neuere repentiþ hir noght
                But avaunteþ hir as tite
                And haþ þerof greet delite.
                If men hir blame for she dide so,
                Anoþer time she shal werse do: 4270
                If men vpbreide and hir bete,
                þe lesse she shal hir foly lete.
                Men shal hir warne twise or þrise
                Wiþ faire wordes, if þei be wise,
                And wiþ ȝifte and faire biheting: 4275
                And she wole not lette for noþing,
                Men shul hir leue and fro hir go—
                It helpiþ not to do hir oþer woo
                For to a womman þat wicked wole be,   f. 63ᵛ
                Of þe deuels wille is she   4280

3369 vnbroyde or] vmbrayde and S, vpbreyde and P.   3371 Thou] Men
P;   warne] wane S.   3372 thow] he P.   3376 helpeth] hit helpis to
P.   3377 Vnto] But P;   that] that of P.

4255 wymmen] *from table* 1171, *om.* L.

And þe devel her wonnes inne
That causeth þat she canne not blynne;   3380
Therfore is noo better wonne
But leue þe devel and here alone.'

Qo. 86ᵃ   'Wat thyng is gelosye to knowe   (87)
           And why is man gelose som throwe?'
                'Off gelosye are maners moo   3385
                To tellen of the[n] oon or twoo.
           Oon gelosye of God hit is
           Whenne a men hereth speke amysse
           Agayn God or agayn his laye,
           As heretykes doon all day: 3390
           There shulde a man be gelous
           And his lay to were desyrouse.
           Ʒyt shall a man gelouse be
           Ouer his frende, and oony have he;
           And þat gelosye is comyng   3395
           Of clene herte and a louyng.
           Ʒit is þere a gelosye
           þat comith of fowle herte and folye
           And of wykked humours also
           That the herte geders vnto: 3400
           That gelosye is not of woman goode
           For hit is full brennyng and wykked mode.
           The herte hit brenneth full of wykked þought;
           Reste in þe body may hit nought;
           Mete and drynke he doþe forsake   3405
           And all his ioye is from hym take.
           Yf a man be in suche a stryfe
           For hir that is his owne wyfe,
f. 51ʳ   Out of his thought he shall hit late
           And þynke þat hit may hym not bate: 3410
           His burthen from his bak he throwe
           And caste hit to þe grounde lowe
           And thynke, yf she wolde goode be,

3380 That . . . she] She dothe his wille and P.   3381 is] Y can P.
3386 then] them BP, þen S.   3392 were] kepe P.   3395 þat] om. S.
3401 That] And P;   not] om. SP;   goode] þicke SP.   3402 For hit] And þat S,
That P;   full] foule P;   wykked mode] wik SP.   3403 herte hit] hart is S, hertis

And þe deuel hir wonneþ withynne
þat makeþ hir she can not blynne;
þerfore þer is no better wone
But late þe deuel and hir allone.'

Ca.º lxxxº   'What þing is gelesie to knowe   (87) 4285
     And whi is man ielous somme þrowe?'
     'Off ielesie beþ maners mo
     For to telle of þan oone or two.
One ielosie is, as 3e shal here,
Whan a man heeriþ men speke here   4290
A3einst God or a3einst his lawe,
As heretikes vsen in her sawe:
þere shulde a man be right ielous
And to kepe his lawe desirous.
3it shal a man ielous be   4295
Ouer his frende, if any haue he;
And þat ielousie is to comende
Of clene herte and louende.
3it þer is a ielousie
þat comeþ of foule herte and folie   4300
And of wicked humours also
þat þe herte gadren to:
þat ielousie is of a womman þikke
And þat is foule brenning and wicke.
þe herte brenneþ so of wicked þoght   4305
þat in þe body may it reste noght;
Mete and drinke þei forgoon as tite
And al ioye and al delite.
And if man be in suche a strijf
For hir þat is his weddid wijf,   4310
Out of his þoght he shal it late
And þenke þat it may him do bate:
His birden fro his bak he þrowe   f. 64ʳ
And caste it into þe grounde lowe
And þenke, if she wole good be,   4315

P;   full] *om.* P.   3405 he doþe forsake] hit (he P) forgos as tyte SP.
3406 is from hym take] and his (all his) delite SP.   3408 wyfe] weddid wyf
P.   3410 bate] abate P.   3412 to þe] into a P.

4291 H *begins again.*   4313 he] to H.

Shulde non here kepe as well as she;
And þenne ay whill he fareth soo　　　　　3415
He seses his sorowe and his woo.
And yif he loue oon wodely
That nought his owne is proporly,
He travayles in gelosy
And brennyng loue and grete foly;　　　　　3420
In angwysshe grete live he shall
And his whyle he tynes all:
He is lyke that man, iwisse,
That nyght and day fyghtyng is
Agayn the wynde hit to take　　　　　　　3425
His owne at his wyll to make,
And euer the lenger he dothe soo
The furthere is þe wynde hym froo.'

Qo. 87ᵃ　　　　'Shall a man love his frende*　　　　(88)
　　　　　　　　And fonde to holde hym to his ende?'　　3430
　　　　'His goode frende a man loue shall
　　　　　With goode herte and clene withall
　　　　　And after his myght do to hym well
And of his charge bere som dele;
For yf he right goode frende be,　　　　　3435
Noo godenesse forgeteth he.
But of diuerse maneres are they all,
Many þat men frendes call.
Summe þere be þat boste can shake
And a man grete chere make　　　　　　3440
And saythe þat he is his frende:
Whill he wote ought in his hende,
He proferes hym his will to do
But there ne is noo triste þerto:
f. 51ᵛ　　　　Whatte he dothe hym rekke ne howe　3445
But that be his owne prowe;
For did he ought agaynes hym,
He sholde fynde hym fell and grymme;

3415 þenne] þenke SP.　　　3416 seses] seches S, sykis P.　　　3417 oon wodely]
inwardly P.　　　3418 nought] *om.* P.　　　3420 And] Of SP; loue] hert
SP.　　　3425 the wynde] *om.* SP.　　　3430 to his ende] in hys hende S.
3433 to hym well] he wylle P.　　　3434 his charge] hoos charite P.　　　3439 boste]

Shulde noon hir kepe so wel as she;
And þenke, euere while he fareþ so,
He sekeþ his sorwe and his woo.
And if he loueþ one hertily
þat is noght his owne propurly,   4320
He trauailleþ in ielousie
Of brennyng herte and grete folie;
In greet angwisshe lye he shal
And his wille he tineþ al:
He is lyke þat man, ywis,   4325
þat night and day fighting is
Aȝeinst þe winde it forto take
His owne at his wille forto make,
And euer þe lenger þat he doth so
þe ferþer is þe wynd him fro.'   4330

Ca.° lxxxj°   'Shal a man loue his frende   (88)
                   And fonde to holde [him] in his hende?'
                  'His good freend a man loue shal
                     Wiþ good herte and clene wiþal
And aftir his might do to him wel   4335
And of charge bere somdel;
For if he right good frende be,
No goodnesse forȝetiþ he.
But of diuerse maners ben þei alle,
Ful manye þat men frendes calle.   4340
Somme þere ben þat wel bost can shake
And to a man faire semblant make
And seie þat he is his frende:
þe while he wote oght in his hende,
He profriþ him his wille to doo   4345
But þer is no trust therto:
What he doþ he ne reckeþ ne how   f. 64ᵛ
But þat it be for his owne prow;
For dide he oght aȝeinst him,
He shulde finde him ful grim.   4350

well P.   3440 grete chere] faire semblaunt P.   3442 wote] hathe P;   hende]
honde hende B.   3445 hym rekke ne] ne reckith P.   3448 fell and] full P.
_____
    4316 she] ȝe H.   4332 him] *from table* 1176, *om.* L, hym H.   4341 shake]
stake H.

For he loueth me lytyll, be my pate,
For well lasse þat wolde me hate.   3450
He þat loveth me for myn
And nought for me, þat is venym;
But he is frende for mannes byhove
And to truste in and to loue
That nouȝt asentes to þe will   3455
Of his frende that may turne to yll,
And s[eru]eth of no losyngerye
But chastyse hym of his foly;
And though he hym a parte misdo,
He ne sayth noo worde therto: 3460
In þat ffrende shall men have fyaunce
And love hym and hym avaunse.'

Qo. 88ᵃ   'May a man his profet do   (89)
     And no travayle haue therto?'

    'Sithen Adam ete thorough wykked rede   3465
    The appel þat God hym forbede,
    Fro þat tyme vnto now
Miȝte neuer man do his prow,
Were he neuer soo mighty,
Withoute travayle of his body.   3470
The worlde þat men on affye
Is but vanyte and folye;
Forthy behoues pore traveyle smerte
In here body, and riche in herte,
Also to þynke how þey shall saue   3475
And multeplie þat they have
And also thynke on heuen kynge
To make hy[m]selue a goode endyng.
Bettyr is bifore to travayle harde
Soo þat the avayle come afterwarde   3480
Thenne of travayle here to slake
And fowle endyng after make;
For withoute summe travayll
May þe worlde no man avayle.'

f. 52ʳ

3449 be my pate] to my state P.   3457 serueth] soroweth B, serues S, seruyth
hym P.   3460 therto] hym to S, hym vnto P.   3468 man] Adam P, om.
S.   3473 pore] om. P;   smerte] and smert P.   3475 Also] As P.

He þat loueþ me for myn
And noght for me, þat is venym;
But he is freend to mannes bihoue
[And] on to truste and on to loue
þat not assentiþ to þe wille   4355
Of his frende þat may turne to ille,
And se[ru]eþ of no loselrie
But chastiseþ him of his folie;
And þogh he partie him misdo,
He seiþ no word þanne him vnto: 4360
In þat frende men shullen haue affiaunce
And loue him and him avaunce.'

Ca.° lxxxij°   *'May a man his profite do*   (89)
                   And no trauel haue þerto?'

          'Sithen Adam eet þorgh wicked reed   4365
              þe appul þat God him forbed,
          Fro þat time til now
          Might neuere Adam do his prow,
          Were he neuere so mighti,
          Wiþouten trauaile of his body.   4370
          þe world þat men on affie
          Is but vanite and folie;
          For hem bihoueþ to traueil and smerte
          In hir body, and riche in herte,
          And to þenke hou þei shul [s]aue   4375
          And multiplie þat þei haue
          And also þenke on heuen king
          To make himself a good ending.
          Better is tofore forto trauel harde   f. 65ʳ
          So þat þe prow come afterwarde   4380
          þan of trauel here to slake
          And a foule ende after make;
          For wiþoute sum trauaile
          þe world may no man availe.'

3478 hymselue] hy selue B.   3479 to] the P.   3480 avayle] prow P, prounde S.

4354 And] *from* H, þat L.   4357 serueþ] semeþ L.   4359 he] þe
H.   4375 saue] *from* H, haue L.

Qo. 89ᵃ   *'Shall men do goode and almessedede*   (90) 3485
                          Vnto pore þat have nede?'
                              'Men shall do goode to poore men
                              That hymselue helpe ne can
                              And what he be rekke hym ne shall
                          But for Goddis loue doo alle.   3490
                          Vnto þe riche is lente rychesse
                          To helpe þe poore þat have distresse:
                          They shall þynke they pore born be
                          Of Adam and Eue as is he;
                          And at his lykenesse are wrought;   3495
                          And þat he hathe his ricchesse nought
                          Of hymselue but of Goddes lone,
                          His body to kepe not aloone
                          But his sowle withall to tylle.

                          And thynke þat he vpon a whyle   3500
                          Shall dye and fare elleswhere
                          And noothynge shall he with hym bere:
                          Oute as he cam, soo shall he fare,
                          Both pore, naked, and bare.

                          Forþy shall he ȝif the pore vnto   3505
                          Also or he go therfroo;
                          For that he yeveth, þat shall he fynde;
                          And þat [he] leueth hym byhynde,
                          That is þe worldes and not his:
                          Thereof shall he have lityll blisse.'   3510

Qo. 90ᵃ   *'How shall a man hym contene*   (91)
                          Whenne he is þe folke betwene?'
                              'A man shall gouerne hym wysely
                              Amonge men and curteysly
                              And with a fayre semelaunt euerywhore   3515
                          And speke at mesure and no more
f. 52ᵛ   And here oþer speke whenne they begynne

3485 T *begins again.*   3486 pore] pore folke T.   3487 to] *add* a T, the
S;   men] man TS.   3493 They (1)] He TSP;   they (2)] that TS, that the P;
pore] boithe S.   3494 is] well as P.   3497 Of hymselue] Not of seluyn
P.   3503 Oute] But TP;   soo] *om.* T;   fare] hens fare T.   3508 he] *from*

Ca.° lxxxiij°   'Shullen men do good and almes[de]de   (90) 4385
                     To þe pouere þat haue nede?'
                          'Men shullen do good to a pore man
                          þat himself not helpe can
                     And what he be rekke he ne shal
                     But for Goddis loue do it al.   4390
                     To þe riche is left richesse
                     To helpe the pore in distresse:
                     Of Adam and Eue alle come we
                     And alle pouere borne we be;
                     At Goddis liknesse we weren wroght   4395
                     And so oure ricchesse haue we noght
                     Of oureself but of Goddis loone.
                     His body may not be kept aloone
                     But his soule þerwith dwelle—
                     þis is soth, as I ȝow telle—   4400
                     And þinke he shal deie and hens fare
                     And whider to wende he not ne whare;
                     And bare he shal hens wende
                     And wiþ him bere no manere þinge
                     Saue a shete him ynne to wynde   4405
                     And al worldly þing leue behynde.
                     And þerfore he shulde, or he went,
                     Parte wiþ suche as God him sent;
                     For he þat ȝeueþ, he shal fynde;
                     And þat he leueþ him behynde,   4410
                     þat is þe worldis and noght his:
                     þerof he shal haue litel blis.'

Ca.° lxxxiiij°   'Hou shal a man gouerne him   (91)   f. 65ᵛ
                     Among þe peple wiþouten grym?'
                          'A man shal gouerne him wisely   4415
                          Among þe peple and curtesly
                     And þat wiþ faire semblant ay
                     And eke in mesure on al way
                     And here men speke or he bigynne

TSP, *om.* B.   3513 gouerne] contene TSP.   3515 euerywhore] euer ay
P.   3516] To whom he speke nyght or day P.   3517 here] he S;   oþer]
men P;   they] he T.

4385 almesdede] *from* H, almesde L.   4397 loone] boone H.   4410 þat he]
from H, *reversed* L.

A[l]though he haue noo delyte þerinne;
For hit is grete curtesye
For to caste vnto hym his ye   3520
That [his speche] holdeþ withall
And his wordis lysten [h]e shall.
Ȝit shall he kepe hym euery tyde
Withouten boste, withouten pryde,
All were he rychere of more   3525
Thenne oþer folke þat þere woore;
For euer þe mightyer he be,
The better sholde he hym byse
For to be curteys and meke
Ȝif he woll his honour seke.   3530
And yf he speke oughwhore,
He shall hym bethynke before
And caste hem in his herte right well
Or þat he speke any dele;
And whenne he shall telle his skyll,   3535
Yeve boldenesse and goode chere thertyll
And be abassed of nooþynge
Whill þat he is in talkyng.
A man þat shall a reson shewe,
And he abasshe hym som threwe,   3540
He may lese his skyll amonge
For men woll say he hathe þe wronge.
Be he amonge folis brought,
There his wisdom helpeth nought
Though he hymselue soore tene   3545
The whyle he is hem bytwene:
As foly amonge wyse men is but lewdenesse,
Soo is wisdom amonge folis expresse.'

Qo. 91ᵃ   'Is a riche man the lesse worthy   (92)
                 Yf he lose his goode holy   3550
                 Or a pore worthy the more*

3518 Although] *from* PS, And though B.   3521 his speche] *from* TS, his spechis
P, he spekeþ B.   3522 he] *from* SP, ye B;   he shall] withalle T.   3525 of] or
T, and SP.   3527] *om.* P.   3528 sholde . . . byse] avise hym shulde hee T;
byse] se P.   3528/9 *add* In what place that he be P.   3530 seke] eke
TSP.   3533 hem] it S, *om.* P.   3536 boldenesse . . . chere] bolde (blode P)

Alþogh he haue no delite þerynne: 4420
For it is greet curtesie
For to caste to him his yȝe
þat he his speche holde wiþal
And hise wordes listen shal.
Ȝit shal he kepe him euery tide   4425
Wiþoute pompe, boste, or pride,
Alþogh he were riccher þan oþer,
And cherisshe hem in manere of his broþer;
For euere þe mightier þat he be,
þe meker to hem be shulde he: 4430
If þat he wole his honour kepe,
He muste be lowely, curteise, and meke.
And loke where he speke shal
þat he biþenke him oueral
Of hise wordes eueridel,   4435
þat þei be spoken in resoun wel;
And whan he shal telle his tale,
Ȝif faire semblant þerwiþale
And be abasshid of noþing
þe while he is in telling.   4440
A man þat shal a resoun showe,
And he abasshe him som þrowe,
He may lese his skile amonge
For a man wole seie he haþ þe wronge.
Be he among fooles broght   4445
þere his wisdom helpeþ noght,
Folily he him conteyne   f. 66ʳ
þe while he is hem bitwene:
As folye among wise is wicke,
So is wisdom amonge foolis þicke.'   4450

Ca.° lxxxv°   'Is a riche man þe lasse worþi   (92)
               þat he forlesiþ his good holi
               Or a pore man worþi þe more

and feire semblaunte TP.   3539 a] his P.   3540 som] in þat T.
3542 þe] no P.   3545] Folehedelye he hym conteyne T, Folely than he hym can
conteyne P.   3546 hem] om. P.   3547 men . . . lewdenesse] is wikke
TSP.   3548 wisdom] foly P;   expresse] thikke TSP.

4423 þat . . . speche] And þat he speke H.

Though rychesse on hym waxand woore?'

'Ay whil the ryche hathe his goode
He fyndes men to do of her hode:
He is called and herde ouerall   3555
And euery man hym trowe shall.
3yf his rychesse falle hym fro,
He leseth honoure and myght also,
Witte, corage, and doughtynesse,
And becomes coward neuerþelese: 3560
At the cownsell shall he be ouerledde;
His wordes shall vnnethe be dradde;
Noo man shall his tales leve
Ne nothyng shall men of hym yeve—
And þe catayll made all this   3565
That he was and now nought is.
The pore, when he waxith ryche,
His ne3tbores gynne to wex hy[m] bryche:
He is holde rightwosse, curteys, and goode,
Though he were a churle of blode;   3570
His worde is herde and trowed right well,
Though lesynges therof be a gret dele;
Frendes he fyndes anoon right
That lete of hym somtyme ful light;
Yf he come oughwhere to mete,   3575
He shall be sette amonge þe grete;
The counsayll shall hym calle astyte
Suche as furste lete of hym li3te.
By the ryche hit fares also
As men see by a marchaunt doo   3580
That boroweth grete gode alday
Of ryche men that l[en]e may,
And [haues] not therof gretly
But travayles and lyves therby;

3554 men . . . her] of doynge ofte (*om.* P) of TP;   hode] blode P.   3555 called]
add wys S;   and herde ouerall] a lord on halle P.   3557 rychesse] goode TP;
falle] *add* alle T.   3559 Witte] With TP.   3561 be ouerledde] be on lowed T,
not be alowyd P.   3562 vnnethe be dradde] nothinge be trowed TP, byneithe be tred
S.   3564 nothyng shall men] no man shall nothyng P;   of hym yeve] hym greve
T.   3565 made all this] makith hit all ywis P, was alle his T.   3566 That]
Than P.   3568 gynne . . . bryche] begynnyth he to vysite P;   hym] hy B, *om.*
T.   3569 rightwosse] wise TP.   3572 lesynges] losynge T.   3576] *om.*

þogh richesse on him woxen wore?'
  'The while þe riche hath good   4455
    He is þanne mighti of mood:
  He is clepid and herde oueral
  And euery man him loue shal.
  And if his good is fallen him fro,
  He leseþ honour and mighte also   4460
  Wiþ corage and doutynesse
  And bicomeþ coward neuereþelesse:
  At counseil he shal not be allowed;
  Hise wordes shullen not be itrowed;
  No man shal his tale leue   4465
  Ne noþing of him men sholen ȝeue—
  And þe catel makeþ al, ywis,
  þat he was oght and now noght is.
  þe pore, whanne he wexiþ riche,
  Hise neighebours byginneþ him to visite: 4470
  He is holden wys, curteys, and good,
  þogh he be a cherle of blood;
  His word is herd and leued wel,
  þogh it be lesing þe moost del;
  Frendes he findeþ anoon right   4475
  þat of him tofore lete light;
  If þat he come owhere to mete,
  He shal be sett amonge þe grete;
  To counseile he shal be clepid tite
  Of hem þat sette bi him ful lite.   4480
  By þe riche it fareþ also   f. 66ᵛ
  As men sen a marchaunt do
  þat boroweþ greet good alday
  Of riche men þat lene may,
  And han noght þerof gretly   4485
  But her trauaile, and liven þerby;

P.   3577 The] To TSP;   shall hym calle] he shall be callid P;   astyte] full skete
PTS.   3578 Suche as] Whiche that T, Of suche that P;   lete of him liȝte] liȝt
(litill T) of him lete ST, of hym light lete P.   3578/9 *add* And now woll bow hym in
the strete P.   3582 lene] *from* P, lyve B, lende T, leyne S.   3583 haues] *from*
S, haue TP, *om.* B.

4485 han] *repeated* L.

And whanne þe ryche his goode woll haue,   3585
Thenne is þe marchaunte but a knave;
And whill he hadde hit vndyr hande,
He was þanne riche and havand.

f. 53ᵛ

Of this worlde hit farith soo
Of all that men may gadyr to: 3590
Hathe he nought but whill he is here
His lyvelode; and be he on bere,
Hathe he no more than he furste began:
He cometh and gothe a pore man.

But the pore þat riche was   3595
Ys holden gentelere, by case,
Th[an he] þat neuer nought hadde
Ne noȝt ne hathe, [for] he is badde.'

Qo. 92ᵃ   'The wykked maner of man I see   (93)
               And wykked custom, whens may they be?' 3600
                  'Of wykkyd wyll, of wykkyd hert,
                     And of males, that gederes smert;
               For man hathe wel þe wete
               To knowe his maner, that evyl is hit,
               And for to leve hit yf he wyll   3605
               And chaunge his maner vnto skyll.
               He þat wykkyd custom hathe also
               No goode may he þynke ne doo,
               Ne his herte in reste be
               For in wykked thought travayleth hee; 3610
               Thorow the which trauayll he wastes thik
               His body and his tyme in wyke:
               As he þat myȝte go by a sty
               That he myȝt sekerly goo by

3588 He was þanne] So was he TP.   3589 Of] In all P.   3593 he (1)] om.
P.   3595 þat] the T;   case] cause S.   3596 gentelere] gentill P.
3597 Than he] from TSP, Thou B.   3598 for] from TSP, om. B.   3600 they]
it T.   3601 of (2)] and TSP.   3602 that gederes] gadred T.   3603 wel]
the wylle and P.   3604 his] his owne P.   3608 may . . . ne] thyng ne may

And whanne þe riche his [good] wole haue,
þanne is þe marchaunt but a knaue;
And þe while he had it vnder hande,
þanne was [he a] riche man and hauande.   4490
Of þis woorld it fareþ so,
Al þat a man gadreþ him to:
In þis worlde, while he is here,
He haþ but his lyflode til he be on bere;
þanne haþ he no more þan he had erst   4495
Whanne he into þis world come ferst:
He cam pore into þis world here
And pore shal wende, wiþouten were,
But if it be of some good deede—
God graunte vs grace þerof to spede.   4500
But þe pore þat riche was
Is holde þe gentiler, in some cas,
þan he þat neuere noght ne hadde
Ne noght ne haþ: þerfore he is badde.'

Ca.º lxxxvjº   þe wicked maners of man þat I see,   (93) 4505
             Wherof come þei?—Telle þou me.'
           'Off wicked wille and wicked herte
             And of malys, þat gadreþ smerte;
           For þat a man haþ wel his witt
           To knowe if hise maners ben wel sett   4510
           And forto leue hem if þei ben ille
           And chaunge hem into a better wille.
           He þat wicked customes haþ also
           No good dede may þenke ne do,
           Nouther in his herte no reste may be   4515   f. 67ʳ
           For in wicked þoghte trauailled is he.
           þoruȝ wicked trauaille bi distresse
           His good he wasteþ in wickednesse,
           As he þat miȝt by a sty
           Go þe weie surely   4520

he P.   3611 the which] wyckid P.   3613 myȝte go] gooth P.

───────

4487 good] from H, om. L.   4490 he a] from H, þe L.   4497/8 And pore
shal wende into þis world here cancelled L.

And goth abowte as vnwyse,   3615
Bothe by downes and dalys nyse,
And nedeles trauayles hym amysse
For all his owne foly hit is.'

Qo. 93ᵃ   '*Sithen iren is soo harde and starke*   (94)
               And for to worke mekel carke,   3620
               How was hit made and wherewith
               Tonges, hameres, and þe styth?'
                    'God comaundid all thynge
                    And all are made of his makyng
f. 54ʳ   And he wiste wherof men had nede   3625
               For to do with ony dede;
               And his massenger he sente
               (The aungel that to Adam wente):
               He badde hym take yren in his honde
               (And þanne was hit nasshe as sonde)   3630
               And þerof first made he a styth
               And hamer and tonge to wyrke with;
               He yede and shope hem euerychone
               And they become harde anoon.
               And whenne he to þe dyluvie cam,   3635
               Noe of suche lomes nam
               That were forge[d] after tho
               And kepte hem and syth made mo;
               And soo fro þat tyme wrought are they
               And shal be to domesday.'   3640

Qo. 94ᵃ   '*Do they amisse þat al day swhere*   (95)
               By here god, whatsoo he were?'
                    'He þat swheres by his god
                    Falsly for he shall be trowed—
                    Whether he goode or wykkyd is—   3645
               He dothe evel and amysse;
               For I trowe there is no man qwyk

     3615 as vnwyse] withowten townes TP.   3616] Bothe bi dales and bi downes
TSP.   3618 all] *om*. P.   3619–40] *om*. S.   3620 mekel carke] moche
werke T.   3621 hit] furste T.   3622 hameres] hamer T.   3624 made]
om. TP.   3627 massenger he] messangers he P.   3631 he] *om*. TP.
3632 to wyrke with] also therwith P.   3635 he] it TP;   cam] *inserted above after*

And gooþ aboute withoute townes,
Boþe bi dales and by downes,
And nedeles trauailleþ him amis
For al his owne folie it is.'

Ca.º lxxxvij º   'Siþen yren is so hard and stark   (94) 4525
And men to worche it haþ greet cark,
Hou was firste made and wherwiþ
Tonges, hamers, and þe stith?'
         'God comaundeth al þing
         And alle þinges beþ of his making   4530
And he wiste wherof man had nede
Forto doo þerwiþ any dede;
And hise messager he sente
(þe aungel þat to Adam wente):
He bad him take yren in his honde   4535
(And þoo it was as neisshe as sonde)
And þerof firste he made a stith
And hamers and tonges to worche with;
And whan he had shapen hem euerichone,
þei bicome harde anone.   4540
And whan it to chaunge cam,
Noe of suche lomes nam
þat weren forged aftir þo
And kepte hem and siþen made mo;
And so into þis time wroght be þay   4545
And so shullen til domesday.'

Ca.º lxxxviij º   'Do þei amys þat alday swere   (95)
By her god, whatso þei here?'
         'He þat sweriþ by his god alday   f. 67ᵛ
         Falsely for he wolde be trowed ay—   4550
Wheþer it good or wicked is—
He doith yuel and eke amis;
For I trowe þere is no man so wicke

---

it T.   3636 nam] manye T.   3637 forged] *from* T, forgeten B, forgyndryd
P;   after] *om.* T.   3639 fro þat] tho this T, tyll this P.   3641 S *begins*
again.   3642 he] thei T.

4521 withoute] in H.   4526 And men] A man H.   4533 messager]
messagers L, messenger H.

That his god holdes wyke
And falsly for coveytyse
Swherys by hym on many wyse.   3650
He is devel and develes lyke
And worse þanne an eretyke
For his god falses he
For thynge that lytel whyle shall be;
And þouȝ his god be false and wyke   3655
And [he] forswheres hym by hym thyke
His neyghborogh for to gyle,
He synnes [gretely] as a vyle:
Lawe ne trouthe hathe he noone
Ne amonge non sholde he gone   3660

f. 54ᵛ   That by his god falsly woll swhere—
He wolde a man with falshede dere.'

Qo. 95ᵃ   'Shall a man of his body   (96)
                    In all thynge be chaste holy?'
                       'Chastite a man shal holde   3665
                       Of his body manyfolde:
                       Of false othes, of lechery,
                    Of all oþer vilony,
                    Of euyl sight, of evel speche,
                    Of evel gett, of handelyng eke,   3670
                    Of slepyng euel; ne euel rede
                    Ne ete ne drynke in euel stede
                    Ne none other thynge do
                    But as right hym yeves to;
                    And þat is euel is goode to fle,   3675
                    And of all shall man chaste be.
                    Sithen God at his lykenesse hathe sente
                    Shap to man and witte him lente
                    Euel to knowe and to forsake,
                    Thenne dothe he amysse therto woll take: 3680
                    That hym therefro holdes all,

3650 many] ony maner P.   3652 an] any P.   3653 For] For to P;   falses]
fals is P.   3655 be] om. P.   3656 he] from TS, om. BP.   3657 gyle]
begile TSP.   3658 gretely] from STP, om. B.   3660 non] no men
TSP.   3670 gett] gate PT, gette S;   handelyng] yuell hankyng (? haukyng)
P.   3671 Of slepyng] Noo (Ne P) slepe in TP;   ne] ne in P.   3675 And]
Alle T;   is(2)] om. P;   goode] om. TP.   3676 chaste] chastised T.

þat bileeueþ [nat] his god is quicke:
And he falsely for couetise
Swriþ by him in any wise,   4555
He is a deuel and a deuel lyke
And werse þan an heritike.
For his god falsith he
For þing þat litel while shal be;   4560
And þogh he to god be false and wicke
And forswerith him neuere so þicke
His neighebore forto begile,
He is a vileyn man and vile:
Feith ne trouthe haþ he noon   4565
Ne among no men shulde suche goon;
For he þat bi his god falsly wole swere
He wolde [a] man wiþ falshede dere.'

Ca.º lxxxixº   'Shal a man in his body
                   Be chast in alle þinges holy?'   (96)
                                                                         4570
                   'Chaastnesse a man shal holde
                   And of his body be not bolde
To vse oþes ne leccherie
Ne none oþer manere of vilenye
Ne yue[l] sight ne yuel speche
Ne yuel going; ne yuel teche   4575
Ne sleepe in yuel ne yuel rede
Ne ete ne drinke in yuel stede
Ne noon oþer yuel þing do
But as right counseileþ to:
For al þat is yuel is good to fle,   4580
For of al yuel a man chast shulde be.
For, sith God of his liknesse haþ sent   f. 68ʳ
Shappe to man and witt him lent
Euel to knowe and to forsake,
þanne doth he amys þat þerto wole take;   4585
And he þat him þerfro holdiþ al,

3678 and] *om.* P;   witte] with TP;   lente] sent S.
hym from alle P.   3681] And he that holdith

4554 nat] *from* H, *om.* L.   4568 a] *from* H, no L.
yue L.   4584 him] haþ H.   4575 yuel (1)] *from* H,

To Goddes company he shall
And tyl his aungels also
When that tyme cometh therto.'

Qo. 96ᵃ

'Whom shall men love with to goo   (97) 3685
And whos company fle froo?'
   'On fayre downes þat may þow mete
   Shal men goo and on herbes swhete:
   There may they goo sekerly
Withouten skathe of here body;   3690
And whosoo on þe fyre gothe,
He brenneth fote and tooes bothe.
By this shalte þou vnderstonde
With whom a man shal be goand:
Goo with the goode to and fro,   3695
So shalte þou not misdo;
And noo man shall to the say,
Where thou gost by þe way,
But worshipp, honour, and goode lose:
Thenne in þe [s]o[f]te dewe thou gose.   3700

But though a man hymselue be gode,
And he turne thereto his moode
To haunte folys companye,
Hym falles þerof but foly
And yvell loose and wi[c]ked name   3705
And vilonye of folke and blame;

And they shall say, "Yede he not þore
But [he] of here maneres woore:
Were he not of here asente,
Oute of here company he wente."   3710
Euery goode man will him flee;

3682 he] come he P.   3687 downes] dewes TP;   may þow] men shall T, may
hym P.   3691 gothe] goos TSP.   3692 bothe] *precedes* fote TSP;   fote] fire
T.   3694 With whom] That when P.   3696 misdo] mysgoo SP.
3698 way] day S.   3700 softe] *from* TS, froste B, *om.* P.   3703 To] *from* TSP,
Tho B.   3705 wicked] *from* TSP, wilked B.   3707 they] *om.* P;   he] yee

To þe blis of heuene goo he shal
And to Goddis aungels also
Whanne þat tyme comeþ þerto.'   4590

Ca.° lxxxx°   'Wiþ whom shal a man loue to go   (97)
               And whom shal he flee fro?'
'In faire dewis, if ʒe any mete,
A man shal goo and bi herbes swete:
þere may he goo sikerly   4595
Wiþouten scaþe of his body;
And whoso on þe fire goos,
He brenneþ bothe foote and toos.
By þis shalt þou vnderstande
Wiþ whom þou shalt be goande: 4600
Goo wiþ the goode to and fro,
So shalt þou mys not goo;
And no man shal axe, as I the seie,
Wheraboute goost þou by þe weie,
But worshipe, honour, and good loos   4605
The ʒeue shal whereuer þou goos:
þanne goost þou in þe dewe ful swete
Whan þou wiþ goode men dost mete.
But þogh a man himself be good,
And he torne so his mood   4610
þat he haunte fooles companye,
It shal him torne to grete folie
And gete yuel loos and wicked name
And miche vilenye and blame;
þanne wole men seie ful tite   4615
To do him repreef and despite,
"And he were good, he ʒede not þere   f. 68ᵛ
But he of her maneres were:
He were not of her assent
But if he in her companye went."   4620
For euery good man wole flee

T.   3708 he] *from* TSP, *om.* B;   here] his P.   3709] Ne shulde he go with
hym per assent P.   3710 Oute] But oute P;   he] shuld he P.

4593 dewis] dawys H.

And þus vppon þe fuyre gothe he.

Therfore shull men the good with goo
And þoo þat are foles flee hem froo.'

Qo. 97ᵃ   'Whether is better, so God the save—   (98) 3715
                Richesse or pouerte for to have?'
                    'Rychesse are here bodyly
                    And ther be also summe gostely;
                    And whoso comyth þat [oon] vntyll
                May have þat other yf þat he will,   3720
                For he may haue that hym is nede
                The soule and body bothe to fede.
                He shall fynde who hym serue shall
                And his comaundemente doo all:
                Euery man shall fonde to do his will,   3725
                And for his rychesse euery dele.
                Ʒif men worshipp þe poore oughte,
                That is but wynde and turneth to nought;
                For of the honoure þat he hadde
                May he nother be fedde ne cladde: 3730
                Therfore to bodyly profyte
                Thenne is hit moore delyte
f. 55ᵛ   Men say, "A riche carle is he,"
                Thenne pore and worshipped be.'

3712 þus] *om.* P.   3713 men] men and wymmen P.   3714 þoo þat are] the
T.   3719 oon] *from* STP, *om.* B.   3723 serue] sayen P.   3725 do] serue
P;   his will] him well STP.   3728 to] *om.* T.   3730 nother] neuer T;
cladde] glad P.   3734 Thenne] Bettir hit is than P;   and] and riche B;
worshipped] worship P.

In companye of foles and shrewes to be;
And þus on þe fire alday gooth
þe goode men þat to shrewidnesse shulde be loth.
For þat men shulde wiþ þe good goo   4625
And fooles and shrewes euere fle hem froo.'

Ca.° lxxxxj° 'Wheþer is better, so God þe saue—   (98)
             Ricchesse or pouert forto haue?'
                 'Richesses ben here bodily
                 And some þere ben also goostly;   4630
             And whoso comeþ þat oone tille;
             He may haue þat oþer if he wille,
             For he may haue þat him is nede
             þe soule and body boþe to fede.
             He shal fynde who him serue shal   4635
             And his comaundement to do al:
             Euery man shal fonde to serue him wel,
             And þat for his ricchesse eguerydel.
             And if men worschepe þe pouere oght,
             þat is but winde and turneþ to noght;   4640
             For of þat honour þat he hadde
             May he neiþer be fed ne cladde,
             But for to haue bodily profite
             It almost is eche mannes delite.
             For as ȝe han herd and seen alday,   4645
             Ricchesse is desired alway;
             For cherles þat to lordes ben bonde
             Ben worshipped in euery londe
             Somme more and some lesse
             After þei han of richesse.   4650
             But he þat into pouerte is cropen   f. 69ʳ
             And þerynne is fully loken
             And can þerwiþ be compotent,
             Shal be to him greet amendement
             Of soules helþe in endeles blisse   4655
             If he his pouert here, ywisse,
             Suffreþ mekely wiþouten grucching—
             þe scourge of God and his chastising;

                        4642 neiþer] neuer H.

Qo. 98ᵃ   'Shall men honoure that are ne do[m]e   (99) 3735
                     Iliche a riche man and a grome?'
                         'All þat deme wyll leely,
                         He shall also debonerly
                         A pore neȝbor do honoure to
                     As he sholde to a riche doo: 3740
                     Not do þe riche sit alway in seete
                     And þe pore stonde on his fete—
                     Do hem bothe alyke to stande
                     Whill they are in deme motand.
                     Ne no moore shall he be dyll   3745
                     To here a pore mannes skyll
                     Thenne he shall be of a ryche,
                     And ouer the poore more bleliche.
                     Dome cam of God: þerfore hit sholde
                     Be deled even, yf men wolde.'   3750

Qo. 99ᵃ   'Delyte the pore in pouerte also   (100)
                     As the riche in here richesse doo?'
                         'A poore man that hathe noo mete,
                         And he his bely ful may gete,
                         He delytes moore þerinne   3755
                     Thenne the ryche with all his wynne.
                     For yf the poore haue his fill
                     Of mete and drynke, he hathe his wyll;

3735 ne dome] ne done B, neye done S, nygh don T.   3737 All] He T, Tho P.
3739 neȝbor] nyghg doon T, men don P.   3741 alway in seete] as (als S, a P) skete
TSP.   3744 motand] metande P.   3745 dyll] of euyl wille P.   3747 ryche] ryche man
P.   3748] For euer the porer the more truthe he han P;   ouer] euer T;   bleliche]

For þus he seith, ful sikerly:
"Whom I loue, him chastise I."'   4660

Ca.° lxxxxij°   'Shal a man worshipe, telle now me,   (99)
    Yliche riche and pouere þat we here see?'
        'Thou þat sittest to deme truly
        Thou shalt als debonerly
    To a pore man honour do   4665
    As a riche þou woldest vnto:
    [Not] do þe riche man sitte þore
    And þe pore man to stonde tofore,
    But do hem bothe yliche stande
    While þei ben in dome pletande   4670
    Ne no more haue yuel will
    To here a pore mannes skil
    þan he wolde of þe riche man,
    For of Adam and Eue al we cam.
    Doome cam of God for þat it sholde   4675
    Be dalt euene, if men wolde.
    For he þat doth þe contrarie
    And from þe trouthe vtterly varie,
    At Goddes dome he shal haue grame
    þat shal him torne to harme and shame;   4680
    For Crist seith, truly to telle,
    Wordes þat ben boþe sharpe and felle:
    "Suche mesure as ȝe meten to men
    Shal be moten to ȝow aȝen."'

Ca.° lxxxxiij°   'Delite þe pouere men in pouert so   (100) 4685 f. 69v
    As riche men in her richesse do?'
        '[A] pouere man þat haþ no mete,
        And he his wombe ful may gete,
    He deliteþ him more þerynne
    þan þe riche man wiþ al his wynne.   4690
    For if þe pouere haue his fille
    Of mete and drinke, he haþ his wille;

---

bebriche T, briche S.   3754 his bely full] fulle the wombe TSP.   3757 fill] wille
P, fill of mete and drynke B.   3758 Of] Ande of T;   he hathe] haue T.

4659 sikerly] secrely H.   4667 Not] And LH.   4678 vtterly] vntreulie
H.   4687 A] from H, om. L.

And þe ryche is hungry ay
To gedre moore þenne he may;   3760
And gedere he neuer soo moche fee,
He may neuer fylled be;
For better at eese thenne is, ywys,
The full man þen þe hungery is.

The poore woll of hunger slake: 3765
The ryche hungereth ay to take.

He þat longe hathe seke layn,
When he is helyd, he is fayn
f. 56ʳ   And in his herte reioiseth more
Thenne [they] þat ay in helthe woore: 3770
Whenne þe sekenesse of þe poore
That hungery is may [recouere]
With mete and drynke þat he gat,
Moore delyte he hathe in þat
Then he þat is in rychesse sadde   3775
That neuer noo defaute ne hadde.'

Qo. 100ᵃ   'Shall a man ought make his rose   (101)
              Of anythynge þat he dose?'
                 'A wyse man shall rowse hym noȝt
                 Of noothynge þat he hathe wrought   3780
                 For mysspa[y]yng were hit Gode vnto
              And his owne dishonour also.
              Be he neuer soo douȝty
              Ne soo stronge of his body,
              And he rouse of his owne dede,   3785
              Men shall scorne hym to his mede;

3761 fee] feys P.   3762] He is bud seldyn while in pes P.
3764 The full man] Wofull P.   3765 slake] swike TP.   3766 to take] elike
TP.   3770 they] *from* PTS, *om.* B.   3772 hungery] hunger T;   recouere]
from S, not keuere BTP.   3777 a man ought] ony man T.   3779 A . . . man]
Theise . . . men TP.   3780 he] thei TP.   3781 mysspayyng] myssparyng B,

And þe riche is hungry ay
To gadre more þan he may
And gadre he neuere so miche fee,   4695
He may neuere fulfilled be,
For bettre at ese men seyn, ywis,
þe ful man þan þe hungry is.
For pouere men, whan þei hungry be
And of mete and drinke may haue plente   4700
Of releef whanne riche men feesten,
þei fillen her wombes and þanne hem resten;
But þe riche men hungreþ euere to and to:
His gredy appetite may neuere be do.
Ensamples herof men may fynde,   4705
Whoso wole loke, of diuerse kynde:
As whanne a man sike haþ laine,
Whanne he is heled, he is ful faine
And in his herte reioyseþ more
þan þei þat euere in hele wore;   4710
For whanne þe sykenesse of þe pouere man
(þat is his hunger) is wel ouergan
Wiþ mete and drinke þat he gat,
More delite he haþ in þat
þan he þat is in ricchesse sad   4715
And neuere no defaute had.'

Ca.º lxxxxiiij   *'Shal a man ought make his boost*   (101)
                  Of þat he dooþ in any coost?'
                        'Wise men shullen boost noght   f. 70ʳ
                        Of noþing þat þei haue wroght   4720
For mysplesing to God it doth
And his worshipe it fordoth.
Be he neuere so doghti a man
Ne so strong of his body þan,
And he booste of his dede,   4725
Men shullen him scorne for his mede;

myspayinge TS, mynstrellis P.   3782 And his] For here P.   3783–4] But be
man neuer so stark of his body / Ne neuyr so semely ne doughty P.   3785 rouse]
rehers P.

4699 pouere] *om.* H.

And þoȝ þey say nouȝt, they hym holde
For a lyere of that he tolde.
But a coward of no bounte,
For men shall wene he douȝty be,   3790
Of mekel moore his rouse woll make
Thenne euer durste he vndertake.
Thenne say summe þat by hym sate
"He is a lyer, he þat:
He was neuer worthe a torde   3795
But a bostmakere of worde."
And [he] þat doughty man is tolde
And is an hardy man and bolde,
Kepe his tonge where he gothe
And lete oþer bere hit forthe: 3800
That is wel more his honoure.
For hit sayeth an olde auctour,
"He þat hymselue rouseth in towne,
With an hors torde men shall hym crowne."'

f. 56ᵛ *Qo. 101ᵃ*   '*Why are houndes faster that done here kynde* (102) 3805
                        Thenne oþer bestes that men fynde?'
                        'Of alle þe bestes þat I wote
                        Ys noone of nature soo hote
                        As is a hounde in his nature;
                        And whenne he sholde make engendrure,   3810
                        Of here hete the grete glowynge
                        Makith hem togedyr fastenyng
                        A[s] two peces of yren fare
                        In fuyre whenne they wellyng are:
                        Lay þat oon þe oþer on   3815
                        And geve hem a dynt anoon,
                        Thorough hete they togeder bynde;
                        And soo fare howndes in here kynde.'

Qo. 102ᵃ   '*That of other mennes wyves coveytous is*   (103)
                Or of his goode, dothe he amisse?'   3820

3787 hym] hem P.   3788 lyere] *add* is he P.   3889 of] is he and of P.
3790 For] All he seithe for P.   3794 a] but a TSP.   3795 torde] stre
P.   3796] But a bost bragger of wor is he P.   3797 he] *from* TSP, *om.* B.
3799 gothe] goos TSP.   3800 hit forthe] his loos TSP.   3801 honoure] *add*

And þogh þei seie noght, þei him holde
For a lier of þat þei tolde.
For a coward of al bounte,
For men shulde wene he doghty be,   4730
Of more his boost he wole make
þan euer he durste vndirtake.
Than sein some þat by him satt,
"He nys but a lier of al þat:
He was neuere worth two toordis   4735
But a boster and ful of wordes."
And he þat a doghti man is tolde
And is an hardy man and bolde
Kepiþ his tunge where he goos
And lete oþer men bere his loos: 4740
þat is wel more his honour.
As seith to vs an oolde auctour,
"He þat himself preiseþ in towne,
Wiþ an hors tord men shullen him crowne."'

Ca.° lxxxxv°   *'Whi ben houndes fastned þat doþ her kynde*   (102) 4745
             More þan oþer bestis þat men fynde?'
                 'Of alle bestes þat I woot
                 Of nature þere is noon so hoot
             As is an hounde in his nature;
             And whanne he shal make engendrure,   4750
             Of her hete þe grete glowing
             Makeþ hem togidre fastnyng
             As two peces of yren doth fare   f. 70ᵛ
             In þe fire whanne þei welling are:
             Leie þat oone þat oþer vpon   4755
             And ȝeue hem a strook anoon,
             þorgh hete þei togidre bynde;
             And so fareþ houndes in her kynde.'

Ca.° lxxxxvj°   *'He þat of anoþer manis wijf coueitous is*   (103) 4760
             Or of his good, doþ he not amys?'

to know P.   3802] For hit is seide in olde daw P.   3805–18] *om.* S.
3813 As] *from* TP, And B;   peces] peas T.   3814 wellyng] leyde P.
3819 S *begins again.*

4729 bounte] bonde H.   4751 þe] here H.

'He that is coveytouse and wode
After other mannes goode,
Other his wyf, wheþer hit be,
Grete synne and amys dothe he;
And suche a man as we of tell   3825
Ys called the devels grype of hell
For þe devel coueytes ay
To drawe vnto hym þat he may.
And for suche a coveytowse is knowen
That moore wolde have thenne his owen   3830
For a man sholde with another do
As he wolde men did hym to:
What man wolde men toke hym fro
His wyf or his godes mo?
I trowe hit sholde his herte be lothe   3835
And right soore make hym wrothe.
Therfore shulde man holde hym euen
As þe aungels doon in heven
There none coueyteth oderes blisse
But holdeth hym apayde with his.'   3840

f. 57ʳ *Qo. 103ᵃ*   '*May noo man askape the dede*   (104)
                          For richesse, might, ne other rede?'
                              'Man is made, as thow has herde,
                                Of foure thynges of this mydelerde:
                                  Of fuyre, water, erthe, and ayre,   3845
Bothe the foule and eke the fayre;
And þese foure ychon be
Contrary to oþer in qualite;
And þe body may not blynne
There these foure ar gadered inne   3850
But togeder haue batayll
Ay vnto some of hem fayll;
And be þat oon clene downe brouȝt,
The body levys longe nouȝt.
Therfore wheresoo a man be—   3855

3827 coueytes] is covetouse TP.   3829 for] *om.* T;   is knowen] is holden T,
knowyng P.   3830] þat wolde more haue of other mennys thyng P.   3832 he
wolde men] men sholde he P.   3833 men] that P.   3836 right soore] myght
sone T, full sone P.   3837 holde hym euen] haue envy P.   3838 doon in

'He þat is coueitous is wood
After oþer mennes good,
Or after his wyf, wheþir it be:
Greet synne and amys doth he;
And suche a man as we of telle   4765
Is clepid þe deuelis gripe of helle
For þe deuel is coueitous ay
To drawe to him þat he may.
þus ben coueitous men knowen
þat wole haue more þan her owen   4770
For a man shulde anoþer do
As he wolde men diden him to:
What man wolde men toke him fro
His wyf ouþer his good euere þe moo?
I trowe it wolde to his herte be loth   4775
And make him right grevous and wroth.
þerfore man shulde holde hem euene
As angels done þat ben in heuene
þere none coueiteþ oþeris blis
But holdeþ hem paide eche of his.'   4780

Ca.° lxxxxvij°   *'May a man þe deth escape here*   (104)
þorgh ȝiftes or prayere in any manere?'
'A man is made, as þou haste herde,
Of iiij þinges in þis midlerde:
Of fire and water, erthe and ayr,   4785
Boþe þe foule and eke þe fair;
And þese foure echone be   f. 71ʳ
Contrarie to oþer in qualite;
And þe body may not blynne
þere þese foure ben gadred ynne   4790
But togidre haue bataille
Euere til some of hem faille;
And whanne þat oone to noght is broght,
þe toþer no lenger lyue may noght.
For whereeuere a man be—   4795

heuen] that are in hevyn an hy P.   3840 apayde with his] paied as he is TP.
3841 askape] escape of dethe T.   3847 be] contrary be P.   3853 clene] clere P.

4769 ben] *om.* H.   4790 gadred] gendred H.

Be hit on londe or on see—
The dethe cleveþ ay by hym
As hit were his owne kyn:
His kynne myȝt he from hym caste
But the dethe cleueþ faste.   3860
Soo þat poore ne richesse
Ne kunnyng ne doughtynesse
None excusacion may make
Whenne God woll the dethe hym take;
For goode and wyke, shrewe and bryche,   3865
Yonge and olde, poore and ryche,

Stronge and febele, foole and wyse,
Grete and smale, may not of thys
Askape þe dethe, that he moste goo
Vnto þe erthe þat he cam froo.'   3870

Qo. 104^a 'Is hit goode to answhere ay   (105)
Hem that foly doone all day?'
　　'So ferforthe a man hym strekes
　　To answhere hym þat foly spekes;
　　But yf his foly sholde hym dere,   3875
Thenne is goode þat he answhere.
Somtyme speketh a fole folily
And no man wote of whom ne why
And ȝif men answhere hym nothynge,
Is noone the worse of his sayyng;   3880
But if men answhere hym there,
They egge hym to speke moore,
And thenne is the fole all hote
Thanne to speke more þanne he wote
And his wordes woll not lete   3885
To confourme with wordes grete.
And soo engendereth grete foly

f. 57^v

3858 kyn] lym TSP.   3859 kynne] lym TSP;   he] *om.* P.   3861 poore]
power T, pouerte S.   3862 Ne (1)] Be P.   3864 woll the] with P.
3869 he] we T.   3870 he] we T.   3871 Is hit goode] Sittith Godde T.
3872 doone] speken T.   3873 So] To TS, The P;   ferforthe] ferthirforthe P;
strekes] mekys P.   3874 hym] hem T;   foly] folishelye T.   3876 Thenne]

Be it in londe, be it in see—
þe deeþ cleueþ euere to him
As it were his owne lym:
A man may no more deeþ from him cast
þan þe lym þat cleueþ to him most fast.   4800
þan may no power ne ricchesse
No kunynge ne doghtinesse
Ne noon excusacioun may he make
Whanne þat deeþ comeþ and wole him take;
For good folk, wickid, and shrewis,   4805
Ʒonge and olde and pouere of good þewes,
þe riche and stronge, mowen not faille,
þe feble, fooles, ne þe wise, saunzfaile,
Greet ne smal: shal noon of þise
For no mede ne none emprise   4810
Ascape þe deeþ, þat he ne mote goo
To þe erthe þere he come fro.'

Ca.° lxxxxviij°   'Is it good to answere ay   (105)
                  Hem þat speken folily al day?'
                    'To ferforþ a man him mekeþ   4815
                    þat answeriþ him þat folily speketh;
                  But if his foly shulde him dere,
                  þanne is good þat he answere.
                  Somtime spekiþ a fool folily
                  And no man wote þe cause why   4820
                  And if men answere him noþing,   f. 71ᵛ
                  Noon is peired of his seieng;
                  But if a man answere him aʒeine,
                  þei eggen to speke þe more in veine.
                  þan is a foole al hoote   4825
                  To speke more þan he wote:
                  þanne his wordes he wole not lete
                  But multiplie hem and hem þrete;
                  And so engendriþ he greet folie

That T;   he] om. T.   3877 fole] man P;   folily] folie TS.   3880 the
worse] of þaim wise S.   3883 all] redy al S.   3886 confourme] conferme
TSP;   wordes] othees S.

4819 folily] foly H.

And grete haterede and envy;
And yf men answhere hym nought,
His iangelyng were to ende brought.   3890

Forwhy, forsothe, he dothe mys
That answhereth vnto folys wordys.'

Qo. 105ᵃ   '*What connyng of all þat þou canne*   (106)
                 Is moste greuous vnto manne?'
                     'Of all connyng that ther is   3895
                      Clergy is beste, iwysse;
                          The soteleste and the moste of witte
                 And the moste worshipp is hit;
                 And hit is cleped arte
                 For it artes in euery parte.   3900
                 Hit is herer into connyng
                 And of all thyng knowlechyng
                 And sonnest may hym avayle.

                 But arte of the moste travayle

                 Than is wrightyng of all þat be;   3905
                 For he þat writeþ may not see
                 Abowte while he is in wrytyng,
                 Ne here, ne speke noone other thyng,

3891] Therfore (Forþi SP) he goth on swerdes ordis (*om.* P) TSP.   3895 con-
nyng] thynges T;   that ther is] the grevousiste TP.   3896] That (Than P) is
clergie ande eke the beste TSP.   3898 worshipp] worshiped S.   3900 artes] is

And grete hatrede and envie: 4830
And if men answere noght,
His iangeling were sone to ende broght.
þerfore to ianglers men shulde noght
Multiplie wordes in dede ne þoght;
For multiplieng of foly wordes   4835
Fareþ as two eggid swordes
þat kuttiþ or kerveþ eueryþing
þat aȝeinst it is countering.
So fareþ the wordes of foly men:
þei spare neiþer freinde ne ken;   4840
þei gnawen and biten whom þei hate
And encrese rankour and bate
And keruen from hem her good name
And done many men tene and shame;
þerfore I rede þat euery man   4845
Speke þe good of oþer þat he can.'

Ca.° lxxxxix°   'Of al þe kunnyng þat we here can,   (106)
                 Whiche is most grevous vnto man?'
                    'Off al kunnyng and moost grevous
                      þanne is þe clergie vnto vs   4850
                    þe sotillest and moost of witt,
                    And most of worship eke is itt;
                    And for þat is it called art
                    For it is art in euery part.
                    He is moste hye in kunnyng   4855 f. 72ʳ
                    For he of alle þinges haþ knowleching
                    And sonnest may him availe
                    If he þerynne truly trauaille.
                    But þe moost trauaile þat is
                    Of alle artis, as I the wis,   4860
                    It is writing of alle þat be;
                    For he þat writeþ may not see
                    þe while he is aboute writing,
                    Ne here to speke noon oþer þing,

art P.   3901 Hit is] His TS, He is P;   herer] heyer P.   3902 And . . . thyng]
And all thyng most P.   3905 Than] That T.   3908 ne speke] speke of P.

4846 he] þei H.

Ne thynke, n[e] luste, ne nought doo
But all oonly thervnto: 3910
Forwhy of all travayles þat there be
Writyng is þe moste, I say the.'

f. 58ʳ   *Qo. 106ᵃ*   *'They that travayle for to wynne*   (107)
                 And cannot live, why woll they not blynne?'
           'Men that trauaille and ease hem nouȝt,   3915
             In grete couaytyse ben they brought
             And grete thraldom live they inne
Whill of laboure þey conne not blynne:
They shull dye and goo therfroo
And all here trauayle and here woo   3920
Shall another make therof hym blythe
[That lytill for the dede shalle hym kythe].
I ne say that in haste
Shall a man dispende in waste,
Ne he ne shall suffere noo miseese   3925
But he shall make hym well at ease;
And neuerthelasse at mesure spende
Of suche as God woll sende:
Ease hem that hemsilfe nought have
And lyff and sowle soo may he save.   3930
But he þat of travayle cannot late
For coueytous of worldis bate
And hathe inow withouten that,
He shall neuer be man fat;
But euer the moore he may wynne,   3935
The moore care is he inne.

Therfore is goode in travayll stronge
A whyle a man to reste amonge.'

3909 ne] *from* TSP, no B;   luste] listen TS, harkyn P.   3911 A *begins again*;   there be] there is P, thou woste TAS.   3912] Than is wrytynge alledermooste TS, I sey writyng is the most A, That is wrytyng most ywis P.   3918 Whill of laboure] Sith A, Sith that T, Siþen þat S, For therof P;   not] neuer P;   blynne] cees þerin A.   3922] *from* P, I ne say B, And so itt ffarith offte sith A;   the] *om.* TS;   dede] did S.   3923 ne say] *add* not STP.   3924 a] no P;   in] hit in P.   3928 Of suche as] And of whiche P.   3929 hem . . . nought] and helpe ham that nought ne P.   3930 he] ye P.   3931 late] cees A.   3932 bate] riches A.   3937 is goode in] in gode is P.   3938 A whyle] Alle wynne TASP.

Ne þenke, ne listene, ne noght ellis do   4865
But only applye his might þerto:
þerfore of alle trauailles þat þou woost
þanne is writing alþermost.'

Ca.° i^C

þei þat traueilen forto wynne   (107)
And kunne not lyue, whi nil þei blynne?'   4870
   'Men þat trauaillen and seseþ noght,
    In grete couetise þei ben broght
And greet trauaile lyue þei ynne
Siþen þat þei kunne not blynne:
þei shullen deie and goo þerfro   4875
And of al her trauaile and al her woo
Shal anoþer make him bliþe,
Spende and waste and reuel swiþe.
But I seie not in haste
þat a man shulde spende and waste;   4880
But he shulde suffre no disese
If wiþ his good he might haue ese;
And neuerþeles in mesure spende
And of suche as God him sende
And ese hem þat nede haue;   4885
And lyf and soule so may he saue.
But he þat of trauaille cannot ceese
For couetise of worldes encreese
And haþ ynow wiþouten þat,   f. 72^v
He ne shal neuere be man fat;   4890
But euere þe more he may wynne,
The more care he is ynne.
þerfore it is good to trauel so
þat after we be hens goo
þat we mowen come to þat rest   4895
þat of al good is þe best.'

Qo. 107ᵃ 'On what manere may hit aryse   (108)
          That men become foles and vnwyse?'   3940
            'On many maneres hit cometh vnto
            That men foles waxen also:
            Somme be symple, as foles born;
          Some for evell here witte hath lorn
          And somme for lesyng of here blode;   3945
          Somme for here braynes waxe all woode;
          Somme for wykked humours withyinne
          And somme for hete that they haue ben ynne;
          Somme for here hertes of febele might
          And somme for evell sight anyght;   3950
          And somme to moche to wake or faste
          That dryeth the brayne at the laste;
          And other maners ar ther moo
          That worcheth vnto man grete woo.'

Qo. 107ᵃ 'Is the soule or þe body woo   (109) 3955
          Whenne eyther shall parte other fro?'
            'Forsothe, hit angerith hem full soore
            And full mournyng ben therfore
            And sofere grete angwysshe and woo
          Whanne þat oon parte is þat other froo;   3960
          And ȝif hit at here will wore,
          They departed neuer more.
          And a yonge man toke a wyff
          That he loued as his lyff
          And she hym moore thenne all thyng,   3965
          Whosoo betwyxe hem made partyng
          And did hem parte agayn here wyll,

3943 Somme] *perhaps* Svmme B;   as] or S.   3945 blode] gode P
3947 for] of TSP;   withyinne] begynne TSP.   3948 ben ynne] within P
3951 to moche] fole P.   3953 other] many TSP.   3955-81 *questions numbered*
107-8 *for* 108-9 B.   3957 angerith] greveth T.   3961 at here] were a

[LIBER SECUNDUS]

Ca.° Primo

'On what manere may it rise   (108)
þat man bycomen fooles and vnwise?'
  'In manye maneres comeþ it to
  þat many men foles waxen so:
  Somme beþ simple and fooles yborne
  And some for yuel her wit haue lorne;
And somme for lesyng of her blood;
And somme for her brain is not good;
And somme of wicked humours bigynne   4905
And somme of hete þat þei haue wiþynne;
And somme for her hertis ben of feble might;
And somme for yuel sightes anight;
And some for wacche and fasting
þat makeþ her hernes to drie and cling;   4910
And manye maneres þere ben mo
þat worcheþ to man miche woo.'

Ca.° ij°

'Is þe soule or þe body woo   (109)
Whan þat one shal parte þat oþer fro?'
  'Forsoþe, it angreþ hem ful so[re]   4915
  And ful of mornyng þei b[en] þerfore
And þoleth greet angwissh[e and] woo
Whanne þat oone departiþ þa[t o]ther fro;
And if it at her wille w[o]re,
Departe here þei wol[de] neuere more.   4920
For and a ȝonge [man t]ook a wijf
þat he loued as [hi]s lijf
And she him more þan al þing,   f. 73ʳ
Whoso bitwene hem made departing
And made hem departe aȝeins her wille,   4925

---

his P.   3962] Neuer wold they partt ensample se here A.   3963 And] As iff
A, As P.   3965 thenne] in P.

4915–22] *bracketed letters obscured by defect in MS* L.   4918 oone] *om.* H.
4921 and] *om.* H.

They wolde bothe lyken full ille.
Also the soule and þe body
Ben spoused togedyr inwardly   3970
And soo grete love togeder holde
That they neuer departe wolde;
And yf they febely have wrought
Sethen they were togeder brought,
Thanne namely is þe sorow all   3975
Whenne þat they departe shall;
For the body roteth allway
And þe soule gothe to payne for ay:
Thenne is no wonder though they be wroth
And dredy of here departyng bothe.'   3980

Qo. 108ᵃ   '*Whether shall a man holde to more—*   (110)
An olde man or a yonge þat woore?'
    'Unto nother shall men holde
    There bothe ben for foles tolde.

f. 59ʳ   For yf the yonge a fole is   3985
And he lerned to do amys,
The hote nature woll in hym glowe
And humours also, as I trowe,
And [h]eteþ his herte and his blode
And makeþ hym iolyf and woode;   3990
And whyll þat hete lasteþ soo,
A shorte reede shulde he assente vnto.
But an olde fole, if there be oon
That hathe lityll hete or noon,
And he be of iolite,   3995
A right kynde fole is hee
For his tyme that he hadde byfore
And now wolde haue another þore;
And the iolynesse men in hym fynde
Is of force and of noo kynde;   4000
And soo is he iolyff amys
For he shewith moore thanne in hym is,

þanne wolde þei boþe like ful ille.
þus fareþ the soule and þe body:
þei ben togidre iweddid iustly
And so greet loue togidre holde
þat þei neuere departe wolde;   4930
And if þei febly haue wroght
Siþen þei weren togidre broght,
þanne namely is þe sorowe al
Whanne þat þei departe shal;
For þe body rooteth away,   4935
þe soule to peine wiþ weilaway:
þanne is no wondre þogh þei be wrothe
And dredeful of departyng bothe.'

Ca.º iij º   'Wheþer shal a man holde wiþ more—   (110)
Oolde or ȝong wheþer it wore?'   4940
   'To noþer shal a man holde
   For boþe ben folie tolde.
For if þe ȝonge be lerned amys
So þat he a folte made is,
þe hoote nature wole on him glowe   4945
And þe hote humours as a lowe
And heeteþ his herte so and his blood
And makeþ him boþe iolijf and wood;
And while þe hete lasteþ so,
A shorte reed shal he assente to.   4950
But oone olde foole, if þer be oon
þat haþ but litel hete or noon,
And he ful of iolynesse be,
A right kynde foole þan is he;
For in his time he was bifore   4955
A foole and now wolde be a more:
þe iolyfnesse þat men in him finde,   f. 73ᵛ
It is of force and not of kinde;
And so he is iolyf amys
For he sheweþ more þan in him is,   4960

om. P.   3996 kynde] *om.* P.   3997 that] *om.* TP.   4001 amys] and amys
P.   4002 thanne] that T.

4926 like] liue H.   4942 folie] foliez H.

As he þat flesshe sethe wolde cunne
With þe clerte of the sunne:
And to suche foles oolde　　　　　　　　　4005
Shall noo wyse man to þem holde.'

Qo. 110ª　　　'Why rayneþ hit in oon yeere moore　　　(111)
　　　　　　　Thenne in another and wherefore?'
　　　　　　　　　'That hit sometyme reyneþ soo
　　　　　　　　　　In oon yeere more thenne in other twoo　　4010
　　　　　　　　　Firste of Goddes wille is fett
　　　　　　　And of gouernayle that he sette,
　　　　　　　As of meuyng of the planetis
　　　　　　　And of þe signes þat hem metis:
　　　　　　　After þe[i] mo[ve hem], lowe or high,　　　　4015
　　　　　　　Make þey yeeres wete or drye.
　　　　　　　All cometh of Goddis will,
　　　　　　　Rayne hit, snewe hit, or be it styll.'

Qo. 111ª　　　'May ony with connyng of clergy　　　　(112)
　　　　　　　A mesell hele other meselry?'　　　　　4020

f. 59ᵛ　　　　　　　'A mesell may men hele, ywys,
　　　　　　　　　With an oynment that is
　　　　　　　　　And is cleped in the clergy,
　　　　　　　"The Oynemente of Philosofy".
　　　　　　　That a mesell wasshe right well　　　　4025
　　　　　　　In water that were warme sumdell
　　　　　　　And bathed hym well all abowte
　　　　　　　And after dryed hym with a cloute
　　　　　　　Ayen the sonne or fire þat brente
　　　　　　　Anoynted hym with that oynemente,　　　4030
　　　　　　　And iiij so moche did therto
　　　　　　　Of iues of sauen and menged it þerto,
　　　　　　　And euery vj dayes so have wrought
　　　　　　　Till xx tymes were ouerbrought:
　　　　　　　That foule skyn of hym shulde pille　　　4035

4003 cunne] sone P.　　　　4004 sunne] mone P.　　　　4005 oolde] tolde P.
4006 man] om. P.　　　　4010 twoo] to P, doo T.　　　　4011 fett] hit P.
4012 gouernayle] generalle T;　　he] is T.　　　4013 of (2)] and of P.　　　4015 þei
move hem] from TP, þe moone B.　　　4018 hit (1)] om. T;　　hit or] om. T.
4025 That] Lete P.　　　4027 bathed] anoynte T.　　　4029 or] of P;　　þat]

As he þat flesshe sethe wolde kunne
At the hete of þe sunne:
And to suche fooles olde
No wise man with hem shulde holde.'

Ca.° iiij°

'Whi reineþ it in oo ȝere more   (111) 4965
þan in anoþer?—Telle me wherfore.'
  'That it somtime reyneth so
    In oo ȝere more þan in oþer to
Firste it comeþ of Goddis wille
And of his gouernaunce, as I þe telle,   4970
As of meuyng of þe planetis
And of þe signes þat hem metis:
After þei meve hem, lowe or hie,
þei maken þe erþe wete or drie;
And al comeþ of Goddis wille,   4975
Reine it, snowe it, or be it stille.'

Ca.° v°

'May any man wiþ kunnyng of clergie   (112)
Hele a misel of his miselrie?'
  'A misel may a man hele, iwis,
    Wiþ an oinement þat good is   4980
And he is called in clergie,
"þe Oinement of Philosophie".
Lat a misel wasshe him right wel
In a water warme somdel
And bare him wel al aboute   4985
And þanne drie him wiþ a cloute
Aȝein þe sonne or fire þat brent
And þan smere hym wiþ þat oignement,
And foure so miche dide þerto
Of iuys of sauein ymengid so,   4990
And euery seuenthe day dighte him also   f. 74ʳ
Til xx be comen and goo:
þat foule skyn shulde of him pile

---

om. P.   4030 Anoynted] Smered T, And smere P.   4032 menged it þerto]
mynge hem soo TP.   4033 vij] vij T, syxte P.   4034 ouerbrought] ebrought T.

4962 At] Ayenst H.   4988 smere] enoynte H.   4990 iuys] yviez H.
4991 also] so H.

And fall from hym withynne a wylle;
And by the xx^{ti} tyde
Sholde hym waxe a newe hide
And he be hole, whatsoo befall,
Of that and of other eueles all.   4040
That oynement is of moore maistrye

But all men may not come þerby.

Whoso in fire hit casteth
And the reke therof vp brasteth,
Also fer as þat reke yeede,   4045
Bothe in lengthe and in brede,
May no wicchecrafte be dight
For it stroyeth all the myght.
And if a man to bataill wente
And anoynte hym with that oynement,   4050
The moste prise sholde he bere
Of all þat togederes were
And moste honoure sholde men hym doo
And moste reuerence vnto;
And if he come amonge his foes,   4055
Were they neuer of soo grete loes
f. 60^r And alle hadde swhoren his dethe,
Shulde noone have might to doo hym qwethe;
And if ony hadde doon a dede
That were the dethe worthy to mede   4060
And hadde en[oynt]ed hym withall
In his name that all deme shall,
Shulde noone have power hym to deme:
All shulde they fonde hym to yeme;
But that he to noon evel assente   4065
For truste of ony oynement.
A woman that conceyve ne might,
And toke of þat oynemente aright
In wille and put hit sotely

4037 xx^{ti}] xxv^{ti} TP.   4039 he] *om.* TP.   4041 moore] many T;
maistrye] myght P.   4042 all men] of hitt alle T;   may . . . þerby] can hit not
dyght P.   4048 stroyeth] fordoth TP.   4050 anoynte] smere P.
4052 togederes] there gadred TP.   4061 enoynted] enioyned B, smered T.

And from him wiþynne a while;
And by þe xxv tide   4995
On him shulde wexe a newe hide
And bi hole, whatso bifalle,
Of þat and yueles alle.
þat oignement is of more maistrie
þan manye men can specifie   5000
But alle men mowen not come þerto
For any þing þat þei can do.
Whoso in þe fire it cast
And þe smook þerof vp brast,
Als fer as þe smoke ȝede,   5005
Bothe in lengþe and in brede,
May no wicchecraft be dight
For it fordoth al þe might.
And if a man to bataille went
And smerid him wiþ þat oignement,   5010
þe mooste pris shulde he bere
Of alle þat þere gadred were
And moost honour men shulde him do
And most reuerence also þerto;
And if he cam among hise foos,   5015
Were þei neuere of so greet loos
And alle hadde iswore his deed,
Shulde noon haue might to do him queed;
And if any haue do a dede
þat were worþi þe deeth to mede   5020
And ysmerid him þerwiþal
In his name þat al deme shal,
þere shulde none haue power him to deme
But alle þei shulde fonde him to ȝeme,
But loke he to none yuel assent   5025   f. 74ᵛ
For trust of þat oignement.
And if a womman conseiue ne might,
And she þat oignement toke aright
Wiþ good wille and putte it sotilly

4065 that] turne P.   4066 ony] that TP.   4068 aright] anon right P.
4069 In wille] om. P;   sotely] previlie T.

5000 manye men] man a man H.   5010 smerid] anoynted H.   5018 haue]
of H.   5021 ysmerid] enoynted H.

In the pryuete of hir body   4070
And bere hit there dayes thre—
Ilke a day that to chaunged be—
And þe fourthe night here spedde
With here husbonde into bedde,
Anoone she shulde conceyve there   4075
But they bothe baren were.
That oynement yet hele can
The goute and all eveles of man.
The makyng of [this] oynement
Of Goddis grace to man is sente   4080
And hit shall sprede ouerall
But euery man ne knowe hit shall;
Ne it may not be made with skyll
But the furste viij dayes of Aprell;
And philosofers sholde hit doo   4085
And with ast[r]onomeres also,
That in þe arte of astronomye
Shulde they worke all ther maistrie
And in certen owres and metes
And certeyn poyntes of the planetes   4090
And of the signes vp an hye
After her mevyng on the sky;

f. 60ᵛ

And in a citee of grete Inde
Betwyxe ij hilles, as we fynde.
Stranon hight that cite right   4095
Aftyr a kyng þat also hight:
That kyng so com of the barntem
Of oon of Noes sones, Se[m];
And he was an astromyer even
And philosofre, þe best might ben,   4100
And in þat cite lete begynne
To worchyn his oynemente withynne;
And therin hit shal be wrought
Vnto the worlde to ende be brought;
And ouerall hit shall be sp[r]edde   4105

4077 yet] that P.   4079 this] *from* TP, *om.* B.   4083 Ne] Yf P.
4086 astronomeres] astonomeres B.   4087 That] Ande T, For P.
4090 poyntes] ouris P.   4092 on] of P.   4095 Stranon] Straman P.
4098 Sem]*from* TP, seven B.   4099 astromyer even] astronomen TP.   4101 in]

In þe priuete of hir body   5030
And bere it þere daies thre
So þat euery day it chaunged be
And þe ferþe night her spedde
Wiþ hir housbonde to goo to bedde,
Anoon she shulde conceiue þere   5035
But if þe boþe barein were.
þat oignement ȝit hele can
þe goute and al yuel of man.
þe making of þis oignement
Of Goddis grace to man is sent   5040
And it shal sprede over al
But euery man it ne knowe shal;
And it may not be made bi skille
But þe firste viij daies of Aprille;
And wiþ philosofres it shal be do   5045
And wiþ astronomiers also,
And in the art of astronomye
þei shullen worche al her maistrie
And in certeine oures and metis
And certein pointis of planetis   5050
And of þe signes vp an hy
Aftir her meueinge in þe sky;
And in a citee of grete Ynde
Bitwene two hilles, as we fynde.
Stranoun hatte þat citee right   5055
Aftir a king þat also hight:
þat king cam of þe barnetem
Of oone of Noees sones, Sem;
And he was an astromien   f. 75ʳ
And philosophre, þe best þat might ben.   5060
At þat citee þei shullen beginne
To wirche þis oignement truly þerynne;
And þerynne it shal be wroght
Til þe world to ende be broght;
And oueral it shal be sprad   5065

om. TP;   lete] dide P.   4102 his] this TP.   4105 spredde] from TP,
spedde B.

5030 hir] his H.   5036 þe] þei H.   5038 and] om. H.   5040 sent]
lent H.

And to diuers londes ledde;
But euery man that wolde hit crave
Shall it not knowe ne hit have.
This oynemente is made alsoo
Of diuerse herbes þat goth therto,   4110
The preciouseeste þat men may fynde
In all the lande of Moche Inde:
Iiij C lx and twoo
Goth to the makyng and noo moo;
And with dragons grece þerto shal be   4115
That men fynde in the iles of the see.
And euer aftyr shall hit dwelle
In the makyng for to welle
Viij dayes, vj, or vij^{en},
After they fynde on the hevene   4120
By the arte of astronomye
And after the signes lowe or hye;
And the fire theruVndir all
Of the herbis and rotis dight he shall
And the herbis þat hit is of dight   4125
Ben kepte honestly aplight
That vnnethes dar ony þem take
Whenne þey þat oynement shall make.

f. 61^r This oynement þanne is of hewe
Betwene broun, reede, and blewe,   4130
A goode odoure to smellen þervpon,
And swhetter hony is ther noon.
Ʒif the weder be [b]right and shire
Vnto it is ouer the fyre,
Rede or blewe hue shall hit take;   4135
And if trowble weder make,
Broune hit shal become of kynde,
Be hit neuer made so mynde.
Whosoo toke in his hande somdeele
And frothed hit with his fyngres well,   4140

4108 ne] ne mow T, ne nouȝt P.   4113 Iiij C lx] CCC seventy T, Thre hundrid
syxti P.   4114 the makyng] om. P.   4115 with] white T, om. P.   4116 A
begins again.   4117 euer aftyr] ouer a fire (while P) TAP.   4122 or] and
P.   4123 fire theruVndir] ferther vndir P.   4124 and] om. TAP;   he] thei
TA.   4125 hit] om. P;   dight] myght P.   4126 aplight] in a plight P.
4127 vnnethes] on erthe P;   ony] none of P.   4133 bright] from TAP, right B;

And into dyuerse londes ylad;
But euery man þat wole it craue
Ne shal not þerof mowe haue.
þis oignement is made also
Of diuerse herbis þat gooþ þerto,   5070
þe preciousest þat men may finde
In al þe londe of Greet Ynde:
þre hundrid fourti and twoo
Goth to þe making and no moo;
And white dragouns grece þerto shal be   5075
And þat men finde in yles of þe see.
And ouer a fire it shal dwelle
In þe makyng forto welle
Viij daies or seuene,
As þei finde by þe cours of heuene   5080
And by þe art of astronomye
And after þe signes lowe or hye;
And þe fire þerevnder al
Of þe herbe rootes dight be shal
And þe herbes þat it is of dight   5085
Ben kept ful honestly, I þe plight,
þat vnneþe dar þei any of hem take
Whanne þat oignement he shal make.
þis oignement is of hewe
Bitwene broun, rede, and blewe,   5090
And a good odour to smelle vpon,
And swetter hony is þer noon.
And if þe weder be bright and shire   f. 75ᵛ
þe whiles it is ouer þe fire,
Reed or blew colour shal it take;   5095
And if trouble wedre it make,
Broun it shal become of kinde,
Be it man to neuere vnhynde.
Whoso toke in his honde þerof somdel
And frote it wiþ his fynger wel,   5100

shire] clere P.   4135 hue] *om.* T.   4136 if] yf in P;   make] they hit make
P.   4138 made so mynde] so wele ffynde A;   made] man T, to man P.
4140 frothed] frote TA, felid P.

5082 or] and H.   5085 is] *om.* H.   5088 Whanne] What H.
5098 vnhynde] vnynde H.

Hit shulde thorogh his handes glide
And come oute on that other side.
This oynemente is vnto man
The dignest thyng that men nempne can:
May noo triacle be therto   4145
For the vertues þat hit may do.'

Qo. 112ᵃ   'Why ne had God man soo wroght   (113)
                  That he ne had synned nought?'
                     'Had God first man [s]o dight
                     That he after synne ne might,   4150
                     Merit were noo man worthy
                  For noo godenesse of his [body]:
                  Alle þe merit ayen sholde goo
                  Vnto God, there hit came froo;
                  And Goddes blisse no man worthy wore   4155
                  But he deserued hit had byfore.
                  And were man made of suche maner
                  That he might noo synne doo here,
                  His goodenesse of hymself were nought
                  But his that hym suche had wrought;   4160
                  For of that þat [t]he behoves nede
                  Art þou worthy to have noo mede.
                  But þe man þat of his wille
                  May do bothe goode and ylle
f. 61ᵛ   And dothe goode, worthy [he] is   4165
                  For to come into that blisse
                  That God hathe ordeyned hym vnto;
                  And for the devel shulde also
                  Shame hym þat God suche oon chees
                  To have þe blisse þat he befor les   4170
                  Thorow werkes of his owne wille—
                  The gode to take and lete the ille.'

                  'Is hit goode to have entirmetyng   (114)
                  Ayenst euery man of all thyng?'

4141 his handes] hym P.   4144 men] I A;   nempne] rekyn AP.   4147 S
begins again.   4149 first man so] so wroght and P;   so] from TAS, do B.
4151 noo] hit to a P.   4152 body] from TSP, mercy BA.   4158 noo] to
S.   4160 his . . . suche] soche as swilke T, yf that suche hym P.   4161 the]

It shulde þorgh his hond glide
And come out by þat oþer side.
þis oignement is here to man
þe worþiest þat men nempne can:
þere may no triacle be þerto   5105
For þe vertues þat it may do.'

Ca.° vj°   *'Whi nadde God man so ywroght*   (113)
              þat he ne hade isynned noght?'
              'Hadde God man first so dight
                 þat he aftir synne ne might,   5110
              Merite to no man were it worthi
              For no goo[d]nesse of his body:
              Al þe merite aȝein shulde goo
              To God, þere þat it come fro;
              And Goddis blisse no man worþi wore   5115
              But he haþ serued it tofore.
              And if man were made on suche manere
              þat he ne mighte no synne do here,
              His goodnesse of himself were noght
              But his þat suche him had wroght;   5120
              For of þat þat þe bihoueþ nede
              Art þou not worþi to haue mede.
              But þe man þat of his wille
              May do bothe good and ille
              And dooþ good, þan worþi he is   5125
              For to come to þat blis
              þat God haþ ordeined him to;   f. 76ʳ
              And for þe deuel shulde also
              Shame him þat God suche oon chees
              To haue þe blis þat he forlees   5130
              þorgh werkis of his owne wille—
              þe good to take and leue þe ille.'

Ca.° vij°   *'Is it good to haue entermetyng*   (114)
               Aȝeinst euery man of eche þing?'

from TSP, he B, þou A.   4165 he] *from* TAP, it B, *om.* S.   4170 befor les]
forlese TASP.   4172] *om.* S;   take and lete] lete and toke A.   4173–4 *q. no.*
om. B.

5112 goodnesse] goonesse L, goodenes H.

'A man þat shall clymbe on a tre,   4175

There hym þynkeþ esiest to be

The frute for to come vnto

3if he woll his profite doo;

But he þat on þe sonnebeme woll clyme,

He may breke his nek sumtyme: 4180

For he þat clymbeþ on hye,

He may happe somtyme to wrie.

Right soo fareth a man vntille

þat entermeteþ hym ouer skyll:

Lete hem þat ben riche and fiers   4185

Entermete þem with theyre peeres

And the poore, I say the,

With suche other as they be.

But the pore to be malapert

That woll alway in his pouert   4190

With the riche entirmete,

He may lese and noothyng gete;

And if þat soo befall

þat the riche hym to counsaill call,

Entirmete he hym of noo more   4195

þanne þat he is icalled fore.

Lete riche with the riche man

Done þe beste þat he can

And worche they goode, worche they ille,

Euer þe poore holde hym stylle: 4200

With his macche aboute he goo

And entermete hym as with þoo,

There dar he haue drede right non

To hurtle his hede ayens þe ston.'

f. 62ʳ

Qo. 114ᵃ   '*Telle me now as for what sake*   (115) 4205

        þat God worlde this wolde make.'

4177 vnto] hym to P.   4178 3if he woll] So will he ffor A;   he] his
P.   4179 woll clyme] clemmys P.   4180 Sumtyme] and hym shendis
P.   4181–2] *om.* P;   on] ouer TS.   4183 Right soo] Also TSP; fareth . . .
vntille] itt ffarith to the man A.   4184 ouer skylle] off more þan he can
A.   4187 I say the] where they fare (fale T) PTAS.   4188 as] there T;
be] are PTAS.   4189 to be malapert] is (as A, is a P) fool apert TASP.

'A man shal climbe vpon a tre   5135
þere him þinketh esiest to be
þe fruite forto come to
If he wole his profite do;
But whoso wolde climbe on þe sonnebeem
And þervpon to honge hemself hem,   5140
He may lightly his necke breke
Or hise ioyntes out of lith steke:
For þat he climbeþ ouer hye,
He may happe somtime to wrye.
þus wiþ a man fare it wil   5145
þat entermeteth him ouere skil:
Lat hem þat ben riche and feers
Entirmeten hem wiþ her peers
And þe pouere, where þei fare,
Wiþ suche oþere as þei are.   5150
But þe pouere is right vnwise
þat wole alweie be so nise
Wiþ the riche to entirmete,
For he may lese and noþing gete;
And if þat it so bifalle   5155
þat a riche man him to counseil calle,
Loke he entiremete him of no more
þan þat he is cleped fore.
Late þe riche wiþ the riche man
Do þe beste þat he can   5160
And weþer þei wirche good or ille,   f. 76ᵛ
Loke þat þe pouere euere holde him stille
And wiþ þe pouere loke he goo
And entermete him wiþ no moo;
For whoso wole hurile wiþ a stoon,   5165
His heed wole breke þereaȝein anoon.'

Ca.º viijº   'Telle me now as for what sake   (115)
                  þat God wolde þis worlde make.'

4190 his] repeated B.   4191–2] And if it befalle soo / That a riche for councell hym
call vntoo T.   4197 with the] repeated B.   4199 worche they (2)] or S.
4201 macche] make A, like TS, pere P.   4203 dar he] they P.   4204 hurtle]
hurte P.   4205 what] whois AS.

5140 to honge hemself hem] wold hong self hem H.   5165 hurile] hurtyll H.

'God made þe world, as was his wille,
The setes of heven to fulfille
Of whiche aungell felle oute byfore
For þe pride þey inne wore;   4210
And for þat the Trinite
Was not worshipped as hit shulde be,
Tanne made he man that blis to wynne
That aungelis had loste for synne.
But al þo þat here ben wroght   4215
Shall not to þat blisse ben brought:
None but tho þat ben worthy
For the gode dedes of here body.'

Qo. 115^a   *'How was þe worlde made as hit is*   (116)
                      And how olde is it?—Telle me this.'   4220
'When aungell had done amys
And was falle oute of the blisse,
God comaunded therto
Be made þe worlde and hit was soo:
Fire and ayre they drewe to the heighte   4225
For they were lightheste of the weighte;
Erthe and water wente down as drestes
And þe water vpon erthe restes;
And all iiij, by and by,
Ben hangyng in þe myddes of þe sky   4230
And fastenyng ne have þey noone
But of Goddis might allone.
God made þe worlde of the lykkenesse
Of an [e]y more or lesse:
By the shelle take I shall   4235
The firmamente þat closeth all;
f. 62ᵛ   By the white the water take I,
That is betwene the erthe and þe sky;
By the yolke, that is vndermooste,

4220 how] whatt A;   olde is] holdes STA.   4223 therto] thervnto
ATSP.   4224 Be] He P;   soo] do P.   4225 they . . . heighte] the (hem
S, *om.* P) highest drowe TASP.   4226 lightheste] lyghter P;   of the weighte] by
ynowe T, inowe S, nough P, as wele is knowe A.   4229 And] Of P.   4234 an

'God made þe world, as was his wille,
  þe sees of heuene to fulfille   5170
Of wicked aungellis þat fel out bifore
For þe priuete þat þei ynne wore;
And for þat the Trinite
Was not worshiped as it shulde be,
þanne made he man þat blisse to wynne   5175
þat aungels tofore losten for synne.
But alle þo þat here ben wroght
Shullen not to þat blisse be broght;
But alle þo þat ben worthi
By good werkes of her body   5180
Shullen into þat blisse wende
Where euer is ioye wiþouten ende.'

Ca.º ixº   '*Hou was þe world made as it is*   (116)
     And hou holdiþ it?—Telle me þis.'
'Whanne aungels hadde done amis   5185
  And weren fallen out of blis,
God comaundid þerto
þe worlde be made and it was do:
Fyre and aire hem hiest drowh
For þei weren light inowh;   5190
Erþe and water ȝede doun as drastes
And þe water in þe erthe restes;
And alle foure, by and by,
Ben hangid in myd the sky
And fastnyng haue þei noon   5195   f. 77ʳ
But of Goddis might alloon.
God made þe worlde of þe liknesse
Of an egge more ne lesse:
By þe egge schelle vnderstonde I shal
þe firmament þat closiþ al;   5200
By þe white wiþynne vnderstonde I
þat is bitwene þe erthe and sky;
By þe ȝolke, þat is innemest,

---

ey] any B, an eye TSP, an egge A.   4238 erthe] ayre S.   4239 vndermooste]
ynnermoste TS, nethirmust P.

———

5188 þe] That H.   5198 ne] and H.

Take I the erthe þat is lowest. 4240
And whanne þe yolke is soden harde,
[A pitte] is in the midwarde:
By that pitte thenne take I helle
For hit is furtheste from the shelle,
And so is helle heuen fro 4245
Firthest pitte in sorow and woo.
And ichon is, þow may see,
That God ordeyned first to be.'

[*'Is ther ony other folke than wee* (117)
That of the sonne haue the claritee?'] 4250
    'Other folk the worlde ben inne
    And ferre from vs they ben atwynne:
    Vnder vs þenne are they tho
That here fete ayens vs goo.
And whoosoo all þe worlde miʒte see, 4255
In oon sonne bothe we be
But sumtyme whenne here is night
Thenne have they the sonnelight,
And here sometyme shynes the sonne
Whanne þat they noone se ne conne; 4260
For whenne þe sonne gothe to reste there,
Halfe prime is hit to vs and more;
And þe roundenesse, iwisse,
Of the worlde makeþ all this.
Oure somer and oure wynter also 4265
Is bothe on vs and on hem vnto
But after þe sonne have his gate,
Whenne here is erly, þere is late;
And in other stedes moo
Of the worlde hit fareth soo 4270
That summe haue somer lawly hete,
That other have wynter colde and [w]ete.
And God hathe of the sonne, ywys,
Made the way that maked all this.'

f. 63ʳ

4242 A pitte] *from* TASP, And rente B.   4245 so] how P;   fro] alsoo T.
4246 pitte] put TP.   4247 þow] as thou TASP.   4248 That] There
TASP.   4249–50] *from* TAS, *lines blank* B.   4254 vs] owren T, oure S, ouris

Take I þe erthe, þat is lowest.
And whanne þat ʒolke is soþen hard,   5205
A pitte is in þe midward:
By þat pitte þan take I helle
For it is ferþest fro þe shelle
And so is helle heuene fro:
þat pitte is ful of sorowe and woo.   5210
And eche þing is, as þou maist see,
As God ordeined it forto be.'

Ca.° x°   'Is ther any oþer folk þan we   (117)
þat haue of þe sunne cleerte?'
                'Other folk þe worlde beeþ ynne   5215
                And fer from vs þei ben atwynne
And vndre vs þanne ben tho
þat her feet aʒeinst oures go.
And whoso al þe world might see,
In oone sunne boþe we be   5220
But alweie whanne here is night
þanne haue þei þe sunnelight,
And here to vs shyneþ the sunne
Whanne þat þei noon se kunne;
For whanne þe sonne gooþ to reste þore,   5225
Half prime it is to vs and more;
And þe roundenesse, ywisse,
Of þe world makeþ al þisse.
Oure somer and oure wynter also   f. 77ᵛ
Is boþe in vs and in hem to   5230
But aftir þe sunne haþ his gate,
Whanne here is erly, þere is late;
And also in oþer stedes mo
Of þe world it fareþ so:
Some han somer resonably hoote   5235
And some winter colde and woote.
And God haþ of þe sunne, ywis,
Made þe weie þat makeþ al þis.'

P.   4255 And whoosoo] For so P.   4262 more] no more TP.   4268 here]
he P;   þere is] here then is he P.   4271 That] But P;   lawly] ffeire and A, of grete
S;   hete] hote TAP.   4272 wete] *from* TASP, hete *(partially erased)* B.

Qo. 117ᵃ   'How longe may the worlde be   (118) 4275
         And how brode and how thik is he?'
           'Whosoo the worlde beholdeth all,
             Hit is rounde as a balle;
             And for hit is rounde, behoueth nede
That all iliche be longe and brede,   4280
And the thyknesse also
Soo is heuen bytwen them twoo.
And thow hit were all playn land
As the palme of myn hande,
And a man sholde euery day   4285
Go certeyn myles day by day
And sholde haue noo lettyng
Of water ne of noone other thyng
The worlde thorogh for to fare,
He shulde neuer be so yare   4290
That he ne sholde make þroghe to goo
A thousand dayes withoute moo:
And the same sholde he fynde þat yede
Owther the thiknesse other the brede.'

Qo. 118ᵃ   'Why shall God wel clenly alsoo   (119) 4295
         The folke of this worlde vndo?'
           'God shall [this worlde] fordo, iwys,
             For a better þenne hit is.
             For were hit nowe þat here stode
A riche palys and a goode,   4300
And the man þat hit langed vnto
Had another hows also
Wel sympeler and las worthy,
And hit felle þenne aventerously
That of the paleys felle a wall   4305
And forlos[t the] stones all,
And that [wall] might he not make
But if he wolde þe stones owtetake
Of the litill howse besyde,

f. 63ᵛ

4283 thow] *om.* S.　　　　4286 day by day] bi the waye TSP, in his way A.
4294 Owther . . . other] Bothe . . . and P.　　　4295 wel . . . alsoo] vtterly ffordo A;
wel] will T, wilne S.　　　4296 vndo] also A.　　　4297 this worlde] *from* TSP, *om.*
BA.　　　4304 aventerously] lightly P.　　　4306 forlost the] for losyng of B, fforlost

Ca.º xjº   'Hou longe may þe world be   (118)
               And brode and þicke?—Telle now me.'   5240
                  'Whoso þe world biholdeþ al,
                    It is rounde as a bal;
              And for it is rounde, it bihoueþ nede
              þat it by yliche in lengþe and brede,
              And þe þicknesse also   5245
              It is euene wiþ hem to.
              And þogh it were al plein londe
              As þe pawme of myn honde,
              And a man shulde euery day
              Go certeine miles by þe way   5250
              And shulde haue no letting
              Of watir ne of noon oþer thing
              þe worlde þorgh forto fare,
              He shulde neuere be so ȝare
              To goo it þorgh, triste wel þerto,   5255
              In a þousand daies wiþouten mo:
              And þe same he shulde finde þat ȝede
              þe þiknesse or þe brede.'

Ca.º xijº   'Whi shal God clenly also   (119)
               þe folke of þis worlde fordo?'   5260
                  'God shal þis worlde fordo, ywis,
                    For a bettir world þan it is.
              For were it so þat here now stood   f. 78ʳ
              A riche paleys and a good,
              And þe man þat it longed to   5265
              Hadde anoþer hous also
              Wel simplier and lesse worthi,
              And it bifel þanne auenturously
              þat of þe pales fel a wal
              And þe stones loste al,   5270
              And þat wal might he not make
              But if he wolde þe stoones take
              Of þe litel hous beside,

the (*om.* P) AP, forles the S, loste the T;   all] of all B, and also alle T.   4307 wall]
from STAP, withall B.

5254 neuere] ne H.   5258 þe] By þe H.   5267 Wel] *om.* H.

I trowe there shulde none other betyde   4310
That he ne shulde his paleis dight
As smertly as he might
And of his howse have lytyll care
But that his paleys fulfilled ware.
He were a fole þat that wolde chese   4315
The better for the wors to lese.
Soo fareth God, I warne the wele,
For of his paleys [fel a] grete dele
And of this worlde hathe he noon dente
But þat that fulfillid be.'   4320

'The foules þat in þe ayre flee   (120)
How ben they bore on lofte an hie?'
  'The thiknesse of the heyre an hye
  Thanne is the moste skele forwhye
  That foules on lofte ben born,   4325
Elles were the flight forlorn.
The ayre is thyk and moyste also
And woll vngo and crepe þerto;
And whanne þe foule is on lofte
And his wynges stereth ofte,   4330
With the warpyng of his wynge
He doothe þe ayre for to mynge
And waxe thyk; and he is light,
And soo gederith the ayre by his might.
And that the ayre is [th]ike above   4335
That may a man lightly prove:
Whoso in his hande woll take
A yerde and smertly hit shake,
Hit shall bowe in the shakyng;
And þat dothe noone other thyng   4340
But the thiknesse of the eyre, that withstondes
The yerde with shakyng of thyn handes.
And soo withstondith hit fowles all
In here fleyng, that they ne falle.'

4317 God] hit P.   4318 fel a] *from* STA, full B, he hathe a ful P.
4319 that] that pales T, þat oþer S, his paleys P, itt A.   4321–44] *om.* S.
4321–2 *q. no. om.* B.   4325 on] of P.   4328 vngo . . . þerto] opyn and ayen

I trowe it shulde none oþer betide
þat he ne shulde his paleys dight   5275
Also smertly as he might
And of his hous haue litel care
So þat his palys fulfilled ware.
He were a foole þat wolde chese
þe better for þe werse to lese.   5280
So fareþ it, I warne þe wel,
For of his pales fel a greet del
And of þis worlde haþ no deinte
But þat his paleys fulfilled be.'

Ca.º xiij º   'þe foules þat in þe eir flie,   (120) 5285
              Hou ben þei bore alofte on hie?'
                 'The þiknesse of þe eir an hy
                 þat is þe moost skile for why
              þat þe foules on lofte beþ ybore,
              Ellis were al her flight forlore.   5290
              þe eir is þicke and moist also
              And wole vndo and close efte to;
              And whan þe foule is alofte
              And hise wynges steren ofte,
              Wiþ þe warping of his winge   5295
              He doth þe eir forto mynge
              And wexiþ þicke; and he is light,   f. 78ᵛ
              And þat him holdeþ in his flight.
              And þe eir is þicke aboue
              And þat may a man lightly proue: 5300
              For whoso in his honde wole take
              A ȝerde and smertly it do shake,
              It shal bowe in þe shaking;
              And þat makeþ noon oþer thing
              But þickenesse of þe eir, þat wiþstandis   5305
              þe ȝerde in shakinge of thine handis.
              And so wiþstondiþ it foules alle
              In her fleyng, þat þei ne falle.'

close to A.   4330 stereth] streyne P.   4334] Ande that hym (hit P) holdeth in
his flight (plight P) TP, And so ascendith to grete hiȝtt A.   4335 thike] like B, thik
TAP.   4341 But] Be P.   4343 fowles] soulis P.

f. 64ʳ *Qo. 120ᵃ*   '*Amonge al othyr telle me yet:*   (121) 4345
                        The rayne þat falleþ, whens cometh hit?'
                          'Rayn is of the water of the [see]
                          And with [bl]aste of wynde amounteth he;
                          And whanne þe wynde hit hathe an high,
The sonne, þat is hote kyndely,   4350
Draweth the water hym faste vnto.
The wynde putteþ after faste alsoo:
As that men may see somtyme
A dewe lyyng to halfway pryme
But whanne þe sonne his hete yeldes,   4355
[The dewe] in townes and in feldes
He takeþ vp and draweþ faste
And cometh to the ayre at laste
And is there þykkyng in clowde:
Thenne comyth wynde and bloweth lowde   4360
And bereþ hit on þe ayre ouerwhere
Till hit be woxen þik and more.
Thanne hit begynneþ to heuy soone:
He may not longe above woone
But fallyn on rayn hastyly;   4365
As whanne þe water is downe clenly,
The clowde beleueþ white and fayre
That is of þe colde of þe ayre;
And þat wasteþ þe sonne þer nere,
And soo becomyth the sky all clere.'   4370

Qo. 121ᵃ   '*Haylstones þat fallen alsoo,*   (122)
                        Whens and wherof comeþ þoo?'
                        'Off water gadered vndyr the sky
                        And of colde and þe ayr on hye.
                        As whanne a cloude is but thynne   4375
And hathe lytell pouer inne,
Above in the ayre flye
Wyndes þat ben colde and drie;

4345 S *begins again.*   4347 see] *from* TASP, wa *(partially erased)* B.
4348 blaste] *from* TASP, waste B;   amounteth] movith P.   4350 hote] *om.*
P.   4352 faste] *om.* A.   4356 The dewe] *from* TSP, That dwelleth
BA.   4357 takeþ] *om.* P.   4362 and] more and S.   4364 He] Ande
TSP.   4368 colde] kelth A, kylthe P.   4369 þat] þan itt A;   þer] beyng

Ca.° xiiij°   '*Amonge alle oþere telle me ȝit:*   (121)
                  þe rein þat falleþ, whens comeþ it?'   5310
                      'Rein is of þe watir in þe see
                        And with blast of winde mounteþ he;
                  And whan þe wynde it haþ an hy,
                  þe sunne, þat is hoot kindely,
                  Draweþ the water faste him to   5315
                  And þe wynde putteþ after faste also:
                  As þat men mowen see somtyme
                  A dewe ligginge til halfwey prime
                  But whanne þe sunne his hete ȝildes,
                  þe dewe, þat is in towne and fildes,   5320
                  He takiþ vp and draweþ fast
                  And comeþ to þe eir at þe last
                  And is þere þikkinge liche a clowde:
                  þanne comeþ windes and bloweþ lowde
                  And possith it in þe eir more and more   5325
                  Til þat it wexe þicke þore.
                  þanne bygynneþ it to heuy sone
                  And may not longe aboue wone
                  But falleþ in rein hastily;
                  And whan þe water is doun clenly,   5330
                  þe clowde bileueþ white and faire   f. 79ʳ
                  þat is þorgh colde of þe aire;
                  And þat is wastid þorgh þe sunne clere,
                  And so bycomeþ þe sky al clere.'

Ca.° xv°   *þe haile stones þat fallen also,*   (122) 5335
                  Wherof and whens comeþ tho?'
                      'Off water gadred vnder þe sky
                        And of þe colde of þe eir an hy.
                  As whanne a clowde is but þynne
                  And haþ litel power him wiþynne   5340
                  And aboue in þe eir þe[r] fly
                  Windes þat beþ colde and dry;

A.   4373 vndyr] on P.   4374 colde] kelthe P;   and] of TASP.
4375 As] And S.   4377] And abowten hit þere flye S.

5309 ȝit] riȝt H.   5325 it] *om.* H.   5338 eir] water H.   5341 þer]
from H, þei L.

And whanne þat clowde sholde in droopes fall,
With colde ben they frosen all,   4380
And þat sholde haue [falle] rayn to grounde
They fallen þenne on stones rounde.'

f. 64ᵛ

Qo. 122ᵃ   'Whedyr be the tempestis all   (123)
                 That sumtyme amonge vs falle?'
                 'In that yeere þat somer is colde   4385
                 And þe moistour manyfolde
                 That is in the ayre holdeth stylle
                 And may not clensed be at wille
                 But gadereth faste and holdith there
                 And ȝit in wynter gadereth more,   4390
                 Thanne befalleþ on summe parte
                 That the erthe is cleue for drie.
                 The swhifte wyndes come þeroute
                 And spredeþ hem wyde ouerall aboute
                 And into the ayre therwith þey take   4395
                 And therof grete tempestes make.'

Qo. 123ᵃ   'Telle me now, for hit is wonder: (124)
                 Of what thynge comyth þe thonder?'
                   'Men may se sommetyme a smeke
                   Rise of the erthe as were a reke   4400
                   And exalt[acions] the[y] hight:
                 Th[o vnto þe] ayre stye vpright.
                 Hote and drye be somme of thoo
                 And somme hote and moyste also.
                 Whan they nygh al[derhigheste] are   4405
                 Of the ayre, there wynde is yare,
                 He þat is hote and drye
                 May the sonner vp stye;
                 And whanne þe hete comyth there,
                 For moistour wynde he gaderith sore   4410

4380 colde] kylthe P;   ben] aier S.   4381 falle] *from* TP, *om.* BA.
4383 Whedyr] Whens T, Wheþen S, Wher A.   4388/9 *add* But gaderith faste and
holdeth stylle / And may not clensed be at wille B.   4392 is cleue] is clove A,
clevith TSP.   4393 swhifte] speryd PT, closed S, *om.* A.   4394 ouerall] where
TAS, owere P.   4395 therwith] ther weye TSP.   4400 erthe] ayre S.
4401 exaltacions they] *from* ATS, exalten the B, exalacones they P.   4402 Tho vnto
þe] The victorye B, Thatt vnto A, Thoo vntill T, For vntill P;   stye] stille P.

And whan þat clowde schulde in dropis falle,
Wiþ colde ben þei frosen alle,
And þat þat shulde falle rein to grounde   5345
þei fallen on stones smale and rounde.'

Ca.° xvj°   'Whennes beþ þe tempestes alle   (123)
                 þat somtime among vs falle?'
                 'In þat ȝere þat somer is colde
                 And þe moisture manyfoolde   5350
                 þat is in þe heir iholde stille
                 And may not be clensid at his wille
                 But gadreþ faste and holdeþ thore
                 And ȝit in þe winter gadreþ more,
                 [þan bifalleþ on some partie   5355
                 That þe erthe cleueth for dry].
                 þe sperid wyndes comeþ þerout
                 And spredeþ hem wide al about
                 And nyhe to þe air her way þei take
                 And þerof greet tempestis þei make.'   5360

Ca.° xvij°   'Telle me now, for it is wondre: (124)
                 Of what þing comeþ thondre?'
                    'Men mowen somtyme se a smeke
                    Arise of þe erthe as it were a reke
                 And exalaciouns þei done highte: 5365   f. 79ᵛ
                 þicke in to þe eyr þei stiȝen vp righte.
                 Hoote and drie ben some of tho
                 And somme moiste and hote also.
                 Whanne þei alþerhiest are
                 In þe eyr, þe windes beþ ȝare,   5370
                 And he þat is hote and drie
                 May þe hastiloker vp stie;
                 And whan þe wete cometh þore,
                 For moisture winde he gadreþ sore

4404 hote] wete P.   4405 alderhigheste] *from* TASP, alle and togedyr B.
4406 wynde is] wyndis AP;   yare] are A.   4407/8 *add* Is caste amonge the
clowdes high T.   4408 sonner] hastiloker SAP, hastlyar T.   4409 hete] wete
SP, moiste T.   4410 sore] thore T.

5355–6] *from* H, And is ywax colde forthy / And stinking also wonderly L (*cf.* 5375–
6).   5374 gadreþ] *from* H, gradreþ L.

And is waxen colde forthy
And thynkeþ also wonderly;
And then is it in sonder caste
And cloudes made with wyndes blaste.

f. 65^r

And exaltacion that is drye   4415
Is caste amonge the cloudes hye
Froo oon to another as a ball
But at the laste oute it shall;
And whan he brekes hit on sonder,
A noyse they make they clepe þe þonder,   4420
For drie amonge the wete woll not
Dwelle whanne þe wete presseth hym oute.
And here an ensampell maiste þou se
On what manere hit woll flee:
Lete a man his handfull holde   4425
Of whete or siluer, whiche he wolde:
The more he þe hande togedre threstis,
The more þe whete oute he brestes.
And soo hit is, vndirstande,
Of that other biforehande.'   4430

Qo. 124ᵃ   'The wynde þat bloweth by banke and see,   (125)
      Whereof euer may hit be?'
'I have tolde herebifore
Exaltacions what they wore;
And he þat is hote and drye,   4435
As I sayde ere, they woll stye;
And whanne hit comeþ the cloudes among,
Yf the cloudes ben stiff and stronge,
They caste þe exaltacion
To and fro, vp and downe;   4440
And for hit is drye, at the laste
Hit turneþ into wyndes blaste;
And where þat exaltacion is wete,
Hit turnith into reyne fote hete.'

4412 thynkeþ] thynkynge T, synkith A, þickened S, styngand P.   4420 they] we
TSP.   4422 oute] o3t S, ought P.   4423 here an] bi TSP.   4428 whete]
whete or syluer P;   he] *om.* TASP.   4429 vndirstande] to vnderstande
STP.   4431 banke] londe TAS.   4436 ere . . . stye] ande (est A, ere S,
eyther P) wole vpstie TASP.   4438 stiff] thik TSP.   4441 laste] last and

And ys ywax colde forthy   5375
And stinking also wonderly;
And þan is it in sondre icast
And clowdes imade wiþ windes blast.
And þe exalacioun þat is drye
Is ycaste amonge þe clowdes hye   5380
From oon to anoþer as a bal
But at þe laste it out shal;
And whanne it brekeþ asondre,
A noyse it makeþ we calle a þondre,
For drie among weet wole noght   5385
Dwelle whan þe wete pressiþ him oght.
And by ensample þou may see
On what manere it wole flee:
Lat a man his hondful holde
Of whete or siluer, wheþer he wolde: 5390
þe more he þe hande togidre þriste,
The more þe whete wole out briste.
And so is it to vnderstande
Of þat oþir biforehande.'

Ca.º xviijº   'þe winde þat bloweþ by londe and see,   (125) 5395
               Wherof euer may it be?'
                  'I haue tolde þe herebifore
                  Of exalaciouns, what þei wore;
               And he þat is hote and drie,   f. 80ʳ
               As I seide er, wole vp stie;   5400
               And whan it comeþ clowdes among,
               And if þei be þicke and strong,
               þei caste þat exalacioun
               To and fro, vp and doun;
               And for it is drie, at þe last   5405
               It torneþ into wyndes blast;
               And were þat exalacioun woot,
               It wolde torne in to rein for hoot.'

done P.   4442/3 add And ther hit is downe caste P.   4443 wete] wotte T,
woot A.   4444] Itt wold into rayn down bete A;   fote hete] as skete S;   hete]
hote T.

5384 A] and H;   a] it H.   5386 oght] oute H.

Qo. 125ᵃ   'Hough cometh wateres on hilles hye   (126) 4445
                  That semed better to be drye?'
                        'Also as the veynes lye
                        To mannys body, lowe or hye,
                        [Also the erthe that we on goo]
                        Is vnder full of veynes also.   4450
                  And opyn the hyde the veyne [vpon],

f. 65ᵛ   The blode sekeþ oute anoon
                  And also vppon the crowne
                  As vppon the fete there adowne;
                  And the veynes þat in the erthe lye   4455
                  Haue water rennyng lowe and hye,
                  Vp and downe, to and froo,
                  As the veynes þat in the erthe goo;
                  And there they the [erthe] feble see,
                  Hye or lowe whether hit be,   4460
                  Hit brekeþ owte and renneþ þore,
                  Hill or dalis whether hit were.'

Qo. 126ᵃ   'The water þat is in þe see,   (127)
                  Why is it salte?—Telle þou me.'
                        'In the myddes of the worlde a see is oon   4465
                  There the sonne brennys euer vpon,
                  And þorough that brennyng hete
                  Ben the watres þat shulde ben swhete
                  Becomen bitter and salt also;
                  And þat see renneth all other vnto   4470
                  And soo ouerall salt hit is,
                  And hete of the sonne makeþ all this.
                  Whether that þe see stylle stode,
                  And were the water fressh and goode,
                  The stynke therof so grete sholde be   4475
                  That all the fysshes in þe see
                  Sholde dye, bothe grete and smale,
                  And that were to man grete bale;

4445 cometh] goth A, issewes T, is S.   4449] from TSP (Also] Right so P), So the
erth whereuer þou goo A, om. B.   4450 vnder full] wondirfull P.   4451 veyne
vpon] from TASP, veynes vpdo B.   4452 oute] the weye T.   4452/3 add And in
streme begynneþ to goon B.   4456 and] or P.   4459 there they] thou that P;
erthe] from TASP, dethe B.   4466 euer vpon] euerylkon T.   4467 that] þe

Ca.° xix°   'Hou renneþ watir from hilles hye   (126)
                   þat semen bettir to be drie?'   5410
                        'Also as þe veines lye
                        In mannes body, lowe or hye,
                   So þe erthe, þat we on goo,
                   Is vndre vs ful of veines also.
                   For peerse a veine on þi body,   5415
                   And þe blood issueþ out ful lightly
                   As wele vpon þe coroun
                   As on þe foote byneþe adoun;
                   And þe veynes þat in þe erthe ly
                   Han rennyng water lowe and hy,   5420
                   Vp and doun, to and fro,
                   As þe veines in þe erthe goo;
                   And þere þei in þe erthe feble be,
                   Hie or lowe, as I seie the,
                   It bresteþ out and renneþ thore,   5425
                   Hil or dale wheþer it wore.'

Ca.° xx°   'The watir þat is in þe see,   (127)
                   Whi is it salt?—Telle þou me.'
                   'In þe midel of þe world a see is one
                   And þe sunne brenneþ euere þerevpon,   5430
                   And þorgh þat brenninge hete
                   Ben þe watres þat shulde ben swete
                   Bycome bitter and salt also;   f. 80ᵛ
                   And þat s[e]e renneþ alle oþer to
                   And so oueral salt it is.   5435
                   þe hete of þe sonne makeþ it, ywis.
                   And were it þat þe see stille stood,
                   And were þe water fresshe and good,
                   þe stenche þerof so greet shulde be
                   þat alle þe fisshes in the see   5440
                   Shulde deie anone, boþe grete and smale,
                   And þat to man were greet bale;

ferventt A.   4470 all] om. P.   4471 ouerall] ouer P.   4472 all this]
mekel of this TS, hit ywis P.   4473 Whether] Were T, Were itt A, Wher S, Were hit
so P.   4474 were] om. A.   4477 dye] add anon TSP.

5434 see] from H, synne L.   5435 oueral] euer all H.   5436 ywis] wisse H.

And on þat londe shulde be suche a stynke

That man wolde not suffre hit for nothynge,   4480

But wynde hit sholde on londe bere
And þat shulde all the world dere.'

Qo. 127^a

'*Telle me now, if þou wote:*   (128)
How oute of erthe spryngeþ water hote?'
    'Watres that alle hote so sprynge   4485
    Have somwhere in here rennynge

f. 66^r

Ouer bristen made his cour[s]
And not full ferre fro the sours;
And thorogh hete of the kynde of brymston
The water becomith warme anoon   4490
And warme spryngeþ oute alsoo:
And whosoo leyde his nose þerto,
He sholde anoon fele ful well
Savour of brymston sumdele.'

Qo. 128^a

'*Amonge all other telle me oon:*   (129) 4495
Whereof comyth þe brymston?'
    '[Q]vyk brymston that men calle
    Comyth of the lightenynges þat down falle
    Vppon roches by the see
Other on hilles, whether hit be.   4500
And soo harde downe ben they caste
With ayre above and wyndes blaste
Thatte they falle the [erthe] withynne
And [in] þat erthe they lye and brenne.
And erthe exust hit hight, forthe,   4505
That is brente soo wondirle;
And that turneþ to brymston
And welleþ vp somtyme goode woon.'

4482 þat] all þat S;   all the world] the folke S, the folke moche P.   4484 How]
om. T.   4487 bristen] brimston TASP;   cours] *from* STAP, cour B.
4488 sours] sens P.   4489 of (2)] *om.* P.   4494 sumdele] fele sumdele
B.   4497 Qvyk] *from* TAP, Ivyk B, white S.   4498 lightenynges þat down]
levenes that ofte TAP, laytes when þai S.   4503 falle] *om.* P;   erthe] *from* TASP,

And on þe londe shulde be
Suche stenche, as I seie the,
þat it suffre shulde no man   5445
For oght þat he do can:
þe winde shulde it to londe bere
And þat shulde þe folke sore dere.'

Ca.º xxjº   *'Telle now me, if þou it woot:*   (128)
            Hou springeþ of þe erthe water hoot?'   5450
       'Water þat al hoot so springe
        Haue somwhere in here rennyng
       Over brimston her cours ymade
       And not ful fer from þe shade;
       And þorgh hete of þe brimston   5455
       þe watir bicomeþ warme anoon
       And warme springeþ out also:
       And whoso leide his nose þerto,
       He shulde anoon fele wel
       Sauour of brimston somdel.'   5460

Ca.º xxijº   *'Amonge alle oþere telle me oone:*   (129)
            Whereof comeþ þe brimstone?'
       'Quicke brimstone þat men calle
        Comeþ of leeuens þat ofte falle
       Vpon roches by þe see   5465
       Ouþer on hilles, wheþer it be.
       And so hard þei ben doun cast   f. 81ʳ
       Wiþ air aboue and windes blast
       So þat þe erthe þei falle withynne
       And on þat erthe þei ligge and brynne.   5470
       þus it is bred ful wonderly
       And in þe erthe norisshed sikerly;
       And þat torneþ to brimstone
       And welleþ vp somtime good wone.'

---

ayre B.   4504 in] *from* TAP, *om.* B.   4505–6] And the erthe drawith forth
therby / Thus is hit ybred full wondirly P.   4506 is] it is TS.

5447 to londe] lowde H.   5464 leeuens] leuez H.

Qo. *129*[a]   'Whereof euer may hit be,   (130)
                     The leven that we as fyre see?'   4510
                        'Cloudes somtyme on the skye
                         Renne togeder vp an hye
                         With soo grete ayre and soo kene
                     That fyre lightenes hem betwene,
                     And þat is þat we lightenyng calle.   4515
                     And somtyme downe woll hit falle;
                     Somtyme sleknes hit on lofte
                     In the cloude, and þat is ofte.'

Qo. *130*[a]   'The water that ebbith and flowith alsoo,   (131)
                     Whens come they and wheder do þey goo?'   4520
                        'Alle þe wateris þat euer be,
                         Alle they come owte of the see
f. 66[v]   And ichon ageyn they goo ·
                     Vnto the see þat they come froo.
                     The wateres þat falle in erthe synketh   4525
                     And as a sp[o]nge the erthe them drynkeþ;
                     And whenne they ben comyn thedyr,
                     In veynes geder they togedyr
                     And they that goo in by oo syde
                     By another oute they glyde.   4530
                     The erthe takeþ and geveþ all
                     The wateres that are on erthe falle.'

Qo. *131*[a]   'Hillis and roches, were they nought   (132)
                     Made furste whanne þe worlde was wrought?'
                        'Fro the furste tyme of Adam   4535
                         Vnto þe tyme þat Noe cam
                         Was neuer hille ne roche withall
                     But as sleight aboute as a ball:
                     Noo reyn fell thanne the erthe vpon;
                     Storme ne tempest was þere noon.   4540
                     But in þe tyme of Noe
                     For the grete iniquite

4510 leven] layte S.   4515 lightenyng] leven TA, leuenes P, layte S.
4521 euer] þer S.   4522-651] *pages missing* A.   4522 see] greitt se S.
4524 see] greitt see S.   4526 sponge] *from* TSP, sprynge B.   4528 In]

Ca.° xxiij°   'Wherof euer may it be,   (130) 5475
               þe lightning þat we as fire see?'
                 'Clowdis þat somtime on þe sky
                 Renneþ togidre vp an hy
               Wiþ so greet ire and so kene
               þat fire lightneþ hem bitwene,   5480
               And þat is þat we lightnyng calle.
               And somtime it wole doun falle;
               And somtime it slakeþ alofte
               In þe clowde, and þat is ofte.'

Ca.° xxiiij°   þe watres þat ebben and flowen alweie,   (131) 5485
               Whens come þei and whidre gon þeie?'
                 'Alle þe watris þat euere be,
                 Alle þei comen out of þe se
               And euerichone aȝein þei go
               To þe see þat þei come fro.   5490
               þe watir þat falliþ into þe erthe sinkeþ
               And as a spounge þe erþe it drinkeþ;
               And whanne it is ycomen þidre,
               þe veines gadren it togidre
               And þei þat goon in by oo side   5495
               By anoþer it doth out glide.
               þe erthe takeþ and ȝeueþ al
               þe watris þat ben and on þe erthe fal.'

Ca.° xxv°   'Hilles and roches, were þei noght   (132)
               Imade whan þe world was wroght?'   5500
                 'Fro þe firste time of Adam   f. 81ᵛ
                 Til þe time of Noe cam
               Was neuere hil ne roche wiþal
               But as sleight aboute as a bal:
               No rein fel þan þe erthe vpon;   5505
               Storme ne tempest was þer noon.
               But in þe time of Noe
               For þe grete iniquite

And for the synne þat man wrought
God sente a flode þat eased nought—
Xl dayes and xl nyght   4545
Was the flode in his might:
All the worlde fordid hit there
Sauffe them þat in the arke were.
And the cours of the flode, so long
In his comyng, was soo strong   4550
That there hit nesshe grounde fonde
Hit frett away erthe and sonde,
Stone and roche, felde and towne:
All was turnid vp so downe.
But whanne þe flode beganne to slake   4555
And litell streme for to make,
Stoones and hepes soo withstode
And turned no more for the flode;

f. 67ʳ

And whanne somme withstode soo,
Moo thenne gadered them vnto.   4560
The nesshe grounde þe water frete:
For noo hardnesse hit lete;
And afterwarde the sonnes hete
And froste and colde togeder gan mete
And drave þe stonis togeder harde   4565
And bicam roches afterward.
Forwhy by the forsayde skyll
That flode made bothe dale and hill.'

Qo. 132ᵃ   *'Shall þe deluuye come any moore*   (133)
            In this worlde that was before?'   4570
        'God hathe hight vnto mankynde,
        As wee in ooure bokys fynde,
        That neuer shal be amongis man
        Suche deluuye as was þanne;
        But if of synne man nought amende,   4575
        Another stroke God wol sende.
        That stroke is a swhirde of wrake

4544 eased] seased TS, resid P.   4546] That was the wreche of Goddes myght
TS, That was the wreche of God almyghtis P.   4547 hit] he P.   4549 flode so
long] flodegange TS, flode goyng P.   4553 roche] rote P.   4557 and] on T, in
S.   4561 frete] flete P.   4563 sonnes hete] stones bete T.   4567] For
this byfore was the skyle P.   4571 hathe hight] yaf hit P.   4574] Suche a

And for þe synne þat man wroght
God sente a flood þat cesed noght 5510
Fourty daies and fourty night,
And þat was þe vengaunce of God almight;
And al þe world he fordide þere
Saue hem þat in Noes ship were.
þe cours of þat flood was so strong 5515
In his time it togidre throng
The erthe þere þe neisshe grounde fond
It freete awey bothe erthe and sond,
Stoon and roche, feelde and toun:
Al was torned vp so doun. 5520
But whan þe flood bigan to slake
And litel streme bigan to make,
Stoones vpon hepis þoo wiþstood
And torned no more for þe flood;
And whanne some wiþstood so, 5525
þanne mo gadred hem vnto.
þe neisshe grounde þe water frett:
For no hardnesse it ne lett;
And aftirwarde þe sunne hete
And froste and colde togidre gan mete 5530
And droof þe stones togidre harde
And bicome roches aftirwarde.
For þat is þe forseid skil
þat flood made boþe dale and hil.'

Ca.° xxvj°   'Shal þe flood come any more   (133) 5535 f. 82ʳ
               In þe worlde as it was bifore?'
                   'God haþ bihote to mankynde,
                   As þat we in oure bokes fynde,
               þat neuer shal be among man
               Suche a flood as tho ran; 5540
               But if of synne man not amende,
               A sharper scourge he shal hem sende.
               þat scourge is a swerd of wrake

deuell as for pride ranne P;   was þanne] thoo raan T.   4576 Another stroke
God] A sharpe scourge he TS, As sharpe a scorge God P.   4577 stroke] scourge
TSP.

5517 þe] is H.   5526 mo] om. H.

That iche shall agayn other take;
And echon shall oþer vndo
And distroye þe [world] also.'   4580

'Whan Noe shoulde to þe arke goo   (134)
And of iche beste toke with hym twoo,
Why wolde he evill bestis take
As scorpyons, addres, or ellis þe snake?'
          'Noe did hym in the arke ley   4585
          For two thynges, I shall þe say:
          That oon for the comaundement
That God hym by the aungell sente
(And his body durste he not breke)—
For he sye ful moche wreke,   4590
Of icheon two God bad hym take
For he wolde not þenne all newe make;
And therfore his comaundement did he,
And of tho came that now be.

That othyr [sk]yll for mannes hele   4595
For but if venemous bestis feele
Were dwellyng in iche contre,
So full of venym the erthe sholde be
That [s]che sholde envenym all thyng—
As froyte and corne—that in here spryng,   4600
And soo sholde therof no man ete
But if he died of the mete.
And the bestes ne leve, ywys,
But of the venem þat in erthe is;
And þey clense the erthe þorough kynde   4605
Of the venem þey þerinne fynde,
And all theyre venem is, forwhy,
Of the erthe þat they leve all by.
For take an edder for asay—
The venemouste þat men fynde may—   4610
And in a vessell þou hit doo

4578] That God wull on man vengeauns take P.   4579 vndo] fordoo TS, fordone P.
4580 world] *from* PTS, werk B;   also] all sone P.   4581–726] *om.* S.
4584 or ellis þe] ande also T.   4585 Noe] Me P.   4589 body] bode T.
4590] *om.* T;   sye] shall shew P.   4592 þenne] hem TP.   4593 comaunde-
ment] bode T, body to dede P;   he] he take T.   4594 And of] For of all P;   that

þat euerich shal aȝenst other take;
And euerich shal oþer fordo
And destroye þe world also.'   5545

Ca.° xxvij°

'Whanne Noe shulde to shippe go   (134)
And of euery beest took wiþ him two,
Whi wolde he yuel beestis take
As scorpiouns, addris, and snake?'   5550
 'Noe dede hem in þe arke leie
 For two þinges, I shal þe seie:
þat oone for þe comaundement
þat God to him bi þe aungel sent
(And his biddynge durst not breke)—   5555
For þat he sawh ful miche wreke,
Two of euerich God bad him take
For he nolde not hem alle newe make;
And for þat his bidding dide he,
Of þilke come al þat now be.   5560
þat oþer skile for manis hele
For but venymous beestes fele
Were dwelling in euery contre,
So ful of venym þe erthe shulde be
þat it shulde envenym al þing   5565
As fruit and corne þat in erþe spring,
And so shulde no man þerof ete
But if he deide for þe mete.
And þise venymous beestis ne lyuen, ywis,   f. 82ᵛ
But of þe venym þat in þe erþe is;   5570
And þei clensen þe erþe þorgh kynde
Of þe venym þat in þe erþe þei fynde,
And of þe erþe and eyre truly
Comeþ al þe venym þat þei lyuen by.
For take an addre forto assaye—   5575
þe venymeste þat men fynde maye—
And in a vessel þou him do

---

now] alle that now T, they that new P. 4594/5 *add* In this worlde as ye mow see T.
4595 othyr] of T; skyll] wyll B, skylle TP. 4597 Were] Here P. 4599 sche]
iche B, she T, they P. 4600 here] erthe T, the erthe P. 4611 þou] do P.

5565 it] *om.* H. 5568 deide] did H.

That no erthe come hym too;
With flessh and brede kepe hit thore
Xv^{en} dayes and no moore:
All his venem shal be goon   4615
And skathe shall he mowe do noon,
For venem may noon in hym holde
But he haue the erthe to wolde.'

Qo. 134^a   '*Whereof euer cometh þe goolde*   (135)
                    That makeþ many a man soo olde?'   4620
                        'Myne of golde, withoute mys,
                            In veynes of the erthe waxand is;
                            And siluer alsoo and metall moo,
                    Alle þe erthe come they froo.
                    But golde and siluer men fynde betwene   4625
                    The erthe, there hit is pure and clene:
                    Men gadereth hit and dight hit soo
                    With arte þat falleþ thervnto.
                    But there men hit moste fynde
                    Is a lande by weste Inde: 4630
f. 68^r   In guyse of bras men fynde hit there
                    By the banke of the see aywhere;
                    But iche man canne hit not dight
                    For to [bri]nge hit to þe right.'

Qo. 135^a   '*Perlis and other stoones moo,*   (136) 4635
                    Whens may þey come all froo?'
                        'Oute of Nigre, þat is a see
                            There cokles ar inne grete plente
                            And hange togeder to and two
                    And vpon the water hove they soo.   4640
                    The rayne falleþ from above
                    And entryþ in hem there they hove;
                    Whanne they have take the rayne a stounde,

4614 Xv^{en}] Fyve P.   4618 wolde] holde P.   4620] That is euery man soo
holde T.   4629 there] that T;   moste] must P.   4630 Inde] in Ynde TP.
4631 guyse] wise T.   4634 to] nothyng P; bringe] *from* TP, hange B.   4635 Perlis]
Carboncles T.   4636 froo] thoo T.   4637 þat is a see] ther is a tre P.

þat none erþe come him to;
Wiþ flesshe and breed kepe it þore
Fiftene daies and no more: 5580
Al his venym shal be goon
And scaþe ne may he do noon,
For venym may noon in him holde
But if þei mighte of þe erthe colde
Gadre her venym more or lesse,   5585
A[s] clerkes in bokes fynde expresse.'

Ca.º xxviijº   'Wherof comeþ the golde   (135)
                 þat is in many a mannes holde?'
                     'Myne of gold, wiþouten misse,
                        In veines of þe erþe liggen, iwis;   5590
                 And siluer and oþer metals mo,
                 Alle þei comen þe erþe fro.
                 But gold and siluer men finde bitwene
                 In þe erthe, þere it is pure and clene:
                 Men gadreþ and dighteþ it so   5595
                 With þe crafte þat falleþ þerto.
                 But þere as men it moste fynde
                 Is lo[n]d bi weste in Ynde:
                 In gise of brasse men fynde it thore
                 By þe banke of þe see euery whore;   5600
                 But euery man can it not dighte
                 Forto bringe it to þe righte.'

Ca.º xxixº   'Charbokles and oþer stones mo,   (136)   f. 83ʳ
                 Wherof may þei come, alle þo?'
                     'Out of Tigre, þat is a see   5605
                        þere cokles beþ ynne greet plente
                 And honge togidre two and two
                 And vpon þe water houe þei so.
                 The reine falleþ from aboue
                 And entriþ in hem þer þei houe;   5610
                 And whan þei haue take þe rein,

4639 hange] gedrith P.   4640 vpon] open on T.   4642 in hem] evyn P.

5586 As] *from* H, And L.   5598 lond] lord L, londe H.   5606 cokles]
cokkes *with 2nd* k *altered to* l L.

They close hem to and go to grounde
And on the grounde lith þey thore   4645
Well an hundred yeere and moore.
And they þat are of that contre,
Whenne þey seke them in the see,
Theyre faces to kevere they begynne
With netes bledres blowen inne,   4650
And in blak þey sowe them also
For the fysshe shall fle þem fro.
Thanne go þey downe them vp to wynne
And perles fynde they them withynne:
White and rounde but nesshe þey be;   4655
But whanne þey come oute of þe see
And the ayre have smeten vpon,
They become right harde anoon.
But tho that are of noo season
No theyre tyme seþþe they yede down   4660
Nought haue fulfilled by the grounde,

They stynke as a pelid hounde.

The charbokeles come alsoo
Of cokles as perles doo;
But charbokeles of smale hayle falle   4665
And in fressh water dwelle þey alle
And they by the grounde woll be
Twoo hundrid wynter well or thre,
And they stynke also and fare amys
Whanne theyre tyme not fulfillid is.   4670
But alle þe reyne ne hayle þat falle
Turne not vnto stones alle.
The rayne that the fu[r]st day falleth
Of the monthe in Genyver þat men callith,
And þe mone [be] in þat signe   4675
That vnto þat thynge be digne,

f. 68ᵛ

4649 kevere] hille T, hele P.   4650 netes] *om.* P.   4652 A *begins*
again.   4654 perles] perlous P;   fynde] wynne T.   4655-6] *reversed*
P.   4655 but] bothe P.   4660 No] By P.   4661 by] they P.

þei closen togidre sone aȝein
And goon doun to þe grounde
Sone wiþynne a litel stounde
And at þe grounde liggen þore   5615
An hundred ȝere fully and more.
And þei þat ben of þat cuntre,
Whan þei seken hem in þe see,
Her visages to hide þei begynne
Wiþ netis bladdris iblowe þerynne,   5620
And in blak sewen hem also
For þe fisshe schal fle hem fro.
þanne goo þei downe hem vp to wynne
And perles fynde þei hem ynne:
White and rounde but nesshe þei be;   5625
But whan þei come out of þe see
And þe eir smyte hem vpon,
Thei become right harde anoon.
But þo þat ben of no sesoun
Of hir time siþ thei ȝede adoun   5630
Ne haue not kepte be þe grounde
Her time fully as it is ffounde,
þei stinken þanne ful grevously
To any manis taast peinfully.
þe charbocles come also   5635
Of cokles as þe perles do;
But charbocles of smal haile falle   f. 83ᵛ
And in þe fresshe water dwelle þei alle
And by þe grounde wole þei be
Two hundrid winter or þre,   5640
And þei stinken and faren amys
Til her tyme fulfilled is.
But al þe haile ne reine þat falle
Torneþ not in to stones alle.
þe rein þat þe firste day falle   5645
Of þe mone þat men Ianuerie calle,
And þe mone be in þat signe
þat vnto þat þing is digne,

Yf that reigne in þe cokkel goo,
Perles of that shall come of thoo;
And hayle þat to falle is woone
The viij day of the moone   4680
In Feuerer, and the moone be right
In a signe that Cancer hight
And the cokkeles þat hayle in take,
Charbokeles therof they make.
But þat rayne and þe hayle eche dele   4685
Falle full seldam, wete yee well.'

Qo. 136ᵃ   'Off this worlde now telle þou me   (137)
                How many londes þerinne be.'
                    'Lande but oon is þere noon,
                     Whooso alle hole myght se þeron.   4690
                    But for departyng of the see,
                That departeþ them in thre,
                Thre landes are þat we calle
                Withoute smale iles alle;
                But all be oo lande togedere faste   4695
                And all vppon oon grounde þay [r]aste.
                And whosoo [m]ought þe londe beholde
                That noo water [lette] ne sholde,
                All hole and oon he sholde hit see,
                And soo God made hit to be: 4700
                The vater aboven asonder hit castith,
                But vnder hoole and [fas]te hit lastith.'

f. 69ʳ Qo. 137ᵃ   'Might any man on drye lande wele   (138)
                Go the warlde aboute euerydele?'
                    'No man in erthe might goo   4705
                     The worlde aboute to and froo
                     For he sholde fynde many lettyng
                And þat of many kynnes thyng.
                He sholde fynde wastnesse ful grete
                There nother were drynke nor mete   4710

4681 be right] bryght P.   4690 hole] *om.* P;   þeron] or gone P.
4691 departyng] the partyng P.   4692 thre] here degre P.   4693 Thre] The
P.   4695] But or they to land gedir faste P.   4696 raste] faste BA, reste
TP.   4697 mought] nought B, myght TAP;   beholde] holde P.   4698 lette]

If þat rein in þe cokkes goo,
Peerlis shullen come of tho;   5650
And haille þat to falle is wone
In þe eight day of þe moone
In Feuerel, and þe mone be right
And in a signe þat Canser hight
And þe cokles þat haile in take,   5655
Charbocles þerof þei do make.
But þat rein and haile eche dele
Falleþ ful selde, wite þou wele.'

Ca.° xxx°   'Of þis world telle þou me   (137)
Hou many londes þerynne be.'   5660
   'But on londe is þer noon,
   Whoso mighte loke þeron.
But for þe departyng of þe see,
þat departeþ hem in thre,
Thre londes þer be þat we calle   5665
Wiþouten oþer smale yles alle;
But al is oo londe togedre faste
And alle vpon oo grounde þei raste.
And whoso mighte þat londe biholde
þat no water ne lette sholde,   5670
Al hole and oone he shulde it see,   f. 84ʳ
And so made it God to be:
þe water aboue asondre it castiþ,
But vndre hole and faste it lastiþ.'

Ca.° xxxj°   'Mighte any man on drie lond wel   (138) 5675
Go aboute þe world euerydel?'
   'No man in erþe might goo
   Aboute þe world to ne fro
For he shulde finde many letting
And þat of many skynnes þing.   5680
He shulde fynde waste cuntrees grete
Wherynne were neiþer drinke ne mete

---

from TAP, light B.   4700 to] gode to P.   4701 asonder] the londe T.
4702 faste] *from* TAP, softe B.   4708 And þat] Of that and P.   4709 wast-
nesse] wyldernessis P, desertis A.

5652 day] *om.* H.   5671 and] all H.

But wylde bestis many oon
For to tere iche a bon.
Were an hundrid men on hym wrought
[And yf that ne let hym nouȝt],
The opyn erthe sholde lettyng be,   4715
That swales and geles ayen þe see.

And many a lettyng yet moo,
If he w[e]ste and e[s]t wolde goo;
And if he goo northe and sowthe,
Other lettyng he fynde cowthe.   4720
For thre wonynges shall he fynde
There no man may lyve of kynde:
Oon is hote and colde ben twoo;
May noo levyng thyng be in tho.
And Goddes will hit is also   4725
That no man be mighty therto.'

'Might ony man sayle night and day   (139)
That hadde þe wynde with hym ay
Soo longe till his shipp wente
Into þe turnyng of the firmament?'   4730
    'A man that in a shipp were,
    Thagh he seyled euermore,
    Yet sholde he not come ner the sky
And I shall telle the forwhy.
The erthe lith rounde as a balle   4735
In middes þe sky, and oueralle
It is yliche fer þerfroo;
And the water is alsoo
f. 69ᵛ   Al aboute in þe erthe standand;

4712 iche a bon] ilkone P.   4713-14] om. A.   4713 hym] oon TP.
4714] from P, blank line B;   that] that thou T.   4715] They apon erthe grete
lettyng shuld be P.   4716 That . . . geles] That swelous ande yevis T, Thatt
swalowith and openyth A, The wordis greuith P.   4718 weste] from TAP, wyste
B;   est] from PTA, eft B.   4719-7203] pages missing A.   4721 wonynges]
yones T, thyngis P.   4726 mighty] ryg heye P.   4727 S begins again;   q. no.

But wilde bestes many one
For to tere in sonder euery bone.
Weren an hundred men wroght   5685
On oone and þat him lette noght,
þe opene erþe shulde letting be,
þat swoloweþ the rage of þe see;
For whanne þe see bigynneþ to flowe,
Be it hie, be it lowe,   5690
þe erþe swoloweþ it aʒein
And makeþ the see lowe and plein.
Ʒit ben þere many lettinges moo,
If he eest or west wolde goo;
And if he goo north or south,   5695
Oþer lettinge þere ben many couth.
For thre yles he shal finde
þere no man may lyue ynne bi kinde:
Oone is hote and colde beþ two;
May no lyuing þing be in tho.   5700
And Goddis wille it is also
þat no man be mighti þerto.'

Ca.º xxxijº   'Mighte any man saile night and day   (139)
þat hadde þe wynd wiþ him ay
So longe þere þe ship cam vnrent   5705   f. 84ᵛ
To þe turning of þe firmament?'
    'A man þat in a ship wore,
      þogh he sailed eueremore,
Ʒit shulde he not come nygh þe sky
And I shal telle þe truly why.   5710
þe erþe lith rounde as a bal
In þe midde þe sky oueral
And ouer al it is þerfro
Yliche, and þe water also
Al aboute þe erþe stonding;   5715
And þat is þorgh Goddis worching.

om. B.   4727–44] *this question (139) occurs twice in S, at 47ʳ. 1 ff. (designated (a)*
below) and at 100ʳ. 17 ff. (designated (b)).   4729 wente] cam vnrent ST.
4734 the forwhy] the cause whie T.   4735 lith] is SP.   4737 yliche] iloke
S(a), þer loke S(b).

    5705 þere þe] þat H.

And though men toke vndir hande   4740
And might sayle an C yere,
He sholde the sky be also nere

As whanne þat he from home wente,
Whanne his hundryd yeere were spente.'

[*'Whi made not God man to bee*   (140) 4745
Aye yonge and iolif and of postee,
Riche ande longe life had hym lente,
Ande atte his deth to blisse haue wente?']
'Had God made man on þat manere
As þat þou foretellest here,   4750
God, as me thynkeþ in my thought,
Hathe þe devell grete wronge ywrought:
For [a þought] he felle to helle
And moo with hym, as I can telle.
Sholde a man be þanne of longe lyff   4755
And be riche, yoonge, and iolyf,
And have here all his delyte,
And sethen fare to heven right?
Noo man is worthy to come there
But he haue doon wherefore.   4760
God hathe grauntid vs vnto,
Forwhy þat [w]e well here doo,
He[l]e withoute sekenesse,
Iolite, delite, and grete richesse,
And lif also withowten ende;   4765
For the dethe that men here to wende
Thenne is, for to rekyn right,

Not ellis but a foules flight

That fleeth here and yoonder oute;
And be a man neuer soo stowte   4770
Ne soo yonge ne fayre tod[a]ye,
Tomorow shall hit all awaye.

4745–814] *om.* S.   4745–8] *from* T, *om.* B.   4753 a þought] allþough B, a
thought TP.   4754 as] than TP.   4758 right] quyte TP.   4762 we]
from TP, he B;   well] wole T, wull P.   4763 Hele] *from* T, He be B, Helle

For þogh a man mighte saile
An hundred ȝere saun faile,
He shulde þe sky no nerrer be
þanne whan he entrid to þe see   5720
Whanne þat he from home wente
And þere his hundred ȝere were spente.'

Ca.° xxxiij°   'Whi made God man not to be   (140)
Euere ȝong and iolyf and of pouste,
Riche and longe lyf him haue lent,   5725
[A]nd at his deeþ to blisse haue went?'
    'Hadde God made man so
        As þou seist me vnto,
þanne, as me þinkeþ in my þoght,
To þe deuel he had wrong wr[o]ght   5730
þat for a þoght he fel to helle
And mo wiþ him þan I can telle.
Shulde a man þanne be of long lyf
And be ȝong, riche, and iolyf,
And haue here al his delite,   5735
And sithen to heuene fare quite?
No man is worþi to come þore
But if he haue ido wherfore.
God haþ grauntid vs vnto,   f. 85ʳ
If þat we wel here do,   5740
Hele wiþouten sikenesse,
Ioye and delite and greet richesse
And lijf also wiþouten ende.
For þe deth þat men herto wende
þanne is it, forto recken aright,   5745
þat man of his lyf haþ no might
And is not but as a foulis flight
Or as a blosme faire and bright;
For as þe foule fleeþ in and out,
So, be a man neuere so stout   5750
Ne so ȝong ne so faire today,
He weloweþ as a flour away.

P.   4764 Iolite] Ioye TP.   4765 lif] om. P.   4769 here] hereyn
TP.   4771 todaye] to dye B, to day P, to deye T.

5726 And: A partially erased L.   5730 wroght] wrght L, wrouȝte H.

I wolde not live a thousand yere
And all my delyte haue here
And thanne vnto heuen goon: 4775
Me were leuer be there anoon,
For oon delite þat fallith þoore
Is worthy a thousand here and more;

f. 70ʳ

And forwhy were hit no biȝate
Thedyr for to come soo late.'   4780

['*Whilke ben the angels, telle me this,*   (141)
That resseyven manis soule to blis?']
'Eche man an aungell kepith hym to
To kepe hym þat he not misdoo;
And whanne þe soule is at þe eende   4785
And shall oute of the body wende,
And it vnto God be dere,
The aungell þat was his keper here
Shall come with grete melodye
And of aungeles a grete companye   4790
And receyve hym to mede
And sith vnto þe ioye hym lede—
After þat tyme, þat is to say,
That Goddys Soone in erthe shulde dey.
But or he dye vpon the roode,   4795
Alle goth to helle, wykked and goode;
But alle alyche shull they nouȝt
Be peyned, but after they haue wrouȝt;
And summe shull be in fre pryson
Tyll tyme of his passion.   4800
But whenne þe grete dome shal be,
Thanne shull men moche wonder se:
Soule and body toge[de]r goo
And togeder suffre ioy and woo.
And shall a soule to helle wende,   4805

The devell þat hym halpe to shende

4778 here] yere T.   4779 biȝate] by yate P, lye yate T.   4781–2] *from* T,
om. B.   4783 kepith] hath TP.   4787 dere] gode here P.   4788 here]
om. T, and his fere P.   4798 peyned] ypunysshid P.   4803 togeder] *from* TP,

I nolde lyue here a þowsand ȝere
And al my delite haue here
And þan to heuen for to goon: 5755
Me were leuere be þere anoon,
For oo delite þat is þore
Is worþe a þousand here and more;
And for drede we come to late
Hie vs þider bitime algate.'   5760

Ca.° xxiiij°   'Wich ben þe aungels, telle me þis,   (141)
               þat resceiueþ a manis soule to blis?'
                  'Euery man haþ an aungel him to
                  To kepe him þat he not mysdo;
               And whanne þe soule at þe lyues ende   5765
               Shal out fro þe body wende,
               And it be to God leef and dere,
               þe aungel þat was his keper here
               Sal come wiþ grete melodie
               And aungels wiþ him greet companye   5770
               And resceiue him in bright wede
               And siþen into ioye him lede—
               After þe time, þat is to seie,   f. 85ᵛ
               þat Goddis Sone in erþe shal deie.
               But or he deie vpon þe roode,   5775
               Alle wendiþ to helle, yuel and goode;
               But alle yliche shullen þei noght
               Be ypined, but as þei haue wroght;
               And some shullen be in fre prisoun
               Til þe time of his passioun.   5780
               But whan þe greet dome shal be,
               þanne shullen men miche wondre see:
               Soule and body togidre goo
               And suffre eiþer ioye or woo.
               But whanne a soule shal to helle   5785
               To þe feend wiþ him to dwelle
               Whiche halpe him his soule to shende
               And broght him to þat sory ende,

toger B.   4805 shall a soule] then shall soules P.   4806 The] To the P.

5761 q. no. xxiiij for xxxiiij L.   5771 bright] gret H.

Shall receyve hym and say hym to,
"Thow dedest as I bad þe doo
Ne my techyng into ille
Hathe made þe thysylfe to spille: 4810
Therfore shalt þow goo with me
Euermore in payne to be."
Thus shall þey be receyvyd alyke—
Goode with goode and wyk with wyke.'

f. 70ᵛ

[*'I pray þe, maistere, þou me seye*   (142) 4815
Whiche ar þe better of þe twey—
Good werkes without chastite
Or wik and chast for to be.']
  'Gode werkys wolde I chese
    Though I chastyte lese: 4820
    For be þou chaste of thy body
And þou werkest wykkedly,
What vertu is þat þow has?
Thy chastite is þanne, percaas,
For sikenesse þat þou maist not dure   4825
Or for colde of thy nature
Or for elde þat þou mayste no moore:
What merite art þou worth þerfore?
And þenne for to sle menne
Or to robbe in wode and fenne   4830
Or thy neighboure begyle qweyntly
Or his goode to forlese falsly:
What is worthe suche chastite
[W]an þow of other haste noo piete?
But þat vnchast lyf ledes,   4835
And ȝif he be goode of all dedes,
That thenne dothe to noo man deere:
Man alone he shall hit bere
And God alone he synnes to;
And þat he may soone fordoo   4840

4808/9 *add* That (Thou P) withstodest not my wille TP. P.   4810] *om.* TP.   4813 alyke] thik TP. 4815–18] *from* S, *lines blank* B.   4815 þou] now T. deye T.   4818 Or wik] Ande werkis wik T. 4823 vertu is] vertues P.   4826 colde] kilthe P.

4809 techyng] rysyng 4815 S *begins again.* 4816 of þe twey] for to 4820 lese] forlese TSP. 4830 robbe] rubbe P.

Shal resceiue him and seie him to,
"Now hast þou done as I bad þe do: 5790
þou wiþstodist not my wille
Neiþer my teching vnto ille.
þerfore shalt þou go wiþ me
Euere in peyne forto be."
þus shullen þei be resceiued þicke—   5795
Goode with goode and yuel wiþ wicke.'

Ca.º xxxvº   'I preie þe, Sydrak, þou me seie   (142)
Which were better of þe tweie—
Gode werkes wiþoute chastite
Or yuel werkes and chast to be.'   5800
'Goode werkes wolde I chese
þogh I chastite forlese:
For þogh þou be chast of þi body
And þou wirche wickedly,
What vertues þat þou has?   5805
þi chastite is þanne, parcas,
For sikenesse þat might not dure   f. 86ʳ
Oþer for colde of thi nature
Or for feintise þou may no more:
What merite art þou worþi þerfore?   5810
And þanne forto goo sle men
Or forto robbe in wode or fen
Or þi neighebore bigile queintly
Or make him his good to lese falsely:
What is worthe suche chastite   5815
Whanne þou of oþer hast no pite?
But he þat vnchast lyf ledis,
And he be good of alle dedis,
His synne doþ to no man dere
But aloone he shal it bere   5820
And God aloone he synneþ to;
And þat he may sone fordo

4831 qweyntly] _om._ P.   4832 to forlese] make hym lese P.   4834 Wan] Man
B, Whan TSP.   4835 þat] thou P.   4836 ȝif he] _om._ P.   4837 That
thenne] His synne TSP.   4838 Man] But TSP.

5807 þat] þou H.   5809 Or] And H.

With almesdede or other þynge.
But he þat is of wykyd beryng
And of wykked dedes leve ne canne,
He synneth bothe to God and man;
And lightere is for to wynne   4845
Foryevenesse of God for þat synne
Thanne of God and of man bothe:
Forwhy that ben to hym wrothe,
The [la]tter may he the pease make.
For goode dede wolde I take   4850

f. 71ʳ
For lyfe in chastyte
Thanne wykkedly worke and chaste to be.'

[*'Now what thinge may it euer make,*   (143)
Erthedyn that makith the erthe quake?']
        'Exaltacions hote and drye   4855
            That ben drawe right vp hye
            And þer with cloudes dreven faste
And harde downe to erthe caste
And into cliftes of the erthe they goo
As þe cloudes shoues hem þerfro;   4860
Comyþ thenne wete wether and rayne
And closeþ the cliftes of the erthe agayne.
The exaltacions dwelle þerinne
Shute and may not owtewynne:
Tyll and froo þey stere hem þere   4865
But oute of þe erthe þey may not eere.
And if þe exaltacions be
Gaderid be grete quantite,
Soo harde meve hem þey shall
That the erthe qwaketh withall;   4870
And summetyme more and summetyme lesse
As hit is of mochilnesse.'

[*'Wherof ben—telle me if thou conne—*   (144)
Eclipses of the mone ande sonne?']

4845 lightere] bettir S.   4846 þat] *om.* TS, o P.   4848 Forwhy that] For the
moo TSP.   4849 latter] *from* TSP, better B.   4850 For] Forþi S, Ande therfore
T.   4851 lyfe in] to leeve TS, to loue P.   4853–4] *from* T, *lines blank* B.

Wiþ almesdede or oþer thing.
But he þat is of wicked bering
And of wicked dedis blynne ne can,   5825
He synneþ bothe to God and man;
And lightlier is it forto wynne
Forȝeuenesse of God for synne
þan of God and of man boþe:
If þei with þee here ben wroþe,   5830
þe latter may he pees make.
þerfore goode dedes I wole take
And for to leue chastite
þan yuel werkes and chaste to be.'

Ca.° xxxvj°   'What þing euere may it be,   (143) 5835
              þe erthequake?—Telle þou me.'
                 'Exalaciouns hoote and drie
                 þat ben ydrawe vp right hie
              And clowdis þerwiþ driuen fast
              And doun into erþe harde þei cast   5840
              And into chynnes of þe erthe þei goo   f. 86ᵛ
              And þe clowdis hem parteþ fro;
              þanne comeþ hoote weder and rein
              And shitteþ the chynnes of þe erþe aȝein.
              þe exalaciouns dwelleþ þerynne   5845
              Yshitte and mowen not outwynne:
              To and fro þei meue hem þore
              But out of þe erthe mowen þei no more.
              And if þe exalaciouns be
              Ygadred þere greet quantite,   5850
              So harde þei hem meve shal
              þat þe erþe shal quake withal;
              But somtime more and somtime lesse
              After þat it is of michelnesse.'

Ca.° xxxvij°   þe clipsis of þe mone and sunne,   (144) 5855
               Wherof be þei?—Telle, if þou kunne.'

4860 As] And in S;   shoues] drevyn P.   4861 wete] hote P.   4865 Tyll] Tyll
to B, to TSP;   stere] move TSP.   4866 oute of þe erthe] therof P;   not eere]
nowhere TP, not where S.   4868 be] there TSP.   4869 meve] ne meue
P.   4873–4] from T, lines blank B.

'The clipses of the mone, þis is noo dowte,   4875
Is in full mone or thereabowte;
   And whanne þe full moone stondith southe,
The sonne is north—this is wel cowthe.
A shadowe on þe erthe riseth soone
And st[ieth] vp above þe mone   4880
And hoveþ lo[nge while] of þe nyght
Betwene here and þe sunnes light,
For light hathe þe mone right noone
But that the sonne here smytes on;
And soo þe mone of his light leueth   4885
For þe shadowe þat hit reveth;
But as she goyng makyth here paas
Forby that shadowe, light she taas.
A clips of the sonne comounly
Is in the newe mone or thereby.   4890
Whanne the mone is newe right,
She is merke withoute light;
And þat tyme þe sonne and shee
By oo side of þe sky shall be
And þe sonnebeme, as hit is wone,   4895
Shulde light downe on þe moone;
But if the mone vndyr a lyne falle
(Lyne of eclips þat wee calle),
Light she takeþ not anoon
Vnto she ferre be goon;   4900
But vntil þat she shall þere houve
Bitwyx vs and þe sonne above,
Hir derkenesse reuueþ fro oure sight
Moche of þe sonnes light:
This is the kyndest clips to se   4905
That may of the sonne be.
Other eclips iij^e we fynde
Of the sonne ayenst kynde:
Ooon cam in tyme of Noe
Ayens þat þe dyluuy shold be;   4910

f. 71^v

4880 stieth] *from* TSP, streyte B.   4881 longe while] *from* TSP, lowe tyll
B.   4883 For] Fulle T.   4884 that] thanne T.   4887 she] the
P.   4888 For] Forthe T.   4900 ferre] forby TS, byforne P.
4901 vntil] stille P.   4905 kyndest] kynde of P.

'The clipse of þe mone, þis is no doute,
Is nyhe þe fulle of þe mone or þereaboute;
And whanne þe fulle mone stondiþ southe,
þe sunne is north—þis is wel couthe.   5860
A shadowe of þe erthe riseþ sone
And stieþ vp aboue þe mone
And houeþ longe while of þe night
Bitwene hir and þe sunnes light,
For light haþ þe mone right non   5865
But þat þe sunne hir smiteþ on;
And so þe mone of her light leues
For þe shadowe þat it reues;
And as she going makeþ her pas
Forþ by þat shadowe, light she tas.   5870
Eclipsis of þe sunne comounly
Is in þe newe mone or fast by.
Whanne þe mone is newe right,
She is derke wiþoute light;
And þat time þe sunne and she   5875 f. 87ʳ
By oo side of þe sky shal be
And þe sunnebeem, as it is wone,
Shal light doun on þe mone;
But if þe mone vnder a lyne falle
(L[i]ne of þe clips þat we calle),   5880
Light she takiþ not anoon
Til she be bifore ygoon;
But while þat she þere shal houe
Bitwene vs and þe sunne aboue,
Hir merknesse reueþ fro oure sight   5885
Miche of þe sunnes light:
þis is þe kinde of eclips to se
þat may of þe sunne be.
Oþer clipsis þre we finde
Of þe sunne aȝeinst kinde: 5890
Oone came in þe time of Noe
Aȝeinst þat þe flood shulde be;

5869 as] *om.* H.   5880 Line] Lune LH;   þe clips] eclipse H.
5883 þere] *om.* H.

Another shal be, sothe to say,
In tyme þat Goddys Sone shall day;
And in þe birthe shall be þe þridde
Of Antecriste, as shal be kydde.'

'*Sterres þat men down se fall,*   (145) 4915
How ffalle þey and whens come þey alle?'
   'Understande, sir, witterly,
     That noo sterres falleþ fro þe sky;
     But I shall say þe what may be
That þe folke soo falland see.   4920
Iit is a [f]yre þat is dwelland
In þe hiest of the ayre brennand

f. 72^r

Althernexte þe spyre of fuyre;
And whanne þe nyght somtyme is clere,
Sparkes of þat fyre soo shere   4925
That moche have of þat matere
Falle and perce þe ayre anight
And come soo vnto ooure sight
And semeth as hit were a sterre
That by the sky glode down yerne;   4930
For a sparkele comyng fro soo hye
Vnto a sterre is full lykely.'

[*'Telle me now, ar we further fare,*   (146)
How many hevenes that ther are.']
   'We saye there be heuenes thre,   4935
     Whereof þat oon is þat wee see
     Turnyng abowte as þe skye;
And þat heven is bodyly
And to oure sight hit is blewe
As hit were of asyr hewe.   4940
That oþer heven is, to telle,
Thereas goode aungell in dwelle:
That is gostely, and is alle
Of hewe þat is cristalle.

4915–16 *q. no. om.* B.   4916 whens come] where becom TS.   4921 fyre]
from TSP, syre B.   4922 ayre] fire P.   4924 clere] shire TSP.
4925 soo shere] clere TSP.   4926 That] Shall P.   4927 perce] parte
TS.   4930 glode down yerne] gold did downe renne P;   yerne] þere S.

Anoþer shal be, sothe to seie,
In þe time þat Goddes Sone shal deie;
And in þe birthe shal be þe þridde   5895
Of Antecrist, as it is kidde.'

Ca.° xxxviij°   'þe sterris þat men sen doun falle,   (145)
                  I preie þe, where bicome þei alle?'
                       'Vndirstondiþ, sire, truly,
                       þat no sterre falleþ fro þe sky;   5900
                  But I shal telle what it may be
                  þat þe folke so falling se.
                  It is a fire þat is dwelling
                  In þe hiȝest of þe eir brennyng
                  Alþernext þe spere of fire;   5905
                  And somtime, whanne þe night is shire,
                  Sparcles of þat fire clere
                  þat miche han of her matere
                  Falle and perceth þe aire anight,   f. 87ᵛ
                  And so it comeþ to oure sight   5910
                  And semeþ as it were a sterre
                  þat by þe sky glood so ferre;
                  For a sparcle comyng fro þe sky
                  To be a sterre is not likly.'

Ca.° xxxix°   'Telle me, or we ferþer fare,   (146) 5915
                  Hou many heuenes þat þer are.'
                       'Sire, þere ben heuenes þre,
                       Wherof one is þat we see
                  Tornyng aboute, and is þe sky;
                  And þat heuene is bodily   5920
                  And to oure sight it is blew
                  As it were of azure [h]ew.
                  þe oþer heuene of to telle
                  Is þere gode aungels dwelle:
                  þat is goostly, and it is al   5925
                  Of hewe as it were cristal.

4933–4] from T, lines blank B.   4935 we] I S.   4937 as] and is TS, that is
P.   4940 asyr] a soure P.   4944 þat is] as it (is S) were TSP.

5899 truly] riȝt truely H.   5922 hew] blew L, hewe H.   5923 heuene]
heuenes L, heuen H.

The thridde that is Goddis se,   4945
There he sitteth in maieste:
There he is in moche blisse
And of hewe of goolde hit is.
Of vij hevenes of we telle
For vij planetes þat thereinne dwelle;   4950
But rightly of hevenes to lere
There be no moo but these iij here.'

[*'Telle me now how high the heven*   (147)
Aboue the erthe is for to neven.']
  'Froo þe erthe soo hygh heven is   4955
  That if there were a stone, ywys,
  In heven beyng there soo
That weyed a C stones and moo

f. 72ᵛ   And it sholde from heven falle
Vnto grounde amonge vs alle,   4960
Hit behoveþ to take vij yeere
Or hit to grounde come here.
And neuerþelese soo ny they be
That yf a goode soule passed fro þe bode,
Froo erthe into heven might steye   4965
With the twynkelyng of an eye.'

Qo. 145ᵃ   '*The firmament þat we ouer vs see,*   (148)
Of what might may hit be?'
  'Whoosoo knewe hit all aright,
  The firmamente is of grete might: 4970
  Euer aboute hit turneth ay
And resteþ neuer, night ne day.
For this worlde had no fastenyng
Ne were his abowte turnyng:
Were hit þat it stille stode,   4975
There is no man ne fissh in flode,
Foule, ne beste, ne noothynge

4947 he] *om.* TSP.   4952 There] So TSP.   4953–4] *from* T, *lines blank*
B.   4955] So high the heven is the erthe froo T, So hye is heuen þe erþe fro
SP.   4956] That if it were now alsoo TSP.   4957] That if (*om.* S) a ston in
heven were TSP.   4958 weyid] peysid P;   C stones] milston P;   moo] more
TSP.   4963 soo ny] so hende T, hefte P;   be] are TSP.   4964 yf] *om.*

In the þridde is Goddis see,
þere he sitteþ in his maieste:
þerynne is þe miche blisse
And of þe hewe of gold it isse.   5930
Of seuene heuenes we of telle
For seuene planetis þat þei in dwelle;
But rightfully of heuenes to lere
Ben no more but þise þre here.'

Ca.º xlº   'Telle me ȝit, wiþ mylde steuene: (147) 5935
              Hou fer is it fro vs to heuene?'
                 'So is heuene þe erþe fro
                  þat if it were now also
              þat if a stoone in heuene wore
              þat weied a þowsand pounde and more   5940
              And it shulde fro heuene falle
              To þe grounde among vs alle,
              It behoueþ to take seuene ȝere   f. 88ʳ
              Or þat it come to grounde here.
              And neuerþeles so nyhe þei be   5945
              þat a good soule might fle
              Fro erthe and into heuene stie
              In þe twincling of an yȝe.'

Ca.º xljº   'þe firmament þat we here see,   (148)
              Of what might may it be?'   5950
                 'Whoso knewe it al aright
                  Of þe firmament þe greet might,
              Euere aboute it turneth ay
              And resteþ neuere, night ne day.
              For þis world haþ no fastnyng,   5955
              And ne were it aboute torning—
              Were it so þat it stille stood—
              þere nis man ne fisshe in flood,
              Foule, ne beest, ne noþing here

TSP;   passed fro þe bode] sholde al yare TS, shall as yare P.   4965 might] om.
TSP.   4967–5142 questions numbered 145–9 for 147–51 B.   4977 noothynge]
add here TSP.
───────────────
5936 is . . . to] it is vnto H.   5959 ne beest] repeated L.

That is in this worlde wonynge
That lyfe hathe þat ought myght stere,
Nere the turnynge of þe ffirmament were.　　4980
All þat euer we stere and goo
Or flette ouer to and froo,
All togeder is vs lente
By the turnyng of þe fyrmament.
Therfore may þou see, iwys,　　　　　　4985
That of moche might hit is.'

Qo. 146ᵃ　　'Telle me now of what might　　　　　(149)
　　　　　That planetis be and what þey hight.'
　　　　　　'Planetys gouerneth all thynge
　　　　　　That leueth or hathe in þe erthe waxyng.　4990
　　　　　And euery planete of his kynde
To norysshe and to yeve his mynde
Of the childe eueriche a litthe
Vnto þe modyr goo þerwith,
f. 73ʳ　　And echon þenne shapyn is　　　　　4995
Of euery lyme þat in hym is.
And of planetes þer be but vijᵉⁿ
And here names woll I nemen.
Saturnus furste we calle:
He is þe higheste of þem alle　　　　　5000
And stalworthest is he;
And he passeþ in his contre
The xij signes by oon and oon,
And he dwelleþ in euerychon,
Er he passe, halfe thridde yeere,　　　5005
And is planete of pouere.
The man þat is boren þerinne,
And he dounward goo to begynne,
Dounwarde shall goo of myght withall;
And if he regneth, regne he shall.　　5010
And þis planete regneþ of pouer
Oones in a xxx yere;
And his regne and his might

4978] om. TSP.　　4980] om. TSP.　　4981 and] or TSP.　　4982 ouer]
eyther T, ouþer S, om. P;　and] or TSP.　　4991 of his] is of P.　　4992 yeve
his] ȝeme has S;　his] in P.　　4995 shapyn is] shapeth his T, shape his S.

þat haþ lyf þat it might stere: 5960

Al þat we here seen stere or goo
Or flete in watir to and fro,
Al togidre is to vs lent
þorgh mevyng of þe firmament.
By þis maist þou see, iwis,   5965
þat of miche might it is.'

Ca.° xlij°   'Telle me ʒit anoon right   (149)
           Of þe planetis, what þei hight.'
             'The planetis gouerneþ al þing
              þat liueþ or haþ in erþe waxing.   5970
And euery planete of his kinde
Norissheþ and kepeþ mannes minde
And of þe child ech a lith
þe while þe moder goo þerwith,
And euerich þanne shapiþ his   5975
Of eche lyme þat in him is.
And of þe planetes þere ben seuene   f. 88ᵛ
And her names I wole neuene.
Saturnus þe firste we calle:
He is þe hiest of hem alle   5980
And most stalworth is he;
And he passiþ in his countre
þe xij signes by oon and oon,
And he dwelliþ in euerichoon,
Or he passe, þe þridde half ʒere.   5985
And þis planet is of suche powere,
þe man þat is bore þerynne,
And he dounward goo to bigynne,
Dounward shal he of might wiþal;
And if he regne, regne he shal.   5990
And þis planete regneþ of powere
Oones in a þritty ʒere;
And his regne and his might

4998 I] you P.   5001 And] For most and P.

5961 stere] om. H.

Is in a signe þat Libra hight;

And downwarde he takeþ his roos   5015

To a signe þat hight Aries.

The secunde planet hight Iubyter:

He is from vs not soo ferre.

Of grete richesse a planete he is,

Of marchaundise, and of grete witt, ywys,   5020

And [amonge men] of goode loos;

[And bi] þe xij signes he goos,

Thanne dwelleth he in echon

[A yere or] he aboute hathe goon.

He þat is born in hym þat   5025

Of xij yeere is he beste of state.

In Cancer he reigneth harde;

In Capricorne he gothe dounwarde.

The þrid planete Mars it hight,

Planete of werre and of fight   5030

f. 73ᵛ   And of blode spyllyng þer [men] deye;

By the xij signes lieth his weye

And ichon a dwellyng he hase

Xl dayes or þat he passe.

He þat is born in þat planete,   5035

Withinne a yere may beete

And xxxiiij dayes therto

His dedes and his will also.

His reigne is in Capricorn

And in Cancer is his might lorn.   5040

The iiij planete is the sonne

And, if thow vnderstonde conne,

Hit is a planete of grete might and lordshipp

Of kynges and of grete worshipp—

Keper of the erthe we hym calle;   5045

And by the signes he passeþ alle

And in echon, whanne he cometh þore,

5014 Libra] *om.* P.   5015 roos] rees PS, ees T.   5017 hight] is T, we call S,
om. P.   5019 he is] is hit TSP.   5020 ywys] *om.* TSP.   5021 amonge
men] *from* TSP, a man shal be B.   5022 And bi] *from* TS, For by P, Moche he
B.   5024 A yere or] *from* TSP, Hye or lowe B.   5031 men] *from* TSP, he
B.   5032 xij] *om.* P.   5034 þat] *repeated* B.   5036 may beete] may be
ete B, he may beyete T, may he byȝete S, may he behete P.   5037 xxxiiij] thre and

Is in a signe þat Libra hight;
And dounward he takiþ his rees   5995
To a signe þat highte Aries.
The secounde planete hiȝt Iubiter:
He is not fro vs so fer.
Of greet ricchesse þat planet is it,
Of marchaundise, and of greet wit,   6000
And among men of good loos;
And by þe xij signes he goos
And he dwelliþ in echoon
A ȝere or he haue aboute goon.
He þat is born in him þat   6005
At xij ȝere is he best of stat.
In Cancer he regneþ harde;
In Capricorne he goþ dounwarde.
The [þirde] planete Mars is it:
In him regneþ many an harde fitt   6010
And of blood spillyng men shul deie;   f. 89ʳ
Bi þe xij signes liþ his weie
And in euery signe a dwelling he has
Fourty daies or he pas.
He þat is bore in þat planete,   6015
Wiþynne a ȝere he may skete
And xxxiiij daies þerto
Alle hise weies fully goo.
His regne is in Capricorne
And in Cancer his mighte is [l]orne.   6020
The iiij planete is þe sunne
And, if þou vnderstonde kunne,
It is a planete of grete worshipe
Of kinges and of lordshipe—
Keper of erthe we him calle;   6025
And by þe signes he passiþ alle
And [in] euery signe whanne he
Comeþ þere, as I telle the,

thritti T.   5043 might and lordshipp] worship TSP.   5044 grete worshipp]
lordship TSP.   5047 cometh] dwellith P.

6009 þirde] from H, om. L.   6020 lorne] from H, borne L.   6024 lord-
shipe] gret lordeschipp H.   6027 in] from H, om. L.

He dwelleþ a moneþ and [no] moore.

He þat is born þerinne, he may euery yere

Chaunge his werke and his manere.   5050

His reigne soo is in Aries
And in Libra he hym abesse.
The v planete Venus is,
Planete of love, delite, and blis.
He þat þerinne born shal be   5055
Feble hert shall haue of vanyte;
But in iij C and xl dayes
May he chaunge all his wayes,
His werke, and his þought holly.
By the xij signes goþe he by   5060
And in echon of tho shall he
Xxvij^{ty} dayes be.
In Piscibus raigneþ he stabely
And down he gothe in Gemeny.
The vj planete hight Mercurious,   5065
That arte and connyng yeveth vs;

f. 74^r By the xij signes lithe his wayes
And dwellith in ychon xvij^{ten} dayes.
He þat is born in hym, he may
Withynne CC and þe iiij^{the} day   5070
Chaunge his corage and his thought
And his werkes þat he hathe wrought.
The moone þe vij^{the} planete is, we say,
Planete of water and of wey;
By the xij signes he goth alsoo   5075
And dwelleþ in ychon dayes twoo.
He that is born in þat planete,
In a moneth may he beete
And chaunge his werke and his will,
Be hit goode, be hit ill.   5080
In Taurus comeþ his regne vnto

5048 no] *from* TSP, *om.* B.   5053 Venus] regnynge T.   5054 delite and
blis] and delite ywis P.   5057 iij C] CCCC P.   5067 xij] vij P.
5068 xvij^{ten}] xvj P.   5078 beete] *from* T, be yeete B, byȝete S, be hete P.

He dwelleþ a monthe and no more
Til his time be fulfilled þore.   6030
He þat is bore þerynne,
He shal euery ȝere wynne
And chaunge his werk fro ȝere [to yere]
So þat he vse noon yuel manere.
His regne is fully in Aries   6035
And in Libra his woning he ches.
The v planete Venus is,
A planete of loue, delite, and blis.
He þat þereynne shal ibore be,
He shal haue miche vanite;   6040
But in CCCC and xl daies
He may chaunge alle his waies,
His þoght, and his werk holy.
And þe xij signes he goþ by
And in euery of hem shal he   6045 f. 89ᵛ
Xxvij daies so be.
In Pissibus he regneþ stably
And doun he goþ in Gemini.
The sixte is Mercurious,
þat art and kunnyng ȝeueþ to vs;   6050
By þe xij signes ben hise waies
And in eueriche woneth he xvj daies.
He þat is bore in him, he may
Wiþin CC and fourty day
Chaunge his corage and his þoght   6055
And his werke þat he wroght.
The mone þe vij planete we seie,
Planete of watris and of weie;
By þe xij signes she goþ also
And in euerichone dwelleþ daies two.   6060
He þat is bore in þis planete,
In a m[onþe] he may wel hete
And chaunge his werke and his wille,
Be it good or be it ille.
In Taurus comeþ hir regne to   6065

6033 to yere] *from* H, *om.* L.   6036 he ches] is H.   6038 and blis] *om.*
H.   6062 monþe] *from* H, maner L.

And abbesses hir in Scorpio.
And all the worlde is not, ywys,
So moche as euery planete is,
Sawfe the thr[ee] þat lowest wone—   5085
Venus, Mercurius, and þe mone.'

Qo. 147^a

'*Telle now þis onys to me:*   (150)
How many maner of wateres þer be.'
    'Many maner of wateres ther be:
        First the water of þe see,   5090
That all other wateres come froo.
Wateres of the welles þere is also,
That theire hewe and þeyre manere
Iiij sithes chaungyng in a yeere.
Welles ben spryngyng elleswhere   5095
Iiij dayes in þe woke and no more.
A flode þere is þat renneth ay
Alle þe wekes vnto Saturday.
A flode þere is in þe est right
And þat renneth euery nyȝt,   5100
And aday hit fryseth faste
But in þe night hit may not laste.

f. 74^v

Yet men may a welle fynde
In the yles of the see of Inde
That whoso put a staff þerinne,   5105
As a fyre þat hit shulde brenne
And hit noothynge sleken canne
But oonly vryne of man.
Other welles be þer moo
And who of the water drynke alsoo,   5110
Of som gode memorye sholde he take
And som for[ȝetfulnesse] sholde he make;
Som amarous woll make man
And som barayn woll make woman
And som woll make iren and stele   5115

5085 three] *from* TP, thridde B, ere S.   5087] Telle me now yutte ones this T, Telle
me now so haue þou blisse S.   5088 þer be] is T, þer is S.   5091–2] *reversed*
P.   5091] *om.* S.   5092/3 *add* Many and somme shall I telle of þo S.
5094 chaungyng] chaunge TSP.   5095 ben spryngyng] of sprynges P.
5097 flode] flume TSP.   5098 wekes vnto] weke but the TSP.   5099 flode]

And abbesseþ hir in Scorpio.
þus haue ȝe now of me, ywis,
Sumwhat þat in euery planete is,
Saue þe thre þat lowest wone—
Venus, Mercurius, and þe mone.'   6070

Ca.º xliijº   'þis oone þing ȝit telle þou me: (150)
                    Hou many maners of water þer be.'
                        'Manye manere of watres þer be:
                            Firste þe water of þe see,
                    þat alle oþer watres come fro.   6075
                    And watris of welles þere ben also,
                    And her hewe and her manere
                    Chaungeþ iiij times in a ȝere.
                    Wellis beþ springing in diuerse place   f. 90ʳ
                    þorgh Goddis vertue and his grace.   6080
                    A flood þer is þat renneþ ay
                    Al þe weke but þe Saturday.
                    A flood þer is in þe est right
                    And þat renneþ euere anight,
                    And in þe day it freseþ fast   6085
                    But in þe night may it not last.
                    ȝit mowen men a welle finde
                    In þe yles of þe see of Ynde
                    þat whoso putte a staf þerynne,
                    As fire hote is shulde brenne   6090
                    And noþing it slake ne can
                    But oonly þe vertue of a man.
                    Oþer wellis þere beþ ȝit mo
                    And who þe watir drinke of tho,
                    Of some good memorie shulde he take   6095
                    And some forȝitfulnesse shulde make;
                    Some amerous wole make þe men
                    And some wole make barein wymmen
                    And some wole make yren and steel

flume TSP.   5100 euery nyȝt] euer anyght T, euer on nyȝt SP.   5101 fryseth]
freshis P.   5104 the see of] om. P.   5109 Other] And thre P;   þer] right T,
ȝet SP.   5112 forȝetfulnesse] from S, forgilten B, for (of P) gentilnes TP.

    6092 vertue] vryne H.

In the fuyre to temper well.
A grete welle ȝit is þere oon
And stondith stylle as ony ston
But whosoo makeþ solas þerby,
Anone it renneth hastely.   5120
Som wateres ben hote of kynde
And somme colde, as men fynde;
And þe kynde of the grounde makeþ all this
There iche a water rennyng is.
But all is at Goddis will,   5125
Bothe rennyng and stondyng styll.'

Qo. 148ᵃ   'Now wolde I wete of the   (151)
                   How many sees þat ther be.'
                      'Sees we fynde there be iij,
                      Whereof þat oon high Becte: 5130
                      All abowte the erthe goth she
                   And is salt, as men may see.
                   The other see the Blak See hight
                   And environneth þat oþer right.
                   The iij is called þe Stynkyng See: 5135
                   Thereinne may no man leuyng be
                   For þe stynke þat þere comyth froo;
                   And þat environth þat oþer twoo.
f. 75ʳ   And God hathe made hem soo to be
                   Of his wylle and his pouste.'   5140

Qo. 149ᵃ   'Why hathe God the world made all   (152)
                   Rounde aboute as a ball?'
                      'Many skilles ben þere why
                      But iij ther ben principally.
                      For his owne liknesse oon   5145
                   Ther noone ende is þerupon,
                   For he ne hadde noo begynnyng
                   Ne neuer shall have endyng;

                   And [s]eke þe worlde neuer so mynde

5119] *om.* P.   5120/1 *add* Swyft as an arow lightly P.   5123 kynde] gynde
S.   5127 the] the see TS.   5130 Becte] Betee TSP.   5133 See] so
P.   6135 Stynkyng] standande S.   5141–74] *om.* S.   5149 seke] *from*

In þe fire to tempre weel.   6100
A greet welle ʒit is þer oone
And stondiþ stille as any stoone
But whoso makeþ solas þerby,
Anoon it renneþ hastily.
Some watris ben hote of kynde   6105
And some colde, as men ay fynde:
þe kinde of þe grounde makiþ this
þere any water rennynge is.
And al it is at Goddis wille,
Boþe rennyng and stonding stille.'   6110

Ca.° xliiij°   'Now wole I wite ʒit of the   (151)
                Hou many sees þat þer be.'
                    'Sees we finde þere ben thre   f. 90ᵛ
                    Wherof of oone hatte þe See Betee:
                Al aboute þe erthe gooþ she   6115
                And is salt, as men may se.
                þat oþer see þe Blak See is
                And environeþ þat oþer, ywis.
                The þridde is callid þe Stinking See:
                þereynne may no lyuynge man be   6120
                For þe stinche þat it come fro;
                And þat environeþ þat oþer two.
                God haþ made hem so to be
                Of his wille and his pouste.'

Ca.° xlv°   'Whi made God þe world al   (152) 6125
                Rounde as it were a bal?'
                    'Manye skiles þer ben why
                    But þre þer ben principaly.
                For his owne liknesse is oon
                There noon ende is vpon,   6130
                For he ne had no bigynnyng
                Ne neuere shal haue ending;
                And þogh men soghte þe world þorgh
                Into Ynde þe ferþest borgh,

TP, eke B;   so] so in T.

6100 to tempre] and tempre it H.   6106 ay] om. H.   6114 hatte] haþ H.

Noone endyng shall men þeron fynde.   5150

Another skele is commodite
Why hit behoueth soo to be;
For all the fourmes þat þou woste
Rounde conteynes althermoste:
Now is it soo at the begynnyng   5155
That the worlde conteyneth all thyng,
Forwhy behouefull was þerto
That hit sholde be rounde alsoo.
The thridde skyll is for the sky
And I shall telle þe how and why: 5160
Lete with wax here be filled a can
And whan hit is filled, broke þan;
The wax shal be of that shapnesse
As was þe canne more ne lasse.
Now is þe sky rounde and fayre   5165
And contenes þerinne fire and aire,
Water and erthe furþest þerfroo,
And al behoueth rounde to be þoo.
The rounde sky þe [f]ire rounde makeþ
And eyre of fyre rooundehed[e] takeþ;   5170

And for the sky, as þow haste herde,
Is rounde, and all ben in hym spredde,
All behoueth hem rounde to be
As þo[u ere on þ]e wax myght see.'

f. 75ᵛ *Qo. 149ᵃ*   '*Why is the mone colde of kynde*   (153) 5175
And the sonne hote, as we fynde?'
             'The sonne þenne is well of hete
             And þe moone of wateres wete:
             Now is þat oon drie and hoote
             And þat other is moyste and wete.   5180

5152 behoueth soo] ouyth rownde P.   5154 conteynes] covetous P.
5157 behouefull] behouelike P, bi hevenlike T.   5168 behoueth . . . þoo] to be rownde
ben thoo T, be ones rownde also P.   5169 fire] *from* TP, sire B.   5170 of] and
T;   rooundehede] roounde he do B, rowndehede P, rowndenes T.   5170/1 *add*
Water withynne (within the P) eyre alsoo / And erth withynne water alsoo (within al tho P)

Ende shulde men none fynde,   6135
As clerkes knowen wel bi kynde.
Anoþer skile is, þe sothe to se,
Whi it bihoueþ so to be:
For al þe formes þat þou woost
Rounde conteineþ alþermost;   6140
For þus it was at þe biginning:
þe worlde conteined al þing,
For þat bihouinge was þerto
þat it shulde be rounde also.
The þridde skile is for þe sky   6145
And I shal telle þe hou and why:
Lat fille here with wexe a canne;   f. 91ʳ
Whan it is fulle, late breke it þanne
And þe wex shal be of shapnesse
As was þe pott noþer more ne lesse.   6150
Now is þe sky rounde and fair
And conteyneþ fire and air,
Water and þe erthe ferrest þerfro,
And al bihoueþ þat rounde be tho.
þe rounde sky þe round fire makeþ   6155
And eir of þe fire roundenesse takeþ;
Watir wiþynne þe air also,
And erthe wiþynne al þo;
And for þe sky, as þou hast herd,
Is rounde, and al is in him sperd,   6160
Hem alle bihoueþ rounde to be
As þou in waxe might ysee.'

Ca.º xlvjº   'Whi is þe moone coolde of kinde   (153)
                And þe sunne hote, as we finde?'
                     'The sunne þanne is welle of hete   6165
                     And also þe mone of watres wete:
                Now is þat oone drie and hoote
                And þat oþer moist and woote.

TP.   5172 spredde] sperred TP.   5173 All] And then P.   5174 þou ere on
þe] þogh oure B, thou ere of the T, thou on the P.   5175 S begins
again.   5175–6 q. no. 149 repeated B.   5180 is] colde S, om. TP.

6149 shal be of] be of þat H.   6158 al þo] also H.   6162 ysee] it see H.

The hete of the sonne doth sprynge
That in erthe is all thynge
But with þat hete may they not dure
But if they have withall moystoure;
And þat the sonne heteth on daylight   5185
The moone keleth vpon þe night
And yeveþ it moystour vnto;
Forwhy all thynges spryngen soo.

Wolde þe sonne vs yeve for ay
His hete bothe night and day,   5190
Man ne beste shulde leve no þrowe
Ne noothyng sholde in erthe growe;
And if the colde of the moone
Sholde euer amonge vs woone
And of the hete haue right noght,   5195
Sholde noo levyng thynge be forthe brought.
Forwhy God hathe ordeyned soo
As the worlde hath mistour to.'

Qo. 150ᵃ   'Now I pray þe, telle me this: (154)
              Whiche is þe moste thynge þat is?'   5200
                 'Of all thynge þat þou woste
                 Goddes mercy is þe moste
                 For noo mowthe may speke, iwis,
              Ne herte thynke how grete hit is
              [Vnto] þoo þat woll hit euer craue   5205
              And euer desyre hit to have.
              Mercy is grettere þanne all erthe may be
              Or all þe water in þe see;
              Hit passith all þe leves þat sprynge
              Of herbes or of other thynge;   5210
f. 76ʳ   [Yee], an hundrid thowsande folde
              Hit passeth all þat I have of tolde.'

5181 doth] dothe make and P.   5182 is] is waxyng and P.   5190 His] In
P.   5191 ne] þe S.   5192 in erthe] om. P.   5193 colde] kylthe P.
5196 levyng] om. P.   5197 God] he P.   5198 mistour] moistour B, myster
TSP.   5204 grete] om. P.   5205 Vnto] from TSP, But B;   craue] grave
S.   5206 euer] om. TSP.   5207 Mercy] Hit TSP.   5210 Of] And

þe hete of þe sunne makeþ al þing
To springe þat is here wexing 6170
But wiþ þat hete mowen þei not dure
But þei haue þerwiþ moysture;
And þat þe sunne heteþ on daylight
þe mone it keleþ on þe night
And ȝeueþ it moisture þerto, 6175
þerfore of hem springeþ so
Alle þinges þat here in erthe ben
And þat waxing here men sen.
For if þe sunne shulde ȝeue vs ay
His hete bothe night and day, 6180
Man ne beest lyue shulde not f. 91ᵛ
Ne noþing growe, God it woot;
And if þe colde of þe mone
Shulde euere among vs wone
And of þe hete haue right noght, 6185
Shulde no living þing be forth broght.
þerfore God haþ ordeined so
Right as þe world haþ mister to.'

Ca.° xlvij°   'Now I prey the, telle me þis: (154)
Whiche is þe most þing þat is?' 6190
    'Off alle þinges þat þou woost
    Goddes mercy is þe moost
For no mouthe may speke, iwis,
Ne herte þinke hou greet it is
To alle þilke þat wole it craue 6195
And desireþ it forto haue.
It is gretter þan al þe erthe may be
Or al þe watir in þe see;
It passiþ alle þe leues þat springes
On herbes, trees, and oþer þinges; 6200
Ȝe, a þousand hundrid folde
It passith al þat I tolde.'

P;   or of] trees and S, and on T, and all P.   5211 Yee] *from* T, ȝe and S, Ye more
then P, Then B.

6173 þat] *om.* H.   6184 euere] neuere L, euer H.

Qo. 151ᵃ   *'Whether may gravell of erthe moo be*   (155)
                  Or dropes of water in the see?'

                     'Gravell of the erthe is wel moore   5215
                     Thenne alle water droppes þat euer woore
                     For alle þat were or yet shal be,
             Alle they comen of the see;
             And for an handfull of gravell
             Behoveth dropes a grete deell,   5220
             For wel smaller [i]s, I hope,
             A gravell þanne a water drope.
             And water may be nowghwhere
             But if erthe be vndyr there;
             And many myles may men goon   5225
             Drye there noo water is on;
             And the see was neuer soo depe aflete
             That depper is vnder þe erthe grete;
             And ȝif water vppon roche stande,
             Vnder roches is þe erthe liggande.   5230
             Now is þe erthe grete and smale
             And wyde strykeþ hym withhalle:
             In many stedes þere water is noon
             Is founde of erthe goode woone.
             Therefore gravell of erthe, say we,   5235
             Been more thenne water dropes be.'

Qo. 152ᵃ   *'Might erthe greete tolde be*   (156)
                  Or water dropes of the see?'

                     'And the worlde suche a thousand were
                     As hit is and wel moore   5240
                     And þat hit sholde laste withall
             Suche a thousand as now shall,
             Xxiiijᵗⁱ oures right
             Ben in þe day and in þe night
             And eche an oure for to twynne   5245
             Sixti poyntes ben þerinne,
f. 76ᵛ   And þogh hit myght soo befall

5215 Gravell] Grete TP;   erthe] eyre P.   5216 water droppes] watris P.
5220 grete] good TS.   5221 is] *from* TSP, as B.   5223 be nowghwhere]
nought here P.   5224 But if] And ȝit P.   5226 on] non TP.
5227 aflete] yflette P.   5228 is . . . erthe] þer is erþe vnder S; þe erthe] *om.*

Ca.° xlviij° 'Wheþer may grauel more be   (155)
      Or droopis of þe watir of þe see?'
       'Gretis of erþe is wel more   6205
       þan alle þe water dropes þat euer wore
      For alle þat were and ʒit sholen be,
      Alle þei comen out of þe see;
      And for an handful of grauel
      Byhoued dropes a good del,   6210
      For wel smaller it is, to hope,
      A grauel þan a water drope.
      And watir may be nowhere
      But if erþe be vnder þere;
      And many myles may men gone   6215 f. 92^r
      On dreie erthe þere water is none;
      And þe see was neuere so deep ywet
      þat ne depper is þe erthe vnder ʒet;
      And if water vpon roches be stonding,
      Ʒit vnder roches þe erthe is ligging. 6220
      Now is þe erthe greet oueral
      And wide strecchiþ him þerwiþal:
      I many stedes þer water is noon
      Of erþe is founde ful greet woon.
      And þerfore þe erthe is gretter, seie we, 6225
      þan alle þe dropes of þe see may be.'

Ca.° xlix° 'Might heeris ought gretter ytolde be (156)
      Or watir droopis ʒit of þe see?'
       'And þe world suche a Ml wore
       As it is and wel more   6230
      And þat it shulde laste wiþal
      Suche a Ml as it now shal,
      Now xxiiij ouris right
      Beth in þe day and in the night
      And euery our forto twynne   6235
      Sixti pointes beþ þerynne,
      And þogh it might so bifalle

T; grete] gryp P.   5232 wyde] *from* STP, wynde B; strykeþ] strekes T,
streccheþ SP. 5234 founde of] sonde and S.   5235 gravell of erthe] the (*om.*
TS) erthe grete PTS. 5237–96] *om.* S. 5246 Sixti] Fourty T.

That in yche a poynte of all
Were bore a thousaunde men and moo
And full of heere were iche of thoo,   5250
Yet sholde the dropes of the see
Be moo thenne sholde þe heeres be;
And ʒit is gravell of erthe moore
Thenne þat all þe dropes were;
And Goddis mercy moste of all   5255
He þat with herte woll to hym call.'

Qo. 153ᵃ   'Now woll I wete witterly   (157)
               How many sterris ben in þe sky.'
                  'Yff alle men oon lyve wore
                   That have be dede here before   5260
                   Sithen þat Adam was forlore
               And all that euer shal be boore
               Betwyx her and þe worlde be g[o]ne
               Were euerychon born anoone,
               So moche folke there nought ne were   5265
               As sterres on þe heven are.
               But for the heighte of the sky
               There may no man se forwhy
               Alle the sterres þat ther be;
               But some aper[t]ly men may see: 5270
               Above with þe sky þey goo
               And hit hem bereth to and froo—
               Whenne som gon vp som downe ar wen[t]e
               With mevyng of the firmament.'

Qo. 154ᵃ   'Canst þou of aungell telle me ought   (158) 5275
               How many God in heven wrought,
               How many be lefte þerinne,
               And how many fel for synne?'
                  'God of his mercy and his might
                   Of aungel [nyne] ordres dight   5280
                   And eche an order made he

5252 heeres] men of here P.   5253 gravell] gret P.   5254 þat ... dropes]
all the dropis that euer P.   5260 be] don T.   5263 Betwyx her and] Now
sithe P;   her ... world] this ande the worldes ende T;   be gone] beganne B.
5264 born] vnborn P.   5268 forwhy] with hye P.   5270 apertly] from TP,

        þat in euery point of alle
        A Ml men were ibore and mo
        And ful of heer were ech of þo,   6240
        ȝit shulde þe dropis of þe see
        Be more þan shulde þe heris be;
        And ȝit is þe grauel of þe erþe more
        þan heeris or watir dropis wore;
        And Goddes mercy is most of alle   6245
        To him þat wole on him calle.'

Ca.° l°   'Now wolde I wite witterly   (157)
        Hou many sterris ben on þe sky.'
        'Iff alle men on lyue wore   f. 92ᵛ
        þat haue ben deed here bifore   6250
        Sithen þat Adam was forþ broght
        And alle þat euer shullen be wroght
        Bitwene þis and þe worlde be gone
        And weren euerichone borne anone,
        So miche folk ȝit not þer were   6255
        As sterres on heuene ere.
        But for þe heighte of þe sky
        No man may see forthi
        Alle þe sterres þat þer be;
        But some openly men mow see: 6260
        Aboue wiþ the sky þei go
        As it hem berith to and fro—
        Whan somme goon vp somme doun be went
        By mevyng of þe firmament.'

Ca.° lj°   'Canst þou of aungels telle me oght (158) 6265
        Hou many God of heuen wroght,
        And hou manye be lefte þerynne,
        And [hou] manye fel out for synne?'
          'God of his mercy and of his might
          Of aungels nyne ordres dight   6270
        And in euery ordre made he

aperly B.   5273 wente] *from* TP, wenne B.   5280 nyne] *from* TP, the B.

6261 wiþ] *om.* H.   6268 hou] *from table* 1329 *and* H, *om.* L.   6270 nyne]
many H.

f. 77^r

Many a legion to be
(And a legion, ywys,
Vj thouȝand and vj C is
And iij score and vj þerto)   5285
And all hym worship for to doo;
But there fell oughte of echon
Als fele as com till oon,
And also many were they tho
As halffeden þe folke and moo   5290
That have be born and born shull be.
And whenne fulfilled is eche a see
[Of] aungell þat fell away,
Thenne shall hit be domesday
That God shall deme bothe goode and ille;   5295
And þat shal be at Goddes wille.'

Qo. 155^a   'Whiche ben moste—of beste or man,   (159)
                Foule other fyssh, þat swhymme can?'
                     'Bestes ben there moo þanne men
                          And foules moo þanne bestes suche ten   5300
                          And for eche a fowle also
                A thousand fysshes ben and moo
                For therof is moste plente
                Of all creatures þat be.
                God made man of erthe slyme,   5305
                And beste of hete he maked [hym],
                Fisshes of water, foule of the ayre;
                And all þat he made is fayre.
                And yif God hem alle hadde wrought
                Of erthe, as þat he did noght,   5310
                They sholde have alle rise alsoo
                At domesday as men shall doo;
                But for erthe is in hem noone,
                Forwhy to nought turne þey ichon.'

5285 iij score] sixti TP.   5288 com till oon] gan gone P;   till] om. T.
5290 halffeden] halfendele TP.   5293 Of] from TP, That B.   5295 God] om.
P.   5297 S begins again.   5306 hym] from TSP, om. B.

Many a legioun for to be
(A legioun, forsothe, is
Vj Ml and CCCCCC, ywis,
And fourty and sixe þerto)   6275
And alle him worshepe for to do;
But þer fel out of echone
þe noumbre of ordre oone,
And as manye were þei tho
As haluendel þe folke and mo   6280
þat haue be bore or shullen be.
And whan fulfilled is eche see
Of aungels þat fellen away,   f. 93^r
þanne shal it be domesday
þat God shal deme boþe good and ille;   6285
And þat shal be at Goddis wille.'

Ca.^{o} lij^o 'Wheþer be moo—of beestis or of man   (159)
Or foules or fisshes, þat swymme can?'
        'Bestes ben ful many þenne
            And of foules ben suche tenne   6290
And for euery foule also
Ben a þowsand fisshes and mo
For þerof is þe moste plente
Of alle creatures þat þer be.
God made man of erþe slym   6295
(And moost to his liknesse made him),
Fisshes of water, foule of ayre;
And al þat he made, it is fayre.
And if God hem alle had wroght
Of þe erthe, as he dide noght,   6300
þei schulde alle haue risen also
At domesday as men sholen do;
But for erthe in hem is noon,
þerfore to noght þei torne echoon.'

6275 fourty] sixti H.

Qo. *156*ᵃ   *'Of alle þe worlde telle me ȝit:*   (160) 5315
          The delitablest stede, whiche is it?'
            'Where a mannes herte is faste
             And for to dwelle were leueste

f. 77ᵛ   There is þe delectabeleste stede
          To hym that he may oon trede.   5320
          For were a man in a contre
          The fayrest þat might be
          And hadde all þat he hadde nede
          Hym to clothe with and fede
          And his herte loved elleswhere,   5325
          Noo delite had he there;
          But ther a man loueth well,
          Thogh hit be fowle iche a deell,
          There is his ioye and his solace
          More thenne in ony other place.'   5330

Qo. *157*ᵃ   *'Wheþer is he hardyer þat gothe anyght*   (161)
          Or he þat goþe by daylyght?'
            'A man þat gothe wykked way
            Ther perell is for to daye,
            And he bo[l]dly þer forth goo   5335
          By light of day, hit semeþ soo
          That he goth hit hardely
          And þat he dredeth noo enemye,
          And if any come goand,
          That he wolde abyde and stande.   5340
          But he þat gothe by nyght,
          That is noon hardynesse of might.
          To defende hym he is not leffe,
          Forwhy he stalkeþ as a thefe:
          In derke he hopith in his thought   5345
          That men shall perceyue hym nought;
          But if he a shadowe shall see,
          His herte shall gaste and he shall flee.
          Yet ben there other as many

5315–30] *om.* S.   5317 faste] leuyst P.   5318 were leueste] hym likid best
P.   5322 The fayrest] That (*om.* P) in the feirest stede (stede that P) TP.
5323 hadde (1)] to P.   5325 his herte] he P.   5335 boldly] *from* TS, bodyly
B, boldith P;   forth] for to P.   5338 noo enemye] not many P.

Ca.° liij°   'Of al þe worlde telle me it: (160) 6305
            þe delictablest stede, whiche is it?'
               'Where a mannes herte is feste
               And forto dwelle were leueste
            þere is þe delectablest stede
            As to him on to trede.   6310
            For were a man in a cuntre
            In þe fairest stede þat might be
            And had al þat he had nede
            Him wiþ to cloþe and to fede
            And he loued to be elleswhere,   6315
            No delite þan hadde he there;
            But þere a man loueþ wel,   f. 93ᵛ
            þogh it be foule e40euerydel,
            þere is his ioye and his solas
            More þan in any oþer plas.'   6320

Ca.° liiij°   'Wheþer is hardier—he þat goþ anight   (161)
            Or he þat gooþ bi þe daies light?'
               'A man þat gooþ a wicked way
               In greet perelle of the day,
            And he boldly þer forth go   6325
            By light of þe day, as many oone do,
            He goþ þanne ful boldely
            And drediþ no manere enemy;
            And if his enemy þanne come goand,
            He dar booldly þanne him wiþstand.   6330
            But he þat gooþ on þe night,
            þat is noon hardinesse of might.
            To deffende him he is not leef,
            þerfore he stalkiþ as a þeef:
            In þe derke he hopeþ in his þoght   6335
            þat men shullen perceiue him noght;
            But if he a shadowe shal se,
            His herte shal t[r]emble and he shal flee.
            ȝit ben þer oþer ful many

5339 goand] etande P.   5340 That he wolde] Theym he wolde boldly P.
5348 gaste] gliste TS, drede P.

6307 feste] best h.   6308 were] wher H.   6338 tremble] *from* H, temble L.

That woll ben holdyn hardy   5350
And ben cowardes moste of all:
Vauacours men hem calle.
Bo[l]dely anyght woll they goo;
They ne recke whosoo seeith hem moo
f. 78ʳ   For with visours ben they dight   5355
That noo man may knowe them aright
And disgise them or þat they goon oute
For to seme hardy and stoute;
And all is but cowardyse
That they doone echon of thyse.   5360
Forwhy he þat gothe by þe liȝte
Is hardyere þanne he by nighte.'

Qo. 158ᵃ   'Whiche is moste proueste and best—   (162)
           That of towne other of foreste?'
                'Prowesse of towne, as I wene,   5365
                Ne was never worthe a bene;
                Hit is no prowesse, hit is folie
           And caytyfhede and misardrie:
           Som man for a worde full ryfe
           Woll drawe vnto a man his knyf   5370
           That wolde neuer doon alsoo
           And they were betwyxe hem twoo.
           But there be thynges iijᵉ
           That makeþ hym hasty to be:
           On therof hit is foly   5375
           That makeþ his herte stye soo hye;
           Another that he hopeþ well
           The folke abowte iche a deele
           Shall sterten on hym and hym holde
           And lat to do þat he wolde;   5380
           The thridde for his brayne is small
           And turned all with wyn and ale.
           And he þat asayled is
           Holdeþ hym stylle in all þis:

5352 Vauacours] Bostoures S.   5353 Boldely] *from* STP, Bodely B.
5354 seeith hem moo] loketh them on TSP.   5362 he] he þat goth TSP.
5363 moste proueste] more prowes TS.   5367 folie] no folie T, but foly thyng
P.   5368 misardrie] musardrye S, myshardy T, manassyng P.   5372 betwyxe
hem] but thei T, but hemself S.   5376 stye soo] skyppe vppe T, skipe on SP.

þat ben holden right hardy   6340
And ben cowardes moost of alle:
Vauacours suche men calle.
Boldely anight wole þei goon;
þei ne rekke who loke hem vpon
For wiþ viseris þei ben dight   6345
For no man shulde knowe hem aright
And disgiseþ hem or þei gone out
Forto seme hardy and stout;
And al is but for couetise
þat þe enchesoun is done of thise.   6350
Wherfore he þat gooþ be light   f. 94ʳ
Is hardier þan he [þat] gooþ be night.'

Ca.º lvº   'Whiche is more prowesse and best—   (162)
                 þat of þe towne or of þe forest?'
                      'Prowesse of towne, as I wene,   6355
                         Ne was neuere worth a bene;
                  It is no prowesse, it is folie
                  And caytifnesse and mishardie:
                  Somme man for a word ful ryf
                  Anoon he wole drawe his knyf   6360
                  þat he durste neuere tofore do
                  And þei were bitwene hem two.
                  But þere ben þinges thre
                  þat makiþ him hasty forto be:
                  þe firste of hem suche folye   6365
                  It makeþ his herte skippe an hye;
                  þe secounde þat he hopeþ wel
                  þat þe folke aboute euerydel
                  Sullen stirte on him and holde
                  And let him to do þat he wolde;   6370
                  þe þridde for his hernes smale
                  Ben torned þorgh wyn and ale.
                  And he þat assailled is
                  Holdeþ him stille in al þis:

5381 brayne is] braynes TS, hernys P.   5382 And] Be T, Ar SP;   all . . . and] full
of of gode P.

    6352 þat] from H, om. L.   6357 folie] but folie H.   6358 mishardie]
mysardrie H.   6363 But] But ȝet H.

He dredeþ that he might hym sloo;   5385
And lordshipp dredeþ he alsoo;
The iij he dredeþ his enemye
For he ne wote if he be doghtie;
His owne loos he dredeþ eke
That makeþ hym his herte meke.   5390

f. 78ᵛ   But were they bothe in the foreste,
There men myght knowe þe beste:
There sholde noo man on them wonder
Ne noo man putte hem in sonder
Ne noo bailleff were there to drede   5395
But the boldere hym forthe bede.
Forthy prowes in towne me calles
Ne is but boste and noothyng elles.'

Qo. 159ᵃ   'Iff a man haue an evill wiff,   (163)
Moch pouert, and ffeble liff,   5400
Oþer an hurtt or maym off lym,
Should anoþer vpbraide itt hym?'
'Iff a man ought saye or obreide
There is noo lakke þat on hym is layde.
If he haue an evell feere,   5405
Soo may God sende to hym here;
If he in pouert fallen be,
So may tomorowe peraventure he
For the whele of aduenture
Will not alway endure;   5410
And if he have ony lakke
Other in body other in bakke
Or ony of his lemys alle,
Vpbroide hym nouȝt, whatsoo befalle,
For he þat sente þat iche a deȩle   5415
May sende hit on the also well.
And therefore lete euery man have fayre speche
That of his speche God take noo wreche.'

5390 hym] *om.* P.   5397 me calles] men (as men P) tellis TSP.   5399 *ques-*
tions written in a different hand hereafter B.   5400 Moch pouert and] Or be pore or of
TS;   ffeble] evill T.   5401] Or haue a wemme in (on S) a lym TS.
5403] Thou shalt not sey and nother vpbreide P;   Iff a] No TS;   saye or] other
TS.   5404 There is] For TSP.   5406 hym] the P.   5408 he] by the
P.   5410] No while stonde (will stande S) nor (ne S) endure TS, No while no wele

He dredeþ þat he might him slo;   6375
And lordshipe dredeþ he also;
þe þridde he dredeþ his enemy
For he ne woot if he be doghti;
His owne loos he dredeþ eke
And þat drede makeþ his herte meke.   6380
But were þei boþe in þe forest,
þere men mighte knowe þe best
þere as no man may putte hem asondre
Ne no man vpon hem wondre
Ne no baily were þere to drede   6385   f. 94ᵛ
But þe boldeloker him forth to bede,
For þat prowesse þat men in toun tellis
Nas but boost and noþing ellis.'

Ca.° lvj°   'If a man haue an yuel wif   (163)
                 Or poure or be of feble lyf   6390
                 Or haue a wem in any lym,
                 Shal a man vpbreide it him?'
                      'No man oght seie or vpbreide
                      For no lak þat on him is leide.
                 If he haue any yuel fere,   6395
                 So may God him sende here;
                 If he in pouert fallen be,
                 So may tomorowe peraventure he
                 For þe whele of aventure
                 Stondinge no while wole dure;   6400
                 And if he haue any lak
                 Other in body or in bak
                 Or in any of hise lymes alle,
                 Vpbraide him not, whatso bifalle,
                 For he þat sente þat eeuerydel   6405
                 May sende it on þe als wel.
                 And for þat euery man faire speke
                 þat for his speche God take no wreke.'

stondith sure P.   5417 lete] *om.* TSP;   have fayre speche] fairely speke
TSP.   5418 wreche] wreke TSP.

   6375 þat] nat H.   6382 men] þei H.   6388 Nas] Is H.   6396 may]
many haþ H;   sende] fede H.

Qo. 160ᵃ   'Shall a man ech man worshippe do   (164)
           And all her will do also?'   5420
           'A man shall doo this with skyll
           If that he might come þertill
           But noo man may ne noo man can
     Doon the will of eche man;
     Neuerþelese do nought amisse: 5425
     Worshipp iche man after þat he is

f. 79ʳ   And fulfille eche mannes wille
     That turneth vnto þyselfe noon ille.
     Doo with goode chere þat þou shalt doo
     To hem þat prayeth the vnto   5430
     And for lityll say not nay—
     Hit may turne þe to goode anoþer day:
     That þou desirest shalt þou thenne fynde;
     Eche man to serue þe shal be in mynde;
     Thyn honour shall wyde wende;   5435
     Euery man shall halde þe goode and hende
     And þou may neuer ille betyde
     Whill thy goode worde gothe soo wyde.'

Qo. 161ᵃ   'Shall he ought forgoten be   (165)
           Thatt to plesure hath serued me?'   5440
     'Iff a man me doo seruise
     Vnto my wyll on my wyse,
     I ought to forgete hit neuer moore
     Thogh the seruise litill woore.
     For he that doothe my lykyng,   5445
     He yeveth me ynogh of his þyng
     And I ought his helpe to be
     Yf he have nede vnto me.
     For euery man þat dothe a goode dede
     Is worthy to haue for his mede;   5450
     And þe goode of suche oon
     Aught I euer to thynke vppon.'

5421 this] alle this TSP.   5429 Doo] Lo P.   5432] To doo hur wille if
(and P) that (*om.* SP) thou maye TSP.   5434 to . . . mynde] shall holde the gode and
kynde P.   5435–6] *om.* P.   5438 soo] to P.   5440 plesure] lykynge
TS.   5442 my] any TSP.   5443 hit] hym T.   5447 helpe] hele

Ca.° lvij°   'Shal men to euery man worshipe do   (164)
                   And al her wille do þerto?'   6410
                        'A man shulde do al þis wiþ skill
                        If þat he might come þertil
                   But no man may ne no man can
                   Do þe wille of euery man;
                   Neþeles, lest þou doo amys,   6415
                   Worschipe euery man after he is
                   And fulfille euery mannes wille
                   þat torneþ to þi soule noon ille.
                   Do wiþ good chere þat þou shalt do   f. 95ʳ
                   To hem þat prayeth þe to   6420
                   And for litel seie not nay
                   To do her wille if þou may:
                   þat þou desirest þan shalt þou fynde;
                   Euery man to serue þe þanne wole be kynde;
                   þin honour shal wide wende;   6425
                   Euery man shal holde þe good and hende
                   And þe ne may neuere yuel betide
                   þere þi good worde gooþ so wide.'

Ca.° lviij°   'Shal he ought forȝeten be   (165)
                   þat to my wille haþ serued me?'   6430
                        'Iff a man do me seruise
                        To my wille in any wise,
                   I oughte to forȝete it neuer more
                   þogh þe seruise ful litel wore.
                   For he þat doth my likyng,   6435
                   He ȝeueþ me ynow of his þing
                   And I oughte his helpe to be
                   If þat he haue nede to me.
                   For eueriche þat dooþ a good dede,
                   He is worthi to haue his mede;   6440
                   And þe good wille of suche oon
                   I oughte euere to þenke vpon.'

P.   5450 for] om. TP, precedes to S.   5451 goode] good wille TSP;   suche
oon] ichone S.   5452 euer] om. P.

6411 þis] om. H.   6426 and hende] frende H.

Qo. 162ᵃ   '*May a man ought hym withhold*   (166)
               Fro women that he hath in hold,
               That he no lecherie do   5455
               Whan he hath grete will þerto?'
                 'Full well a man may holde hym stylle
                 And withstonde his owne wille
                 Fro lecchery, if þat he will,
               Thoght he grete will haue þertyll: 5460
               Lete hym caste in his thought
               How fayre God hathe hym wrought

f. 79ᵛ   At his owne liknesse to be,
               And that soo fayre agayn to see
               Sholde be kepte clene alsoo   5465
               That noo filthe ne come therto.
               Were now soo þat the kynge
               Yave me a robe of his clothyng,
               Full clene I wolde hit kepe and bright
               And worshipp hit at all my myght   5470
               For moche worshipp to me hit were
               A kynges clothyng for to bere.
               Also sholde hit here byfall:
               Of Goddis clothyng ben we all
               And if we thynke to holde hit clene,   5475
               Oure [f]owle woll þat was soo kene
               Shall goo away and passe for nouȝt
               And kendell no moore in oure þouȝt.
               The moore þat men a fyre leyeth in,
               The more hotter woll hit brenne   5480
               And hit wol not leue brennyng
               But men hit slek with somþyng:
               Right soo brenneþ leccherye
               In men þat yeveth hem to folye
               And if he woll þat hit be laide,   5485
               Thynke on God, as I have sayde.
               Also ther shall in his þoght be
               What mede cometh of chastyte

5453–92] *om.* S.   5454 he] here T.   5459 þat he will] he will thus doo T.   5460 þertyll] thertoo P.   5464 agayn] a thynge TP.   5466 filthe] flesh P.   5468 clothyng] weryng P.   5473 here] higher T, *om.* P. 5474 Goddis] gode P.   5476 fowle] sowle B, foule TP.   5477 goo] deye T,

Ca.° lix°   'May a man oght him wiþholde   (166)
                 From a womman þat haue him wolde,
                 þat he no leccherie do   6445
                 Whan he haþ gret wille þerto?'
                    'Ful wel he may holde him stille
                    And wiþstonde his owne wille
                 From lecchery, if þat he wil,
                 þogh he grete wil haue þertil: 6450
                 Late him caste in his þoght
                 Hou fare God haþ him wroght
                 And at his owne liknesse to be,   f. 95ᵛ
                 And þat so faire a þing to see
                 Shulde be kepte clene also   6455
                 þat no filþehede cam þerto.
                 Were now, sire, þat a kyng
                 Ȝaf me a robe of his cloþing,
                 Ful clene I wolde kepe it and bright
                 And worshipe [it] wiþ al my might   6460
                 For miche worshepe it to me were
                 A kinges cloþing forto bere.
                 þus to vs, sire, it is bifalle:
                 Of Goddis cloþing we ben alle
                 And if we þenke to holde it clene,   6465
                 Oure foul will þat was so kene
                 Shal wasshe away and passe for noght
                 And brenne no more in oure þoght.
                 þe more þat a man a fire leiþ ynne,
                 þe more and þe hotter it wole brenne   6470
                 And it wole not leue brennyng
                 But men slake it wiþ somþing:
                 þus brenneþ the synne of lecchery
                 In a man þat ȝeueþ him to foly
                 And if he wole þat it be leid,   6475
                 þenke on God, as I haue seid.
                 Also shal in his þoght be
                 What mede comeþ of chastite

vanesh P.   5480 more] more ande T, more and the P.   5485 he] ye P.
─────
     6444 haue] *repeated* L.   6452 haþ] *repeated* L.   6460 it] *from* H, *om.* L.

And ȝif he be thanne in synne,
What payne shall his sowle ben ynne;   5490
And thus may he kele fote hote
His brennyng will þat was soo hoote.'

Qo. 163ª   'Grettest delite þat is   (167)
Which is it?—Now tell me þis.'
          'We fynde ther be delites two: 5495
          Bodily and gostly alsoo.
          The bodely woll not laste:
          That men doth þeron is owte caste.
f. 80ʳ   Hit fareth as þe candell light
          That now brenneth fayre and bright   5500
          Now thenne is hit oute as tyte—
          Soo fareth bodely delyte.
          Gostely delyte is on other wyse
          As delite in God and in his seruise.
          And þoo þat deliten hem þerinne   5505
          For to kepe hem oute of synne,
          Wete þou well þat they þoo
          In þe moste payne of þe woo
          That they suffere here soule to saue
          Full grete delite therinne þey haue.   5510
          And whoosoo þerinne is brought,
          That delite ne keleth nought:
          Hit waxeth euer froo lasse to moore
          Ay till a man come thoore
          There noon ende ne may be—   5515
          That is bifore the Trinite—
          And there shall his delite be tolde
          Moore than here a thousand folde.
          Forwhy the moore delite that is
          Is to delite in God, ywys.'   5520

Qo. 164ª   'Tell me now iff that a man   (168)
Shall ouȝtt delite hym with woman.'

5489 thanne] taken TP.   5491 fote] full T.   5492 will] loue P.
5493 S begins again.   5500 fayre and] ferlye TS, fairely P.   5508 moste] om.
TSP;   of] and S.   5510 therinne] pyne S.   5512 ne keleth] he listith
P.   5513 Hit] He T.   5514 Ay] And P.   5515 There . . . ne] That ende

>   And if þat he be take in synne,
>   What peyne his soule shal be ynne;   6480
>   And þus may he kele, God it woot,
>   His brennyng loue þat was so hoot.'

Ca.° lx°   'The grettest delite þat is,   (167)
>   Whiche is it?—Telle me þis.'
>   'We fynde þer ben delites two: 6485
>   Bodily delite and goostly also.
>   The bodily delite wole not last   f. 96ʳ
>   þat manye her þoght done on cast:
>   It fareþ as þe candels light
>   þat now brenneþ fers and bright   6490
>   And now is it out as tite—
>   So fareþ here bodily delite.
>   Goostly delite is anoþer wise
>   As delite in God and in his seruise.
>   And þilke þat deliten þerynne   6495
>   For to kepen hem out of synne,
>   Wite þou wel þat þei tho
>   In þe peyne of sorwe and wo
>   þat þei þolen her soules to saue
>   Ful greet delite þerynne þei haue.   6500
>   And whoso is þeryn ibroght,
>   þat delite he leseþ noght:
>   It wexith euere fro lesse to more
>   Euer til a man come þore
>   þere noon ende may be—   6505
>   þat is bifore þe Trinite—
>   And þere shal his delite be oftolde
>   More þan here by a þowsand folde.
>   þerfore þe most delite þat is
>   Is to delite in God, ywis.'   6510

Ca.° lxj°   'Telle me now if þat a man   (168)
>   Shal delite him oght with a womman.'

ther T.   5519 moore] moste TSP.   5521–668] om. S.   5522 ouȝtt]
nought T.

6503 It] And H.

'Delite with women are ther tway
And why they be I shall the say.
   That oon is gostly with chaste lyf   5525
As a man with his owne wyff:
Flesshly knowe here will he may
Childeren to wynne to Goddes pay;
And for that ilke tyme þat he
Wote þat she with chylde be   5530
He shall hym holde fro hir holly
Till hit be born of hir body—
This is delyte of chastite,
That digne and honest ought to be.

f. 80ᵛ   Bodily delite ther is also   5535
That noo tyme hathe rewarde vnto
But euery tyme that will hym takeþ
His flesshly luste he not forsaketh:
That is puerly lyff of bestes
That nother is goode ne honest [i]s;   5540
And suche a delite with woman to have
Sholde noo man of hir hit crave.'

Qo. 165ᵃ   *'Iff an hoost anoþer mete,*   (169)
     Shall he anon on hym shete?'
    'Come an oste with all her mayne   5545
And another come hym agayne,
Smyte anoon shull they nought:
Here cheueteyn shall have aforethought
And be wel avysed and wyse
And ouersee his enemyes.   5550
And if he haue hope in his mode
That his party may be goode,
He shall ordeyne his folke wysly
And be vigerous and hardy
And his enemyes asayle   5555
As hit fallith to bataille.
And if he aperceyuant is

5524 why] whiche TP.   5527 knowe] knowyng P;   will] wele TP;   he] y P.
5529 for] fro TP.   5534 honest] heyest P.   5539 puerly] the poure P;   bestes]
beeste TP.   5540 honest is] honestes B, honeste TP.   5541 to have] *om.* TP
5542 of . . . crave] haue that good can TP.   5547 anoon] a not T.   5548 afore thought]

'Delite wiþ womman þer beeþ tweie
And whiche þei beeþ I wole ȝou seie.
þat oon is goostly wiþ chast lyf   6515
As a man wiþ his owne wyf:
Fleisshely knowe hir wel he may
Children to gete to Goddis pay;
And fro þat same time þat he
Wote þat she wiþ childe be   6520
He shal from hir absteine truly   f. 96ᵛ
Til it be bore of hir body—
þis is delite of chastite,
þat worþi and honest ought to be.
Bodily delite þer is also   6525
þat no time haþ reward to
But euery time he wole take
His flesshely lust and not forsake,
And þat is pure lyf of beest
þat is nouther good ne honest;   6530
And suche delite with womman
No man shulde haue þat good can.'

Ca.° lxij°   'If an oost anothir mete,   (169)
          Shullen eiþer on other anoon shete?'
'Iff a[n ooste] come wiþ al her mayn   6535
And anoþer hem mete agayn,
Smite anoon shullen þei noght
Til eiþer cheueteins haue ful þoght
And be ful avised, iwis,
And eiþer ouerese her enemys.   6540
And if he haue hope in his mood
þat his partie may be good,
He shal ordeine his folke wisely
And be right kene and hardy
And hise enemyes fersely assaile   6545
As it bifalleþ to bataile.
And if he perceyuing is

forthe hote T.   5549 be] om. P.   5550 his] furste alle his T.   5554 be
vigerous] so rigous T.   5556 As] Ande T.   5557 aperceyuant is] aperceyuyd is P,
wole perceyve this T.

6535 an ooste] from H, a man L.   6539 be] he H.

That the febeler side be his,
He shall comforte his folke ilk a deell
And make goode visage and bere hym well   5560
And fare as he hadde noon awe
And in the meane tyme lete hym withdrawe
And holde hym faste togeder soo
That noon outray oþer froo.
Yf his fleyng may not avayle   5565
But that other hym assaile,
Vigorously þanne þat he withstonde
And herte his folke to be doande:
The febele syde perchauns so may
With lytill stroke skape away.'   5570

f. 81ʳ *Qo. 166ᵃ* *'Which membris off the man ar tho*   (170)
Thatt he worst myȝtt fforgo?'
          'A man might noo lym forbere
          But if hit hym gretly fordere,
          And som oon might he wors forgoo   5575
Thanne he might other twoo:
For thogh he forgoo fote and hande,
Eres and eyen þogh h[ym] wande,
Yet may he be full hote of herte
And leve many a day in qwarte;   5580
But were tethe and tonge forgon,
Good lyf after hadde he noon
For tho ben þe moste, hardely,
That helpeth to susteyne þe body.
The tonge the mete turneþ all   5585
And þe teth þat cheweth hit small;
Firther the tonge is made alsoo
As to God worshipp for to doo
And þe teth grynt the mete small
That the body leueth withall;   5590
And for that a man may noȝt
Withouten this forthe be brought.

5562 the meane tyme lete] alle that TP.   5566 that other] there on P.
5567 þanne þat he] he them T, he than P.   5570 stroke] scathe TP.
5574 fordere] dere T, shuld dere P.   5578 hym] *from* TP, h B.   5586 And]
Vndir P;   cheweth hit small] chewe it shalle TP.   5587 Firther] Ande TP.

þat þe febler partie be his,
He shal comforte his folke euerydel
And make good visage and bere him wel   6550
And fare as he had none awe
And slily him wiþdrawe
And holde hem togidre faste so
þat nouþer outraye oþer fro.
And if his fleing may not availe   6555 f. 97ʳ
But þat þe oþer wole him assaile,
But strongly þan he hem wiþstand
And chere his folk wiþ glad sembland:
The feble side perchaunce so may
Wiþ litil helpe scape away.'   6560

Ca.° lxiij°   'Whiche membris of þe man ben tho   (170)
                þat he mighte here werst forgo?'
                    '[A] man might no lym wel forbere
                    But if [it] shulde him gretly dere,
                And some one he might werst forgo   6565
                Than he might som other two:
                For þogh he forgoo foot and hond,
                Eren and yȝen þogh him wand,
                Ȝit may he be ful hoot of herte
                And lyue many dayes in querte;   6570
                But were teeþ and tunge forgone,
                Good lyf after had he none
                For þilke ben moost, verrily,
                þat helpeþ to sustene þe body.
                þe tunge þe mete turneþ al   6575
                Vnder þe teeþ þat it chewe shal
                And þe tunge is made also
                Worshipe to God forto doo;
                þe teeþ grindeþ the mete smal
                þat þe body lyueth wiþal;   6580
                And for þat a man may noght
                Wiþouten þise ben forth ybroght.

5588 As to] Vnto TP.   5592 this] tethe P.

6563 A] *from* H, *om.* L.   6564 it] *from* H, *om.* L.

Therfore tounge and teth ben tho
That a man may worst forgo.'

Qo. 167ᵃ   'The ffirst instrument off melodye, who made itt   (171) 5995
                 And how came itt into his witt?'
                        'Oon of the children of Noe,
                        Iafeth, the yongest of þe iijᵉ,
                        He contreved and wroght
                 As God hit sente in his thoght.   5600
                 And of the sowne he hit toke
                 Of trees that the wynde shooke
                 And also of wateres sown
                 That ranne alday fro hilles down;
                 [Som] was lowe and som hye   5605
                 And þerof fonde he melodye:

f. 81ᵛ   An instrumente he made anoon
                 That melodye to worke vpon.'

Qo. 168ᵃ   'A man þat is born dome and deeff and may not se,
                 Whatt spech in his hertt þinkith he?'   (172) 5610
                        'A man þat is born today
                        Dowme and defe and not se ne may,
                        No maner langage may he lere
                 Bycause þat he may not here:
                 Thanne behoveþ hym of kynde   5615
                 In his herte to haue mynde
                 Of the speche that Adam spak
                 Or he Goddes comaundement brak—
                 That is the lernyng that God yave man
                 First whan he to speke began.   5620
                 And ȝif a tre frewte bere,
                 Be hit appill, be hit pere,
                 The frute moste take kynde and hewe
                 Of the roote þat hit on grewe;
                 But the kynde of the tre   5625

5593–94] om. P.   5595 off melodye] om. T.   5597 children] sonnes T,
eldris P.   5603 of wateres sown] aftir sum P.   5604 alday] harde TP.
5605 Som] from P, Some sowne T, And B.   5609 A . . . dome] He þat domme is
T.   5612 and not] that TP.   5613 maner] om. TP.   5616 In] Nedis in
T, Nedely in P.   5618 comaundement] byddynge T, body P.   5619 the
lernyng] Ebrew TP.

þerfore tunge and teeþ ben þo
þat a man may werste forgo.'

Ca.º lxiiij°   'þe firste instrument, who made it   (171) 6585
                 And hou come it in his wit?'
                   'Oone of þe children of Noe,
                   Iapheth, þe ʒongest of the thre,
                 He cont[r]y[u]ed it and wroght   f. 97ᵛ
                 As God it sente in his þoght.   6590
                 And of þe sounde he it took
                 Of trees þat þe wynde shook
                 And also of water soun
                 þat ran fro þe hul adoun;
                 Some sounde was lowe and some hye   6595
                 And þerof he fond melodie,
                 And instrument he made anoon
                 þe melodie to worche vpon.'

Ca.º lxv°   'He þat is dumbe and deef and may not see,   (172)
                 In his herte what speche þinkeþ he?'   6600
                   'A man þat is bore today
                   Dombe and deef and see ne may,
                 No langage may he lere
                 For þat he may noon here:
                 þanne byhoueþ him of kynde   6605
                 In herte nedely haue mynde
                 Of þe speche þat Adam spak
                 Or þat he Goddes heste brak—
                 þat is Ebrew, þat God ʒaf man
                 Firste whanne he to speke bigan.   6610
                 And if a tree any fruyt bere,
                 Be it appel or be it pere,
                 þe fruite mote take kynde and hewe
                 Of þe roote þat it on grewe;
                 But þe kinde of the tree   6615

6589 contryued] *from* H, conteyned L.   6591 sounde] *from* H, secounde
L.   6595 lowe] *from* H, lowde L.   6597 And] An H.   6599–600] *written in right margin* L.

Shall [chaunge] ȝif hit ymped be.
And but a man have ympyng
Of langage thorogh lernyng,
The furste speche have he shall
That man was furste lered withall.'   5630

'Why be some cloudis off the skye   (173)
                White and some blak þerbye?'
                    'Clowdes somtyme be right thynne
                    For litell water that is them inne.
                    Thanne comeþ the light of the day   5635
                And the sonne that shyneth ay
                And yeveth on the [clowde] light:
                The clowde that is of lityll might
                Is thorowshined þerwithall
                Forthe white he shewes withall,   5640
                For thorogh water men may se
                If that hit noȝt depe be.

f. 82^r   The clowde that blakke is to ooure sight
                Is thyk of water and of might
                And for the thiknesse þat hit hase   5645
                May noo liȝte þerþorogh paase;
                Forwhy he haldes hit drye
                Not full moche vp an hye
                And for hit is thykke and lowe
                Behoveth hit blakke vnto vs showe.'   5650

'May no creature þat God wrouȝtt   (174)
                Wote Goddes will ne his þouȝtt?'
                    'God made neuer creature—
                    Aungell, ne man, ne other, sure—
                    That might wete Goddes þought   5655
                Ne his wyll till hit was wrought.
                Whanne he onythynge woll do,
                He saith, "Be made," and hit is doo;

5626 chaunge] *from* TP, *om.* B.   5628 thorogh] thought oute P.
5629 have] lerne P.   5632 White] *om.* T.   5633 be] of P;   thynne] renne
P.   5635] *om.* P.   5636 shyneth] shewyth P.   5636/7 *add* Makith hit
white and gray P.   5637 clowde] *from* TP, sonne B.   5638 of] full of
P.   5640 For the] Ande therfore T;   shewes withall] shewe hym shall
TP.   5644 thyk of] like P.   5647 he haldes hit] holdith it on TP.

Shal chaunge if it ymped be.
And but a man haue ymping
Of langage þorghout lernyng,
þe firsthe speche haue he shall
þat man was first lerned wiþal.' 6620

Ca.° lxvj° *'Why ben some clowdis of þe sky* (173)
Whyte and som blak þerby?'
       'Clowdis somtime beeþ right þynne
       For litel water þat is þerynne.
þanne cometh þe light of þe day 6625 f. 98ʳ
And þe sunne þat shyneþ ay
And ȝeueþ on þe clowde light,
And þe clowde þat is of litel might
Is þorghshyned þerwiþal:
White þerfore he him shew shal, 6630
For þorgh waater may men se
If þat it noght deep be.
þe clowde þat blak is to oure sight
Is liche watir and of oon might
And for þe þiknesse þat it has 6635
May no light þerþorgh pas;
þerfore holdeþ it not drie
For it is fer bynethe þe skye
And for it is þikke alowe
Blak byhoueþ him to to vs showe.' 6640

[Ca.° lxvij° *'May no creatour þat God wroght* (174)
Knowe Goddis wille ne his þoght?']
       'God made neuere creature—
       Aungel, ne man, ne oþer figure—
þat ne knoweþ not Goddis þoght 6645
Ne his wille til it was wroght.
Whan he wole anyþing do,
He seide, "Be it made," and it was so;

5650 hit] *om.* P; vs] *om.* P. 5654 sure] figure TP. 5655 might wete] wite
shall not P. ˙5656 hit was] he haue P. 5657 Whanne] What P.
5658 doo] soo TP.

6633 blak] deepe H. 6639 alowe] and lowe H. 6641–2] *from table* 1365–6
and H, *om.* L. 6645 not] *om.* H.

But or he in werke hit fulfille,
There may noo man wete his wille.   5660
God knowith the thoght of euerychon
But of his þoght ne wote right noon
Saue the Holy Trynyte,
For al oon ben they thre.
Somtyme wote man what God doo wyll—   5665
That is he þat he sendeth vntyll
By an aungell [to] telle hym his thoght;
Elles is þer noon wote hit nought.'

Qo. 171[a]   '*Yitt wold I wete, iff I may,*   (175)
           Iff man shall worshippe God allday.'   5670
    'Alle men sholde with right soo do
        But her might is not þerto,
        For tho body is febyll of myght
    And behoueth somtyme [reste] be right;
    And but hit reste may haue,   5675
    Longe may he not the liff saue.
    And forwhy God honoure he may
    A certeyn owres of the day;

f. 82ᵛ   And in certeyn tyme he shall
              Trauayle to holde the lyff all;   5680
    And somtyme reste shall he take
    The body stalworth with to make,
    For after mete and drynke is reste
    To noreshyng of the body best.
    And whanne he shall God worshipp do,   5685
    Loke all his herte be therto;
    For he that seyth to God his bede,
    And his þought be in other stede,
    The tounge were as goode be stylle
    For hit axeth with noo goode wille: 5690
    Forwhy þat God worshipp shall,
    Spekeþ tounge, herte, and þou3t withall.'

5659 But...werke] For or he P.   5660 noo man] nothynge TP.   5661 thoght
of] lawes P.   5662 ne ... noon] knoweth not one T.   5667 to] *from* TP, *om.*
B.   5668 hit nought] owght TP.   5669 S *begins again.*
5674 reste] *from* TSP, þerfore B.   5677 he] thou P.   5678 A] At P, In
S.   5681 he] be P.   5683 is] gode P.   5684 of] *om.* P;   best] hit is
best P.   5690 goode] *om.* TSP.   5691–714] *om.* S.   5691 þat] whan
thou T.   5692 withall] ande alle TP.

But or he his werke gan fulfille,
Might no man here knowe his wille.   6650
God woot þe þoghtes of echone
But his þoght wote creature none
Saue þe Holy Trynyte,
For alle in oone ben þei þre.
Somtime wote man what God do wil,   6655
And þat is he he sendiþ vntil
Bi aungels to telle him his þoght;
Ellis is þer noon þat woot oght.'

[*Ca.° lxviij°*] '*Now wolde I wite, if I may,*   (175)
If man shal worshipe God al day.']   6660
      '[A]lle men shulde wiþ right do so   f. 98ᵛ
      But her might is not þerto,
For þe body is feble of might
And somtyme moste reste wiþ right;
And but it reste here now haue,   6665
Longe may he not þe lyf here saue.
And þerfore God honour we may
At certeine houres of þe day;
And in certeine tyme he shal
Trauaille to holde þe lijf wiþal;   6670
And somtime reste shal he take
þe body þerwith strong to make,
For after mete and drinke is rest
To norisshe þe body it is þe best.
And whan he to God worshepe shal do,   6675
Loke þat al his herte be þerto;
For he þat seith to God his bede,
And his þoght be in oþer stede,
þe tunge were as good be stille
For it axeþ wiþ no wille: 6680
þerfore he þat God worshipe shal,
Speke wiþ þe tunge, herte, þoght, and al.'

6659–60] *from table* 1367–8 *and* H, *om.* L.   6661 Alle] lle (*initial* a *for rubricator*
om.) L.   6665 now] may H.   6668/9 *add* And in certeyn houres of þe day
L.

Qo. 172ª   *'Wheroff may itt be and why*   (176)
                      Thatt eyen sometyme wepe blithely?'
                        'Somtyme hereth a man a þyng   5695
                        That is not to his likyng
                        Or a thyng of grete pite:
And he of tendre herte be,
The herte makeþ anoon righte
And casteþ water to þe sight;   5700
So wepen þe eyen also smerte
And all makeþ tendernesse of herte,
And of that herte shall seldom
Euell will [o]r fe[l]lenesse com.
And tho eyen þat wepen ofte   5705
Aledeþ the herte and doith hit softe,
For the hete þat þe herte feles
With the teeris gretly keles.
But he þat noȝt woll may not wepe,
Grete felnesse in his herte doth kepe   5710
And of his hard herte thanne is he
And of noo mercy ne piete;
But he that to wepe is redy,
In hym is pite and mercy.'

f. 83ʳ *Qo. 173ª*   *'Whatt maner ffolke ar men hold to*   (177) 5715
                      In this world worshippe to do?'
                        'Euery man shall principally
                        Worshipp God, þat [is] an hy,
                        That hym made and shall vnmake
Whan that talent shall hym take.   5720
His wyff shall man worshipp also,
For oon body be they twoo.
His lorde also worshipp he shall
That he serueth and dwellith withall.
Father and modyr alsoo shall he   5725
Worshipp before al þat [b]e.

5694 wepe] greeten T.   5699 makeþ] mekith TP.   5701 So wepen] To
helpe P.   5704 will or] willer B; or] of P; fellenesse] feblenesse B, fellenes
TP.   5705 tho] *om.* T, to the P; ofte] faste P (ofte *written above*).
5706 Aledeþ] Alleggith T, Al gothe to P.   5711 his] *om.* TP.   5715 S

Ca.° lxix°   *'Wherof may it be and why*   (176)
              þat yȝen somtime wepen blepely?'
                    'Somtyme a man hereþ a þing   6685
                     þat is not to his liking
              Or elles a þing of grete pite:
              And he þanne of tendre herte be,
              þe herte m[e]keþ anoon right
              And þat castiþ watir to þe sight;   6690
              þanne wepeþ the yȝen ful smert
              And þat makeþ tendernesse of þe hert,
              And of þat herte shal seldome
              Euel wille or felnesse come.
              And þe eyȝen þat wepen ofte   6695 f. 99ʳ
              Melteþ the herte and makeþ it softe,
              For þe hete þat þe herte feleþ
              Wiþ the teris gretly keleþ.
              But he þat may not lightly wepe,
              Greet heuynesse in herte he kepe   6700
              And of harde herte þanne is he
              And haþ nouþer mercy ne pitee;
              But he þat to wepe is redy,
              In him is pitee and mercy.'

Ca.° lxx°   *'What manere of folke ben men holden to*   (177) 6705
              In þis worlde worshipe to do?'
                    'Euery man shal principaly
                     Worshipe God, þat is an hy,
              þat him made and shal vnmake
              Whanne he wole mannes lijf slake.   6710
              A man shal his wyf worship also,
              For oo body and flesshe þei ben boþe two.
              His lord also worshepe he shal
              þat he dwellith wiþ and serueth wiþal.
              Fadir and moder also shal he   6715
              Worshipe bifore alle þat be.

begins again.   5718 is] *from* TSP, *om.* B.   5722 oon body] on obedyence
P.   5723 lorde] lovers T.   5726 be] *from* ST, he B, shalbe P.

———

6684 bleþely] besily H.   6689 mekeþ] *from* H, makeþ L.   6692 þat] *om.* H.

Yet shall he worshipp furthermore
That hym goode doothe with worde and core.
Suster and brother and his kynne
Vnto worshipp he ought to haue mynde inne;   5730
And euery man, if that he myght,
Ought he to worshipp with right.'

Qo. 174ᵃ   '*The largest man, which is he*   (178)
               Thatt now in this world may be?'
          'A large man þat haue shall,   5735
            Though he þe worlde seke ouerall
            Shall he neuer fynde ne see
That of his owne may large be.
For of noone larges tolde hit is
A man to yeve þat noght is his,   5740
For alle þe largesse þat men telles
Of God þey ben and of noo man elles;
And all þat a man is sente
Of Goddis love hit is hym lente,
For naked heder vs he brought   5745
And of ooureselfe we haue nought
And naked away shall we wende:
With [vs] we bere noght at the ende;
And if hit ooure owne were,
Thanne might we with vs bere.   5750

f. 83ᵛ   And God vs leveth goode forwhy
That we hit spende worthyly
Ouresilf at mesure for to fede
And helpe þe poore þat have neede;
And sethen we be holde þerto   5755
The poore for to helpe alsoo,
Soo noo man may make hit soothe
That it is his largesse þat he doþe:
Therfore knowe I noo large man
That of hymselfe hathe ought wane.'   5760

5727 he] the P;   furthermore] for hur mede TS, ferther mede P.   5728 and
core] or dede TS, and dede P.   5729 and (2)] in P;   kynne] kynde TS.
5730 he . . . inne] owght by (be P) mynde TP, my3t he be mynde S.   5733–822] *om.*
S.   5737 neuer] non TP.   5745 vs] is TP.   5746 ooureselfe we haue]
hymself ne (he P) hathe TP.   5747 we] he TP.   5748 vs] hym B;   we bere]
he berith TP.   5749 ooure] his TP.   5750 we with vs] he it with hym

Him shal he worship, as it is kid,
þat good him dooþ or good did.
Brothir and sister and al his kyn
To worshipe hem oweþ him;   6720
And euery man of þat he might
He oweþ to worshipe as it is right.'

Ca.° lxxj°   '*þe largeste man, whiche is he*   (178)
                þat in þis world now may be?'
                'A large man þat haþ shal   6725
                þorgh þe worlde seke oueral:
He shal noon finde ne see
þat of his owne may large be.
For of no largesse tolde it is   f. 99ᵛ
A man to ȝeue þat is noght his,   6730
For al þe largesse þat men of tellis
Comeþ of God and of no man ellis;
And al þat a man is to sent
Of Goddis lone it is him lent,
For naked he is hidre broght   6735
And of himself ne haþ he noght
And naked away shal he wende
And berith noght ellis with him at þe ende;
And if it his owne were,
þanne might he it wiþ him bere.   6740
And God him leneþ good forthy
þat he it spende worþily
Himself in mesure forto fede
And helpe the pouere þat haue nede;
And sithen he is holde þerto   6745
þe pouere forto helpe also,
þanne may þer no man make his roos
That it is largesse þat he doos:
þerfore knowe I no large man
þat of himself ought may or can.'   6750

TP.   5751 vs leveth] hym lennythe T, he leuyth (? lenyth) P.   5752 we] he
TP.   5753 Ouresilf] Hymselfe TP.   5755 we be] he is TP.   5757 hit
soothe] his roos TP.   5758 it] *om.* TP;   his] *om.* TP.   5760 hathe ought
wane] ought may or can TP.

6721 of] if H.   6729 of] *inserted above line* L.

Qo. 175[a]　　　'Shall a pore man owhere　　　　　　　　(179)
　　　　　　　　　Putt a rich man hym beffore?'
　　　　　　　　'Iff hit be soo þat they tweye
　　　　　　　　Goon togeder by the weye,
　　　　　　　　The pore man shall euermore　　　　　　5765
　　　　　　　　Put the riche man bifore;
　　　　　　　　And at here table sekerly
　　　　　　　　The poore may not sit soo hy
　　　　　　　　For if a richer come þan he,
　　　　　　　　Hym behoueth flitt his see,　　　　　　5770
　　　　　　　　And thenne woll men more þynke hit were
　　　　　　　　That he had sette hym elliswhere.
　　　　　　　　But ben they bothe in bataill
　　　　　　　　And shull theyre enemyes assayll
　　　　　　　　And þe pore withouten drede　　　　　　5775
　　　　　　　　[Before] þe riche forth hym bede,
　　　　　　　　The pore man is also doughti
　　　　　　　　As is þe riche of his body
　　　　　　　　And with þat forth puttyng percaas he may
　　　　　　　　Gete more worshipp þanne þe riche þat day.'　5780

Qo. 176[a]　　　'Is itt to a man any syn to ete　　　　　(180)
　　　　　　　　Ech þing þat he may gete?'
　　　　　　　　　'God hadde to man suche loue
　　　　　　　　　That he made to his behoue
　　　　　　　　　Foules and fisshes in þe see,　　　　　5785
　　　　　　　　Beste and frute in erthe to be;
f. 84[r]　　　　And whanne þat he man hathe wroght
　　　　　　　　And vnto paradyse hym brought,
　　　　　　　　He made hym lorde of alle thise
　　　　　　　　Hem to putte in his seruise　　　　　　5790
　　　　　　　　And for to vse hem to his foode.
　　　　　　　　For God made all thynges goode
　　　　　　　　And sethen he yave hem leue þertill,
　　　　　　　　He doith noo synne, me þynkeþ by skyll,
　　　　　　　　That of alle thynge eteth　　　　　　5795

5762 a rich man hym] hym a riche man T.　　　5767] Ande be thei atte a (the P)
mangerye TP.　　　5768 The poore] Therfore P;　　may . . . soo] sette hym not to
TP.　　　5769] And yf a riche man come then sit mote he P.　　　5770 Hym
behoueth] Then behouythe the poure to P.　　　5771] Ande wel more menske (worship
P) hym (hit P) were TP.　　　5775 And] There TP.　　　5776 Before] *from* TP,

Ca.° lxxij° 'Shal a pore man owghwore   (179)
     Putte him a riche man bifore?'
     'Iff it be so þat þe tweie
     Go togidre bi þe weie,
     þe pouer man shal euermore   6755
     Putte þe riche man him bifore;
     And if þei be at feste or mete,
     þe pouere shulde desire þe lower sete
     For [i]f a richer come þan he,
     Him bihoueþ to leue his see,   6760
     And more worshepe to him it were
     þat he hadde not sette him þere.
     But and þei ben boþe in bataille   f. 100ʳ
     And her enemyes sholen assaille,
     þogh þe pouere wiþouten drede   6765
     Bifore þe riche wole him forþ bede
     For a pore man may be als douty
     As a riche man of his body
     And wiþ þat putting forþ he may
     Gete more worshipe þan þe riche may.' 6770

Ca.° lxxiij° 'Is it any synne a man to ete   (180)
     Al þing þat he may gete?'
     'God haþ to man suche loue
     þat he made to his bihoue
     Foule in eir and fisshe in þe see,   6775
     Beestis in erþe and fruite on tree;
     And whan þat he hadde man wroght
     And into paradys him had broght,
     He made him lord of alle þise
     Hem to putte in his seruise   6780
     And forto vse hem to his fode.
     For God made alle þinges gode
     And sithen he ȝaf hem leue þertil,
     He doth no synne, me þinke by skil,
     þat of alle þinges eteth   6785

Than B.   5777 is] may be T.   5780 þat day] may P.   5781 itt . . . man]
a man in T.   5786] Beest on erthe and fruyte on tre P.   5787–8] *reversed*
P.   5793 leue] *om.* T.

6754 þe] þei H.   6759 if] *from* H, of L.   6765 þogh] There H.

At mesure whanne he hit geteth.
For what he eteth with goode will
Ne may dere hym neuer ill,
Thogh hit adder were or snake;
But if he ayen herte it take,   5800
Thogh hit be þe beste men fynde,

Hit dothe noo goode to his kynde.'

Qo. 177ᵃ   'Shall a man anoþer greete   (181)
                  All day whan he metith hym in the strete?'
                      'To often a man not grete þou shall   5805
                      As þou metest aday withall;
                      But if þou in þy hous be
                  Amonge thy folke and thy meyne,
                  Gretyng shalt þou seye hem thore
                  Twyse vppon þe day and no moore: 5810
                  On morowe whanne þou comest hom amonge

                  And on even at þy bedde gonge.

                  And if þou mete þy frende in þe strete,
                  Oones on þe day þow shalt hym grete;
                  And þou shalt saye hym þat gretyng   5815
                  After the tyme of yooure metyng—
                  At morn or at even, whethir hit be.
                  And yif he furste grete þe,
                  Grete hym ayeen courtesly:
                  Men shall þe say worshipp þerby.   5820
                  But þou hym shalt but oones grete
                  On a day, þough þou hym ofte mete.'

f. 84ᵛ Qo. 178ᵃ   'How shall a man his children demene   (182)
                  So thatt itt hym affter queme?'

        5798 dere hym neuer] neuer don hym TP.   5804 metith . . . strete] may hym
        mete T.   5805 To] So TP.   5820] Men wull of the worship seye P.
        5823 S begins again;   demene] yeme TS.

In mesure as he it geteth.
For what he eteþ wiþ good wille,
It may neuere do him ille,
þogh it were addre or snake;
But if he it aȝeinst herte take,   6790
And þogh it be ȝit þe best
þat men may fynde, eest or west,
Good shulde it neuere do to his kinde,
As men may it write finde.'

Ca.º lxxiiij°   'Shal a man anoþer grete   (181) 6795
         Alday whan he him mete?'
      'So ofte a man not greet þou shal   f. 100ᵛ
       As þou metest him alday wiþal;
But if þou in thyn hous be
Among thi folke and thi meyne,   6800
Gretyng þou shalt seie to hem þore
Twies on a day and no more:
Amorwe, whan þou comest hem among
(þogh þou in bedde be neuere so long),
þou shalt hem grete wiþ good wille   6805
And þei sholen answere aȝein þertille;
And whan þou goost to bed at night,
To God comende hem and þat is right.
And if þou mete þi frende bi þe strete,
Oones a day þou shalt him grete;   6810
And þou shalt him seie þat gretyng
Aftir þe time of ȝoure meting—
At morwe, at euen, wheþer it be.
And if þat firste he grete þe,
Grete him aȝen curtesly: 6815
Men sholen seie þe worship þerby.
But þou shalt him but ones grete
On þe day, þogh þou him mete.'

Ca.º lxxv°   'Hou shal a man his children ȝeme   (182)
         So þat þeraftir þei may him queme?'   6820

6800 thi (1)] om. H.   6802 on a] oo H.   6806 þertille] þe til H.
6819 Hou] om. H.

'Iff þou haue children, kepe hem well 5825
Till they be of age somdele
And þenne, if þou love them dere,
Putte euerych of them som crafte to lere
Soo þat they mowe hem kepe all
Afterwarde, and nede fall. 5830
For well is þat euery man
That in nede a crafte can:
His connyng is ethe to bere;
Hit woll helpe and noothynge dere;
There is noo tresour therageyn. 5835
Tresour woll ay awayward fayn
And whanne þe tresour is goone all,
Crafte agayn hit brynge shall.
Daunte þem noȝt whill they be yonge,
But sharpe wordes of thy tonge 5840
Say vnto them euer amonge:
Soo shull they drede for to do wronge.
With thy childre do þou shall
Soo men doth a grene yerde withall:
Hit may be wreþen whill hit is grene 5845
As a man woll haue it to beene,
And be hit drye, soone woll hit breke—
A with thereof no man shulde make.
Soo shulde men children worche in youthe
Till þat they som goode cowthe; 5850
For þat yoonge takeþ comounly,

In age hit fyndeþ redyly.'

Qo. 179ᵃ   'Shall a man haue more love tyll   (183)
His wiff or his child by skill?'
'A man shall loue aboue all thyng 5855
God, his maker, heuen kynge
And thenne next his owne body

5827 And þenne] om. P;   love] haste T, has S.   5829 hem kepe] hem warysshe
TS, wirchyn P.   5833 His] om. P.   5839 Daunte] Banne S, Koye P.
5840 But] But with T.   5845 wreþen] wretyn P.   5846] How so men will
withouten teyne S, How to men it wolde oute tene P;   haue . . . beene] withowten

'Iff þou haue children, kepe hem wel
Til þei ben of elde somdel
And if þou loue hem hertily and dere,
Do eche of hem som crafte to lere
So þat þei mowen be kept alle   6825
Aftirward, whatso bifalle.
For wel is þat ilke man
þat in nede any crafte can:
His kunnyng is light to bere
For it wole helpe and noþing dere;   6830
þer is no tresour theraȝein—   f. 101ʳ
Al oþer tresour is but veyn.
And whan þi tresour is goon al,
Crafte aȝein it bringe shal.
Cherisshe hem not while þei be ȝonge   6835
But wiþ sharpe wordes of þi tonge:
Seie to hem sharply euere among
And so shul þei drede to do wrong.
Wiþ þi children þou do shal
As wiþ a ȝerde men done oueral: 6840
It may be writhe while it is grene
If men wolé, wiþouten tene;
And it were drie, it wolde crake—
A withþe shulde no man þerof make.
So shulde men children teche in ȝouthe   6845
Til þat þei sum good kouthe;
For þat þat ȝonge children taken,
Good and vertuous hem it maken:
In [eelde] þei fynden it redily
þat ben wel taght comounly.'   6850

Ca.° lxxvj°   'Wheþer shal a man more loue haue til—   (183)
                His wijf oþer his children be skil?'
                    'A man shal loue ouer al þing
                    God, his maker, heuene king
                    And þanne, next his owne body,   6855

tene T.   5847 And be] were TSP;   breke] crake SP.   5849 men] ye P;
worche] writhe TSP.   5851 yoonge] they yong P.   5852 hit fyndeþ] he
fyndeth it TSP.   5853 ff.] *missing* P.   5853 Shall] Wheder shall TS.

  6827 ilke] *om.* H.   6849 eelde] *from* H, helle L.

And thenne his wyf principally;
His children ought a man, þorogh kynde,
For to love and have in mynde.   5860
But whan God firste made Adam
And Eue of his body nam,
He gaue hym hir vnto his feere
And badde hym for to haue here dere;
Than in þat geuyng made hee   5865
Man and his wyff oon to be;
And if þou and þy wyff be oon
And þat partyng is there noon
Ne noon other may forsake
Vntill dethe yoour oon take,   5870
Thanne ought þou þy wyff to loue moore
Thanne alle þe children that thyn woore.
If þou forlese þy goode wyff,
Thanne lesest þou the solas of þy liff;
And if þou thy children forgo,   5875
Of þy wyf may þou wynne moo:
Therfore shalt þou thy wyff loue moore
Thanne þy childe and holde [in] oore.'

'Iff I had no fadir born   (184)
Ne no modir me befforn,   5880
How should Y haue born be
In this world to here or se?'
   'Longe or God þe world wrought
   Or man or beste þerinne brought,
   Thanne wiste he alle þat sholde be born   5885
And whiche saued and whiche forloren
And all theyre names and þeyre thoght—
God [hadde] he ben elles nought.
Wherefore he wiste well of the
That þou shuldest born be;   5890
And sith þou nedelyng sholde be born,
Thogh thy father þe beforn

5859] To his childer aȝt man be kynde S.   5860 For] Hem S.   5865] þen
at þe bigynnynge made he S;   geuyng] greuyng B, gevynge T.   5866 oon] alle
one TS.   5872–7] om. T.   5878 in oore] moore B, in ore TS.   5879–
922] om. S.   5882 to here or] or here T.   5888 hadde] from T, om. B.

His wyf euer principally;
Her children oghte men of kynde
Forto loue and haue in mynde.
But whan God first made Adam
And Eue of his body nam,   6860
He ȝaf him hir to be his fere
And bad him forto loue hir dere.
In þat bigynnyng þanne made he
Man and wijf al oone to be;
And if þou and þi wijf be one,   6865 f. 101ᵛ
Parting bitwene ȝow is þer none
Ne noon may oþir forsake
Til þat deeth it [wol make]:
þanne owest þou loue þi [wife] more
þan þe children þat þine wore.   6870
If þou leesist a good wijf,
þou leesist þe ioye of þi lijf;
And if þou [þi] children forgo,
Of þi wijf þou may wynne moo:
þerfore shalt þou þi wijf loue more   6875
þan thi children, as I seide ore.'

Ca.° lxxvij°

'If my fadir hadde not be borne   (184)
Ne no moder hadde be me biforne,
Hou shulde I borne haue bene
Or þis world here haue sene?'   6880
  'Longe or God þe world wroght
  Or man or beest þerynne brought,
þo wiste he alle þat shulde be borne
And wich saued and whiche forlorne
And alle her maners and her þoght—   6885
And ellis had he God be noght.
Wherfore he wiste wel of thee
þat þou shuldest borne be;
And nedly sithen þou shuldest be born,
þogh þi fadir þe biforne   6890

6864 al oone] aloone L, all one H.   6868 wol make] *from* H, for sake *marked for*
correction L.   6869 wife] *from* H, children L.   6873 þi] *from* H, *om.*
L.   6882 Or] And H.

f. 85ᵛ

Ne thy modyr þat was also
Had neuer this worlde come vnto,
Anothyr fadre hadde þou hadde   5895
And modre þat þe fed and cladde.'

Qo. 181ᵃ   'The child thatt hath his ffull shappe   (185)
            In the modir, by whatt happe
            Itt is sometyme brouȝtt to nouȝtt
            And may nott leve ffurth to be brouȝtt?'   5900
                'By thre skyllis may hit come to
                Why hit is don for alsoo:
                Oon may than be Goddis wille,
            That he woll þat he shall spille;
            Anothir skill alsoo þer is   5905
            Why hit forfareth somtyme amys:
            The febill nortour in the wyff
            That hit may not com to lyff,
            For the feblenesse of the wykked nature
            Makeþ þat the seede may not endure.   5910
            Febleness of raynes is þe þridde,
            As in woman is betidde—
            Som woman with childe may be
            And soo febele of raynes is she
            That she ne is nought of þe might   5915
            Of the childe to sofere þe wight:
            The modre steres and turneþ aboute
            Soo þat the childe falleþ oute;

            Whan hit is owte, þenne is hit [l]orn,
            And soo þan is hit dede born;   5920
            And þorow grace of Goddis might
            The modre spereth anoone right.'

Qo. 182ᵃ   'Women thatt in this world are,   (186)
            Be they all affter o manere?'

    5894 neuer] neyther T.   5900 leve] alyfe T;   to] om. T.   5903 Oon . . .
be] Som (? Oon) man may it by T.   5909 nature] nurture T.   5916 sofere]
holde T.   5919 lorn] born B, lorne T.   5923–56] follow 5398 S.
5923 are] add here TS.

      Ne þi moder þat was also
      Hadde neiþer this world ycome to,
      Anoþir fadir þou shuldest haue had
      And a moder þe to haue clad.'

Ca.° lxxviij°   *'þe childe þat haþ ful þe shap*   (185) 6895
      In þe moder, by what hap
      Is it somtime broght to noght
      And may not alyue for[th] be broght?'
      'It may be þre skilles come to   f. 102ʳ
      Whi it is fordone þanne so: 6900
      One is by suffraunce of Goddis wille
      þat suffreþ hem here to spille;
      Anoþer skile also þer is
      Whi it fariþ somtime amys:
      þe feble norisshing in þe wyf   6905
      þat it may not come to lyf,
      For þe felnesse of wicked norture
      Makeþ the seed it may not dure.
      Feblenesse of reines is þe þridde,
      As whan a womman is so bitidde—   6910
      Some womman wiþ childe may be
      And feble of reynes eke may be she
      þat she is not of þe might
      þe peine of childinge to suffre right:
      þe modir steriþ hir and turneþ aboute   6915
      So þat þe childe falleþ oute
      Of þe chaumbre þat lieth ynne;
      Wiþ greet peyne þei parte atwynne:
      Whan it is out, þanne is it lorne
      Whan it is þan so deed borne;   6920
      And þorgh grace of Goddes might
      þe modir closiþ anoon right.'

Ca.° lxxix°   *'Wymmen þat ben in þis world here,*   (186)
      Ben þei alle of oone manere?'

  6898 forth] *from* H, *for* L.   6917 lieth] he lieþ H.   6921 Goddes might]
God almy3tt H.

'Women are made all after oon   5925
In flessh and blode, hide and boon;
And all þe lemes þou sees on bere,
Euerychon suche lemes were;
And [men feles oon vppon]
May men fele on euerychon.   5930

f. 86ʳ

But of complexion are þey sere
Of word, of wyll, and of maner;
But all o delite men fynde
Whenne hit comeþ to dede of kynde.
Ofte of wateres may þou see   5935
That of diuers hues þey be
But in thy mouthe and þou hem take,
All as water shull þey smake;
Soo doo women, where þey fare:
All of oon sauour they are.   5940
But ther be som men þan
That thynkeþ swhetter oon woman
Thanne he doþe other fyftene

And may by iij þynges, I wene:

Oon is yif she be fayre and white,   5945
For a man hathe moore delite
In hir þat is bright of blee
Thanne on a lothliche on to see;
Another is for here noble wede,
For a man had leuer geve mede   5950
To hire þat honestly is rayed and dight
Thanne to a poore a ragged wight;
The iij skele is when a man
Soo grete loue hath to a woman
That hym thynke noon soo swhete to holde,   5955
For "Love hathe [no] lak," seith the olde.'

5926 and blode] *om.* T.   5929 And] *add* that TS;   men . . . vppon] *partially
erased* B.   5935 Ofte] As S.   5940 sauour] *add* and complexion S.
5941] But some men hit are nought ane T.   5944] Ande that may be thre thynges

'Wymmen ben made euere after oone   6925
Of flesshe and blood, hide and bone;
And suche lymes as oone haþ here,
Alle oþer han in suche manere;
And þat men feleþ vppon oone
Men mowen it fele on euerychone.   6930
But of compleccioun be þei sere
Of worde, of wille, and of manere;
But in alle oo delite men fynde   f. 102ᵛ
Whan it comeþ to dede of kynde.
Wellis of watris þou may see   6935
Of diuers colours þat þei be
But if in thi mouth þou hem take,
Smel of watir all þei make;
So do wommen, where þei fare:
Alle of oo sauour forsoþe þei are.   6940
But som men þere ben ʒit þan
þat þinkeþ swetter sum womman
þan he dooth oþer fiftene,
þogh one of hem mighte him sustene
Of al þing þat longen him to.   6945
Of suche condicioun some ben, lo,
And þat may be þorgh þinges þre
þat many wymmen wiþ endowed be:
Oone is if she be faire and white,
For a man haþ more delite   6950
In hir þat is bright of ble
þan in a loþely for to se;
Anoþer skile is noble wede,
For a man had leuere ʒeue mede
To hir þat is clenly dight   6955
þan to a pouere ragged wight;
þe þridde skile þat whan a man
So grete loue haþ to a womman
þat him þinkeþ none so swete to holde,
For "Loue haþ no lak," as seiþ þe olde.'   6960

mene (sene S) TS.   5951 honestly . . . and] is noblye T, noblye is S.
5955 swhete to holde] faire to biholde S.   5956 no] from TS, om. B.

6927 And] In H.

Qo. 183ᵃ   'Iff thy ffrende haue wiff and meane   (187)
                    And they ou3tt misdo þat þou se,
                    Shall þou itt vnto thy ffrende seye
                    And his wiff and his meane bewreye?'   5960
                        'And þy neighbour haue a wyff
                        That be wykked and of evill lyff
                        And þou may hit vndertake
                    That she wronge dooth agayne here make
                    Or distroyere of his goode be   5965
                    And þou may hit wete or se,

f. 86ᵛ   Warne hym soo preuely and soo stille
                    That he smyte in noone evell wille.
                    But say hym that he loke þerto
                    Soo þat they noo more doo soo;   5970
                    And make [he] hym wroþe at the firste
                    Whenne þat he soo hit hathe wiste,
                    Thanne shall [hym thi] wordes qweme
                    And þanne he [shall better] hym yeme
                    And saue his goode þat sholde away   5975
                    And if þow noo worde hym say,
                    For men se[y]en in oolde sawes,
                    "By goode neighbours goode day men dawes."'

Qo. 184ᵃ   'Iff a man anyþing shall do,   (188)
                    Shall he hym ou3tt hast þerto?'   5980
                        'Iff thow caste to doo a goode dede,
                        Hastely þerto þou þe spede
                        For goode dede shall haue noo respite:
                    He dothe hit twyes þat dothe hit tyte.
                    But thynke þou evel dede to do,   5985
                    Haste þe nooþynge þervnto:
                    Bethynke the firste in þy herte
                    That hit þe nought after smerte.
                    For if that þou take goode hede,
                    Euell haste is all vnspede: 5990
                    In litell tyme may befalle þe

───────────

5957-78] *om.* S.   5963 þou may hit] she T.   5971 he] *from* T, *om.* B.
5972 soo it hathe] the sothe T.   5973 hym thi] *from* T, they my B.   5974 he
. . . hym] he þat bitte hym B, shall he hym the better T.   5977 seyen] sethen
B.   5978 day men] *reversed* B, daye me T.   5984 tyte] light T.

Ca.° lxxx°   'If þi frende haue wif and meyne   (187)
                And oght be mys þat þou maist see,
                Shalt þou to þi frende seie
                His wijf and mayne to bewreie?'
                     'Iff þi neighebore haue a wyf   6965
                     þat be wikkid and of yuel lyf
                And þou may it vndirnym   f. 103^r
                þat she do wrong aȝenst him
                Or distroyer of his good be
                And þou it mighte wite or see,   6970
                Warne him so priuely and stille
                þat he take it wiþ none yuel wille.
                But seie him þat he loke hir to
                So þat she no more do so;
                And if he make him wrooþ at þe firste   6975
                Whan þat he þe sothe haþ wiste,
                þanne shullen ȝe him wiþ wordes queme
                And þanne shal he bet him ȝeme
                And saue his good þat shulde awaie
                And if þou no worde him saye,   6980
                For men sein in olde sawes,
                "By good neighebore good day men dawes."'

Ca.° lxxxj°   'If a man anyþing shal do,   (188)
                Shal he him haste þerto?'
                'Iff þou þinke to do good dede,   6985
                Hastifly þerto þou þe spede
                For good dede shal haue no respite:
                He dooth it twies þat dooþ it as tite.
                But and þou þinke an yuel dede to do,
                Haste þe noþing neuere þerto   6990
                But biþenke þe first in þyn herte
                þat aftir it makeþ the not to smerte.
                For if þat þou take good hede,
                Euel haste is but al vnspede:
                For in litel time it may befalle þe   6995

6962 be mys] by nyȝt H.   6968 þat] And H.   6978 he] ye þe H.
6984 he] om. H.

That thyne herte may chaunged be
So þat þou shalt þe withholde
Fro þat þou furst haue doon wolde,
And þanne [shalt] þou like well   5995
þat þou ha[ste]dest the noo dele.'

Qo. 185[a]   '*Shall he þat any good can*   (189)
              In this world loue ech man?'
              'Gostly for goode love shalt þou
                   Euery man, and I shall say þe how: 6000
                   Till his soule noon evill wyll
              Moore þenne þou wilte þyn owne vntill.

f. 87[r]   But bodely þy love shall be
              To euery man as he loueþ the:
              Love he þe, loue hym agayn   6005
              And of his companye be fayn;
              Hate he the, hate hym alsoo
              And do to hym as he wolde to þe do.
              Come þou to þy frendes howse,
              The woll not he from þens refowse;   6010
              He will receyve þe with blisse
              And for þe þe merier he is;
              ჳif þou onythyng hym crave,
              With goode will þou might hit haue:
              Suche a man shalt þow loue agayn   6015
              And his will to do be fayn.
              If thow come vnto þy foo,
              That wolde [see] þe leuer hange þen goo,
              Dispite of hym may þou gete
              Or þou eyther drynke or ete: 6020
              Froo suche a man most þou nedes flee
              And hate hym as he doþe the;
              For in olde sawes men say, ywys,
              "He þat loueþ þere most h[at]e is,
              Ayenste þe streme he roweth soore   6025
              And to forlese hath he no moore."'

5995 And . . . þou] And if þanne þou B, Ande shall thou T, And þou shalt þen
S.   5996 hastedest] haddest to B, hasted TS.   5997–6050] *om.* S.
6004 as he] that T.   6010] There ne bostow owte fous T.   6018 see] *from* T,
om. B.   6020] Er than ony drinke or mete T.   6024 most hate is] he is hat
T; hate] he B.   6025 he] who T.

þat þyn herte may ichaunged be
So þat þou shalt þe wiþholde
Fro þat þou firste done haue wolde,
And þan shalt þou like ful wel
þat þou ha[sti]dist þee þerto no del.'   7000

Ca.° lxxxij°   *'Shall he þat any good can*   (189)   f. 103ᵛ
               In þis world loue euery man?'
               'I shal seie þe euery man hou
Goostly for God loue shalt þou:
To his soule haue noon yuel wil   7005
No more þan þou wilt þin owne til.
But bodily þi loue shal be
To euery man as he loueþ the:
And he loue þee, loue him agein
And of his companye be ful fein;   7010
If he hate þee, hate him also
And do to him as he wolde do þe to.
If þou come to þi frendes hous,
þere shalt þou not be daungerous;
He shal resceiue þe wiþ blisse   7015
And for þe þe lighter isse;
If þou anyþing him craue,
Wiþ good wille þou might it haue:
Suche a man shalt þou loue aȝain
And his wille to do be right fain.   7020
And if þou come to þi foo,
þat had leuere see þe hange þan go,
Despite of him maist þou gete
Raþer þan any drink or mete:
Fro suche a man shalt þou fle   7025
And hate him as he doth þe;
For in olde sawes seiþ men þat
He þat loueþ þere þat is hat,
Aȝenst þe streem he roweþ sore
And for to lese haþ he no more.'   7030

7000 hastidist] haddist L, hastidest H;   no] neuer a H.

Qo. 186ᵃ   '*The ffolke off thys world echon*   (190)
                Be they comune affter oon?'
                   'Betwene hem is cominalte
                   In som þynges, as þou mayste see,   6030
                   For all ben þey bore in care
             And alle shall they hens fare
             And alle shall þey rote away
             And alle shall þey ryse at domisday.

             Betwene þem i[n] somþyng   6035
             Is diuersite, for some is kyng

             And some poore, beggyng mete;
             Some leve by þat þat þey may gete;
f. 87ᵛ   Some goon cloþed and som bare;
             And of diuerse maneres men are,   6040
             Of diuerse will and of diuerse þouȝt—
             Hereinne [comen] be they nouȝt.
             And all here is diuersite,
             Soo shall in other worlde be:
             Som shall into payn be broght,   6045
             To beye þe worke þat he hathe wroght;
             And soome shall into þe payne of hell,
             There withouten ende to dwelle;
             And some shall into heven blisse
             That noothynge here haue doon amysse.'   6050

Qo. 187ᵃ   '*Do men to the rich honour echon*   (191)
                And to the pore right noon
                In thatt oþer world also
                As thatt men here in this do?'
                   'A riche man moore honoure shall have   6055
                   In another worlde þanne he can crave
                   And the pore moore shame suffere and þole
             Thanne ony man dothe in this hole:
             The riche shall there honoure fynde

6028/9 *add* The folke of this worlde ilkon / Thei ben comen after oon T.   6035 in]
from T, is B.   6042 comen] *from* T, oon men B.   6043 all] *as* T.
6046 beye] obeye B, bye T.   6051–132] *follow* 5956 S.   6057 suffere and]
om. TS.

Ca.° lxxxiij°   *Þe folke of þis world echone,*   (190)
       Ben þei comounly of wille one?'
         'Bytwene hem is comoun hate:
         For some þinges þere is debate.
       For alle ben ibore in care   7035   f. 104ʳ
       And so sholen þei hens fare
       And alle sholen þei roote away
       And shullen rise at domesday.
       And bytwene hem in many a þing
       Is diuers[it]e bitwene oolde and ȝing: 7040
       Some ben kynges bolde and stoute—
       To hem pore men muste often loute;
       And some here muste begge her mete
       And some lyuen bi þat þei mowen gete;
       Somme goon cloþid and some bare;   7045
       And of diuers maners also some are,
       Of diuerse wille and of diuerse þoght;
       And of comune stature ben þei noght.
       A[nd] as here is diuersete,
       So shal þere in þe oþer world be: 7050
       Somme shullen into peyne be broght,
       To bigge þe werke þat þei haue wroght;
       And some into þe peyne of helle,
       Wiþouten ende þere to dwelle;
       And shullen into heuen blisse   7055
       þat here haue not done amys.'

Ca.° lxxxiiij°   *'Do men honour þe riche echone*   (191)
       And to þe pouere man right none
       In þat oþir world also
       As men in þis worlde here do?'   7060
         'A riche man more honour shal haue
         In heuene þan he þere can craue
       And he þat of vertu is pore and lame,
       He shal suffre þere greet shame:
       þe riche for vertu shal honoured be   7065

7033 comoun] comme H.   7037 away] alway H.   7040 diuersite] *from* H,
diuerse L.   7041 kynges bolde] of kynges blood H.   7049 And] *from* H, As L.

And þe poore be put behynde;   6060

But they haue noo man þere dere
After þat he was riche here.

Vndirstonde now, if þou canne,
Alle þe richesse of the man
Is the soule, þat hym is inne;   6065
And if hit be clene of synne,
Hit is noble and hit is riche:
Him shall aungeles a be liche
And worshipp hym as his men
For his richesse so goode ben.   6070
The poore soule, that synfull is,
Shall nother haue honour ne blisse:
The aungell turne theyre faces þerfroo
For hit for pouerte goth to woo;

f. 88ʳ   Worshipp getiþ hit right noone.   6075
Were hit riche, it hadde goode woone,

But his richesse was all spente
And from hym clerely all is wente
Whenne he Goddes comaundemente forsooke
And to dedely synne hym toke.   6080
Therfore after his richesse were

Is worthy he to be honowred there.'

Qo. 188ᵃ   'Shall the ffadir bere any burþen grym   (192)

6068 a be liche] *one word* B, alle to briche T, all be bryche S.   6069 hym] don T,
done hym S;   men] knaves TS.   6070 so goode ben] that he hauys TS.
6072 nother] no more S.

And haue ioye gret plente;
þe pouere shal þere no ioye finde
For he to vertu was vnkynde.

For as a man loued here,   f. 104ᵛ
Vice or vertu, wheþer it were,   7070
He shal hereafter resceiue:
Ioye or peyne he may [nat weyue]
But suffre he shal wheþer it be,
Ioye or peine, as I seie the.

But vnderstonde, if þou can,   7075
Al þe ricchesse here of man
Is þe soule him wiþynne;
And it be clene out of synne,
It is noble, faire, and riche;
For he shal be aungels liche   7080
And more worþi shal he be
þan any aungel, as I seie þee.

þe pouere soule, þat synful is,
Shal haue neiþer ioye ne blis:
Aungels shal tourne her face him fro   7085
And it shal for pouert goo to wo;
Worshipe getiþ it right noon
But it shulde haue had greet woon
If it had loued vertu here
And hatid synne on al manere—   7090
But his ricchesse al he spent
And from him clenly it went
Whan þat he Goddis heest forsook
And to synne him bitook.

And þerfore aftir his ricchesse,   7095
Be it more, be it lesse,
He shal þere honoure[d] be
þorgh Goddis might and his maieste.'

Ca.º lxxxvº   '[S]hal þe fadir bere any gilte   (192)
                    For þe sone þogh he be spilte   7100

7072 nat weyue] *from* H, *om.* L.   7074 as] or H.   7076 Al] *marked by raised*
dot on each side L.   7083 synful] symple H.   7091 al] as H.   7092 And
. . . it] All . . . is H.   7097 honoured] *from* H, honoure L.   7099 Shal] *from* H,
Thal L.

For the sonne or the sonne for hym?'

'The fader of the sone shall bere   6085
Noo birthen þat hym may dere
Ne the sone nought charged is
What þat þe fader doþe amys:
Euery man of his owne synne
Is charged þat he dieþ inne.   6090
But for þe sone þe fader may
Be charged ofte and euery day
As yf þat the soone misdo
And þe fader wote þat hit be so
And chastiseþ not hym of his synne   6095
And sofereth hym to be withynne,
He synneth also as well as he
And for hym shall he charged be—
The soone for his dede doyng
And þe fadre for his sufferyng;   6100
But the fadre is charged noȝt
Of that þat his soone hath wrouȝt
But thereas he might haue do hym lete
Yf he hadde awe vnto hym seete
But sofered, ther [i]s he nede   6105
Charged for his soones misdede.'

Qo. 189ᵃ   *'Tho þat sle men and ffordo*   (193)
Take þey þere syn them vnto?'
'Nay, synne þat oon man hath wroght
May charge another noght.   6110
f. 88ᵛ   Noo man by right may other s[l]oo
For noo misdede ne for no woo
But if hit bi lordshipp bee
That of God hath þe pouste
Iustise for to do and right—   6115
Therto is hym yoven myght.
And if a man for wraþþe and hate
Slee another goyng in þe gate,
The synne of the dede chargeþ nought

6088 what] with TS.   6105 is] *from* TS, as B.   6111 sloo] *from* TS, shoo B.

Or þe sone ʒit for him
For hise defautis vgly and grym?'
 'The fadir for þe sone shal bere   f. 105ʳ
 No burthen þat him may dere
Ne þe sone chargid not is   7105
With þat þe fadir doth amys:
Euery man of his owne synne
Is chargid þat deieþ þerynne.
But for þe sone the fadir may
Be chargid ofte euery day   7110
As if þat þe sone oght mysdo
And þe fadir woot þat it be so
And chastiseþ him not of his synne
But suffreþ him to lye þerynne,
He synneþ als wel as he   7115
And for him shal chargid be—
þe sone for his dede doyng
And þe fadir for his suffring;
But þe fadir is charged noght
Of þat þat þe sone haþ wroght: 7120
þat he of might him haue lett
If he wolde awe to him haue sett
But suffrid him, þanne is he nede
Chargid for—his sones misdede.'

Ca.° lxxxvj° 'þei þat sle men and fordo,   (193) 7125
    Take þei her synne hem vnto?'
   'Nay, synne þat a man haþ wroght
   May charge anoþer right noght.
No man wiþ right may oþer slo
For no mysdede ne for no wo   7130
But if it by lordshipe be
þat of God haþ the pouste
As iustice forto do dome and right—
þerto to him is ʒouen might.
And if a man for wratthe or hate   7135
Slee anoþer in greet hate,
þe synne of þe dede chargeþ noght   f. 105ᵛ

7111 As] And H. 7135 or] and H. 7136 hate] debate H.

Hym that h[ym] to dethe brought   6120
But what he did, euell or weell,
Shall becleue hymself eche deell.
[M]oght thanne be of Goddis mercy
That he þat is slayne wrongfully
May of somme synne relesed be   6125
For the sharpe dethe þat he
Ayens right was broght vnto;
And he þat hym slowe alsoo
Encreseþ þe synne where he goo
By alsoo many as he doþe sloo—   6130
For gretter synne noȝt telle I can
Than wilfully to slee a man.'

Qo. 190ᵃ   'Which is more sorowe, so þinkith the—   (194)
              Thatt þou herist or þat þou doyst se?'
                   'Sight of eye is more verier   6135
                   Thenne þat a man hereth with eare
                   For þat a man [seeth] furste with eye,
              That may be noo flaterie:
              For he sethe all þe dede doyng
              And all þe sorow of þat thyng,   6140
              That moste goo right nere þe herte
              And doith hit alþermoste smerte;
              For olde men sayn, and ȝit it newes,
              "That eye ne seith þe herte ne rewes."
              But þat a man is tolde vnto   6145
              He wote neuer if hit be soo
f. 89ʳ   And þogh he trowe he saye aright,
              Yet hit dereth not vnto þe sight;
              For þe herte thynkeþ, as hit wolde,
              "Is noone perchaunce as he tolde"—   6150
              And þus comforteth he witterly
              Alle þe wittes of the body.
              Sight of eye is bodyly
              And heryng of ere is gostly:

6120 hym (2)] from TS, he B.   6122 becleue] cleue bi TS.   6123 Moght]
Noght B, Nought may T;   Moght . . . of] He may be at S.   6124 he þat] om.
S.   6125 May] He may S.   6132 wilfully] wrongfully S.   6133–
82] om. S.   6135 is more verier] wole more dere T.   6137 seeth] from T,

Him þat him to deeth haþ broght
But wheþer he deie yuel or wel
It shal cleue bi him eche a del.   7140
But þanne may he þorgh Goddis mercy
þat is yslawe wrongfully
May of somme [synne] relesid be
For þilke sharpe deeþ þat he
Aȝeins right was broght vnto;   7145
And he þat him slowh also
Encresith his synne where he go
By as many as he sleeþ so—
For a gretter synne telle I [ne] can
þan wilfully to slee a man.'   7150

Ca.º lxxxvijº   'Whiche is more sorowe, as þinkeþ thee—   (194)
               þat þou herest or þat þou may see?'
                  'Sight of yȝe wole more dere
                   þan þat a man hereþ wiþ his ere
               For þat a man seeþ wiþ his yȝe,   7155
               þat may not be no faiterie:
               For þat he seeþ al þe doing
               And al þe sorowe of þat þing,
               þat muste goo right nyhe þe herte
               And þat makiþ it moste to smerte;   7160
               For olde men sein, and ȝit it newis,
               "þat yȝe seeþ þe herte rewis."
               But þat a man is tolde vnto
               He not wheþer þat it be so
               And þogh it be so he seie aright,   7165
               Ȝit deriþ it not to þe sight;
               For þe herte þinkeþ, as he wolde,
               "It is not perchaunce as he tolde"—
               And þus comforteþ he vtterly
               Alle þe wittes of his body.   7170
               Sight of yȝe is bodily   f. 106ʳ
               And hering of eere is goostly,

om. B;   furste] om. T.   6150 Is] perhaps Ie B.

    7143 synne] om. LH.   7144 deeþ] om. H.   7149 ne] from H, om. L.
7165 he] om. H.   7171–2] om. H.

Right as þe wynde, soo is heryng   6155
That is herde and yse nothyng.
Therefore more sorowe is to see
Thanne to here, whatsoo hit be.'

Qo. 191ᵃ   'Might men any ffolke now ffynde   (195)
              Thatt etith and drinkith ayen kynde?'   6160
                  'He þat travayleþ day and night
                     To make his neighbour with vnright
                     For to lese his goode, þat he wanne
                  With travayle and crafte þat he canne,
                  And þat he sholde his lyff with lede   6165
                  For to cloþe with and fede,
                  Me thynkeþ he biteth hym full soore—

                  That eteþ hym as þoh hit wore.

                  ʒet is þere another maner
                  A man to ete another here: 6170
                  Yf he a lesyng on hym lye,
                  Wherfore he hath grete vilonye,
                  Or seith hym evell behynde his bakke
                  Or before men makeþ hym lakke,

                  With his tonge he dothe hym ete   6175
                  Thogh he to hym noo toth do lete;

                  And he þat sleeþ a man alsoo
                  And ne hathe noo skyll þertoo
                  Or for y[ift]e þat hym is hight,
                  Forsothe he eteth hym right   6180
                  And mo maners þer ben of mete
                  That a man may another ete.'

6160 and drinkith] other T.   6175–76] He etith hym withowten meth / Though
he nought bite hym with his teth T.   6179 for yifte] from T, foryeve B.

Right as þe winde by hering
Is herd and seen noþing.
þerfore it is more sorwe to see   7175
þan to here, whatso it be.'

Ca.º lxxxviijº   'Might any man folke now fynde   (195)
            þat etiþ anyþing aȝenst kynde?'
            'He þat trauailleþ day and night
                To greue his neighebore wiþ vnright   7180
            To make him lese his good, þat he wan
            Wiþ trauaile or craft þat he can,
            And þat he shulde his lijf wiþ lede
            Forto cloþe him wiþ and forto fede,
            Me þinkeþ he biteth him ful sore   7185
            And freteþ and gnaweþ him wel more
            þan eting of mete discretly
            Or any oþer þing done vertuously.
            Ȝit þer is anoþer manere
            A man to ete anoþer here: 7190
            If he a lesinge on him lie,
            Wherfore he haþ greet vilenie,
            Or spekiþ him yuel behinde his bak
            Or bifore men make him a lak,
            He etiþ him, and þat is noght—   7195
            He dredeþ not God, þat hem wroght.
            To speke men shame it is ful hard:
            þei shullen forþinke it aftirward—
            þogh þei wiþ teeth biteþ not hem,
            On hem þei maken manye a wem.   7200
            And he þat sleeþ a man also
            And haue no skile so to do
            Or for ȝifte þat is him behight,
            Suche eten men wiþ vnright.
            And many mo maneres þer beth of mete   7205   f. 106ᵛ
            þat many men wiþ oþer ete
            Whiche shal be founde vnsauoury
            At oo day and ful perilously.

7189 manere] manerere L.   7196 hem] hem boþe H.   7203 for ȝifte] one
word L, for yifte H.   7205 many] om. H.   7207 vnsauoury] vnsauerly H.

f. 89ᵛ *Qo. 192ᵃ*   'Which is the worst þing off thes þre   (196)
Mordre or theffte or a baratour to be?'
                 'A baratour is wykyd to be   6185
                 For he makeþ often medelyng to be se:
                 He is abowte day and night
            To make coun[tecke] at his might,
            And soo many þorogh his reede
            Might be cause of mannes dede;   6190
            Therefore hit is grete folye
            Suche oon to haue in companye.
            [þefte] is hit as moche synne
            For he þat will neuer blinne
            For to stele his neighbour froo   6195
            That he hathe beden for full woo,
            And soo shall he ayeyn hym dryve
            In woo and in travayll to lyve
            Or to begge for euermore—
            Loke what synne he dothe þoore.   6200
            But the moste synne of all þoo
            Is man to mourdre and to sloo,
            For he fordothe þat iche stature
            That God made after his figure
            And roueþ lyff there hit shulde be   6205
            And Goddes seruise soo letteth hee:
            Mannes lykenesse sloo ne shall he noght
            Ne noon but he þat hym wroght.'

6183–208] *follow* 6132 S.   6186 medelyng . . . se] medle S, melle T.
6188 countecke] counsaill B, contecke TS.   6189 many] he may T, it may
S.   6190 Might] *om.* TS;   cause] encheson TS.   6193 þefte] *from* ST,
ȝet B.   6195 neighbour] neȝbores goodes hym S.   6198 to] all his S.
6208] But þo that hymself haþ wroȝt S.

þerfore men shulde suche me[te] ete
As þei mighten truly gete,   7210
And reuerence and worshipe do
At eche mele, whan þei come þerto,
To God, þat is of mightes most,
þat is Fadir and Sone and Holy Goost,
And ete oure mete in charite: 7215
þis is Goddes wille þat it so be.'

Ca.º lxxxixº   'Whiche is þe werste þing of þese thre—   (196)
Morthur or þefte or baratour to be?'
   'A baratour is yuel to be
      For he makiþ ofte medle: 7220
He is aboute day and night
To make contacke wiþ al his might,
And so may by his wicked reed
Enchesoun be of som mannes ded;
þerfore it is greet folye   7225
Suche oone to haue in companye.
Thefte also is myche synne
For he þat wole neuer blynne
For to stele his neighebor fro
þat he haþ geten wiþ trauaille and wo,   7230
And so shal he aȝein him driue
Into woo and trauaille forto liue
Or to begge for euermore—
Now loke what synne he doth þore.
But þe moste synne of alle þese þre   7235
Is murþur and slaghter, as I seie the,
For slaghter fordoth þat stature
þat God made after his figure
And reveþ lijf þere it shulde be   f. 107ʳ
And Goddis seruice also lettiþ he: 7240
Mannes liknesse slee shulde noght
Noon but he þat here it wroght.'

7209 mete] *from* H, men L.

Qo. 193^a   'Foryevith God with good chere   (197)
             All the synnys þat a man doth here?'   6210
                  '[I]ff alle þe dropes in þe see
                   And all þe grete þat in erthe may be
                   And all þe leues þa men couthe nempne
                  And all þe sterres of heven even
                  And all þe fissh þat swhymme can   6215
                  And all þe heres of beste and man
                  Were alle in oon summe broght,
                  The tenþe parte ne were they nought
f. 90^r   Of the mercy of God of heven
                  For þat may no man somme neven: 6220
                  Hadde a man done all þe synne
                  That all þis world durste begynne,
                  And he had sorowe in [h]erte þerfore
                  And wolde leve and doo no more,
                  God wolde of hym haue mercy   6225
                  And foryeve hit hym redily
                  And woll hym knowe of his meane
                  And of his turnyng right glad to be.
                  But he þat lesseþ nough[t] his synne
                  Ne nought þerof woll blynne   6230
                  Nother he woll mercy craue,
                  He is worthy noone to have—
                  For whosoo axith vnworthily
                  Hit may be wernyd skylfully.'

Qo. 194^a   'Why travaileth a man so   (198) 6235
             In this world as some do?'
                  'For twoo þynges principally:
                   That oon to susteyne þe body,
                   That other þat hit stalworth be
                  To serue God in Trinite   6240
                  As in prayer and in almesdede,
                  For þoo woll þe sowle fede—
                  And noȝt to gadre to his hande
                  To leue his children or his freande.

6209 ff.] *follow* 5996 S.   6211 Iff] Off B.   6214 even] *om.* TS.
6217 summe] synne S.   6223 herte] *from* TS, erthe B;   þerfore] before T.
6229 lesseþ] angris TS;   nought] *from* TS, nough B.   6232 He] *from* T, For he

Ca.° lxxxx°   *'Forȝeueþ God wiþ good chere*   (197)
                   Alle þe synnes þat a man doþ here?'
                   'Iff alle þe dropes in þe see   7245
                   And al þe grauel þat in erþe may be
                   And alle þe leues þat men kunne neuene
                   And alle þe sterres þat beþ in heuene
                   And alle þe fisshes þat swymme can
                   And alle þe heres of beest or man   7250
                   Weren alle in oone summe ibroght,
                   þe tenþe deel were þei noght
                   Of þe mercy of God of heuene
                   For þe somme þerof may no man neuene:
                   For hadde a man do al þe synne   7255
                   þat al þis world might begynne,
                   And he were sory in herte þerfore
                   And wolde leue and do so no more,
                   God wolde of him haue mercy
                   And forȝeue it him redily   7260
                   And wole knowe him for oon of his meyne
                   And of his torning bliþe wole be.
                   But he þat langriþ not his synne
                   And þerof wole not blynne
                   Noþer wole he mercy craue,   7265
                   þanne is he worþi noon to haue—
                   For whoso it askeþ vnworþili
                   Hit may be warned him skilfully.'

Ca.° lxxxxj°   *'Why trauailleþ a man so*   (198)
                   In þis world as somme men do?'   7270
                     'For two þinges principally:
                     þat oone is to sustene þe body,
                   þat oþer þat it stalworþe be   f. 107ᵛ
                   To serue God in Trinite
                   As in prayers and almesdede,   7275
                   For þo wole þe soule fede—
                   And not forto gadre to his ende
                   And leue it to his children and to his frende:

B, Ne he S.   6235–58] *om.* S.   6236 as some do] that is so woo T.
6243 hande] ende T.

7250 or] and H.   7263 langriþ] angreþ H.

All this travayle shulde be here   6245
To saue þe soule þat God loueþ dere
And to doo all þat we fynde
As the empte doþe in his kynde:
By someres day he gadereþ all
That he in wynter by live shall—   6250
He woll not soo longe abyde
That it come to þe wynter tyde.
Alsoo shulde a man lere
To teele his sowle whill he were here—

f. 90ᵛ   Abideth he til he hens fare,   6255
Cold wynter he fyndeth and care:
Wherefore sholde he so trauayle
That it hym after availle.'

Qo. 195ᵃ   *'Tell me now, withoute mys:*   (199)
Which is the derkest þing þat is?'   6260
 'Wykkedder þyng may noon be
  Than wykked man in his pouste
  For the soule þat is in hym
She is bothe merke and dym.
And a wikked man myght soo bynne   6265

How derke his soule is for synne,

So foule a thyng he shold se hit
That he sholde forlese his witt:
Forwhy is there noo derkenesse
Ayens a man in wikkednesse.'   6270

Qo. 196ᵃ   *'The good werkis and the yll*   (200)
Thatt a man doth off his will,
Wheþer come they off God hym to
Or off hymselff þat he doth so?'
 'Understande well, ywys,   6275
  That of God noon evill is:
  Of hym is all holinesse

6259 S *begins again.*   6261 Wykkedder] Derker S.   6265 bynne] hym (*om.*
T) *within* ST.   6271–456] *om.* S.

Al his trauail shulde be here
To saue þe soule þat he boght dere.   7280
Ensample herof we fynde
Of þe ampte in her kynde:
In somer daies he gadreþ al
þat he in wynter lyue by shal—
He wole not so longe abide   7285
þat it come to þe winter tide.
Also shulde a man lere
To tille his soule while he is here;
And if he abideþ til he hens fare,
He shal finde colde winter and bare: 7290
þerfore schulde he sore trauaille
þat it him might aftir availe.'

Ca.° lxxxxij°   'Telle me now, wiþouten mys: (199)
                   Whiche is þe derkest thing þat is?'
                       'Derker þing may noon be   7295
                       þan wicked man in his pouste
                   And þe soule þat is in him
                   So is boþe derke and dym.
                   And if a wicked man might
                   Se him wiþynne fully aright   7300
                   Hou derke his soule is for synne,
                   I trowe of synne he wolde blynne:
                   A foule þing he shulde se it
                   Wherþorgh he lightly might lese his witt:
                   þerfore þere is no derknesse   7305
                   Aȝeinst a man in his wickidnesse.'

Ca.° lxxxxiij°   'þe good werkes and þe ille   (200)   f. 108ʳ
                   þat a man doth of his wille,
                   Wheþer come þei of God him to
                   Or of himself þat doth hem so?'   7310
                       'Vnderstonde þou wel, iwis,
                       þat of God noon yuel is:
                       Of him is al holynesse

7279 trauail] truauail *with* 1st u *marked for deletion* L.   7280 he] God H.
7292 it] it hit L.   7300 aright] and riȝt H.

And all fayrehede and goodenesse,
And for goodenesse man he wroght
To paradise whenne he hym brought.   6280
He yave hym witte, as was his will,
For to knowe bothe goode and ille
And whanne a man had knowlechyng
Of bothe, thenne was he at his chesyng
Whether he wolde take vnto;   6285
And þan began he evill to do
Whanne þat he þe goode lete
And bote in the appel þat he eete;
And sethen he might do what he wolde,
And he luste to þe wykked hym holde,   6290

Of hymsilfe euerydeell hit is
Though he did also amys.
To helpe he hadde an enmy
And soo dothe bothe þou and I:
Thre we have yche a day   6295
Vs to tempte all þat they may—
Oure owne fflessh, þe world, þe fende—
Echon wolde have vs in her hande;
But for we knowe amonge all þis
Whiche is better and whiche worse is,   6300
Thanne is þat wikkednesse all dede
Of hym þat doth hit and [no]ght at nede.
If a man were wel bethought
To thynke on hym þat made þem of nought,
He sholde have grace well to wyrke   6305
And of idelnesse to be yrke;
For of God comeþ goodnesse withynne
And of oouresyluen euell and synne.'

'Wher hideth hym þe day ffro the ny3tt   (201)
And the ny3tt ffro the daylight?'   6310
        'That tyme þat þe world was dight
Of his worde and of his might,
The elementes were menged echon

6285 take] take hede T.   6299 among] *om.* T.   6301 all dede] ilke a dele T.
6302 noght] might B;   at nede] doo well T.   6304 thynke on] thanke T.
6306 idelnesse] wickidnes T.   6311 þe world was] God the worlde T.

And al fairhede and goodnesse,
And for goodnesse man he wroght 7315
To paradys whan he him broght.
He 3af him wit, as was his wille,
For to knowe boþe good and ille
And whan a man had knowleching
Of bothe, þanne it was at his chesing 7320
Wheþer he wolde take him to;
And þo bigan he yuel to do
Whanne þat he þe good lete
And bote an appul þat he ete;
And siþþe he might doo wheþer he wolde, 7325
And he wolde to þe wicke him holde,
Of himself euerydele it is
þat he dide so amys.
To helpe he hadde an enemy
And so han boþe þou and I: 7330
þre enemyes we haue euery day
Vs to tempte al þat þei may—
Oure owne flesshe, þe world, þe fende—
Echone of þise wolden vs shende;
But for we knowe among al þis 7335
Euel and good and what yuel is,
þanne is þat wickednesse euerydel
Of him þat dooþ yuel and might do wel.
For if a man were wel biþoght
To þanke him þat made him of noght, 7340
He shulde haue grace wel to wirke   f. 108ᵛ
And of wickidnesse be right irke;
For of God goodnesse comeþ vs to
And of ouresilf þe yuel þat we do.'

Ca.º lxxxxiiijº   'Where hideþ the day him fro þe night   (201) 7345
     And þe night fro þe daies light?'
      '[T]hat time þat God þe world dight
      Of his word and of his might,
      þe elementis weren made echone

7343 goodnesse] goodnesseþ L.   7345 Where] Wheþer H.   7346 And] Or
H.   7347 That] *from* H, hat (*gap for rubricator, not completed*) L.

And light on erthe was þer noon.
Thanne departed God in sonder   6315
And echon sette other vnder;
Thanne made he sonne and moone to light,
That oone on þe day, þat other on þe night.
The sonne gothe abowte euermore
To geve light here and euer[y]whore: 6320
Whenne vs liȝt sendeth, thenne hit is day
And night whanne he is away;
And whanne he departeth us froo,
Aboute þe erthe moste hym nede goo
And the erthe, þat is soo rounde,   6325
Reueþ vs þat ilke stounde

f. 91ᵛ
The light that wee hadde of hym,
And þenne is vs þe night dym.
Whanne the sonne is aboute wente
And ayeen is to vs sente,   6330
As soone as he apperith vnto vs onyþyng,
We say hit is in the dawnyng;
And as he risith ay and ay
Soo waxeth vnto us þe clere day:
Thus departeth þe day and þe night   6335
Bi reson of þe sonnelight
And euer whan þat oon comeþ vpon,
The oþer soone parteþ anoon.'

Qo. 198ᵃ   'How holdith þe planetes hem all   (202)
             In the skye thatt they ne ffall?'   6340
             'Whanne God had dight þe firmament
             And stabeled euery elamente
             On þe sky vnder þe heuene,
             Made [he] þe planetes seuene
             And he made also vpp an hy   6345
             Alle þe sterres on þe sky;
             And euery planete soo hathe his
             Spere there his goyng is.
             The moone soo is loweste of all,
             The highest Saturnus we call;   6350

6320 euerywhore] euerwhore B, elliswhore T.   6331 he . . . vnto] she sheweth
T.   6338 soone parteþ] partith vp T.   6344 he] *from* T, *om.* B.

And light on þe erþe was þer none.   7350
þo God departed hem asondre
And sette eche element oþer vndre;
þanne made he sonne and monelight,
þat one to þe day, þat oþer to þe night.
The sonne gooþ aboute euermore   7355
To lighte here and elleswhore:
Whanne he lightneþ vs it is oo day
And on þe night þe light is away;
And whanne he departeþ vs fro,
Aboute þe erthe him bihoueþ to go   7360
And þe erþe, þat is rounde,
Bynymeþ vs þat ilke stounde
þe light þat we hadde of him,
And þan to vs is þe night [dym].
Whanne þe sonne is aboute ywente,   7365
Aȝein to vs he is isente;
As sone as he shewiþ anyþing,
We seyn it is in þe dawening;
And as he riseþ hye and hye
So wexeþ to vs so clere deye: 7370
þus departeþ þe day and night
By resoun of þe sonnelight
And euere whan comeþ þat oone,
þat oþer departeþ fro vs anoone.'

Ca.° lxxxxv°   'Hou holdeþ the planetes alle   (202) 7375 f. 109ʳ
               On þe sky þat þei ne falle?'
                  'Whan God had made þe firmament
                  And stabled euery element
               On þe sky vnder heuene,
               He made þere the planetis seuene   7380
               And he made also vp an hy
               Alle þe sterres of þe sky;
               And euery planet so haueþ his—
               A speere þere þat his going is.
               þe mone also is lowest of alle,   7385
               Saturnus þe hyest þat we calle;

And alle have þey here steryng
Ayens þe sky in his goyng
And euer þe highere þat he be,
The moore to goon þanne hathe he:
Somme hath a yeere and som twoo   6355
In his spere abowte to goo
And somme abowte to goo also
Doith but a moneth þerto.
And all ben þay of oon kynde
Of the ffirmament, as we fynde,   6360
And have togeder a fastenyng
Soo þat there may be noo partyng;

f. 92ʳ   And also God ordeyned hem alle
That [n]oon may from other falle:
Soo may noone falle fro other well   6365
Till God þe worlde fordo euerydele.'

Qo. 199ᵃ   'How may men the houris knowe aright   (203)
              And the poyntys off day and ny3tt?'
              'In what lande þat þou in be
              Thow maiste easely knowe and see: 6370
              Sone þow the sonne se may,
              That is a poynte of the day;
              And whanne þe sonne to reste is goon
              Thow woste hit neighhit ni3t anoon;
              And the ni3t with þe day   6375
              Hathe but xxiiijᵗⁱ owres ay,
              And euery oure hathe noo more
              But a thousand poyntes and foure scoore.
              And þis þynge may þou well
              By a candell prove hit euerydele,   6380
              Be þe day shorte or longe by skyll—
              The ought not mysse yf þou will:
              Reken þe day after hit is
              And þe night also reken not mys
              And euery houre reken we may   6385
              Whan hit sheweþ and passeþ away.'

6359 oon] the T.   6364 noon] oon B, non T.   6369 þat þou] the regne
T.   6374 neighhit] is T.   6379 þis þynge] theise poyntis T.
6382 ought] thar T.   6384 reken not mys] after it is T.   6385 reken we] wyte

And alle haue þei her stirynge
Aȝens þe sky in her goynge
And euere þe hiȝer þat he be,
þe more to goo þan haþ he: 7390
Somme haþ a ȝere and some two
In his spere aboute to goo
And some aboute to goo also
Do but a monthe trauel þerto.
And alle ben þei of þe kynde   7395
Of þe firmament, as we fynde,
And alle han togidre a fastnyng
So þat þer may be no parting;
And also God ordeyned hem alle
þat noon may from oþer falle: 7400
þus may from oþer noon falle wel
Til God fordo þe world euery del.'

Ca.º lxxxxvjº   'Hou may a man knowe þe houres aright   (203)
                     And þe poyntes of þe day and night?'
                     'In what lond þou ynne be   7405
                     þou maist lightly knowe and se:
                     As sone as þe sunne þou se may,
                     þat is a point of þe day;
                     And whanne þe sonne to rest is goon,   f. 109ᵛ
                     þou woost þat it is [n]ight anoon;   7410
                     And þe night with þe day
                     Ne haþ but xxiiij houres ay,
                     And euery hour haþ no more
                     But a þousand pointes and foure score.
                     And þeise thinges may þou wel   7415
                     By a candel preue euery del,
                     Be a day longe or short wiþ skille—
                     þou maist not misse but if þou wille:
                     Reken þe day after þat he is
                     And þe night also rekene, iwis,   7420
                     And euery hour wite þou may
                     Whan he come and passeþ away.'

thou T.   6386 sheweþ] comyth T.
_____
7410 night] right L, nyȝt H.

Qo. 200ᵃ   'All the sterris vp an hye,   (204)
                 Turne they aboute vppon the skye?'
                    'Tournyng be sterris ay
                     For as þe sky gothe, soo goo thay,   6390
                     And for the turnyng of the sky
                 Is þat they goo soo hastely.
                 But oon is there that semeth nou3t
                 Vnto ooure sight that hit gooth ought,
                 And 3it is he alway steryng   6395
                 In a serkle abowte turnyng;
                 And fful well stereth he
                 That oon ende of the axel tre
f. 92ᵛ   That the worlde all stereþ vpon,
                 And yit there semeth his steryng noon.   6400
                 And for he the axel tre is by
                 And turneþ hym soo narowly,
                 Till sight semeth he þerfore
                 Euer in oon stede as þogh he woore;
                 And therfore shipmen by the see,   6405
                 In what place that they be,
                 By night have grete knowlechyng
                 By hym and by his shewyng:
                 And þerfore the shipmen alle
                 The lode sterre they hit calle.'   6410

Qo. 201ᵃ   'Shall euer in this world be   (205)
                 Werre and contecte as men may se?'
                    'At the begynnyng, whan þer were
                     Foure men in the worlde and noo more,
                     Was there werre and felonye   6415
                 And manslaughter for enuye;
                 And hit shall neuer seas
                 Ne in the world be in peas.
                 For were the world peas holly,
                 Men might hit calle skylfully   6420
                 Paradys and ellis noght,
                 For there was neuer werre ywroght
                 But loue, peas, and charite

6397] For ful nere stondith hee T.   6399 stereþ] turneth T.   6400 And yit]
Therfore T.   6408 shewyng] shynynge T.   6416 for] ande T.   6418 Ne
in] Till T.

Ca.° lxxxxvij°   'Alle þe sterres vp an hy,   (204)
                   Torne þei aboute on þe sky?'
                        'Tornyng beth þe sterres ay   7425
                        And as þe sky gooth, so goon þay,
                   And for þe torning of þe sky
                   Is þat þei goon so hastily.
                   But oone þere is þat semeth noght
                   To oure sight þat he gooþ oght,   7430
                   Alþogh he is euer sterning
                   And in a cercle aboute torning;
                   For ful euene stondeþ he
                   In þat oon ende of þat extre
                   þat al þe worlde torneþ on: 7435
                   þerfore in him semeth stering noon.
                   And for he þe extre is by,
                   He torneþ him so narowly
                   To sighte semeth he þerfore
                   As þogh he euere in oo stede wore;   7440
                   And þerfore shipmen by þe see,
                   In what stede so þei be,
                   By night þei haue greet knowleching   f. 110ʳ
                   By him and by his shewyng:
                   þerfore þe shipmen alle   7445
                   þe loode sterre þei hir calle.'

Ca.° lxxxxviij°   'Shal euer in þis world be   (205)
                   Werre and contekte as men now see?'
                        'At þe bigynnyng, whan þer wore
                        Foure men in þe world and no more,   7450
                   Ther was werre and felonye
                   And mansleyng and envie;
                   And it ne shal neuere cees
                   Til þat þe worlde be al in pees.
                   For were þe world in pees holy,   7455
                   Men mighte calle it skilfully
                   Paradys and oþer noght,
                   For þere was neuere werre wroght
                   But loue and pees and charite

And þo may noȝt holly here be.
But in þis worlde ben werres twoo: 6425
Gostly and bodyly also.
The gostly werre may noo man see,
That is of the deuell and his meayne:
Night and day on man he werres;
In alle þat he may he hym deres.   6430
Bodyly werre alle furst beganne
Tha[t] is betwyxe manne and man
And þat shall neuer to ende come
Till hit be at the day of dome.'

f. 93ʳ *Qo. 202ᵃ*   *'Wratheth God hym ouȝtt ffor man þat is dede* (206) 6435
                         Whatt deth so he dye, good or quede?'
            'Thogh God sawe all the worlde brenne
            And all the ffolke dye þat ben þereynne
            And drye alsoo all þe see,
In God shall noo wraþþe be: 6440
In hym may be noon evel moode
For noothyng of this worldes goode.
Mannes dethe dereth God noo more,
What dethe he dyeth or whoore,
Than it dothe þe for to brenne   6445
An hill þat many emptes were ynne:

No more doþ God, þe soth to say,
What tyme a man shall here dey.
Noo suerer þyng than is þe dede
But of the tyme can noo man reede   6450

And forwhy what tyme he dye shall
God greveþ hym nooþyng þerwithall;

6432 That] *from* T, Than B.   6435 man þat is] mannes T.   6439 alsoo]
ilke daye T.   6446/7 *add* Hit is to the no maner grucchynge / The pyne that thei
suffer in brennynge T.

And only þilke mowen not here be.   7460
But in þis world beþ werres two:
Goostly werre and bodily also.
þe goostly werre may no man see,
þat is of þe deuel and his meyne:
Night and day on men he werris   7465
And in al þat he may he hem derris.
Bodily werre þat firste bigan
Was bytwene man and man
And þat shal neuere to ende come
Til it be þe day of dome.'   7470

Ca.° lxxxxix°   'Wreþþeth God him oght for mannes deed   (206)
               What deth so he deie, good or queed?'
                  'Thogh God sawe al þis world brynne
                   And alle þe folk þat ben þerynne
               And dreied euery del þe see,   7475
               3it in God schulde no wraþþe be
               For in him may be noon yuel mood   f. 110ᵛ
               For noþing of þis worldes good.
               Mannes deth deerith God no more,
               What deeth so he deie owhore,   7480
               þan it doþ the forto brynne
               An hille þat many amptes beþ ynne:
               þe peyne þat thei þole in brennyng
               Ne greueþ a man no manere þing;
               No more it doth God, þe soþe to seie,   7485
               What time a man here shal deie.
               No sikerer þing is þan þe deth
               But whan a man shal 3ilde þe breth
               No wight can telle þat is livyng
               But he þat is euerlasting,   7490
               þat is þe Fadir wiþ the Sone
               And þe Holy Goost, þat wiþ hem wone;
               þerfore þat time he deie shal
               God greueþ him noþing withal.
               þerfore siþen no man knowe ne may   7495

But sethen man wote not soo moche prowe
To wete whanne he shall dye ne howe,

Loke he be redy, as I rede,   6455
Thenne dare hym noght þe dethe drede.'

Qo. 203^a   '*Tell me now, ffor I am in a were,*   (207)
Off the dignest day off the yere.'

'Off all þe yeere þe digneste day
So is holden þe Saturday,   6460
Whanne God had heuene and erthe wroght
And all thyng þerinne brought
And all hadde he wroght hem tho
In vj [dayes] and noo moo.
On þe Sonday he began   6465
And þe vj day made he man;
And whan þat man was made euery lym,
The vij day God rested hym—
For werihede toke he noo reste
Therfore he chese that day for þe beste   6470
And bad man þat day to be in peas
And of all bodely workes to seas—
Therefore þe digniest day of all
The Saturday men hit calle.
But at that tyme shull men see   6475
That Goddis Soone shall man bee
That he shall dye and sethen rysee
The iij day on all wyse:
That vpriste shall men worship ay
And þat shal be the Sonday;   6480
And sethen shall men calle
The Sonday best of alle.'

f. 93^v

6455 as] aye T.   6457 S *begins again.*   6464 dayes] *from* TS, planetes
B.   6470 Therfore] But for TS.   6472 bodely] *om.* TS.   6475 as that]
a TS.   6481 calle] euer calle TS.

þat deeþ þat to him is comyng ech day,
He shulde be redy euery hour
And drede of deth þe sharpe shour:
þerfore be redy euere, I ȝou rede,
Whereeuer ȝe be and in what stede.'   7500

Ca.º Cº   'Telle me, for I am in were,   (207)
þe worþiest day of þe ȝere.'
'Iff God wole, þat I shal do,
And of his helpe I preie þerto.
Sire, of al þe ȝeer þe worþiest day   7505
We shulde it holde þe Satirday,
Whanne God had heuen and erþe wroght
And alle þinges þerynne ybroght:
In sixe dayes and no mo
He made fully alle þinges tho;   7510
And þe Sonday he bigan   f. 111ʳ
And þe sixte day he made man;
Whan man was made eche a lym,
þe seuenþe day God restid him—
For werihede toke he no reste   7515
But for he chees þat day for beste
And bad man þat day be in pees
And of alle hise werkes forto sees—
þerfore þe Saturday of alle
þe worþiest day we it calle.   7520
But suche a time men shullen se
Whan Goddes Sone man shal be
þat he shal deie and sithe arise
The þridde day after in al wise;
And þat vprist men sholen worshipe ay   7525
And þat shal be þe Sonday;
And þan shal men þat day calle,
þe Sonday, þe beste day of alle.'

7505 Sire] ffor H.